Culture Work

Culture Work

Folklore for the Public Good

Edited by
TIM FRANDY and B. MARCUS CEDERSTRÖM

THE UNIVERSITY OF WISCONSIN PRESS

Publication of this book has been made possible, in part, through support from the Department of German, Nordic, and Slavic+ and the Anonymous Fund of the College of Letters and Science at the University of Wisconsin–Madison.

The University of Wisconsin Press
728 State Street, Suite 443
Madison, Wisconsin 53706
uwpress.wisc.edu

Gray's Inn House, 127 Clerkenwell Road
London EC1R 5DB, United Kingdom
eurospanbookstore.com

Printed in the United States of America
This book may be available in a digital edition.

Library of Congress Cataloging-in-Publication Data

Names: Frandy, Tim, editor. | Cederström, B. Marcus, editor.
Title: Culture work : folklore for the public good / edited by Tim Frandy and B. Marcus Cederström.
Description: Madison, Wisconsin : The University of Wisconsin Press, [2022] |
    Includes bibliographical references and index.
Identifiers: LCCN 2021054502 | ISBN 9780299338206 (hardcover)
Subjects: LCSH: Public folklore. | Public folklore—Wisconsin.
Classification: LCC GR67 .C85 2022 | DDC 398.09775—dc23/eng/20211214
LC record available at https://lccn.loc.gov/2021054502

*For our public folklorist teachers and mentors
and the culture workers whose work inspires us today.*

Contents

Acknowledgments

A work like this does not create itself. This work depends fully on the shared vision of more than three dozen contributing writers, a team at the University of Wisconsin Press, and the support and guidance of our teachers, our peers, and our students.

In particular, we'd like to thank our public folklorist mentors in Wisconsin, whose guidance helped teach us how to do culture work: Thomas A. DuBois, Christine Garlough, Janet Gilmore, James P. Leary, Richard March, Ruth Olson, Anne Pryor, and Mark Wagler. We'd like to also thank the broader network of folklorists and collaborating community members in the Upper Midwest, both past and present, who have inspired us and shaped our work and who are too numerous to name.

We'd like to thank Nathan MacBrien, Amber Rose Cederström, and Holly McArthur from the University of Wisconsin Press for helping us usher this manuscript forward, along with the keen insights of Lisa Gilman and our other anonymous peer reviewer whose comments on our draft manuscript helped create a better finished product. We also are indebted to the work of Ariana Pedigo, who assisted with the bibliography, and indexer Elizabeth Reuter.

We'd like to thank the countless public folklorists who shaped us and our work. The annual meeting of the American Folklore Society (AFS) is host to dozens of panels and forums that discuss the fascinating, innovative, and inspiring work our colleagues and friends are engaged in. Most of these people are employed in public folklore positions outside the university: at museums or cultural centers, arts or humanities councils; as festival organizers; in PreK–12 education; as fieldworkers or contract workers; in nonprofits; in media production; and much more. Through the publication of this book, we wanted to bring some of these conversations to a larger audience, to our students, to people outside our small discipline.

We'd like to thank each and every one of our contributing writers, whose patience and hard work have been essential in crafting this work. The reality for many public folklorists (which represent about half of the workers in our field) is that on-the-ground labor takes precedence over publishing about it in traditional scholarly formats. The very people doing public culture work are often underpaid, overworked, and stretched thin. To write a chapter about that work is no small task and one that usually lies outside professional job duties. Similarly, for academic folklorists who do public work, public work is institutionalized as secondary in importance and too often remains an uncompensated labor of love. We are thankful that the many contributors to this volume shared our belief that it was both important and timely to discuss their work in print and to bring these conversations from AFS to a larger audience in a centralized and systemized manner.

And, of course, we'd like to thank our families: Amber Rose Cederström, Oskar Cederström, Elizabeth Reuter, Andrew Fisher, and Cedar Frandy, for their enduring patience and support as we have wrestled with this work.

Culture Work

Introduction

TIM FRANDY and B. MARCUS CEDERSTRÖM

In 2016, a group of folklorists from the University of Wisconsin–Madison (UW–Madison) presented a poster at an on-campus symposium dedicated to interdisciplinary public scholarship. Our team (Marcus Cederström, Colin Connors, Thomas DuBois, and Tim Frandy) had since 2011 been working in Waaswaaganing (Lac du Flambeau, Wisconsin) with local Anishinaabe artists, educators, and cultural leaders to assist with cultural revitalization efforts, most of which were in partnership with National Heritage Fellow Mino-giizhig (Wayne Valliere). In addition to Wayne, our small and rotating team included people like Wayne Valliere Jr., Iris Carufel, Lawrence Mann, Geoff Valliere, Carol Amour, Doreen Wawronowicz, Leon Valliere, and Greg Johnson. Together we were building birchbark canoes with dozens of community participants (Cederström et al. 2016; Frandy and Cederström 2017). We were revitalizing winter competitive sports and building traditional tools of hunting and trapping with schoolchildren (Cederström, Frandy, and Connors 2018). We were also working with the community to run wild ricing camps, build different kinds of lodges, tan buckskin, and make lacrosse sticks to play traditional lacrosse. We weren't simply documenting or presenting or preserving culture. We were experimenting with revitalized traditions in new contexts and how we could create new meanings (or awaken very old meanings) with the community through traditional arts programming.

It was—and still is—the sort of invigorating collaborative partnership that is a reminder of the power of public culture work: the kind of culture work that involves creating long-term, flexible, community-initiated, and community-driven projects in which community members have decision-making authority (Cederström et al. 2016); the kind that involves collaboration and alliances that build local capacity to sustain a project, effectively working folklorists out of a job (Cederström, Frandy, and Connors 2018); the kind that involves developing new cognitive frameworks to approach problems and amplifying and validating local worldviews and knowledge traditions to outsiders (Frandy 2015; Frandy and Cederström 2017).

The poster we were presenting was on the positive social effects that these cultural revitalization efforts had on the community's health and wellbeing, especially in young people who face great challenges in coping with the many forms of racism and bigotry that pervade white American society. For instance, we found that when youth really understood the sophistication of Anishinaabe hunting tools or watercraft, it helped them develop resilience while facing racist stereotypes of "primitivism" that pervade American culture even today. The poster session was predictably awkward, as is often the case. People drop by and stare at the poster. We give elevator speeches, and if people scrunch their faces into a position that might reflect interest, we keep talking. They try to think of questions to at least appear interested and sometimes just say "thanks" or wander off without saying a single word.

After we explained the project to one individual in some detail, how the provision of Western health care in Native communities has traditionally worked to erase traditional culture and how cultural and health interventions could be developed as mutually rein-forcing concepts (thereby having a compounding effect on community wellness), they turned to us and asked, "Well, what did you actually do?" The question flummoxed us. "Well, all of this," we stammered. "We did all of this together." For some reason, this person was not impressed with the amount of shoveling we did as we built snow-snake courses, nor with the difficulties of trying to teach archery to a ten-year-old who has never shot a bow before (and who, not without good reason, refused to take off his mittens in the sub-zero temperatures), nor with the number of mosquito attacks we endured in wetlands as we felled and quartered black ash trees to help teach young people how to make traditional lacrosse sticks, nor with the grants we wrote to help support this work. We worked hard on these projects alongside the community members.

We most certainly did not impress this person, nor did we change their mind. The more we insisted our work was community driven, it appeared (at least) that their conviction grew that we'd done nothing at all and simply were piggybacking on a community project of little to no research merit. Several years later, we still ask ourselves how important we are in this work, what our role is in this work, and how we can build better practices to enable community-driven and desired cultural shift in those communities.

For us, though, this episode illuminates what culture work is all about. Culture work is about the humility of understanding that the work we are doing is not about us. It's about working with the community to co-create something more impactful than that which any of us could do on our own. It's about critical reflection and dialogue with the commu-nity to understand what we're doing together and why we're doing it. It's about having in-tegrity and using our labor to uplift our community collaborators rather than to seek status for ourselves through this work. It's about recognizing and rejecting the authority that we've wrongfully inherited as university folk, produced and reproduced through the con-tinuation of colonial, racist, elitist, and patriarchal educational systems. It's about realizing that—in the words of the community elder and educator Carol Amour—"we are all teach-ers and all learners here" and that education is about creating knowledge and meaning to-gether, not listening to the person with the most degrees.

Culture work can mean many things and take shape in many ways. On the ground, as we see in this book, we might work with a community to document an event or teach others to do so or administer a folk arts apprenticeship program or assist an applicant in writing for one. We could connect fieldwork surveys with the development of museum exhibitions or facilitate a community-driven revitalization of Francophone songs. We might create a structure to digitize deteriorating magnetic tapes or analyze jokes collected during fieldwork through a linguistic lens in order to better understand performative ethnicity. We might run folklife festivals, find stages or recording studios for musicians, conduct research that meets a community-identified interest, or think critically about what made a particular project a success so that we can replicate and improve upon it.

All these facets of culture work are interconnected. We need people to document in order to build folklife archives and collections. We need people to organize, maintain, and enable access to these collections to reuse them. We need individuals trained to use these collections to put them into use for the best interest of the community. We need experts—whether trained at a university or, sometimes more important, trained in their community—who collaborate with professionals in museums, on state arts boards, at schools, and more, to bring their expertise into our work and to advance our shared vision. We need people to reflect critically on this work, to help us understand why something works or does not, and to challenge us to do better. Culture work is expansive, cross-disciplinary, and happening inside and outside institutions. And the more we embrace the interconnectivities of our work, the better our potential to create enduring, high-impact projects that are transformative to artists, audiences, and public humanists alike.

As folklorists, we are trained at universities to do all (or at least most) of this. And then we go on to train still more students to do all of this. When we encounter a community with a specific cultural need, we can work with a community to creatively address it. When working with Wayne Valliere, we didn't just build birchbark canoes; we helped build a program based on community need to develop more canoe builders. We connected him to universities, media, and grant funding. We brought university faculty and staff to Waaswaaganing to work in the woods with Native people, and we brought middle school students from Waaswaaganing to UW–Madison to build the canoe and experience our campus. We built a large public event around a ceremonial launch. We documented everything, amplified it, and helped build the capacity in the community to continue that work as more and more students and new canoe builders worked on the next generations of *wiigwaasi-jiimaanan* (birchbark canoes). We used the program as a way to explore issues of differences between Indigenous and non-Native approaches toward sustainable environmental management (Frandy and Cederström 2017) and of approaches toward decolonizing the hidden curricula of schools that serve to reinforce white and colonial norms (Cederström et al. 2016; Cederström, Frandy, and Connors 2018). And, most important, we connected Valliere to apprentices who were excited by all this work and began working to learn the craft themselves.

All of this is certainly in line with decades of public folklore work that predates it. There are a number of different terms to describe these sorts of efforts: public folklore, public-interest folklore, applied folklore. In other disciplines, we find translational research, community-based participatory research, or community-centered research. These terms all have their merits and different shades of meaning. We, however, are partial to the proletarian implications and humble nature of the phrase "culture work." We like its broad interdisciplinary overtones and its ability to describe how folklore and other humanities matter in other disciplines like health, ecology, social work, and education. And we like that it is not bound to the language of the historic divide between "public folklore" and "academic folklore" in our field but rather engages more broadly with the continuing endeavors our discipline has faced to better engage with inequality and political representation (Ferrell and Goldstein, forthcoming). We'd like to gently nudge at least our own language beyond this dichotomy and beyond strict disciplinary silos that limit us in more ways than we might be aware.

Our vision for this book, however, is still very much in the lineage of public folklore work. That work has been prominent in our field for nearly fifty years, and its roots trace back more than a century. Folklorists and ethnologists played major roles in the creation of open-air museums in the 1880s and 1890s in Scandinavia. Folklorists were employed in the Federal Writers Project in the 1930s to document American cultures in a broad survey project. Public folklorists were responsible for the development of the Festival of American Folklife (later the Smithsonian Folklife Festival) in 1967. Public folklorists such as Archie Green and Bess Lomax Hawes played pivotal roles in the creation of the American Folklife Center at the Library of Congress and in the expansion of a national network of state folklorists. Public folklorists used these statewide networks to build traditional arts apprenticeship programs, statewide honors, and thematic projects. Since the 1980s, especially with the founding of the Philadelphia Folklore Project, public folklorists have worked deliberately to connect traditional arts with social justice and activism (Kodish 2011). This culture work was happening outside the university in public and private spaces, in collaboration with local leaders and community experts. Today, we build on these and other intertwined legacies of culture work, as we continue to try to meet the needs of the communities we work within in order to create—to invoke Henry Glassie's (1995, 395) definition of tradition—a (better and more desirable) future out of a (continually reimagined) past.

This book comes from our work at UW–Madison, where the historic divide between public folklore and academic folklore hybridized in productive and powerful ways in the formation of the UW–Madison Folklore Program and the Center for the Study of Upper Midwestern Cultures (Widmayer and Cederström 2020). As UW–Madison alumni, we have been inundated with calls to honor the Wisconsin Idea: the notion that the boundaries of the university are the boundaries of the state. The idea, first articulated by University of Wisconsin president Charles Van Hise in 1905, was physically inscribed into our everyday life on campus. Today a monument to the Wisconsin Idea sits perched atop Bascom Hill, the symbolic and administrative center of the campus. Wedged between Bascom Hall and North Hall, a boulder and plaque feature the words of Van Hise: "I shall never be content until the beneficent influence of the university reaches every home in the state."

Such ideals are aspirational, if still unfulfilled. Enshrining an idea in stone perhaps more signifies our failures to live up to the ideal than our success at abiding by it. After all, the university still stands upon stolen Ho-Chunk land named Dejope ("Four Lakes"), with its buildings situated upon razed effigy mounds—historical atrocities for which no number of commemorative plaques will atone. And the university has advanced ethnocentric and racist theory deeply damaging to Native peoples, including Van Hise's famous contemporary at UW–Madison, Frederick Jackson Turner, whose "frontier thesis" romanticized colonization and genocide in the American West. Steeped in the discourse of beneficent public-facing scholarship, yet also in the realities of our institution's failures, we took interest in the kinds of public work that is ground up, community centered, and humble in its approach.

The Wisconsin Idea looms large: in our lives, in the state of Wisconsin, and in this book. We see value not only in the aspirational nature of the Wisconsin Idea but also in the myriad creative ways it can be put into practice by public humanists. We see it in the everyday research, public programs, and productions that folklorists and community members co-create every day. As Christine Garlough and Anne Pryor note in "Fearlessly 'Sifting and Winnowing': Folklore and the Wisconsin Idea," three themes emerge in the work of folklorists from UW–Madison: "inclusivity, civic engagement, and locatedness," all of which are "applied to folklore studies in order to fundamentally embrace the idea that public institutions are responsible to their community" (2011, 247). This Wisconsin method focuses on doing folklore work of the community, for the community, and with the community and on the vast number of creative possibilities that such processes and products entail for culture workers. For us, this is why folklore and culture work more broadly matter.

We also see it in the classroom. While pK–12 classrooms as well as classrooms on campus are not necessarily the first places we think of when we discuss public folklore, folklorists like Kaitlyn Berle, Paddy Bowman, Linda Deafenbaugh, Tim Evans, Ruth Olson, Anne Pryor, Lisa Rathje, and Mark Wagler have made them places of public culture work. Janet Gilmore writes about the Wisconsin Idea in the classroom, stating that "a mischievous public folklorist twist encourages a reverse flow of knowledge from outside the classroom into the classroom, which then loops back out again, affording a greater sense of exchange, collective knowledge-building, and social equity between the state's people and the University" (2011, 257). The use of such "looping effects" through institutions is a feature of many of the projects detailed in this volume.

We see the Wisconsin Idea within our own institutional history, as Widmayer and Cederström lay out in their history of folklore at Wisconsin (2020, 214), from John Bascom, who is credited with the idea and served as president of the university from 1874 to 1887; to his successor, Thomas Chamberlin, who said that "scholarship for the sake of the scholar is simply refined selfishness. Scholarship for the state and the people is refined patriotism" (1890, 10); to, finally, Charles Van Hise, who in 1905 gave the speech in which he made clear that the "beneficent influence" should extend well beyond campus.

Although our own "beneficent influence" might not be what Van Hise envisioned more than a century ago, we still see clearly that the culture work we do—as freelancers and contract workers, at institutions like arts boards, museums, universities, or any of the multitude of cultural organizations represented in this book—unequivocally must advance the interests of our collaborators and their community (while keeping in mind, of course, the heterogeneous constitution of any community). That is what culture work can be—what public folklore can be.

We believe that the work folklorists do on the ground and in communities can make a concrete difference in the quality of life people live. Although public folklore is not fully immune from extractive, racist, colonial, heteronormative, and misogynistic practices, it can be purposed to counter and combat these same forces in our society. We've seen firsthand how culture workers can help improve our health care systems, our environments, our educational systems, and our policies and practices for better co-management of the intercultural world we all live in and must share. While there is still significant work to be done within our own field to achieve equity, diversity, inclusion, and justice, make no mistake: we believe in this field's transformative powers and importance in creating a better world.

In his work on Indigenous research methodologies, *Research Is Ceremony*, Cree scholar Shawn Wilson writes that within Indigenous and constructivist research paradigms,

> the interaction between the investigator and the subjects is the key to this epistemology, with reality made up of socially constructed concepts that are shared. The goal is a coming together between researcher and subjects to create a mutual reality and to find common meaning in the natural world. . . . The aim of the research is to come to a consensus among researcher and subjects on a construction that is better informed than it was before. In both critical theory and constructivism, knowledge in itself is not seen as the ultimate goal, rather the goal is the change that this knowledge may help to bring about. (2008, 37)

If this is true about academic research, it is especially true for culture work. As culture workers, we do work that can exist only in partnership with communities; our communities are our peer reviewers, and our work cannot hide behind the paywalls and the specialized discourses of academic journals. While we work with communities to co-create culture, we simultaneously reflect—again in partnership with community collaborators—on what we have created. This can be a transformative process for everyone involved. As Wilson notes, "If research doesn't change you as a person, then you haven't done it right" (135).

Historically, universities and a variety of cultural institutions have been divided about the notions of research and outreach, of scholarship and service, of what is considered academic and what is considered public. Public work has been historically devalued in our field and beyond, as something "lacking" scholarly merit. And this stigmatization of public folklore has largely been entangled with academe's historical and enduring misogyny, elitism, and racism. Looking down on public work has been and continues to be looking down on the work of women, the work of scholars of color, the work of the working class, and the work of queerfolk.

As a field, we can and must do better. We stand firm in our convictions that the best scholarship and public work exist without ego, gatekeeping, and top-down modes of research and engagement. We remain committed to decentering ourselves, to using what privilege we have to elevate those who have less. We call for culture workers to remain humble, to let our work bend us on the slow march toward equity and justice, and to allow our work to transform us. When done well, public culture work can change lives, draw people together, help people cope with trauma, or just create a little bit of good in this world. We must recognize that public culture work is of equal merit with traditional academic "research." With our framing of this book as culture work, we aim to suggest that good research is public work and that good public work is research—that public work and academic work are two wings on the same bird. When both are working in tandem, culture work takes flight.

How Culture Work Works

This book presents a series of short, thematically arranged chapters that all represent inter-connected aspects of culture work. Together, this presents a lateral (but certainly not com-prehensive) cross section of the many innovative and essential culture works occurring today in our field—in all their complexities, challenges, and potentialities. Some chapters fall under classic notions of public folklore; others test the boundaries of the term by stretching it into the academic, the applied, the interdisciplinary, and the entrepreneurial. We have arranged the chapters to be in dialogue with one another: building on one an-other, complicating one another, teasing out new models of how we might work.

We have chosen to organize this volume around six themes, which we believe tell a story about our vision for culture work: where it is from, how we engage with it, and what it is for. The first two sections work in tandem to engage with existential questions about public folklore work and practice. These founding questions and answers serve as the origins of this work. "Public Folklore, Cultural Equity, and Collaboration" explores how the prod-ucts and processes of public folklore practice can advance cultural equity. "Beyond Preser-vation and Conservation" looks more specifically at the challenges that face the classic ethnographic model of documentation, preservation, and curation, inviting critical reflec-tion on our traditional public folklore methodologies. Together, these sections speak to the need to reevaluate the past, present, and future of public work both in our aspirations and in our practices on the ground.

The next two sections look at two of the most common practices employed by public folklorists. The first, "Amplifying Local Voices," involves the presentation, curation, and amplification of local voices to advocate for community needs, and the problems that emerge in tandem with amplification and ethnographic representation. The second, "Cre-ating Community," explores more directly how folklore is purposed intentionally to make sense of community, to intensify relationships, to create new economic realities in which communities can continue to exist, or to ground people to place in ways that address a community want or need. If the first is largely directed at representing community to out-siders, the second is much more dedicated to looking at the ways folklore galvanizes com-munity from within.

Finally, our last two sections focus on how public folklore intersects with history, heri-tage, and tradition. "Engaging with the Past" looks at the ways public folklorists engage with the historical past and create heritage to benefit communities in the present. And the book's final section, "Creating the Future" (a nod to Glassie's classic definition of "tradi-tion"), looks specifically at using folklore to build the world we want to live in. These tempo-ral framings (looking backward and looking forward) play upon some of the oldest academic concepts of our discipline (heritage and tradition) that still shape our work today in subtle and sometimes problematic ways as we apply them to real-world settings.

We make no pretenses that these concepts are monolithic or that they represent the en-tirety of culture work today. Rather, we feel this organization helps illuminate the existen-tial questions that gave rise to the Wisconsin method of folklore practice; the repertoire of tools, projects, and collaborations that helped shape it; and our aspirations for the future of the field. Further, these notions broadly speak to the challenges many public folklorists face today, the tools we use to address them, the reasons we engage in this work, and the exciting potentialities that emerge from this work.

We hope that we have constructed a work that will provide concrete examples and accessible theory grounded in practice. We hope that the projects in this volume will inspire readers to try to embark on their own public culture work. We hope that we have created a volume that will provide food for thought and new working and replicable models for public folklorists and community scholars currently engaged in the field. We hope that we have created a book that is of value to scholars interested in public humanities theory. And we hope that we have created a book that is at once engaging and compelling, as we continually grapple with existential questions about the value of the humanities in the twenty-first century.

PART I. PUBLIC FOLKLORE, CULTURAL EQUITY, AND COLLABORATION

Public folklore has historically been inclusive of many practices. Public folklorists conduct ethnographic documentation of cultures, sometimes focused and sometimes in broader surveys, which are stored in archives and collections. We couple this documentation with contextualizing research for varying audiences into a variety of products: an exhibit in a museum; a radio show or podcast of traditional music; a narrative stage, musical performance, or a craftsman's demonstration at a festival; a film or a website; a traditional artist's visitation of a classroom; and so much more. We help fund these projects, writing grants with communities, working at funding agencies, or pitching in out of pocket. We work between community members, artists, cultural institutions, educational institutions, and state and federal agencies to try to help our collaborators achieve a shared vision for their community and their work. In doing so, we often take the role of community organizers—to borrow an analogy rooted in labor studies—working within a community in order to help a community organize itself, find its own power and sovereignty, and work to advance its own self-interest.

The authors in this section speak to the opportunities and the challenges in this type of work. They speak to the detailed, on-the-ground work that must be done, while also noting the important, big-picture approach that culture workers must take to ensure that the public work truly is community driven. They detail how public folklore work, when done right, can enact meaningful change in the world, advancing cultural equity.

We open the section with an essay by James Leary, who reflects on transforming one fieldwork visit into something of value to an individual musician—and in fact an entire community—over the span of decades. Leary details the ongoing developments that have emerged from fieldwork decades ago, as opportunities and challenges dictate the winding path we sometimes take in our work as jacks of all trades and how there is value in returning again and again to the communities with which we have built relationships.

In her discussion of one of the United States' flagship institutions of traditional culture, the National Endowment for the Arts' National Heritage Fellowship program, Cheryl Schiele looks at the ways the program was conceived as a tool of amplification for traditional artists, despite major concerns that it would contribute to discord in these communities. Looking at a survey of National Heritage Fellows, she demonstrates numerous ways that the program has in fact amplified interest in and community around traditional arts and outlines continued challenges for the program.

David Fakunle's chapter looks at the use of storytelling from the African oral tradition with individuals in recovery from manifestations of trauma, including substance and alcohol abuse, in West Baltimore. In learning to acknowledge their stories and in being encouraged to share their stories with others, people learn to represent themselves in ways that are humanizing, empowering, and ultimately healing. Such efforts show the interdisciplinary potentials of the field of folklore and offer exciting pathways for the future of our field.

Mary Twining Baird's essay, which reflects on a collaboration during her fieldwork in the South Carolina Sea Islands, challenges our conceptions of our own value as culture workers. Pressured to collect and categorize African American folklore by her graduate advisers, Twining Baird found herself engaged in the community's struggles for civil rights and in helping it navigate new aid programs, while also documenting and learning from the traditional, collaborative, and community-oriented cultural practices of the Islanders.

In Claire Schmidt's chapter on Wisconsin prisons, she reflects on the shadow of the Wisconsin Idea in prisons. Looking at these enclosed spaces, which have radically different meanings for those who are confined inside them, those who work inside them, and the communities that house them, Schmidt argues for the value of extending documentation efforts into these spaces to better understand what the Wisconsin Idea means to the practices of the criminal justice system and how we can do culture work within these spaces.

The final chapter, written by Carmen Beaudoin Bombardier, Kim Chase, Robert Desrosiers, Andy Kolovos, and Lisa Ornstein, involves a revitalization of Francophone singing traditions in Vermont, crafted collaboratively between the French heritage community and the Vermont Folklife Center. This large-scale project involved pairing handwritten French-language songs with melodies, translating them, and re-creating the contextual singing environment of the traditional soiree within the community. Such projects represent a deliberate intervention to change the contexts in which the soiree exists, in order to reanimate not simply the singing style but also the sense of relationality that singing soirees formerly entailed.

Together, these pieces suggest that our value as culture workers is in part dependent on our ability to employ diverse tools to achieve our abstract ends of supporting traditional culture and achieving cultural equity through our methods of community collaboration. This is how culture works, not simply by presenting folklore publicly but rather by encouraging and revitalizing the contexts in which folklore lives to help give it renewed power and life in the here and now.

From a Potato Hole, Part 2

Collaboration, Repatriation, and Cultural Equity

JAMES P. LEARY

JAMES P. LEARY

DEBTS TO THE DEAD

Folklorists who have done fieldwork for many years, who have co-created images and recordings of traditional artists, who have prized human experiences over conceptual cutting edges, inevitably commune with and owe debts to the dead. Moved by the eloquent egalitarian inversion of James Agee and Walker Evans, such folklorists are compelled to do ongoing culture work that praises—in measures at once dispassionate, critical, exuberant—little-known yet famous people whose more than nominal existence in the historical record might otherwise vanish (Agee and Evans 1941). And debts assume greater dimension when public funds finance fieldwork.

Bess Lomax Hawes (1921–2009) and Archie Green (1917–2009), champions of the ongoing renascence of public folklore work that emerged in the 1970s, both understood the publicly supported fieldworker's obligations. Each had come of age in the 1930s when President Franklin Roosevelt's Depression-era public programs, particularly the Works Progress Administration, hired unemployed citizens "who collected songs, noted life stories, photographed everyday scenes, and documented vernacular landscapes" (Green 2000, 5). Archie observed philosophically: "The use of public funds for the common good is as old as our republic. . . . The songs, stories, dramas, rituals, amulets, artifacts, beliefs, and practices that intrigue us are also instruments in the construction of common wealth" (Green 2000, 6). Bess mused sagely: "When you talk with somebody about their folklore, you move quickly and often imperceptibly into a realm of deep intimacy . . . you're very apt to have made a new friend with all the responsibilities, as well as the delights, that friendship brings" (Hawes 2007, 68).

Like many "baby boom" generation folklorists, I had the honor and pleasure of knowing and working with both Bess and Archie during the last thirty-five years of their respective lives. Like many, I owe them debts that can best be paid forward. Upon becoming director of the National Endowment for the Arts (NEA) Folk Arts Program, in 1977, Bess set about establishing state folklore programs nationwide, while fostering grassroots grants initiatives that served metropolises and hinterlands alike. Consistently seeking out, encouraging, and enlisting younger folklorists, she recommended me in 1978 when a would-be grantee, Northland College in northern Wisconsin, needed a hired hand to help document diverse ethnic musicians along the south shore of Lake Superior. Subsequently I was able to borrow state-of-the-art equipment—a stereo Nagra reel tape recorder and two Sennheiser microphones—from the American Folklife Center (AFC), a division of the Library of Congress that largely owed its existence to Archie's shrewd, sustained, enlightened lobbying.

That crucial extended ethnographic experience—distinguished by collaborative documentation, funded by fellow citizens—generated further personal obligations that persist roughly four decades later. Many intensified yet broadly representative incidents from my 1979–81 fieldwork, supported by NEA/AFC, still resonate, including one entwined especially with issues of responsibility, repatriation, and cultural equity. In the early 1990s I sketched it at Burt Feintuch's behest. During his tenure as editor of *Journal of American Folklore*, from 1991 to 1995, Burt solicited succinct reflections on cultural conservation from public folklorists for an imagined special issue of *JAF*. Despite his best efforts, the plan never coalesced. Fortunately, coeditors Betty Belanus and Gregory Hansen solicited brief essays soon after from public folklorists "recounting a pivotal moment in their careers that epitomized something good, or particularly revealing" for a "Public Folklore" issue of *Folklore Forum* (Belanus and Hansen 2000, 2). Thanks to them, my orphan contribution, "From a Potato Hole," was published in 2000 and is embedded here, with elaboration ensuing.

In January 1981, I drove through whirling snow to Herbster, Wisconsin, a run-down fishing and logging village settled by Finns on Lake Superior's shore. I was working on an NEA-funded project to document traditional music and I had heard about an old accordion player.

"He lives just behind the abandoned grocery store, you'll probably find him home." I did. But before I could introduce myself, Bill Hendrickson told me, "I've been waiting for you. Come along." Hendrickson led me from his front porch around the side of the house to the cellar door. We descended, bending our necks to avoid suspended cabbage heads, dodging crates of potatoes. In near darkness I glimpsed a weathered piano accordion, a cheap tape recorder, and a dusty box of tapes. Hendrickson showed me his hands, twisted by arthritis, and explained that his hearing was fading. "I have to play loud, and my fingers don't work so good anymore. Down here I don't bother my wife."

Down in the cellar Bill Hendrickson was taping all the tunes he knew before they slipped from his memory or through his gnarled fingers. When he could no longer play them, he could hear them. And when he could no longer hear them, others could.

Driving home that day, I pondered Hendrickson's commitment. I thought about his unexpected greeting: "I've been waiting for you." Over the next few months, I recorded his biography and many of his tunes on high-quality equipment provided by the Library of Congress. I photographed him and copied his old photographs. Near the end of the grant period, I welcomed Hendrickson to a local archive where his collection had been deposited, and I organized a concert where he "played out" for the first time in forty years. Eventually I produced a recording that included one of his tunes.

Ever since, I have had the good fortune to encounter others who have been "waiting." Some wait for help finding markets, others for venues to enlighten outsiders, or for opportunities to inspire their own people. Nearly all seek some recognition that their art is worthy of practicing and preserving.

Public folklorists have the power to foster that recognition. We possess the wherewithal to be true public servants and, hence, whole folklorists. By combining our academic training as scholars and fieldworkers with our grasp of grants, bureaucracies, and the nuances of cultural productions, we are able not only to inform the general public regarding cultural traditions but also to serve as documentarians, archivists, consultants, mediators, producers, and advocates for those who practice traditions. And we do this best collaboratively, when we simply add our expertise and energy to extant desires and activities.

Put another way, we can find a better recorder than Bill Hendrickson's noisy model, a better archive than a dusty cassette box, a better stage than a potato hole. By serving those who wait, we also enhance our emotional, intellectual, political, and occupational survival. Whether based in the academy, in a state agency, in a private non-profit organization, or in the ranks of the self-employed, public folklorists are as potentially disenfranchised and endangered as the cultures and people with whom we work. In our often paradoxical and Sisyphean efforts to conjure centers out of edges, to make margins meet mainstream, we are best sustained by the support, understanding, and critical appraisal of people like Bill Hendrickson. They are not concerned with the shifting hierarchies of disciplines or with which theories currently comprise the cutting edge. They are not convinced by arguments that "fine art" is any more fine or universal than their own. Nor do they buy the notion that a folklorist's work is trivial or always "fun." Because they are serious about what they do, they are serious about what we do. And by helping them, we help ourselves.

Pointed, polemical, complying with the coeditors' call, intended to capture a moment and convey its larger implications tersely, the foregoing exhumed piece raises questions aplenty. What more do we know about Bill Hendrickson? The particular project that brought us together? The occasion for which Bill played again publicly? The related archival collection? The LP and booklet in which his performance figured? Further developments in our digital era? Ongoing issues of responsibility, repatriation, and cultural equity? I welcome the opportunity to offer more expansive answers, both belated and current.

Bark Point and Bill Hendrickson

The two interviews I did with Bill in 1981 were group sessions, instances of publicly funded "survey" fieldwork sacrificing depth for breadth, necessarily focused on acquiring brief, mostly music-related biographical information, as well as on recording performances, song and tune titles, and their provenance for future productions (Hendrickson 1981). Depth was further hindered by my relative inexperience as a documentarian and by my at-the-time rudimentary understanding of the Finnish American diaspora. What we know about Bill, consequently, owes something to those 1981 interviews but more to the man himself. In the late 1970s he wrote a series of reminiscences (Hendrickson n.d.), which were generously provided to me by his son, John William Hendrickson. Combined with data from public records and published scholarship, they offer an illuminating sketch.

William H. "Bill" Hendrickson was the child of poor yet gritty, resourceful immigrants. His father, John Hendrickson (1866–1950), grew up in Kukkola, a tiny hamlet in Finnish Lapland, on the eastern shore of the Tornio River, which forms the border between Finland and Sweden. The eldest of Heikki and Anna Kukkola's eleven children, four of whom died in infancy, John ran away from home at age twelve to herd reindeer in Sápmi (Lapland). His "parents were very religious and very strict," probably aligning with the pietistic Laestadian Lutheran movement that flourished in the Tornio Valley. When his employer died, in the mid-1880s, John toiled on fishing boats along the coast of northern Norway. Fellow fishermen were Sámi and Kven (Norway's ethnic Finns), many of whom not only flocked from the Tornio Valley to Arctic fishing grounds in the Tromsø and Lofoten areas but also made their way—like John in 1891—to the Upper Peninsula of Michigan. There he adopted the surname Hendrickson, a patronymic formed from a Swedish version, Hendrick, of his father's parallel Finnish name, Heikki. After a short stint cutting firewood on the Keweenaw Peninsula, John Hendrickson labored in an iron ore mine near Ely, Minnesota. In 1893 he married Josephine Salmela (1863–1919), a Norway-born ethnic Finn. The couple had three daughters before moving to Bark Point in Bayfield County, along the Wisconsin shore of Lake Superior, where Bill was born in 1901, followed by two more daughters.[1]

The Finnish settlement of Bark Point and adjacent Herbster was deemed "at the end of the earth" in John I. Kolehmainen and George W. Hill's vivid survey (1951, 52–53). Seventeen Finnish families arrived by boat from Duluth between 1900 and 1910, with the Kauppis, Riipis, Okkonens, and Hendricksons—all dissatisfied with mining and living conditions around Ely—first among them. Acquiring stump-strewn, logged-off public lands in parcels of from twenty to forty acres, they eked out a living like the Hendricksons, who farmed and took in boarders, with John earning cash in winter lumber camps, by offloading freighters in an era when Lake Superior rather than roads connected communities, and by fishing commercially with gill nets and set hooks. Young Bill did farm chores, attended school through eighth grade, then joined his father fishing from his early teens through his late twenties, when additional opportunities emerged.

Dismayed by unfairly priced groceries and dry goods, Finns created the Finnish Farmers' Cooperative Mercantile Association in the early twentieth century, with a network of locally run outlets, open to all comers, throughout the western Great Lakes region. In 1915, the Orchard Valley Co-op store in Herbster was launched. Subsequently, *Pelto ja Koti* (Farm and Home), a socialist monthly published in Superior, Wisconsin, to serve the cooperative movement, reported in its August 1917 issue that nineteen settlers in the Bark Point/Herbster community were entering into an agreement with the flourishing Iron River Co-op "about 27 miles" to the south, to establish a Herbster branch: "Erikoisena etuna on, että kauppa pääsee heti sellaisen voimakkaan liikkeen yhteyteen kuin Iron Riverin liike on, siten saaden nauttia suuresta ja hyvin järjestetystä ostovoimasta" (The special advantage is that the store immediately gets connected to a powerful store like Iron River's, thus enjoying great and well-organized buying power) (Anonymous 1917, 255; see also Alanen 1975, 111–17; Lawless and Reynolds 2005, 40). The results were less than rosy, as

Bill Hendrickson and Peter Soronen display their catch, mid-1920s. (Copy photograph by Sue Ellen Smith. Courtesy of University of Wisconsin–Madison Library.)

Iron River's Co-op "took too large a margin of the profits" (Anonymous 1917, 255). In the early 1920s, with local roads built and automobiles accessible, Herbster shareholders sold out to one of their own, Victor Korppas, who ran the store from 1924 until Bill Hendrickson bought it in spring 1928.

The Depression era's hard times followed. With his father's help, Bill ran the store, continued to fish commercially, logged and milled lumber, and bought and sold land to make a living. In 1937, he married Aileen Irene Kallio (1904–94), the daughter of Finnish immigrant farmers who, like the Hendricksons, had left fraught working conditions in Minnesota's iron ore mines, traveling by boat to settle northwest of Washburn, east of Herbster/Bark Point, in Bayfield County. Their children, John and Irene, were born in 1938 and 1940, respectively. Seeking prosperity, Bill leased his store following World War II, and the family moved to Idaho. With Roy Wegelius, a trucker and fish dealer and a neighbor from Herbster, he purchased eighty timbered acres in Clearwater County, near Orofino, where he logged and established a sawmill before selling his interests in the early 1950s to work once again as a Herbster-based logger and storekeeper.

Music, song, and sociability complemented hard work in the Herbster/Bark Point Finnish settlement. Bill recalled that his dad, like several neighbors, "played mouth organ" and "could sing real good." He learned Finnish songs and tunes from his parents, from neighbors at local house parties, from Finnish 78 rpm records brought in by boat from Duluth, and from lumberjacks like Bill Kauppi and Uno Okkonen, who sang "dirty ones" that "come over from Finland." When Bill showed promise on a cheap harmonica, his dad bought him a "two-row 'cordeen,'" and he swapped tunes with Eino Okkonen, a lifelong pal and fellow button accordionist (who figures prominently in Janet Gilmore's contribution to this volume). In 1919, community members banded together to build Bark Point's "Finn Town Hall," featuring a stage for plays and musicians, "a darn good lunch room" in the basement, and sufficient floor space for public meetings, basketball games, and dances that attracted folks of various cultural origins from nearby settlements along Lake Superior: Herbster, Cornucopia, Port Wing.

Dance musicians included both locals and such regional Finnish performers as the legendary recording artist Viola Turpeinen, a piano accordion virtuoso from Iron River, Michigan, who began making records for Victor in the late 1920s and toured the Finnish hall circuit through the 1950s (Leary 1990). Like Hendrickson, Turpeinen first learned to play a button accordion limited to two keys, but she made her virtuoso's mark with the more modern, versatile, fully chromatic piano accordion that became the prevailing instrument for professional musicians in the 1920s. Dazzled by her playing, Bill and Eino pooled their resources to buy a used piano accordion from a traveling performer (Leary 2012). From the late 1920s through the 1930s, they sometimes entertained hall dancers, taking turns as solo piano accordionists. Their harmonica-playing neighbor Helmer Olavi Wintturi reminisced that, in their youth, Eino was "a great one for waltzes, fox trots, and two steps," while Bill preferred "peppy" Finnish polkas, jaunty schottisches, and haunting mazurkas (Wintturi 1981).

Thriving through the 1930s, Bark Point's Finn Hall was eventually torn down, after falling into gradual disuse as the immigrant generation aged and youngsters left seeking

Bill Hendrickson with his co-owned piano accordion, 1920. (Copy photograph by Sue Ellen Smith. Courtesy of University of Wisconsin–Madison Library.)

employment or for military service during World War II. Bill's public playing diminished too, as family and work responsibilities increased. Yet he continued to play for his own interest, sometimes at home, sometimes during idle storekeeping spans. In the late 1960s, when inexpensive cassette tape recorders became available, Bill bought one and began recording songs and tunes recalled from his youth (Hendrickson 2019).

COLLABORATION ELABORATED

Bill Hendrickson's performances and related reminiscences would have remained hidden treasures if not for the fortunate coincidence of NEA Folk Arts grants programs and a pair of regionally grounded entrepreneurial visionaries at Northland College in Ashland, Wisconsin: Stuart Lang and Marina Lachecki. A history professor on the verge of an extended fundraising career for private colleges in the Upper Midwest, Lang founded and directed Northland's Special Student Programs (1978–84), winning and overseeing grants focused on Native American Studies, community education, folk arts, and more. Lachecki, a native of the region captivated by its musical diversity and inclined to public service, currently serves as a United Church of Christ pastor, but in the late 1970s she was Northland's Community Specialist.

From July 1979 through June 1981, Lang and Lachecki secured and coordinated two consecutive one-year NEA Folk Arts grants focused on "Ethnic Music in Northern Wisconsin and Michigan." Year one emphasized infrastructure, training, and preliminary documentation, as Lachecki especially consulted with diverse community members regarding leads on local Croatian, Czech, Finnish, French Canadian, German, Hungarian, Italian, Norwegian, Ojibwe, Polish, Russian, Slovak, Swedish, and Swiss performers; enlisted the Northland music professor Joel Glickman and several undergraduate students willing to conduct fieldwork; and, following recommendations from NEA Folk Arts staff, brought in veteran professionals on staggered, short-term bases to offer training, establish documentary and archival practices, and do collaborative field research. They included three ethnomusicologists: Fredric Lieberman of the University of Washington, editor of *Ethnomusicology*; Thomas Vennum Jr. of the Smithsonian Institution; and Frank Gillis of the Archive of Traditional Music at Indiana University. Richard March, prior to his hiring as Wisconsin's first folk arts coordinator; Ellen Stekert of the University of Minnesota; and I served as consulting folklorists. I subsequently took a year's leave from the University of Kentucky faculty to work full-time for year two. With assistance from a talented Northland student, Matthew Gallmann, I continued with field documentation, oversaw completion of the resulting archival collection, and worked with local organizations to involve traditional musicians in a series of public events. Overall, more than one hundred musicians or ensembles from thirteen ethnic traditions were documented on more than one hundred hours of recordings, augmented by field notes, tape indices, and photographs (Leary 1981b; Gilmore et al. 2007).

Our awareness of and contact with Bill Hendrickson occurred in a circuitous, fortuitous, incremental fashion familiar to field researchers. During my two-week, year-one consulting stint, Joel Glickman and I traveled to the fishing port of Cornucopia, Wisconsin, on July 31, 1979. We informed a luncheon gathering of local seniors about our project, then met with my childhood pal Phil Stack, who was living in the area that summer. A friend of Phil's in turn told us about a harmonica-playing Finn—Helmer Olavi Wintturi (1910–82), the son of Finnish immigrants hailing respectively from Kaustinen and Seinäjoki in Ostrobothnia—who lived westward along Lake Superior in the Bark Point/Herbster area. Once there, a local bartender directed us to Olavi's place, where we spent three pleasant hours touring his farmstead, photographing, interviewing, and recording tunes (Glickman 1979). I visited him again on August 8, 1979, for another recording session; and then returned in year two on January 7, 1981. During that third visit, Olavi encouraged me to talk with his brother-in-law, Eino Okkonen, and with Eino's old friend and fellow accordionist Bill Hendrickson. And so I found Bill in the cellar that afternoon among cabbages, potatoes, canned goods, and audiocassettes.

Six days later Matt Gallmann and I interviewed both Bill and his friend Eino, at the Okkonen's home. At the time I had a Marantz Superscope cassette recorder, but I was looking ahead to the arrival of professional equipment, thanks to a gratis loan program from the American Folklife Center. January 13 served, consequently, as a rehearsal for a follow-up session with the aforementioned stereo Nagra open-reel recorder and Sennheiser microphones. In the meantime, Bill and I exchanged correspondence regarding both Finnish tunes he might play and relevant photographs we might copy.

On February 17, Matt and I returned and recorded a score of tunes from Bill, all but one instrumentals, which spanned his repertoire. The dozen Finnish numbers included unnamed dance tunes—a waltz, two schottisches, a mazurka, and more—circulating in aural tradition; a pair of "dirty" lumberjack songs with the informal titles "Mama näki" (Mother saw) and "Kymmenen sormea" (Ten fingers); the stirring marches "Kerensky," associated with Alexander Kerensky, a leader of the Russian Revolution ultimately ousted by Lenin's Bolsheviks, and "Vapaa Venäjä" (Free Russia), the marching song of "Red Finns" during the 1919–20 Finnish Civil War; "Raatikkoon" (To Ghost Mountain), a twin-tempo couple dance popular in Finnish halls on both sides of the Atlantic; and pieces learned from 1920s recordings by well-known Finnish Americans. Among them were Juha Koskelo's version of J. Alfred Tanner's "Orpopojan valssi" (The orphan boy's waltz) (Columbia E-9032, 1923); Leo Kauppi's 1926 waxings of "Maailman Matti" (Matti of the world) (Columbia 3032-F) and "Kuuliaiset Kottilassa" (The dutiful at Kottila) (Columbia 3040-F); Hiski Salomaa's "Tiskarin polkka" (The dishwasher's polka) (Columbia 3045-F, 1927); and the accordionist Viola Turpeinen's driving "Kauhavan polkka" (The Kauhava polka) (Victor 8058, 1928). Not surprisingly, considering heavily Swedish Port Wing just to the west, Bill played the ubiquitous schottische "Johan på Snippen" (Johan of the snipp), as well as the enormously popular "Nikolina," recorded in 1917 and several times thereafter by the Swedish immigrant Hjalmar Peterson, who performed as Olle i Skratthult (Olle from Laughtersville). Bill also offered a reel from an Irish fiddler, Dan Daly, and even sang a fragment from Daly's version of the British broadside ballad "William Taylor" (Laws 1957, 208). And he favored us with "Little Brown Jug," "Mocking Bird Hill," and "Loose Talk," from American country music sources.

Soon after, I wrote field notes and created a tape index for the recording session, while making a cassette tape "listener copy" that corresponded to the original reel-to-reel "preservation

From left to right: Jim Leary, Bill Hendrickson, Aili Hendrickson, and Marina Lachecki examine
an archival index card for documentation on Bill. Northland College Archives, August 1981.
(Photography by Janet C. Gilmore. Courtesy of University of Wisconsin–Madison Library.)

copy." In July 1981, Washburn, Wisconsin, held its quinquennial "Homecoming." Established in
1929 as a reunion for the area's far-flung and rooted folks, the Homecoming was an opportunity to feature local Finnish musicians. I organized and emceed an outdoor session featuring
reminiscences from and performances by the brothers Reino and Hugo Maki from Washburn's Finn Settlement, as well as their Bark Point/Herbster neighbors Olavi Wintturi and
Bill Hendrickson. As hundreds thronged appreciatively around Washburn's City Hall, Bill
summoned fiery tunes and vivid recollections conjuring bygone Finn Hall dances.

In August 1981, Marina Lachecki and I invited all the musicians figuring in 1979–81 NEA
Folk Arts grants to the opening of the Ethnic Heritage Sound Archive and Resource Center, situated in the Wisconsin Historical Society's Area Research Center at Northland's
Dexter Library and housing original and user copies of recordings, tape indexes, field
notes, and photographs documenting their musical lives and performances. Bill and his
wife, Aili, attended, and they were gratified to see his tunes and musical memories archived
for posterity. Thanks to the Wisconsin-born ethnomusicologist Philip Bohlman and his
mother, Florence Bohlman, funds from the estate of her parents, Vere P. and Rosa M.
McDowell, supported Lachecki as part-time archivist in 1981–82 "to index the collection's
recordings and further the archive's mission to make the collection available to the area's
residents, recorded musicians, and researchers" (Gilmore et al. 2007).

In 1984, I received a related grant from NEA Folk Arts to produce a double LP and an accompanying booklet distilling significant performances from and providing lyrics, translations, song and tune notes, biographies, and context for the 1979–81 recordings. Mastered by Dave Hill of Inland Sea Recordings in Superior, Wisconsin, and issued in 1986 by the Wisconsin Folklife Center (soon to become the Wisconsin Folk Museum) in partnership with Northland College, *Accordions in the Cutover: Field Recordings of Ethnic Music from Lake Superior's South Shore* included fifty-eight performances, twenty by Finns, two of them instrumental renditions of "Vapaa Venäjä." Lyrics for this march urged common folk to break the emperor's chains and seek freedom. Since the Russian Revolution also ended Czarist rule over Finland, "Vapaa Venäjä" resonated strongly with immigrants who had left an oppressively colonized Finland only to struggle for survival in America. Continuously performed, including in the twenty-first century by the Finn Hall Band of Minneapolis, it appeared four times on 78 rpm recordings by immigrant artists, with versions by Otto Pyykkönen (Columbia 3003-F, 1924) and Jukki Ahti (Victor V-4068, 1930) the best known. Hendrickson's powerful rendition invokes the feel of Ahti's recording.

When producing *Accordions in the Cutover*, I consulted and corresponded with key participants, some of whom helped with transcribing and translating non-English lyrics. And the completed double LP and booklet were sent to each performer. For years thereafter, I thought foolishly that my work on this project and my obligations to the friends and acquaintances with whom I had worked were completed. But inevitably, as the poet W. B. Yeats put it, "things fall apart." Bess Lomax Hawes's prophetic public folklore admonition echoed too, as eventually "all the responsibilities, as well as the delights, that friendship brings" took hold.

Repatriation and Cultural Equity

In the decades that followed summer 1981, a series of changes threatened prior carefully established archival and commemorative efforts with the same fate that had befallen Bark Point's razed Finn Hall. By 1996, the Wisconsin Folk Museum, producer and distributor of *Accordions in the Cutover*, was plagued by debts and ceased existence. The original reel-to-reel tapes held in Northland College's archives had begun to deteriorate, requiring specialized preservation processes. Northland College had transferred "files, slides, copy cassettes, and other related materials to the Northern Wisconsin Heritage Connection," which in turn made a deposit agreement with the Wisconsin Historical Society's newly established "History Center and Archives at the Northern Great Lakes Visitor Center to provide access to the collection" (Gilmore 2007). And, in 2009, the Northern Wisconsin Heritage Connection disbanded as an organization. What to do?

In summer 1996, Steve Sundell, Wisconsin Music Archives curator at University of Wisconsin–Madison's Mills Music Library, and I made the six-hundred-mile roundtrip journey to Northland College, where, thanks to Marina Lachecki's assistance and advocacy, we acquired all the 1979–81 original field recordings for the Mills collection. By that time I had worked with Mills to create the beginnings of a professionally equipped and staffed "sound lab" for creating multiple, backed-up digital copies of historic analog recordings in a full range of formats. Meanwhile, with Janet Gilmore's assistance, ownership of the Wisconsin Folk Museum's stock of documentary LP and cassette productions was transferred to the Folklore Program at the University of Wisconsin. In 2009, the Wisconsin Historical Society became the custodian of files, photographs, and other materials formerly entrusted to the defunct Northern Wisconsin Heritage Connection. Thanks to prolonged efforts by Mills Music Library and the Center for the Study of Upper Midwestern Cultures, Mills acquired the aforementioned documentation from the Wisconsin Historical Society in 2015.

Such concerted, convoluted efforts, successful though they were, nonetheless amounted to little more than shifting stuff from one potato hole to another. To boot, *Accordions in the Cutover* was out of print. Confronted again with what to do, we sought public funding.

During his sometimes fraught 1997–2001 tenure as chair of the National Endowment for the Humanities, the folklorist Bill Ferris sought, through a matching grants program, to create ten major regional public humanities centers situated throughout the United States, with each center engaging in education and outreach through research, public programs, and the use of new technologies. Although vigorously opposed by high-culture advocates across the political spectrum, as well as by antipluralists from the ideological right, Ferris nonetheless succeeded ultimately in opening up NEH considerably to applications from public folklorists and their populist, pluralist, globally engaged, yet regionally grounded allies. At the University of Wisconsin, thanks to support from the College of Letters and Science, we successfully won federal grants and UW Alumni Research Foundation funds to create the Center for the Study of Upper Midwestern Cultures (CSUMC) in 2001. A coalition of folklorists and linguists, CSUMC is committed to research, archival collections development, and collaborative public programs focused on the languages and folklore of our region's diverse peoples. Subsequently working with UW's Mills Music Library, we won a three-year grant from the Preservation and Access division of NEH in 2016.

Our grant, Local Centers/Global Sounds: Historic Recordings and Midwestern Musical Vernaculars, has resulted in free searchable public access—maintained and backed up by the UW Digital Collections Center—to thousands of sound recordings, tape indexes, field notes, and photographs documenting "the Upper Midwest's culturally diverse traditional musicians" (https://uwdc.library.wisc.edu/collections/localcenters/). In fall 2017, the first of many collections, "Ethnic Music in Northern Wisconsin and Michigan," was launched; it included the full booklet and sound files for *Accordions in the Cutover*, all the aforementioned 1979–81 documentation created with NEA and Northland College support, and, of course, the sessions with and images of Bill Hendrickson and his friends from the Herbster/Bark Point Finnish Settlement. Through ongoing outreach efforts, we are actively spreading the word about each component of the larger collection. Commencing by contacting musicians' communities and such descendants as John William Hendrickson, who kindly, invaluably provided otherwise elusive documents illuminating his father's life, we are also encouraging educators, researchers, and contemporary performers to draw on the collection in myriad ways.

Who knows what comes next? Perhaps the foregoing forty-year saga has concluded, or perhaps unforeseen developments loom. The latter seems more likely. Paraphrasing an old gendered proverb, a public folklorist's work is never done. I doubt we'd want it any other way.

Rescuing voices and artistry otherwise consigned to potato holes, conserving and repatriating related documentation, and, most important, arguing for the enduring worth of the lives and deeply humanistic productions of "ordinary" yet also "famous" men and women requires painstaking effort, public support, many partners, and years of persistence. Indeed, it requires the essential culture work that public folklorists can do, have done, and must continue to do. Otherwise, how else can we as citizens of a diverse, stratified, and sprawling nation know fully who we are? Bill Hendrickson and his spirit and others like him will always be waiting for our best efforts.

NOTE

1. All direct quotations in this section, unless otherwise indicated, are drawn from Bill Hendrickson's reminiscences and my interviews with him. Further information is drawn from both cited sources and public records accessed through FamilySearch.org and Ancestry.com.

The National Endowment for the Arts National Heritage Fellowships

A Reflection on the Roots and Impact of a National Cultural Heritage Honorific Program

CHERYL T. SCHIELE

The National Endowment for the Arts National Heritage Fellowships program is an essential primer on cultural heritage in the United States. In its maturity, the program's ideals stand confidently next to venerated fellowship programs that recognize excellence in arts and culture. As master artists, Heritage Fellowship recipients illuminate the fruits of human tenacity and serve as cultural custodians. Reflecting on the program's impact, I am drawn not just to its origin story but to how the Arts Endowment's development elevated folk and traditional arts in the US arts ecology.

HISTORY

1965–76: An Arts Agency for All Americans

Before establishing the National Endowment for the Arts and its sister agency, the National Endowment for the Humanities, in 1965, US government policymakers began exploring arts policy for the first time since the Works Progress Administration (WPA) of the 1930s. The Arts Endowment's founding differed from those of the WPA's Federal Arts Project and Federal Writers' Project. The New Deal programs employed jobless artists and writers during a national economic crisis (Bauerlein and Grantham 2009, 1). The newly established Arts Endowment characterized its goals as providing access to artistic excellence for all Americans (Bauerlein and Grantham 2009, 6).

Leading up to the nation's Bicentennial celebration and tasked with strengthening its support of culturally relevant expression of American life, the Arts Endowment buttressed multicultural and traditional arts activities, including jazz, folk, and ethnic music, folk arts and crafts, and expansion arts directed at minority and ethnic groups (Binkiewicz 2004, 186). Since folk arts was listed as an artistic discipline in the legislation that created the agency, the formation of an official division suggested that the Arts Endowment assuredly "opened its doors to greater aesthetic diversity, [paying] greater attention not only to contemporary art but also to traditional folk art" (Binkiewicz 2004, 186).

1976–82: Bicentennial Shift

In the late summer of 1976, the folklorist, folk singer, and educator Bess Lomax Hawes was winding down her term as deputy director of the Smithsonian Institution's Bicentennial Festival of American Folklife on the National Mall and intended to return to a teaching post at California State University–Northridge. Instead, she switched gears after being invited to join the staff of the National Endowment for the Arts. Hawes's personal decision coincided with critical inflection points, both professionally and nationally.

Hawes followed in the footsteps of Alan Jabbour, a folklorist and noted fiddler who directed the agency's folk arts program fund from 1974 to 1976. During Jabbour's tenure, folk arts projects were integrated into larger disciplines (e.g., visual arts, music, theater). In 1976, he left the agency to lead the newly established American Folklife Center at the Library of Congress, a federal institution for the preservation and study of folklore whose creation was boosted by increased interest in American ethnic and regional diversity in the run-up to the Bicentennial (Groce n.d.). At the Arts Endowment, Hawes's leadership adeptly ushered in a stand-alone Folk Arts Program by 1978.

A conversation about Japan's Living National Treasures program between Bess Hawes and the Arts Endowment's second chairperson, Nancy Hanks, sparked the idea behind the National Heritage Fellowships. After World War II, Japan's years of reconstruction in its government and economy led to rapid industrialization, and Western popular culture gained greater influence on its society to a worrying degree. In 1950, the Japanese government enacted the Cultural Properties Protection Law to support and designate culturally significant and centuries-old artforms as Important Intangible Cultural Properties (IICP). The tradition bearers of IICP, popularly known as Living National Treasures, received a yearly stipend to sustain cultural knowledge and skills through personal development, transmission, public performance, documentation, and archival efforts.

Adapting this idea to a US model was not without debate, but it appealed to staff and panelists, who deliberated over the issue for five years. Questions arose early about the adverse effects of singling out an individual with a prominent honor and monetary award. At present, the Arts Endowment defines folk and traditional arts as artistic disciplines and traditions "learned as part of the cultural life of a community whose members share a common ethnic heritage, cultural mores, language, religion, occupation, or geographic region. These traditions are shaped by the aesthetics and values of a shared culture" (National Endowment for the Arts n.d.[a]). If these overarching principles were realized, then how would highlighting individual accomplishments support the elevation of shared culture? Bess Hawes inscribed the oral history of the period: "Would not this public recognition have a dampening effect on the artists not selected and, thereby, on the art form itself? Would it not create jealousies or stimulate unhealthy competition? . . . We considered the effect of such an award on an individual carver in a remote New Mexico Hispanic village, as well as on Serbian American urban steelworker/musicians in a neighborhood band. . . . I believe I am accurate in stating that in all these many discussions nobody ever exactly wanted to do it, but everybody thought it ought to be tried" (2008, 164).

Daniel Sheehy, who worked under Hawes and who later became the program's director (1992–2000), reflected on the discussion in the 2017 documentary *Extraordinary Ordinary People*: "There was a real concern for the benefit of the field that if we're going to recognize individuals, it better be done right and in a way that it doesn't have the opposite effect. And frankly, it must be said that the power of Bess Lomax Hawes's personality, her charm, but at the same time with a certain kind of enormous presence, was a powerful argument in support of the [idea]" (Govenar 2017).

In 1980, the debate was resolved when the National Heritage Fellowships were established under chairman Livingston Biddle, third chairman of the Arts Endowment. In 1982, fifteen traditional artists were inducted as the first class of National Heritage Fellows, the highest honor awarded to folk and traditional artists by the US government.

PROGRAM MANAGEMENT

Founding Principles

Ultimately, Bess Hawes's version of a US "living national treasures" program differed from Japan's focus on sustaining inherently Japanese cultural practices. At the time, the Arts Endowment supported transmission of cultural knowledge through direct apprenticeship grants before the program was moved to the state level. The National Heritage Fellowships program was designed as a celebration of traditional arts within a culturally pluralistic society. Cultural equity, a trademark of the program from its inception, implicitly propelled inclusivity into the national arts ecology.

In the Heritage Fellowships' fourth year, Bess Hawes opened the program book with a director's message that captured the burgeoning excitement of the program's attributes. She noted that as a new endeavor, the Heritage Fellowships were "the most appreciated and applauded," positing that "perhaps because they represent to Americans a vision of themselves and of their country, a vision somewhat idealized but profoundly longed for and so, in significant ways, profoundly true. It is a vision of a confident and open-hearted nation, where difference can be seen as exciting instead of fear-laden, where men and women of good will [*sic*], across all manner of racial, linguistic and historical barriers, can find common ground in understanding solid craftsmanship, virtuoso technique and deeply felt expression" (Hawes 1985, n.p.).

In this vision lies the complexities of a culturally pluralistic society perpetually under construction. It provides a space for common purposes, similarities, and differences. Hawes's vision can be seen today when the Fellows meet one another in Washington, DC. At the National Heritage Fellowships Concert, the audience can also witness goodwill in an exuberant fashion. A glowing review of the 2008 concert extolled the finale's spontaneous performance by all the recipients dancing together as "one of the most miraculous things" seen on stage (Gauvreau Judge 2008).

Nomination Process

Though the nomination process has changed through the years, the guidelines have remained largely the same and are untethered to conventional grant application requirements. The Arts Endowment accepts nominations from the general public, apart from nominating oneself. In other words, one does not need to be a folklorist or have a graduate degree, nor does one need to be affiliated with a nonprofit organization or personally affiliated with a nominee to submit a nomination.

The staff assembles a review panel of cultural experts—folklorists, cultural anthropologists, ethnomusicologists, traditional artists (including past Heritage Fellows), and one layperson—to review the submissions. The panel discusses and evaluates nominees according to several criteria: artistic excellence, significance within a particular artistic tradition, and contributions to living cultural heritage (National Endowment for the Arts n.d.[a]). In the first decade, as many as seventeen Fellowships were awarded in a single year, but the number has hovered between nine and twelve a year for the past two decades. The panel's recommendations are reviewed by Arts Endowment senior staff and the National Council on the Arts and approved by the agency's chairperson. Beginning in 2000, the agency added a Bess Lomax Hawes Award designation to one of the Fellowships. Recipients of the Bess Lomax Hawes Award are individuals who embody Hawes's remarkable comportment, vision, and advocacy as a folklorist, teacher, documenter, and promoter. In the director's message of the 2000 program book, Daniel Sheehy summarized this singular distinction as an "award [that] honors individuals who have had major positive impact on American folk and traditional arts in ways other than their own artistry" (2000, n.p.).

The elements to ensure an in-depth review include a nomination letter that makes a compelling argument, comprehensive biographical information, informative letters of support, and high-quality work samples. Framing a traditional artist in the context of their tradition is vitally important. The configuration of a nomination is not inconsequential, and, though the nominator does not receive compensation for making one, a successful nomination proves to be its own reward. Each spring, successful nominees receive a phone call from Washington, DC, notifying them of once-in-a-lifetime recognition for the gifts they have bestowed upon the nation. It is, for some, a complete surprise. In recent years, US senators and congressional representatives have assisted the Arts Endowment with notifying their constituents of the honor and grant award.

Honoring Traditional Arts

From the outset, the Arts Endowment created a way to honor and draw public attention to the excellence and representative diversity of folk and traditional artists. In the early years, the monetary award began at $5,000 and then was increased three times, to $10,000 (1993–2002), $20,000 (2003–8), and $25,000 (2009–present). The ceremony and performances were originally held in conjunction with the Smithsonian's Festival of American Folklife on the National Mall. Subsequently, the festivities moved to different Washington, DC, area venues and expanded to include a formal banquet, currently held in partnership with the Library of Congress and its American Folklife Center in the Great Hall of the Thomas Jefferson Building.[1]

Since 1983, the National Council for the Traditional Arts (NCTA), a nonprofit arts organization and producer of the peripatetic National Folk Festival, has deftly managed the events surrounding the ceremony, and the Arts Endowment has secured private funding to support formal activities, publications, and multimedia projects. Throughout the years, a combination of public and private events, formal and informal, has been integral to honoring and drawing public attention to the Heritage Fellows.

Typically, the Fellows attend a White House or Capitol Hill awards ceremony, embassy receptions, and a formal banquet, and perform or demonstrate their traditions in a public concert. The concert has been held at Ford's Theater, the George Washington University Lisner Auditorium, the Music Center at Strathmore, and Sidney Harman Hall, home to the Shakespeare Theatre Company. Both American Routes, with host Nick Spitzer (the concert's master of ceremonies from 1997 to 2014), and WDUQ Radio have created radio broadcasts and specials for later broadcasts. Most recently, during the COVID-19 pandemic, the Arts Endowment produced a one-hour film to celebrate the Fellowships in an online broadcast, forgoing in-person events. This marked the first time in the program's history that honorees were unable to travel to Washington, DC.

Many staff and contractors at the Arts Endowment, the NCTA, and the American Folklife Center have facilitated an atmosphere of intimacy and grandeur for the honorees. In turn, Heritage Fellows have reciprocated with gifts of extraordinary cultural wisdom that connect everyone through their songs, crafts, and stories—especially at times of national crises.

When the September 11, 2001, World Trade Center and Pentagon terrorist attacks occurred, the Heritage Fellowship festivities were scheduled for the following week. Barry Bergey, who worked under Bess Hawes and later became a folk and traditional arts director (2001–14), recalled: "In my conversation with the artists in the days following the tragic events, I sensed their resolve to carry on. . . . On the night of the concert, after a moment of silence, taiko master Seiichi Tanaka performed a cleansing ceremony using flute and bell, and following a procession and ritual drumming, the National Heritage Fellows assembled on stage as the audience welcomed them with a thunderous ovation" (2002, 3).

In 2017, bomba and plena master Modesto Cepeda attended the festivities between two major hurricanes. He and his daughters arrived just in time to attend the orientation. They were unsure whether the rest of the family would make it after Hurricane Irma grazed Puerto Rico, causing flooding and a major power outage. Fortunately, his multigenerational family of more than twenty people arrived that evening, tired from the journey but ready. Once orientation introductions and formalities were out of the way, spontaneous plena music and dancing erupted from the Cepeda family. Buoyed by their unflagging spirits and excitement for the days ahead, the cordial orientation became a celebration with dancing and singing. When the family returned to San Juan at the end of the week, Hurricane Maria followed. In the aftermath of back-to-back hurricanes, Cepeda and his daughter Gladys formed their own relief effort for the Villa Palmeras community in San Juan, home to their bomba and plena school (Jervis 2017).

IMPACT

Let Me Count the Ways

Between 1982 and 2021, the Arts Endowment awarded 458 National Heritage Fellowships. Though that number is significant, it is also deceptive. Even as it swells from year to year, 458 is an accounting figure, and it cannot fully reveal the scope of the program. As an independent federal agency, the Arts Endowment judiciously tracks the number of grants awarded, in addition to producing detailed financial and congressional reports. If we dig deeper, we find that an informal count shows that roughly 225 unique cultural traditions have been honored, as well as master traditional artists in all fifty states, the District of Columbia, and four US territories (Guam, Northern Mariana Islands, Puerto Rico, US Virgin Islands).

Viewed as a collection, each yearly class of Heritage Fellows has a magnifying effect on cultural identity and place. Human migration and immigration patterns across states emerge, revealing noteworthy familial and occupational folklife, as well as local and regional cultures that inform national and international histories. Viewed in relation to one another, as surveyed by Steve Siporin, author of *American Folk Masters: The National Heritage Fellows*, recipients may be categorized as inheritors, innovators, or conservers. Viewed as a whole, the Heritage Fellows have a democratizing effect that raises their communities to national importance. Measuring impact may be harder to quantify but easier to illustrate when you assess the value of local culture, language, community, personal and professional feats of excellence, and legacy.

The initial concerns about how the Fellowships would be accepted by the artists and their communities dissipated within the first decade. In a retrospective, Barry Bergey captured this in his introduction to the class of 1990 Fellows. He highlighted Douglas Wallin, an Appalachian Ballad Singer from Marshall, North Carolina: "In the early years of the nomination process, someone had nominated the Sodom-Laurel areas of Madison County, North Carolina, an area rife at one time with unaccompanied ballad singers in the Anglo tradition. Ballad collector Cecil Sharp visited this region . . . and described it as 'a community in which singing was as common and almost as universal a practice as speaking.' Douglas Wallin, whose mother had been documented by Sharp, served as a representative of this tradition" (Bergey 2011, 26).

A year earlier, in 1989, the Arts Endowment awarded the National Heritage Fellowship to a group for the first time. The Fairfield Four, a quartet-style, African American gospel ensemble from Nashville, Tennessee—the number of whose members ranged from four to seven throughout the years—received one Fellowship as an ensemble. Two years earlier, in 1987, the husband-and-wife team Emilio and Senaida Romero, tin embroiderers from Santa Fe, New Mexico, received a Fellowship together. To date, thirty-six Fellowships have been awarded to duos, trios, ensembles, spouses, sisters, and brothers in crafts, music, dance, and oral traditions.

The Fellows often interpreted the Fellowship as posthumous formal recognitions of their cultural forbearers. At the 2004 banquet, Gerald Bruce Miller, a Skokomish elder, stated, "I want to extend my gratitude on receiving this award to all of our ancestors who left us the gifts that we exhibit today; the gift of the song, the gift of the dance, the gift of the story, and the gift of creativity. As long as we keep these traditional arts alive, we speak for our people" (Bauerlein and Grantham 2009, 59). In 2005, Michael Doucet, a Cajun fiddler and composer, reflected, "You know, it's interesting—it's a national award but it really comes down to your community and what you do for your community. I was very fortunate to be around when a lot of people born before 1900 were still alive—the 'old-timers,' as we call them now. I think that's where most of my inspiration comes from. It's really a process of a continuation—I wouldn't be getting this award if it wasn't for people who came before me" (Bauerlein and Grantham 2009, 59).

Recognition of this kind may also validate and bring about clarity of purpose, commitment, or recommitment to maintaining a practice in a dynamic world and in sometimes challenging circumstances. There are countless stories of how this has come to pass, including in the areas of professional and personal support, new traditions, language preservation, and legacy.

PROFESSIONAL AND PERSONAL

1990 National Heritage Fellow Natividad "Nati" Cano (1933–2014)

The mariachi band leader Nati Cano received a National Heritage Fellowship for his mastery in the mariachi tradition as well as for his teaching in his community and for sharing with audiences worldwide. Cano, a musician since age six, learned mariachi from family members and eventually toured professionally in Mexico. In 1961, he settled in Los Angeles and formed the group Mariachi Los Camperos. Cano opened La Fonda restaurant in 1967 and expanded the reach of his band and mariachi by providing a place to perform regularly. Before receiving the National Heritage Fellowship, he performed around the world as part of a group and with pop stars like Linda Ronstadt. Revered among mariachi musicians and students, Cano was a mentor, competition judge, and benefactor to mariachi festivals and "mariachi-in-education" programs. He received a 1990 National Heritage Fellowship at age fifty-seven. Already a venerable figure, after receiving the honor, Cano demonstrated a deeper dedication to mariachi traditions. In 2000, he created the City of San Fernando Mariachi Master Apprentice Program, which is still active today. He won a United States Artist fellowship in 2006 and a Grammy award in 2009. Since his passing, his group, Mariachi Los Camperos de Nati Cano, continues to perform and teach to honor his legacy.

1995 National Heritage Fellow Wayne Henderson

Recognized worldwide as a master luthier whose clients include the late Doc Watson and Eric Clapton, Wayne Henderson has also made a significant contribution to his community. Born and raised in Grayson County, Virginia, a rural hotbed of great old-time musicians and singers, Henderson learned to play the guitar from family and friends at a young age. In the mountains of southwest Virginia, he developed a unique and masterful picking style while playing with and admiring the guitarist and singer E. C. Ball. The son and nephew of craftspeople and something of a craftsman himself (he whittled and made his own toys), Henderson felt compelled to make his own guitar. He admired a Martin guitar like the one Ball owned, so his father introduced him to a luthier in North Carolina. From that point forward, building guitars became his life's passion while he maintained a thirty-two-year career as a mail carrier for the US Postal Service. In a 2015 interview, he recalled how he enjoyed working for the postal service, saying, "I got to travel around through up every hollow in here. . . . I knew everybody and I got to do it in my own community right here" (Reed 2015). The same year he received the Fellowship, he inaugurated the eponymous Wayne Henderson Festival, which includes a contest whose winner receives a Henderson guitar; all the proceeds go to a youth education scholarship fund. Henderson chose to build a new workshop with his Fellowship grant funds. He acknowledged that he "[used] that Heritage Award every day, ever since 1995" and continued, "I've certainly made use of it. I wouldn't've had that nice shop out there if it hadn't have been for that . . . that's a cool thing and I've always appreciated that" (Reed 2015). After finishing her degree in environmental law and discovering the resale cost of her father's guitars (more than $20,000), Henderson's daughter, Jayne, asked him to build her a guitar for resale so she could pay off her student loans. Instead, he taught her how to build one. Jayne took to the task and now builds guitars in the studio alongside her father (Henderson and Henderson 2016).

2013 National Heritage Fellow Sheila Kay Adams

A seventh-generation ballad singer, storyteller, and musician, Sheila Kay Adams received the National Heritage Fellowship at a significant point in her life. Born and raised in the Sodom Laurel community of Madison County, North Carolina, an area renowned for unaccompanied ballad singing, she learned songs from her great-aunt Dellie Chandler Norton, who taught her the old style of "knee-to-knee," or sitting across from another person with knees almost touching. She also learned songs from other notable singers in the community, including Dillard Chandler and the Wallin family (including 1990 Fellow Douglas Wallin). A respected clawhammer banjo player and storyteller, Adams had a deep knowledge of her community and heritage that allowed her to carve out a career in music, publishing, and some film work. In 2009, tragedy struck when her husband and musical partner took his own life as a mental health complication of Lyme disease, which had infected his brain. In a 2013 interview with the Arts Endowment after receiving news about her Heritage Fellowship, Adams recalled this painful time, saying, "My world fell apart right there. Everything about my world just went" (Reed 2013). Four years after her husband's death, Adams was in a different place. The Heritage Fellowship, she explained, "came at a time when I was healed enough from that trauma to be able to accept it because I had just made the decision to move on, to try to move on with my life. . . . I don't know how many recipients of the NEA award have ever said this award validated my existence on this planet and really truly and honestly from their heart meant it, but for me, this award validated my existence" (Reed 2013).

New Traditions
2005 National Heritage Fellow Chuck Brown (1936–2012)

Recognizing Chuck Brown, affectionately known as the Godfather of Go-Go, was a bold nod to an innovative African American vernacular musical tradition. In the early 1970s,

Chuck Brown developed a new sound called "go-go," a funky percussive groove blending Latin beats, jazz, and soul. Go-go's development at that time defined a cultural community in and around the District of Columbia, a dynamic city whose rapid shift in racial and economic demographics was just beginning (Tatian and Lei n.d.). After performing in a few local bands, Brown founded his own, the Soul Searchers. They enjoyed a few hits from their first two albums, *We the People* and *Salt of the Earth*. In 1978, he released his third album, *Bustin' Loose*, as Chuck Brown and the Soul Searchers. The single of the same name went to the top of the Billboard R&B charts and lifted Chuck Brown and go-go into the national spotlight. The virtues of go-go music as a traditional art form lie in its close ties to the community. Brown's signature live performances featured call-and-response interactions with the audience, coupled with driving, continuous percussive beats that glued people to the dance floor. "The popularity of the new sound spread quickly and resulted in a fierce competition between local D.C. bands. In fact, there were dozens of go-go bands that popped up . . . in the mid-1980s" (Reynolds and Zimmerman 2015). When Brown accepted his 2005 Heritage Fellowship as a cultural heritage pioneer, go-go music stood forty years strong. Since his death, the Chuck Brown Band has continued to perform regularly, carrying forward its founder's legacy. Go-go music and culture have been enveloped in the District's identity and have continued amid the economic development and gentrification that have displaced many Black Washingtonians. In April 2019, a grassroots campaign called #DontMuteDC mobilized to assert the District's cultural identity following a new resident's noise complaint that temporarily "muted" an electronics store, considered a fixture in the Shaw neighborhood, that was known for playing go-go music outdoors since 1995. In February 2020, galvanized by residents, musicians, and politicians, Mayor Muriel E. Bowser signed legislation that enshrined go-go as the official music of the District of Columbia.

LANGUAGE AND LEGACY
2006 National Heritage Fellow Esther Martinez (1912–2006)

Like many Native American children in the 1920s, Esther Martinez, also known as P'oe Tswa (Blue Water), was forced into a government boarding school for Native children. The goal of these institutions was to rupture the students' ties to their Native language and culture. In practice, the school punished Martinez when she spoke Tewa, her native tongue, spoken in Ohkay Owingeh Pueblo. But she persevered and retained her language despite the hardships. She returned to Ohkay Owingeh, married, raised a family, and taught Tewa language and culture to her family and community. Martinez became a custodian of the Tewa language, through storytelling, teaching at the San Juan (OhKay Owingeh) Day School, and developing a compilation of Tewa dictionaries for each of the six Tewa dialects. In her seventies, she presented Tewa stories in English, sharing the Tewa way of life to general audiences at festivals around the country. Revered as an elder in the community for her many decades of tireless advocacy, Martinez received the National Heritage Fellowship for language preservation and storytelling at age ninety-three. Sadly, on the trip home from the ceremonies, Esther Martinez died in an automobile accident when a drunk driver struck the family's car. Congress renamed a bill after her posthumously and passed the Esther Martinez Native American Languages Preservation Act in 2006. Administered by the Administration for Native Americans (ANA) in the Department of Health and Human Services, the Act offers three-year grants to support community-driven language immersion and restoration programs in Native schools, early childcare centers, or cultural centers. At ANA's 2017 Native Languages Summit, held at the Indian Pueblo Cultural Center in Albuquerque, New Mexico, recipients of the Esther Martinez Immersion Grants celebrated the tenth anniversary of the Act's ratification. grantees and reflected on and shared their work, triumphs, challenges, and best practices.

I had the pleasure of introducing Matthew Martinez, grandson of Esther Martinez, before his presentation at the opening of the summit. When we chatted briefly before the presentations, Matthew and I reminisced about the 2006 Fellowships, which included the soul and gospel singer Mavis Staples as a recipient. Martinez spoke fondly of Mavis and her sister Yvonne. Staples and his grandmother were paired in a dressing room at the concert venue. He recalled that his grandmother enjoyed Mavis's humming. "Perhaps it was comforting, which created an automatic bond," he posited. "I think because they were together as Fellows but, more importantly, as an inherent recognition of their spirits by their artistic and activist pathways they followed and created." After Martinez's death, Arts Endowment staff attended the funeral, and the Fellows reached out to the family. Staples continued to keep in touch. When scheduled to perform in New Mexico, she would invite the family to attend her show. "We joined her backstage to visit and share memories of time in DC and life in general," Matthew recollected.

LEGACY WITHIN THE PROGRAM

There are several honorees who have familial and generational connections to previous Fellows. Mavis Staples was the first recipient to represent familial ties when she received a 2006 Heritage Fellowship eight years after her father, Roebuck "Pops" Staples (1998). The conjunto musicians and brothers Santiago Jimenez Jr. (2000) and Leonardo "Flaco" Jimenez (2012) each received the Heritage Fellowship, as did the Ghanaian drummers and brothers Obo Addy (1996) and Yacub Addy (2010). As another example of generational connections, Bounxeung Synanonh, a Laotian khaen player and 2016 recipient, accompanied a 1991 recipient, Khamvong Insixiengmai, a Laotian Lum singer, at his Heritage Fellowships concert. The Yiddish musician Michael Alpert, a 2015 recipient, performed with Beyle Schaechter-Gottesman, a Yiddish singer, poet, and songwriter, at the 2005 concert for her Fellowship. The Tlingit ceremonial regalia maker and 2016 recipient Clarissa Rizal apprenticed under Jennie Thlunaut, a 1986 recipient, when Thlunaut was in her nineties and Rizal in her twenties.

In an example of cultural heritage transmission conjoined, family members of two 1982 Heritage Fellows designed and fashioned new award medallions in 2016. A citizen of the Osage Nation, the late Georgeann Robinson, received a Heritage Fellowship for her intricate ribbonwork stitched by needlepoint onto clothing worn by Osage people for important social gatherings. Drawing inspiration from one of Robinson's designs, Jami Powell, Robinson's great-granddaughter and a scholar and documenter of Robinson's legacy, worked with her mother, Lisa Powell, Robinson's granddaughter, on a lanyard for a medallion.

NEA National Heritage Fellowship award designed by Lisa Powell and Jami Powell (lanyard) and Carlton Simmons (medallion). (Photograph by author.)

The late Philip Simmons, a master blacksmith, received a Heritage Fellowship for his ornamental ironwork. A notable feature of Charleston, South Carolina's visual and cultural aesthetic, Simmons's remarkable wrought-iron gates, fences, balconies, and freestanding sculptures grace many of the homes, gardens, and businesses in the city and its surrounding areas. Carlton Simmons, an apprentice to his uncle Philip at age thirteen, designed a heart motif medallion with the signature scrolling filigree found in Philip Simmons's designs. The new medal linked the legacies of Georgeann Robinson and Philip Simmons to each other and those legacies to present-day recipients, combining past, present, and future (National Endowment for the Arts 2016).

FUTURE

Challenges

In addition to the National Heritage Fellowships, Japan's Living National Treasures program inspired similar systems worldwide, including in South Korea, Thailand, and the Philippines, among others (Stefano 2019). Between 1993 and 2003, the United Nations Educational, Scientific, and Cultural Organization (UNESCO) conducted a program called Living Human Treasures (LHT), modeled after the Important Intangible Cultural

Properties systems of East Asia. Along with honoring master traditional artists, the primary goal of LHT was to "ensure the transmission of knowledge and skills which these bearers master and to thus ensure the perpetuity of the expression of the intangible cultural heritage concerned" (United Nations Educational, Scientific, and Cultural Organization n.d.). Following UNESCO's guidelines, member states and territories customized systems built on the tenets of safeguarding cultural heritage by providing a financial subsidy to support skill-building, transmission, documentation, dissemination, and archiving. Although UNESCO no longer actively manages the program, the guidelines are still available on its website, and new LHT systems are still being enacted throughout the world.

Upon adopting the LHT guidelines, the Conseil québécois du patrimoine vivant (CQPV) in the province of Quebec, Canada, announced its first class of Maîtres de traditions vivante (Masters of Living Traditions) in May 2020. Accompanying the announcement, the CQPV held a colloquium to discuss the impact of these systems, focused on six programs from around the world (Burkina Faso, Chile, the Flanders region of Belgium, France, Japan, and the United States). Many of these national programs provide yearly stipends that run for from one to three years, and recipients have deliverables and requirements related to transmission, documentation, and promotion. The US model differs in that its one-time grant award is unencumbered by requirements or obligations upon acceptance. Instead, the Fellowship serves as a recognition of the importance of maintaining intangible cultural heritage; by default, though not expressly so, the program catalogs cultural practices in the United States. Interestingly, the Arts Endowments' folk and traditional arts division has supported similar safeguarding tenets of LHT, such as transmission, documentation, and dissemination, on a much broader and decentralized scale for more than forty years.

Largely thanks to a network of statewide folklife programs that were launched in the lead-up to the creation of the National Heritage Fellowships, folklorists and public folklore specialists situated at state arts agencies, universities, humanities councils, and nonprofit organizations have conducted extensive fieldwork across the nation since the 1970s. Tasked with sustaining traditional arts through apprenticeship grants, exhibitions, publications, festivals, and collaborative partnerships, state folklife programs provide a robust influx of nominations derived from this fieldwork (Molloy and Murphy 2017, 36). Presently, a rough estimate puts the number of apprenticeships managed throughout any given year at five hundred. As such, nominations and recipients are likely to be from states and regions with a solid folklife program.

At its start, there was worry that the program might exhaust the number of candidates for the Fellowship. Though this has not been the case, the number of nominations has fallen. In 2020, panelists reviewed only 106 nominations as opposed to a pool of 200 or more in the 1990s and early 2000s. This decline, even as the number of statewide folklife programs rises, is concerning.

Furthermore, a general analysis of demographic figures reveals interesting data on cultural heritage and gender gaps. While a thorough analysis of ethnicity or race has never been conducted, there are striking features that one can draw from the data recorded. Broadly, men have been nominated and ultimately received the accolade twice as often as women. As an example of cultural analysis, Latinx and Southwest-region Hispanic cultural traditions represent roughly 13 percent of all Fellowships awarded. Of that 13 percent, 22 percent focus on Mexican/Chicano traditions, 22 percent on Tejano traditions, 20 percent represent Puerto Rican traditions, and 20 percent represent New Mexican/Coloradoan traditions. The remaining 16 percent (in order of prominence) represent Cuban, Brazilian, Peruvian, and Argentinian traditions.

Increasing and diversifying the pool of nominations will aid in closing such gaps. Without nominations of Guatemalan or Salvadoran traditional artists, for example, there will not be Heritage Fellowships recognizing these cultural heritages. Moreover, raising the visibility of the program in a saturated online environment and soliciting more nominations from underrepresented demographics will be consequential.

Prospects

The National Heritage Fellowships is approaching its fortieth year, and consideration of past accomplishments will be valuable. Nevertheless, it will be equally important to evaluate the effectiveness and impact of the program on master artists and living cultural heritage.

Overall, the goal of bringing greater visibility to cultural knowledge and practices by highlighting extraordinary individuals and groups has garnered a great deal of local interest, while mainstream media attention has ebbed and flowed. There is still more that could be done to gain high-profile visibility like that accorded the MacArthur "Genius" Fellowship and to maintain a connection to and draw on Heritage Fellows as ambassadors of the program. In the past few years, Fellows from previous years have been asked to participate in the ceremony and banquet as performers and/or guest speakers.

In 2019, the Arts Endowment examined folk and traditional arts grants and fellowships awarded from 2013 through 2015 in a report called "Living Traditions: A Portfolio Analysis of the National Endowment for the Arts' Folk and Traditional Arts Program." The report included a policy action item about the program's impact: "Host a national gathering of National Heritage Fellows in 2022 to mark the 40th anniversary of the program, in advance of the Semiquincentennial (America 250). This gathering would celebrate the strength and diversity of the nation's many cultural communities, would generate symposia and other public events focused on cultural sustainability and social cohesion, and would gather information about how the Heritage Fellowships have positively affected individuals and their cultural traditions" (National Endowment for the Arts 2019, 3).

Throughout the years, stalwart ethnographers, documenters, curators, and folklorists have developed programming and collections about the Heritage Fellowships. There are several major works in the form of publications, articles, documentaries, educational guides, and museum and online exhibitions, including but not limited to *American Folk Masters: The National Heritage Fellows*, a publication by Steve Siporin; Masters of Traditional Arts books and educational guides by Alan Govenar of Documentary Arts and Paddy Bowman of Local Learning; the story map *Masters of Tradition: A Cultural Journey across America*; an interactive online portal by Marjorie Hunt and Arlene Reiniger at the Smithsonian Center for Folklife and Cultural Heritage; and the *Folk Masters: A Portrait of America*, a publication by Tom Pich and Barry Bergey. To dig through any one of these collections is a feast for the senses that may reveal enlightening observations. In 2016, Clifford Murphy, folk and traditional arts director (2015–present), proposed that the "nation of immigrants" trope cannot encapsulate the "complex tale of community journeys . . . we are also a nation of indigenous peoples, a nation of migrants, refugees, and descendants of enslaved Africans" (2016, 7).

As one takes in their breadth and diversity, the National Heritage Fellowships illuminate a national identity stitched together like a handmade quilt. I am reminded that quilting is sometimes a communal effort, as it is done by 2015 Heritage Fellows Mary Lee Bendolph, Loretta Pettway, and Lucy Mingo of Gee's Bend, Alabama. Sitting and singing together, the quilters of Gee's Bend strengthen a quilt by cutting away tattered edges and reinforcing weak spots. Every stitch supports the backing and batting to the top layer's mosaic patchwork, providing texture and pattern, seen and unseen.

In his ceremony remarks, 2017 Heritage Fellow Phil Wiggins, a country blues harmonica player and longtime musical partner of the late John Cephas (1989 recipient), referred to this analogy when he spoke about the patchwork quilt his mother had given him to take to college. "That patch quilt is an amazing symbol of this country that we call home," he explained. "I'm so happy to be a part of this celebration because it celebrates what that patch quilt symbolizes, it symbolizes the patch quilt of beautiful deep cultures from all over the world that came to make up this country, that we call home."

Note

1. The National Heritage Fellows Collection is archived at the American Folklife Center of the Library of Congress.

The Lion's Side

DiscoverME/RecoverME and the Utilization of Storytelling for Emotional Transformation

DAVID OLAWUYI FAKUNLE

Until the lion tells his side of the story, the tale of the hunt will
always glorify the hunter.

—Zimbabwean proverb

The story that I love to tell at the beginning of workshops or sessions is called "The Precious Stone." In the story, there was an elder woman who would walk through the forest every day, taking in all the ambience it had to offer. They said it was in the forest where she felt closest to the Divine. On one journey she came across a stone unlike any she had ever seen before—she immediately knew there was something special about it. So she picked it up, put it in her pouch, and kept walking. As she continued her daily pilgrimage, the elder woman came across a young man, and as the young man approached, she could see that he was hungry, tired, thirsty, and in need of assistance. Once they connected, the young man begged for any help the elder woman could provide, but those desires went away the moment he laid eyes on the precious stone. He then asked if he could have the stone, and without any hesitation, thoughts or words, the elder woman took the stone out of her pouch, gave it to the young man, and kept walking. As they were heading in opposite directions, the young man was infatuated with his new stone and thought to himself that all his wishes would now be possible . . . but after a while he stopped. After a brief moment, in which some say he took in the forest's ambience for the first time, the young man ran to catch up with the elder woman and asked her one question: "May I have whatever it is inside of *you* that allowed you to give me this stone so freely?"

Regardless of the many times I have told that story, it never fails to remind me of those "elder women" in my life that shared their "precious stones" with me, be it their knowledge, their wisdom, or simply their love. I am unapologetically a product of those precious stones, many of which remain the guiding principles in my life today and the foundations of the work I do. If not for all the things inside them that allowed them to give to me so freely, I would not be who I am, nor would DiscoverME/RecoverME exist. I am honored to share our story, and perhaps you will find the genesis of this journey through art and public health to be quite an interesting tale.

PROLOGUE

It goes by many names: serendipity, the alignment of the universe, karma, good luck, God's favor. I believe in it all. As such, it is important to acknowledge that this story was written long before I ever realized. It started with my aunt Val, who is the first great storyteller in my life. During the more than thirty years of her recovery from substance abuse, my family and I have supported her, and many years of my childhood included Saturday afternoons at her Narcotics Anonymous meetings. Laying around at home watching television was preferable for me, but instead I was fortunately exposed to the healing properties of storytelling through the narratives of women undergoing their journeys to and through recovery. There was nothing like Aunt Val's anniversary of sobriety, where sponsors, sponsees, family, and friends from all over Baltimore would crowd into a dingy basement on Maryland Avenue, just to hear her *tell her story*! The message was always powerful and important for those in recovery, but it was her energy and charisma that made her captivating. Even to this day as an adult, hearing Aunt Val recount her life before, during, and after addiction is an experience I cherish.

Perhaps the reason I enjoy telling "The Precious Stone" so much is because I have my own version of the story, in which a powerful elder woman gave of herself so freely to me: her love, her wisdom, her dedication, and her near-infinite repository of tales. That woman's name is Mary Carter Smith, whom many Black storytellers in the United States and I reverently call "Mama Mary." Back when I was ten, driven by simple juvenile jealousy, I had the gall to tell a story I had heard a week or two before on *Griot for the Young and the Young at Heart*, her radio show on Baltimore's WEAA 88.9 FM: The Voice of the Community. Unbeknownst to me, Mama Mary was in the audience to hear it. She was so impressed that she mentioned this little boy on her radio show the following week. It was not too long afterward that she invited this little boy onto her radio show to read stories. Not too long after that I was performing with her, telling the stories she taught me . . . and I have been honoring her memory ever since. She was the grandmother figure I needed, and she gave me much more than I could have imagined. Part of me believes she knew what I could become, even if she would not be here to see it herself. But I know her spirit watches over me . . . it must, for I will always need her guidance. I said at the celebration of her would-be one-hundredth birthday that I would never let her down . . . and I mean it with every fiber of my being.

THE BEGINNING

I told them, they are on the ground floor of something potentially extraordinary
and revolutionary, and I sincerely want them to seize this opportunity. I think they are
starting to believe me now.

—Project Tell-a-Tale notes, December 20, 2013

Once upon a time, as many stories begin, I was in my first year of doctoral study at the Johns Hopkins Bloomberg School of Public Health, taking a course titled "Gaps and

Opportunities in Public Mental Health: A Systems Approach." Unlike my other courses that were heavily focused on theory, construct, and analysis, this course was practical and introduced students to the harsh reality of treating mental health in the United States. As part of the course, I was required to participate in a practicum that would pair me with a local organization that addressed mental health challenges, and many of the projects involved the skills I was learning as a budding public health researcher. However, my instructor found out that I was a storyteller—this was never confirmed, but I am certain the teacher's assistant, who was also my officemate, told the instructor about my ability, which she found out through a talent show held earlier in the term. Again, serendipity. As a result, a special project was offered to me: to partner with Recovery in Community (RIC), a substance abuse recovery center located in West Baltimore, to teach their clients storytelling. I admit, I was hesitant only because as a new doctoral student in the best public health school in the world (they will tell you, trust me), I felt compelled to remain focused on opportunities that would enhance my skills as an epidemiologist. But it did not take much for the instructor (e.g., providing the course grade) to convince me to give it a try.

As simple as it may have sounded to the instructor, it presented quite a challenge to me. While I was a seasoned storyteller, I had never taught other people how to tell stories in the formal sense. When I think back to learning under Mama Mary, I realize that my skills came from reading stories, telling them, and receiving feedback. I did not think that would necessarily work well with adults in recovery, so I went to the one person I knew could help me figure it out: my mother. A storyteller in her own right, my mother had experience teaching the art as part of a student literacy program and therefore could assist me in creating an instructional approach for the basics of storytelling within a finite period. After much discussion, we crafted a sixteen-week curriculum that, despite the limited time presented during the course, we felt would at least show the feasibility of teaching storytelling in the recovery space. Most important, the course would provide a healthy environment in which individuals could comfortably express their innermost thoughts and emotions with the intent to bring perspective, inspiration, and hope for fellow individuals who might be enduring similar circumstances in silence.

The next major step was to solicit buy-in from RIC. The existing relationship my instructor had with the center bought me only so much leeway. The sad truth was that, despite being a Black man born and raised in Baltimore and having engaged in work focused on elevating people in my city for much of my life, I found that my association with Johns Hopkins University immediately introduced doubt and suspicion about my intent. I was not naive to that reality and understood the reaction, as Hopkins's institutions have a tumultuous history of exploitation, mistrust, and outright dehumanization of Baltimore's Black citizens, particularly those living in East Baltimore—where I am from. The story of Henrietta Lacks is the most well known of the injustices perpetrated under the Hopkins name (Skloot 2010), but it seems like every family in Baltimore has its own tale. My mother recalls being warned not to stay out at night unless she wanted people from Hopkins to snatch her up. To this day, she believes there was some truth to that warning. Skepticism acknowledged, I assured both RIC's executive director and the clinical director that this project was not for research purposes but solely to benefit the clients: no recordings, no notetaking, no personally identifiable information—just me and my stories. After clarification was provided and permission granted, I was finally given the opportunity to share my proposal with the Level 4 clients, people furthest along in their recovery journey.

When my mother, Aunt Val, and I first met with the Level 4 clients, many things were immediately apparent. First was their inquisitiveness: they asked many questions about the project, all of which I was happy to answer. Second was their perceptiveness, as many of the clients asked about my expectations of them for this class project. I said that they would not have to do anything that made them uncomfortable, nor would I proceed with any aspect of the project without their awareness and understanding, which they appreciated. In retrospect, it was an example of how individuals from historically divested environments may consciously or unconsciously feel obligated to cater to positions of perceived power, including researchers. Given the history of oppression and marginalization in the United States—white people against people of color, wealthy against the poor, educated elitists against common folk—there is validity to the idea of inherited generational trauma. Therefore, it was important to explicitly state and exude the belief not only that they had power but that it was respected and that the only thing the project aimed to accomplish was to strengthen that power for the benefit of themselves and others going through an experience that could literally mean life or death. Additionally, it was important to share the reverence we had for both storytelling and the journey of recovery, and that is why it was imperative that Aunt Val share her story along with ours. As they say, we had skin in the game, and someone with her credibility within "the rooms" could not be ignored. With optimism and excitement, the clients unanimously gave us permission to work with them.

I was somewhat nervous the first official night of Project Tell-a-Tale, especially because my mother was away in Morocco. But the anxiety quickly receded as I began the instruction. The clients really enjoyed a story I told called "The Real Meaning of Peace" and appreciated the message, which they picked up very quickly. That did not surprise me, given their experiences. There was real wisdom surrounding me. We then talked about the actual plot of the story, after which I encouraged the clients to retell the story in their own way. One woman agreed to tell, but it was not the story I told: it was her own. I was immediately captivated: her delivery, her tone, the content. It had everything that makes a good story, and, most important, it was *her* story . . . just like Aunt Val's at her anniversary of sobriety. I gave her the highest praise because I knew that is what the clients needed to hear. That was the point, and I told them so. It is that kind of story that could help bring someone into recovery and therefore a story that needs to be told and heard. I truly believe that was the turning point of the meeting, the point where everyone "got it."

Clients talked about the importance of honesty and being real about their stories. One gentleman talked about how he was able to bring silence over a typically rowdy Narcotics Anonymous meeting with his story, so it became apparent that these were the people that could drive this project to great heights. One woman talked about how she grew tired of hearing sob stories in NA meetings, which I could understand. Substance abuse takes people to depths that should never be seen, so negativity is fairly pervasive at meetings. I realized it may be more beneficial to talk about the stories of recovery, about redemption. I also discussed the power of emphasizing positive qualities in a person that are inherent, even during substance abuse. They really enjoyed that. I encouraged them to incorporate a virtue into their stories, because it could be the message that best reaches the audience. That night was memorable and set the tone for our relationship, because there was an acceptance that I truly wanted what was best for them as *they* dictated it.

Discoveries through DiscoverME/RecoverME

My mother and I continued to have sessions at RIC long after the course ended (I received an "A," by the way). Much like the forest was for the elder woman in "The Precious Stone," that rowhouse at 31 North Fulton Avenue became my refuge every Thursday evening . . . and the clients became my healers. To this day, I say I received more from them than they ever received from me: as someone going through the rigorous grind of a doctoral program, the pending birth of my first child, the myriad opportunities that fell at my feet, and just the curious journey that is life, those two hours I spent with them were my moments of peace, understanding, comfort, and love. The clinical director, who probably exhibited the most skepticism about me at the beginning, became a mother figure in my life and still is. The clients were my biggest cheerleaders, my wisest teachers, my most steadfast support. It was the space where I shared my fears, confusion, frustration, and dreams. Conversations that I longed to have with my mother, subjects I never felt comfortable broaching with my now-wife, tears I never knew I needed to shed, I was happy to bring to the clients . . . because they always helped me. They always loved me. They showed the benefits of being open with all of who I am. I grew to appreciate that my RIC family did not care about my degrees, my accolades, or my prestige. I could not hide behind any persona or created perception about myself, nor did I want to. I was not Dr. Fakunle: I was just David. It was experiential evidence of what makes DiscoverME/RecoverME effective: the accepted vulnerability of the facilitators. Even the word "facilitator" is taken lightly because for anyone who has experienced a session, *everyone* participates. There is no hierarchy, no power dynamic, just a group of people trying to figure it all out together while using stories as our vessels. The role of the facilitator is merely to serve as a catalyst through the folktales they share, and it is magical how people become empowered to share their own stories. I can attest.

As the journey continued, my mother and I realized that the fluid nature of substance abuse recovery was not conducive to utilizing a stringent curriculum. Level 4 clients were allowed more freedom to participate in programming as they saw fit, which meant that some would be in and out of our sessions for weeks at a time. There was also the consideration of people who would participate in the sessions under court order for drug and/or alcohol-related offenses, meaning that their time at RIC and with us was limited. Additionally, we realized that there was no need to "teach" storytelling. Rather, our value came in the consistent utilization of storytelling as the modality by which clients could connect with their own life stories. If there was any teaching from us, it was to recognize and acknowledge the positive intrinsic qualities exuded by characters within the stories we facilitators told, in the clients' personal narratives, and in the actions of others. For many it was a revelation how we were able to see the good in them no matter how deprived of positivity they felt their story was, but once it was revealed they refused to let it go. As a result of these iterations, the sessions became continuous, with no beginning or end, and people could join and leave as they liked. A healthy consequence was that clients were empowered to take greater charge of our sessions, including getting new participants up to speed about the stories we were discussing. There were nights where my mother and I did not tell any stories but rather asked a question that became the discussion of the evening, nights when the clients had a story they felt compelled to share. It was truly a potpourri of art, culture, philosophy, religion, spirituality, comedy, history, sociology, public health, and rhetoric.

Stories from Their Hearts to Ours

There are two stories that my mother and I recall as if it were yesterday: one was told and one was experienced in real time. There was one client, Ms. Carmen (name changed out of consideration), whose natural talent for storytelling was quickly apparent to us every time she spoke. During one session she crafted a narrative about a woman being stuck in the rain with her children. As much as she did not want her kids to get wet, there was nothing she could do because *she* was the cause of the rain. Desperate, the woman went to her mother for help. The mother was more than happy to bring her grandchildren out of the rain but informed her daughter that she must address the cause of the perpetual downpour before she could retrieve her children. The woman went through the process, and eventually the rain ceased. Finally, she returned to her mother's house under clear skies and with an umbrella by her side. With appreciation and pride, the grandmother gave her grandchildren back to her daughter, and they were able to move forward with a brighter journey. That story was how Ms. Carmen described the work she had done to overcome her struggles with alcohol abuse, losing and ultimately regaining custody of her children. To this day, I have yet to hear a narrative that so beautifully and clearly captured an essence of addiction's impact—and recovery's impact—on oneself and those one loves. The other stories imprinted in my memory is that of Mr. Rob (name changed out of consideration). Mr. Rob joined our sessions after spending twenty-six years in prison. I cannot and do not want to imagine what horrors he saw and experienced during his incarceration, and so it was no surprise to me that during the first several sessions, Mr. Rob would not say *a word*. My mother and I would always encourage him to share, but he refused, so we decided to let him know that we and the group would be open to his insight when he was ready. After some time of adjustment and growing comfort with us and life outside prison, Mr. Rob finally spoke. It was not many words, but it was the highlight of that evening! Soon Mr. Rob would say a little more and a little more, and after a while we could not get him to stop talking! He smiled, he laughed, and he shared his wisdom with us and the group. For as much as he did say, we did not get all the details of his incarceration, nor did we press him about that time. I was just grateful he trusted us enough to say anything. However, it further empowered me to believe in what this work could do. If storytelling can help a man achieve some semblance of emotional freedom, after spending more than a *quarter century* locked away from society and surviving some of the worst manifestations of what humanity does to its own, then I was confident that storytelling could help *everyone*.

What Remains to Be Discovered

As many revelations as there were during the first years of DiscoverME/RecoverME, there were just as many questions. The first question that came to mind was whether anyone else had done similar work, and whether (and especially how) they went about chronicling it. My initial searches resulted in a limited number of articles, with most focusing on the utilization of storytelling in support groups, particularly for cancer patients. Surprisingly, despite the inherent nature of storytelling within twelve-step programs for substance abuse recovery, there were less than a handful of papers that investigated its impact. I am certain now, as I was then, that the lack of literature around storytelling's utility as a healing practice is tied in large part to my second major question: how exactly do you measure the influence of storytelling on healing?

One may wonder why this question is so difficult to answer, and the reason is because of the unhealthy overreliance on "objective" quantitative data. The relative ease of converting information to numbers has unfortunately led to a notion within the sciences that if it cannot be added to an equation, then it does not exude rigor or impartiality. However, as I hope every person in the sciences would agree, there is only so much of the human experience that can or *should* be quantified. Rather, it must be qualified. The initial push aside, much of the impetus of DiscoverME/RecoverME was the fact that people, let alone those experiencing substance abuse and recovery, are too often and too easily quantified, which removes so much of their quality. I remember telling RIC clients that in my field, people would see only their age, race, sex, and the fact that they were current or former drug users. I would then ask, "Is that all there is to you?" Every single time, I received the answer "no." I have resisted the temptation to utilize traditional instruments that aim to "quantify" qualitative experiences such as surveys and questionnaires because they would introduce my personal biases and perspectives as the researcher and would not allow for the depth and dynamics needed from participants to truly understand what it is about storytelling that aids the healing and recovery process. However, I am encouraged by the effectiveness and efficiency of group concept mapping technology, which was developed to allow for rigorous quantitative analysis of authentic human reflections and perspectives. It is good to know that other researchers recognize the importance of conducting precise and meticulous research while honoring the law of humanity, to which we are all bound.

How the Story Continues Today

> We don't know how the story will end, but we do know that you have richly blessed our lives . . . thank you for your time. Thank you for your commitment. Thank you for showing your love and concern.
> —The Recovery in Community (RIC) Family

I always had the feeling DiscoverME/RecoverME could be something special, but I never imagined that it would be as impactful as it is, especially as such a young organization. My mother and I continue to serve people looking to recover from any manifestation of trauma, be it adults dealing with diagnosed mental disorders or youth on the brink of intense interaction with the criminal justice system. Additionally, we have had opportunities to introduce people to the art and science of storytelling via workshops, allowing us to partner with educational institutions, nonprofit organizations, governmental agencies, social change initiatives, health systems, and even an international conglomerate. In many presentations I play a video that we put together of some RIC clients telling bits and pieces of their narratives, which we did to help get financial support to create a book of their stories from the sessions. We didn't make enough to do the book, but that video is the lasting tangible legacy of DiscoverME/RecoverME's genesis at RIC. Whenever my audience and I watch the video and I get to see the faces of so many who gave this idea an opportunity to flourish, it brings me to tears. Aside from my eternal gratitude to those prophets and prophetesses, I miss them. I hope their lives are better and happier, because I know mine is due to their imprints on our hearts. The overwhelmingly positive responses to our work have inspired me to focus my public health research on storytelling, not only as a healing practice for mental and emotional health but also as modality by which rich qualitative data are acquired from populations, particularly those most subject to historically systemic oppression. Thus, my career now explicitly operates at the intersection of arts and health; I am someone who both does it and studies it.

When this journey first began, my confidence in the efficacy of storytelling as a public health tool was largely supported by my lived experiences seeing the art used extensively in my aunt's recovery process from a major public health issue, substance abuse, and by the depth of my professional expertise. Among the philosophical tenets of the African oral tradition that I learned to exude is the concept of "ubuntu," a Zulu word meaning "humanity," which is widely interpreted and applied as "I am because we are, and because we are I am." Many moments in my life, not just my aunt's recovery, served as profound examples of how storytelling operated as a modality by which human beings could remind themselves and others of their common humanity. As my marriage between art and science commenced, I became more skilled at acquiring support for storytelling that was written in my new empirical language. Some of the initial evidence I found discussed storytelling's impact on people dealing with cancer diagnoses and treatment (Chelf et al. 2000; Høybye, Johansen, and Tjørnhøj-Thomsen 2005; Crogan, Evans, and Bendel 2008). More specific to my endeavors, I found literature that explicitly discussed storytelling as an integral part of the twelve-step model of recovery (Jensen 2000; Nowinski and Baker 2012). Several years into this work I continue to discover how much research has been conducted on storytelling, including understanding the African oral tradition in particular, the use of storytelling to address health equity, and its application in approaches that visualize qualitative data (Banks-Wallace 2002; Banks 2012; Pavlovskaya 2017; Teixeira 2018; Fakunle et al. 2021). Learning of this literature and utilizing storytelling as a research methodology corroborated what I quickly identified during my doctoral study: there is a noticeable gap in our understanding of public health issues, because there is a noticeable gap in our engagement of the *public* in public health. Storytelling is a technique that can be implemented to better understand how people react, respond, and navigate many health challenges, be it the pandemic of COVID-19 or the pandemic of systemic racism. Storytelling encourages researchers and practitioners to focus not just on the what, when, and where but also on the how and why. With a fuller view of the spectrum of the factors and results that affect and are affected by public health, we are better equipped to address and ultimately eliminate our challenges.

Throughout our time, many people have asked us why storytelling works so well. It blows their minds that something so simple has such powerful properties when it comes to understanding and navigating the human experience. My answer is always the same: we just do what our ancestors have always done. We do not believe that we created something novel but rather believe that we simply reminded people of the abilities they always possessed. Culture and folklore have always provided avenues by which we as its utilizers and bearers can help ourselves and others figure this thing out called life. With the billions of iterations of existence and through those who have chronicled some of them, we believe that humans have the same core desires: to be acknowledged, to be understood, to be respected, to be appreciated, to be loved. Storytelling is a consistently available and dynamic path by which we can work toward achieving these desires, and DiscoverME/RecoverME is obligated to those who help us to help as many as we can to tap into this ancient but perpetually relevant energy. The Hawaiian epistemologist Dr. Manulani Meyer put it best: "Aloha (knowledge used in service to others) is intelligence with which we meet life . . . isn't it a radical idea? It's a rigorous idea, it's a liberating idea, when you teach yourself [and others] and you exhibit the intelligence of loving. It's the new old intelligence that the planet is asking for" (keyele 2010).

Notes from the Field

Activism, Folklore Research, and Human Rights on the South Carolina Sea Islands in the 1960s

MARY TWINING BAIRD

We were a group of Johns Islanders and culture workers in Washington, DC, seated around a group of tables, after attending the 1984 National Heritage Fellowships recognition ceremony. Ms. Janie Hunter, Moving Star Hall Singers, lifelong resident of Johns Island, South Carolina, stood up and broke into song: "It is late in the evening and the sun is going down." Her lovely minor-key song cut through the discussion that rankled among us. It was her gentle way of bringing us back to ourselves—a reminder that the important thing was that we respond to her call in African fashion, as we agreed to go forward together. She was composing the song as she sang, so as we hummed it as one, the atmosphere changed completely. It is scenes like this, all of us united in song, awakening in this realization together, that I cherish and remember—and not so much the contentious attitudes of my professors who were striving to have us produce what the editors of this volume describe as "impenetrable discourses" to gather dust on shelves.

ACADEMIC FOLKLORE

I was a graduate student under Richard Dorson at the Folklore Institute, Indiana University, beginning in 1966, and, although we shared an interest in African American folklore, our approaches were vastly different. Richard Dorson followed a scientific method developed by Antti Aarne (1973) of Finland and brought to the United States' academic community by Stith Thompson for the classification of themes found in the world's folktales. Dorson relied on this system, which lent credibility to the whole enterprise of collecting and categorizing folk narrative, as a means to understand folk cultures, including African American folklore. I felt that Dorson did not have a notion of the powder keg on which he was standing when he went into the field to collect African American folktales (1967) as the civil and human rights struggle was getting under way.

Dorson's acolytes were expected to follow the safe model of doing the classificatory work in whatever cultural milieu they researched. I, however, was more interested in branching out into a concept of folklife research and engagement, which included more diverse and holistic aspects of the people's lives and culture than narrative categorization.

I learned of folklife studies from Guy Carawan, a folk musician who had been active on Johns Island, South Carolina.

As my interests diverged into folklife and community activism, Dorson made clear that he did not believe that I was a genuine folklore scholar. Much like Stith Thompson, who did not understand the breadth and depth of the folklore of the African world, Dorson believed there was simply not enough worthy of study. While taxonomic work was clearly valuable and added to the information about the folk stories of world cultures, Dorson and I were on a collision course from the outset.

I had done much of my fieldwork before I went to the Folklore Institute to earn my doctorate, and therein lay a problematic beginning for our relationship. Dorson doubted both my talents as a folklorist and the value of the folklore of the Sea Islanders I wanted to work with. He said I should go back to the Islands and be nice to the benighted residents; his attitudes were that specific and that insulting, racist toward the Islanders and sexist toward me. It is in this strained context, the struggle between my training and my personal convictions to do right, that my work on the Islands takes shape.

THE CALL OF THE SEA ISLANDS

Watching television in Denver, Colorado, in 1965, I saw the scenes on the road in Alabama with the dogs and police literally hounding the young people, causing John Lewis and others terrible harm—physical damage that took a long time to heal from. I was shocked to my core and resolved to do something to help. I had learned what the folk musicians and activists Guy and Candie Carawan were doing to register people to vote, and I resolved to join in that effort or some other community work. I contacted the Carawans, and they gave me addresses and numbers for Esau Jenkins, an activist in Charleston, South Carolina, so that I could join the movement down there. I drove to the J and P Café and Motel that Mr. Esau ran with Mr. John Polite down near the foot of the bridge that crossed the Ashley River. There, Islanders were waiting for a ride home from work onto the Islands while having a bite to eat and a cup of coffee. I was about to launch into a life-changing experience.

Informed by their own experiences and expertise, the Islanders took action in a variety of ways. Some drew on their African heritage. Others used the dominant political systems of the day to fight the very oppression that those systems upheld. In the 1950s, when rural communities with limited means were left to their own devices for solutions that most Americans took for granted, school segregation, for example, was required by law in South Carolina. The Reverend Joseph Delaine, along with other activists, fought the school board to obtain a secondhand school bus for the children of his community in South Carolina after a child drowned after falling out of one of the boats, poled along in the water by older children as their only transportation to school. The Reverend Delaine organized the Clarendon County residents to fight for educational equality. Petitioning Clarendon County school superintendent R. M. Elliott got the group nowhere, and, with help from the NAACP, a case was brought to trial. Judge Julius Waties Waring, a white man from a prominent local family, recommended to Thurgood Marshall that the case be tried as a desegregation case, knowing that in doing so, it would most likely be sent to the Supreme Court. Known as *Briggs v. Elliott* (1952), the school segregation case came before a three-judge panel that ruled 2–1 that school segregation was legal. Judge Waring was the dissenting vote. The ruling led to the case being combined with several others into *Brown v. Board of Education of Topeka* (1954), in which the Supreme Court found school segregation to be unconstitutional. The Delaine family and the Warings had to move to New York City as a result of the backlash. When it came time for Judge Waring's funeral some years later, the African American turnout was huge. They never forgot the unpopular stand he had taken for them.

In Charleston, South Carolina, African American leaders in the 1950s and 1960s had a history of holding concealed meetings to strategize politically around elections and other affairs. They knew they were risking their lives and livelihoods to meet and strategize to work against a dominant society that has oppressed them and their families for far too long. At this time, the leaders in the African American community were trying to support whichever white politicians would best advocate for African American communities. At the time, African Americans in South Carolina were not credited as human beings possessing a sense of dignity with emotions, desires, and aspirations, individually or collectively. Even having toed the line and measured up to the standards of the dominant white society, they found it was not sufficient to win them full citizenship and the human rights to which they knew they were entitled. Some believed that the Islanders needed charitable help or, in Dorson's case, having folkloristic research done, rather than political maneuvering. However, as became clear to me in my continued work in the Sea Islands, by collaborating with community members, standing beside them and participating and listening, I was able to serve the community.

INTO SERVICE IN THE COMMUNITY

In 1966, when I was able to obtain housing on Johns Island, I brought my two-year old son, Tim, to be with me and my housemate, a divinity student who had been recruited by the Reverend Charles Sherrod from Union Theological Seminary in New York City. Tim happily sat on many laps in the car as I drove and joined in when he was in the midst of dancing teens; he was a fine ambassador in plastic pants. I conducted fieldwork on the Island with Tim in tow part of the time. I came to see clearly the brilliance and resilience of a culture that created community through reaffirmations of folklore and folklife that had been handed down to create humane security and dignity in the face of unrelenting racism. I participated in cooperative activities in Island occupations that highlighted the collaborative nature of Islanders' association patterns, which sprang from their African heritage as they worked and played.

Since there had been no anthropologists or folklorists in the area for some time, I initially thought that some descriptive ethnography could be useful to the field. Questionnaires and other more formal approaches were not useful to me as they made the Islanders nervous. Instead, I employed participant observation methods, which allowed me to serve some of the needs of the community as well. As I was further integrated into the Islanders' culture, my comprehension deepened of their lives and lifeways. The more subtle aspects of what they did, why they did it, when and then how, were perceptible only in daily association patterns. I sat next to them as they worshipped, danced and sang with them, learned how to make nets, ate oysters, mourned, celebrated, and conferred with them as the opportunity presented itself. When I could participate, I did; I observed when taking part was not appropriate; I took notes when I could and stepped out when propriety indicated.

As a folklorist, I knew how important it was to learn the customs and mores of the Sea Islands in order to understand their culture. Without that cultural understanding, I would have been unable to actually work with and for the community. At that time, most of the available books were written by Euro-Americans who had their own set of mores and beliefs. If they were Southern, it was even more complicated; part of the task was to untangle attitude from actual fact. It was possible to glean information from these written sources by sorting out the habitual mode of regarding anything about the African American Islanders in negative terms. A lot of this was due to white Southerners' need to devalue the Islanders and protect themselves against a perceived threat. South Carolina had not forgotten the Denmark Vesey and Nat Turner uprisings, nor the fact that Africans had fought for the Union side in the Civil War. White Southerners were desperately clinging to the "Lost Cause" and the perceived injustice of the North's winning of what they described as the "War between the States."

In addition to reading all that I could about the community, I also worked with the community, especially various activists and community leaders, like Mr. Esau Jenkins. One day Mr. Esau Jenkins came along the sandy drive to my house, blowing his horn to warn us of his approach, to tell me about the War on Poverty office in Charleston, which needed another driver for the Head Start program. It was one of President Johnson's edicts to initiate a transport system (for which no money had been allotted) to get the children to the small schools in buildings, which themselves were in-kind contributions provided by the communities. Johns Island is the second-largest island on the East Coast, so we needed to cover many miles to get those children to school and back every day. There were few cars on the Island, and each one was loaded to capacity, taking workers and students off the island to jobs and schools. Mr. Esau volunteered me, and I was drawn into the community's solution. He drove one side of the island, and I drove the other. Some of the parents had not had much schooling, and they were most anxious to have the children participate. The kids wanted to stay home and play. At first, there were tears, but once they found out the schools would have familiar singing games, dancing, and lunch, among other things, they acclimated quickly. One day, on the drive home, they serenaded me with an unending rendition of "Batman and Robin" as we drove.[1]

Along with the schools, churches were, and continue to be, an important place of community. While living on the Sea Islands, my housemate and I attended church services. We picked up on the sermon topic from the ministers, who told the congregation that we would be coming around to pick them up at the end of their driveways or roads (called "gaps" on the Islands) to register to vote and to eventually go vote. While they rode in the back seat, Islanders went over the candidate list, showing the aspiring voters the basics of voting literacy or, failing that, where to make their mark. They coached each other, in a true enactment of the "each one, teach one" movement of an earlier time. The more experienced among them were selecting their teaching venue wherever they could find it. More formal classes in literacy were under way at the same time as they were trying to catch up after the shameful marginalizing they had undergone for most of their lives. They could not wait until they had all learned to read to be able to vote. As Ms. Janie Hunter of Johns Island would sing, "When the Lord get ready, you got to move" (Carawan and Carawan 1994, 165).

As I continued to work with community members, it became clear that I could be of more significant use in the community than driving students to school and adults to register and vote. I helped out with the young people who had suffered culture shock from the integrated schools, where there were only one or two African American children among two thousand students. We took the traumatized young people to the beach, where they figured out a way to upset the guards on the beach. We linked arms in pairs, Black and white, and kept strolling across the so-called barrier between that part of the beach that was open to whites and the side that was open to Blacks. We went back and forth to the frustration of the lifeguards, who really did not know what to do about it. Having had a good laugh at their consternation, we got in the vans and left, not wishing to have a confrontation with the police. The young people enjoyed that after what they had gone through at the schools. Some had suffered nervous breakdowns as a consequence of being on the front lines of a struggle, seemingly unsolvable even by the time they reached adulthood. We also invited them to cookouts (oyster roasts and crab boils) to help them relax. We had meetings where they could talk over plans for the future as their education was on hold for a recovery period.

With the War on Poverty and the Civil Rights Act in effect, President Johnson's new programs were being staffed by people new to the community. Members of the teams knew little about Sea Islanders' lives and culture, and they had difficulties understanding the language as well. Again, it was here that the role of a folklorist in understanding a community's culture and taking part in that culture was so important. By working with the community, I was also able to serve as a sort of cultural translator, using my own position as an educated white person to amplify the needs of the community to the young members of the government teams. At the same time, I was also participating in Island life, interviewing people in the hinterlands about getting them signed up for health insurance, Social Security, and other badly needed services that had not heretofore reached these deeply rural areas. I was receiving a wealth of information about these people's lives while ensuring that I was giving back in whatever way I could.

According to the reading I was doing, a number of people had come to the islands over the years and taken information and material for books or publications, but not all had given much back to the Islanders; if they did, most did not write about it. There are a few exceptions. Fanny Kemble, for instance, did her best to help the people her husband enslaved, in spite of his obdurate racist objections. His heartless behavior toward the enslaved families on his plantation ultimately brought the marriage to an end (Kemble 1961). Lydia Parrish, author of *Slave Songs of the Georgia Sea Islands* (1965), had a praise house built for the residents on St. Simons Island as part of her song collecting activities. Examples of collaboration and community, though, were few and far between as I continued my own research and work with the Sea Islanders.

ENTER MS. BESSIE JONES

Ms. Bessie Jones came at the behest of the Newport Folk Festival's Revival of Folk Music initiative. She was a resident of the Georgia Sea Islands, a member of the Sea Island Singers from St. Simons Island, known for her stage presence, personality, sense of humor, and wealth of games, songs, and stories. She was brought to the Charleston area to travel around to various Head Start schools and other community organizations (with no means of transportation provided). As I had done for voters and students, I was ready to provide transportation to Ms. Jones. In doing so, I learned the games and dances that she taught to the children as she traveled through the community (Jones and Lomax Hawes 1972). She was a teacher who understood the African heritage of the Sea Island people, and she was a valuable mentor to me as I saw firsthand the important role that culture played in the lives and education of community members. By recognizing and legitimizing the Sea Islands' culture and traditions, Ms. Jones was helping to lift up the students with whom she worked so closely. It was a lesson in what collaborative culture work could mean and accomplish.

Once I had worked together with Ms. Jones and the young people on games, transportation, voting, registration, Social Security, government teams, and more, we became kin; my sons were accepted as godsons by a family in the River Road community on the Island. By becoming part of the kinship system, I was able to better comprehend the structure of the culture: people's interactions, and the contexts and contents of the songs, and my kin's relationships to these traditions. The girls I met in the afternoons after school liked to include their friends', relatives', and my names in the songs they sang, using formulaic structure and improvisations. West African praise singers use such compositional devices in the inclusion of names.

Here, again, the importance of understanding a community, working with a community, and being part of a community in order to enact change driven by that same community were all clear to me. The Sea Islanders have been faced with solving problems on their own in marginalized circumstances for hundreds of years. What for many folklorists of the time served as the basis for scientific collection and categorization served for locals as the creative solutions to everyday problems—solutions that highlighted a collectivity that took root in West African custom. Africans brought these communal solutions with them in the forced migrations from Africa. They arrived with a method involving "we," not "I."

These solutions were characteristically part of a living African diasporic culture, and they were rooted in working for the collective wellbeing of the community. Each proof of African heritage was a gem to be treasured in those days as there was skepticism about Africanisms. The Sea Islanders maintained many of these West African traditions. For example, they used the net knitting technology and the casting of nets that young West Africans still use today. They made coiled basketry as it is made in West Africa now. They used the social patterns of the rotating credit associations to do their banking, just as their long-distant cousins in African village associations do today. One particular aspect, which I would continue to learn about, was the ways in which community members utilized clothing and household cloth pieces to fashion quilts that were reproductions of the silk and cotton woven cloth they had known in West Africa. Specifically, the women manufactured bedclothes, layered apparel styles, nets, okra soup, and dolls for the household and family. The children would participate, sometimes quite young children, sitting up under the quilting frame to retrieve dropped thread spools and performing other small services for the quilting ladies. In the quilts and quiltworks, women reproduced some of their memories of African patterns with cloth pieces cut and set together not only to make the bedcovers they needed but also to reaffirm the woven patterns of their West African origins (Twining 2016, 204–10). Inside the coverlets and quilts, they put old jackets, pants, or whatever would provide warmth. In doing so, they recycled old clothing and household fabrics to make the quilts. The African heritage was evident in the colors and the way the pieces of cloth were put together to reproduce what their forebears had known in West Africa. I went to West Africa to do research into the roots of the quilting patterns and found the images that the enslaved Africans had brought with them in their minds. Making the quilts, they sit together, the family contributes old materials, and their knowledge from their African ancestors inspires the patterns, so they bring together a combination of color and conversation about and a contribution to the comfort and life of the family. The cooperative and reciprocal lifestyle was a powerful life and professional lesson for me and one that I learned thanks to the help of Esau Jenkins.

The concept of Africanisms, such as these, seemed impossible to the doubters like Dorson and Thompson, given the distance, passage of time, and the racist attitudes toward Black cultures held by many white people at the time. It was revelatory for me to understand the tenacity of people and cultures; I knew the Islanders and what they were capable of, and I began to comprehend the connection between the models from the home cultures and the lives they had made for themselves over here. Their isolation on the Islands contributed to the retention of and the reaffirmation of their culture.

What became clear during my time on the Sea Islands was the importance of truly collaborative endeavor—work that was not extractive but additive; commitment that rejected racist beliefs and structures; obligations that embraced community-led and community-driven projects; work that amplified culture. That type of work is what led me to continue to conduct fieldwork and to continue to build relationships with the people I met. At the time, some older scholars had reservations about my approach, which was viewed as radical and nonscholarly. However, driving voters to registration and polling sites, driving students to Head Start, and driving Ms. Jones to schools throughout the region was one aspect of my fieldwork that reinforced the importance of public engagement and the power of public culture work. Educational opportunities, voting rights, desegregation, and the many issues we continue to deal with today were and are tied intrinsically to the cultures that we as folklorists work with. Acknowledging that and working with communities to address those and other issues was one lesson among an abundance that I learned from the many community members with whom I was privileged to work on the Sea Islands.

CONCLUSION

In spite of being offered a job as a librarian at Haut Gap High School on Johns Island in the Charleston County system, which would have placed me right where I could have continued the fieldwork I was doing, I returned to graduate school at Indiana, somewhat reluctantly. As I departed in 1966, not for the last time, I felt I had stepped up to help out when I could, gathered a great deal of information, and become a member of the community that helped serve the community based on its expressed needs. Back in Indiana (MA 1968; PhD 1977), I found a more receptive climate and recognition for the fieldwork I had done and was invited to present to the graduate classes and seminars about it, a great change from the earlier Dorson opprobrium.

Whereas Dorson advocated for the extraction of folklore to contribute to the building of the tower of knowledge, the cooperative model practiced on the Islands wanted to purpose these same energies into the sustenance of their own lifeways. They could do this by better understanding the resiliencies of these practices as what we considered at the time to be surviving Africanisms. They could do this by devoting my labor (and my vehicle) to efforts the community valued: education, voting efforts, and civil rights. They could do this by enlisting me as a cultural translator for them. They could do this by welcoming me into the community—as an ally, as a friend, and even as family—so I could better serve in these roles. The cooperative model within the culture of the Islands was rooted in African autochthonous and diasporic societies—truly the most appropriate way for me to interact with these communities on their own terms.

It was in the working relationship with Mr. Esau and Ms. Jones and in the collective methods of the African-descended Islanders that I came to understand that our responsibilities as folklorists is not to the academy but rather to the community that takes us in. As Ms. Jones taught dancing games, she also taught us life lessons. As I continued teaching and writing about the games in other communities throughout my life, I understood the implications and the significance of the collective accomplishments of the games and play in the children's lives (Twining 2016). The children learned their own skills in teaching one another, the value of their beautiful synchronic movement, and the cooperation that made it possible as they matured in dance, work, and other collaborative endeavors.

Today, Charleston and the world continue to face issues similar to those that we worked to address in the 1960s. Standing beside people as they grapple with issues seems to be the order of the day and a move forward and outward among constituent elements of our society. The overt actions and underlying problems of racism are still present and human interrelationships more intense than ever. Furthermore, we are informed about events as news and information are instantly transmitted, since they can no longer be seen as simply regional but have national and worldwide impact. The consequences are more profound, and the scope has expanded as more is revealed. To combat this, we must continue to recognize the value and importance of cultural knowledge and traditions. As folklorists, we must recognize that the importance of the work we do has also been augmented in significance as we seek to understand the major concerns in other people's lives through collaboration. The disciplines of study and research in different cultures need to heed the lessons of such cooperative and humane activity, if our own culture and the investigations of others are to survive in a rapidly changing world.

NOTE

1. One of my more amenable professors at Indiana University cited a similar story that involved many Congolese men riding in the back of the truck he was driving, singing "Ho Ho, Tuna Bwenda Ho Ho" for most of the ride home.

Prison Landscapes and the Wisconsin Idea

Shaping the Study of a Public Occupational Culture

CLAIRE SCHMIDT

T he state of Wisconsin has been actively engaged in culture work and public folklore since the beginning of the twentieth century. While we might associate the
rise of public folklore with the 1970s and public humanities with the 1990s and
early 2000s, the progressive ideology of the Wisconsin Idea has involved citizens in scholarship and culture work for more than a hundred years. Conceived by the Progressive-era
governor Robert ("Fighting Bob") LaFollette and University of Wisconsin president
Charles Van Hise and eponymously codified in a 1912 book by Charles McCarthy, the Wisconsin Idea envisioned the state as a "laboratory for democracy," and Van Hise famously
vowed, "I shall never be content until the beneficent influence of the University reaches
every family of the state" (University of Wisconsin–Madison n.d.). According to the Wisconsin Idea, knowledge must be sought and shared in order to improve the health, quality
of life, and environment of the people of Wisconsin. When the American Council of
Learned Societies argued in 1989 that it was essential for scholars and scholarship to connect with the public in innovative and meaningful ways, breaking down walls between society and scholars, four generations of Wisconsin scholarship had endeavored to do just
that. In this chapter, I examine the Wisconsin Idea and its implications for culture work
through two decades of ethnographic fieldwork with prison workers shaped by my experiences as a multigenerational product of this ideology. There is a great deal to be gained by,
as Schiele writes elsewhere in this volume, "bringing greater visibility to cultural knowledge and practices by highlighting extraordinary individuals and groups." Applied collaborative research between corrections workers and public folklorists is necessary to address
workplace conditions and social justice.

I am the fourth generation in my family to attend the University of Wisconsin–Madison,
hub of the Wisconsin Idea that has shaped my life and my research. My great-grandparents,
both from immigrant families, met there. My grandparents met there. My parents met
there. I met my husband there. No one in my family has attended a college other than the
UW. When I entered an out-of-state graduate program, I broke a tradition that defined
family identity.

When I was little, my mother was finishing college at UW–Madison. She was a journal-ism student and writer and took me to readings by Wisconsin writers, including one at Edgewood College that featured Ben Logan, Robert S. Gard, and Lenore McComas Coberly. That night, a woman read a story about a farm wife and some hippies. The story revolved around Alma Ruth, the trauma of losing her brother in Bataan, and the clash be-tween the rural farming community and the back-to-the-land, Vietnam-protesting hippies who moved in and pestered her to teach traditional rural ways of life. My eight-year-old self recognized my parents in the hippies, my grandmother in Alma Ruth. Thirty years later, I googled "Alma Ruth and the hippies," and I found the story that McComas Coberly (2005) had read while I sat in her audience. It's a story about insiders and outsiders, us and them. On the way home from the reading, my mother told stories about how the old farmers talked about her and her friends with that same curiosity and suspicion. *Those hippies! What do they eat? What do you think they're doing right now?*

At that same reading was Robert S. Gard—a force inside and outside the university in the collection and dissemination of regional writing and folklore. While he read to us about people, places, ghosts, and traditions, my skin crawled, my heart beat fast, I was choking on homesickness for the home I was in. I met Robert Gard; he shook my eight-year-old hand and autographed my book. I read the Gard and Leland George Sorden books over and over and learned about the Ridgeway ghost, the Hodag, the WPA, and farm women who wrote and acted in plays in their spare time—all of which seemed both outlandish and familiar. Despite pretending to be too cool, I listened to *Down Home Dairy-land* on public radio and swooned over storytellers at school assemblies.[1]

A decade later I was sitting in the Humanities building at UW in John D. Niles's ballads class. It was the most influential class of my life. I was already in love with the material, transported by the combination of music and word, connecting Yo Mama jokes and rid-dling in *The Hobbit,* and one day we had a guest lecturer, and it was this guy, Jim Leary.

And Jim was playing us ballads from Wisconsin and telling us stories. The places, the music, the jokes—these were *mine.* Mine. I was seeing myself again, reflected back. I saw my dad's beard, my uncle's accent, and my grandmother's Ole and Lena jokes. And I was choking back tears because I knew this music, I knew these place-names and these stories. I wanted to run away and never come back; I wanted to shout, *Stop, this is mine! Hey! Every-body! I know this stuff!* And, just like when I was eight, I was homesick for a place I hadn't left. My throat hurt; my muscles were twisted from the sheer power of this experience of being seen, of seeing my experience recognized in the academy. Like Leary, I was and am in love with the idea of being from Wisconsin. Thus, I took it for granted that I had talents, and that I had a right to develop those talents, and that the state—and the university—existed to serve me and every other Wisconsinite.

So here's the thing. The stories I carried were from this landscape. The improvisational taxidermy of the tavern where my uncle watched Packers games. The incessant festivals (The Wilhelm Tell Fest! Heidi Fest!) and polka emanating from New Glarus, where my mother ran the newspaper. The apocryphal stories of julebukking in Oregon, where I went to high school. The beads and arrowheads you could still find on The Ledge outside Wau-pun, where my parents used to drink and smoke in their own high school days. The farms that the Wisconsin Idea scholar Edward Janus describes as "the creation of a new agriculture for a new kind of human being, the yeoman farmer-entrepreneur-intellectual: an intelligent, thoughtful, educated, and diligent professional agriculturalist" (2011, 4). This landscape was *covered* in institutions.

In her book *Reading Places: Literacy, Democracy, and the Public Library in Cold War America*, Christine Pawley writes, "Institutions—a form of organized sociability—constituted the building blocks of the towns and villages that American settlers (mostly white and of European origin) established in the heartland during the nineteenth century. Some were commercial, like banks and insurance companies, while others were cultural and cooperative, like churches, schools, and public libraries. All made use of print, a technology that settlers employed to establish their communities as permanent features of the landscape, and that depended on other technologies like the railroads (and later the highways), to knit communities together in increasingly interdependent relationships" (2010, 13–14). Pawley does not mention prisons, but they, too, as institutions, work to knit together communities in interdependent relationships across the state.[2]

So that landscape—*my* landscape—of trees and cows and black earth and rivers—that same landscape holds prisons. Boscobel—where my great-great-grandfather Grandpa-Dan-the-railroad-man kept a mistress—holds the Supermax prison, politely known as the Wisconsin Secure Program Facility. My uncle's northern Wisconsin paradise of hunting, fishing, and cross-country skiing was made possible by his job at "Camp Gordon"—where inmates from overcrowded prisons in Waupun were sent to work the managed forest and grow their own food (Bureau of Correctional Enterprises 2003). When I took the Greyhound from Madison to Duluth, I rode with parents, grandparents, siblings, and spouses making the long, uncomfortable trip to visit family at the New Lisbon Correctional Institution, the Black River Correctional Facility, the St. Croix Correctional Facility, the Stanley Correctional Institution, or the Flambeau Correctional Center.

Gard's landscape of cheerful farmers, intrepid woodsmen, and goofy immigrants existed, but it was just one layer of the land. Despite the Wisconsin Idea's efforts to create an educated, active, enfranchised citizenry, crime, addiction, disease, and defect stand as ongoing and inevitable barriers to the fulfillment of the Wisconsin Idea. We have to remember that the exalted and enlightened Professor Van Hise supported the 1913 law authorizing forced sterilization of inmates in Wisconsin's institutions (Buenker 1998).

Five generations of my family reaped the benefits of the Wisconsin Idea, and five generations of my family have made a living working in Wisconsin's criminal justice system, or, in the case of a great-grandfather, as an unwilling guest of state hospitality. One great-grandfather was a lawyer; another was a Lutheran minister turned forger. My mom's dad was a prison social worker specializing in work with violent sex offenders. My dad's dad was a guard—a correctional officer. My uncle was an officer, union steward, and parole agent. My godfather was a guard. My godmother was a guard and prison librarian. The kids I grew up with, camped with, babysat, became guards. My neighbors were prison nurses. My landlord was a prison doctor. My best friend was a patient care technician with forensic patients at Mendota. Those of us who went to college went through the UW system, and we absorbed the Wisconsin Idea while paying tuition with the help of the prison-industrial complex.

The Wisconsin idea proposes a public landscape populated by educated, enlightened, and empowered citizens. The lived landscape, the whole environment, is populated by a more complicated set of individuals than the enlightenment-driven, assimilationist-focused ideology hoped for (Pawley 2010, 67). The Wisconsin Idea was born of reform ideology, and that is visible in many historical features of Wisconsin corrections, from the spacious campus of Oshkosh Correctional Institution or the wooded cabin system in Oakhill to the prison farms of Oregon and Fox Lake. However, this pastoral landscape of rehabilitation, fresh air, homegrown food, and righteous labor imagined by progressive corrections policy is at odds with the prison-industrial complex. By this I mean private, for-profit prisons as well as the private industries that supply goods and services to public institutions for a profit. Amid the economic ruins of 2009, the US prison industry made three and a half billion dollars in revenues (Camplin 2017, 27). Corporations like Aramark, A'Viands Food and Services Management, ABL Management, Canteen Correctional Services, and Trinity Services Group reap profits through prison food. As the number of incarcerated Americans has risen, so have profits. While the Wisconsin Idea was anchored firmly in benevolent capitalism, the opportunity for individuals to rise in their social standing and material comfort through corrections has not paid out. Profits go out of state; they do not stay in the local community as envisioned by the architects of progressive corrections models (Yanarella and Blankenship 2006, 113). And while my grandfather once supported a wife and two children on one Department of Corrections social worker salary, erosions in benefits and the rising cost of living make it hard to pay the bills today in a two DOC-salary house.

If prison work is necessary in Wisconsin, then under the aegis of the Wisconsin Idea it is the responsibility of researchers to conduct their research with the active engagement of the rank-and-file workers who perform that work. If we agree with the Wisconsin Idea that citizens have a responsibility to be active and engaged citizens and a right to the benevolent influence of the university and if we agree that, in Christine Pawley's words, "a service relationship should exist between the university and the state by which the expertise of social scientists, economists, legal scholars, and scientists should be brought to bear on solving Wisconsin's problems" (2010, 79), then we can start this process by understanding prisons as inhabited landscapes and listening to the voices of those who inhabit those landscapes. This matters, because the United States continues to maintain the highest prison population rate in the world (World Prison Brief n.d.). Prison affects all of us in the United States, though not all equally. Corrections work is public work. Culture work with prisons has the potential to serve the different publics—inmates, workers, policymakers—that have a stake in corrections.

Prisons are difficult places to document. In some ways, prisons and those inside them are painstakingly documented. Ask a DOC employee about documentation ("paperwork") and you'll get stories of absurd forms, incoherent reports, and lots and lots of wasted time. Ask an ethnographer or member of an Institutional Review Board about documentation in prison and you'll have a conversation about ethics. In addition to the obvious concerns about security and safety, inmate populations are protected because there are constraints on an inmate's ability to give voluntary, uncoerced consent to participate in research. That said, inmate culture has been documented from a wide variety of disciplinary perspectives. It is not terribly difficult to visit a prison; these are public institutions and there are clear protocols. Different institutions and administrators vary, but watchfulness and suspicion are the norm. When I expressed a desire to set foot in a prison to a correctional officer collaborator, he said, "Well, the thing is, people are really going to wonder *why* you would want to do that. What's your agenda? They're going to be looking for your hidden motive" (personal communication, 2015). Prison employees tend to be suspicious of outsider interest, which is often puerile and ill informed. Employee populations have aroused far less interest; prison employee culture and behavior seem to be of concern to a limited number of researchers within the field of corrections whose goals do not usually include an understanding of creativity, aesthetics, or artistic communication. The desire to document prison workers working is logical, but reality is complicated. It is rarely practical or desirable, from a CO's point of view, to be followed around by a stranger with a camera.

The ethical concerns of prison research are enormous, but the ethical issues of *not* documenting prison work are serious. Prison workers are public employees; their public service, however uncongenial to outsiders, requires understanding, and that understanding requires documentation. As Garlough and Pryor observe, "Institutions like the University of Wisconsin Madison . . . have the responsibility to help the community be itself, in all its diversity, without denying its conflicts or incommensurabilities. In doing so, a common history is evoked, while simultaneously refusing to take any single 'we' for granted" (2011, 248).

In my own documentation of prison worker culture, I have collaborated with workers outside the walls of the institution. After all, the Wisconsin landscape shapes, and is shaped by, prisons. Most correctional facilities in our state were built, at least in part, by inmate labor (Bureau of Correctional Enterprises 2003). Prison boundaries permanently block off spaces. Roads, snowmobile trails, even deer trails circumnavigate the fences that separate prison from not-prison. Communities' understanding of landscape is shaped by ideas about prisons. Those of us who grew up in prison-centered towns or families interpreted our landscape through a prison worldview. Escapes, riots, work-release groups all impacted how we navigated nonprison space. Our boogie men, our dangerous places, owed much to stories that came home with family members who went to prison every day.

The Wisconsin landscape wields what Larsen and Johnson (2017, 11) call "agency of place"—the active role that landscape plays and place as a conscious being. Both inmates and officers talk about the personality and character of individual institutions and the communities that house them. These personalities are made up not exactly of people, but of the collective experiences of people in the context of the land. The "more than human world" (Larsen and Johnson 2017, 3) is a public financial endeavor, as Yanarella and Blankenship remind us, writing,

> Prisons also have unsettling social consequences for the communities that view them only in terms of investments in a strong economic future. Prisons have been historically tied to the advancement of a just, fair, and rational criminal justice policy in a civil democratic society. Viewing them only in terms of economic development ignores the fact that the raw materials being transformed within the prison walls are one's fellow citizens. There is no way to escape

the reality that the "success" of this economic development strategy hinges on the suffering of one's fellow citizens—both the victims and perpetrators of crime. Whatever social benefits flow from it, the corrections industry is a component of an economy built on human misery. (2006, 121–22)

As Laura McAtackney has observed regarding the Long Kesh/Maze prison landscape in Northern Ireland, a prison can have "as much significance as an imagined landscape as it does as a physical entity" (2007, 42). How outsiders imagine the landscape of public institutions like prisons, whether as economic cash cows, or as an inhabitable symbol of racism, or as a nightmare fantasyland of violence, is often dependent on media depictions.

Since many Americans will never set foot in a prison, their understanding of the landscape and its effects comes sometimes from roadside views but most pervasively from glimpses of this forbidden landscape on TV news or fictionalized accounts. Fictional stories of prisons and prison work are not enough; they project a single narrative, unconnected to lived experiences. Each CO, social worker, dentist, bookkeeper, and inmate carries his own accounts of prison stories, rituals, and tricks, and those voices are not heard by the public that pays their salary.

For insiders—workers and inmates—the prison landscape dictates movement, access, information, and freedom. If prisons sit on the land like a black hole, a bowling ball distorting the rubber sheet of interpreted land, the prison itself is all about people coming together in space and time. Public folklorists have a role to play here, especially because, as Leary notes elsewhere in this volume, they are experts at partnership and persistence. Prison workers know what they do; folklorists can listen and broker connections that lead to amplification of the voices behind prison walls. Leary reminds us that public folklore works collaboratively, lending energy and expertise to existing desires and efforts.

What I know about prison workers is that they know more about prison culture and prison life than I do and that prison workers want their hard-earned knowledge to be seen, heard, and used. Larsen and Johnson write about the challenge of "being-together-in-place" and write that

place calls us to the challenge of living together. At root, this is a challenge of worldviews involving many different ways of being whose relationships are interdependent yet asymmetrical, sometimes harmonious, and other times in conflict, and that for this reason require definite protocols for balance and understanding. Place calls out to the struggles of coexistence in this pluriverse, a world of many worlds. . . . Place is not just a site of forced engagement, but is actively initiating and sustaining coexistence struggle in lands that have been exploited and degraded but that are still claimed by the Indigenous peoples who assert their belonging, guardianship, and sovereignty. (2017, 1–2)

While we might think of a correctional institution as, as Massey writes, "settled, enclosed and internally coherent," it is in reality "a meeting place, the location of the intersections of particular bundles of activity spaces, of connections and interrelations, of influences and movements" (1995, 58–59). Movement of inmates, officers, and other staff from space to space is continuously negotiated with others. Inmates and workers negotiate this movement every day, and they know more about permeability and incoherence of institutions than the policymakers and administrators who fondly design mechanisms to order and contain.

Prisons are landscapes, and movement from one space to another is tightly controlled. As Laura McAtackney reminds us, it is essential to understand the balance between "the built environment, designed to control and its every day experience and use by those who live within it" (2007, 39). Boundaries that separate one space from another are selectively permeable. While only some people have access to the prison landscape, that place carries meaning for others. For example, in theory, outsiders can visit prisons. In practice, outsiders can enter certain places but not others, and efforts to integrate family life and prisons seem surreal to outsiders. While my father went bowling, square dancing, and attended church services in prisons as a child, he never visited cells, never saw the hole. In my research, the children and spouses of prison workers talk about "this far, and no further." They talk about where they *could* go and where they couldn't follow their fathers, mothers, husbands, wives, children. The prison landscape offers Appleton's (1975) preferred landscape of "prospect and refuge" (to see without being seen) in unequal quantities to workers and those they supervise. It would be hard to find an occupation where us-versus-them is a more integral part of occupational identity.

Control over boundaries is contested by both formal authority and informal authority—by both officers and inmate leaders. For inmates, a legal conviction determines where they go after the limbo of a county jail or other detention center. Their new place in geography depends on the severity of the crime and the determination of best placement. Their specific cell or ward or cottage can hinge on their specific type of crime—sex offenses against minors, for example. For other inmates, placement depends on the ways they interact with their world, as in the case of transgendered people. The type and amount of supervision determines inmates' freedom to move between spaces. Informal authority holds perhaps equal power; prison space is segregated according to ethnicity, color and creed. Gang affiliation and other inmate-driven power structures control who has access to which spaces and at which times. Corrections workers know that understanding boundaries is key to successful institutions. Like the Sea Islanders Twining Baird describes elsewhere in this volume, people who live and work in prisons have been creatively solving problems on their own for generations.

Culture workers understand the interplay between written and unwritten rules and the "locatedness" of culture (Garlough and Pryor 2011). The set of formal expectations inherent in corrections work is tied to the demands of the land, whether haying season, the call of Lambeau Field, or deer camp. This is most commonly found in scheduling. Haying season is for many a tortuous experience because of the demand for sequential days of dry weather in order to cut, rake, and bale hay. Requesting days off in January for a hypothetical first crop of hay in June, a second in July, and a third in September demands a tolerance for the financial and emotional crush of a week of solid rain during your week of vacation. Employees respond to the demands of the institution in ways that are shaped by cultural landscape; understanding behavior requires an understanding of culture.

As prison workers transfer between institutions, they must learn the landscape of the new prison campus as well as the surrounding community: taverns, churches, seasonal municipal and ethnic traditions, and the benefits and hazards imposed on the job by the surrounding environment. Sometimes that is felt in conflict between institutional employees and the outside community. Waupun was a case in point when, in the mid-twentieth century, grocery stores charged one price to farmers and factory workers and another price to state workers, resulting in state workers starting their own in-home grocery stores. Efforts to build a diverse staff sharing ethnic and cultural backgrounds with inmates have been met with limited success, as officers of color found transfers away from family and historical communities into predominantly white small towns to be more hostile and isolating than any DOC promotion was worth.

Expressive occupational culture is shaped by landscape. Inmate escape stories are one of the most popular genres of prison worker narrative shared with outsiders. In these stories, landscape holds agency and is often the protagonist. Escaped inmates are thwarted by mosquitoes and skunks in the dense woods and present themselves back at the institution, begging for rescue. Escaped inmates are outwitted by the "Haha" wall—the optical trickery of landscape, and guards enjoy watching rebellious inmates smacked down by the landscape—so foreign to the inmates and so familiar to staff, whose personal life is spent in the woods, fields, streets, and businesses surrounding their institution.

Practical jokes among prison staff depend on landscape—whether sewing an officer's coat sleeves shut in the dead of winter, or sending a fellow officer off on rounds with a gay pride sticker stuck to his back, or turning on the radio, turn signals, hazard lights, and windshield wipers before handing off the perimeter car. Stories of pranks illuminate the relationship between occupation and environment.

The very notion of "work" changes depending on the landscape. The Wisconsin Idea posits that work is good and leads to personal gain (Janus 2011, 4). This is just not sufficient for correctional work. In a prison context, good "work" is not "work"—when prison work is going well, prison staff don't need to do much. Success (safety, predictability, calm) means not having to work hard and thus a feeling of not having to "earn their pay that day." When an institution is poorly run (understaffed, inexpertly organized, unpredictable), riots or other dangerous situations happen, and *that* creates a lot of work.

Adlai Stevenson famously said, "The Wisconsin tradition meant more than a simple belief in the people. It also meant a faith in the application of intelligence and reason to the problems of society. It meant a deep conviction that the role of government was not to stumble along like a drunkard in the dark, but to light its way by the best torches of knowledge and understanding it could find" (Stark 1995, 2–3). Problem-solving among the state, nonprofits, labor organizations, and educational institutions is possible and necessary. As Gilmore writes, "This dynamic brings a greater sense of exchange, collective knowledge building, and social equity between the state's people and the university" (2011, 257). No one knows more about how prisons work than the people who eat, sleep, and work there. Nobody else understands how both banal and fascinating corrections work can be. Any research concerning our institutions must partner with the people who staff our institutions.

There is an urgent need right now for collaboration between public folklorists and correctional workers because the experiences of workers impact anyone connected with the prison landscape. This is not an easy time to work in a Wisconsin prison. For decades, the union was the official mouthpiece for rank-and-file corrections workers. Collective bargaining, born of the Wisconsin Idea and the Progressive era, meant that the common economic and social goals of DOC employees were heard loudly at the state and national level. Union stewards were powerful leaders and spokespeople within the network of Wisconsin COs. Nonunion employees (social workers, doctors, bookkeepers) often complained that the union was too powerful, offered too many protections for spoiled workers.

Today, that union is broken. When Act 10 (Buhle and Buhle 2011) stripped public employee unions of collective bargaining rights, membership collapsed and experienced COs fled the DOC in droves rather than work in increasingly unpredictable, unprotected conditions. Working in prisons was already a fraught profession; it has become much harder to hire and retain good workers, which means forced overtime, inexperienced staff, and high stress. In 2019, the Wisconsin DOC logged $60 million in overtime costs due to understaffing (Associated Press 2021); in late 2020, during the COVID-19 crisis, hundreds of Waupun inmates had to be relocated due to dangerous overcrowding and understaffing (Hamer 2020). Talented professionals leave the profession when working conditions become unbearable, and essential knowledge and experience are lost. High turnover, inexperience, and lowered standards are bad for inmates. A skilled, experienced, workforce that feels heard and valued means better conditions for inmates.

Correctional officers and inmates are hypervisible to each other but not to outsiders. We know that there is tremendous public curiosity about prisons and prison work. That means there is an audience hungry for stories. Rather than feeding that hunger for prison stories with screen-based fictions, public folklorists can help public employees find a better stage than the "potato hole" of prison (or its adjacent bars) on which they can tell their own stories. That public stage means dialogue between storyteller and audience, and that is essential for meaningful change. This work, like Fakunle's storytelling and recovery work, can have life- or death-level impacts for vulnerable populations.

Folklorists can ask workers what questions we *should* be asking about corrections work. Michael Owen Jones points out: "Stories, language, rituals, customs, festive events, and other forms of folklore develop directly out of individuals' experiences on the job and with one another. Therefore, they are likely to point to sore spots and reveal problems, on the one hand, and, on the other, indicate positive attitudes and supportive conditions or suggest solutions to issues" (1993, 175).

Public folklorists and public employees can work together to make visible this profession, its problems, and its unexpected joys. Respect for occupational knowledge means collaborative work in order to improve the health, quality of life, and environment of this group of workers, which also means the health, quality of life, and environment of the populations these workers supervise. We know that prisons are at the center of racial and economic injustice. We know that reform of the criminal justice system is necessary. Van Hise tasked the University of Wisconsin system to train specialists to serve the government and the people of Wisconsin by involving them democratically in reform. Before we can reform a system, we must understand how it works.

Notes

Many thanks to research assistants Katanna Davis and Tyesha Rhodes.

1. See Richard March's chapter for more on *Down Home Dairyland*.

2. And it seems important to me to say here that my grandmother was this same Dr. Pawley's cleaning lady for twenty-five years. Only in researching this chapter did I realize that Christine, whose house I had helped my grandmother clean, was also Dr. Pawley, expert on literacy, libraries, and the Wisconsin Idea. It seems fitting that the woman whose books I dusted during my vacations now helps me understand the underlying political ideologies that shape my scholarship. It may also explain my preoccupation with work, class, and power structures.

Revitalizing Franco-American Song

CARMEN BEAUDOIN BOMBARDIER, KIM CHASE,
ROBERT DESROSIERS, ANDY KOLOVOS, and
LISA ORNSTEIN

In 2018 the Vermont Folklife Center (VFC), in partnership with culture bearers and traditional music scholars, undertook a project to call attention to the continuing presence of Franco-Americans in Vermont by highlighting a key aspect of Franco-American cultural practice: communal singing.[1] Toward this end we produced a series of six weekly "singing schools" that provided face-to-face instruction in an informal context modeled after traditional Franco-American *soirées*. To support the Singing Schools, we developed a website and print songbook (Beaudoin Bombardier, Chase, and Ornstein 2018) that included musical notation, French-language transcription, phonetic rendition, English-language translation, and audio recordings. A crucial aspect of the project focused on making the language and content of the songs accessible to non-French speakers—those of Franco-American heritage and otherwise—to further support the goal of broadening awareness of the role of Franco-Americans in the history of Vermont.

Titled "Revitalizing Franco-American Song in the Champlain Valley of Vermont," the project had its roots in the VFC Archive and developed in part as a way to open up accessibility to several collections of French-language songs held in the archive. Beyond this, the project also served as an example of the intersection of folklore and ethnographic archives with public programming and the value of collaborative engagement with members of the cultural communities represented in our collections. This essay provides an overview of the project and its outcomes, exploring the challenges we encountered—what we frame as the divide between intention and execution—and our successes, as well as providing background on the content, communities, and individuals from which the effort emerged.

TEXTS, SOUND, AND SHARED SONG

Communal singing has played an important role in many Franco-American families in Vermont since large-scale immigration from Quebec to the United States began in the mid-nineteenth century and continues to hold relevance in the present day. Some Franco-American singing families preserved their repertoires, including material such as popular commercial songs, children's rhymes, French and Québécois folk ballads and the classic call-and-response songs—"Chansons à répondre"—in notebooks and on scraps of paper.[2]

Frequent, informal performance with family and friends kept the melodies associated with these *cahiers* in living memory.[3] But what happens to lyrics when no one remembers the tune? What are words—words intended to be sung—when there is no longer a melody to accompany them? Poetry, perhaps, depending on one's perspective. Perhaps a reasonable term is "potential music"—lyrics waiting to be reunited with melody and shared once again as song.[4]

The Vermont folk singer Margaret MacArthur often talked about a treasure gifted to her in the early 1950s by one of her neighbors in Marlboro, Vermont—a late eighteenth-century manuscript of a song called "The Marlboro Medley," written in 1789 by a local man.

"The Marlboro Medley" details wares bought and sold in the town of Marlboro early in its history, and the writer was even conscientious enough to note the song's tune title in the upper right corner of the page: "Black Joke." The problem for MacArthur was that although she had a title for the melody, she could find no one who knew the tune. So "The Marlboro Medley" sat dormant until Joe Hickerson of the Library of Congress turned up the associated melody in the Archive of Folk Music, and MacArthur was able to bring the song back to the world.[5]

Thinking about this issue from the perspective of a musician like MacArthur is one thing—how do I sing this song? How can I perform this song? Thinking about it from the perspective of archival access is another—here is a text; draw meaning from it as you will. When presenting the written text of a song, what exactly is an archive providing to someone who wants to know more than just the lyrics? And what is an archive actually preserving if the melody that makes the lyrics a *song* is unknown? Furthermore, what if the language of the text is incomprehensible to the reader?

The VFC Archive holds several versions of the French Canadian song "Rame, rame" (Row, row), donated to us by the Franco-American musician and cultural advocate Martha Pellerin. Someone being presented with this image might very well recognize it as a song. Someone holding the physical notebook that contains it and several other similar inscriptions would probably get the gist pretty quickly. But could that person sing it? Without melody, one is once again faced with "potential music." Put the words and the tune together and you have something very different—for the active researcher, the casual browser, and the person who wants to learn the song to sing it.

The VFC Archive houses approximately six thousand recordings of interviews and music, roughly twenty-five thousand photographic images, and several hundred feet of manuscript materials. The majority of VFC's holdings were created by representatives of the organization itself—audio interviews, print transcripts, and photographs generated by staff members in the course of their work—but the archive contains many donated collections as well.

One of the most significant bodies of donated material in the VFC Archive consists of three distinct family collections of Franco-American manuscript songbooks and audio recordings: the Martha Pellerin Collection, the Beaudoin Family Collection, and the Desrosiers/Joyal Family Collection. Over nearly a decade, VFC has worked to make them available online via an Omeka-based digital archive. Our intention in putting them online was to make them as broadly accessible as possible. We had done the same with a collection of field recordings of English-language songs created by Margaret MacArthur, and we

Rame, rame

Refrain:
Rame, rame, rame donc
Le tour du monde (bis)
Rame, rame, rame donc
Le tour du monde nous ferons

I
On est parti tôt ce matin
Le vent du nord caresse nos mains
Plus de soucis, loin des rivages
Tout n'est que rêves et lendemain.

II
Sourire aux lèvres, le cœur léger
Fini le temps de s'attarder
Suivons l'air du goéland.
Dans son élan de liberté.

III
Après le jour, viendra la nuit
Et les étoiles nous guideront
Les anges viendront nous rencontrer
Portant nos cœurs dans l'immensité

IV
Un soir ils nous verront passer
Ramons à fond sur les nuées

Manuscript of "Rame, rame." (Martha Pellerin Collection, Vermont Folklife Center Archive.)

viewed this project as related to that effort—albeit with an added goal: making these materials accessible to people of French Canadian heritage who wanted to learn these songs and sing them. The project itself, although time consuming, as is the case with all detailed cataloging, was satisfying, in part because the materials were discrete and could be easily divided into individual textual units.[6] All and all, the archive staff were pretty pleased with themselves—until the archivist Andy Kolovos had a somewhat painful heart-to-heart with his colleague the musician, folklorist, and archivist Lisa Ornstein. Their (heavily edited) conversation went something like this:

ANDY: So what do you think?
LISA: Well, Andy, it's just a lot of lyrics, you know?
ANDY: Yeah! Isn't that great?
LISA: But without the melodies, how will people be able to sing them?
ANDY: Oh.

And with that—and with support from the American Folklore Society—Kolovos and Ornstein hatched a pilot cataloging project for French Canadian song materials aimed in part at connecting the lyrics in one collection—the Beaudoin Family Collection—to the tunes that made them songs. The Beaudoin Family Collection consists of audio recordings, manuscripts, photographs, and ephemera documenting the musical life of two brothers, Louis and Willy Beaudoin, and their families. In the 1970s and 1980s, Louis, Willy, and their wives and children shared music informally with friends and neighbors and performed professionally at local venues, regional and national festivals, and, significantly, as a part of Jimmy Carter's inauguration in 1977. After Louis's death, in 1980, family members continued their performance tradition and remained professionally active until the early 2000s. The manuscripts in the collection include two song notebooks that contain a combination of orally transmitted materials, lyrics garnered from nineteenth- and twentieth-century sheet music, and lyrics transcribed from early twentieth-century commercial recordings.

Ornstein has known the family for decades and was excited to dive in and work through the two manuscript songbooks in the collection. We incorporated a model of community collaboration based on work by Glenn Patterson and Laura Risk (2014) for a project in the Douglastown community in Quebec. As Ornstein pointed out, an important part of our work was to connect lyrics with associated melodies. Because of the complexity of the project and the number of individual song texts, Ornstein and Kolovos were forced to make decisions on how best to bring together melody and lyrics. In the case of songs derived from commercial sources such as sheet music and 78 rpm recordings, we sought to identify the tune to which they were sung and, when possible, included a link to a cataloged example that also presented audio or a scan of the notated melody. We did so most often through the Virtual Gramophone: Canadian Historical Sound Recordings database of Library and Archives Canada (n.d.).

The song "Les Montagnards" (The mountaineers) provides an example of the process. Working from the manuscript, Ornstein identified "Les Montagnards" as a song written by the French composer Alfred Roland in 1832 under the title "Tyrolienne des Pyrénées" (Yodel of the Pyrenees). She then sought out examples to which we could link and located a version recorded by the French Canadian performer Joseph Saucier in 1910 for Columbia (issue # E464; matrix # 8045), hosted through the Virtual Gramophone project of Library and Archives Canada (Saucier 1910). We then added the URL for the audio recording to our database record.

This approach worked well for songs that had been published or recorded in one form or another, but it was no help for songs that have not been recorded or for which we could not locate a recorded version. Still, considering our constraints, we successfully brought together melodies and lyrics.

In addition to recognizing the limitations of their approach, Kolovos and Ornstein realized that connecting lyrics to their associated melodies addressed only part of the challenge. A second important consideration that informed our project is particularly pointed for ethnographic collections: content stripped of cultural context. Without knowing the music, one cannot sing the song. Without cultural context, the embedded meaning of the song to the person who inscribed it, the social functions of the song, and a host of ethnographic data are lost. As folklorists, we see the complex interplay of these sites of contextualization—the situational, the cultural, the linguistic (to name just a few that we encountered in this particular project)—as crucial to understanding expressive culture from the perspective of those who enact it. And as ethnographic archivists, we believe that a central part of our role involves maintaining as much information about these sites of use and performance as possible, preserving context along with text. VFC has done this most often through interviews with culture bearers, creating a wrapper, if you will, of ethnographic data around materials in the collection so that some understanding of what these things meant—and possibly still mean—can persist in time.

The tense issue—*meant* versus *mean*—is important as we preserve and present archival materials to the public. The majority of the songbook manuscripts in our collection date to the mid-twentieth century and were created by people who died long before these objects came into our possession. As a result, the materials are subject to multiple levels of contextualization and interpretation—foremost those embedded in the period of their creation and active use but also, significantly, to later interpretive frames that historicize them, that classify them and their content as a part of academic exercise, or that see them as family heirlooms tethering past and present.

Songs in Context

As mentioned earlier, these sorts of materials and the activity they supported—communal singing—were once integral to social interaction among many Vermonters of French Canadian origin. In the words of our late colleague Greg Sharrow, the *soirée* as event—and song as a crucial component of it—served the roles of "simultaneously affirming connections within family networks, strengthening relationships between families, and asserting French identity and the continuity of French culture in the Anglophone world of their new home" (2012). And well into the mid-twentieth century, Vermont was not always a welcoming place to French Canadians, so gatherings like these of family and friends, particularly outside the "p'tit Canadas" of Winooski and Burlington (Beattie 1989, 1992; Chase 2016), provided oases of cultural immersion and cultural reinforcement.[7]

Martha Pellerin—the creator of the Martha Pellerin Collection and an important advocate for Franco-American culture in Vermont who passed away in 1998—shared a description of such an event in an interview with Sharrow in the 1990s. Note that Martha was born in 1961 and refers to her childhood in the 1960s and 1970s:

> The soirées when we were kids . . . very often we'd start off early evening with a meal with whoever's there. And then people would just keep showing up during the evening and the party would just get bigger and bigger and bigger. It wasn't unusual to have sixty people in the house for a soirée. These parties always last until the wee hours of the morning. And everybody in the family has a song that's significant to them. When my mom got up to sing, you pretty much knew that she was going to sing one of maybe three songs. And that was pretty much the same with everybody. It's comforting because you know you're going to hear that, that song, and you expect it. (Pellerin 1997)

Building on Sharrow's work to further contextualize our archives, Andy sat down with Bob Desrosiers, donor of the Desrosiers/Joyal Family Collection, while he played a tape made at a house party in the 1970s that featured his grandfather singing "La Gangarla" (Adam's apple). (Chase and Desrosiers determined that *gangarla* is a word of Basque origin [Azkue 1905].) As Pellerin notes, in Franco-American families individual relatives often had "a song that's significant to them" that they could be depended upon to sing at gatherings. "La Gangarla" was such a song for Desrosiers's grandfather, and, as indicated by Desrosiers (not to mention as evidenced on the recording), he was far from a virtuoso singer. Desrosiers shared that his grandfather's anticipated performances of "La Gangarla" were greeted with equally anticipated laughter, teasing, and abuse, marking this almost ritual exchange as a fundamental component of family gatherings. How does this knowledge change the understanding of the song? And what else can these ethnographic insights add to our collections?

Desrosiers has a large collection of recordings made at *soirées* by his father and his uncle, many of which he donated to VFC. They range from open reel recordings made in the 1960s to cassettes recorded in the 1970s, and they provide a wonderful window into this aspect of the social world of immigrants and first-generation Franco-Americans in the Lakeside neighborhood of Burlington, Vermont. When Andy asked him why he thought his father documented these events, Bob said, "My father made the early recordings to send to my uncle who was a lifer in the Air Force. After my uncle retired and was back in the area I think that he made some of the other tapes. I doubt there was any thought of posterity. Even I didn't think of what was being lost until almost all of the singers were gone" (personal communication, 2018).

So, at least initially, these tapes were about including his uncle in family activities remotely—and a great example of the use of recording technology to extend the family circle to include those geographically absent from it.

Here Desrosiers reflects on the song "Chanson du Jour de l'an" (Song for New Year's Day):

"Chanson du Jour de l'an" is a song that is sung only on New Year's Day. New Year's was always a big deal. People would go house to house to visit relatives and friends, maybe sing a song and definitely have a drink. It got pretty interesting by the end of the day. The gist of the refrain is that "It's the time of the new year. We shake hands and embrace. It's the time to take advantage of. It comes but once a year." The verses go through the preparations made for the holiday. The last verse says, "There are those who smell of pipe smoke, others of onions. But I tell you right now, most smell of the drink." (personal communication, 2018)

For the past few years, Desrosiers has recorded himself singing songs from his family repertoire that exist only as transcribed lyrics. To date he has uploaded approximately 125 songs, about 50 of which include lyrics. He continues working on deciphering lyrics and recalling melodies for the remaining songs. Desrosiers's digital efforts are yet another way to add voice to inscribed text.

These house parties were—and still are, when they occur—social events tied to shared identity—broad ethnic identity certainly, but in practice the scope of house parties was more intimate and tied to closer networks of kinship, friendship, geography—including specific sites of origin in Quebec as well as more immediate geographies such as neighbor-hood, parish, and town of residence.

Today nearly a quarter of Vermonters (22.3 percent) are of French Canadian descent (Myall 2012). We argue—echoing perspectives expressed by the Vermont singers Michèle Choinière and Deb Flanders in their *Native Daughters* project (2005)—that we can no lon-ger treat the cultural practices and perspectives of Franco-Americans as something distinct from or outside "Vermont culture" but rather need to see them as an important component of it.[8] The cultural heritage of Franco-Americans is a crucial aspect of the contemporary iden-tity and culture of the state. And this is where the Revitalizing Franco-American Song in the Champlain Valley of Vermont project emerged.

REVITALIZING FRANCO-AMERICAN SONG

The Revitalizing Franco-American Song in the Champlain Valley of Vermont project sought to overcome the limitations of our archival approach and the language barrier to promote, present, and revitalize Franco-American song as a vital cultural asset for all Vermonters.

The project itself was built around developing a "Franco-American Singing School" that ran for six weeks over fall 2018. It was executed through a partnership between two organ-izations (the Vermont Folklife Center and Young Tradition Vermont), two culture bearers/performers (Carmen Beaudoin Bombardier and Kim Chase), and the folklorist/archivist/musician Lisa Ornstein. Young Tradition Vermont managed administrative activities such as overseeing registration and organizing classes. Beaudoin and Chase focused on select-ing the repertoire and developing the pedagogical approach. Ornstein worked with the song texts selected by Beaudoin Bombardier and Chase, transcribing music and lyrics and—crucial to our thinking—creating both phonetic renditions of the songs and, with Chase, English-language translations of them to make both the sound of the language and its content more accessible to non-French speakers. With all these materials, VFC created a print songbook for use in the classes and a website that featured all the print materials as well as audio recordings of Beaudoin Bombardier and Chase performing the songs. To be very clear, the book and website were viewed not as the end product but as supplementary to our efforts to ensure that these songs were accessible. We intended the Singing School as the primary output, and we created the resources to support the goals of the school, not as an end in themselves.

So why a "singing school"? We could have tried to accomplish our goals by creating a web-based resource, but our experience has shown that web-based resources are seldom used. We also could have just created a print songbook and included with it access to audio recordings—but how many people would buy it, and how much impact would it have?

As our plans developed, we thought about the school from several perspectives, the most important of which was the creation of a learning environment that mirrored as much as possible the social contexts in which these songs have been shared historically. To this end, the classes met at Beaudoin Bombardier's house on the South Side of Burlington rather than at a more public location. The Singing School was certainly not a *soirée* in the classic Franco-American/French Canadian sense, but we hosted it in a home so that it could provide some direct exposure to aspects of the *soirée* experience and embed the learning of the material within a social context. In addition, by facilitating a collective learning experience, we hoped to encourage participants to continue the transmission of the songs and the other cultural traditions that emerged through the classes. By teaching both the songs and the context, we hoped to foster an understanding of the intersection between text and context and expressive form/culture and to foster the replication of *soirées*, music, and song.

However, this effort to present a culturally immersive social learning environment addressed only one of our goals. How could we make clear the idea that Franco-American culture is not on the margins but rather something that has shaped the history of Vermont? And how could we make this experience accessible to others? Opening up a window of understanding into expressive cultural forms that are inextricably tied to language necessitates diminishing the barrier that language often presents. Through the project, we had two primary ways of overcoming this—textual and interpersonal. From a textual perspective, we saw the creation of phonetic renditions of the French-language lyrics and translations of the songs into English as crucial to making the sound of the language and its meaning accessible to non-French speakers. Lisa Ornstein developed the phonetic system for the project by drawing on a system created by Ann Savoy for her book *Cajun Music: Reflection of a People* (1984).

From the perspective of interpersonal engagement, we provided the opportunity for dialog with the instructors as another important avenue for connecting participants to cultural context and Beaudoin Bombardier and Chase's personal cultural experiences. Both women have extensive experience with public presentation and interpretation of Franco-American culture and identity. Beaudoin Bombardier, with her long history of performance, and Chase, with her career as a public school French teacher, are articulate and engaging and know how to work with groups.

These three elements—a social pedagogy of traditional song; the scaffolding for non-French speakers to help overcome language limitations; and the presence of engaging and articulate culture bearers to assist in the navigation of tradition, language, and culture—are key aspects of the project.

So how did it work out? One key change turned out to be demographic—our original intent was to focus on young people within the scope of Young Tradition Vermont's mission: ages twelve to thirty. After we opened enrollment, we were overwhelmed by interest from adults and decided to broaden the scope. The twenty-five available slots filled quickly as well, despite intentionally limited advertising. The class held its first meeting on Monday, September 17, 2018, and met once a week for six weeks with fifteen to twenty-eight people filling Beaudoin Bombardier's living room and three-season porch for ninety minutes. Rather than the dialogic exchange between teacher and students we imagined, the class was filled with group sharing of cultural experiences and discussions of songs, of the French language, of holidays and traditions—so our nod toward immersive learning was enriched immeasurably.

Reflecting on the Singing School, Beaudoin Bombardier notes that one of the things she likes best about sharing her music is giving people who grew up singing these songs a chance to re-experience them. Not surprisingly, many of the attendees were Franco-

Class in session. Beaudoin Bombardier's group in foreground, Chase's group beyond glass doors on three-season porch. (Photograph by author.)

Americans who embraced the opportunity to reconnect with their cultural heritage. Chase shares that singing these songs with the students, people who value the music so much that they dedicated one night a week for eight weeks to engage with it, was both humbling and validating—"a true joy." Most of all, she loved hearing the thrill in the voices of participants who suddenly recalled singing a particular song at some forgotten, happy time in their lives. In addition, she loved hearing the stories, anecdotes, and other versions or verses of the songs brought to the gathering.

One particularly gratifying comment came from a participant, Ian Drury, Martha Pellerin's son, who enrolled in the class with his three children, ages eight through the early teens. In a Facebook post following the class, Ian expressed his appreciation for the chance the Singing School provided for the next generation to connect with the music he had grown up performing: "So thankful for this opportunity to have my children be around this music and tradition in a way that they can learn the songs themselves. Thank you Lisa Ornstein for your phonetic work. It was really helpful to my kids:)."

Another participant, who attended sessions with her elderly mother, reflected, "I wanted to do an activity with my mom centered around our heritage. It brought us even closer and we look forward to sharing it with our family. Thank you so much for creating this opportunity!" Finally, one other participant shared, "I got to sing many songs that were sung in my family growing up and also several songs totally new to me. All of this happened in a lighthearted and fun way in Carmen's living-room, just as [it] might have happened in times gone by."

But not everyone who took part in the Singing School had cultural connections to French Canada—and this was very much our hope. It was especially satisfying to Beaudoin Bombardier that people not of French Canadian descent wanted to learn these songs and sing them. One non-Franco participant, the traditional musician and teacher Brian Perkins, reflected on the Singing School this way:

> To be able to enter Carmen's house and hear her sing and tell stories from her family's repertoire tremendously enriched my connection to the local Franco-American singing tradition. I was able to learn valuable repertoire and cultural context that I have used in my teaching in the Burlington school system. Particularly, the experience has allowed me to better connect French-speaking New Americans to the historical Franco-American traditions of our region. For the future I feel I am connected to tradition bearers who can continue to educate me and guide me in understanding a very local cultural tradition. (personal communication, 2020).

Perkins, the teacher, became once more a student. Then, wearing the shoes of an educator, he carried what he learned to his own students, contextualizing and recontextualizing it to make the songs relevant and meaningful to them.

We concluded the Singing School, appropriately, with a *soirée* at Kim Chase's house. Participants gathered there and spent the evening sharing food and singing the songs they learned together.

The Revitalizing Franco-American Song in Vermont project began with a question that emerged while we were cataloging collections of Franco-American song in the Vermont Folklife Center Archive: for the sake of users of these collections, how can we connect transcribed lyrics with the melodies that make them songs? In wrestling with this problem, Kolovos and Ornstein found solutions suited to the texts in the archive but also opened up more questions related to cultural context, performance, and the continued meaning of these songs within living tradition. To bridge the distance between archive and living cultural practice, Kolovos and Ornstein reached out to Carmen Beaudoin Bombardier and Kim Chase and, ultimately, Young Tradition Vermont to develop a way to connect culture bearers with the public and to inspire deeper engagement with Vermont Franco-American singing traditions, an effort that led to the Franco-American Singing School. Through the Singing School we created an environment that fostered direct personal connection and group interaction: social learning for a social music. By bringing together Francos and non-Francos, we hoped to educate participants about a potentially unfamiliar cultural context while simultaneously stressing the potentially unrecognized familiarity of much of the culture from which it emerged. Taken together, we made a small step in a larger effort. By contextualizing Franco-American music within a discourse of the traditional music of Vermont—rather than as distinct from it—we begin to assert the deep significance of Franco-American experience in the culture and history of the state.

Dénouement

Each spring, Young Tradition Vermont selects a significant figure in the history of Vermont Traditional music to honor through a tribute concert that caps off the group's annual Young Traditional Weekend. For 2019, Young Tradition chose to recognize Martha Pellerin. As a part of the event, students from the Franco-American Singing School, including Martha's son and her three grandchildren, took to the stage alongside Carmen Beaudoin Bombardier and Kim Chase to perform two songs—"La Boiteuse" (The hobbling lady) and "J'entends le moulin" (I hear the mill).

Notes

1. Partners included the musician, folklorist, and archivist Lisa Ornstein; the culture bearers Carmen Beaudoin Bombardier and Kim Chase; and the Vermont nonprofit organizations Young Tradition Vermont and the Vermont Folklife Center. The project was supported by a grant from the Champlain Valley National Heritage Partnership, a program of the Lake Champlain Basin Program.

2. Items of this sort in the Vermont Folklife Center Archive range from hardbound notebooks, school composition notebooks, and small notepads to the blank backs of calendar pages and loose sheets of paper.

3. *Cahiers* is the word commonly used both in Quebec and in Franco-American New England to refer to notebooks of family songs and memorabilia.

4. See Bucky Halker's chapter in this volume for more on "potential music" or what Halker calls "song-poems."

5. MacArthur performed the song frequently live and recorded it for her 1989 album, *Vermont Ballads and Broadsides*. The Library of Congress's unit dedicated to folk materials has borne the following names: from 1928 to 1955 it was called the Archive of American Folk Song; from 1946 to 1955 a parallel section, the Folklore Section, existed as a part of the music division; from 1955 to 1981 it was known as the Archive of Folk Song; from 1981 to 2003 it was called the Archive of Folk Culture; and since 2003 it has been known as the Archive of the American Folklife Center. Here we use the name current at the time MacArthur reached out to them.

6. Of course, projects like this are never truly done. We continue to revisit and correct all the mistakes made the first time around.

7. Vermont State Advisory Committee (1983) includes a discussion of discrimination against and stereotyping of Franco-Americans in Vermont.

8. Michèle Choinière is from a Franco-American family from St. Albans, Vermont, and Deb Flanders is an English-language singer and the grand-niece of Helen Hartness Flanders, who collected English-language songs in Vermont from 1930 to 1960. Her collection, the Helen Hartness Flanders Ballad Collection, is held by Middlebury College. The project and resulting recording were important efforts to assert the place of Franco-American traditional music within the broader scope of Vermont traditional music rather than as just an adjunct to it. Their effort informed our thinking on this project.

PART II. BEYOND PRESERVATION
AND CONSERVATION

Folklorists both create and draw from collections for our work, conducting research in archives to provide necessary context for our work, while also creating collections of our own with our documentation. Whether archived interview indexes and photographs stored in acid-free paper boxes or on external hard drives or a museum's physical objects stored off site in a climate-controlled environment, collections are left behind for others to work from, learn from, improve upon, and even use as the basis from which to create something new. Collections are also subject to deterioration over time. These are the pathways we leave others to find in the future.

As folklorists, we need to think critically about the tracks we leave and follow, on the collections we make and use. Collections are far from neutral renderings: they can be assembled and purposed in ways that amplify racism, colonization, and misogyny. We must reflect on how to care for them, how to repatriate them (when necessary), and even when to let go of them. We might spend years organizing them, compiling metadata around them, and making them public. Quality collections management assists folklorists and communities in the future. For instance, both archival and museum collections have been of fundamental importance for some Native American communities in their cultural revitalization efforts. Crafts can be reverse engineered; ethnographic fieldnotes may shed light on lost cultural knowledge.

Despite the many changes in our field over the past two centuries, building collections, maintaining collections, and using collections has remained central to folklore studies since its inception. Yet documenting and archiving culture little more assists in its survival than pinning a butterfly into a collection helps secure the survival of the species. This section looks at a sampling of contemporary challenges that ethnographers, archivists, and curators face in going beyond preservation and conservation.

Nicole Saylor reflects on the federally funded documentation conducted by folklorists throughout the United States and looks toward the challenges of the preservation of mass volumes of ethnographic data. Saylor provides an introduction to the creation of public folklore infrastructure in the United States and brings perspective to the challenges archivists face in managing and recirculating the documentation work that folklorists do.

Terri Van Orman's chapter visits the midsize cultural center Folklore Village, in southwestern Wisconsin. When Van Orman stepped into her role as director, she inherited unsorted (and therefore unusable) collections of vinyl records, folk dress, and even a historic but disassembled and partially rotted log home. These three examples help show how even disordered collections can be organized, made public, and put into service of the community.

The essay by Nathan Gibson and Anna Rue explores another sort of unsorted collection: a box of homemade field recordings of live musicians by the late citizen-ethnomusicologist Arnold Munkel. With cassettes spliced together and lacking song titles or performer information, Gibson and Rue faced the challenges of organizing the cassettes, digitizing them, and eventually building a public portal to access these recordings—while negotiating complex legal issues of informed consent surrounding their fair use.

Robert Teske's chapter discusses his work with James Leary and Janet Gilmore in documenting Wisconsin folk art to create a series of exhibits for the Kohler Art Museum. Although each exhibit surpassed the previous one in terms of success, the fieldworkers faced increasing top-down pressure to conduct fieldwork a certain way. Teske details how he accepted the position as director of the Cedarburg Cultural Center and realized the importance of installing folklorists in administrative positions to help advance the larger vision of the field beyond the necessity of documentation, preservation, conservation, and even presentation.

In Janet Gilmore's chapter, she reflects on collaborative fieldwork and the documentation process through a look back at fieldwork completed in the 1980s. Gilmore examines how memory and even technology alter the ways in which these working documents are used in public presentations and programming and the re-creation necessary for archivists, researchers, and community members as they continue to learn from and make use of the documentation and preservation of traditions.

Diana N'Diaye's contribution on the Smithsonian Folklife Festival looks at the way governments use the folklife festival model to amplify the work of folk artists through cultural heritage tourism. In doing so, N'Diaye takes us beyond preservation and conservation by noting the importance of collaboration to respectful and effective amplification.

The chapters in this section suggest that documentation for the sake of preservation is met with countless challenges, but with those challenges come opportunities, sometimes decades down the road. These pieces collectively advocate for not only the continued investment in, engagement with, and collaborative use of archival collections but also the continued reevaluation of how we build collections to meet our future needs.

Securing a Future for the Nation's Folklore Documentation Heyday

NICOLE SAYLOR

All across the United States, there are little-known collections of field notes, photographs, sound recordings, and moving images that document traditional cultures and communities from the mid-1970s through the mid-1990s. Created by an impassioned group of academically trained folklorists at the height of federal funding for folklore, these collections have the power to inform those outside a culture and inspire those within it. Not since the better-known Works Progress Administration era of the 1930s have a nation's cultural workers amassed such an incredible range of visual and sonic documentation of Indigenous and immigrant communities and their musical and artistic, occupational and recreational, and religious and spiritual traditions.

Collectively, this documentation represents important segments of the cultural legacy of the United States. Captured were the songs, stories, sayings, dances, customs, beliefs, foodways, and handwork from many communities: occupational folklore of New York's subway workers and California's migrant workers; Irish step dancing, Brazilian capoeira, Puerto Rican bomba, and square dance calls; poetry from American cowboys, fishermen, ranchers, and Native Americans; stories and images of bay houses on Long Island, sharecropper cabins in the South, and adobe houses in the Southwest. The documentation was created at a time when popular and traditional music were becoming interwoven. Fueled by the proliferation of mass media, the nation was gaining exposure to musical offerings beyond the classic Anglo- and African American southern preoccupations of revivalists. Ethnic musical traditions such as conjunto and polka were reaching broader audiences, and klezmer was experiencing a fervent revival.

Today, the collections are at risk of being lost. Housed in archives, museums, arts agencies, nonprofit organizations, universities, and private homes across the United States, many of these late twentieth-century collections are contained on recording formats highly susceptible to degradation and obsolescence. The contents of many collections aren't well described or are stored in places that lack the capacity to digitally preserve them, let alone make them accessible onsite or online for research.

Providing ongoing care is an ethical imperative when documenting communities that agree to share their traditions and cultures. Inaccessible or deteriorating collections threaten to damage relationships between institutions and communities. Inaction jeopardizes long-term access to a national trove of one-of-a-kind field recordings of oral narratives, songs, and other vibrant forms of cultural expression.

Archivists and folklorists have been working at this problem from different angles for well over twenty years. They have held conferences and convened experts to establish digital preservation and descriptive standards. They have sought grant money to survey collections and experiment with consortial solutions. And, in some cases, they have catalyzed wholesale audiovisual digital preservation efforts at institutions where some of these collections are housed.

Likely the first coordinated exercise in the United States to address folklore archives from a perspective of a professional archivist was a 1991 effort between the New York Folklore Society (NYFS) and the New York State Archives, which resulted in a conference, a survey, and a published report (Kolovos 2010). Subsequent gatherings, such as the Folk Heritage Collections in Crisis initiative at the Library of Congress in 2000, yielded published proceedings in the form of a Council on Library and Information Resources (CLIR) Report in 2001. In fact, early publications from the American Folklife Center at the Library of Congress, such as *Folklife and Fieldwork* and *Ethnographic Collections in the Archive of Folk Culture*, served as de facto handbooks for the archival arrangement of folklore materials for many folklorists in the United States. In the nonprofit sector, Preserving America's Cultural Traditions (PACT) started in the 2000s and turned its focus to addressing the archival needs of organizations with folklore collections. The American Folklore Society has been actively involved in furthering the work started by PACT through the National Folklore Archives Initiative (NFAI). Meanwhile, institutional archives were scaling digitization and beginning to fold in ethnographic audiovisual materials. For example, spurred by an archivist at the Archive of Traditional Music at Indiana University (IU), in 2013, IU president Michael A. McRobbie announced the Media Digital Preservation Initiative (MDPI), which was charged with digitally preserving and providing access to all significant audio, video, and film recordings on all IU campuses by the IU Bicentennial in 2020.

The audiovisual portions of folklore collections raise broader—and daunting— preservation concerns. A 2015 study concluded that of the more than 537 million sound recordings housed at collection-holding organizations across the United States, more than 250 million audio items are preservation-worthy and have not yet been digitized. The estimated cost to digitize all of the preservation-worthy items is at least $20 billion (Lyons, Chandler, and Lacinak 2015, 17). Even once audio materials are digitized, it is hard to glean meaningful information about their content, unlike textual materials, which can often be made full-text searchable. Institutions scaling digital preservation of these formats are working on ways to incorporate manual descriptions from experts along with automated solutions so that value can be derived from these collections, which would otherwise lead to lack of interest and use (Dunn et al. 2018, 7).

The distributed nature and disparate locations of late twentieth-century collections create additional challenges. Grants to fund ethnographic fieldwork were awarded to many state arts agencies and small nonprofit organizations, whose primary responsibility was to develop exhibits, festivals, documentary sound recordings, radio shows, films, and other programs and publications. The fieldwork was considered source material and often repurposed across projects. With few exceptions, archiving of these collections was never a well-supported activity within those organizations.[1] Because of the distributed and often hidden nature of this documentation, no one has been able to establish a true baseline data set outlining the location and ownership of the nation's publicly funded folklore collections and the extent to which they are preserved and accessible. A series of successful grant-funded national and regional surveys of folklore collections helped bring about subsequent initiatives to catalog key collections in a central online database. These efforts reinforced the need for collection creators to secure a future for their at-risk collections. One encouraging outcome is that most major folklore organizations created during the funding heyday have entered into negotiations or signed agreements to transfer their collections to institutional archives at universities and federal and state repositories where trained archivists collect, preserve, and make accessible unique collections using infrastructure with ongoing funding support.[2]

These collections are entering archives at a time of increasing concern over the longevity of physical audiovisual materials, which has prompted several institutions to embark on projects to digitize audiovisual materials for long-term preservation and improved access. At the same time, institutional archives are seeing a rapid rise of born-digital audiovisual ethnographic content, which has its own stability issues and competes for institutional resources aimed at stabilizing, preserving, and making accessible archival collections.

To avoid permanently losing the collections generated during the heyday, archivists and folklorists must employ steadfast commitment, creative and strategic planning, and a significant investment of time and human capital. As important, they must work to connect these materials back to the communities where they matter most.

THE RISE OF THE HEYDAY

The genesis for the robust funding era is marked by activities that crystalized around the 1976 US Bicentennial celebration at the annual Smithsonian Folklife Festival, which lasted three months. Some years later, the folklorist Bess Lomax Hawes (1921–2009) recalled that "almost every person I know who is active today in the area of public folklore participated at least in some small fashion in the 1976 Festival. Historians will eventually look at the far-reaching effects of the 1976 Festival of American Folklife" (Pettan and Titon 2019). The same year, the American Folklife Center (AFC), where I now work, was established at the Library of Congress by an act of Congress to "preserve and present" folklife. A year later, in 1977, Hawes moved to the National Endowment for the Arts (NEA) as its Folk Arts Program director; there she would build a well-funded national network in support of traditional arts helmed by folk arts coordinator positions in state arts councils. Hawes, who served as director from 1977 to 1992, grew the program's annual budget from $100,000 to more than $4 million. She established a network of state-based folk arts programs in fifty of the fifty-six states and territories covered and apprenticeship programs for traditional arts in more than forty states (Smithsonian n.d.). A wave of academically trained folklorists entering the field undergirded this flourishing movement (Feintuch 1988, 70).

The Bicentennial celebration marked a time when the country was turning away from notions of a melting pot toward a celebration of the diversity of its peoples. With this came a drive to document the variety of cultural practices. It was fieldwork that enabled state arts agencies and nonprofits to engage with underserved communities. Fieldwork was often undertaken as a way to identify traditional artists to present at festivals or participate in folk arts apprenticeship programs. The resulting documentation focused on the transmission of knowledge and creativity that allowed traditions to be learned and passed onto others. It became a resource for cultural communities and the public.

A distinguishing aspect of folklore documentation from this era is the presence of a creative intention to document events, social customs or practices, traditional beliefs, oral histories, narratives, and other community-based activities into a multisensory collection, one that can be seen, read, heard, and touched (Hoog 2018). The result was a proliferation of field notes, photography, sound recording, and moving image materials that often became the responsibility of the folklorists or the institutions that hired them (Gilmore 2015).

The practice of preserving ethnographic research is a central characteristic in folkloristics in the United States, something that distinguishes it from other ethnographic disciplines such as anthropology (Kolovos 2010, viii). Yet care for these collections was uneven across the organizations sponsoring the documentary projects. Places such as the Western Folklife Center and the Vermont Folklife Center, where professional archivists cared for the collections generated by those institutions, were the exception. The folklorist Janet Gilmore describes working as a contract folklorist in Wisconsin during this time: "The typical public folklore project of this era—in my localized experience—had a number of qualities that have contributed to what has been called our twenty-first century crisis in folk heritage collections (Council on Library and Information Resources 2001). Even though these projects were often better funded than most projects today, they still struggled with inadequate budgets, dubious infrastructure, and ambitious goals that depended on temporary workers and further grant funding to achieve fully" (2015, 102). She noted that long-term conservation of project documentation was often a low-level concern for sponsoring organizations and temporary workers.

Meanwhile, the AFC adopted a centralized approach to conducting field surveys using federally appropriated funds. During the first full year of AFC operations, it launched two field documentary projects, the Chicago Ethnic Arts Project and the South-Central Georgia Folklife Project, where teams of fieldworkers went into communities to document music, verbal arts, material culture, occupational culture, and the like. In his twenty-five-year retrospective on the AFC, Alan Jabbour (1996) remarked that the field projects spanned the entire first generation of the Center's existence, having in a sense defined the Center. Between 1977 and 1997, AFC conducted approximately twenty-five ethnographic field projects and cultural surveys in various parts of the United States.

Like all heydays, the era of flourishing funding ended. With the changes in congressional leadership in 1995, federal funding priorities shifted and pressure mounted to defund and privatize federal arts agencies, including the NEA.[3] Support for large-scale ethnographic surveys receded across federal agencies. At the AFC, a shrinking budget gradually led the Center to focus on its collections-based functions. The last field survey of any size was conducted in 1997.

Now, AFC channels its documentary impulses into providing ethnographic training expertise and awarding annual grants to fieldworkers for ethnographic projects that adhere to a set of topical and technical guidelines. The archive's role has grown to accommodate more than the documentation generated at the behest of the Library, whether it be the 1980s–1990s field surveys or early twentieth-century wax cylinders made by the archives founder Robert Winslow Gordon or the many disc recordings created during the John and Alan Lomax era. Increasingly, the archives are becoming home to collections generated by documentarians and nonprofit organizations created during the NEA public-funding heyday.

ATTENTION TURNS TO PRESERVATION

A lot of the documentation created from this time was captured on polyester-backed audiotape, a medium we have since learned is prone to develop "sticky-shed syndrome"—a condition that causes damage to tape during playback unless it is desiccated or "baked" at low temperature in special ovens prior. Before the advent of polyester tape, audiotape was commonly backed with acetate, a medium prone to developing its own problems over time, including "vinegar syndrome," severe shrinkage, brittleness, deformation, and eventual delamination. A recent report on AFC's AV collections noted: "Though there is no hard onset date for these issues, when they do occur they often begin between 20–30 years after tape production, except in cases where materials have been stored in poor conditions or in the case of certain low-quality tape stocks, which may accelerate onset" (American Folklife Center 2018). There was also the short-lived and problematic DAT format, which is prone to playback errors and data loss. Needless to say, all formats used during that era are distinctly on the obsolescence and degradation path.

While funding for ethnographic projects began to shrink, an awareness was already growing about the fragility of the audiovisual formats used in documentation from this era and the need to enlist the help of archivists. Quite likely the first coordinated exercise in the United States to address folklore archives from the perspective of professional archivists was a late 1980s grant-funded project to survey folklore archival collections in New York state, conduct a conference, and produce *Folklore Archives and the Documentary Heritage of New York State*, a foundational document that began to apply seriously archival methods to folklore archives (Kolovos 2010, 146–49). That project was followed in 1994 and 1998 by two practical handbooks for managing folklore archives, which became widely referenced by folklorists looking for advice on how to handle their research collections. The work at AFC influenced the work in New York state, which drew on professional archival methods in instructional guides, including *Folklife and Fieldwork* (Winick and Bartis 2016) and *Ethnographic Collections in the Archive of Folk Culture* (Hall 1995).

In 2000, AFC issued a call to action. The *Folk Heritage Collections in Crisis* report, which was based on a 2000 symposium and national survey commissioned by the AFC and the American Folklore Society, concluded that hundreds of thousands of historic ethnographic audio recordings were in danger. According to the report, "Both the local documentary sound materials and professional archival audio collections are at risk of deterioration and terminal neglect as America enters a new century" (Council on Library and Information Resources 2001, 1).

A survey conducted ahead of the conference was aimed at providing a baseline data set about the nation's recorded folklore. Of the three hundred respondents to the survey, more than three-quarters reported that 25 to 50 percent of their collections were "seriously deteriorated." In addition to problems such as "sticky shed," other problems associated with the audio collections include inadequate storage conditions and cracked wax cylinders.

Not only was the documentation deteriorating but also the people conducting the Collections in Crisis survey revealed uncertainty about the overall scope of folklore and ethnomusicology recordings, where recordings were housed, and how accessible they were: "Although the results are profoundly interesting and paint [a] vivid picture of the state of collections, not enough data were gathered to serve the stated purpose. Rather, this survey reveals where the state of knowledge ends and ignorance begins" (Council on Library and Information Resources 2001, 59–60).

A flurry of other initiatives followed the symposium. From 2002 to 2004 the Smithsonian Institution and the AFC jointly conducted Save our Sounds, a project to develop preservation standards for ethnographic audio records. Years later, the Archives of Traditional Music at Indiana University and the Archive of World Music Harvard University Libraries embarked on a project called Sound Directions: Digital Preservation and Access for Global Audio Heritage, funded by the National Endowment for the Humanities (NEH), to test emerging standards and develop best practices for audio preservation.

In his dissertation, the folklorist-archivist Andy Kolovos noted: "Projects like *Save our Sounds* and *Sound Directions* were possible in large part due to the relatively easy access these institutions have to four key things that most public sector folklore organizations lack: trained staff dedicated to audio preservation, quality analog playback and digital conversion equipment, large-scale information technology (IT) support, and ready access to dedicated funds" (Kolovos 2010, 221).

EXPLORING CONSORTIAL SOLUTIONS

As a handful of public institutions were focusing more attention on digital preservation, concerns throughout the public folklore sector continued to build. Private nonprofit folklore organizations and folklorists whose folk arts programs had suffered under state budget cuts grappled to sustain stewardship of their ever-growing collections, which were expanding exponentially with the mainstreaming of born-digital recording and photography devices.

In Wisconsin, the folklorist Janet Gilmore recognized a growing need to preserve folklore fieldwork in her region. Toward that end, in 2002, through her work at the Center for the Study of Upper Midwestern Cultures at UW–Madison, Gilmore led a Heritage, Preservation, and Access grant from the National Endowment for the Arts to begin to identify, locate, describe, inventory, and make more accessible public folk arts project collections generated during the heyday in Wisconsin and border states (Gilmore 2015, 100). It would be the first of a series of grants Gilmore and her colleagues received in support of this work. Her approach to identifying collections was to assemble a list of NEA Folk Arts grant awardees in the region starting in the mid-1970s. Under Gilmore's direction, I was hired in 2005–6 to conduct a regional survey, contacting award recipients to find out what had become of any fieldwork associated with their grant-funded projects. In all, I conversed with more than eighty folklorists, archivists, anthropologists, and other cultural workers and visited twelve sites to assess collections. At the end of the year-long project, we had discovered more than fifty discrete collections in more than twenty locations, including institutional repositories, private and public nonprofit organizations, and private hands. We found that collections fared better (though they still could benefit from more attention) when housed at an institutional archive, yet most collections were still kept by the agencies or individual folklorists who created them. Sometimes the reason was that the owners were still drawing upon the source materials for contemporary work. Yet, too often there was not a clear plan for what would happen to this documentation once a folklorist retired or an agency folk arts program was dismantled. The reasons were threefold as I wrote following the survey:

> 1) Sometimes the folklorist simply hasn't made identifying a permanent archival home a priority (this was evident in lack of response by some would-be survey participants), but more often than not it is because of 2) a feeling that mainstream repositories do not value and understand folklore fieldwork and therefore would not provide proper care for these collections. Stories were common of fieldwork collections in mainstream repositories languishing from neglect, or being destroyed by an archivist imposing traditional (i.e., history-based) archiving principles onto folklore. Fieldworkers feel a huge sense of ownership and of responsibility to the people documented in their collections. This makes them extremely discriminating, if not at times possessive, about who is entrusted as stewards of their work. 3) Still other agencies such as the Illinois Arts Council Ethnic and Folk Arts Apprenticeship Program, and individuals like Philip Nusbaum, former Minnesota State Arts Board folklorist, have been unable to interest their state's institutional repositories in acquiring their collections. (Saylor 2006, 9)

Gilmore's approach to identifying hidden folklore collections by working from grant cards is compelling but difficult to scale. At AFC, as a proof of concept, we recently scanned in a box of grant cards from the late 1980s and scraped the data into tab-delimited form to attempt to scale such a preliminary analysis. While distinctive field survey projects are usually easy to identify, it is difficult to surmise from grant card information whether fieldwork was associated with any of the many festivals, apprenticeship projects, and other public engagement projects. Finding a way to analyze grant data to aid in identifying these collections would be an interesting avenue of inquiry for a motivated researcher.

In the mid-2000s, Preserving America's Cultural Traditions (PACT) conducted a survey of its members' documentary collections. PACT, a loose affiliation of private nonprofit organizations and university-based public programs doing public folklore, formed to strengthen relationships with federal entities such as the American Folklife Center and the Smithsonian Center for Folklife and Cultural Heritage and to share information about preservation and access issues related to the members' accidental archives.

Survey funds were administered by the Fund for Folk Culture, with money from the GRAMMY Foundation (Kolovos 2008). The archivists Andy Kolovos and Steve Green visited eleven PACT-member sites: Alabama Folklife Association, Birmingham; Alliance for

California Traditional Arts, Fresno and San Francisco; Center for the Study of Upper Midwestern Cultures/Folklore Program, University of Wisconsin–Madison; Center for Traditional Music and Dance, New York; City Lore, New York; Institute for Community Research, Hartford, Connecticut; Institute for Cultural Partnerships, Harrisburg, Pennsylvania; Michigan State University Museum, East Lansing; Philadelphia Folklore Project, Philadelphia; Vermont Folklife Center, Middlebury; and Western Folklife Center, Elko, Nevada.

According to the preliminary report to the GRAMMY Foundation, the survey found more than 8,500 audio recordings, 3,000 videos, 234,000 still images, and an untold number of manuscript materials at seven of the eleven sites surveyed. The totals do not reflect collection counts at three large nonprofit folklore organizations: CityLore, Vermont Folklife Center, and the Western Folklife Center. While many key recommendations from the report mirrored those in the *Folk Heritage Collections in Crisis* report (e.g., create cataloging standards, develop a shared catalog), it also called for the creation of shared storage and centrally supported online access for digital collection materials from PACT-member organizations (Kolovos 2008).

Today, consortial work to preserve folklore archives is happening through the National Folklore Archives Initiative (NFAI), an effort, coordinated by the American Folklore Society, to provide access to information about ethnographic collections held by folklore programs at academic institutions, community-based cultural and ethnic organizations, nonprofits, and state government–based arts and cultural agencies in the United States. An NEH grant helped NFAI create AFS Folklore Collection Database (FolkloreCollections .org), a site hosted by Indiana University that contains general information from a national survey of folklore archival repositories and collections. Grant money was used, in part, to pay staff at some locations to add specific information about collections to the searchable online database. AFS is currently executing a Council on Library and Information Resources (CLIR) Hidden Collections grant to digitize and make accessible online digital collections from some NFAI participants, starting with the Vermont Folklife Center and the Oregon Folklife Network at the University of Oregon.

PRESERVING FOLKLORE COLLECTIONS AT SCALE

The Library of Congress's 2012 National Recording Preservation Plan estimated that there remain fifteen to twenty years to digitize audio and moving image materials before most are lost to obsolescence and degradation (Nelson-Strauss, Brylawski, and Gevinson 2012, 2). At AFC, the archives turn one hundred years old in 2028. We have an ambitious goal to ensure that the collection of more than 160,000 physical audiovisual carriers remains accessible into the next hundred years.

During the fall of 2017, we conducted a comprehensive survey and assessment of AFC's physical audio and moving-image assets and made recommendations to inform future planning. We work closely with the Library's National Audio-Visual Conservation Center to prioritize onsite digitization that can be automated, such as VHS tapes, as well as digitization of the most fragile formats, including wax cylinders and acetate discs. In parallel, we have dramatically scaled up our use of external contracted digitization services, starting with audio reels, audio cassettes, and other magnetic media formats. The effort has dramatically increased preservation and access to important historic recordings. As of this publication, AFC estimates that only about 20 percent of its analog audiovisual carriers remains to be digitized. In many cases, older discs and cylinders that have not yet been transferred directly to digital are accessible via digitized copies of preservation reels made decades ago.

More broadly, the cultural heritage sector is making it a priority to develop comprehensive plans for media preservation. An early and staunch advocate for this work is Mike Casey, director of technical operations for the Media Digitization and Preservation Initiative at Indiana University (IU) and former associate director of the Archive of Traditional Music. Since the university president announced, in 2013, a $15 million investment to comprehensively digitize analog audiovisual materials across the IU system, 99 percent of the audio and video holdings (323,220 of 325,000) and 60 percent (15,044 of 25,000) of film holdings have been digitized. In a presentation Casey has been giving for years, "Why Media Can't Wait: A Gathering Storm," which is full of ominous claps of thunder and lightning bolts to drive home his point, he articulates the problem with a few keywords: "large numbers, obsolescence, degradation, high research value, and short time window" (Casey 2015, 14). His warnings, along with his proven successes in scaling up audiovisual digitization, have inspired many to pick up the digital preservation charge in earnest. For example, in 2018 the Southern Folklife Collection at the University of North Carolina was awarded a $1.75 million Andrew W. Mellon grant to digitize its more than 300,000 recordings (Nickel 2019). At the University of Wisconsin, grants from NEH are helping fund the Local Centers/Global Sounds initiative, which seeks to digitize and make available online more than a thousand commercial recordings of ethnic American music along with more than eight hundred hours of home recordings and fieldwork from the Upper Midwest.[4]

ALIVE IN MANY HANDS

In the *Folk Heritage Collections in Crisis* report of 2001, the acoustical engineer Elizabeth Cohen wrote: "our collections are far more likely to survive the scars of mayhem if they are robust and alive in many hands" (Council on Library and Information Resources 2001, 21). What good is all of this preservation effort if people don't know about these collections or use them?

Folklore documentation from the public funding heyday does have some advantages over pre-heyday ethnography. In many cases, signed permission forms exist that enable subsequent use and permit online access to the documentation. Also, many people who created and participated in the fieldwork are still living, and many have turned their attention to their own legacy and giving back to the communities they documented.

At AFC, we have embarked on a multiyear project to digitize and make accessible all AFC field survey field notes, slides, sound recordings, and moving images from the mid-1970s through the mid-1990s. To date, we have made freely accessible online cultural documentation from a diverse range of communities and geographic regions, including Lowell, Massachusetts; the Blue Ridge Parkway; greater Chicago; Montana; Rhode Island; South Central Georgia; New Mexico; and Colorado.

This documentation is extraordinary, and unfortunately, underused because of the lack of information about the collections and their research value available to the public. It also illustrates what is so dynamic about survey documentation. The fieldworkers focused their lenses and microphones on the transmission of knowledge and creativity that allowed artistic creation to be learned, made, and passed onto others. Documenting the creative process required fieldworkers to get close to the making of the art, which means getting close to the makers of the art by establishing a trusted relationship with the people and their expressive culture being documented.

Not only is this large body of digital materials being made available online, but AFC is also devoting staff time to encouraging the creative use of these collections in new projects and programs within the source communities. Working alongside the Chicago-based folklorists Lisa Rathje and Susan Eleuterio, AFC's Michelle Stefano has introduced the collection to state, regional, and local stakeholders in Chicago, including community-based cultural organizations (Stefano 2018).

They convened state, regional, and local stakeholders, including community-based cultural organizations, in 2018 to generate ideas for how to make use of the 1977 documentation. Some outcomes of that gathering include the creation of a photographic exhibit in a community museum in Chicago and the creation of a digital map highlighting the collection.[5]

Some organizations from this era have established partnerships with institutional archives to enable preservation and access of important fieldwork from this era. The partnerships sought out in recent years by the Tennessee Arts Commission and Maryland Traditions Archives are but a few examples.[6]

The Road Comes into Existence

At IU, Casey has added a new ending to his "Why Media Preservation Can't Wait" presentation. It is a quotation from the writer Lin Yutang that reads: "Hope is like a road in the country; there was never a road, but when many people walk on it, the road comes into existence." The quotation is a nod to other digital preservation "roads" that are appearing at institutions such as the New York Public Library, the University of North Carolina, the Smithsonian, Stanford, and the Library of Congress. Casey writes: "We cannot see a path to take us where we want to go and yet, as we join with other like-minded collaborators, the road rises before us and becomes real" (M. Casey 2018).

The folklore community needs to keep walking—if not running—its roads into existence. No one path or one archive is going to ensure that folklore materials are preserved and available for future generations. No one survey is going to identify all stray collections made during the public funding heyday and now lingering in basements and forgotten office filing cabinets, let alone appraise their condition or value to communities. There is an abundance of work right in front of us. Time is short to preserve the audiovisual materials created during the heyday from the mid-1970s to the mid-1990s. Time is short to glean all that we can from ethnographers who made the documentation and the tradition-bearers who shared their stories. We must push for radical collaboration between folklorists and sustainable archives, each group doing what it does best—connecting with communities and preserving collections. These efforts must be intertwined. It is imperative that we stretch to find the necessary money to fund preservation digitization and connect these materials to people who will create and learn from them.

NOTES

1. The Western Folklife Center and Vermont Folklife Center each had a trained archivist on staff and invested in an archival program. The Traditional Arts Program, located within the Michigan State University Museum, has a climate-controlled facility and trained staff.

2. The term "archives" is contested. Here, I am referring to a group of primary original, unique materials that are maintained using the principles of provenance, original order, and collective control. See Theimer (2012) for more.

3. For more about the culture wars of the 1980s, see Ault (1999); Hall (2010); Jensen (1995).

4. See Nathan Gibson and Anna Rue's chapter in this volume for more.

5. The story map "Homegrown Pride: Mapping Chicago's Community Cultural Centers" is accessible at https://arcg.is/TOr00.

6. Tennessee State Library and Archives is home to folklife materials from the Tennessee Arts Commission, which can be found at https://teva.contentdm.oclc.org/customizations/global/pages /collections/tacfolklife/tacfolklife.html. A detailed collection finding aid describes the Maryland Traditions Archives, housed at the University of Maryland-Baltimore County, https://lib.guides.umbc .edu/marylandfolklife.

Collections

Opportunities and Responsibilities

Terri Van Orman

Nonprofit organizations may find themselves caretakers of collections that are publicly inaccessible and improperly stored but nonetheless valuable—whether monetarily, academically, culturally, or artistically. Pressed for time, space, staff capacity, and money, these caretakers often find themselves at a loss as to how to process collections and make them available to a wider audience. Nonetheless, it is our responsibility as public folklorists to do our best to make sure that our collections are not only organized and well cared for but also available to the public, in order to fulfill our obligations to improve quality of life for others at a community, local, state, national, or even global level.

This chapter examines the case study of a cultural organization located in southwestern Wisconsin, Folklore Village, the collections it holds, and the steps that have been taken to organize the objects, and provide access, both physically and digitally, to the cultural treasures held within, as well as the steps that remain.

HISTORY OF FOLKLORE VILLAGE

The story of Folklore Village is related strongly to the story of Jane Farwell, the organization's founder. Born in 1916 and growing up on a farm near rural Ridgeway, Wisconsin, Jane would not normally have been afforded the type of worldly experience that she eventually embraced. However, her younger sister Philippa was hearing impaired, and it was decided to send the girls to Doty School in Madison, which taught deaf students lipreading and speaking, not just signing, as they did at the State Deaf School at Delavan. From grade school on, the two girls would ride the Greyhound bus to Madison, with seven-year-old Jane as "guardian" for her four-years-younger sister. After Jane graduated from Central High School, her aunt insisted that she attend Antioch College in Yellow Springs, Ohio, where the older woman was an instructor. Antioch was quite progressive in its time, allowing Jane to create her own major in rural community leadership, a degree that required internships. One of her internships was located at Hartley House, in New York City's Hell's Kitchen neighborhood, where the international folk dance movement was in full swing. She befriended Michael and Mary Ann Herman, who were the most notable folk dance instructors in New York at the time and who became her mentors (Miller 1992). Jane vowed to make folk dance the focus of her recreational leadership practice, and upon graduation, in 1938, she traveled the rural parts of America, teaching her distinctive brand of recreation:

In the early 1940s, she was Extension Recreation Specialist in West Virginia for the State University, and was associated with the Oglebay Institute at Oglebay Park. She directed recreation programs for more than 50 camps and conferences in Ohio, New York, Maryland, Pennsylvania, and West Virginia. . . . From 1947 to 1955, she established the country's first recreation leaders' laboratories and folk dance camps. In the years that followed, these institutes trained hundreds of camp counselors, Boy Scout, Girl Scout and 4-H leaders, physical education instructors, and folk arts instructors. Jane is credited as one of the founders of the modern folk dance movement, whose enthusiasts in the United States became [sic] to number in the thousands. (Houston 2018)

In between jaunts to teach folk dancing, Jane would return to her parents' farm in Ridgeway, where she met a young agriculturalist from Germany who had come to intern with Jane's father. They fell in love, married, and moved to Ostfriesland, Germany, to live on his family farm. Jane continued to teach folk dancing in Europe and, from what can be discerned, traveled broadly with her folk dancing. In 1956, she and fellow folk dance leaders Michael and Mary Ann Herman, Ralph Page, and Nelda Drury were chosen by the United States Department of State to teach folk dancing in Japan. In conjunction with the Japanese State Department Ministry of Education, Asahi Press, and the national YMCA of Japan, and in the spirit of reforging fellowship among humanity after World War II, the group was sent on a six-week, twenty-three-city tour teaching forty-six folk dances from sixteen nations (B. Casey 1981, 18). It was one of the Japanese people's first exposures to international folk dancing, an activity where common people get together to explore and enjoy the folk dances and sometimes other aspects of folk culture, including costuming, foodways, music, and craft of many ethnic groups and countries.

After ten years, Jane's marriage dissolved, and, in 1966, she returned to her family farm in Wisconsin. Since 1947, she had organized the annual Festival of Christmas and Midwinter Traditions near her home in Ridgeway, inviting her many friends to come and share folk dancing, music, crafts, and food. In 1967, local fans of her Christmas Festival pooled their money and purchased the 1893 one-room Wakefield Schoolhouse, which had just gone on the market after being retired when school districts consolidated. The schoolhouse was actually adjacent to her family's farm, as it was positioned on a small piece of land that Jane's grandfather had originally deeded to the county to build the school. It was at the Wakefield Schoolhouse that Folklore Village began and where Jane finally had a home to express her notions about folk festivals, community, recreation, folk dance, and the land. For example, in 1974, Jane and a group of young members of her youth dance group traveled from Ridgeway to Europe to perform on the stage in Leiden, Netherlands (*Monroe Evening Times* 1974). The organization celebrated its fiftieth anniversary in 2021.

In the 1970s, young people from Madison and beyond heard about the organization and clustered around the charismatic Jane, who taught them about music, dancing, folk culture, gardening, and cooking, forging a community that continues today. By the late 1980s, the group had outgrown the tiny one-room schoolhouse and realized its dream of building a much bigger activity center. Farwell Hall opened in 1987, complete with a sprung wooden dance floor with a parqueted Moravian Star in the center, handcrafted woodwork, blacksmith-forged chandeliers, a certified kitchen, office spaces, and classrooms.

In 1993, when Jane Farwell passed away, she deeded her family farm and all the buildings to her beloved organization, Folklore Village. Today the organization sits on ninety-four acres, with sixty-six acres of restored prairie, and boasts Farwell Hall; the late nineteenth-century Farwell family farmhouse; several outbuildings, including a large garage; the 1882 Plum Grove Chapel; the 1893 Wakefield Schoolhouse, which is flanked by two rustic bunk-houses; and currently being restored, the 1848 Aslak Lie House.

The organization's programming through the years has changed to stay relevant, and today it offers five annual dance and music festivals: a Spring Scandinavian Weekend, a Cajun Weekend, an English Country Dance Weekend, a Fall Swedish Weekend, and the Festival of Christmas and Midwinter Traditions. There are also concerts featuring musical tradition bearers, school field-trip programs for children, free concerts for local seniors, monthly open mics, barn dances featuring live string bands, and special seasonal "socials," including a Maypole Dance, a hand-cranked Ice Cream Social, a Sankta Lucia processional, and a German Christmas Tree celebration. Newest on the docket of activities is a folk school, with six instructional sessions teaching a variety of craft, music, dance, and cooking techniques.

Prior to Jane's passing, Doug Miller was hired as the organization's executive director in 1991. He and his family served the organization with distinction until his retirement, in 2012. At that time, the board of directors chose to further professionalize the organization, hiring an interim director, while they hammered out the first policy and procedures manual in preparation for the next permanent director of Folklore Village.

PHONOGRAPH RECORDS COLLECTION

Upon my arrival as the new executive director of Folklore Village, in 2014, I found much to discover and to resolve. The first matter concerned a flood that had happened in the basement of the late nineteenth-century farmhouse and the insurance claim that sought to replace the furnace, the hot-water heater, and the holding tanks, which were destroyed as a result of turning off the heat to the building during the previous extreme winter in order to save money. This economic plan resulted in the discovery of forty inches of water in the basement when the house reopened in the spring. The claim triggered an insurance auditor visit and a tour of all the facilities. The tour prompted a threat to cancel insurance coverage unless Folklore Village fulfilled a set of repairs and other requirements. One requirement was to remove the numerous cardboard boxes that were parked directly next to the furnace in Farwell Hall—all of which were discovered to house phonograph records.

The furnace room was not the only place where phonograph records were discovered—they were in a closet next to the sound system in the main hall, they were in the library, they were in the garage, and they were in the farmhouse—some loose, some in boxes or bins, and some in record-carrying cases. There were 78s, 45s, LPs, and EPs, some quite old. Many were fouled with mice leavings or mold, and quite a few of the 78s were cracked or broken. There were at least three thousand discs. What started as a requirement for keeping insurance coverage turned into the unearthing of a chronicle of the music that accompanied dancing during the height of the international folk dance heyday and the records which Jane Farwell carried with her as she crisscrossed the country teaching.

Fortunately, at the time, Rich March, the retired folk arts coordinator for the Wisconsin Arts Board and a polka specialist, was serving on our board of directors, and he was kind enough to come and help me survey the collection. Were the recordings valuable enough to save for any reason, or were they destined for the dump? Recognizing many of the recording artists, he advised, and I agreed, that the collection needed to be saved. But the question was how to find the money to sort, clean, resleeve in archival sleeves, notate in a database, file properly on a shelf to be easily located, and share them with the public?

Several grant possibilities were considered, and finally a grant request to the GRAMMY Foundation (now the GRAMMY Museum) provided the funding to purchase a record-cleaning machine and archival sleeves for the discs and to hire a team of interns to do the work. Christopher Bishop and David Natvig from the University of Wisconsin–Madison Department of Scandinavian Studies (now Department of German, Nordic, and Slavic+) came aboard, with Chris ending up doing the lion's share of the work. Later, Abby Wanserski, a graduate of UW–Madison's School of Library and Information Studies, joined the team to help us clean up and professionalize our database. Finally, when the databases were complete, we dedicated a page on our website to hosting them (The Jane Farwell Collection of Recorded Music), and I took the opportunity to link as many of the out-of-copyright songs and tunes to those that had already been digitized via the Internet Archive and other sources.[1] Accordingly, the collection, which had formerly been at risk, was now not only clean and safe but also accessible to the public as well.

The final result is a collection of records that includes among the old family phonograph records and folklore-related record donations from libraries a chronicle of the music of the international folk dance phenomenon. According to Mirjana Laušević's *Balkan Fascination*, international folk dance–themed events and activities mushroomed after World War I, especially during the Depression and the New Deal era. International folk dancing was used to symbolically promote peace among the peoples of the world (Laušević 2007, 135). During that particular period of international folk dancing (1930s–1970s), teachers who traveled carried their phonograph records (and often their portable record players) with them. An entire recording industry emerged, including specialty labels such as The Folk Dancer, Folkraft, MacGregor, Western Jubilee, Windsor, Kolo Festival, and Michael Herman's Worlds of Fun—as well as specialty subsets from the big labels like Capitol, Columbia, Decca, Imperial, and RCA Victor. All of these produced records exclusively for various styles of folk dancing and square dancing. There were even records produced under the Folklore Village label, featuring young amateur musicians from the ranks of the fledgling organization. These folk dance bands often sported fanciful names such as Jack Barbour and his Rhythm Rustlers, Bill Mooney and His Cactus Twisters, and the many versions of the Michael Herman Folk Orchestra, as well as the polka band favorites Six Fat Dutchmen and Fezz Fritsche and his Goosetown Band. There are Balkan Tamburitzan,

Scandinavian, South African, and Mexican recordings and appearances by the Choir of the
Red Army of the USSR. A bonus to this particular collection is that Jane Farwell apparently purchased recordings in Europe during the ten years that she lived in Ostfriesland
and brought home records that were rare or unavailable in the United States (Miller 1992).

Those who would like to access this collection may now make an appointment with
Folklore Village staff to spend time in the library and physically play the discs, or they may
opt, wherever they are, to hear the linked selections, connecting to their digitized versions
online. International folk dancers, whether from the Folklore Village dance community or
from any other dance community in the world, may access many recordings in the collection for teaching, dancing, or simply touching memories from an earlier time in their lives.
And ideally, the collection can be used as a resource for anyone who would like to study
the history or music of international folk dancing or perhaps even the life of Jane Farwell.

THE ASLAK LIE HISTORICAL HOME

Not long after my arrival, I was contacted by scientists from the University of Wisconsin–
Platteville concerning some logs, which I knew to be located in a pasture just south of the
old family farmhouse on the campus of Folklore Village. The logs were from the first story
of a historic home, originally located in Klevenville, Wisconsin, which had been be-
queathed to Folklore Village in 2003. It had been disassembled and transported to the site,
but the plans for rebuilding had stalled due to lack of funding. The scientists were conducting a drought study in the area and believed that the oak logs were quite possibly the oldest
felled logs in the area on which they could conduct core sampling. The house itself had
been built in 1848 and was one of the first homes built during expansion in this territory.
Of course, I granted them permission, and since I had not had a chance to survey the logs
myself, I took their visit as my opportunity to do so. What I discovered were logs that had
been covered in tarps years earlier. The tarps had developed rips due to many seasons of
severe weathering, which had allowed rainwater to get in but not to evaporate. Small seedling trees were growing out of depressions in the logs, and the surfaces of many felt "corky"
to the touch.

I met with the scientists, Dr. Evan Larson and research assistant Sara Allen. My concerns
were not theirs. They conducted their core samples to mixed results, as some of the samples
simply crumbled upon extraction. They did acquire enough ring data to more closely understand drought patterns in the eighteenth century and early nineteenth century. One log, they
verified, had its genesis as a seedling in 1713 (Larson, Allen, and Underwood 2021). That
meant the tree was 135 years old when it was felled and had lasted another 166 years as a log.

I was thrilled with this information, which added interest to the reading materials that
I had discovered in my office concerning the history of the house and its builder and
owner, Aslak Lie. Lie was born in 1798 in Aurdal, Valdres, Norway. His was a family of poor,
landless laborers who moved between farms every year or two. A fascinating character, he
learned to read and write, likely through the ambulatory school system, despite being of
rural peasant class, and became a corporal in the military. Lie married Marit Knudsdatter
Dølven, a bride from a far higher class, and became a celebrated craftsman in Norway. During his time there, he built two log homes and constructed freestanding cabinetry pieces

that are still held in Norwegian museums today (Bakken 2000). At the age of fifty, he and his family decided to emigrate to Wisconsin. Upon arriving, he, his brother, and two of his sons-in-law carved out a shallow basement in a rock outcropping at the home site and spent the first winter underground. When spring arrived, the men got to work, building the first floor—a two-room, log-only cabin. Later, a timber-framed second story was erected, with an attached *sval* (literal translation "cool" or "cool air," denoting an unheated space) that covers an outdoor stairway connecting the two stories. One can only guess Lie's surprise when he realized that in Wisconsin, he would have primarily oak logs available rather than the softer fir and spruce logs from which he had built his previous two homes in Norway. Because of this, he was forced to alter his building style to employ dovetailed, squared-off logs, with mortar in between, rather than the more tightly fitted, rounded log construction technique to which he was accustomed. Once settled in Wisconsin, he made his mark again as a craftsman, creating freestanding cabinets that are currently in the Wisconsin Historical Society collection and in that of the Minneapolis Museum of Art (Holzhueter 1986).

But my immediate concern was with those logs. Would we be able to use them to rebuild the home once funding was procured, or would we simply have to burn the materials and chalk it up to poor project management?

I knew of a man in the Folklore Village community named Nels Diller who might be able to answer that question. I was aware of a piece of his handiwork—a *stabbur* that graces Main Street in Mount Horeb, Wisconsin, which is as fine a piece of architectural woodworking as any I had seen. And I had heard through the grapevine that he was one person in the community who had been disgruntled by the progress of the rebuilding of the Aslak Lie house. So I called him, and he agreed to come over and check out the logs. Equipped with an architectural reconstruction document that had been produced on December 15, 2008, and armed with a crew of strong volunteers, he uncovered every log, checked for rot, and stacked them in a way that was more conducive to drying. At the end of the work session, he had marked each log in the document's schematic drawing to indicate whether it was missing and needed to be re-created, could be used only as a template, or was usable. He announced that the project was still feasible. Moreover, he had just retired and was looking for a "project." He asked to volunteer to head up a crew of additional volunteers to rebuild the house. Having studied Norwegian log cabin building techniques in Telemark for two summers prior to building his lovely *stabbur*, Nels could not have been more perfect for the job. I reminded him that we had only $5,000 for the project and that the 2008 estimates to complete the building were in the range of $140,000 (Pape 2008). We agreed that somehow, we would work it out.

And so far, we have done just that. With Nels's expertise, knowledge, and patient nature, the project has progressed slowly—as could be expected, especially since we were restoring ancient oak logs using primarily hand tools. He has worked with a variety of volunteers, interns, and students, teaching as he proceeds and making sure that the work satisfies his high standards of quality and workmanship. One year he had an apprentice funded by the Wisconsin Arts Board. We have invited adult students to come learn Norwegian log cabin building through our Sustainability Weekends and through our new Folk School program.

The American Scandinavian Foundation provided the stipend for Nels's teaching fee for two folk school classes. Also, in recent years he has been able to hire summer interns thanks to a grant from a private donor who has an interest in the project. We received an unexpected inheritance that promises to help us secure supplies that must be purchased, such as caulking, window glass, and finishing materials when the time comes. As a donation, a farming couple who are our neighbors allowed the volunteer crew to fell oak trees in their forest, supplying the wood for the missing or damaged logs and for interior boards. In 2019, we laid the last log of the first story, which was my only wish—to complete that first floor (the building's original form) and get those logs off the ground so that they would not degrade any further. Behind the scenes, staff has been fundraising and keeping permits and paperwork in order. Obtaining building permits and driveway permits and meeting with inspectors and Township officials—something Aslak Lie did not have to deal with in 1848—are the invisible tasks that ensure that the construction can go ahead unhampered.

As is so often the case, the building has taken on a life of its own, and the volunteer crew and Nels have decided that they will complete the building in its fully finished form, complete with second floor and *sval*. The materials for the second story have been stored indoors and so are in somewhat better shape than the logs were. Construction of the timber-framed second floor will go much faster. The plan is to totally construct the framework, currently housed in a large barn nearby, inside the building in order to ensure that everything fits together properly before having to put it together ten or twelve feet above the ground. The cedar shake roofing shingles have been purchased. The pier foundation footings for the *sval* have been poured. What was once designated as an "impossible" project by skeptics is fully under way and slowly reaching fruition. Without adequate upfront funding, we have relied on interested volunteers and student builders, as well as the generosity of our neighbors. Through human capital, our community has come together to safeguard the anticipated completion of this building.

Once finalized, the house will serve as a testament not only to the skill and fortitude of Aslak Lie, a distinctive mid-nineteenth-century immigrant craftsman from Norway, but also to the cohesion and dedication of the Folklore Village community. It will provide classroom space for Folklore Village's expanding Folk School programs, perfect for green woodworking, and other nonmechanized craft work, and as an interpretive space to tell the story of Aslak Lie.

INTERNATIONAL FOLK DANCE COSTUME COLLECTION

Folk dance costuming has played an important role in the international folk dance movement, and Folklore Village founder Jane Farwell often donned costuming from the area of the world whose dances she was teaching. Likewise, contemporary folk dance groups continue to wear coordinated ethnic costuming during dance presentations. Folklore Village boasts three large closets full of vintage ethnic dance costuming. Many costumes are complete, including the dress, skirt and blouse, or trousers and shirts, and their accompanying vests, belts, jewelry, shoes or boots, and hats.

Currently not inventoried and in at-risk status, the costumes are stuffed into the closets, many on wire coat hangers or in common cardboard boxes, with some in protected custom-made garment bags. The scope of the collection is not known, but it is clear there are some real treasures here above and beyond typical inexpensive theatrical wear. Many of the garments are constructed of hand-woven fabric and decorated with handmade lace and/or embroidery and beading. Likewise, many of the garments are not American-made reproductions but come from the country of their ethnic origins.

Funding is needed to examine the entire collection, check it for cleanliness, put together what complete outfits are available, document the pieces according to material and fabric techniques as well as ethnicity represented and/or country of origin where known, photograph for a dedicated page on our website, and then store in acid-free wrapping paper and boxes. Several funding requests for this initial work have been denied. Much of this work could be done with volunteers, as our community includes several fabric and costuming specialists. But the archival storage materials must be purchased. A new strategy is to go ahead and cull unimportant items in those closets, keeping the valuable, the genuine, or the artistically accurate handworked pieces. We are currently partnering with folklorists from UW–Madison to create a paid, grant-funded internship in order to photograph the resultant distilled collection for a dedicated page on our website. Our thoughts are that if they see the quality of the collection via the photographs online, granting organizations will be more likely to consider donating funds for the proper storage materials than if they see only a mass of disorganized hangers, boxes, and piles of clothing. This is our next major collections project.

Although Folklore Village has never been known as a repository of collections, we aim to change that notion with this round of work. Other in-process collections work includes restructuring, organizing, and committing to a publishable database our books and periodicals library, which has become overgrown and chaotic; documenting a small dolls collection; and archiving a collection of folk dance monographs, music, instructional materials, and ephemera. One of the many aspects of collections work is knowing what to keep and what to part with. Through collaboration with community members, students, universities, and other cultural organizations, we are working constantly to improve our collections and meet our organizational mission.

Conclusion

The hands-on practice of public folklore is a profoundly rewarding vocation, albeit often a difficult one as maintaining these types of organizations can present extreme challenges to sustainability. When it seems as if all your working hours are spent just trying to keep an organization properly administered and funded, where are the time and money to support keeping collections in good shape and making them accessible? And for what reason?

One reason is joy. As cultural workers—whether folklorists, historians, cultural anthropologists, or other sustainers of culture—we tend to love tangible and intangible cultural heritage: music, whether performed live or recorded by some means; food, whether shared with fellow community members or gathered together in a cookbook; objects, most often handcrafted, be they musical instruments, garments, pottery, weavings, metalwork, vernacular architecture, or woodcarvings; storytelling, whether time-tested or springing fresh from the heart of experience. It is an act of delight to gather groups of these expressions of humanity together, especially when they have a deep and profound meaning for a community or represent a particular cultural movement, time, or place when people gathered together to display and articulate.

But with these joys come responsibilities. To gather these human manifestations for one's own enjoyment may be pleasurable, but when the collections belong to a nonprofit organization, the onus is to make them publicly accessible, especially if by doing so one's mission is authenticated or even expanded. Too, the sense of community can be bolstered, whether through memories of earlier times together or by banding together, particularly in volunteer work, to make sure a precious collection is well cared for and brought to a place where it can be used. No one benefits when antique ethnic costuming is jammed so tightly on wire hangers in closets that no one even knows what is in there, when beautiful weathered oak logs are rotting in a meadow, or when boxes of old recordings are simply home for mice nests. But when cleaned, organized, cataloged, photographed, displayed, and/or rebuilt, the collections can be shared by others, whatever their interests. Family members can delight that their ancestral home is once again standing and that their remarkable great-grandfather's story will be told. Community members can remember when they danced to that tune or even played that tune and wore that costume to perform a folk dance. Scholars may study the international folk dance phenomenon, the music that was created expressly for it, and understand the desire to wear the clothing from the country whose dances you are stepping.

Digital tools have made it much easier to share all aspects of folk culture with a wider audience. An Aslak Lie descendant can monitor progress on the house through pictures on our website and through Facebook updates. A woman in Japan who learned as a young girl to folk dance from Jane Farwell can queue up some of the tunes that she danced to in 1956 from our website in the comfort of her living room. A textile major can come and study a particular type of old lace or the proper hat to accompany a traditional outfit from Valdres or can simply view an object via a photograph on our website. Travel need no longer be a prerequisite to community cohesion, familial memories, or scholarly pursuits.

Despite any difficulties inherent in the process, by cleaning, cataloguing, preserving, and, most important, sharing our collections, we make the world a richer, more varied, and more interesting place to be.

NOTE

1. The Jane Farwell Collection of Recorded Music is available at https://folklorevillage.org/jane-farwell-collection-recorded-music/.

"We Have All Been Neighbors Here"

Preservation, Access, and Engagement with the Arnold Munkel Collection

NATHAN D. GIBSON and ANNA RUE

I n 2010, Mills Music Library and the University of Wisconsin–Madison acquired the private recordings and collection of Arnold M. "Charlie" Munkel. A welder, mechanic, and World War II veteran from Spring Grove, Minnesota, Munkel was also a dedicated fan of Scandinavian American old-time music and an amateur field recorder. For more than thirty years, he traveled throughout the Upper Midwest recording hundreds of old-time musicians. For many of those musicians, Munkel's recordings are their only known recorded output. Munkel's open reel and cassette tape recording efforts were extensive and documented approximately twenty years of the Norwegian American Folk Music Festival in Decorah, Iowa. Several years after his death, his collection was brought to Mills Music Library, where it was digitized and made available to the entire world via the University of Wisconsin's streaming digital collections. To our knowledge, this is one of few instances where a research university has processed, accessioned, digitized, and streamed an extensive private fieldwork collection with little documentation and zero permissions. In this chapter, we explore what we received and who made it, how we processed and provided access to it, the ethical dilemma and legal implications involved in our decision to stream this collection, and why it remains relevant to the musicians and communities in the Upper Midwest.

MILLS MUSIC LIBRARY AND ETHNIC AMERICAN MUSIC

The first mention of a music library on the University of Wisconsin–Madison campus appeared in 1900 as part of a remodeling project in the music school, though a dedicated music library was not formally established and named after the former music school director, Charles Mills, until 1939 (Mills Music Library Special Collections n.d.). By the early 1970s, the library had outgrown both the music school and its space in the humanities building, and the basement of Memorial Library was cleared out to house a rapidly growing music collection. Today, Mills houses more than a quarter of a million physical items in addition to another quarter of a million music items in special collections.

As the collection grew, the areas of interest and specialization changed to accommodate the varying needs of the music school, though in the previous four decades special attention had been paid to collecting the diverse ethnic musics that prospered in the Upper Midwest. In the nineteenth and early twentieth centuries, hundreds of thousands of immigrants came to Wisconsin and brought with them their languages, religion, food, dress, folk customs, and, of course, music. Large influxes of German, Polish, Irish, Norwegian, Finnish, Swedish, Swiss, Czech, and other immigrants settled throughout the region and altered the musical soundscape of the Upper Midwest.[1] For much of the early twentieth century (roughly 1893–1942), various record labels recognized and recorded these musicians and marketed their music as "ethnic music" or "foreign language music."

After World War II, when the United States witnessed a patriotic push against pluralism and foreign language recordings in the music industry, many folklorists took up the task of recording ethnic musics. Alan Lomax, Sidney Robertson, and Helene Stratman-Thomas (the latter's collection is housed at Mills) traversed the Upper Midwest and recorded extensively, though only their English-language recordings were issued or published during their lifetimes (Leary 2015, 3–4). In the mid-1970s, the music librarian Steve Sundell founded the Wisconsin Music Archives (WMA) and began building a collection of Wisconsin-related music materials at the University of Wisconsin–Stevens Point that largely focused on these ethnic field and commercial recordings. His collection was then brought to Madison and merged with the Wisconsin music collection at Mills Music Library in 1984.

Today, the mission of the WMA is to actively collect and preserve (and to provide access to) the music of Wisconsin and the Upper Midwest. The mission is stated broadly enough to provide flexible interpretations for future library staff, though over the years that mission has been interpreted to mean the intensive collection of ethnic American music of the Upper Midwest. Mills now houses more than ninety thousand 78s, with approximately twenty thousand of those being foreign series or ethnic 78s, as well as several fieldwork collections (Mills Music Library Special Collections n.d.). It is one of the largest ethnic American music collections, and we are among a handful of institutions creating free and open access to such collections.[2]

Among the most frequent and enthusiastic UW–Madison faculty members to use these collections was James "Jim" P. Leary, the folklore and Scandinavian studies professor emeritus and cofounder of the Center for the Study of Upper Midwestern Cultures. The ethnic music collections at Mills played crucial roles in his radio productions of *Down Home Dairyland,* a radio program he cohosted with folklorist Richard March that explored the traditional and ethnic musics of the Upper Midwest, as well as his many music-centric publications, perhaps, most notably, *Folksongs of Another America: Field Recordings from the Upper Midwest, 1937–1946* (2015).[3]

In addition to using the ethnic music collections already held at Mills, Leary began amassing his own collection of fieldwork as well as the personal and private collections of aging regional musicians and their heirs. The fieldwork from his *Down Home Dairyland* productions and with members of the Goose Island Ramblers formed the foundation of what quickly became a plethora of more than twenty individual and private collections documenting a varied mix of vernacular musics found in the Upper Midwest: Cornish, Croatian, Czech, Finnish, French Canadian, German, Hungarian, Irish, Italian, Norwegian, Polish, Russian, Slovenian, Slovak, Swedish, Ukrainian, and more. In total, the collections represented more than twenty-five languages and included more than a thousand handpicked, commercially released ethnic 78s and more than eight hundred hours of original field and home recordings made between the 1950s and the 1990s.

To arrange, describe, digitize, and create online guides for these recordings (and related ephemera, including label scans, fieldwork notes and indexes, and photographs) and to stream them to the general public, Leary and Jeanette Casey, head of Mills Music Library, drafted the Local Centers/Global Sounds grant. Pitched as a three-year collaborative grant between Mills Music Library and the Center for the Study of Upper Midwestern Cultures (including their campus partners), the grant was successfully funded by the National Endowment for the Humanities in 2016. Nathan Gibson was hired in January 2017 as the ethnic American music curator and was responsible for rebuilding an in-house audio preservation studio and doing the digitization transfers.

In September 2017, the online portal for the Local Centers/Global Sounds: Historic Recordings and Midwest Musical Vernaculars was launched, and collections are routinely added as they are ready. At present, fifteen different collections are now searchable and streaming that call attention to the often neglected but incredibly important living traditions that shape the national soundscape and immigrant experience in America. As the project unfolded, one realization quickly emerged: one of these collections was not like the others. It was mysterious, even legendary, in status before it arrived on our doorstep. Many people knew it existed, but nobody knew what was in it. And nobody knew where it was—until Leary dropped it off on the Mills loading dock in September 2010.

In the four unmarked boxes were 150 audiocassettes, 36 five-inch reels, dozens of concert programs and personal notebooks, as well as portable reel-to-reel and audiocassette recorders. What we lacked were any permissions or hints at why these recordings were made and for whom they were made. They sat in a box, unprocessed, until NEH funding made it possible for Mills to devote personnel time and library resources to process them. To truly appreciate the unique character of this collection and to understand its cultural and regional significance, we need to return our attention to the music and the man behind the recorder.

Arnold "Charlie" M. Munkel

Arnold "Charlie" M. Munkel was born in Caledonia, Minnesota, in 1918 and lived the majority of his life just thirteen miles away, in Spring Grove, Minnesota. In 1941, he was drafted into the US Army and served in the 7th Armored Division as part of the European Campaign in World War II, earning a Bronze Star for his heroic service in the war. By 1943, Munkel married Marion Klinge, also of Caledonia, and began a decades-long career as a mechanic and welder for the Houston County Highway Department in Minnesota. He was an active member of the Spring Grove community, maintaining memberships at the local Sons of Norway Lodge and the American Legion, and was heavily involved in organizing Spring Grove's annual Syttende Mai, or Norwegian Constitution Day celebration.

Those who knew "Charlie," as he was called among friends and family, were also well aware of his love for Norwegian American old-time music. He was known for frequenting live traditional music performances in southeast Minnesota and northeast Iowa, including the annual Nordic Fest celebration in Decorah, Iowa. Local musicians recalled how he would travel to old-time music festivals and live music events throughout the Driftless Area with his reel-to-reel recorder and microphone and sit near the stages taping dozens of music performances. We are less sure, however, about how Mr. Munkel shared or used his recording collection. In an interview with the Decorah-based fiddler Beth Hoven Rotto (2013), Rotto recounted how she once tried to ask Arnold Munkel if she might take a closer look at his collection. "I went to his house one time, and I knocked on the door . . . and I said, 'I know you've got the best collection of the local music in here and I would love to come and hear some of your music.' [Imitating Arnold Munkel:] 'Oh . . . well you come back sometime, and we'll do that,' and I was like, 'Well, I'm just wondering if we could do some of that [now].' Well, he went on about his service in the military and I never got in the door. And then he passed away." When Munkel passed away, in 2003, with no children to inherit his belongings, Beth and others who knew of his recordings were left wondering what had happened to them. The fear was that they had been thrown away or discarded.

In Munkel's case, the collection was picked up by relatives and stored in a closet. Seven years after his passing, some of his surviving relatives began reaching out to find a permanent home for his materials. They eventually contacted Jim Leary, who in turn contacted Jeanette Casey, about accepting the donation at Mills Music Library. In 2010, Leary transported several boxes of Munkel's original reel-to-reel and cassette recordings, recording equipment, and manuscript materials to Madison. The boxes lay dormant for some time, but the majority of the collection is at last available to the general public to view and stream online—an invaluable resource for those interested in old-time music traditions in the region in general and among Norwegian Americans in particular.[4]

While the details surrounding this collection and the collector are still rather vague and frequently invite speculation, the recordings in Munkel's collection relate very well to a number of productions by Upper Midwestern old-time musicians and organizations that put out regional and ethnic old-time recordings. Albums like *Accordions in the Cutover: Field Recordings of Ethnic Music from Lake Superior's South Shore*; *Tunes from the Amerika Trunk: Traditional Norwegian-American Music from Wisconsin Vol. II*; the fiddler Leonard Finseth's albums *The Hills of Old Wisconsin* and *Scandinavian Old Time Folk Fiddler from Wisconsin*; the many records of LeRoy Larson's Minnesota Scandinavian Ensemble; and Anne-Charlotte Harvey's *Memories of Snoose Boulevard: Songs of the Scandinavian-Americans* reflect the same era and generation of musicians represented in the Munkel tapes. Furthermore, old-time music productions are still emerging out of the traditions that musicians on these recordings and in the Munkel Collection maintained. Albums like *My Father Was a Fiddler* and *Decorah Waltz*, by Foot-Notes Band from Decorah, Iowa, and *Minnesota Fiddle Tunes Project* and *Reviving the Wisconsin Barn Dance Music of Leonard Finseth*, by the Minneapolis-based musician Mike Sawyer, continue to delight fans of old-time music in the region and attract new audiences.

Munkel's recordings also overlap with a number of other music collections held at Mills Music Library and the Wisconsin Music Archives. These collections were created by other Norwegian American old-time musicians, and Mills Music Library has digitized some of them as part of the Local Centers/Global Sounds project: the Robert Andresen Collection 1976–94, the Leonard Finseth Collection, the LeRoy Larson Collection, the Bruce Bollerud Collection, and the Minnesota Folk Arts Program (Phil Nusbaum) Collection, 1959–2000.[5] Many of the musicians Munkel recorded appear in these other collections, among them Leonard Finseth of Mondovi, Wisconsin, William "Bill" Sherburne and his band from Spring Grove, Minnesota, LeRoy Larson and Bob Andresen from the Minneapolis area and Duluth, Minnesota, respectively, and dozens more. An extensive list of active Norwegian American old-time music performers in the Upper Midwest is reflected in these collections, and Arnold Munkel's recordings make up one of the most complete representations of those performers who were actively playing in the Driftless Area between the late 1960s and the early 2000s.

With so much overlap represented in all these collections, the value of Munkel's personal collection resides in his extensive and complete documentation of live performances in the area. His tapes capture more than thirty years of performances that only someone living in that area would have been able to document, for example Leonard Finseth playing a wedding dance at Geno's Pub in Whitehall, Wisconsin, on October 12, 1974. At the beginning of this recording, we hear Munkel explain that he was there for the dance after Finseth himself mentioned the event in a chance meeting weeks before. Munkel, his wife, and a friend showed up to the dance, admitting to the recorder, "We kind of surprised him by coming up here" (1974).

In addition to all the recordings he made at events like the Whitehall wedding dance and recordings of jam sessions at local bars like the Viking Bar in Spring Grove, Munkel consistently appeared at the Norwegian American Folk Music Festival, a musical event held as part of the annual Nordic Fest in Decorah, Iowa. Nordic Fest began in the late 1960s and was part of a growing number of ethnic heritage festivals in the United States. Adopting the common focus of similar local festivals across the nation, Nordic Fest organizers made the community the heart of the event, being careful not to commercialize it and to concentrate instead on celebrating Norwegian American folklife and folk arts (Rue 2018).

Beginning in the fest's second year, the Norwegian American Folk Music Festival was a major part of festival programming, featuring dozens of musicians from the surrounding communities, some who traveled from further afield like North and South Dakota, and an annual guest musician or group from Scandinavia. The Folk Music Festival no longer exists in a formal way—it ended in the early 2000s—but in the years that it ran it reflected the significance of the Norwegian American musical traditions of the region. Year after year Arnold Munkel recorded the Folk Music Festival performances and took meticulous notes of the performers, instruments played, the occasional tune, and sometimes details such as the temperature and humidity on the day of the performance. These recordings provide an unusually complete picture of this festival and a time in which dozens of old-time musicians populated the valleys and ridges of the Driftless Area.

Yet when the unmarked boxes initially arrived, in 2010, we had no idea what to expect other than an email from Jim Leary warning that "there's a lot of junk amidst his materials." Like many archives that ingest private collections, and particularly ethnographic collections obtained with little paperwork and no permissions from the collector, the boxes sat on a shelf untouched for years.

Challenges to Ingesting and Creating Access
to Private Collections

Eventually Anna Rue acquired access to the collection for her dissertation, "From Revival to Remix: Norwegian-American Folk Music and Song" (2014), and in 2016 she was hired by Mills Music Library to compile a collection guide. Once a description of contents was available, staff set out to scan, digitize, barcode, sort, and rehouse the physical materials. The question then was how to group similar items—by format, date, location, or other means? Several possibilities were discussed, though in the end a decision was made to group items on the basis of "events." Each concert, festival, and so on constituted one unique event, and photos, programs, notes, and recordings that corresponded with other items from the same event were then grouped together.

The next step, and perhaps the most exciting, was to listen to and discover all that Munkel had recorded. To expedite the processing of this collection, the open reel tapes were sent to the folklore archivist Steve Green in South Carolina, and the Mills efforts were focused on rehousing and digitizing the more than 150 (mostly ninety-minute) cassette tapes. What we quickly discovered while digitizing is that, although we sorted the collection on the basis of the various events he documented, Munkel himself did not categorize his tapes by event. On many occasions, there were three or four different events on one tape. Sometimes the tape case would note the different occurrences, other times not. Sometimes we would find handwritten notes about these recordings in a separate program guide, and we would have to pair them up ourselves after listening to the tapes. Usually the tapes would include live recordings. Sometimes the tapes also included dubs of commercial LPs. And sometimes those dubs of commercial LPs were of live recordings. Other times Munkel sourced the recordings from live TV or radio shows. It got hairy pretty quickly as we tried to determine the sources of each recording. Our intent was to omit the commercial recordings and to make streamable the original and unique fieldwork.

What we uncovered were several hundred hours of amateur fieldwork recordings that presented us with several archiving challenges. Among the more pressing challenges was the need to minimize the varying quality of the recordings. As it turned out, Jim Leary's warning of "lots of junk" turned out to be particularly true, not because of the content but rather due to blown-out recording levels, wavering tempos from dying batteries, and assorted recording errors that rendered a small percentage of the audio unlistenable.

Another challenge was identifying the songs within the collection. In an effort to preserve as much tape as possible for music, Munkel made a habit of cutting off all in-between-song chatter by the musicians. The minute applause began, he would hit stop. The start button would usually be hit once the band had played the first few notes of the next song. While he was able to fit a lot more musical content on each tape this way, it presented a real challenge for us as we attempted to find accompanying song details from cassette inserts or concert programs and to create tape indexes. While we have received some help from community members and from area musician Beth Rotto in naming the instrumentals, for some tunes we still know nothing more than "Unidentified Norwegian-American Waltz."

Easily, the biggest challenge was determining what is officially "in the collection" and what should remain private. It's ultimately subjective, and members of the Mills Music Library staff have gone back and forth several times with specific items. What about Munkel's fiddle rehearsal tapes, which were never likely meant for a public audience? What about his whistled renditions of fiddle tunes, which he often recorded during his trips home after a show to help commit the tunes to memory? What about his recording a TV show about Stonehenge and then recording a twenty-minute story of the time he visited Stonehenge with his military commander? What about including stories of him reading poems and short stories from the local newspaper? What about music recordings that are so murky that you can't really understand what is going on? What about commercial recordings he dubbed to cassette so that he could learn those tunes? Of course, all content is digitized, as digital formats will far outlast their eventually obsolete physical counterparts, but difficult decisions persist as we attempt to determine what constitutes the official or accessible versions of the collection.

Collection editing is vital because we want this collection to be used by musicians in the region and to be an academic resource. But we also want to be sensitive because we are treading new ground. We don't have written permissions from the musicians or audience members or even from Munkel himself. The collection was donated by his nieces and nephews, and, without the aforementioned permissions, some might say we shouldn't even bother processing it. From a financial standpoint as well, the amount of time put into this collection from many employees (the authors, music technical services librarian Matt Appleby, Steve Green, digital services librarian Jesse Henderson, and more) would likely preclude us from doing a similar project again in the future. And yet, we maintain that the collection is immensely valuable, and, as stewards of the collection, we aim to create free and open access to it and to engage multiple publics.

Creating public access to university collections is nothing new at Wisconsin. In what has come to be known as the Wisconsin Idea, UW–Madison has led several pioneering efforts to ensure that the university serves the greater state of Wisconsin. As far back as 1919, via the AM radio station WHA (now part of Wisconsin Public Radio), UW–Madison was among the first universities to broadcast lectures so that the general public could hear them. The UW General Library System was also among the first university libraries to sign on with Google Books and to allow books to be scanned for future access.

Continuing in this tradition, Mills Music Library is among a select handful of institutions creating online access to ethnographic fieldwork collections, including the audio. With the Munkel collection, we are moving ahead into quite murky access issues, as the material is largely unpublished recordings, privately recorded, without written permissions. The Mills approach thus far has been to focus on how we can appropriately make this material accessible and how doing so might benefit the greater public. There are, of course, risks involved, the risk of embarrassing people who don't think their performances are great; the risk of potential illegal or inappropriate reuse of our online content; the risk of unidentified underlying compositions; and the risk that folks might not want their music to be freely available online.

Furthermore, Arnold Munkel never knew this would end up in our hands. Are we following his wishes or intent? For what purpose and whose benefit did Munkel create all these recordings? Ethical and legal dilemmas abound. In assessing the potential risks and benefits, we looked at other digital collections, the Music Modernization Act of 2018, best-practice guidelines, and our fair-use assessment for streaming ethnic American 78 rpm discs. We went back to the overall goal of the Local Centers/Global Sounds project: "to offer free public access to the Upper Midwest's diverse historic sound recordings of roots music for purposes of recognition, repatriation, and revitalization" (Casey and Leary 2016).

Our decision was to provide access to the documentation and the accompanying audio content. Our intent remains to learn from, enjoy, and preserve the collection for the benefit of the Spring Grove / Decorah communities, the Norwegian American community, and Upper Midwest old-time music communities, as well as the larger academic community. We want to preserve and present as much of the collection as possible so that the potential engagements and points of contact are as broad as possible.

In addition to streaming the collection, we're also in the business of building up our collections with connections. The coauthors (frequently joined by Marcus Cederström, our Nordic Folklife project colleague) have now presented the Arnold M. Munkel collection to audiences at Nordic Fest, the Ygdrasil Literature Society, the Society for the Advancement of Scandinavian Study, and the American Folklore Society.

Relevance and Significance of the Munkel Collection

Judging from reactions from our recent presentations, many of Munkel's recordings continue to be relevant for musicians and scholars, as well as Munkel's extended network of family and friends. His collection provides us with a record of an early ethnic music festival that served as a precursor to other ethnic music festivals, such as Nisswa-stämman held in June every year in Nisswa, Minnesota. It encapsulates the live music scene among Norwegian Americans at a time when house parties were becoming less common, the most active musicians were aging, and old-time music was being consciously revitalized by staged festival performances. The recordings he made also expand on the scholarship and traditions that Norwegian Americans have been contributing to for decades. LeRoy Larson of the Minnesota Scandinavian Ensemble wrote about Scandinavian American dance music and in his research conducted fieldwork and collected tunes from many musicians found in Munkel's recordings (1975). Foot-Notes of Decorah have been keeping the old-time music repertoire of the Driftless Area alive since the 1990s, and several other projects led by musicians have recently emerged to transcribe old Norwegian American tune books from the region.

Of course, there are issues with Munkel's documentation, such as his habit of cutting his recordings off between tunes and eliminating whatever contextual information may have been provided by MCs or the musicians themselves. But what we're left with are the tunes themselves, the voices from the audience, the periodic shuffle of feet from the dancers traveling across the floor, and occasionally Munkel's own voice describing the circumstances of the event, telling a humorous story, reading a poem or two, or signing off by whistling a favorite old-time tune. The composite of these recordings paints a lively picture of the Norwegian

American old-time music scene in the Driftless Area over three decades. It's an unlikely collection from an unlikely man, given to Mills Music Library and returned to the community via the online streaming services of UW–Madison's Digital Collections Center.

Arnold Munkel's collection is useful not only as a resource for scholars interested in the folk musics of the Upper Midwest or musicians looking to expand their repertoires but also as an educational tool. Already there are plans for students to utilize these recordings in various ways. Undergraduates in several folklore courses at UW–Madison are becoming familiar with ethnic music collections at Mills through course projects and assignments. For example, a folklore field school in the summer of 2019 centered on documenting traditional arts in the Norwegian American community in the Driftless Area. Students in that class became acquainted with the Munkel collection as a way of introducing them to the distinct music traditions of the area.

We've also spread the news during our outreach presentations in the region to make people aware of these online resources. Inevitably, at every presentation, members of the audience reveal a personal connection to this collection. In 2019 we gave a presentation on Munkel's life and collection to a Norwegian American Literature Society, and we played a selection of Leonard Finseth playing the wedding in Whitehall, Wisconsin. Three members in the back of the room shared that they grew up down the road from that dance hall and had fond memories of attending dances there as children. When we gave a presentation at Nordic Fest, in Decorah, Iowa, an audience member said he had been friends with Arnold Munkel and shared fond memories of him during our discussion. We get particularly excited, though, when we hear about his music reaching younger audiences. Sandy Good, a music instructor from Decorah who played with many of the old-time musicians in the Munkel recordings, wrote to Anna Rue after viewing the digital collection through the Local Centers/Global Sounds site:

> Thank you so much for sharing that link with me. I have explored it briefly this morning and find it absolutely fascinating! You people have put a lot of work into this; I hope our younger people will recognize it for the treasure it is! I know my husband will be absolutely amazed that this music is preserved and now available for everyone to hear; he was involved with many of those house parties. I will be sharing this music with my students. Thank you again for your hard work on this project and for sending me the link to access it.

The personal impact that this online resource is having in the community surrounding Decorah and Spring Grove is amazing to see but difficult to measure because of the online format. In most cases we hear these stories when we're at outreach events, but occasionally we just get lucky. As part of the Driftless Area field school that Anna Rue, Marcus Cederström, and Nathan Gibson co-taught in 2019, we enlisted the help of Carolyn Solberg, a Decorah resident known for baking superb *kransekake* (a Norwegian style of almond cake baked in rings and stacked in a conical formation, commonly served at weddings and holiday celebrations). We spoke with Mrs. Solberg, who also happens to have been Anna's third-grade teacher, about being interviewed as part of the course's fieldwork activities, and in those initial conversations we discovered that she was related to Arnold Munkel. He was her Uncle Munkel. We were thrilled at the connection, and she had no idea that he had left behind such an extensive collection of recorded music or that it had been acquired by Mills and was now streaming online. We left her with information about how to access the Local Centers/Global Sounds website and turned our attention back to planning the field school.

When the course trip rolled around, a small group of students and instructors arrived at Carolyn's house. She welcomed us at the door clad in a spotless apron and led us to her dining room, where we found an impressive spread of cookbooks, newspaper clippings, baking logs, baking tools, and food samples—complete with hand-drawn labels—all neatly displayed on her dining room table. *Kransekake* ingredients were set out and at the ready for the demonstration. After an hour of our students interviewing Carolyn about growing up in Spring Grove and her knowledge of Norwegian baking (and enjoying her many baked treats), she had this exchange with Anna about the Munkel Collection on the Local Centers/Global Sounds site:

> CAROLYN: You know I went into the website.
> ANNA: Oh, you did?
> CAROLYN: And there's something else on there, Anna.
> ANNA: What?
> CAROLYN: My uncle [Arnold Munkel] is telling about where they're playing and who's play-ing, and my sister . . . was listening to some of this and he [Munkel] says, "Well, we're at the Viking Bar and Bill Sherburne is [playing], and so-and-so is on the piano, and Arnold Myhre is on the drums." And that's my dad.
> ANNA: (in astonishment) No—
> CAROLYN: Yes. [*Chuckles*] (Field recording, June 19, 2019)[6]

Carolyn Solberg's father, Arnold Myhre, was not a working musician, and, as is the case for many of the performers Arnold Munkel recorded, there are no professional or circulating recordings of his performances. In fact, in a recent personal exchange about the collection, Carolyn wrote, "I know of no other recording of my Dad. I only know that he enjoyed play-ing drums with the folks at the Viking Bar in Spring Grove." This is undoubtedly true for others who pop up in Munkel's recordings, as many of the moments he captured were at community dances and gatherings where local musicians provided the evening's entertain-ment. Recordings like these help us stay connected to those neighbors and loved ones who have been recorded, but they can also help us understand the breadth of the musical life in a community like Spring Grove and consider the ways in which the music in this area has been sustained and the ways it has continued to evolve.

Beyond the confines of the university, this collection will help many individuals remem-ber their families and neighbors through their music and also resonate with new and younger audiences. Through the Local Centers/Global Sounds site and because of this project, old-time music is being introduced to new generations of young people in the region and teach-ing them something about the place they call home.

Notes

Special thanks to the head of Mills Music Library, Jeanette Casey, as well as other General Library System staff who helped process and present the collection: Matt Appleby, Steve Green, and Jesse Henderson. Our thanks and gratitude also go to Carolyn Solberg and Beth Hoven Rotto for their insights into this collection and its significance.

1. For an introduction to ethnic recordings in the United States, see Gronow (1982) and Spottswood (1982). Perhaps the most complete picture of early ethnic music in the Upper Midwest is Leary's GRAMMY-nominated compendium, *Folksongs of Another America: Field Recordings from the Upper Midwest, 1937–1946* (2015).

2. For more on the Wisconsin Music Archive, see Hathaway (1989). Other institutions streaming notable fieldwork collections to the public include Brown University Library's Ghana Field Recordings collection; Cornell University's Indonesian Music Archive; Missouri State University's Gordon McCann Ozarks Folk Music Collection; the University of New Mexico's John Donald Robb Field Recordings; Vanderbilt University's Global Music Archive; and the Library of Congress's Alan Lomax Collection of Michigan and Wisconsin Recordings, to name a few.

3. See March's essay on *Down Home Dairyland* elsewhere in this volume.

4. The Arnold Munkel Collection is available online at https://uwdc.library.wisc.edu/collections/localcenters/munkel/.

5. Online finding aids for these collections can be found at UW Digital Collections, https://digicoll.library.wisc.edu/cgi/f/findaid/findaid-idx?page=home;c=wiarchives;cc=wiarchives.

6. The recording referenced here was made by Arnold Munkel at the Viking Bar in Spring Grove, Minnesota, on April 14, 1973, and can be found on the Local Centers/Global Sounds site, https://search.library.wisc.edu/embed/audio/LocalCenters08/eu92-4A1.

Running the Show

Documenting and Exhibiting Wisconsin Folk Art

ROBERT T. TESKE

I n October 2006, the American Folklore Society held its annual meeting at the Hyatt Regency Hotel in Milwaukee. One evening during the course of the meeting, the Milwaukee County Historical Society, where I served as executive director, hosted a reception for those attending the conference. William Ivey, president of the American Folklore Society at that time, thanked our organization for hosting the gathering and encouraged the folklorists in attendance to consider doing what I had done—using my folklore training to pursue a leadership position with a historical or cultural organization rather than accepting a staff position at a larger institution in order to have greater control over the nature and the quality of the programming offered. While I was somewhat embarrassed to have been recognized so graciously by a past chairman of the National Endowment for the Arts (NEA), I realized that his recommendation had merit. Indeed, my two previous positions with arts and cultural organizations in Wisconsin bore him out. I had been able to present more and better folk arts programming as executive director of the Cedarburg Cultural Center than I had been able to develop as an associate curator of exhibitions at the John Michael Kohler Arts Center, and I had been able to do so largely because I was "running the show" rather than scrambling to find space for my programming ideas amid a larger selection of competing proposals. In order to illustrate these alternatives more fully, let me offer a more detailed accounting of the organization and presentation of a series of traveling Wisconsin folk art exhibitions developed over a ten-year period at these two institutions.

FIRST OPPORTUNITY: A SURVEY OF WISCONSIN FOLK ART

After five years of teaching folklore courses at Wayne State University and Western Kentucky University and another five years serving as an arts specialist with the Folk Arts Program of the National Endowment for the Arts, I returned to my native Wisconsin in 1985 when I was offered a position as associate curator of exhibitions at the John Michael Kohler Arts Center in Sheboygan.

My wife, Heather; our nine-year-old son, Chris; and I arrived back home in February, just in time to help install the exhibit *Hmong Art: Tradition and Change* at the Arts Center.

The Folk Arts Program had funded the show, and it was during the development of the center's application that I had met Ruth DeYoung Kohler and learned that there might be a curatorial position available on her staff if I was interested in returning home. The chance to return to the Midwest, to aid in the care of our aging parents, and to work with an established group of folklorists like Jim Leary, Janet Gilmore, Ruth Olson, and Rick March made that decision an easy one. However, I quickly discovered during the long hours associated with the installation of the Hmong exhibition that mounting an exhibition was much harder work than funding one.

Despite the many challenges associated with *Hmong Art: Tradition and Change* (a newly arrived ethnic community spread widely across the United States, a significant language barrier, artists unfamiliar with the Western system of exhibitions, and curators unfamiliar with Hmong culture), the show proved to be the most popular ever mounted by the John Michael Kohler Arts Center. The warm reception afforded the Hmong traditional art exhibition prompted Ruth Kohler to ask me to write a grant application requesting funds to support field research in preparation for an exhibit of Wisconsin folk art. Given the sophisticated approach to Hmong traditional arts demonstrated in the previous exhibit and the fact that the Kohler Foundation was at that time a leader in preserving Wisconsin folk art environments, I did so without hesitation. Thanks to my five years' experience reviewing 150 grant applications per quarter, my application to the Folk Arts Program was fully funded, and we were able to hire Jim Leary and Janet Gilmore to conduct a year's fieldwork to identify artists whose work should be included in our survey exhibition. We were off and running—or so I thought!

Because the Hmong art exhibit had been carefully researched and meticulously mounted, I assumed that the development of a Wisconsin folk art exhibition would proceed similarly—especially since trained folklorists had been involved in writing the grant and carrying out the research. However, I was soon disabused of that assumption. As I recall, contract negotiations with Gilmore and Leary regarding fieldwork expectations were contentious, largely as a result of the Arts Center's efforts to retain complete control of the process. Monthly meetings to evaluate the work being done—which I found to be of the highest quality—were equally challenging.[1] Although I assumed the approach to the Hmong art exhibition would govern the preparation for the Wisconsin folk art show, I soon realized that the exceptional work of artists from throughout the state seemed a little too "homespun," a bit too "everyday," for the Center's staff, whose tastes in folk art typically ran closer to Eugene von Bruenchenbein's chicken-bone sculptures or the figures at Fred Smith's Concrete Park in Phillips. In retrospect, it seems to me that the Hmong costumes, jewelry, and needlework presented in the earlier exhibition were sufficiently "exotic" in and of themselves to merit acceptance in an institution devoted to fine art and contemporary crafts, while the Ho-Chunk baskets, Polish papercuts, and African American quilts from Wisconsin lacked the element of the "extraordinary."

Despite such obstacles, Leary and Gilmore stayed the course, and—largely as a result of their fieldwork—the Arts Center received a second grant to mount *From Hardanger to Harleys: A Survey of Wisconsin Folk Art* in March 1987. The exhibition would also tour to the State Historical Museum in Madison and to the Milwaukee Public Museum. Intended as a sampling of the rich and diverse traditional art forms still actively practiced throughout the entire state, the exhibit included more than 271 pieces of folk art from a wide range of different communities. An introductory section explored the notions of tradition and creativity within tradition, and subsequent sections showcased work from numerous ethnic, regional, and occupational communities. These included Selma Spaanem's Norwegian Hardanger lace, Willie G. Davidson's Shovelhead Wide Glide, Adolph Vandertie's elaborate woodcarvings, Ethel Kvalheim's Norwegian rosemaled *tyne*, Gerald Hawpetoss's Menominee beadwork, Latvian mittens created by three generations of the Upeslaja family, Anton Wolfe's Czech concertina, Ethel Storm Whitewing's Ho-Chunk baskets, and Allie Crumble's necktie quilt, which featured the neckwear of all the male members of Milwaukee's Metropolitan Baptist Church.

While the folklorists involved in the project would have preferred to feature a motorcycle customized by one of the bikers Gilmore and Leary identified rather than a "commercially customized" ride by Willie G. Davidson to demonstrate the continuity of folk tradition in contemporary culture, and while a number of the artists would have preferred a more traditional Easter table than one set with Kohler family china and stemware surrounding Ukrainian and Czech decorated eggs, *From Hardanger to Harleys* surpassed the Hmong art exhibition as the most popular in the Arts Center's history and enjoyed a successful run in Madison and Milwaukee. The overall success of the effort did not, however, erase the disappointment that Leary, Gilmore, and I shared as a result of the tumultuous preliminary process. Following the opening of the exhibit, Gilmore and Leary presented me with a copy of the book *Kohler on Strike: Thirty Years of Conflict*, by Walter Uphoff, which documented similar but more protracted labor issues workers had experienced with the eponymous plumbing ware manufacturer. The idea that we needed to find a venue that offered us as folklorists more complete control of the fieldwork and exhibition process was crystal clear and fully appreciated.

Second Chance: New Venue, New Exhibitions, and New Programs

The alternative venue we were looking for appeared a short time later in the form of a job posting in the *Milwaukee Journal*, which my wife, Heather, brought to my attention. A newly formed cultural center in Cedarburg was looking for its first full-time director, and when I applied for the position, I was delighted to discover that they were interested in focusing not only on Cedarburg's long association with fine arts and artists but also on the history of the community and its strong German cultural heritage. I jumped at the chance to take the position despite the challenges associated with heading up a new organization, figuring that this might well be the place where my folklore colleagues and I would be able to more fully control the projects we wanted to undertake.

The Cedarburg Cultural Center turned out to be just what we were hoping for. After taking the position in 1988, I was able to organize several series of folk music and dance performances with generous support from Richard March and Anne Pryor at the Wisconsin Arts Board. As an initial offering, the Cultural Center hosted a series of Sunday-afternoon community band concerts on the City Hall lawn next door. These concerts were followed in the 1990s by performances of Irish dance, klezmer music, and a host of other genres in a newly renovated theater and gallery space. All of these traditional performing arts programs were very well received alongside a wider range of contemporary jazz and popular music performances presented by the Cultural Center. But even more than serving as a venue for traditional performing arts, the Cultural Center offered the opportunity to organize, present, and then travel a number of exhibitions highlighting the traditional arts and crafts of Wisconsin's folk communities. Since the NEA still had sufficient funds to support projects of this type, I turned my attention to finding a suitable subject almost immediately after taking the position, and of course I reached out once again to Jim Leary and Janet Gilmore for their advice and assistance.

Happily, both Gilmore and Leary were willing to undertake another exhibit project. In fact, as I recall, they were the ones who suggested focusing on Wisconsin's traditional musical instrument makers as the subject of our first major exhibition at the Cedarburg Cultural Center. With their assistance, I submitted a grant application to the NEA Folk Arts Program, and—despite the fledgling nature of the organization—the NEA provided full support in the amount requested. While securing the funding for the exhibition was critical to the success of the project, a number of new challenges still loomed. As Jim started the fieldwork, I was confronted with a variety of issues that an established organization like the Kohler Arts Center would have already addressed. At the most basic level, I needed to select and purchase exhibit display cases and panels that could be easily transported to several tour locations and that would adequately protect the instruments included in the display. I also needed to learn how to mount photographs and label text to the panels in a professional and durable fashion. Since the NEA grant also included funding for an exhibit catalog, I needed to find a designer who could lay out the text and photographs that the field researchers and I prepared and selected and who could see the catalog's production through the printing process. Once those tasks were completed, I needed to become familiar with promoting the exhibition and preparing contracts for the other institutions that had chosen to host the show on tour. And, finally, as the only paid staff member of the Cultural Center, I needed to figure out how to transport the show from location to location without laying waste to the grant budget!

Remarkably, I was able to accomplish these various tasks in the time available with the assistance of a committed group of volunteers, the donated services of an exceptional designer in the community, and the aid of a number of museum professionals at other institutions. *In Tune with Tradition*, as the exhibition was called, opened in March 1990 and traveled to four other venues around the state. The show included the work of seventeen folk artists representing a wide range of ethnic, regional, and occupational communities, all diligently documented by Leary and photographed by Lewis Koch. Among the instruments presented were Louis Webster's Woodland flutes, Ron Poast's Hardanger fiddles, Epaminontas Bourantas's Greek bouzoukia, Nick Vukusich's Croatian tamburitza, and Konstantins Dravnieks's Latvian *kokles*. Despite the fact that Mr. Dravnieks lived in Thiensville, no more than five minutes from the Cultural Center in Cedarburg, I would never have known of his exceptional work had it not been for the breadth and depth of Leary's fieldwork—fieldwork that was critical to the success of the musical instrument exhibit and that is the foundation of all successful folk art projects. *In Tune with Tradition* was well received around the state and highlighted the critical role of the contemporary craftsmen throughout Wisconsin in creating the "tools of the trade" that made it possible for other members of their communities to continue their musical heritage. In his review of the exhibition, published in the *Journal of American Folklore,* the folklorist Tom Vennum noted that "the exhibition also attests to the close cooperative network of folklorists in the state" (1991, 345).

In private conversation with Jim Leary during the site visit upon which his review was based, Vennum even labeled the folklorists involved in its production as "the great team," a reference to Richard Dorson's laudatory designation of the early British folklorists (1951, 1968), underlining the importance of cooperative relations that extended back beyond even the creation of the *Hardanger to Harleys* exhibition.

The second traveling folk art exhibit organized by the Cedarburg Cultural Center and based on the field research of Jim Leary, Janet Gilmore, and Mary Zwolinski was titled *Passed to the Present.* It was carried out in partnership with a group called Wisconsin's Ethnic Settlement Trail, a cultural and tourism organization that was dedicated to highlighting the numerous ethnic communities that had developed along the old Highway 41, now Interstate 43. The show included the Slovak wheat weaving of Sidonka Wadina from Lyons, the Ukrainian Easter eggs of Betty Piso Christensen from Suring, the Danish heart baskets of Albert Larsen from Racine, the Czech cattle feed baskets of John Arendt from Luxemburg, and the German folk music of the Alte Kameraden Band of Freistadt. The catalog that accompanied the exhibition, like the one published in conjunction with *In Tune with Tradition,* featured an article by Jim Leary and the photographs of Lewis Koch. The exhibit was presented in Cedarburg and at five other venues in Milwaukee, Sheboygan, Green Bay, Sturgeon Bay, and Oshkosh during 1994 and 1995, following the path of the ethnic settlement trail itself and providing access to the exceptional artwork created by members of those communities to their friends and neighbors. Fortunately, the organizational and administrative challenges that had been addressed in preparing *In Tune with Tradition* posed less of a problem the second time around. We were able to make use of the same exhibition furniture for installing the show and the same publication designer in preparing the catalog. In addition, we were able to better manage the transportation of the exhibition between the participating venues. Only a small problem with the mounting of a few photographs that had not been adequately stopped required attention during one of the transition periods between presentations. Yet, while the distances traveled between locations were not great, relocating a show six times in two years was no small feat for an organization with a staff that had increased to only four people by this time.

The third and final traveling folk art exhibition organized and presented by the Cedarburg Cultural Center was carried out in conjunction with Wisconsin's Sesquicentennial in 1998. Like many other states, Wisconsin chose to participate in the Smithsonian's Folklife Festival on the National Mall as a means of bringing its 150th anniversary to the attention of a national audience. The Wisconsin Program of the Festival was then transported back to Madison, where it was restaged for the home audience. In conjunction with the festival's presentation in Madison and at other venues throughout the remainder of the year, the

Sidonka Wadina, Lyons, Wisconsin. *Slovak Wheat Weaving*, 1990s. From the Cedarburg Cultural Center exhibition *Wisconsin Folk Art: A Sesquicentennial Celebration*. (Photograph by Lewis Koch.)

Cultural Center's exhibit *Wisconsin Folk Art: A Sesquicentennial Celebration* offered a complementary look at the material culture of the state's folk communities. Based once again on the fieldwork of Jim Leary and Janet Gilmore, assisted in this instance by their colleague Ruth Olson, the sesquicentennial folk art show included roughly one hundred pieces. These were divided into four major sections: *Keeping Tradition, Celebrating Community, Expressing Ethnic Identity,* and *Living On the Land/Living Off the Land.* Under the heading of *Keeping Tradition,* the exhibit explored the ideas of consistency, continuity, and creativity in traditional art forms. Under *Celebrating Community,* it examined calendar and life-cycle celebrations, as well as social symbols representing smaller groups within particular communities. Under the heading *Expressing Ethnic Identity,* the exhibit investigated traditional art forms as expressions of ethnicity, offered a series of cross-cultural comparisons, and considered examples of creolization. Finally, under the heading *Living On the Land/Living Off the Land,* the exhibition considered folk art associated with occupations such as lumbering, farming, and commercial fishing, as well as such recreational activities as hunting and sport fishing.

Funded primarily by a grant of $85,000 from the Folk Arts Program of the National Endowment for the Arts—the largest NEA project grant awarded to any organization in the state during that year—and by a generous grant from the Wisconsin Arts Board facilitated by Richard March, the sesquicentennial folk art exhibit benefited from the skills of a professional exhibit designer and the fabrication of more substantial display cases and wall panels by a local firm owned by a member of the Cultural Center's board of directors. The show also benefited greatly from the established relationships between the members of the field research team and the state's many folk artists and between the Cultural Center and other presenting institutions, several of which had hosted previous traveling exhibits developed by the Center. *Wisconsin Folk Art: A Sesquicentennial Celebration* earned the Cultural Center the Governor's Award in Support of the Arts in 1998—symbolized, appropriately enough, by a Norwegian ale bowl carved by Phillip Odden, whose work appeared in the show—as well as the Reuben Gold Thwaites Trophy from the Wisconsin Historical Society for the Outstanding Local Historical Society of the Year. No other organization had ever received both awards over the history of their presentation, much less both in the same year. The recognition seemed a clear confirmation of the significant role a small organization with a clear focus on a particular art form might have in bringing that subject matter to the attention of a statewide—even national—audience.

CONCLUSION

None of the folk art exhibitions organized by the John Michael Kohler Arts Center or the Cedarburg Cultural Center would have been possible without a solid basis in thorough field research. In that field research, we were able to share contacts, learn from experts about the state's folk communities, and document and present the intricacies of the traditional arts and crafts practiced throughout the state. Thanks to the efforts of regional public folklorists, Wisconsin has a record of those traditional arts and crafts still practiced by its residents during the last years of the twentieth century, a record that appears in print and in photographs in the catalogs that accompanied all the exhibitions and also in the copious field notes that have been preserved at the Kohler Arts Center and in the Archives of the University of Wisconsin Library System. The lesson here is clear and easily comprehended: an investment in field research and documentation—and the preservation of that research in publicly accessible repositories for subsequent use by other individuals and organizations—is absolutely critical to the creation of exhibitions, festivals, performances, and other public programs offering access to the traditional arts.

What also became clear over the decade was the fact that having complete organizational control over how research and exhibition work were to be carried out ensured the creation of better products. I would certainly not deny that other folklorists in other states created excellent exhibitions and programs while working with or for host institutions not directed by academically trained colleagues in the field. Indeed, a number of colleagues mounted exceptional state folk art exhibitions while serving as folk arts coordinators at state arts agencies committed to supporting all forms of performing and visual arts. I would submit, however, that having someone "running the show" who shares the same background and perspective as others working on the exhibitions considerably eases the flow of the work and strengthens the final product. Had I not been the executive director of the Cedarburg Cultural Center, I doubt that the organization could have seen its way clear to offering the number of exhibitions and performances by traditional artists that we eventually did, especially with the organization's other obligations to contemporary artists in the community and to the community's history. Had I not been the executive director, I doubt that we would have been successful in touring the exhibitions to venues both large and small around the state in order to best share the work with members of the artists' home communities and the larger population as well. And had I not been the executive director of the Cultural Center, I doubt that the organization would have garnered the statewide recognition from both arts and historical organizations that it did. Consequently, I suggest that an increased effort on the part of folklorists to pursue leadership positions in organizations such as museums, arts centers, and community organizations would help to ensure that our best work reaches public audiences in a manner we can proudly celebrate.

NOTE

1. See Janet Gilmore's chapter in this volume for more details.

The Bobbing Boat

Lasting Impressions, Rejuvenated Memories, and Intriguing Prospects

JANET C. GILMORE

ublic folklorists, as well as independent folklorists like me, customarily receive invitations to revisit fieldwork and the resulting documentary experiences, exhibit productions, research, and publications from decades past. Colleagues seek advice with projects, site visits, and grant application reviews; scholars, journalists, and script writers ask for specialized knowledge; and former interviewees, community members, and descendants want to continue discussions or request access to recorded material. In ethnographic and historical realms where the fruits of memories are the stuff of scholarship, both folklorist and collaborator and their professional reputations rely on finely tuned memories and generous, hospitable, and trustworthy exchanges in perpetuity to "balance out the conflicting essentials" of our work—in a form of what Bess Hawes calls "payback" ([1992] 2007, 68–90; cf. Gilmore 2011, 258)—even when fieldwork-dependent jobs require hundreds if not thousands of interview and institutional contacts over the years. Documentary recordings in numerous formats clearly serve as aide-mémoire, and well-kept ones even better, especially when little gray cells go rogue. Many public folklorists keep informal collections of these increasingly digital records handy for quick reference; they may not automatically go into a formal archive, nor once there become processed and readily accessible. Where field collections receive processing into archival collections, some folklorists actively reuse them, sometimes threatening collection integrity and preservation. Keeping and accessing these records are part of our folklorist identities, forever reminding us of the generosities we have experienced and the debts we owe. Records remain open invitations to return when there's still time, to reconnect and enjoy each other's company, while continuing to learn more deeply—even when returning them for destruction upon family request (Toelken 1998).

This essay reflects on a public contestation I brought on myself at a 2018 Folklore and the Wisconsin Idea symposium among fellow folklorists and colleagues. It challenged my long-term memory and grasp of related specialized research knowledge, adequacy of records unviewed in decades, and personal archival collection practices. The experience prompted a journey back into the languishing records to reacquaint myself with interrelationships involved—individuals, sponsoring organization, and documentation, in a fraught context, where an influential late 1980s public folklore survey project undermined classic ethnographic field methodologies and tested fieldworker confidence in the documentary results. The investigation restored faith in my aging memory and the continued utility and practice of robust field documentation. It also reminded me how instrumental the experience had been in securing more effective labor conditions, documentary interactions, and results in later projects and in decades of productivity that built on them. Yet it unfurled darker sides of ethnographic endeavors that we folklorists struggle with continuously, uneven relationships among documenters and documented, perpetually incomplete documentation frozen in time, awareness of how many important aspects of context, circumstances, sociable and personable exchanges, including later recall, reflection, and storytelling, are left out (cf. Toelken 1998, esp. 386–87). The worthiness of what we produce to outlast an immediate public program remains justifiably suspect, serving, as it does, as a value-added object created from an outsider's momentary glimpse, which can be so bound up in fieldworker ego, as I show in this essay. We must keep discussions flourishing in ongoing relationships aiming to achieve closer partnerships that coordinate and define the extent and scope of documentation and public engagement—honoring the community spirit I now see more clearly in the case of the Okkonen bobbing boat.

Setting the scene at that public 2018 symposium contestation had been several days of academic presentations, some by coworkers from statewide public folk arts field surveys in the 1980s supported by National Endowment for the Arts Folk Arts grants (NEA-Folk Arts), state arts program involvement, and local organizational project sponsorships. As the gathering progressed, I began noticing my colleagues' variations in recall of similar events. I pondered the selections, intensifications, and omissions of distinctive information that they chose to reveal or leave out—in word choices, referents, associations, chronologies, and descriptions of events and outcomes. Each of us could position ourselves differently, I realized, and each voice had a distinctive style and legitimacy that relied on many contextual factors, including distance in time from recalled events. Uncomfortably, I wondered if we were also showing the trickery of our memories as they became more formulaic and fantastic in a retreating past and as we resorted to selected versions of the very evidence we had been party to experiencing, discussing, and creating. Together, however, they could build an interesting corpus of testimony, no matter how fantastically painted or bowdlerized, for future generations to contemplate, question, critique, and apply selectively.

When I reached the closing session of the symposium, I received another, closer test while observing Jim Leary, my folklorist spouse, present his career retrospective—a story I've seen acquiring an increasingly classic form. Sitting at the presenters' table in front of the audience, obliquely viewing the projector screen, I found myself watching the accompanying slides with a surreal sense of disconnection and lack of recognition, even though I had seen many of these images before, sometimes when they were taken, sometimes when on duty as a folklorist, sometimes when not. "What dark church basement lunch event could this be?" I wondered as I examined one image. Likely it was in Wisconsin, but where? Perhaps up north, I surmised, ruminating over several possible locations. But I just couldn't place it, although it seemed like it had to be a community organizational get-together and fundraiser of some kind in Wisconsin, perhaps the aftermath of a wedding or funeral event. Most maddening, who was that dark-haired woman conversing hospitably with an older fellow across the table? Their exchange was definitely the focus of the slide—a photographer's field opportunity to show attendees arranged in folding chairs along both sides of long rows of cafeteria tables filling the lighted basement. Was she an unknown associate from my colleague's past? Why couldn't I recognize her?

The scanned, digitized versions of the slides' original film were sometimes not immediately recognizable, and, in any case, it had been a long time since I had viewed them—if I even had viewed them before. Already I knew that the scanning and the computer on which they were displayed that afternoon had left them rather dreamlike: blurry, more intensely and darkly shaded, and sometimes stretched horizontally. As the presenter lingered on the basement lunch image, I finally realized the identity of that unfamiliar woman with such dark hair: Who else could be wearing that one-off dress of her own making? I was shocked to realize that I was the woman in the photo, more than four decades younger.

Another image appeared, much more recognizable, an instance of one fieldworker with camera capturing the other, fixed behind her camera, their small daughter caught jumping in the foreground, ghost-like in a boat shed's dappled light. The enthusiastic little one certainly assumed the lens was focused on her! I understood a little better what was happening: disguised ethnographic opportunities to show us at work in the field—though not with my awareness or consent at the time, nor for the unfolding presentation. To my right, on the slide's left, was an upended wooden skiff with its interior facing the camera. There, the wide-angle camera lens, coupled with the laptop's horizontal stretch and projector lens warp too, grossly exaggerated its dimensions into a much wider-based triangular shape than I recalled. Jim located us fellow fieldworkers "beside the bobbing boat," wrenching this one to certain attention and concern after my increasing discomfort about where the presentation was headed. "That's not the bobbing boat!" I blurted with displaced frustration, astonished and without restraint. Ironically, I couldn't recognize myself immediately in the earlier slide, but I could the skiff in this one. "Yes, it is," batted back the presenter. "No, it's not!" I continued, stunned. "Yes, it is!" the presenter insisted, the fixity of his assurance staggering. As the drama intensified, I realized it had been a while since I had been focusing on traditional commercial fishing skiff forms, constructions, and uses—and particularly this one's. But right then I would have to summon courage and knowledge on the spot in a public defense of my indignant interruption. In an impromptu performance, I explained to the varied audience—mostly unfamiliar with "boatological" description that translates intimacies of boat forms into specialized terminologies, written texts, and drawings—just how that skiff could not be the bobbing boat. Without the benefit of a comparative image, at first, or blackboard and chalk in the meantime, I used the available table top as a prop to show how the sturdily built skiff we were viewing onscreen could not be the smaller, more lightly built bobbing boat. Without the effect of performed boat plans, this inset follows the flow of details presented to compare the two vessels' dimensions, construction, and uses, mostly in that order. As I explained:

Janet photographs Okkonen-Wintturi boat shed with fishing skiff (*left*) and fieldworker Bella in foreground. Herbster, July 29, 1986. (Photograph by James P. Leary, Wisconsin Folk Art Survey. Courtesy of John Michael Kohler Art Center.)

The c. 8-foot by 32-inch table top, I surmised, was similar in horizontal length, breadth, and four-sided shape to the bobbing boat's "deck plan" and relatively flat bottom. Its sides at both bow and stern were separated by flat boards (transoms) that gave the effect of a boxy oblong rectangle with squared ends. Compared to the skiff, the bobbing boat's sides looked proportionally higher. The skiff's deck plan, in contrast, achieved a shallower triangular effect, its bow coming to a point and its stern ending in a flat transom broader than either of the bobbing boat's.

Fewer, wider boards made up the bobbing boat, and skeletally, its ribs (interior framing) were angular, boxier, fewer, and compound in construction. While both boats' flattish bottoms spoke to their maneuverability in shallow inshore waters with heavy loads of fish and gear, the bobbing boat's lengthwise sides each extended down into a runner at the bottom, stably elevating the boat's bottom from the ground. This smaller boat's handle could be rapidly inserted into the stern or removed as needed, making it versatile for winter fishing on and around untrustworthy inshore ice. The amphibious design afforded pushing the boat across ice to get to open water or ice-fishing locations through the ice, yet enabled oar-powered transport by water between floes or if the ice failed.

The heavier, longer, triangular skiff, on the other hand, curved smoothly and continuously from its edge-to-edge narrow lengthwise planked sides around to the bottom. Numerous closely placed steam-bent ribs hugged the plank interiors down each side, rounding the bilge and crossing the bottom. A simple single keel extended along the bottom from bow to stern.

Stern view forward of bobbing boat deck plan with Eino standing to the side. Herbster, July 29, 1986. (Photograph by James P. Leary and Janet C. Gilmore, Wisconsin Folk Art Survey. Courtesy of John Michael Kohler Art Center.)

> The skiff had taken more care and time to build and, while shaped for good loads and shallow inshore waters, the keel indicated deeper water use, the stern transom its propulsion by outboard motor, and the smoothness of the interior attempts to minimize entanglements with gear—more effectively than the bobbing boat's.

As I finished, Jim projected an image of the bobbing boat to the group, acknowledging his lapse and my gist. Whether by the serendipity in the fieldwork moment, or terminology, form, or function, or possible Old Country cold-climate connections, this artifact had impressed us both during our shared ethnographic event. However, I remained apprehensive and shaken.[1] Once I returned home that evening, I immediately visited my project files to check how closely the information I presented matched the original records and reflected each fieldworker's contributions.

Before I examine how my testimony held up and what more it unleashed, I must qualify distinctive aspects of the shared field experience during which Jim and I encountered the bobbing boat, on July 29, 1986. Acting as the two specialized folklorists for the year-long 1985–86 fieldwork phase of the Wisconsin Folk Art Survey project (WFAS), we were visiting the gracious and sociable Helvi and Eino Okkonen at their home place in the Bark

Eino showing how to push bobbing boat with handle inserted in stern transom. Herbster, July 29, 1986. (Photograph by James P. Leary and Janet C. Gilmore, Wisconsin Folk Art Survey. Courtesy of John Michael Kohler Art Center.)

Point-Herbster area near Lake Superior in northern Bayfield County (see Okkonen n.d.). As most ethnographic fieldworkers know well, working in the field is an adventurous, emergent, and immersive experience that, despite training and tenets, requires negotiation of many simultaneously happening parts, on the spot—and it inevitably results in "ambiguities of memory and the recording of memory" (de Caro 2008, 54). This event was just that, complicated from the beginning by the overarching political characters of the project itself, which aggravated the ordinary hubris I feel as an ethnographic fieldworker. We also had both met or known of Okkonens through prior research in the area, making this summer interview visit a more challenging sociable one, heightened by the presence of our two-year-old.

I have been drawn to add in selected personal, subjective, social, and contextual information here that I still remember, in part as an obligation to create a little fuller record but, importantly, to acknowledge more of the people with whom I engaged and from whom I learned so much more than may have been obvious during fieldwork or in the busy exhibit production aftermath over ensuing years. In exposing embarrassing yet quirky aspects of myself as a public folklore survey fieldworker, perhaps I provide an instructive view, seen more keenly from this distance. In this way, I also respect the wisdom of Barre Toelken, one of my earliest professional folklorist guides, for emphasizing our need for "professional commentary on the validity and necessity of subjective involvement in the analytical discussion of cultures" (2003, 1).

BOBBING BOAT INTERVIEW CONTEXT

When Jim and I visited Helvi and Eino in summer 1986, they were in their early seventies and eighties, respectively, downright spritely, regular social dancers at Finn Hall, their minds active and engaged. In build, energy, reserved humor, and even aspects of semiformal dress, Eino, bespectacled, with a slightly balding ring of white hair, reminded me of my elderly male relatives, especially ones with Norwegian heritage, with whom I had felt awkward and reserved. My memory of Helvi is much less vivid, but she too wore glasses, a little more fashionably framed than Eino's, her hair more bountiful than his, wavy and shoulder-length in an aging honey brown. Her full-skirted dress with cardigan spelled "company visiting" to me. The pair enjoyed singing to Eino and friends' music, and were adept at late-going card-playing with friends. Both were quite attentive to our quest amid the flowing circumstances, and Helvi actively distracted our daughter at times to make her feel welcome yet special despite her parents' distracted focus.

Jim had enjoyed prior field and programming experiences with the pair during an ethnic music project in northern Wisconsin and Michigan in 1980–81, when I had also met and heard of them. For Jim, the 1986 repeat visit with kindly associates required a new and different focus in need of representation. He had already produced a substantial, well-developed, and personable field report and formal sound recording that we could use as a starting point (1981a; see also Gilmore et al. 2007), influencing what we recorded on this visit, who was recording what, and why we had sought Eino's commercial fishing and boat-building expertise and related occupational material culture for the survey.

For me it was a boon to follow up on how Eino, a second-generation Finnish American born in the area in 1903 (d. 1996), had worked much of his early life in local commercial fisheries, participating with his father, friends, and relatives in building and replacing small and larger fishing vessels as needed. Importantly, he also kept an abundance of related occupational artifacts in one shed and shared another housing old boats with Helvi's brother, Olavi Wintturi, then recently deceased. As part of my 1980–81 year in northern Wisconsin, while finishing my dissertation on Pacific Northwest commercial fishing folklife (Gilmore 1999), I had informally been observing and photographing comparable vessels, gear, workers, occupational events, and installations along Chequamegon Bay and Apostle Island shorelines and checking out surveys, exhibits, or reports of local fishing people, boatbuilders, and researchers. Eino's example could help with my quest during the WFAS to represent "coastal" commercial fisheries bounding Wisconsin along the Mississippi River, Lake Michigan, and here, Lake Superior.

Visitors had lingered with our hosts in the drive as we arrived at the residence, after we had first inspected the boat shed some miles away, scene of the skiff photography. I recall everyone then trekking across the lawn to a shed containing fishing nets, gear, and other tools. Dark, somewhat claustrophobic, and saturated with the familiar essences of aging tarred twine and departed fish, the space was complicated by so many people. I lurked barely inside, Jim bantering with the crowd about the artifacts there. Here I first heard about "the bobbing boat," eagerly expressing interest at this serendipitous moment. Soon, Eino led me to the vessel at yard's edge, uncovering it for inspection and discussion. With only one guest left, we retired to the house where—despite ongoing conviviality in the kitchen—I managed to interview Eino in an urgent, focused, bare-bones way, handwriting notes about his long commercial fishing and boatbuilding career; specifics about both small boats' compositions, functions, and dimensions; and similar aspects of larger vessels he had experienced and participated in building. In and around this event within an event, Jim and I variably photographed the boat and Eino with it or various fishing equipment, interchanging cameras depending on the situation, since one held the required black-and-white film, and the other the necessary color slide film.

WISCONSIN FOLK ART SURVEY CONTEXT

Jim and I considered ourselves fortunate to become the fieldworkers for the WFAS project, sponsored by the John Michael Kohler Arts Center (JMKAC) in Sheboygan, Wisconsin. Our "trained folklorist" status was essential for a project receiving NEA-Folk Arts grant funding; fieldwork required a public programming result. The exhibit, *From Hardanger to Harleys: A Survey of Wisconsin Folk Art* (Teske 1987), opened in JMKAC's main art exhibition gallery in 1987, stopping in 1988 at the Milwaukee Public Museum and then at the Wisconsin Historical Museum, in Madison, and inspiring a northwestern Wisconsin version at Chippewa Valley Museum in Eau Claire.

Jim and I split one full-time job, each favoring varying balances of genders, ages, ethnicities, folk arts, and geographical areas in our research. We ordinarily worked alone, and we both coordinated with fellow folklorist and colleague Bob Teske, a JMKAC curator of exhibitions. We all worked under the Center's then director, Ruth DeYoung Kohler II, aided by a director of special projects, Joanne Cubbs. A folklorist colleague, Richard March, then Wisconsin Arts Board folk and ethnic arts coordinator, provided project advice and support.

Our work contract immediately cast us into extensive preexisting museum legalities, including copyrights, artist quotas, and an art-object-focused selection mode, evident in my Okkonen fieldwork report. Over a year's time, we were expected to document four times the eighty artists the art museum exhibition curators anticipated representing to fit the final exhibit's gallery space and provide an acceptable ratio for review and selection. We soon demonstrated that an average of twenty-six or more artists a month, more than one a work day, including extensive travel throughout the state, would not result in equitable representation of artistic expressions, social, occupational, and cultural groups flourishing in the state, nor their historical backgrounds and geographies, nor provide the quality and quantity expected of all visually artistic works we represented in photography. By the time we were visiting the Okkonens in far northern Wisconsin that summer, we had negotiated an agreement to cover two hundred artists altogether, in requested types of photographic shots, colors, and numbers—still requiring too many professional folkloristic methodological concessions.

These types of projects were often expected to result in "merely" working documents, less authoritative work in progress that was suggestive, prepared for discussion, awaiting further decisions for limited uses and access. They were not really expected to be seen in the globally accessible digital forms we now see emerging from them. Our awareness of their limitations and, often, lack of accessibility lent us and the people represented some protection from being seen and read in absolute, reductive, and somewhat incorrect terms.

Nevertheless, the labor conditions and unreachable expectations placed on our reluctantly meager documentation added underlying tension and angst to our fieldwork, encouraging subversive thoughts and acts of resistance.[2]

Redemption and New Insights in the Field Documentation

I approached my field documentation copies when I arrived home that post-symposium evening with a sense of impending doom and disappointment in the records left behind. My first challenge was just finding the field report, although the JMKAC project corpus had inhabited its own file drawer for decades, maintaining much of its "respect des fonds" original order. It was both extensive in scope and somewhat varied in organization due to differing fieldworker organizational styles and intermittent ongoing uses. I first checked my section of interview files, where an intuitive sense guided me to a "Janet's Interviews" folder. I had originally placed in it all reports for interviews I had conducted, but as the number of reports increased, it came to harbor a smaller selection. I was relieved to find the Okkonen field report there, suggesting I had claimed it as mostly "mine," in alphabetical order amid those for other men I had interviewed during the project. My first impression of the report was one of impoverishment, the results of the political economies of this type of work (Hawes 2008, 147–48), intensified by the fieldworkers' shared aesthetics of thrift. But I was relieved to see a miniature deck plan sketch with key measurements of the bobbing boat on my one-page outline of attached field notes, an almost autonomic relic of my boat and architectural documentation training. Crouched over the file drawer with poor lighting and deteriorating eyesight late in the evening, I was quickly finding hope in plenty of information requiring careful reading.

Over the next several days, I dug into the documentary remains of the Okkonen site visit, refreshing my familiarity with the scope and organization of the documentation. With intuitive detective powers I scoured the field report, moving next to comparative photo and slide evidence, then photo and slide logs, and Jim's handwritten tablets of fieldwork notes. Clues followed basic expectations of interrelated project reporting for multiformat public folklore project documentation, but as I had found in trying to prepare metadata for digital collections of old project remains in recent years, I often had to rely on trip and supply expense accounting records to verify more esoteric evidence—and, yes, I had kept them as self-employment work logs over the years, including breakdowns of expenses and justifications required by some contracting organizations and tax authorities. I needed them all for the Okkonen review. For some older projects like this one, and even a few recent ones, I had been happy to shed some detailed reporting formats when I could— but here I found new utility and appreciation for more detailed trip logs or sketches, for example, as I encountered the ambiguities that de Caro notes. While he also counsels "We cannot get it all" in his lovely and astute poem "Oral History" (2008, 57), I would argue that we folklorists must aim to achieve a good balance in our field documentation and adequate production of checks and balances for everyone involved!

In the all-important three-page single-spaced typed field report I first viewed (Gilmore and Leary 1986), I found expected information as remembered but now recognized ambivalences and absences. The first page presented customary folk arts survey interview metadata borrowed from Leary's January 13, 1981, Okkonen interview report, but with categories customized for the JMKAC survey project (see Gilmore 2015, 104–5). We had listed both of us as interviewers, in alphabetical order, with no distinction other than order to show which of us might have claimed the lead and authored the majority of the report. While the form offered space for "Other Pertinent Data and Comments from Field Experience" where more social and interview context could have been elaborated, there were only two sentences culled from Leary's earlier report about the prior project's connection. The next page and a half were devoted to the bobbing boat and skiff information that I sought and the bottom third of the third page to exhibit recommendations.

Using the related sketch, photos, slides and their logs, and a trip log reduced the report's ambiguities while also revealing more. The strength of the report could be the minimalist object-focused documentation and written description and discussion of the vessels and related fishing gear that I had likely mostly produced. But I found it sadly lacking in depicting the character of the fieldwork experience and especially of Eino as a Bark Point Finnish American commercial fisherman-boat builder who had given form and substance to the bobbing boat within a context of collaborative community labor during a particular era of his life. When I turned to the photographic record, I realized that our inventory was also incomplete. Because all originals were housed at JMKAC and access had been irregular over the years, we had kept a small selection of copy slides in a dedicated WFAS slide container. Some were missing from where they were supposed to be. The black-and-white contact sheets also proved inadequate for reviewing some details of the vessels, individuals, and actions portrayed.

To the good, however, our photo and slide logs were robustly descriptive, often beyond some details in the field report, and provided evidence of who likely took each shot and prepared the description for each image—mine typed, Jim's hand printed. Handwritten field notes for the Okkonen interview were absent from Jim's interview tablets, organized consecutively by interviewee and date, suggesting that he accepted his prior project's fieldwork as enough and/or that he had entrusted the reporting to me.

Remarkably, a call to JMKAC archivist Brian Rusch resulted in good-quality digitized versions of most images taken for the report, as well as scans of the report and related logs. That good fortune illuminated aspects of the specific boat forms (some I had recalled, others not), what and how much we had documented, who might have been doing what in the images—including Leary's capture of Janet and Bella measuring the bobbing boat—and which fieldworker was using which camera at which time. All restored a more comprehensive sense of what had unfolded, despite limitations.

Here also were the measurements I had been so obsessively seeking, and they roughly confirmed the table top as a good example! As I pored over the drawing and the report's description, I could see that I had measured the boat's lengthwise bottom centerline, which from flat bow to flat stern totaled eight feet, tapering out to ten feet overall at the top of those two transoms. The widest, or beamiest, part of the boat's breadth measured thirty-six inches on the bottom and flared out to forty-seven inches at the top of the sides. The ovoid shaped bottom was, to quote my report, "26 inches . . . at the stern spreading to 34 inches" at the top "and 20 inches . . . at the bow spreading to 24 inches" at the top. The two sides measured seventeen inches high. It continues: "the boat featured cedar planking (edge-to-edge), oak frames . . . runners and portions of the hull . . . covered, like all of the skiffs and the fishing tugs, with tin sheeting, to protect the wood from ice."

By comparison, the skiff received less detailed technological description in the report, just the key overall length dimension of sixteen feet—a classic western Great Lakes maximum length that required no official state licensing (cf. Gilmore 1998, 469, 473)—and the details that it followed "the same shape, size, and construction" that Okkonens privileged for building their smaller commercial fishing vessels during the first half of the twentieth century: "oak frames inserted in a shell of cedar planking formed with the use of battens . . . except that his [Eino's] father lapped the planks together [in "lapstrake" fashion with continuities to older forms] rather than placing them edge to edge" for the earliest skiff that Eino learned to fish when in his teens. Larger skiffs like these he built with his father "for fishing herring and lake trout with gillnets as well as set hooks (lake trout only); they powered these boats with single cylinder Elto outboards. In the early fall, they would float the nets in deeper water, while in the spring they would bring the nets in close to shore to fish the bottom, where the fish were spawning."

The report placed the skiff in a chronology of like boats, including a forty-foot fishing tug Eino, his brother, and his father helped a professional builder complete in 1930, followed by a twenty-four-foot by eight-foot flat-bottomed pound net skiff that Eino, his brother, and two Johnson brothers built when they took up pound-net fishing in 1939. Eventually, instead of using the tug to tow the skiff into shallow pound-netting waters, they built yet another thirty-foot skiff, following the earlier sixteen-foot model, for towing the pound-net skiff (cf. Gilmore 1998, 460–61).

The bobbing boat description stands apart, more personally depicted as a boat type essential for protection while ice fishing commercially every winter day possible, and one that Eino could have built with the help of a friend or relative several times over his occupational life—the last, and the one we witnessed, in the 1940s. He would fish with others for self-protection, "setting up a wind-break near their two holes . . . His largest catch one day was 105 pounds of lake trout (33 fish) which sold at $.28 per pound—a big take at the time . . . they would take a boat and oars, in case the ice began to break up, which it occasionally did." In parentheses I note that Eino and his friend Bill Hendrickson "tell a riveting story of such an experience," but my cryptic handwritten field notes suggest we'd gotten too absorbed in the story to record more at the time (cf. Hendrickson n.d.).

The report goes on to speculate about the design heritage and antecedents for both bobbing boat and skiff types, invoking the possibility of a Finnish immigrant connection for the former but a more complex American immigrant syncretism of historical forms and traditions for the skiff. It also places Eino's combined commercial-fishing and boat- and gear-building example in a broader community context of common commercial fishing practices just as it also intimates patterns specialized to western Great Lakes waterways occupational cultures—all contentions worthy of further research, clarification, and correction.

The final section of this rather clinical, impersonal, historical-archeological-geographical, structural-functional, and reductive boat-focused reporting recommends the bobbing boat over the skiff for possible exhibition, because of its better condition, smaller size, appeal with "its runners and removable handle," and the way in which it "represents one of several typical ways of handling the problem of being out on the ice." It also recommends older traditional fishing gear from Eino's trove as an accompaniment.

Only the cedar net floats and tarred linen fishing line wound on a hand-carved oak bobbin made it into the exhibit (Teske 1987, 70, 100, 189–90), passing JMKAC curatorial standards. The workboats, by comparison, had apparently looked banged up and beaten, disheveled workhorses in storage, not ready for show. The bobbing boat as a work platform could have set a contextual scenario to stimulate viewers' imaginations about what it expressed relationally with the gear, especially with a fresh coat of paint for display. Yet it was a feat that Okkonen's legacy became part of the exhibit and exhibit catalog at all, where it now stands for posterity and equity in Great Lakes maritime occupational expressions, a testament to Eino's community artistry and stewardship. Although unsure what opinion Okkonen held of the matter, I suspect he was pleased to speak for his community in helping out someone who'd helped before in gathering fellow musicians together at a local public performance.

My review of these impoverished field circumstances, reductive results, languishing personal field collections, and aging memories has left me feeling surprisingly inspired, as we contemplate what we are about as folklorists and ethnographic fieldworkers. I was humbled, grateful, and relieved to recapture familiarity with our personal archival trove of WFAS project field documentation—still in pretty good original order after all. I was thrilled that my Okkonen field reporting upheld critical details of the boat descriptions I hazarded at the symposium, restoring professional and personal confidence in my recall but also making me pay closer attention to inadequacies in reporting and memories. While I was clearly a researcher with research agendas beyond, indeed almost in spite of, the limitations imposed by the JMKAC project scope, my commitment to minimum adequacy in boatological description left a reasonably useful record for comparative research purposes and improvement.

I realize now that the Okkonen experience ushered in a remarkable period of small-boat fieldwork for me on several interrelated projects, in the Great Lakes and Pacific Northwest regions. The vessels' small size made them eminently accessible, and I found their fisherman-builders well networked, cordial, generous, and instructive, well beyond initial interviews. Some contributed to strings of interrelated research projects that resulted in fuller documentation, public productions, exhibits, artifact and digital collections, publications, university teaching, festival camaraderie—and enduring social kinships. The limitations of short-term underfunded projects with grand ambitions could thus improve focus and depth in later projects and move into more expressive performative directions of inquiry that more fully engaged and empowered the individuals involved. My convictions about using one project's results to build into next projects in a larger context of research practice often secured a return to individuals for further collaboration, more insights, stronger relationships, and, ultimately, more accurate and fairly shared results, perhaps with greater community impact. In some cases, I became, and came to behave, like family, listening, learning, and relating more deeply and comfortably—and I had a much harder time assuming roles of fieldworker or documentarian as we brought stories "to dramatic reality . . . in a living cultural context" (Toelken 1998, 386).

I see much creative re-creation ahead for archivists, researchers, and interviewee's descendants who face the often spare and disparate documentary recordings and employment records made by many public folklore project fieldworkers, solo or in teams, from the
late 1970s into the early 1990s, the pre-Mapplethorpe era at the NEA, heyday of the large
statewide folk arts surveys. For original fieldworkers and collaborators alike, these esoteric
"fossilized" records can ascertain and restore bits of fading memories and reestablish information and interpretations that years later may not be independently evident in the old
records. At the same time, gaps in adequacy and slants in orientation may become clearer
to the fieldworkers and the people they collaborate with, including later researchers, exposing interesting critiques yet raising further questions and germs of ideas that may encourage follow-up on this patchwork of old, partial, and inadequate records and the people
they represent.

Notes

1. Readers may recognize the porous and gray areas of personal-professional relationships
among spouses and partners working in the same occupational sphere, especially when sharing
project work effort at the same moment. As in any fieldwork, important gender, power, status, and
other "colonial" and systemic differentials condition the experience, documentary ownership, production, legalities, and degrees of collaboration and access. Here, I felt them all.

2. Comparing notes with other contract workers, we learned effective ways of designing documentary projects with classically meager public support and joined them, often at American Folklore Society sessions and Independent Folklorists Section meetings, in articulating fieldwork
dynamics, ethics, labor rights and relationships with sponsoring organizations, dimensions of project time and planning, factoring in the value of our own efforts and the important voluntary contributions of our collaborators (cf. Lux 1990; Suter 1994).

The Smithsonian Folklife Festival Model as Transferable Technology for Cultural Heritage Craft Tourism in Local Museums

DIANA BAIRD N'DIAYE

Watching expert masons build a house using materials, methods, and aesthetic principles that are a continuation of architectural traditions of archaeological and historic sites like the fourteenth-century great Mosque in Timbuktu (Arnoldi 2012); purchasing silver jewelry and blends of incense from the workshops of traditional Omani artisans and savoring the aromas of coffee from Haiti and groundnut stew from Senegal; joining a Bermudian kite-making workshop; and attending a demonstration on Armenian rug weaving are all experiences of cultural heritage craft tourism in their respective locales. They also have all been re-created or evoked as part of Smithsonian Folklife Festival visitor experiences. At the level of state and regional governments in the United States and around the world, participation in the Festival and adoption of Folklife Festival paradigms have impacted cultural policy and tourism practices. Such participation often has involved the negotiation of turf and subsequent collaboration among ministries of culture, tourism, craft, and cultural industries and—of course—the primary involvement of individuals within their local communities. At another level, involvement with the Folklife Festival stimulates conversations about changing and conflicting notions of heritage, authenticity, and cultural citizenship.

WHAT IS THE FOLKLIFE FESTIVAL?

For more than five decades, almost every year during the last week of June and the first week of July, up to one million visitors—including residents of the Washington, DC, area, international tourists, and members of Congress and other government staffers—have traditionally converged on the front lawn of the nation's capital to attend the Smithsonian Folklife Festival. The Festival is organized and presented in the context of the Smithsonian Institution, composed of a system of national museums and research centers. Like museum exhibitions, the programs are researched and curated around specific themes. Unlike conventional museum exhibitions that are object centered, however, programs at the Festival strive to create an opportunity for visitors to learn about another culture or their own cultural heritage through interactions with artists and other cultural creators. In the edited volume *Folklife in Museums* (Dewhurst, Hall, and Seeman 2017), several authors point to dialogue and community engagement in planning and participation as hallmarks of desirable folklife presentations. These are also notions that apply to well-conceived cultural tourism projects.

In 2020, for the first time, because of COVID-19, the Folklife Festival was produced virtually. This format, used in both 2020 and 2021, was curated and produced under the supervision of Festival director Sabrina Motley in a virtual space with moving presentations that captured the essence of the Festival in the flesh. While the immediacy of scent and touch and ambiance could be reached only in the imagination, virtual visitors were treated to powerful sights, sounds, and meaningful discussion online. This pivot, though not the optimal way to "visit" the Festival or to experience interactive cultural heritage tourism, nevertheless opened many new opportunities. One of these was the production of an online Festival Marketplace; another was the creation of virtual stages that could link participating artists on different continents in discussion, demonstration, and performance. This virtual tourism, during a time of restricted travel, can provide an intimacy of experience with artists that has the potential to prepare tourists and artists for flesh-and-blood visits to places and people that they have met online.

The event, which began in 1967, has been a tourism destination and a major showcase for cultural heritage crafts, introducing large audiences and potential consumers to traditional artisans from communities around the United States and around the world. Historically, crafts persons have participated in the Festival each year in the context of three or four thematic programs taking place on the United States National Mall in front of the Smithsonian. Since the Smithsonian Institution comprises a system of national museums, these Festival programs have sometimes been referred to as "living exhibitions without walls" but might be better described as cultural conversations. As Senator Mark Hatfield from Oregon once said, "No curator can convey through a glass display case what the people can say to us directly" (Kurin 1998).

The Folklife Festival program themes are typically developed by the Center's Festival and curatorial staff in collaboration with lay and academic scholars, educators, artists, and others from the communities to be represented. Financial, in-kind, and logistical support from governments, nongovernmental organizations (NGOs), private donations, and many volunteers play crucial roles in making the Festival possible. In the case of the Haiti Program in 2004 and 2010, donations of free shipping of artisans' supplies, materials, and crafts for exhibits from a local business came just in time during moments of economic, political, and environmental crises in Haiti. Haitian crafts accounted for more than $46,000 in Marketplace sales paid directly to artisans for the 2004 Festival. In addition, as noted in an essay by Richard Kurin, then Undersecretary of the Smithsonian, the fortuitous timing of the Haiti Festival Program during a World Bank Donor's conference, prompted commitments of aid to Haiti in 2004 of more than $1billion. As remarked by James Wolfensohn, president of the World Bank at the time, the fine work presented by Haitian craftspeople at the Festival demonstrated the capacity, potential, and resilience of the Haitian people in general (Kurin 2011).

Smithsonian Folklife Festival programs may focus on the cultural heritage of a region (The Silk Road, 2002), a nation (Armenia, 2017), or a neighborhood (Anacostia, 2012). Other programs have focused on a cluster of occupations and occupational arts (*The Will to Adorn*, 2013; *The Circus Arts*, 2018) or the traditions emerging around a culture or theme. For example, as early as 1994, the Smithsonian collaborated with the Inter-American Foundation to produce a program on the theme of culture and development. The program highlighted ways in which communities in the Caribbean, Latin America, and South America built upon the traditions of their localities to develop literacy programs, sustainable agriculture projects, and craft cooperatives.

In the course of fulfilling its mission, the Smithsonian Folklife Festival works with traditional artisans in several ways. First, in the research stages of planning a program, Festival curators and researchers identify crafts traditions that are important to a community and locate and interview local practitioners and document their work in photographs and in audio recordings. At a program review, the Folklife Festival curatorial team (made up of Smithsonian staff, local curators, and advisers) reviews the research and selects the crafts traditions and craftspersons that will be highlighted in the program as representative of the community. During the production phase, crafts reflective of the local heritage of the communities to be featured at the Festival are selected for the Marketplace. In 2015, the initiation of a Cultural Sustainability division at the Center for Folklife and Cultural Heritage incorporated cultural tourism, design and marketing training, and assistance for artisans through training initiatives and other entrepreneurial programs geared toward nations and communities that also participated in the Folklife Festival.

MUSEUMS CAN DRAW TOURISTS TO LOCAL IN-COMMUNITY MARKETS

Since the beginning, the Smithsonian Institution's Center for Folklife and Cultural Heritage (CFCH) has provided a venue for the sale of the work of artists represented at the annual Smithsonian Folklife Festival at its Festival Marketplace. Showcasing heritage arts and featuring the work of cultural practitioners are both part of Smithsonian Folklife Festival's mandate to educate and display culture of, by, and for the people.

Over the ten days of the Festival, artisans demonstrate their knowledge and skills, share stories about their personal histories and their arts, and converse with visitors about issues that affect their lives and livelihoods. As comments in Smithsonian Festival surveys reveal, visitors experience the invited crafts persons as embodying the living cultural heritage of their communities, and the Festival offers them the opportunity to interact with artisans from all over the world (Smithsonian 2016). In the 2002 Silk Road Program, the 2004 Haiti Program, and the 2004 First Americans Festival, Festival organizers experimented with creating opportunities for small entrepreneurial craft businesses. Artisan groups like the Self-Employed Women's Association (SEWA), a women's trade union from India, and NGOs such as Aid to Artisans and Amazon Alliance have all participated as independent operators in Festival-sponsored markets. In 2001, the Bermudian cedar carver Llewellyn Emery described the challenges faced by traditional cedar artisans in the aftermath of a cedar blight in the 1940s that wiped out much of the wood used in framing houses, building boats, and making furniture as well as smaller items that tourists took home as mementos of their visits to the island. Cedar workers in Bermuda now rely on recycled and imported cedar and have begun to experiment with more accessible woods.

In earlier Festivals, the Marketplace sold the recordings and books of featured participants. Over the years, the Marketplace increased its inventory by including the crafts of Festival artisans such as basketry, weavings, and carvings. In recent years, the Marketplace has developed into a larger operation that includes many artisanal crafts (e.g., jewelry, ceramics, sculpture, textile arts, paper products, metal arts), food products such as coffee and tea, bath and beauty products (homemade soaps and lotions), and children's items (dolls, toys, clothing). The Marketplace features products related to the Festival programs that are unique, handmade, affordable, and typically available only in their respective countries or communities. In 2018, the *Crafts of African Fashion* Project functioned as a capsule Festival program. During the run of the Festival, weavers, dyers, and a leatherworker demonstrated and discussed their métiers and the community context in which they practiced in their homeland, while also selling their work. Companion events at the National Museum of African Arts and the National Museum of African American Art provided opportunities for participants to talk more about the role of artisans in fashion. During the program, the leatherworker Soumana Saley recounted his efforts to begin and sustain a school for traditional artisans and their apprentices, who work in the courtyard behind the National Museum of Niger in Niamey. The revenue from the crafts sold at the Festival, more than $5,000 in two weeks, paid the salary of teachers at the school for the next year (personal communication, 2019).

Throughout programs such as those described, the Folklife Festival Marketplace has maintained its mission of sustained development of artisan crafts around the world. Like the Festival Marketplace, large and small museums can feature local crafts in shops. Museums can take an active role in making links with artisans by hosting lecture demonstrations linked to their holdings. Museums can also collaborate and cosponsor events, tours, and publications that inform tourists about the history and cultural context of the places they can visit within their local communities. At events in which museums and the local community partner, staff can also suggest and model respectful and dignified ways for visitors to act within a community setting.

THE HALLMARKS OF THE CLASSIC FOLKLIFE FESTIVAL MODEL

Ethics and principles place local communities at the center of the Folklife Festival as primary stakeholders. In short, when the Festival is doing its job, there is what James Early, a former cultural policy director at the Smithsonian, called "No Folklore without the Folk." The Festival places an emphasis on self-representation. Scholars act as facilitators, foregrounding the expertise of Indigenous and traditional experts—though in some cases they are both. Unlike conventional exhibitions, the Festival focuses on tradition bearers and traditions rather than sites or objects to convey an understanding of the cultures represented. In this way, the Festival Model is consistent with the spirit of UNESCO's 2003 Convention on Intangible Cultural Heritage (Keitumetse 2006).

Master artisan Capuchi Bobbo demonstrates Ewe-style Ghanaian weaving at the 2018 Smithsonian Folklife Festival. (Photograph by author. Courtesy of Smithsonian Center for Folklife and Cultural Heritage.)

Cultural heritage tourism policy frequently notes the involvement of or benefits to "local communities." However, the term can be nebulous. Given the multiplicity of cultural identities and the differing social and economic statuses of individuals and groups within any given locale, the ways in which community membership is defined can have serious social, political, and economic impacts on individuals and groups. For example, groups and individuals with more class, caste, and gender privilege may act as gatekeepers for the cultural production of those with less privilege, though they are not the primary cultural producers.

As centuries of disagreement over issues of identity and ownership can attest, defining "community," like defining "culture," can become an inevitably messy if not unfortunately bloody process. "Community" can refer to residents of a particular town, neighborhood, or ethnic or other grouping of people who are designated by those who create or execute tourism policy as beneficiaries or whose ways of life are (more nefariously) seen as "attractions." Communities are groups of people who have shared history, experience, practice, knowledge, values, and aesthetics. There are important principles that underlie these references to communities, especially the *definition of "community" based on a shared history of knowledge and practice*. Another term that is often used vaguely in creating tourism policy or mission statements is community "agency," that is, a recognition of the importance of participation in all aspects of the process of documenting and safeguarding heritage art by practitioners, including conveyors, creators, and audiences/users.[1]

In the best of all possible worlds, respectful and community-driven tourism supports efforts of Indigenous cultural groups and individuals to continue to value, practice, nurture, and transmit the vitality of forms of traditional knowledge, skills, and expressive culture that embody their identities, with the proviso that these practices do not impinge on essential human rights. Best practice dictates that diversity, equity, accessibility, and inclusivity are considered in planning for community cultural tourism and that the agency of all artists and other cultural practitioners at heritage tourism destinations is fully recognized. Furthermore, artists and cultural practitioners should be fully engaged in the planning of public activities, and they should be compensated adequately for their engagement with tourists. It is important that national and local governments proactively create sustainable programs and projects that nurture the continued vitality of heritage arts within their borders. It is worth noting that governments often underfund the heritage arts of groups that are considered to be less powerful than others in society. Last but not least, respect and appreciation for heritage arts should become a part of the education of youth both within schools and less formal educational settings.

For the Festival model to work, active collaboration among stakeholders, including government policymakers, research professionals, cultural practitioners, private-sector organizations and/or agencies, and members of civic society is necessary in initiatives directed toward safeguarding heritage arts in the context of cultural tourism. This collaboration involves opening communication, collectively brainstorming ideas, establishing partnerships, negotiating, and defining stakeholder roles. Projects can begin, as they often do at the beginning of the Folklife Festival process, by identifying and convening and soliciting cooperation from multiple stakeholders. Curators then make a research plan on the basis of input from multiple sources. Research contracts are awarded to local researchers. Smithsonian staff curators provide orientation for local experts and researchers in field research methods adapted to Festival programs. These local researchers often come to the Festival as "presenters" (introducing traditional artists and giving visitors an idea of the larger historical and cultural framework). The research process identifies community assets and needs. The curators brainstorm what to represent and who can do what, along with mapping environmental impact and concerns. The Smithsonian Folklife Festival models the creation of an infrastructure for craft tourism in several ways. Planning often begins with consultations with a broad swath of actors, including artisans, artisan support organizations, scholars and curators, tourism and government officials, educators, and potential funders or donors. These conversations cover the goals of the tourism effort, community assets, and the capacity of the local community to support visitors. The next step often involves training both community-based and local academic researchers in how to document local traditions and cultural practitioners with an eye toward presenting heritage crafts in new ways and, importantly, deciding which crafts are most appropriate to be presented to visitors. At the same time, local organizers work to make plans for the infrastructure needed to accommodate visitors. Furthermore, plans can include selecting and training community members to represent their work and their stories to unfamiliar audiences and supplying initial resources. For example, a Smithsonian Folklife Festival program in the United States was followed by a restaging of a "Homecoming" in Bermuda and the incorporation of several of the participating artists in ongoing cultural programming on Wednesdays, when cruise ships reached Bermudian shores.[2]

An excellent example of the Festival model working at its best was in the 2018 *My Armenia* program. The program was produced in the context of a much larger and well-funded initiative sponsored by USAID and led by Halle Butvin, director of special projects at the Center for Folklife and Cultural Heritage. In 2018, the *Armenia* project was the most ambitious and comprehensive pre- and post-Festival effort and signaled the development of a new Division of Cultural Sustainability at the Center, one that built on staff knowledge and expertise along with the reputation of the Festival to build capacity, nurture, and support community-based heritage tourism projects in Armenia. My role in the project, working with fellow veteran Folklife Festival curator Dr. Betty Belanus, was to provide an orientation for Armenian scholars and researchers in the specialized research required for Festival production. That research was used before, during, and after the actual Festival program on the Mall in the development of tourism experiences with local artists, artisans, and performers. Visitors to the Folklife Festival Program on Armenia learned about traditions of embroidery and other forms of needlework through demonstrations and workshops. Visitors to Armenia were invited to local festivals where these arts offered as part of the cultural experience. These opportunities had been available in a few places in Armenia already, but the expansion of craft experiences at festivals was enhanced and multiplied through the practice gained by Armenian artisans, researchers, and coordinators at the Smithsonian Folklife Festival. In an article about the project written in 2021, Yuri Horowitz, the newly appointed cultural tourism specialist at the Center, wrote that the effort "includes working with nearly 150 local partners to create signature tourism experiences connected to artisans, foodways, local history, regional museums, festivals, and more" (Horowitz

2020). Unfortunately, however, funds have often not been forthcoming for the intense robust engagement that was possible with Armenia.

The Smithsonian Festival model is a technology of development for cultural heritage
tourism, and the Festival model includes a variety of positive aspects, many of which have
been mentioned. There are also, of course, experiences throughout the Festival's history
that present object lessons—pitfalls to be avoided at all costs in order not to fail. One such
lesson is to ensure that those involved in the Festival never impose the program on the
community without its consent and explicit participation. On occasion we have hired researchers, curators, administrators, or other staff who did not show proper respect for the
cultural artists and community whose creative works they were charged to assist, an issue
we take very seriously. There have also been plenty of examples where active collaboration
between government sectors was difficult or impossible. There are also times when, despite the good intentions of those involved, the Festival presentations leaned toward colonial,
voyeuristic display rather than the ideals of community self-representation and interaction
for which the Festival strives. The Festival is constantly changing, and we are constantly
learning from our successes and our mistakes.

Those successes and mistakes of the Festival model have been interrogated in several
books and articles. In *Curatorial Conversations: Cultural Representation and the Smithsonian
Folklife Festival* (Cadaval, Kim, and N'Diaye 2016), for example, Festival curators provide an
in-depth and reflexive look at the history and practice of the Festival from their perspective
and address many of the contradictions between the Festival's intentions and outcomes.[3]

CONCLUSION

Cities, states, and nations are drawn to participate in the Smithsonian Folklife Festival
because they are looking for ways to stimulate the growth of cultural tourism in their own
localities. They see the Festival as a means to attract international visitors, to test the market for traditional cultural industries, and, sometimes, to jumpstart the process of research
for inventories of intangible cultural heritage. UNESCO, the World Bank, and other agencies have encouraged national governments to inventory "representative items of intangible heritage" and to utilize local culture as a resource in development. Cultural tourism is
furthermore linked to the development and representation of identity and citizenship,
which may incorporate an acknowledgment of "cultural diversity" as an asset.

The museum-based Smithsonian Folklife Festival is seen by many ministries of tourism
as a way to introduce a large and diverse audience to the features that make their countries
unique as cultural destinations. Ministries of culture also look to the elements of Festival
representation for clues as to how to develop their own events and to "learn the ropes" of
cultural representation through traditions on display. At the level of local governments,
participation in the Festival and adoption of Folklife festival paradigms sometimes impacts
cultural policy and tourism practice. Such participation often involves the negotiation of
turf and subsequent collaboration among ministries of culture and the tourism, craft, and
cultural industries. At another level, involvement with the Folklife Festival stimulates
conversations about changing and conflicting notions of heritage, authenticity, and cultural citizenship.

Museums today face pointed challenges in incorporating intangible cultural heritage into their purviews, engaging meaningfully with local communities whose tangible heritage museums are charged with preserving and presenting, and fulfilling a role as tourism destinations: educating visitors, tourists, and residents alike about the cultural heritage of their environs.

As conventionally object-based institutions still emerging from the legacies of colonialist and postcolonialist interpretations, as well as from voyeuristic approaches to various cultures, museums often face an imbalance between their historic mandate to conserve, interpret, and display the objects they hold and their legitimate responsibility to present local communities in ways that dignify and amplify many voices rather than objectify and essentialize. When tourists begin and end their cultural exchange with the objects in the museum and their exchange of money in the museum shops, both they and the local communities whose heritage is represented in the museum are quite literally shortchanged.

Museums and other cultural venues and events can play a dynamic role beyond their conventional place in tourism as destinations using modalities similar to those of the Folklife festival. One obvious means of utilizing the model is through its replication at museum sites. Several countries have restaged Festival programs back home. Gathering traditional artists from across an entire nation for a museum-based festival focuses attention on the national significance of traditional artists and can be viable as a high-profile event. As incubators for cultural tourism, museums, communities, NGOs, and collaborating government agencies can work hand in hand to develop tourist experiences that are principled, respectful, fulfilling, informative, and multivocal, as well as reciprocal, and that bring economic benefits to the people as a whole and lead to return visits.

Notes

1. For a slightly more expansive discussion of community in the context of the UNESCO Convention on Intangible Cultural Heritage, see https://ich.unesco.org/en/convention.

2. See https://folklife.si.edu/bermuda-connections/smithsonian for a Cultural Resources Guide developed in conjunction with Bermuda researchers and educators following the 2001 Bermuda Connections Program at the Smithsonian and the 2002 Bermuda Homecoming Program in Bermuda.

3. For more on the craft and tourism at the Festival, see Diamond and Trimillos (2008).

PART III. AMPLIFYING LOCAL VOICES

One of the most foundational elements of public folklorists' work involves finding a bigger stage and audience for traditional culture. Although folklorists may be more comfortable with the notions of "presentation" of folklore or "representation" of culture, we maintain at least some concern about these terms and the ways that "celebrate diversity" and "raise awareness" models of culture work tend to exoticize and tokenize the real-world experiences of our human kin by hiding their actual lives behind colorful and accessible displays of staged folk culture often meant for public consumption. Doing so runs the risk of ignoring and even erasing the multitude of different approaches, beliefs, expertise, and experience that makes traditions so rich and ever-changing.

Culture workers, especially those doing public culture work, must recognize those risks and acknowledge that the institutions in which many of us work are efficient at erasing the voices of the people with whom we collaborate—from classrooms, scholarship, grants, exhibitions, and public productions in general. Often, we have at least some degree of institutional leverage and systemic privilege with which we can amplify these voices through our work. Because of our emphasis on ethnography, folklorists are in a prime position to amplify the voices of community members. We believe that the broader term "amplifications" serves to remind us of our most important motivations for working with communities, and we feel it centers our collaborator's agency, rather than the affective experiences of a casual viewer.

Thomas DuBois and Marcus Cederström's chapter focuses on two collaborative projects with musicians to revitalize Finnish American immigrant songs. Examining the many different forms amplification can take, both in-person and online, DuBois and Cederström present one model that couples research with public programming and production to center the experiences of Finnish and Finnish American folk musicians as they work with and in the Finnish community on both sides of the Atlantic.

Richard March, in his essay on the history of his radio program *Down Home Dairyland*, discusses challenges and changes to the way he presented Wisconsin musical traditions. The essay surveys the technical and logistical challenges to changes in programming, format of delivery, and even recording spaces as he literally amplified the sung voices of Wisconsinites throughout the southern part of the state.

In her study of the Missouri Traditional Arts Program, Lisa Higgins details an effort to document individuals who participated in the arts apprenticeship program, to understand its impacts on their lives, while also examining the relationship folklorists have to those artists. The genealogical nature, as Higgins puts it, of traditional arts helps demonstrate how one person's impact on an arts community can be amplified over time for artists and folklorists alike.

Jared Schmidt's chapter on a rosemaled pair of hot-pink pumps looks at the transformations of a material object as it takes on ever-deepening layers of cultural significance. The rosemaled pumps tell a story about a community in change and how that change is explored at a local museum. A selected amplification of a single artistic vision can single-handedly complicate the ways that communities perceive themselves.

Hilary-Joy Virtanen's contribution on Finnish American labor songs looks at the musician Oren Tikkanen's performance of labor songs and his exploration of traditional cultural practice as a way to better understand the history and heritage of Michigan's Copper Country. Through careful translation and edits, Tikkanen uses traditional Finnish American music to bolster his community's sociohistorical understanding of not just the past but also the present and the future.

Collectively, the chapters look at the complex role that amplification efforts can play in the delicate balance between forms of cultural representation and social power. Amplification, when used strategically, can help enhance the way communities understand their places, their histories, their traditions, and themselves—and create better opportunities for outsiders to recognize and value their perspectives.

Songs of the Finnish Migration

Amplification and Revitalization

THOMAS A. DUBOIS and B. MARCUS CEDERSTRÖM

On an unseasonably warm October day in Minneapolis, Minnesota, in the midst of a global pandemic, Ralph and Jaana Tuttila's ensemble Laulu Aika met in a backyard to perform six songs to be recorded by the documentary filmmaker Cris Anderson. Masked and physically distanced, Laulu Aika, Finnish for "song time," performed these Finnish and Finnish American folk songs from the bilingual anthology *Songs of the Finnish Migration*, a work edited by the authors of this chapter, Thomas A. DuBois and B. Marcus Cederström (hereafter referred to as Tom and Marcus). The recorded performance was part of a larger project centered on sustaining and amplifying Finnish folk songs in the Upper Midwest that had crossed the Atlantic and that involved musicians from both Finland and Finnish America, scholars, community members, and a variety of cultural organizations.

Laulu Aika's backyard performance is part of a case study of how public-minded folklorists can engage with folk musicians, institutions, and people within a given cultural community to amplify and support their acts of cultural celebration, preservation, and maintenance, particularly with an aim toward revitalizing, sustaining, and extending a particular genre of folklore in that community in the future. The community in question: Finns and Finnish Americans; the genre of folklore: vocal songs related to the lives and experiences of Finnish migrants to the United States at the turn of the twentieth century. Through their work to translate, contextualize, and promote the adoption into active performance of songs included in Simo Westerholm's 1983 foundational anthology *Reisaavaisen laulu Amerikkaan: Siirtolaislauluja*, the folklorists aimed to use what this volume's editors term "institutional leverage and systemic privilege" to amplify the voices and promote the creative engagement of community members with an important but relatively inaccessible element of their cultural heritage. The translation of Westerholm's monolingual Finnish anthology, *Songs of the Finnish Migration* (DuBois and Cederström 2019), provides sheet music and bilingual singable translations of the eighty-five songs originally selected and anthologized by Westerholm, providing background information regarding Finnish migration to North America and Finnish American music making at the turn of the twentieth century that Westerholm did not include for his original Finnish-language

audience. The events organized in connection with the publication of the translation promoted the adoption of songs from the anthology into the active repertoire of folk music
performers in both Finland and Finnish America and amplified the creative innovations of
performers engaging with these historical sources in new ways. Where a close literal translation of the anthology would have served the interests primarily of scholars, Finnish
American or otherwise, the production, promotion, and performance of singable translations, as well as the events organized once the translation was published, aimed to empower performers to use the anthology in creative and independent ways. This case study
documents ways in which performers approached the anthology's materials since the
translation's publication, including during the COVID-19 pandemic of 2020 and 2021.

The project described builds on annual cultural festivals that developed in tandem on
two sides of the Atlantic, in both Finland and North America. In 1940, in the aftermath of
the 1939–40 Winter War, Finnish Canadians organized the first Finnish Canadian Grand
Festival in Sudbury, Ontario, aimed at raising relief funds to send to Finland (Toiviainen
2011). While the original flyer for that "Laulu ja Soitto Juhlat" (Song and playing festival)
depicted a singing Väinämöinen playing a five-string kantele—images evoking the long-
standing Finnish attention to the Eastern Finnish and Karelian song traditions celebrated
in Elias Lönnrot's Finnish national epic *Kalevala* and the lyric anthology *Kanteletar*—in
practice, the musical performances and folk dances performed in annual Finn Grand Fests
ever after included or even emphasized the group dancing and the fiddle-dominated *pelimanni* musical traditions of Western Finland, the homeland of most Finns who migrated
to Canada and the United States in the nineteenth and early twentieth centuries.[1] Locally
organized Finnish Canadian annual festivals stabilized through a permanent Finn Grand
Fest steering committee in 1961 and the establishment of the Kanadan Suomalainen Kulttuuriliitto (Finnish Canadian Cultural Federation) in 1972 (Toiviainen 2011).

As Ronald Cohen (2003) shows in his history of the American folk music revival from
1940 to 1970 and as James Leary points out in his *Folk Songs of Another America* (2015, 3),
American public interest in folk songs at the time of the first Finnish Canadian Grand Festival tended to focus on songs performed in English, exemplars of anglophone vocal traditions celebrated in works such as John A. Lomax's 1910 *Cowboy Songs and Other Frontier
Ballads* and John Lomax and Alan Lomax's 1934 *American Ballads and Folk Songs*. As Leary
(2015) shows, fieldwork recordings of non-English folk song performances became an interest of scholars collecting for the Archive of American Folk Song (established in 1928),
with substantive collections of Finnish American songs being assembled in the Upper
Midwest of the United States in the late 1930s and early 1940s, although these did not generally lead to publications or publicly available recordings. In contrast, as the Finnish musicologist Pekka Gronow (1982) has shown, the fledgling American record industry of the
early twentieth century embraced "ethnic music," producing some eight hundred recordings of Finnish performers for the Columbia and Victor labels in the first half of the twentieth century, marketed principally to the Finnish American community, a wealth of
materials that was often overlooked as "neglected heritage" (Gronow 1982, 12; DuBois and
Cederström 2019, 142).

Toward the end of the 1960s, however, particularly with the foundation of the Smithsonian Folklife Festival, in 1967, folk music in languages other than English began to gain greater prominence (Kurin 1997, 1998; see N'Diaye in this volume). In Finland, attention to West Finnish folk song and instrumental music received a similar boost with the establishment of the Kaustinen Folk Music Festival, in 1968, and the Kansanmusiikki-instituutti (Folk Music Institute) in Kaustinen, in 1974. Decisive, too, was the creation of the folk music ensemble Tallari as a nationally funded musical organization, tasked with "preserving and promoting Finnish folk music and making its various genres known both in Finland and abroad through concert and performance activities as well as educational and research activities" (Träskelin 2021). Simo Westerholm, the compiler of *Reisaavaisen laulu Amerikkaan*, became deputy director of the Folk Music Institute in 1974 (Leary 2019, 220) and worked with Pekka Gronow to produce and rerelease albums of earlier Finnish American 78s (Leary 2019, 220–21). Gronow's anthology of Finnish migrants' songs—culled from archives, preserved broadsides, and transcribed ethnic 78 rpm recordings—included not only song texts but also musical transcriptions and chord notations. The aim of such accompanying apparatus was to allow Finnish performers to incorporate the songs into their repertoires. Although the anthology had a strong reception in Finland, in the United States it remained mostly unknown.

In 1983, Finnish Americans in Minneapolis emulated the long-standing Finnish Canadian Grand Fest, the well-established Smithsonian Folklife Festival, and the Kaustinen Folk Music Festival to organize the first-ever FinnFest USA, an annual event that has taken place each year since, except for 2020, when it was canceled because of the COVID-19 pandemic. FinnFest USA is an immersive Finnish-created exploration of all things Finnish and Finnish American. Broader in compass than a folk festival, it is made up of a diverse array of Finnish-related events, including lectures, folk music and dancing, symphonic concerts, banquets, sporting events, theatrical performances, art installations, church services, and the sale and purchase of Finnish foods, crafts, and souvenirs. Longtime FinnFest organizer and participant Marianne Wargelin once called it a "Chautauqua." As Susanne Österlund-Pötzsch (2003) has shown, FinnFest serves as a vehicle by which Finnish Americans can learn about their heritage and find elements of Finnish folklore to incorporate into their performative lives. Tom is a longtime participant and sometime organizer of FinnFest USA, having presented at many iterations of the festival, including presentations based on the work for *Songs of the Finnish Migration*.

In 2005, at the urging of Jim Leary, Tom started the translation project. At the advice of Vern and Anja Sell—fellow Madisonians who had long been involved in the translation and publication of classic Finnish art ("Lied") songs—Tom determined to produce "singable" translations that would allow a performer to sing the song in the original Finnish, in English, or in some mixture of the two. In 2005, he presented some of his first translations of songs from the anthology at the Marquette FinnFest and promised that the translation project was well under way and would soon reach completion. Over the subsequent many years, he worked with then graduate students Sara Tikkanen, Hilary Virtanen, and Marcus to prepare digitized versions of the music that Westerholm had provided in the anthology, to create transcriptions of the original Finnish texts, and to produce first drafts of English translations. It was only after Marcus completed his doctoral dissertation, in 2016, however, and took up an appointment as community curator of Nordic-American folklore as part of the project Sustaining Scandinavian Folk Arts in the Upper Midwest (SSFAUM) that Marcus and Tom began to work in a concerted fashion to bring the project to print. Crucial in that process was the assistance of Jimmy Träskelin (hereafter Jimmy) of the Folk Music Institute, a frequent collaborator with the musical group Tallari. Jimmy worked to secure the translation and publication rights of the songs and to provide the layout for the volume that would eventually appear in 2019 as a copublication of the Folk Music Institute and the University of Wisconsin Press.

A goal of the SSFAUM project has been to encourage and facilitate intergenerational transferral of traditional art forms in Nordic-American communities. This includes the intergenerational transfer of artistic skills, as well as ethnographic and public programming and production skills. In connection with Finnish American music making, that transferral involved amplifying the creative contributions of active musicians in both Finland and America while also ensuring that the lyrics would be accessible to singers who might not speak Finnish. It was an exciting side development of the collaboration among Tom, Marcus, and Jimmy in producing the translation that Jimmy and two of the members of Tallari (Katri Haukilahti and Sampo Korva, hereafter Katri and Sampo) decided to record a selection of songs from the anthology and to reproduce in their liner notes not only the original Finnish lyrics but also their singable English translations. The resulting album, *Lähtölaulu: A Song of Departure*, appeared in 2019 (Träskelin). The album draws materials directly from *Songs of the Finnish Migration* but adapts them, as we describe here, in interesting and independent ways.

In his introduction to the anthology's section "Levyllä. On the Turntable" (DuBois and Cederström 2019, 140–41), Marcus notes that Westerholm's collection included only one song performed by a woman (Viola Turpeinen's "Unelma-valssi/Dream Waltz"). Nonetheless, Jimmy, Sampo, and Katri chose in their album to explore and highlight many of the anthologized songs that narrate the experiences of women as well as men. In the context of a migrant crisis in Europe and North America, they produced an album that uses the anthologized songs of past Finnish migrants to comment on the "dreams, disappointments, joys and sorrows" of the migration experience (Träskelin 2019). Their eight-song album, all drawing from *Songs of the Finnish Migration*, includes "Juhannuksen aikana/Over Midsummer," "Viola Turpeinen tanssit Kiipillä/Viola Turpeinen at the Dance in Cape Ann," "Lähtölaulu/Song of Departure," "Unelma-valssi/Dream Waltz," "Laulu/Song of an America-Widow," "Siirtolaisen ensi vastuksia/The Immigrant's First Difficulties," "Amerikan liikkojen tanssilaiva/American Girls' Dance Floor," and "Kotimaani ompi Suomi/My Homeland Is Finland."

The album opens with "Juhannuksen aikana/Over Midsummer," but, significantly, with changes. Where the anthologized song, performed by Tiila Ilkka in 1950, begins:

Juhannuksen aikana on ilma lämpimämpi
Viirentoista vanhasta on tyttö lempivämpi

Midsummer has come and now the sun shines ever brighter.
Maiden when she's fifteen well it's easy to delight her
                    (DuBois and Cederström 2019, 126)

Jimmy chose to change the album version of the lines to become:

Juhannuksen aikana on ilma lämpimämpi
Amerikan rannoilla on pojat lempivämpii

Midsummer has come and now the sun shines ever brighter.
On the shores of America the boys will sure delight her.
                    (Träskelin 2019)

Jimmy contacted Marcus and Tom about the lines during the production of the album and asked for help in coming up with a singable English version of the new line, which, although a departure from Westerholm's text, meshes well with subsequent verses of the song as portraying the words of a jilted lover. Jimmy was worried that the anthology editors would disapprove of his editorial changes, but to Tom and Marcus they represented a creative response to the song rather than some sort of violation of its integrity, a collaborative effort, despite the song's being published. In fact, even after *Songs of the Finnish Migration* was published, the editors viewed the translations as a work in progress, something to be changed as musicians and community members engage with the songs, perform the songs, and make the songs their own.

The collaborators made other alterations as well, including substituting a different melody for "Amerikan liikkojen tanssilaiva/American Girls' Dance Floor" and selecting only portions of Westerholm's often lengthy texts for incorporation into the album tracks. The ensemble's haunting rendition of "Laulu/Song of an America-Widow" highlights the situation of a woman left behind after the migration of her husband to America and brought the song into a performative space where it could influence or inspire subsequent performers. That song was also selected by Laulu Aika for performance in 2020, as we will note later.

Where Jimmy, Katri, and Sampo recorded their songs exclusively in Finnish, when they came to the 2019 FinnFest USA in Detroit, they were eager to sing in both Finnish and English. As part of the overall publication project, Tom and Marcus wrote grants to finance Tallari's trip to FinnFest and arranged a short performance tour in the Upper Midwest that included performances in Madison, Wisconsin; Hancock, Michigan; and Chicago, Illinois. At FinnFest and at Madison, joint events were staged in which Marcus, Tom, and Jim Leary introduced songs and the book while Jimmy, Sampo, and Katri performed and led the audience in alternating Finnish and English singalongs (Cederström et al. 2019; DuBois et al. 2019).

In collaboration with Linda Pensala of the Finnish American Society of Milwaukee, Tom and Marcus worked with Jimmy to organize a reprise of that combined book introduction and song event on Zoom. This event included subtitled song renditions by the ensemble and a live performance (Cederström et al. 2020). In a context in which many of the event's participants were homebound because of the pandemic, the event was viewed as an exciting respite and one that was gratefully received by an audience scattered across the United States and Europe. For this event, the band performed additional songs from the anthology, including Hiski Salomaa's 1930 "Lännen lokari/Logger of the West" and Kosti Tamminen's 1927 rendition of William Larsen's "Työttömän valssi/Waltz of the Un-employed 'Come Around Again.'" In conversation with the band, Tom suggested "Lännen lokari" as a Finnish American song that was composed in Chicago and that had traveled across the Atlantic already in the 1940s, making it well known in Finland today but rela-tively obscure in its country of origin. Tom also suggested "Työttömän valssi" as a song that would work well for an audience conversant in both English and Finnish, since it pre-sents humorous takes on the meanings of the English phrase "Come around again." The verses recount the song's protagonist hearing the phrase when looking for work, when standing in a soup line, when being propositioned by a married woman, and finally when seeing a former boss reduced to poverty. Although the song is included in Westerholm's original anthology, Jimmy, Sampo, and Katri had not engaged with the song before. With its enjoyable waltz timing and wry macaronic humor, the song seemed extremely appeal-ing to the performers, who indicated that they would make it a part of their standard per-formance repertoire from then on. While speaking to the sensibilities of Finnish American workers around the time of the Great Depression, its message of worker solidarity and speaking back to entrenched power carried present-day resonance. And in a modern Fin-land, in which most people have a strong command of English, the song's humor is com-prehensible in a different way from when it was first performed in the 1930s.

These collaborations with Jimmy, Katri, and Sampo helped the songs reach new ears on both sides of the Atlantic, through performances at FinnFest and performances at the Kaustinen festival and elsewhere on the band's concert circuit in the United States and Finland. However, in working to support the intergenerational transmission of the songs in the United States, Tom, Marcus, and the SSFAUM team recognized the need to work specifically with Finnish American musicians. Jim Leary, a founding member of the SSFAUM team and also a member of the FinnFest USA board, orchestrated the coopera-tion that would bring a *Songs of the Finnish Migration* event back to FinnFest in its virtual form in 2021 (Cederström et al. 2021).

Project members Anna Rue and Marcus also worked with Ralph and Jaana Tuttila, lead-ers of the St. Paul/Minneapolis-based band Laulu Aika, and the filmmaker Cris Anderson to adapt and record six songs from the anthology to be made publicly available online. In discussion with the band, Marcus suggested a variety of songs that would be representative of the bilingual anthology, while also introducing audiences to the varied experiences that many immigrants faced. While four of the six songs describe various aspects of the labor conditions that Finnish migrants faced in the United States, the songs also describe love and loss and longing, all issues that many people dealt with on a daily basis during the pan-demic, in which numerous people were confined to their homes.

Ralph (harmonica, mandolin, vocals) and Jaana (bass and nyckelharpa) were joined in the performance by band members Lotta Kiuru-Ribar (fiddle, harmonica, vocals), Johanna Lorbach (fiddle, vocals), Eric Platt (mandolin), Tamara Baker (triangle, tambourine), Dan

Kiuru-Ribar (guitar), and Samuel Breyer (cello). Laulu Aika includes Finnish-born performers such as Lotta Kiuru-Ribar, Finnish American performers such as Ralph Tuttila, and other
members of the band with less direct connection to Finland.

Working with Mike Rivard and Cris Anderson of the Minneapolis-based Cris Anderson
Productions, and with field audio and mix by Vladimir Garrido-Biagetti, those leading the
project believed that the process of performing safely during a pandemic was a priority. Laulu
Aika, like many bands, had a number of gigs prudently canceled because of the pandemic in
consideration of both audience and band members. This gig, however, was different. Meant
to be filmed and shared exclusively online, we were able to reduce the health risks by simply
removing an in-person audience. To further reduce the health risk, the performance took
place outdoors, itself a decision that carried a lot of uncertainty because of the weather in
October in Minnesota. In addition, band members, when not singing, wore masks, and the
recording session was socially distanced, with band members maintaining much distance
from one another, much more than they normally would. The result, thanks to Cris Anderson and his team, was a recording session that adhered to local health ordinances, ensured
that the band members and the documentary crew remained safe, and created a snapshot of
how bands could jam, rehearse, and even perform during the global pandemic.

While the recordings were an important reminder of the artistic challenges that folk
musicians faced during the pandemic, the team arranged for these music videos not as a
commentary on art in the time of COVID but as resources that could be used in the classroom, in online programming, in online posts for a general audience, and by the band itself
as it saw fit. The videos were published on the University of Wisconsin–Madison's Center
for the Study of Upper Midwest Cultures (CSUMC) YouTube channel. The performances
are subtitled in Finnish, but the English translations from the anthology, as well as additional contextual information, are included in each video's description. Using grant funding for the public production and programming meant to amplify Nordic American folk
arts, the performers and the video production team were paid for their work. While this
was especially welcome in a time when nearly all in-person public performances had been
rendered impossible by the pandemic, use of grant funding to remunerate documentarians, artists, musicians, culture workers, and interviewees has been a standard part of the
SSFAUM project since the project's inception. Paying artists is integral to the continued
sustainability of folk arts.

On February 24, 2021, Marcus wrote a short article for the SSFAUM website, Nordic
Folklife, with a brief description and analysis of each song along with links and embedded
videos of the performances. Each recorded song is introduced to readers: "Kaivantomiehen laulu/The Digger's Song," Hiski Salomaa's "Lännen lokari/Logger of the West,"
"Laulu/Song of an America-Widow," Arthur Kylander's "Lumber-Jäkki/Lumber-Jack,"
Ernest Paananen's 1930 "Muistatko vielä illan sen/Do You Still Remember That Night?,"
and another by Hiski Salomaa, the well-known "Tiskarin polkka/The Dishwasher's Polka."
Along with the background text drawn from the anthology, Ralph introduces the songs
briefly in the associated YouTube videos (Cederström 2021).

On February 27, 2021, the joint FinnFest 2021-SSFAUM online concert "*Songs of the
Finnish Migration* with Marcus Cederström, Tom DuBois, and Laulu Aika" took place, with

Anna Rue as host and Tom, Marcus, Ralph, Jaana, and the Laulu Aika band members taking part. Marcus and Tom briefly discussed the anthology, but the focus was on Laulu Aika and its work with songs from the anthology. After a short interview, the band members performed songs from the anthology, tunes from their instrumental repertoire (e.g., "Ruiskukkia/Rye flowers"), and traditional folk songs not included in the anthology (such as the ever-favorite "Löylyä lissää/More sauna steam"). That online event brought in nearly two hundred audience members who saw a live performance by Laulu Aika and could explore further thanks to links to all the music videos. In response to Marcus's interview questions, Ralph and Jaana described their work in the band Finn Hall as well as their later establishment of Laulu Aika, and they spoke of their joy in playing not only Finnish music but also Swedish and Mexican music. They underscored the intercultural and intergenerational aspects of their band, the band's personal connections to the songs it played, and the thrill members felt at being together again as a band, if only for a short time, to play music with masks on in a socially distanced, windows-open, Minneapolis home, as the vaccination rollout continued.

That personal connection was especially evident when, in addition to the songs from the anthology that had been prerecorded, the band played a rendition of "Kauhea tapaturma kaivannossa/Tragic Mine Accident." Ralph spoke poignantly of his experience of coming upon the song in the anthology. Originally published as a broadside in 1899 in commemoration of a mine accident that occurred on December 31, 1898, in Ishpeming, Michigan, the song led Ralph to feel an immediate connection to this tragedy that had occurred in his boyhood hometown but that he had never heard about. The published version of the song contains nineteen four-line verses and is set to a melody that Westerholm drew from another song related to tragic events from the 1880s (DuBois and Cederström 2019, 77). Ralph and the band adapted the song to a different, haunting melody that Ralph's mother used to sing to him in his childhood; they performed only the first verse of the song in Finnish and then sang in English after an extended instrumental interlude. This abbreviation and adaptation, along with the personal connection that Ralph felt to the substituted melody, transformed the song into a new entity, yet one with clear and conscious connection back to the original broadside and the Finnish American workers killed on that New Year's Eve 123 years earlier. The resonance of the rendition in the context of the pandemic, which had claimed hundreds of thousands of lives, added a new dimension to the powerful song.

Viewers joined in from across the globe and were eager to catch the names of the songs and tunes performed. The Zoom Webinar event was recorded and later shared on the Nordic Folklife and FinnFest USA sites as well as on the CSUMC YouTube channel. Together, the videos, the online article, and the online concert formed a repository of Finnish American music in the here and now. While showcasing historical connections to music depicting the challenges that faced Finnish migrants a century ago, these events also captured the current experiences of people working to revive and retain folk music in the midst of a global pandemic. Marcus, Tom, and Anna were able to contextualize this work by bringing it to students at the University of Wisconsin–Madison and to an ever-growing network of people interested in Nordic and Nordic American cultural expressions. Today the videos are being used in the classroom, Laulu Aika displays the videos prominently on its website, and the YouTube channel continues to garner new views every day, introducing the music to a broader audience.

In his 1983 anthology, *Reisaavaisen laulu Amerikkaan*, Simo Westerholm aimed to provide the descendants of the great Finnish migration to (and sometimes back from) North America something similar to what Elias Lönnrot had sought to provide Finns of the early nineteenth century in his *Kalevala* and *Kanteletar*. By procuring, preserving, and then presenting disappearing or forgotten songs from the community's past oral tradition, both Westerholm and Lönnrot believed a common heritage could be documented, celebrated, and ultimately sustained. In this way, Westerholm, like Lönnrot before him, was involved in a process of amplification and intervention. But publication of songs, with or without musical notation, cannot fully satisfy the goals of amplification if the language of the songs remains opaque or if the publication exists only in a research library or archive. The *Songs of the Finnish Migration* project aimed, in a sense, to revitalize the songs Westerholm had documented and published, bringing them to Finnish and Finnish American communities in new ways, with background information that would contextualize the songs and a bilingual singable translation that would encourage performance in English and Finnish. The project resulted in a bilingual anthology, of course, but that, too, does not ensure that the songs will become part of people's active performance repertoires and identity. Bringing those songs into performance at well-known community events like FinnFest extends and enlivens the published records. To date, the wider project has resulted in an album by Finland's nationally funded folk music ensemble, six music videos by a Finnish American band, an online concert publicly available after the fact, several public presentations, and an online article contextualizing and analyzing the music videos for a general audience. Every step of this unfolding process helped support artists who are working to revive and sustain Finnish and Finnish American music traditions while sharing their work with thousands of people around the world.

The case study described here centers on public programming and production based on one anthology, but it has become a model that SSFAUM has begun to use in other areas of its project, both musical and related to folk art. Specifically, the SSFAUM team has applied lessons learned during the pandemic to replicate this successful model through a combination of in-person and online, digital and physical, and written and oral approaches to amplify folk arts and to work toward their revival and sustainability. The team has applied the model to other musical projects, such as the work of Maja Heurling and Ola Sandström, which has included streaming online concerts, in-person events, as well as presentations and publications about revitalization and folk music. Similarly, the team has partnered with Duane Lahti to highlight his vernacular architectural work and with Gloria Johnson to highlight her Finnish baking, both in Oulu, Wisconsin. This has resulted in physical and digital exhibitions, presentations for general audiences, as well as short films featuring their work. By amplifying the art, the artists, and the research in multiple forms and forums, the team has made availability a priority and, in doing so, introduced a variety of folklife traditions to a broader audience.

NOTE

1. For a discussion of this "younger folk song tradition," see Asplund and Hako (1981).

The Down Home Dairyland Story

Richard March

In the fall of 1986, I drove with my colleague Jim Leary forty miles southeast from home in Madison to take in a rare musical experience. We had noticed in the Wisconsin Polka Boosters newsletter that the New Jolly Swiss Boys—Syl Liebl Jr.'s band from Coon Valley, Wisconsin—would be performing in the VFW Hall in Janesville, Wisconsin. Syl Liebl Sr., the legendary concertina player, would be sitting in. We jumped at the chance to hear and meet this immensely influential but now mostly retired musician.

Janesville's VFW Hall sits atop a high hill overlooking the sprawling General Motors plant, the small city's largest employer. In the distance, the rolling green countryside is dotted with dairy farmsteads, massive barns flanked by towering silos. The VFW is a friendly gathering place for the farmers, autoworkers, and others from the area to nurture their ethnic traditions and celebrate weddings, anniversaries, and community events like this day's polka dance.

The dance was in full swing when we arrived. The final flourish of a Dutchman-style polka was just fading and the spinning dancers' skirts still settling as we walked in. The two Syls and the Swiss Boys were on stage, taking a short pause, preparing to play a set of waltzes momentarily. Eager to meet the elder Liebl, we strode toward the stage. By the time we reached the middle of the dance floor, I had been recognized by Archie Baron, a dairy farmer and the polka promoter who had booked this dance.

"Hey, Rick, it's great to see you here," he beamed. "Would you like an introduction?" Assuming he was going to introduce me to Syl Liebl Sr., I nodded assent. Archie sprang to the stage, snatched a microphone from its stand, and announced, "Hey, everybody, look who's here—Rick March of *Down Home Dairyland* radio!" I stood frozen in surprise as a hearty ripple of applause filled the hall.

For about two months, the Wisconsin Arts Board (WAB), where I worked as the traditional and ethnic arts coordinator, collaborating with WORT, Madison's listener-supported community radio, had been producing *Down Home Dairyland* (DHD), at that time a three-hour Monday morning show. The show featured the traditional and ethnic music of the Upper Midwest with an emphasis on polka. It hadn't yet occurred to me that we might have listeners in Janesville. The incident marked my in-person debut as a radio personality in Wisconsin, as it was also, in a way, for Jim Leary. In a couple of years, he would join me as on-air cohost and coproducer of the show after it moved from WORT to Wisconsin Public Radio.

Since beginning work for the Wisconsin Arts Board in 1983, I had often found it hard to explain to people from outside the orbit of ardent arts supporters just what I did at WAB and how it might relate to them. I had been hired in a 1980s wave of the establishment of folk arts administrator jobs, most commonly based in state arts agencies. The creation of these positions had been an initiative of the Folk and Traditional Arts program of the National Endowment for the Arts. Bess Lomax Hawes, the director of that program in those years, stated to me her concern that, given the political vagaries of Washington, DC, the federal folk arts program might be abolished "with the stroke of a pen." Decentralizing folk arts support and infrastructure to the states would be likely to enhance the prospects for the continuation of these programs.

The original model for these folk arts administrator positions was a folk arts grants officer who would solicit applications and oversee an approval process to award grants to non-profit organizations. As a musician myself and an enthusiast for Midwestern old-time dance music, I hoped music would be included in the supported activities. I sought out the traditional musicians to explain how, through the grants process, the WAB might assist them. The typical response was a blank stare. Even though their bands were scarcely making any profits, they were decidedly not incorporated nonprofit organizations. Nor did they want the bureaucratic hassles involved in incorporating to be eligible to receive and manage grants.

"So what would help you?" I asked. Many musicians informed me that what they needed was improved exposure in the mass media. The Federal Communications Commission had recently eliminated requirements for local programming content as one condition of licensing radio and TV stations. Local old-time music TV and radio programs had been a common way to meet that condition. Once they were no longer required, those music programs dropped like flies. Radio stations cut local music and increasingly embraced nationally produced music formats—Top 40, country music, classic rock, and the like. "Help us get on the air, so people can hear our bands, and we'll do the rest" seemed to be the persistent message from the musicians.

I detected an opportunity with WORT. The Madison community radio station featured five weekday morning folk music shows from 9:00 a.m. to noon. Five different volunteer programmers came in one morning per week to serve as deejays. A couple of them were my friends. A couple of times I had been invited to do guest spots on their programs, to devote a half hour or so during their shows to airing the ethnic Upper Midwestern traditional music that my folk music programmer friends were largely unaware of.

In 1986, I learned that the Monday morning host was moving away from Madison and relinquishing his time slot. He had featured Irish music exclusively. I met with WORT's program director, Steve Gotcher, who waxed enthusiastic about my idea for a show devoted to the local region's traditions. My boss, Arley Curtz, the WAB executive director, was worried, however. This was quite a departure from grant officer work, and the idea of having a state arts agency provide, instead of a grant, a direct artistic service, in this case a radio program to a community station, was unconventional. Moreover, Arley was concerned that WORT had a bad reputation with conservative legislators. He fretted, "What if a legislator finds out that the Arts Board guy is on 'the hippie station'?" But I pushed for the idea, and ultimately Arley relented but directed me not to mention my Arts Board connection on the air.[1]

One of my WORT volunteer programmer friends, Karen Gogolick, taught me how to operate the sound board in the studio, and in a couple of weeks I was on the air. Each of the daily morning shows had a title. I concocted the name *Down Home Dairyland* to be reminiscent of *Dairyland Jubilee*, a local old-time music TV show very popular in south-central Wisconsin during the 1960s and 1970s.

Initially there weren't any polka albums in WORT's record library, so each Monday I toted to the station a heavy suitcase filled with LPs from my personal collection. I needed about sixty tunes to fill the three hours of the morning's program, so usually I hauled twenty-five to thirty LPs of artists like Whoopee John, Karl and the Country Dutchmen, Louie Bashell, Concertina Millie, and Barbara and the Carousels. They were albums that I had scrounged from tattered stacks in thrift stores or eagerly bought from the musicians themselves at their gigs; only rarely had any been purchased in commercial record stores, where polka albums had become virtually absent.

Instantly the show was controversial. Steve Gotcher felt blindsided. He thought "local" meant that I was going to be playing a lot of material from Madison-area singer-songwriters, and he leaned on me to include that sort of material. I stuck to my original idea. WORT held monthly meetings of a "Community Action Council," a group of active WORT listeners, mostly young and many of them in tune with hip current styles. They offered commentary on the station's programming. I didn't attend, but I received notes on the comments offered. "Too much polka!" read one. "Not enough polka!" responded another, reflecting in the first comment the commonly held disdain for polka as out-of-date and associated with uncool ethnics and elderly but in the second comment an indication that a segment of WORT's core audience, Madison "hipsters," had decided polkas were cool because, like rhinestone-encrusted glasses frames, they were "retro," although that term was not yet current.

When the next "pledge rapping" fundraising drive came around, *Down Home Dairyland* easily met its funding goals. As Wisconsin Public Television also was to discover later, once Jim Leary and I persuaded them to produce polka TV specials, polka enthusiasts responded with alacrity to pledge support for such shows. For the first time, WORT was getting pledges from polka-loving farmers in Arlington, Lodi, and other rural communities near Madison but also from a segment of WORT's core audience.

I continued the trek to the WORT studios for more than a year, but, perhaps surprisingly, I began to feel limited by the need to spin discs for a full three hours of air time weekly. I wanted to produce more focused programs about regional music traditions, but it proved difficult to program three hours of music and also to create a focused segment in the limited amount of time I was able to devote to the radio efforts.

Then, in 1987, another opportunity arose. Tom Martin-Erickson, a cohost of the *Simply Folk* folk music program on Wisconsin Public Radio (WPR), approached me. "Rick, we've noticed what you have been doing on WORT and wonder if you would be interested in bringing your music to WPR in a shorter format?" *Simply Folk* aired from 5 to 8 p.m. on Sundays. Recently Tom's cohost, Judy Rose, had produced thirteen special half-hour segments called "Wisconsin Patchwork," drawing from the field recordings collected in the 1940s by the University of Wisconsin music professor Helene Stratman-Thomas.

The "Wisconsin Patchwork" segments are an excellent example of the Wisconsin Idea, the notion that the University of Wisconsin should serve the entire population of the state by offering educational opportunities.[2] Since its inception in 1917, WPR had provided informative and educational programs to serve Wisconsinites. The "Wisconsin Patchwork" segments aired from 7:30 to 8:00 p.m., the last half hour of the *Simply Folk* program. Martin-Erickson offered me that time slot for *Down Home Dairyland*. The underlying idea would be to continue in the vein of "Wisconsin Patchwork" but now to reveal the present status of the type of musical traditions Stratman-Thomas had documented more than forty years earlier.

Extensive new field research would be needed to do an adequate job of accomplishing that task. My administrative duties in my Wisconsin Arts Board job didn't allow me enough time to carry out all that research myself. Fortunately, Jim Leary was available to be hired on contract to do it. In 1988, I sought and received a grant to fund the research from the National Endowment for the Arts Folk and Traditional Arts Program. Funding continued for three years. During that time, the *Down Home Dairyland* project stimulated a splendid burst of new fieldwork by Leary and me on Wisconsin's traditional music. In the first 40 *DHD* programs, we used audio segments from 136 field interviews with musicians. Leary recorded 86 of the interviews, I managed to find time to conduct 29 interviews myself, and Leary and I jointly recorded an additional 9—a total of 124 interviews. The remaining 12 were drawn from archival sources. We conducted the interviews in every region of Wisconsin with practitioners of musical traditions from Native, African American, Latinx, Asian, and European American communities.

We had a goal that the music traditions aired on *Down Home Dairyland* reflect the cultural diversity of Wisconsin. The 1990 US Census, conducted shortly after the inception of *DHD*, showed the racial composition of Wisconsin to be 92 percent white. However, this huge portion of the state's population certainly did not consider itself culturally homogeneous—a result of the state's large numbers of New Immigrant settlers. That same census also asked respondents to identify their cultural identity. Only 1.57 percent indicated nonhyphenated "American" or "United States" as their identity. Thus, more than 98 percent of Wisconsinites cited a specific cultural identity like Norwegian American, Slovak American, Mexican American, Italian American, African American, Irish American, and so on.

Each of the dozens of cited cultural identities is manifest in a range of homemade traditions, including musical. And in terms of music, the two most commonly cited identities, German American and Polish American, are further subdivided according to the Old World region of origin of their Wisconsin communities. For example, the Pomeranian-Germans of Cedarburg and Freistadt in southeastern Wisconsin played music in groups like the Alte Kameraden that is noticeably different from the Bavarian-German music of the Hacker Family, also southeastern Wisconsin residents. And their music differs too from the German-Bohemian sounds popularized throughout the Upper Midwest region by Minnesota's Whoopee John Band.

The regional identity of the northern Polish Kashubians who settled around Stevens Point in central Wisconsin is evident even in the name of the local Kaszub Aces band, while southern Polish Gorale communities around Armstrong Creek in northeastern Wisconsin nurture the old stringed-instrument traditions of their European region of origin. Numerous Polish American bands around Wisconsin play the very popular, Americanized "Dyno" style initiated by Eddie Blazonczyk, who is of Gorale-Polish descent.

Leary and I strove to acquaint listeners with the sometimes obvious, sometimes subtle differences that distinguish the musical traditions of scores of Wisconsin communities, broadening an understanding of the immense diversity of the state's musical practice and of the persistence of many Old World specificities through generations in Wisconsin.

To put our sonic treatises on the air, I needed to acquire additional radio skills to produce the focused programs. Leary and I listened to the full taped interviews and selected pithy segments to include in programs. The two "Simply Folk" hosts, Tom Martin-Erickson and Judy Rose, offered me a radio apprenticeship. Each spent several hours at the tape-editing deck instructing me in their art: marking the reel-to-reel mylar tape with a white china marker, slicing out and splicing together the selected sentences. I realized that I must have passed through a radio rite of passage after my first solo job editing a program. Tom or Judy must have mentioned it to other WPR staff, because I was greeted in the hall with comments like, "Hey, you did it. Get any razor cuts? Need any Band-Aids?" I was in the radio producer club now.

From 1989 to 1991, during one quarter of the year, thirteen new DHD programs were broadcast statewide in *Simply Folks'* last half hour; then the same programs were rerun in the same time slot for another quarter. Thus, we were on the air for half of each year. In the third year, we made fourteen shows so that the total number would come to an even forty *DHD* programs. The reason we aimed for forty shows was that Leary had conceived of a project: to produce an educational curriculum package consisting of twenty audiocassettes with a half-hour *DHD* program on each side. The cassettes would be accompanied by a book (Leary and March 1996), a listener's guide, and for each program there would be an essay containing further information that elaborated on the program's contents. By this time, Leary was working for the University of Wisconsin–Extension, and such a project fit well in the scope of the Extension program's typical activities, which work to bring the university's educational services to all state residents. This was the Wisconsin Idea in action, as we amplified the voices of the musicians we worked with, while ensuring that those voices, along with additional research, were easily accessible to people throughout the state.

Leary and I split the essay-writing duties roughly fifty-fifty. I wrote nineteen, and Leary penned twenty-one. As with all publishing projects, the writing, editing, and media production efforts took some time. The book *Down Home Dairyland: A Listener's Guide*, with its accompanying binder of cassettes, was published in 1996. The obsolescence of audiocassettes that occurred in the ensuing years prompted the reissue of the audio component on compact discs (CDs) in 2004.

Around the time of the inception of the listener's guide project in the early 1990s, a big change for *DHD* was proposed by Wisconsin Public Radio. WPR was implementing a split of its services into two networks, the News and Classical Music Network and the Ideas Network. The content offered by the two networks is fairly evident from the titles—there would be NPR News and classical music on one network, whereas talk shows hosted by WPR hosts dominated on the other. About half of the WPR stations around the state would broadcast the programming of one or the other network. In most of the state, it would be possible to pick up a signal from both of the WPR networks. The weekend programming was more diverse, and *DHD* was on the air on Sunday evenings. Even though it was a music show, it certainly wasn't classical; management decided to put *DHD* on the Ideas Network.

Along with this change, the program director felt that *DHD* would have to become a regular program, on the air fifty-two weeks a year in its own time slot, Sunday at 8 p.m. They would require that we produce thirty-nine new programs per year (thirteen reruns could be aired during the summer), and we would need to have recognizable elements—a consistent format with a standard intro and signoff. Leary and I embraced the new challenge. Previously *DHD* programs had begun with an evocative interview segment focused on someone featured in that program, a different person for every show. For a consistent intro theme, I found a recording by a polka band called the Mitternachters, "Milk Cow Polka," that began with the sound of a cow lowing, then that of a stream of milk hitting the bottom of a tin milk pail; next, a button accordion kicked in—perfect for a Dairyland show (although the band happened to be from out of state).

Leary and I had already decided to create a format that eschewed the typical solemn public radio tone, a trend we amplified when we established the year-round program. Leary's uncle who worked in the Omaha stockyards was skilled in imitating a calf's bawl as a way to call a cow. On a visit, Leary recorded his "calf bawl," which we henceforth played just before the exit theme, "Franczeska Polka," by our friends, the Madison musicians the Goose Island Ramblers. "OK, calf, it's time to go . . ." Leary or I would intone before reading the credits.

We tapped into a sound-effects CD created for radio dramas, using an old-fashioned telephone ringtone to play prior to the occasional clip we aired from a telephone interview. More frequently, on almost every program we had a "From the Vault" feature: echoing footsteps, a creaking door, and a cavernously reverberating voice calling "From the vault." Leary, pretending to be out of breath from running back to the radio studio out of the "vault," the basement music archives at Mills Music Library, would then introduce an old 78 rpm disc from the 1920s or 1930s that he had selected.

DHD was one of the most lighthearted programs on WPR. In between polkas, Leary and I engaged in spontaneous-sounding patter, most of which actually was semiscripted, and Leary demonstrated an uncanny ability to come up with a witticism at the end of each show as we signed off, for example "This is Jim Leary, dancing with a broom," referring back to the "broom dance" tune we had played earlier in that program.

To market the program, we produced quarterly brochures listing and briefly describing the next three months of weekly programs. For the brochure's cover, I asked my friend the political cartoonist Mike Konopacki to create a logo for the program. He came up with an anthropomorphized cartoon bull wearing a German Jaeger's hat playing a big Chemnitzer concertina, a bovine Dutchman musician. The brochures were mailed mostly to Wisconsin media outlets. They got results. The very popular Madison alternative weekly *Isthmus* and the *Milwaukee Journal-Sentinel* consistently listed *Down Home Dairyland* among their recommended weekly radio highlights. *DHD* developed a devoted audience.

From the beginning on WPR, Leary and I understood the archival value of *DHD* programs. Each show was a little audio essay on a particular aspect of Upper Midwestern traditional music. The original reel-to-reel tapes all have been archived in Mills Music Library and are now available to students, researchers, and the general public. In the original dozen-year run of *DHD*, more than 350 programs were archived, and since its revival in 2016 (discussed later), an additional 260 programs have been accessioned into the collection.

Change comes to all things. In 1996, after seven years of involvement with *DHD*, Leary found that increased job responsibilities prevented him from continuing to work on the program. I soldiered on, producing and hosting the program myself until the year 2000. In 1999, the longtime WPR director Jack Mitchell retired. Mitchell was a nationally significant public radio pioneer who had always been highly supportive of including *DHD* among WPR's offerings. His replacement, Dana Rehm, came from Seattle. It soon developed that during her relatively short tenure as WPR director, she favored cutting several locally produced WPR shows to make room for nationally syndicated programs. She decided to cut *DHD* in 2000, replacing it with a program of Celtic music. Because of her lack of familiarity with the regional culture, she may not have understood that recordings largely from Scotland and Ireland did nearly nothing to satisfy an audience's interest in Upper Midwestern music. It is ironic that in the same year that the Wisconsin polka audience lost *DHD*, I worked with Wisconsin Public Television to produce a special TV program, "Polka 2000," which the same polka audience predictably supported, swiftly exceeding on-air fundraising goals.

Time passed. It seemed that *DHD* was dead. It had been off the air for nearly a decade when I took early retirement from WAB in 2009. I was eager to have time to pursue a couple of long-postponed book-writing projects on Midwestern musical traditions, polka, and tamburitza. By 2015, both books—*The Tamburitza Tradition* and *Polka Heartland*— had been written and published. Publicity for the polka book caught the attention of a volunteer committee that was establishing a new community radio station, WVMO, located in Monona, a close-in Madison suburb. The program director offered me the opportunity to revive *Down Home Dairyland* in a one-hour format. He didn't have to ask twice. I snatched up the Sunday 7:00 p.m. time slot.

By this time, the development of more accessible, user-friendly technology made it possible for me to produce the *DHD* programs at home using only my laptop computer and a handheld digital recorder. Audio editing software had replaced the razor blade, tape, and splicing block. Each week, I produced digital files of the program and emailed them to the station.

Newly available federal funding for local radio has prompted community groups across the nation to establish small nonprofit stations like WVMO. The Wisconsin managers of these stations had an active network of communication, and they soon heard about *DHD*. In the early months of 2016, stations in Amery, Janesville, Oshkosh, Stevens Point, Sun

Prairie, and Waupaca also asked for the program, and I gladly provided it to them. Each station made its own decision regarding the day and hour to schedule *DHD*.

Since most of these local stations instituted live-streaming of their broadcasts on the Internet, *DHD* can be heard worldwide. I created a *Down Home Dairyland* Facebook page where I listed each station's scheduled time of broadcast. Thus, listeners can choose from four or five different time slots to tune into *DHD*, and several Internet listeners have left comments and queries on the Facebook page.

Now, in 2021, *DHD* continues. The program survived a couple of sea changes. The first was my departure from Wisconsin. My wife, Nikki, and I decided to move to Portland, Oregon. When they heard about my impending move, a couple of the station managers urged me to continue to make the show. I said I would try. In September 2016, we moved into an apartment on a noisy thoroughfare. There was no quiet space to record programs. The stations played reruns for a while. But by December of the same year, we had moved into a house with a quiet room for a radio studio. I resumed creating new programs and sending them to the stations.

Each *DHD* program has a focused theme. By June 2017, living in a different region, I began to lose inspiration. Ideas for program themes were not occurring to me. I pondered ending the show. Before I could make a final decision and notify the stations, I received an email from John Quirk, the station manager of WSNP in Stevens Point. John wrote, "Hi Rick, I figure you would be interested in this," and he attached a promo he had put out: "June is Dairy Month, and we're going to celebrate Wisconsin's Dairy Industry by playing the 'Down Home Dairyland' Polka Program from Noon on Friday through Midnight Sunday night! . . . So call your Babcia [Grandma in Polish] and tell her to tune in to WSNP-LP 105.9 FM all weekend! It's going to be non-stop Happy Music for three days!" It would be sixty hours straight, apparently using nearly the entire archive of *DHD* programs WSNP had accumulated since 2016. I slapped my forehead and realized that with that kind of enthusiasm for the show, I couldn't quit producing *DHD* yet. And then ideas for new programs began to come to me again.

Since its inception, in 1986, *Down Home Dairyland* has been a remarkably successful public folklore project. It focuses on music traditions that are very dear to the communities that participate in and perpetuate them and that are often symbolic of their sense of identity. Effective public folklore programming needs to be presented in a location and a medium familiar to the intended audience. For example, staging the Smithsonian Folklife Festival in the season and location of a well-established pattern of summer tourism to the National Mall museums in Washington, DC, has resulted in good attendance. Radio, on the other hand, does not typically bring together communities. Radio programs are created in a studio and broadcast to listeners who typically hear them in their own homes or cars. Radio is not like a concert or festival that brings various people together. It's not the right medium for that. However, radio, and *Down Home Dairyland* in particular, is a familiar and readily accessible medium to its core community audiences and just where they would expect to hear the music.

Associated as various polka traditions are with rural farmers and urban working-class immigrant or ethnic communities, they have drawn little interest and often overt scorn from wider mainstream American culture. *Down Home Dairyland* offers validation of the worth of these musical expressions. Having had its origins and continuing to broadcast on the public radio/community radio platform, *Down Home Dairyland* carries a degree of the sociocultural and intellectual status that public radio enjoys. Not only does this type of radio platform validate the polka to its own community, but also it provides an avenue of discovery to audiences interested in diverse cultural expressions that might otherwise never hear polka.

Moreover, it is important that each program is thoughtfully conceived: that the music is curated for quality and contextualized in terms of its cultural locus. A *DHD* program needs to be educational, but at the same time it has to be an entertaining radio show. It needs to be accessible, and, as a music program, it needs to amplify the work of the artists, which is why most of the air time is devoted to complete performances of songs. I limit my comments to one minute and usually less, brief and to the point remarks that reveal something about the music's ethnic, regional, or historical provenance, about the artists' significance and influence, or about connections to other musical genres.

Quality public folklore programming requires the involvement of a trained folklorist who has strong knowledge of the particular tradition. A folklorist who is a skilled woodworker can create a better program about decoy carving than someone who lacks that skill. A folklorist who is a skilled cook can create better foodways programming than a noncook. When it came to *Down Home Dairyland*, a deejay with little knowledge of the polka traditions could not create this type of program. I can't play the trumpet, but right here it is necessary for me to blow my own horn. For decades I have worked hard to learn about and been fortunate to participate in the polka tradition in a variety of roles—as a musician (on button accordion and tenor banjo), as a researcher and writer of articles and books on the topic, as an organizer of folk festivals and concerts that included polka and of community-originated events like the Squeezebox Jamboree. I have served as the compiler of compendium CDs for Smithsonian Folkways and served as a consultant on numerous media projects dealing with polka.

Working on my own and also for several years with coproducer Jim Leary, we produced more than five hundred *DHD* programs beginning in 1986. While I can't make a credible claim that *DHD* reversed the diminishing toehold of polka in radio, nonetheless the musicians appreciated being featured on the program. Musicians often expressed to me their appreciation of the program, which helped promote and amplify their own art. Ethel Bergum, a Norwegian American accordionist who was on a show, composed a new tune that she titled "Dairyland Polka" in honor of *DHD*.

As was mentioned, all the *DHD* programs have been archived at Mills Music Library of the University of Wisconsin–Madison, where we hope they will serve as a resource for future researchers. In the meantime, in my home studio I continue to produce five programs per month for the several Wisconsin community stations that happily broadcast them to their listeners.

Yep, calf, it's milking time. Gotta go. This is *Down Home Dairyland*, I'm Rick March saying goodbye 'til next time.

NOTES

1. About six months later, I was able to answer Arley's query about a legislator. I was playing mandolin in an Irish band for a St. Patrick's Day dinner in the small burg of Lyndon Station, northwest of Madison. The local state representative and later state senator Dale Schultz was in attendance. On a break, I chatted with him. "So you're Rick March!" Schultz exclaimed. "I keep hearing raves about your program from folks down around Loganville and Reedsburg."

2. The Educational Communications Board, which included Wisconsin Public Radio and Television as major undertakings, is a university entity.

Then and Now

Public Folklore and the Folklorist in Missouri

LISA L. HIGGINS

Once, at an annual conference of the American Folklore Society (AFS), I took the opportunity on the hotel elevator to introduce myself to Bess Lomax Hawes (1921–2009), the first director (1977–92) of folk and traditional arts at the National Endowment for the Arts (NEA). After skimming copies of old AFS conference programs, I am reminded that the year was likely 2003, when AFS convened in Albuquerque and the theme was "Folk Culture and the Public Domain." At that time, I had been working my dream job as director of the Missouri Folk Arts Program (MFAP) for four years, and I had been working in public folklore programs, starting as an intern with MFAP, for ten years. A little online research tells me that, in 2003, Bess Lomax Hawes was about eleven years post-NEA retirement. Though I could see that she was a bit frail physically at eighty-two years, there was no doubt that Ms. Hawes, as I called her then (and still refer to her now), was still very sharp intellectually. We finished our brief conversation outside the elevator, and I closed by personally thanking her for her vision at the NEA. Ms. Hawes launched many of her brilliant ideas into nationwide projects.

In a 2019 Folk and Traditional Arts Fact Sheet, the NEA notes that it "piloted the first state folklife programs at state arts agencies in 1974, leading to a robust network of state folklife programs and partnerships with deep regional resources and archives" (National Endowment for the Arts n.d.[b]). And, in a "Legacy Honoree" profile of Ms. Hawes, the Smithsonian Center for Folklife and Cultural Heritage reports that "her efforts to create state-based folk arts programs were successful in fifty of the fifty-six states and territories. Her State Apprenticeship Initiative helped create programs for traditional arts in over forty states" (Smithsonian n.d.). It was for this reason, her championing of state-based folk arts programs, that I stopped to acknowledge Ms. Hawes that October afternoon: "I know that if not for you, there would be no Missouri Folk Arts Program, nor a director, and I thank you for that."

I do not recall much else specifically of our conversation, though I know it included mutual admiration for Barry Bergey, a predecessor to my own MFAP predecessor. Bergey served as Missouri's first state folklorist, then left his home state in 1985 to work by Ms. Hawes's side in Washington, DC. Though I do not recall our exact words, I will always remember her bright, smiling eyes and that we sealed our brief exchange about our occupational heritage with a warm clasping of all four hands. Effectively, I trace my experiences and knowledge as a public folklorist from Ms. Hawes and Barry Bergey to Peggy Bulger, who hired me to work as a public folklorist at the Southern Arts Federation, and to Dana Everts-Boehm, who immediately preceded me at MFAP and who guided me in the early 1990s as my internship supervisor. Ms. Hawes and Bergey sculpted the programs I inherited, while Bulger and Everts-Boehm provided me with hands-on experiences in the field that steered my career away from academia and into the public sector. Bulger, via our work at a regional arts organization serving nine southern states, also introduced me to the network of outstanding folklorists working in the public sector via the Folklorists in the South Annual Retreat, collaborative regional projects, and the nascent "Publore" email listserv (launched in 1996). I am cognizant of these public-sector role models and their legacies in my own career, then and now, especially after more than twenty years as the director of the Missouri Folk Arts Program.

No matter the sector, folklorists seek to comprehend cultural legacies. In interview and fieldwork settings (to be honest, in most exchanges about culture), we public folklorists often ask folk artists a version of these questions: "Where did you learn this tradition, and from whom did you learn it?" Sometimes those artists reply with a variation on the brief answer "self-taught." With a little nudging, the tradition bearers usually begin to recite something akin to their artistic lineage.

At the Missouri Folk Arts Program, we ask a version of these questions of master artists and their apprentices when they apply to participate in our Traditional Arts Apprenticeship Program, one of more than forty such state projects strongly encouraged by Ms. Hawes. In answer to the legacy question, one fiddler charted his cultural lineage to an aunt who played old-time music and inspired him so much that, as a teenager, he often walked a few miles each way to learn more tunes and perfect his bowing from an influential fiddling neighbor. Conversely, this fiddler himself easily influenced dozens of musicians of more than one generation in seventy years of playing at dances, festivals, and with friends in his kitchen. His story is not atypical. Another participant, a gospel singer, pianist, and preacher's kid, who started singing as a child in the Sunshine Children's Choir, gives credit to her father, the church pianist, and God for passing down the tradition. As she grew, she observed and learned from a few powerhouse female vocalists within and beyond her congregation. Over the decades, she has returned that legacy one hundredfold to younger vocalists and pianists. The traditional dancers that I know almost always credit a family matriarch (mother or grandmother or aunt, mother and grandmother and aunt) whose footsteps the young dancers shadowed at age three, or five, or eight; they also point to revered dancers in their barrios, parishes, or blocks. Now, they teach dozens of peers and youngsters in their studios and homes, dancing side by side at festivals and other celebrations.

In my career as a public folklorist, I have heard and read dozens of answers to those two legacy questions from MFAP applicants, as well as in other states when I served on application review panels. A decade or so ago, I began to conceptualize a cultural lineage or ancestry of culture. After one too many professional development workshop leaders urged me to develop an "elevator speech" about my work and MFAP's projects, I developed an elevator quip, as most Missouri elevators don't have many floors. I tell the uninitiated that "folk arts are arts with a genealogy," invoking both past and present, then and now, in creative expressions. With the current proliferation of genealogy websites and TV commercials for DNA tests, my little definition can easily elicit "aha" moments. Simplifying the concept of folklore and metaphorically comparing it to tracing a family lineage tends to evoke understanding better even than our field's classically succinct definitions of folklore: "artistic communication in small groups" (Ben-Amos 1971, 13). These "aha" moments between this folklorist and people outside my occupational in-group are conversation starters. This verbal cue creates an opening for me to expand my audiences' perceptions of "folk arts." Their narrow preconceptions typically involve rural folk painters and living history reenactors wearing overalls and straw hats or prairie dresses and bonnets. I know my little definition can be reductionist, even flawed in the wrong context. For instance, listeners might construe my definition as implying that cultural legacies are linear and occur only in biological families. However, when my audiences' preconceptions crack open for a moment, I often find that I can illustrate my metaphor more fully with an array of specific examples of traditional artists in Missouri: yes, the longbow fiddler and paper piece quilter; also, the urban Black gospel singer, *cumbia* dancer, and low-rider car builder. When conversations continue outside the elevator, I can elaborate on MFAP projects, which even today are grounded in Ms. Hawes's first two NEA initiatives: to establish state folk arts programs and then statewide folk arts apprenticeships.[1]

In Missouri, the apprenticeship program, first called Folk Arts Apprenticeships, has a direct legacy to Ms. Hawes, as she personally picked up a telephone around 1983 and called leaders at the Missouri Arts Council and the Cultural Heritage Center at the University of Missouri.[2] She strongly encouraged them to apply for new grant funding to pilot an apprenticeship project in Missouri. After decades of the Traditional Arts Apprenticeship Program (TAAP), artists have indeed built greater visibility for their traditions—and sustained them for next generations. To date, MFAP has coordinated more than four hundred apprenticeships supporting more than two hundred master artists who have taught more than five hundred apprentices (some master artists have taught more than one apprenticeship, and some teach more than one apprentice in a year, especially, for instance, in dance). As I write this, Missouri's TAAP is in the midst of its thirty-sixth year, supporting ten more teams.

In fiscal years that end in a 0 or a 5, we at the MFAP try to celebrate the project with special programs; a traveling exhibition was curated in 2000, and an online exhibition was created for 2005, for instance. Prior to and during the thirtieth anniversary of Missouri's apprenticeship program, in 2015, my coworker Deborah Bailey and I spent many hours reviewing archival materials, reading old reports, updating spreadsheets, and talking with previous TAAP artists. Most often, we (and they) reflected on the role of master artists in the decades-long project. Throughout that anniversary year, we worked with Missouri State Parks and Historic Sites to celebrate the milestone and to share stories about two dozen previous TAAP master artists in a series of six public events in five regions of the state. That special cadre of master artists represented all three decades of TAAP and included the only two surviving artists from 1985, the inaugural year. The featured artists of

the thirtieth-anniversary events hailed from most regions of the state and practiced a diversity of genres (including gospel, old-time, Irish, and jazz music; Mexican paper flower
folding; blacksmithing; johnboat building; Ioway applique and beadwork; quilting; boot-
making; South Sudanese drumming; and regional storytelling). They also represented an
array of cultural communities in our state—some long established and others much newer.
Several previous apprentices also performed and demonstrated alongside their teachers,
or sometimes in their stead, during these events.

After the thirtieth anniversary wrapped, we found ourselves once again interested in
exploring stories about TAAP from the apprentices' perspectives. Apprentices, we have
found over the years, tend to be much more transient than their teachers, making it harder
to locate and contact the younger artists. Their addresses and names change, sometimes
multiple times. Still, in the counting and accounting of the thirtieth anniversary, we realized that around twenty previous apprentices had subsequently returned to TAAP to apply
for funding with students of their own. We wondered what these artists had to say about
the project's impact on them, then and now.

With these questions about the impact of apprenticeships in mind, in 2016, MFAP staff
sought to document apprentice stories to satisfy our curiosity, to record their stories for
posterity, and to formally introduce a new perspective on the apprenticeship program.
Over the years, we have grown quite familiar with the stories from the master artists and
ways that they tell us that TAAP sustained their traditions and their own selves. A series of
narrative histories with a key cadre of TAAP artists was born. That first year, we presented
MFAP's first "Then and Now: Apprentice Journeys" series of events at the Museum of Art
and Archaeology in Columbia, Missouri, with master artist John P. Williams, who was the
final apprentice to the late, great Boone County old-time fiddler Pete McMahan (1918–
2000). Williams was such a young apprentice when he first participated in TAAP that he
recalled how his mother would drive him fifty miles each way to meet with Mr. McMahan.
The two fiddlers had met a few years earlier at the annual Bethel Youth Fiddle Camp in
Shelby County. McMahan eventually saw promise in Williams, and both families committed to the apprenticeship. For "Then and Now," with Williams, we videorecorded his interview privately in our offices; then he joined his own apprentice and a legendary rhythm
guitarist to play a well-attended concert of "Little Dixie" regional old-time tunes in the
Museum galleries.

For the second 2016 event, master artist Loretta Washington, who previously apprenticed with Missouri's beloved master storyteller Dr. Gladys Caines Coggswell, joined us
during a special set at the annual St. Louis Storytelling Festival. Washington, unlike Williams, is not at all shy about telling her story or telling it publicly. She knows how to work a
stage, and she not only participated in the interview but, befitting the partnership with the
festival, shared some family stories and a song in a quick set that followed her interview.
Later, staff worked to edit both interviews to approximately ten minutes to post on MFAP's
YouTube channel. In each year since, MFAP has collaborated with partners and artists to
present two "Then and Now" events annually—ten so far, with more in the works for the
future. Whenever possible, MFAP strives to conduct these narrative history interviews
in public settings. For instance, we continued to partner with the storytelling festival to

present three more narrative histories on stage in 2017, 2018, and 2019. Like John Williams, though, some of the artists are understandably too shy to talk about themselves in a public forum, and we have found ways to accommodate them with private or semiprivate interviews with very small audiences. In 2020, both "Then and Now" interviews were collected remotely via Zoom to accommodate pandemic guidelines.

The core of the "Then and Now" series is the narrative history, set up similarly to a folklife festival narrative stage where a folklorist interviews a tradition bearer in public for an audience. In this case, either Deborah Bailey or I enter into conversation with these artists from the get-go. We invite them to participate, find a mutually suitable date and location for the event, share the core questions with the artists, and speak with them at length prior to the actual event, taking notes to use as prompts to cue key stories and details. Once on stage (or in a more private setting), we ask each artist the same seven open-ended questions:

1. What motivated you to learn to be a traditional artist?
2. Tell us about your apprenticeship with the master artist. What would you say was the most important thing you learned as a TAAP apprentice?
3. What was the most challenging aspect of the apprenticeship experience?
4. What did you learn about teaching during your time as an apprentice?
5. Tell us about the apprenticeship/s you taught. What would you say was the most important thing you taught your TAAP apprentice?
6. What does the master–apprentice relationship mean to you, then and now?

We have seen some similarities in answers, perhaps reflecting an almost universal tenaciousness required not only to complete an apprenticeship but to continue to pursue excellence and ultimately to commit to teaching others. A common denominator these artists recall as apprentices, despite their diversity of traditions, places, heritage, and ages, has been intrepidity.

All the "Then and Now" artists so far seem to have struggled early on to find a place in the tradition and as traditional artists. John Williams first played violin with a Suzuki children's program before he found his love of old-time fiddle practically in his own backyard at that annual youth fiddle camp, just one county north of his home. Williams also recalls that Mr. McMahan was impatient with his young apprentice often in 1998 (and still in 1999), which actually encouraged Williams to practice harder. Loretta Washington remembers hearing stories as a very young child at the feet of her great-granny on a front porch in the rural "bootheel" region of southeast Missouri, while the rest of her family toiled daily in the fields. Despite being a quick study, Washington struggled to identify herself as a storyteller for decades, even once she understood that her granny's valued role had a name. Washington attributes her self-identification as a storyteller, as well as the confidence she found in claiming that role, to weekly apprenticeship lessons around the master artist Gladys Caines Coggswell's kitchen table in Frankford in 2003.

Similarly, Bernard Allen yearned to learn how to build a fiddle, screwed up the courage to ask a local luthier he admired—and was promptly rejected. Doggedly, Allen found a book, made a fiddle, and returned to the luthier's workshop, where Allen was matter-of-factly criticized, as well as minimally encouraged. The gig maker Ray Joe Hastings asked his mentor Paul Martin several times to teach him how to forge Current River fishing tools, but Mr. Martin finally agreed to teach Hastings only in order to earn the apprenticeship stipend in 1996. Martin earmarked those earnings for his anticipated burial costs. Some artists, like the Irish step dancer Helen Gannon and Gladys Coggswell, hustled to carve out the time away from family and in the midst of paid work to pursue their dreams and take their traditions to a whole new level. Others, like Mike Massey, already a fine leatherworker with a viable business, humbled himself enough to step back and relearn from a much more seasoned master artist. The lessons these artists learned in apprenticeships, they told us in the interviews, always came back into play in the lessons they taught later.

Now, as master artists, they evoke a similar theme in their "Then and Now" answers: sustaining their tradition with confidence. For instance, the luthier Bernard Allen actually did his apprenticeship in wood joinery with James Price, PhD, a local master of many regional traditions, as well as an accomplished archaeologist who served the region well in his roles at the Ozark Scenic Riverways National Park until retirement and since. During his narrative history with Deborah Bailey, Mr. Allen recalled of his 1987 apprenticeship: "He [nodding at Dr. Price, who was a member of the small audience] said something to me, and it stuck with me. I tell all my apprentices, 'It's easy to take wood off, but it's hard to put it back on.'" That motto, and metaphor, is an important one to Allen. He points out that in lessons with Dr. Price they used only hand tools. In his work as a stringed instrument builder, however, and as someone who now teaches others to build string instruments, Allen uses both hand and power tools. No matter which he uses or teaches an apprentice to use, Allen instills in his students the importance of developing the patience to plan ahead and to move through the project with care and foresight. These components, he observes, are key to the apprentices' successes. While Allen knows they will make mistakes, as he did many years ago with his first fiddles, he also told us in his narrative interview that teaching the "process" is the most important outcome of the apprenticeships:

> I think it gives you confidence to try it, and that's what I told all my apprentices, too. You're going to have the confidence now. If someone has a fiddle that needs repairing, you know you can do it because, if you can build one, you can sure repair it. And, if you build one from scratch, like they did, well, you know every little part of that instrument. That's the biggest thing. The process, and the knowing that you can do it, and getting confidence that you can do it. Building confidence.

Thirty-two years after the apprenticeship, Bernard Allen still acknowledges the roots of the tradition grounded in the hours that he and Dr. Price spent together in the workshop. And, as a traditional artist does, Allen took the practice to a new level. He kept to the roots and, with confidence, grew his skills in some different directions on the basis of his own needs and aesthetics.

Similarly, the storyteller Deb Swanegan, who works in a vastly different art form, sees a sense of confidence, of knowing, as the key to the master artist–apprenticeship relationship:

> Gladys was the person to plumb the well, to make me understand that there's more wonderfulness in the well, and so that's the beginning. So, now, I see stories all around me. I love to sit and just listen to other people, just to be still and to hear their lives' journeys and their experiences, and then share them where I can. Whereas before, they were just people talking. And, very selfishly, I listen to my family's stories, but now I'm intrigued by other families' stories and other experiences and just looking around.

Both in luthiery and in storytelling, and in all the other genres, these former apprentices tell us how they not only learned the basic and advanced techniques of the art forms but also saw the bigger picture of the art forms within their traditions. And they gained confidence. The luthiery apprentices can put together and pick apart a fiddle, and the storytelling apprentices can put together and pick apart a narrative. All these former apprentices, though, with the immersion in lessons, reached an understanding of the connectedness of those traditions, much like those instruments that carry a community's melodies or the stories that carry a community's memories.

The Irish step dancer Helen Gannon shared her "Then and Now" narrative history on stage in 2019, noting early in the interview: "I got the impression at that time that you become a master, but it's not just for you. It's for you to pass on to the next generation." After she and I completed our live interview on stage at the community radio station's stage, several students from St. Louis Irish Arts, which she helped to establish more than four decades ago, performed and danced in her honor. Gannon, now around eighty years old, emigrated from Ireland in the 1970s. She told us, too, that the Traditional Arts Apprenticeship Program (TAAP) was crucial to grounding her family members in their heritage, while they made a new home in their adopted city. Just as her students ended their performances that night and just before Gannon took a quick turn on the floor to dance a jig, she spoke to the audience, including her students. She reminded them to stay connected and to sustain these traditions: "It's like I told you; you can't leave until you share it!" She has no plans to leave us any time soon, and she has no plans to quit sharing her Irish traditions. Gannon has a strong desire to reciprocate for what she learned from the master artist Maureen Hall, her TAAP mentor, and from the Missouri Folk Arts Program, which she credits for supporting her and members of her St. Louis Irish Arts community since 1988.

Collecting "Then and Now" narrative histories has been one of the more profound components of my most recent work. Over the years, state folklorists and culture workers have periodically assessed Ms. Hawes's apprenticeship initiative formally and informally at state, regional, and federal levels.[3] The goals and outcomes tend to assess public sector programs' stewardship of public funds, as well as quantifying apprenticeships, project administration, participation, and outreach, for instance (Auerbach 1996, 53–63). For grant makers, these assessments are necessary to justifying, sustaining, and growing allocations. Professionally, I intend for Missouri's "Then and Now" stories to deepen our understanding of the apprenticeships and to create reflexive space for individual artists' qualita-

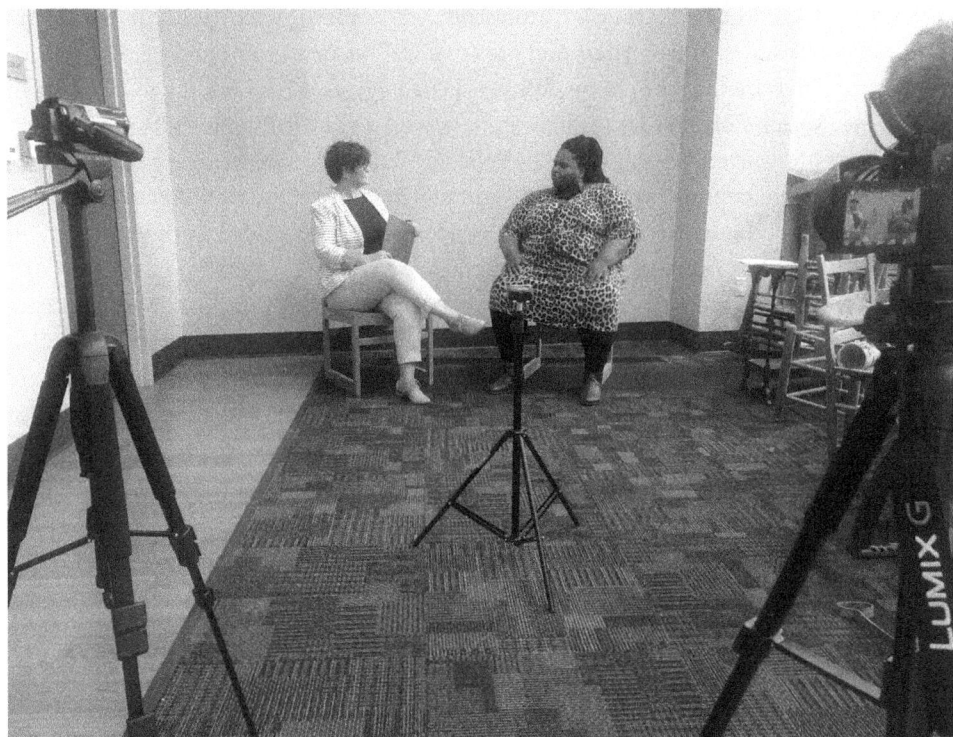

Recent master storyteller and previous apprentice Angela J. Williams joins Lisa Higgins to share a narrative history in Kansas City, Missouri, June 18, 2021. Williams is the third apprentice to Dr. Gladys Caines Coggswell to participate in "Then and Now." (Videographer Rachel Krause of Banjo Creative. Copyright Rachel Krause, 2021.)

tive assessments of the project. Through "Then and Now," these former apprentices may discuss their journeys to new layers of artistry. In the course of storytelling, they assess their own legacies and the legacies of the decades-long work that Bess Lomax Hawes began. Just as folk arts are arts with a genealogy, so too does our work as folklorists reflect our own genealogies.

Personally, I continually find that "Then and Now: Apprentice Journeys" resonates with me as a mid- to later-career public folklorist. When I returned to Missouri in 1999 to direct the MFAP, I recognized that my internship—my apprenticeship—had given me hands-on training, introduced me to colleagues in the public sector, and helped me gain confidence in my ability to work within my chosen field. Upon my return, I also found that organizationally MFAP's internship program had lapsed. So, I made a point to immediately connect with the Folklore Studies program in the University of Missouri's English Department, and we welcomed our newest interns, or apprentice folklorists, in 2000. Through 2016, we worked with graduate student interns, as well as work-study students. The Museum of Art and Archaeology, our department, even helped find funding for graduate student worker stipends, which we offered to interns who had completed two consecutive semesters. Now, many of those former MFAP student workers are employed in the field of folklore, in adjacent fields, and beyond. They are professors and lecturers, public folklorists and university administrators, grant writers and poets, as well as an attorney and a nonprofit administrator. They are branches in my folk arts genealogy, and I am finding more seeds to plant, as we search near and far for new student workers. MFAP's internship program at University of Missouri ended only when the Folklore Studies program waned, in 2016. Now, we are finding ways to continue with graduate and undergraduate student workers from other departments and other universities; recent opportunities have included work with Missouri Valley College, Western Kentucky University, and University of Louisiana-Lafayette.

Before Ms. Hawes's tenure at the NEA, she served at the Smithsonian as a deputy director, where she worked with "hundreds of folklorists" to plan and produce the 1976 Bicentennial Festival of American Folklife. She wrote in 1992, "Almost every person I know who is active today in the area of public folklore participated at least in some small fashion in the 1976 Festival. Historians will eventually look in wonder at the far-reaching effects of the 1976 Festival of American Folklife" (Smithsonian n.d.). With awards and accolades and the spontaneous "thank you" on a random elevator, Bess Lomax Hawes must surely have known the tall legacies that grew from the seeds she planted way back then.

NOTES

1. Recently, the NEA succinctly defined the apprenticeships in a new publication compiling research on recently funded folk and traditional arts projects in the United States, as supported by NEA state partnership grants and direct grants to organizations: "Apprenticeships are time-honored programs allowing master artists to train apprentices, often over an extended period of time, who will then go on to teach others and share what they have learned with their own communities. Formal learning programs of this nature are instrumental in passing on cultural knowledge to the next generation. Apprenticeships build greater visibility for specific traditions while sustaining these traditions for future generations" (2019).

2. The Missouri Arts Council (MAC), now a division of the Office of the Lieutenant Governor, has supported the apprenticeship program since its inception. While Missouri's Cultural Heritage Center was dismantled in 1993, MAC and the University of Missouri worked with the Museum of Art and Archaeology to establish the Missouri Folk Arts Program, with staff and components that were previously funded under the auspices of the Center.

3. Each year at the Missouri Folk Arts Program, outside evaluators visit a sampling of apprenticeship teams to assess their work, and staff visit during lessons to document and assess the team. With the pandemic, staff has implemented a new self-evaluation as well. In 2001, the folklorist Jon Kay conducted a regional assessment for South Arts that included state apprenticeship projects in the nine southeastern states, and in 1996, Susan Auerbach assessed several state apprenticeship programs via a National Endowment for the Arts grant to the Fund for Folk Culture.

Applying Ethnicity

The Case of Olga Edseth's Hot-Pink Rosemaled Pumps in Mount Horeb, Wisconsin

JARED L. SCHMIDT

In 1998, Olga Edseth visited a garage sale near her hometown of Mount Horeb, Wisconsin. During this shopping excursion, the then eighty-four-year-old Edseth came across a pair of hot-pink pumps. She picked up the pair of size eight shoes, paid fifty cents, and brought them home. Two decades later, these same shoes would be displayed as part of the first special exhibit at the Mount Horeb Area Historical Society's (MHAHS) Drift-less Historium (a portmanteau of history and museum). What makes this pair of second-hand pumps worthy of preservation and presentation as a symbol of the village's Norwegian and Norwegian American heritage? In the comfort of her home, Edseth had rosemaled the pumps, permanently transforming them into a piece of ethnic art.

By focusing on Edseth's rosemaled pumps, this essay explores a series of intertwined goals. On the surface, my first objective is to trace how an everyday pair of pumps can be transformed from a retail object into ethnic folk art. When she rosemaled these shoes, Edseth added a fresh layer of distinctly Norwegian symbolism. She creatively expressed a connection to, negotiation with, and ownership of her ethnicity, and her place in the larger community (Stern 1991). I situate these shoes within the context of Mount Horeb as it continues to navigate its own Norwegian and Norwegian American heritage. Specifically, this essay examines the role of local museums in exhibiting and analyzing pieces of art from the area, transforming them into what Barbara Kirshenblatt-Gimblett refers to as "objects of ethnography" (1991). The selection and presentation of a particular piece of folk art, such as a pair of rosemaled shoes, may influence how a community sees itself and engages with its traditions. At the very heart of this essay, though, is Edseth herself. As an artist who deeply loved her family, friends, and community, she fully embraced her heritage in rural Wisconsin. I construct a biography of the artist and explore how her legacy, through a pair of hot-pink pumps, is represented within the larger context of a village that heavily markets the Norwegian American aspect of its ethnic heritage.

Pumps as a style of footwear bridge centuries, continents, and genders. Low-cut, seamless, flat-heeled shoes, pumps are typically made of leather with a thin sole and heel and can be easily slipped on by the wearer. Pumps came into high fashion in sixteenth-century

France and were worn by men and women in Europe and colonial America. These shoes were often decorated, adorned with buckles and lace. Pumps dropped from fashion following the French Revolution but made a prominent return to mainstream American and British women's fashion during the mid-twentieth century. Because of their versatility and their ability to pair with most types of attire, pumps became a symbol of the professional woman (McDowell 1989; Walford 2007; DeMello 2009; Johnston 2017).

Edseth's shoes themselves are manufactured hot-pink leather and have a two-inch heel. No records exist concerning who originally purchased them, where they were purchased, or their retail price. Branding information is not visible as a Dr. Scholl's cushioned insert has been glued into each shoe's insole. The pumps do appear to have been well cared for as they are in excellent condition, suggesting they were either worn infrequently or much loved. The Dr. Scholl's insert implies that they were worn enough to justify permanently incorporating additional comfort.

In 1998, Edseth's pumps underwent their most dramatic transformation, going from a commercialized fashion product turned garage-sale bargain item to a piece of Wisconsin ethnic folk art. Folk art in Wisconsin can be viewed both as a reaction to technological innovation and as artistic reinterpretation as individuals seek to engage with a sense of identity (Leary and Gilmore 1987). Edseth's shoes represent the pervasiveness in which rosemaling has become a powerful symbol of identity for Norwegian Americans (Gilmore 2009). They are emblematic of immigrant folk art in the United States. In these painted pumps we see an artist's passion for her heritage, blending hues of home, love, and revival into her art. The shoes represent the larger history of an artistic form, one developed to grace the walls of religious and domestic structures, providing vibrancy and color to a dark Norwegian winter landscape. Edseth's pumps are part of a larger artistic lineage of reinvigorating and revitalizing a tradition in decline. Rosemaling, then, becomes a bridge between the old and the new.

Rosemaling, or "flower painting," developed in eighteenth-century Norway and represents an infusion of artistic motifs. This painting style is rich with Renaissance-era geometric designs, "zigzag" borders with interweaving patterns inherited from Viking and Norwegian carving traditions. Depending on style, rosemaling features a variety of Baroque scrolls and rococo C-stems, and organic tendrils and acanthus leaves that dance within the designs to give each painting a body and a sense of weight. Rosemalers commonly use an earth-toned color palette of varying shades of reds, blues, whites, and greens. Rosemaling heavily features stylized two-dimensional floral motifs, characteristic signatures of this art form (Kitchell Whyte 1971; Martin 1989; Nelson 1989; Ellingsgard 1993, 1995; Nelson 1995; Gilmore 2009). Distinct stylistic variations developed throughout the Norwegian landscape, reflecting the tastes and talents of artists and clients and bearing the names of the administrative districts in which they flourished (Gilmore 2009). The two most prominent forms of rosemaling in Norway and America are Telemark and Hallingdal (Ellingsgard 1995). Rosemaling would increasingly leap from walls into the domestic sphere, gracing ale bowls and utensils, a trend that expanded as the practice was brought to the United States (Martin 1989).

The nineteenth century saw an influx of Norwegian immigrants to the United States, particularly in the Upper Midwest, and from 1820 to 1975 approximately 885,000 individuals made the journey (Leary 2006b, 892). By 1900, Norwegians represented Wisconsin's third largest ethnic group, behind the Germans and Poles (Zaniewski and Rosen 1998). While Norwegians may have largely settled near one another to form ethnic enclaves, they underwent degrees of cultural shifts. Immigrants selectively maintained traditions during more pressing economic changes and increased access to mass-marketed goods. Among these was the highly commercialized and deeply valued practice of rosemaling.

Interest in rosemaling grew in America largely because of the dynamic work of a Norwegian immigrant, Per Lysne (1880–1947). A trained painter, he gained fame for his innovative and prodigious painting techniques, especially with respect to smorgasbord plates, in his Stoughton, Wisconsin, studio (Martin 1989; Gilmore 2009). Lysne not only greatly expanded the visibility and artistic potential of the medium; he also inspired others to take up paint and brush. Rosemaling as practiced in Norway was a male-dominated industry. The rosemaling revival in the United States, however, saw women become the predominant tradition bearers beginning in the 1930s. While men still practice rosemaling today, they are by far the minority. As women's leisure time increased and they began rosemaling, the need for teachers and instructional materials also grew. This need was eagerly met as the art form spread across the Upper Midwest and the rest of the United States well into the 1960s (Martin 1989). While some artists I have spoken with are wary about rosemaling's future, dedicated artists continue to teach, innovate, demonstrate, sell, and compete. Rosemaling has proliferated to become a symbol of highly marketable Norwegian ethnic identity (Gilmore 2009).

Although Norwegian immigrants settled in both urban and rural areas, James P. Leary observes that "the small towns and hinterlands of the Upper Midwest are the Norwegian American Heartland" (2006b, 893). Mount Horeb is one such community, and has formally emphasized its strong sense of Norwegian ethnic heritage. Kirshenblatt-Gimblett suggests that heritage is the "present having recourse to the past," and as groups give the past a "second life" they create something new. Critical to this heritage production process, she suggests, "to compete for tourists, a location must become a destination. To compete with each other, destinations must be distinguishable, which is why the tourism industry requires the production of difference" (1998, 152). Barbro Klein observes further that heritage is "selected or appointed in complex processes" and this is a political process that involves many stakeholders (2000, 25). Beginning with the open-air museum Little Norway, Mount Horeb has continuously engaged in the process of selecting symbols and giving them new "life" through the heritage production process. This includes rosemaling public surfaces like the Open House Imports gift store on Main Street and sponsoring the tongue-in-cheek Scandihoovian Winter Festival (Gilmore 2009, 27, 31–32; Mount Horeb Historical Society 1986, 108–9).

Latching on economically to tourism can subject communities to the whims of cultural fads, economic swings, population shifts, and infrastructure changes. Beginning in the 1980s, Mount Horeb began feeling these shifts, with the most threatening being the construction of the Business Highway 18/151 bypass (Gilmore 2009). Following the practice of other communities that had faced similar fates, Mount Horeb organizers selected to rebrand the village around a central theme to drive marketing campaigns in an effort to draw in tourists and unify the community (Engler 2000; Gradén 2003). Mount Horeb rallied once more behind images of Norwegian ethnic identity, selecting the troll as its mascot. Much like theme towns of similar ilk that draw upon their ethnic heritages, Mount Horeb now bears the moniker "The Troll Capital of the World." Dozens of carved troll statues playfully line the village's major thoroughfares and occupy businesses (Martin, Anderson Kramer, and Schmidt 2020). Dining establishments like the Grumpy Troll Brew Pub, complete with troll statue brandishing a brewer's paddle, invite tourists to literally drink in the local heritage. This thematic re-creation further enacts transplanted and reinvented Nordic traditions, creating an ethnic landscape whose canvas includes *bunads* (Norwegian folk dress), rosemaling, and trolls waiting to join you in a selfie. While outsiders may view this community as eccentric, it speaks to the dedication and creativity of its residents' regard for a sense of Norwegian heritage.

Coming of age in Mount Horeb during the dynamic reinvention of rosemaling in Wisconsin, Olga Edseth found her artistic niche among her fellow Norwegian American neighbors. The daughter of first- and second-generation Norwegian immigrants, Edseth was born in 1914 and raised in Dodgeville, a rural community near Mount Horeb. Growing up surrounded by her ethnicity, Edseth, according to her daughter Carol Hoeritz, did not speak English until she began elementary school. Hoeritz recalls that when she visited her grandparents' home, Norwegian was spoken extensively, and her mother and father used Norwegian to speak in secret in front of her and her siblings (Hoeritz and Horneck 2018). Brian Bigler, MHAHS volunteer artifact curator, also comments on Edseth's speech, noting that she was "very Norwegian in her talk and everything . . . she still had an Old Country accent" (2017). Marg Listug, manager of the Livsreise-Norwegian Heritage Center in Stoughton and a close friend of Edseth, recalls in an email that during their final visit, "my husband started conversing with her in Norwegian and then she brightened up and spoke to him for almost an hour—pulling the long unused Norwegian words from her memory."

Edseth, according to her granddaughter Jean Horneck, was a "true Norwegian," "very involved and inspired by her culture. It's what she lived for" (Hoeritz and Horneck 2018). Susan Hefty, Hoeritz's oldest daughter, stated in an email to me that "she always held her Norwegian ancestry on a high pedestal." Throughout her life, Edseth made frequent trips to Norway and especially her ancestral province of Telemark, where she would stay with distant relatives. Listug noted in an email that Edseth "tried hard to keep abreast of modern Norway when her health became such that a trans-Atlantic flight was not possible anymore. She cut articles about Norway from magazines and newspapers and glued them into scrapbooks." Edseth regularly prepared lutefisk and lefse and donned her *bunad*.

Edseth most strongly expressed her ethnic identity through rosemaling. In 1946, she began teaching herself rosemaling by copying a design from a postcard in her mother's collection. She applied the design to a wooden plate that her husband, Earl, had lathed from an orange crate. Throughout Earl's life, he carved and constructed many of the wooden pieces Edseth rosemaled. This included a wheeled wooden cart where she kept her art supplies and which, appropriately, she also rosemaled. She never had a studio in her house; rather, she wheeled her cart into the room with the best light as the day progressed. Edseth was hooked on rosemaling from the very start, working long, focused hours. When asked what Edseth preferred to paint, Hoeritz commented, "For herself she worked on plates that my dad made. Then as there were grandchildren she tried to [paint] trunks . . . she loved to do the trunks, even for her nieces and people like that. She enjoyed birdhouses, too, that was a specialty, and Christmas ornaments" (Hoeritz and Horneck 2018). Among the "oodles" of objects their grandmother rosemaled for family members, Hefty specifically notes a pair of wooden skis, jewelry boxes, and a small trunk she used as a card box at her wedding. Listug recalled in an email that Edseth "loved vivid colors—not necessarily the traditional reds and blues. I have a box she painted for me as one of the many gifts I received from her over the years and it is really wild; the background color is watermelon pink. [S]he was definitely her own person and broke the rules for rosemaling if that suited her at the moment."

Although Edseth never actively sold or promoted her work, her talent received recognition. As Mount Horeb increasingly embraced its Norwegian heritage, the village featured her designs on street banners. The Sons of Norway also presented Edseth with an International Heritage Award (Madison.com 2017). Her passion for Norwegian folk art also led to articles in multiple publications. Philip Martin's *Rosemaling in the Upper Midwest: A Story of Region and Revival* (1989) features three pieces rosemaled by Edseth. On the page opposite the preface is a ceramic vase (6), and later in the book are pictures of a small frying pan (66) and a dustpan (75). Edseth is even featured wearing her Telemark-style *bunad* in the third edition of Janice Stewart's *The Folk Art of Norway* (1999). Both daughter and granddaughters note that Edseth was exceptionally creative. Over the course of her sixty years of rosemaling, she painted whatever object she felt might benefit from a flourish of color. Horneck recalls, "She painted all of my life. She did a lot of stuff for us as we were growing up. [We would] bring it to grandma, 'Would you paint it for me?' I always loved it" (Hoeritz and Horneck 2018). Hefty echoes this, stating in an email, "As a child and young adult we couldn't wait to give her another piece of plain woodenware to see what fantastic rosemaling would be displayed on it. She was a true artist and would also include scenic pictures." Her artistic career demonstrates the continued American expansion of this folk art tradition, its incorporation into daily life, and her lifelong association with this form of art.

Given Edseth's inclination to paint whatever struck her fancy and the fact that she lived in a community that increasingly promoted its Norwegian American heritage, it is not a surprise that she felt it natural to transform a pair of hot-pink pumps into a form of heritage on the go. Beginning at the shoe's toes, tendrils of blue, green, and yellow acrylics overlap on a race to a heavily stylized Telemark flower whose roots reach downward along the heel, grounding her and her art to the landscape. As if to commemorate this stretching of a dynamic artistic tradition, Edseth wrote across the sole of the left shoe, "The first pair of shoes I ever rosemaled."[1] Through the application of folk art, these pumps become distinct, something set aside from the potential normal biographical trajectories of their "peers." Furthermore, the pumps become desirable heritage objects, the promotion and performance of which may be actively encouraged by local institutions such as museums (Dicks 2000; Smith 2006, 2015).

Although Edseth contributed to Mount Horeb's public development and promotion of its Norwegian American ethnic heritage through her art, she rarely parted with her work, reserving items as gifts for family and close friends. However, in 2003, Edseth approached MHAHS volunteer curators about gifting several objects for preservation in their collection. Among the objects donated were her rosemaled pumps. Through its inclusion in MHAHS's

Rosemaled pink pumps by Olga Edseth. (Photograph by Jennifer Bastian. Courtesy of the Mount Horeb Area Historical Society.)

collection, Edseth's art was further validated and ascribed additional value rooted in the institutional authority ascribed to museums. The ethnologist and Nordic scholar Lizette Gradén (2013) observes that when community residents give gifts to museums through donations, they can in turn shape how a community perceives and presents its own heritage. This may be especially salient where smaller, "local museums" as sites of influence and memory making are concerned (Levin 2007). Institutions such as the Vesterheim, in Decorah, Iowa (Rue 2018), and the Ulen Museum, in Ulen, Minnesota (Cederström 2018), play significant roles in the creation and maintenance of heritage-driven narratives at the heart of "Nordic places." Museums have played a long and significant role in presenting the Mount Horeb area's Norwegian heritage (Dregni 2011; DuBois 2018; Mount Horeb Area Historical Society n.d.) and its connection to folk art (Gilmore 2015). Edseth's pumps became an agent in the ongoing discourse about the present and future performance and exhibition of Norwegian heritage in her community.

In preparation for the Historium's reopening in 2017, staff recognized the need for a special exhibit to alleviate pressures from completing the larger permanent exhibits. While the Historium's staff members did not focus expressly on Norwegian heritage or folk art like their predecessors, they did call upon their vast collection to develop a folk art exhibit heavily featuring Norwegian cultural symbols. According to executive director Destinee Udelhoven, as time progressed, the exhibit, "Creators, Collectors, and Communities: Making Ethnic Identity through Art," grew into a chronological exploration through material culture of how Mount Horeb "became the Trollway."

Even though Udelhoven notes that the area has been home to a variety of ethnic groups, the exhibit explored "how the Norwegian-ness of the area crystallized" (Bigler, Udelhoven, and Buysse 2019). Bigler describes the exhibit as demonstrating "how we evolve from some ethnic beginnings and turn [ourselves] into a commercial way of looking at that" (Bigler, Udelhoven, and Buysse 2019). The objects were selected on the basis of their connection to folk art and the reinvention of identity over time. The exhibit was divided into four parts oriented counterclockwise with a divider wall in the exhibition hall's center: "The Old World in the New," "Made in America with Foreign Parts," "Heritage Memorialized," and "Trolltown, USA." Museum staff also partnered with the University of Wisconsin–Madison throughout the stages of development. Students, including myself, enrolled in an art history course under the direction of Dr. Ann Smart Martin to write object interpretive labels and an accompanying e-book featuring in-depth object studies.[2]

The "Heritage Memorialized" section of the exhibit demonstrated how the role of the community's folk art revivals during the 1970s and 1980s played into the village's sense of identity. Uniting artist and artwork in the display, the exhibit reminded guests of the role an individual can play in shaping a community (Mount Horeb Area Historical Society 2017). While the exhibit also featured Swiss and German folk art, nineteen of the twenty-three objects in this section were Norwegian or Norwegian American; thirteen featured rosemaling. The number of rosemaled objects speaks to the presence of this folk art during this period of identity negotiation. Artists in Mount Horeb were inspired by Little Norway as well as competition for tourists driven by ethnic heritage-centric neighbors like New Glarus and Stoughton. Udelhoven makes a critical comment speaking to the community's psyche, the power of history, and heritage on museum displays: "We maybe subliminally assumed that we needed to include rosemaling because that's what people knew would be Norwegian" (Bigler, Udelhoven, and Buysse 2019). She further notes that with rosemaling, you can "glance at it and know that it is Norwegian." As Janet C. Gilmore has observed, rosemaling has become a pervasive and easily recognizable symbol identifying Norwegian ethnicity (2009). By heavily featuring rosemaling in the exhibit, the Historium reinforced and perpetuated the idea that rosemaling equals Norwegian to visitors of varying ages.

Bigler observes that rosemaling brought many Mount Horeb residents a degree of fame in the community (Bigler, Udelhoven, and Buysse 2019). Hoeritz confirms this thought. Even though she has not resided in Mount Horeb for many years, "people that I run into, even my classmates when I go to the reunion and things like that, they all know my mother—she's famous, you know. I mean, it's a small town, but she made a name for herself" (Hoeritz and Horneck 2018). Access to locally known artists' creations helped shape the object selection process, because MHAHS wanted to "represent people that people could relate to" (Bigler, Udelhoven, and Buysse 2019). Three objects painted by Edseth were selected for display: her first rosemaled plate, a hand-carved wooden basket she purchased in Telemark and rosemaled in Mount Horeb (MHAHS 2003.020), and, of course, the hot-pink pumps. These objects, according to Bigler, reveal an artistic "evolution" from her first attempt at rosemaling to a "very refined idea of the art. I mean, she really took it on. And I think just the genuine sort of folky appeal that she gave. I mean, she was still Norwegian" (Bigler, Udelhoven, and Buysse 2019). Positioned behind the objects is an equally vibrant portrait of a smiling Edseth embodying her culture by wearing a *bunad*.

Regarding why Edseth's rosemaled pumps were selected, Bigler recalls, "I liked the fact that they were something non-traditional that was rosemaled. I liked that the best. I knew that somebody...would walk away remembering something from the exhibit" (Bigler, Udelhoven, and Buysse 2019). These shoes provide what Bigler calls a "wow moment," helping alleviate the potential "mundanity" of the exhibit. This "mundanity" may be broken as guests might literally walk into the exhibit case displaying the shoes. When designing the exhibit's layout, Bigler felt that "space was a problem, but you always want something to step out, to kind of protrude in your way a little. . . . In this case, you know, [the shoes are] right there. I think of them like Judy Garland's ruby slippers from the *Wizard of Oz*. You go to the Smithsonian and there they are, they're right in front of you. So, you can see [Edseth's] work, which is interesting, but then there's this" (Bigler, Udelhoven, and Buysse 2019).

Though entertaining in their appearance, Edseth's pumps represent a balancing act of ethnic expression and historical period in Mount Horeb. When displayed, the shoes produced a double take among guests and evoked a smile. Udelhoven, for example, often overheard people express surprise when they saw the shoes in an art-based exhibit. "I also think that [the shoes] shows how much a part of [the artist's] life these things are," she suggests (Bigler, Udelhoven, and Buysse 2019). They are a symbol of their time, a love letter to an artform that brought incredible joy to Edseth's life and that continues to connect her to family and friends after her passing, in 2012. Furthermore, the shoes become symbolic of the twentieth- and twenty-first centuries' heritage production process with an emphasis on local identity. Spanning two centuries of artistic expression through rosemaling and featuring traditional objects, including an immigrant trunk circa 1835, dishware, and a pair of pumps, the Mount Horeb exhibit presented the legacy and value of this art form. Edseth's shoes further reveal both the enjoyment folk artists can have when they stretch their medium to familiar objects and the ongoing discourse about what it means to be a Norwegian American today.

The rosemaled pumps serve as a potential nexus for conversations about how best to display Norwegian American identity, particularly for a village that has a rosemaled water tower and that bills itself as "The Troll Capital of the World." The shoes, in conjunction with the trolls, according to Bigler, suggest that "we can step out and have a little humor about this all," and, one could argue, this benefits the community (Bigler, Udelhoven, and Buysse 2019). While the shoes, Udelhoven notes, may be "one of the flashier pieces we have" and might potentially be good for museum literature, she makes a critical observation: "I think that the struggle with those shoes, too, is that it kind of seems to be like, what the Chamber, for instance, would want us to be. I think it's not what some of the more serious people may want us to be. So those shoes are kind of like a weird representation of the friction between people and what they think Norwegian culture should be. It's kind of like they are an artifact that stands for these two kinds of thoughts about Norwegian-ness, serious versus light" (Bigler, Udelhoven, and Buysse 2019).

Going forward, the museum is carefully considering options for promotion and display. They must negotiate respecting Edseth's legacy and her family. Edseth was very proud of her work. Knowing that her artwork is viewed as worthy of preservation and display brings a sense of pride to her family and functions as an extension of her desire to pass on as well as to save a tradition she held near to her heart. The Historium's staff also needs to contend with the seriousness with which people take rosemaling and their heritage amid the playful approach to Norwegian-ness the village currently espouses. Thinking about the legacies of artists in a museum setting, especially in a smaller community, is an important and complicated process.

Rosemaling transformed the "life" of these hot-pink leather pumps, sending them on an unforeseen trajectory at the time they were initially produced. Through becoming a walking statement of ethnic pride, the shoes serve as a window into the practices of folk artists like Edseth, who explore their heritage at the shadow's edge of the economic and political power of the state capital in Madison. Furthermore, they are a time capsule of artistic revival and how an artist negotiates and performs her own sense of heritage through creative means. Rosemaling also saved these shoes from the literal and metaphorical trash pile of history. The bright blue and green acanthus leaves, highly stylized flowers, and rococo-C stem motifs covering these pumps imbue them with a cultural and historic value worthy of gifting to a museum. Without the application of rosemaling, it is unlikely that this pair of shoes would have been preserved for future generations. Now, future patrons will be able to glean knowledge about a beautiful Norwegian/Norwegian American art form at a specific point in Mount Horeb's history and the life of local artists like Edseth. Perhaps they too will stop and admire these striking ethnic fashion statements. The future of Edseth's rosemaled hot-pink pumps looks bright.

Notes

I am sincerely grateful to Carol Hoeritz, Jean Horneck, and Susan Hefty for sharing their heartfelt and loving memories about Olga. Thank you to MHAHS's Driftless Historium's Destinee Udelhoven, Johnna Buysse, and Brian Bigler, for the opportunity to work on the "Creators, Collectors, and Collaborators" exhibit and for their continued support. I extend my appreciation to Dr. Ann Martin for connecting me with MHAHS and for her guidance throughout the various stages of this project. Thank you to Marg Listug, manager of Livsreise, for the opportunity to present a version of this research at her museum and for telling me about her friend. Finally, thank you to my family and friends for their editorial guidance and for the time spent listening to me excitedly talk about a pair of hot-pink rosemaled pumps.

1. Horneck notes that Edseth did in fact rosemal several more pairs of shoes. She recalls having her grandmother decorate a pair of canvas shoes for her own daughter to match Norwegian-themed attire for Stoughton's Syttende Mai (Norwegian Constitution Day) celebration. She comments that people offered to purchase them from her. Horneck owns several pairs of rosemaled shoes made by Edseth.

2. The e-book features colored images of the objects exhibited, as well as their labels and in-depth object studies. It can be accessed at https://wisc.pb.unizin.org/mthoreb/.

"Let the Blood Roses Grow"

Workers' Worldviews in the Music of Oren Tikkanen

HILARY-JOY VIRTANEN

It was at a lively concert at the University of Wisconsin–Madison where Oren Tik-kanen performed Finnish American traditional songs, drawing from a body of music that had developed since his childhood in Calumet, in Michigan's Copper Country. It was not the first time I had seen Oren perform. We have collaborated on various public programs and productions in the Upper Peninsula for years as part of my work as a public folklorist in my home region. His final piece, "Kaivantomiehen laulu" (The digger's song), reflected the musings of a copper miner working underground but wishing to be with his wife in a warm bed and cursing the bosses whose greed kept him virtually chained there. As the song ended with the rousing words "If the choice is to struggle in sunshine and air / or slavery way down below / If it must come to battle, then battle I will / and I sing, 'Let the blood-roses grow!'" I turned to a colleague and whispered, "Should we clap or put our fists in the air?" In that moment, like so many others, the roles of folklorists and community blur together in ways foundational to effective and participatory culture work.

"Kaivantomiehen laulu," written by Finnish immigrant Santeri Mäkelä in 1903 and published in the Finnish American songbook *Työväen Laulukirja* in 1907 (Golubev and Takala 2014, 98–99; DuBois and Cederström 2019, 75), represents one aspect of Finnish American music that Tikkanen has incorporated into performances since the 1970s.[1] Labor and proletarian music is a well-recognized aspect of the Finnish repertoire, cultivated on both sides of the Atlantic as Finns sang about battles with the traditionally powerful farmwives and clergy of Finland and also the new power class created by global industrialism.

Finns arrived in the Upper Midwest starting around 1865 (Holmio 1967, 125–26), with most coming between 1880 and 1920, attracted by mining jobs that would inspire songs such as "Kaivantomiehen laulu." In Houghton County, they became the largest ethnic group by 1910 (Bureau of the Census 1913, 606), but their numbers didn't translate into social prestige or power. Finns were considered strange due to traditional practices such as sauna (Lockwood 1987; Berkovici 1925, 101–2, 113) and were even seen as not really white because of national romantic (and later eugenic) ideas that labeled them as having Asian origins as far flung as Mongolia (Kivisto and Leinonen 2014; Keskinen 2019).

Their political activities contributed significantly to their social conflicts. Coming to blows with bosses over exploitative labor practices and with police in response to local political suppression (Puotinen 1977; Kaunonen 2010; Virtanen 2020), Finns were well known in many parts of the United States for their leftist politics (Karni and Ollila 1977; Kostiainen 2014). Finnish songlore records their experiences in ways more evocative than newspaper reports or court documents (see Leary 2014; DuBois and Cederström 2019). In some cases, it provides the only direct evidence of historical events as told from a vernacular perspective (Virtanen 2010).

Immigrants came with songs that revealed unfair social stratification in their home country (see Leary 2014; DuBois and Cederström 2019). Finns translated songs from the labor and socialist movements, including "La Marseillaise," "The Internationale," and songs by Joe Hill of the Industrial Workers of the World (Green et al. 2007, 16; Leary 2010; Halker 2017). They also created their own Finnish-language songs illustrating workers' lives, from the miner to the female domestic servant (see DuBois and Cederström 2019, 176–77). Later, the IWW songwriter T-Bone Slim, born Matti Valentine Huhta, presented original English-language works, such as "Mysteries of a Hobo's Life," which crossed ethnic lines and were immensely popular among IWW members in the 1920s and 1930s (Rosemont 1992, 7–8; Green et al. 2007, 20–21).

These songs have remained in the repertoires of performers and on the record players or MP3 players of listeners today. Some have disappeared only to be rediscovered later, and others have been reconfigured to bring new meaning to timeless issues and concerns.[2] They have a circuitous history that led to their inclusion in Oren Tikkanen's performances. This history was not influenced by the presence of workers' songs in Oren's everyday consciousness but developed over time from a relationship to these songs and the ideas they conveyed.

A YOOPER CREOLE

I'm half Finnish, and my mother was a red-headed Scots-Irish from Missouri, and my parents met in Detroit before World War II. Everybody was moving to Detroit from everywhere. And so I think of myself as a Yooper Creole and I just love the . . . Creole nature of America and how music comes in. I like to play Finnish music on the banjo and, you know, I like to mess up tradition as much as possible.

—Oren Tikkanen, interview (2018)

Born in Alabama, where his father was stationed during World War II, Tikkanen spent part of his childhood in Detroit before returning to the Copper Country in the late 1940s. Periods of adulthood spent in Detroit, Duluth, and Minneapolis kept Oren in this world of Upper Midwestern music (Tikkanen 2019). Over the decades, Tikkanen has become well respected among musicians and folklorists alike, and his relationships with people in both communities have had a profound positive impact on the performance and teaching of regional traditional music and on the effect of public humanities in his community.

The Creole of ethnic groups—and music styles—that surrounds Tikkanen was largely bound together by the work that immigrants and their descendants had in common. Mines

Oren Tikkanen performs at the 2019 Juhannus Midsummer Festival, Toivola, Michigan. (Photograph by author.)

initially attracted mass immigration, and until they closed permanently in the late 1960s, mining was often a first job for the area's young men and even a career for some. Working underground created an experiential bond between people whose first generations were separated by language and custom and whose subsequent generations became bound by shared work, education, neighborly relations, and intermarriage (Lankton 2007, 15–16). In addition to the Indigenous Ojibwe people whose land the settlers took, Finns joined already-established Yankees, Cornish, Irish, French Canadians, and Germans in the mines, as part of the second wave of immigrants from Eastern and Southern Europe that also included Italians and Poles, Jewish peoples from several locations, and Slavic, Germanic, and Hungarian peoples from the Austro-Hungarian Empire.

Just as these people worked together, so too did they strike together. Between 1872 and 1906, notable labor actions took place in the Copper Country eight times, and the biggest and deadliest of all, the 1913–14 Copper Country Strike, forever altered the ways in which worker–management relations and political leftism are viewed in the area (see Puotinen 1977; Kaunonen 2010; Ross and Galdieri 2013; Silvers 2013). The Copper Country Strike is still regularly discussed in the community, and the implications of its aftermath continue to resonate today.

Music is a tangible reflection of community diversity, creating points of contact across ethnic lines over time (Leary 1987, 2006c, 2014). The reflections of toil in music brought work and play together. Songs such as "Kaivantomiehen laulu" reflect the importance work has in our lives; the Finns were not the only musicians in the area playing it (Tikkanen 2014). Northern and Eastern European polkas and waltzes were combined with French Canadian quadrilles. Later developments in a uniquely American, and particularly Midwestern, music brought early country music sounds, especially with the advent of recorded and broadcast sound.[3]

Oren's initial experiences with music were, like those of many who came of age in the 1960s, centered around rock and roll. He acquired a guitar and a mandolin in his youth, performing in a band with Bill Ivey, a Calumet resident and future folklorist, and developing a repertoire of dance music encompassing primarily popular rock and country music, as well as jazz and bluegrass (Tikkanen 2018). Much like the Copper Country accordionist Art Moilanen before him (Leary 1987), Oren performs covers and parodies of popular songs as well as original compositions of his own. "Pennies from Heaven," for instance, becomes "Heikki Lunta," a song about a local Finnish American folklore character. Though he was exposed to traditional music in his youth, it was only when he lived in the Twin Cities as a student in the 1970s that Oren incorporated it into his repertoire, including labor music: "The history of this area, as far as the Finns go, is very interesting. By the time I grew up, there was very little of the political aspect. And I found out that most of the Reds and the Progressives had either been chased out or discouraged to the point that they left after the 1913 Strike. And so it's when I moved to Minnesota that I found out about the workers' tradition amongst Finnish Americans and the Wobblies and all of that juicy stuff" (Tikkanen 2018).

For Oren, Minnesota was the gateway to Finnish American traditional music (Tikkanen 2019). He began to collaborate with the musician Al Reko, with whom he recorded several albums, as well as with the Finn Hall band and the Kisarit folk dance group. It was at this time, too, that he began to learn about the leftist tradition, which at first were tied to the broader experience of Finnish Americans nationwide but which soon also connected him to hometown historical events.

When Oren returned to the Upper Peninsula in the 1980s, he maintained relationships with Minnesota performers and expanded his network to include Copper Country musicians in a variety of genres. He also developed relationships with professional folklorists and cultural arts communities in the United States and Finland. This not only resulted in his becoming well respected among music lovers and folklorists alike but also enabled Tikkanen to receive support in the form of apprenticeship grants and honorific awards that highlighted his importance to regional folk culture. As a traditional musician, Tikkanen created work that reflected contemporary—and changing—representations of the past, which is a noticeable feature of life in today's Copper Country, where heritage tourism and local history programs bring the past into dialog with the present every day.

Interestingly, Oren lives in a community with a high level of social conservatism, in which labor history has an ambiguous place, though it has affected the lives of many of the area's current and former residents. Many residents have ancestors who died in mines, and even today postmining environmental degradation has lasting effects on public health. The leftist elements of the turn-of-the-century community are not as prominent as they once were, and it can feel dangerous to view socialists and IWW members in a positive light when the dominant local discourse at the time—not to mention at present—was openly and violently hostile (Puotinen 1977; Kaunonen 2010). That Oren maintains his popularity is a tribute to his open, accepting personality and to the fact that he knows when to play certain songs and when not to.

THREE LABOR SONGS FROM TIKKANEN

The early 2010s was an interesting point in local history as it came up on the period of preparations for a large international ethnic heritage festival, FinnFest USA 2013, which took place in the nearby university towns of Houghton and Hancock. The year 2013 was also the centennial of the tragic Italian Hall Disaster, which happened in Calumet and is one of a number of labor-related tragedies that unfolded in the early twentieth century, along with the Triangle Shirtwaist Factory fire, the Ludlow Massacre, the Bisbee Deportation, and the Everett Massacre. Although the Copper Country Strike of 1913–14 that precipitated the Italian Hall Disaster was the labor history focal point that year, Oren also remembered earlier events. At this time, I worked in public programming and outreach at Finlandia University in Hancock, and a large part of my job between 2011 and 2013 was planning and coordinating more than 150 lectures and twenty-four films as well as overseeing prefestival fundraising and promotional activities, on which Oren and I often collaborated. Local labor history was in the air; one of our many collaborations occurred at FinnFest, and Oren's songs were an outlet for reflecting on this.

One song that Oren performed multiple times in these years was his own composition from 1981 that commemorates the 1872 labor strike at the Calumet and Hecla mines in Calumet. Oren was inspired to write a humorous tune about a true event detailed by the historian Arthur Puotinen (1979). In "The Finnish Women," a group of miners' wives prevent the mass arrest of their striking husbands by barricading the road. The song ends with a punchline reflecting stereotypes of Finnish women as headstrong and bold, also acknowledging the important role women played in local labor actions.

"Kaivantomiehen laulu," the second song, details the everyday musings of the Finnish miner as experienced by Santeri Mäkelä in the first years of the twentieth century, when he worked in iron mines in the Gogebic Iron Range, south of the Copper Country.[4] Oren's interaction with this song is different from his creation of "The Finnish Women." It is a song that he first experienced in its original Finnish language, a tongue in which Oren is not fluent but in which he has gained what can be considered a musical fluency. It is also a song that, with the help of a nonlyrical translation provided by a Finn Hall member, Dennis Halme, Oren has translated into a lyrical English version (Tikkanen 2014).

Upon first reading the lyrics, Oren was able to discern that the song was about a miner. The process of lyrical translation was helped by Oren's father's stories of working in the mines. As he said in his FinnForum X presentation (2014), "My limited Finnish language skills prevented me from understanding the complete text of the song, but I knew it was

about working in the mine, and that it had a local connection. I could see that the song referred to the utter blackness of working underground, a condition to which I had heard my
copper-miner father, Harold Tikkanen, refer many times." The common experience of
mining united Oren, his father, and Santeri Mäkelä through song and story. What was
more visceral to Oren, and what he better understood through watching a performance of
the song by a student ensemble at Helsinki's Sibelius Academy and seeing Halme's translation, was the very leftist, revolutionary sentiment that the song also conveyed (Tikkanen
2014):

Kapitaali mun orjakseen ostanut on
Käsivarteni ja verenkin
Oi Luoja, oi luoja, sua kiroa en,
En kiroa kohtaloain
Minä kiroan valtoja tyrannien
Ja vapauttain ikävöitsen
Minä ikävöin vapautta ihmiskunnan
Proletaarien sorrettujen
Minä ikävöin taistohon tuimimpahan
Veriruusuja katsomahan

Capital has bought my servitude
My arms and even my blood
Oh creator, oh creator, I curse you not
Nor do I curse my fate
I curse the power of tyrants
And I long for my freedom
I long for the freedom of humanity
And of the oppressed proletariat
I long for the sharper struggle
to see the blood roses

For Tikkanen, as he worked to create a singable translation, the challenge lay in making a
version that not only fit meter and rhyme conventions, dispensed with the original version's
repetition of each verse, *and* reflected Mäkelä's original imagery and "mood" but that also
would "hold the attention of a 21st-century audience" (Tikkanen 2014). This audience, particularly in the local context, would have problems with direct translations of words rendered
(accurately) as "capital/capitalism," "wage slavery," "tyrants,'" and "oppressed proletariat" and
with a direct call for entering a "struggle," all of which would result in "blood roses." As Tikkanen himself says, Americans have been conditioned to have "knee-jerk" responses to phrases
such as these, making it hard for audiences to hear the message of the song and to "consider
the ideas on their own merits" (Tikkanen 2014). He reshaped this narrative by substituting
words like "bosses" for "capitalist," for instance. He did, however, keep the phrase "blood
roses" in his translation despite "personal reservations about referring to potentially fatal

gunshot wounds as 'blood-roses blooming'" (Tikkanen 2014). By keeping the metaphor in place without interpretive translation, he allowed listeners to interpret for themselves. He did, however, use light and darkness metaphors in the song more than is done in the Finnish original, highlighting the common experience of dark work in the mine against "the metaphor of overcoming the darkness of ignorance with the illumination of knowledge and new ideas" (Tikkanen 2014). This is an excerpt of his translation alongside the Finnish original:

Niin musta on, musta on ikuinen yö	It's blacker than ink, it's darker than night
ja kellot lyö kaksitoista	And there is the 12 o'clock bell
Vain torkkuen toverit istuskelee,	It's here that we earn our poor daily bread,
hikikarpalot kulmillansa.	This pit in the deep heart of hell.
[there is no Finnish equivalent stanza]	I could stay in darkness and do as I'm told
	remaining where I'm working blind.
	But I see a light that is showing the way
	to the freedom of all humankind.

While in 1903 Santeri Mäkelä may have foreseen a bloody struggle for miners and other wage slaves, by the end of 1913 it was in full swing in the Copper Country and in other parts of the United States, a situation that would continue well into the twentieth century.

The last of Oren's three songs was written by the American folk music legend Woody Guthrie. "1913 Massacre," released in 1941, is a variant of the Italian Hall story, inspired by Ella Reeve Bloor's autobiography, *We Are Many* (Ross and Galdieri 2013). While the song brought the Italian Hall Disaster story to a wider audience, the song's proworker stance, best reflected in the final verse, "See what your greed for money has done," is an indictment of the mine owners and the instigator of the incident, who has never been conclusively identified.

Like many, Oren grew up ignorant of local labor history (Ross and Galdieri 2013).[5] The Italian Hall Disaster garnered national headlines when, on Christmas Eve 1913, a union Christmas party at the Italian Mutual Benefit Society Hall was disrupted, with deadly results. An unknown person entered the event and falsely cried out that there was a fire. A stampede for the staircase at the front of the building led to the deaths of at least seventy-three individuals who were crushed and suffocated in the stairwell. The majority of the victims were children; a majority of the victims were also ethnic Finns (Kaunonen 2010; Lehto 2013).

The Calumet and Hecla mine, which employed, among many others, Oren's father and around which many of the events of the strike centered, remained open until 1968. The strike was something people spoke of, as folklorists have discovered through fieldwork in the area (Ivey 1970; Dorson 2008, 215; Heimo 2017), but they did so in hushed voices, and younger people became less and less exposed to the stories, especially if they had no family who had died in the incident.

As a teenager, Oren attended dances at the Calumet Eagles Lodge: "Nobody ever told me it was the Italian Hall. I used to go up and down those stairs, nobody ever told me that those were the stairs. Nobody would talk about the Italian Hall Disaster. You know, that

73 people died on those stairs" (Tikkanen 2018). Proposals to demolish the building brought a new awareness of the disaster to the people of Calumet; though many wanted to preserve the building in some way, others wanted it demolished, and this in fact took place in 1984. As Oren's brother Tom, former director of Main Street Calumet, says, the "ghosts" of the disaster contributed much to the prodemolition movement (Ross and Galdieri 2013). By this time, Oren was cognizant of the building's history, and in 1989 he performed at the dedication ceremony for the Italian Hall memorial site, singing "1913 Massacre" as individuals selected by their age and gender to represent each of the lost souls of that tragedy came onto the stage and were handed a white flower (Ross and Galdieri 2013).

In 1992, the US Congress established the Keweenaw National Historical Park to preserve the local mining heritage and to share the "copper story" with the world (See 2013, 117–18; National Park Service n.d.). This park is a collaborative effort between the National Park Service and nonfederal museums and sites associated with aspects of local history. Its creation has contributed to local industrial heritage tourism, and, in the leadup to the centennial of the Copper Country Strike, it contributed to public commemoration of the difficult and tragic events. Oren naturally had a part in these activities. As a federal agency, the National Park Service must take a neutral tone when describing such visceral topics. Private citizens like Oren, however, are freer to share their thoughts.

Over the past few decades, Oren has often been present to perform Guthrie's "1913 Massacre," just as he did at the commemoration of the Italian Hall memorial site in 1989. As the centennial of the disaster approached, in 2013, however, Oren created his own variant of the song, once again making space for a personal reflection on historical events and on public history as a phenomenon. On Christmas Eve 2013, the centennial of the Italian Hall Disaster, my family and I spent an evening at Oren's home with a small group of friends. In acknowledgment of the anniversary that hung in the air all around us, Oren performed his own version of "1913 Massacre."[6]

At FinnForum X, Oren described his process for reimagining Guthrie's song in a locally relevant way using multiple subjective viewpoints in order to better represent local understandings of the event and to more strongly incorporate Big Annie Clemenc, one of the most prominent female supporters of the striking miners who is understood to be the woman in Guthrie's version of the song trying to tell people there is no fire.[7] As he said at FinnForum, "For the most part, I'm attempting to get more of the historical account into Woody's song and I don't think the original spirit is changed" (2014). Oren's version is meant to augment Guthrie's version, exchanging a story described by one local resident in the film *1913 Massacre* as "despicable" for a version that not only reflects a more nuanced local understanding of the incident but also incorporates historical sources that were not available to Guthrie when he wrote the song (Ross and Galdieri 2013). For Oren, "this is not a criticism of Woody. . . . If he had the sources we now have—even Arthur Thurner's *Rebels on the Range*—he might have come to the same conclusion that I have" (Tikkanen 2014). Oren's conclusion, then, is this:

> It seems clear that the Citizens' Alliance, capitalizing on the Dally-Jane murders in early December 1913, had created, with the compliance of local authorities, an armed force of 2,100

"deputies."[8] These "deputies" (along with the hired "security advisers" from the Waddell-Mahon company and others) treated strikers roughly and established a palpable sense of intimidation by searching people's homes, raiding union stores and offices, and making public threats of deportation. The Citizens' Alliance quickly and efficiently created a mode of fear among many of the strikers—*and their families*—which instantly heightened into terror when someone yelled "Fire!" at the Italian Hall Christmas Party. (Tikkanen 2014)

The Italian Hall Disaster and the shift from being the source of copper for the entire world to being an economically depressed area continually struggling to reinvent itself casts a shadow over the Copper Country today. In the film *1913 Massacre*, a group of townspeople listens to Woody Guthrie's song and then discusses their reactions with the filmmakers. The indictment of the mine companies, their executives, and the local bosses doesn't sit right with some of the listeners, who seem to feel almost as though Guthrie is criticizing them and their working-class miner ancestors. One man responds, "When you're talking about Calumet, you're talking about Silicon Valley, 1900. It was a good company. And it was a good workforce. *We're all good people*" (emphasis mine). Another listener, after revealing that his father was the last miner to die on the job at Calumet and Hecla shortly before the 1968 strike and the mine's final closure, counters a warm memory of the mine with his memory of the loss of his father, finally summing up with this thought: "There's so much history up here. . . . I don't know, maybe that's all we have left."

For Tikkanen, reframing the narratives of labor struggle through song rehumanizes the real people who lived through—and died in—these events. Annie Clemenc, alluded to but not named by Guthrie, is envisioned by Tikkanen in bitter mourning over the deaths of so many children. The rumors that the company held the doors to the hall closed and allowed so many deaths to happen, embraced as the truth by Guthrie, are redescribed by Tikkanen to reflect what was surely an atmosphere of fear and confusion felt by party attendees as well as by first responders, many of whom would have been distrusted police and deputized private citizens. His version allows the anger and sorrow to come out just as they did in Guthrie's original, but, coming from a community perspective, his version also invites fellow insiders to reflect on what Oren says and what they believe about not just the Italian Hall disaster but also the nature of the labor and class struggle in the Copper Country up to the present.

OREN TIKKANEN: COPPER COUNTRY TROUBADOUR

For Oren, a life steeped in music in a region brimming with a sense of shared culture and history has resulted in a repertoire that brings traditional cultural practices into dialogue with the present and the future. He contributes to a durable record of traditional music as it has existed in his lifetime by recording repertoires, stories, and interpretations of history and culture, both his own and those of many others. He has mentored two generations of traditional music and dance practitioners, offering formal and informal apprenticeship opportunities, providing venues for performance of song and dance, and kindling in young artists an interest in exploring these traditions on their own. He has engaged with two generations of folklorists and folk cultural researchers, including my own mentors and colleagues Jim Leary, Yvonne Lockwood, Michael Loukinen, and Dan Truckey, and now me. Because of him, other folklorists have developed new insights into the various cultural traditions in which Oren engages, and he has helped us contribute to an understanding of human culture through our academic work and through the public folklore programs in which we also engage, providing traditional artists, including Oren, with financial support for apprenticeships and public recognition for all the good works he has done.

In the Copper Country, history is personal for those like Oren and me, who come from long-established local families and who are engaged in exploring the past through our endeavors. Our engagement with songs, narratives, material culture, and even the landscape are imbued with several generations of incorporation into the Copper Country. It is in Oren's recognition that his father's experiences in the "darker than night" mines of Calumet were echoed in the smoldering song left to us by Santeri Mäkelä. It is in the eerie sensation I experienced a few years back when the current owner of my great-great-grandparents' farm showed me a Young Communist League membership card signed by my great-grandfather, a man I knew until his death in 1997 and who I suspected had a red past. In those moments, I cannot feel that it is a coincidence that I have always been drawn to the stories, songs, and struggles of the working class. It is also in these moments that I feel that it is no coincidence that I have had the good fortune to know and work with Oren. As he once said, "Music that comes out of working-class people, and country people, and people in the cities who are further down on the socioeconomic rungs, it has a kind of depth, and sound . . . and reality" (Durocher 2014). In this, I wholeheartedly agree.

One of Oren's informal apprentices, Matthew Durocher, made a film as a college student to describe the social world Oren has created through music. In *Concentric Circles*, Durocher interviews Oren and other local musicians who perform with him, revealing the ways in which people are drawn to create, reinterpret, and carry forth music for themselves and, one hopes, for future generations. Oren's work sparks his creative spirit and his desire to engage the ideas and experiences of people from the past. Whether working with the compositions of others or with compositions of his own, Oren imprints impressions and understandings of the past that come from all around to create a dialogue between history and the present. As Oren tells Durocher in the film, "As far as trying to preserve [folk music], I don't think of myself as a preservationist, although I suspect someone could call me that. I think of myself more as just trying to keep it going."

Notes

1. Born in Vimpeli, Finland, in 1870, Mäkelä lived in the United States briefly, returning to Finland by 1908 and serving as a member of parliament in the Social Democratic Party. Following Finland's independence in 1917 and the Finnish Civil War in 1918, Mäkelä, as a prominent member of the losing Reds, fled to Soviet Russia. Though he was active in the development of the Soviet Union throughout the 1920s, he, like many other Finnish communists in 1930s Russia, was a victim of the Great Purge, dying in 1937 or 1938 (Saarela 1997; see also Tikkanen 2014).

2. Heimo (2017) discusses this process with online commemoration of the Italian Hall Disaster, including various uses of the song "1913 Massacre." None of this discussion, however, mentions local performances and alterations of the lyrics as described in this essay.

3. Leary (2006c, 9–11) calls this regional musical aesthetic *polkabilly*, describing the repertoire of Bob Andresen by saying in part that his Wisconsin Norwegian ethnic repertoire is only one part of a more dynamic range that includes "Germanic, Slavic, Finnish, Canadian, and metis songs and tunes" as well as "Anglo-American music—whether fiddle tunes, post–World War II country music, or 1960s roots rock." This same musical sensibility applies to Oren Tikkanen.

4. In his 2014 presentation for FinnForum X, "Challenging Icons: Rewriting Woody and Santeri," Tikkanen also presents another song about everyday issues in the local mines with the song "The Thirty-First Level Blues," by Vladimir Floriani Jr. and Jim Floriani, ethnic Croatian copper miners employed in Ahmeek, Michigan. This song was recorded by Alan Lomax during his Upper Midwest song-collecting trip in 1938 and details daily work on the thirty-first level of a Calumet and Hecla mine, approximately three thousand feet underground. While the song does refer to the mine as a "slave camp," much of the tone is similar to that found in any number of American songs concerning work and general dissatisfaction with it.

5. This is also discussed in an interview with John Prusynski (2018).

6. Oren also later presented these lyrics at FinnForum X (Tikkanen 2014). He represents the idea that someone (not identified directly but arguably someone who supported the mining company) deliberately yelled, "Fire." Because Oren presents a very incendiary—and very anticompany— version of what happened at Italian Hall, he understands its locally sensitive nature. In an interview conducted by John Prusynski at which I was also present, my request for Oren to perform this particular song was declined, in part because of this variant's sensitive nature.

7. Annie Clemenc, daughter of Slovenian immigrants, has been described both firsthand and in later legend surrounding the strike by figures ranging from Ella "Mother" Bloor to Richard Dorson. While Dorson (2008, 215–16) reports negative anecdotes about her, modern representations of Clemenc have showed her in a much more positive light, and she is generally recognized as one of the heroines of the strike, including by Oren himself.

8. The Citizens' Alliance was a vigilante group established in November 1913 to "eliminate the Western Federation of Miners [the union representing the strikers] from the area." Less than a month before the Italian Hall Disaster, the Alliance's newspaper reported that 6,132 people had joined (Puotinen 1977, 158). The Dally-Jane murders occurred in the nearby community of Painesdale, in which three miners who did not participate in the strike were killed by members of the Western Federation of Miners who were "bent on scaring off scabs" (Lankton 1991, 234–35).

PART IV. CREATING COMMUNITY

Folklorists work within communities to selectively strengthen and sustain them through cultural maintenance efforts and through creating better environmental and economic conditions in which traditional culture can thrive. Sustaining folklore and folklife is not simply about the sustaining of material products, narrative forms, customary practices, or aspects of folk belief. Rather, the sustaining of these forms helps intensify a community's relationships and relationalities *through* the practice of folklore. In other words, communities sustain folklore, but folklore is equally necessary to sustain communities.

Public folklorists and culture workers have long understood this and for decades have worked with projects that elevate traditional cultures, that focus on its transmission, that sustain selected traditions, and that help build or support the contexts in which traditions exist to make them more viable in ever-changing communities. The chapters in this section look at a sampling of community-based projects that involve folklorists and the distinctive kinds of professional tools and methods we employ.

In her chapter, Anne Pryor looks at her own community of curlers and at the importance of certain social customs and traditions within the community. As a folklorist-curler, Pryor discusses her project to document her own curling club's history and customs and to use this documentation project to create a stronger sense of identity for the curling club and the many new curlers who may understand the game but not the sport.

Mirva Johnson, in her piece on the Oulu Heritage and Culture Center, details the founding of a cultural center as an extension and repatriation of the open-air museum concept. Johnson explores the origins, products, and visions of this Finnish American center and explores how the process of creating heritage infrastructure has allowed the community to remain resilient in the face of outmigration.

In her chapter on Sámi American folk arts, Sallie Anna Steiner details the "lost" Sámi American community's reclamation of its Indigenous identity. Through traditional crafting and the intercultural dimensions that revitalized crafting often entails, individuals are able to transform their sense of self, their sense of relationalities, and to create an emergent community where there formerly was none.

In her essay on identity, mining, and the creation of an arts community on Minnesota's Iron Range, Rhonda Dass explores the different iterations of a community marketing and branding its own local culture as an avenue for improved economic and cultural sustainability. In doing so, Dass explores the complex dynamic between local identity and tourist marketing and how a community continually redefines itself to retain not only its sense of self but also its economic viability.

Yvonne Lockwood's contribution examines the history of a fish festival in Michigan in creating community and details her efforts of working with a 4-H club in documenting the event. Lockwood looks at how the festival has worked to define the community's distinctiveness to outsiders and to itself and shows how it responded to challenges to the community and its traditions.

In the final essay of the section, Ayako Yoshimura explores the role of ethnic grocery stores as "third spaces," neither fully public nor private, yet essential in maintaining community. She offers an in-depth resource guide for their documentation, with emphasis on the ways material culture reflects the intangible cultures that use these spaces. Yoshimura suggests how the documentation itself of "third spaces" plays an important role in cultivating critical community resources for ethnic or other marginalized communities.

These chapters showcase how community building must occur at systemic levels, balancing cultural and social factors alongside economic and environmental ones to encourage the smart growth of a community. Perhaps most central to this work is the notion that communities don't simply create folklore but rather that folklore works as a critical vehicle for the maintenance and creation of community.

Stacking Brooms

Curling Camaraderie and Folklore in a Time of Transition

ANNE PRYOR

B eing a folklorist means that one is trained to observe culture; to identify cultural identity as it is performed and displayed; to recognize group boundaries that embrace, question, or reject a tradition as representative; to look beyond the moment to how a group has carried its culture over time and perhaps in multiple places; to learn a people's way of being in the world. Employing this set of skills does not stop when one is "off duty." In a laundromat, a bar, a gas station, a hotel, a garden, a curling club—one doesn't stop being a folklorist just because one is not "working."

I find deep satisfaction in being part of a profession that advocates for cultural democracy, that works toward understanding and respect across divides, that seeks to strengthen the cultural commons, and that thus engages in promoting social and cultural justice. Toward those ends, facilitating dialogue and interactions *between* cultural groups is a frequent role for public folklorists, achieved in myriad ways, including festivals, exhibits, essays, performances, presentations, films, and recordings. In such settings, we facilitate cultural sharing and learning.

Of equal importance to cross-cultural understanding is self-cultural understanding (Pryor 2004; Wagler, Olson, and Pryor 2004). Learning about one's own culture, finding out that familiar practices are actually cultural constructions, and understanding oneself as a cultural being are critical early steps in learning about other cultural groups and practices. This focus is especially key in folklore and education efforts through which students and their teachers learn about local cultural communities, starting with their own.

During my twenty-year tenure at the Wisconsin Arts Board, one ongoing project was providing professional development opportunities to K–12 educators across the state. This most often took the form of a cultural tour for teachers organized by a long-term partnership group, Wisconsin Teachers of Local Culture (Pryor et al. 2011). After participating in one of these tours, seeing how local culture could be uncovered in multiple types of communities, the gifted and talented coordinator for a northern Wisconsin school district was inspired to investigate the local culture of her hometown. I worked with her and her students to help them develop a Rhinelander Cultural Tour, a student-led tour that featured local people and places that contributed to Rhinelander's community and culture. At the end of this two-year process, this educator confided to me that she had been on the verge of leaving her small city for someplace more interesting, someplace that had more to offer. What changed her mind was discovering the richness in Rhinelander's hidden gems. She wrote this note to me on the back of a folder, which I have kept and treasured for many years: "Since I've started working with you, I've started looking at my town and my life differently. Before, I was scornful and bitter about being so far away from 'the culture.' Now I notice things differently. Everything is a story and everything is real."

Other teachers on other WTLC cultural tours experienced similar revelations, declaring that they had learned to see their communities with new eyes after having participated in this public folklore project. It is that sense of revelation I aim to bring to curling now, by using public folklore tools within curling communities to foster cultural self-awareness. Helping cultural communities lift the veil of familiarity that can obscure seeing one's own traditions has always been a part of public folklore's mission, and applying it to a cultural community to which I now belong is an unexpected but delightful application of my professional skills to an adopted recreational activity.

This essay is written at a time of transition. I am transitioning out of a career as a public folklorist at a state arts agency, one of the most iconic yet rare positions in the field. As of 2020, all fifty-six states and territories partnered with the National Endowment for the Arts through a governmental arts agency, yet only twenty-eight of them had a staff position dedicated to folk and traditional arts. I was one of the lucky few in the nation who was employed in one of these positions, as a folklorist hired to document, support, and present the traditional arts of a state. It was a great job that didn't pay well but that was deeply rewarding and nearly constantly fascinating. Since leaving that position, I have sought opportunities to continue to serve the common good by employing my highly particular ethnographic skill set in new settings.

An avid curler since 2007, I have slowly been learning the depth of transition that the sport of curling is experiencing. In typical traditional style, I am learning through oral transmission, from anecdotal comments, fully narrated stories, overheard discussions between experienced elders, and more recently—due to targeted efforts on the topic—recorded interviews. I didn't understand the casual comments at first, made during conversations around a table after a curling match by a thoughtful person with perspective wrought from many decades in the sport. But with more years at those tables and more opportunities to personally witness changes, I have come to understand the concerns that some members of this cultural group have about the future of the sport we love.

This essay is a reflection on what I have learned about curling so far—some of its many cherished traditions, variations within one specific tradition (broomstacking), and social changes that are potentially threatening its viability. It is also a reflection on the power of public folklore in an unexpected setting. The skills and training I bring to the curling community are welcomed and valuable there. They also are bolstered by collaborations with my fellow enthusiasts, who bring their own set of complementary skills. Together we work to expand curlers' awareness of the deep culture that buoys our sport in an effort to preserve the best of what we have inherited from centuries past.

THE SPORT OF CURLING

The most common type of curling match involves two teams of four players each. They play on a sheet of ice about 150 feet long by 15 feet wide with a bullseye-like target "house" at each end. Over the course of eight "ends," every player has two turns per end to deliver one of sixteen stones, each weighing about forty-two pounds and each made from granite harvested from an offshore Scottish isle (Butler 2003). A released stone slides down the sheet toward the far house, according to the strategy of the "skip." The skip stands in the far house calling instructions to the team, telling the thrower what kind of curl and weight to give the delivery and telling the other two teammates when they should sweep the ice in front of the stone as it travels. A typical game lasts around two hours. Skillful play requires good strategic decisions by the skip, accurate delivery by the thrower, vigilant reading of the ice and traveling stone by the sweepers, and constant communication among all team members.

When the sport started, in the sixteenth century, curling was played outdoors on natural ice with stones of the players' own making, of iron or wood. Most historians of curling agree on the game's Scottish origins due to physical evidence, such as the oldest extant stone (dating from 1511) and supported by written evidence such as the earliest recorded notation of a curling match (Kerr 1890; Hansen 1999). At least three clubs, all of which are located in Scotland, claim to be the oldest curling club in the world.

Curling grew in popularity and by the eighteenth century had expanded across lowland Scotland. It was spread to other parts of the world by Scottish emigrants and troops and did especially well in climates that provided winter conditions consistently cold enough for annual play. Canada is now the world's stronghold of curling, with an estimated 90 percent of all curlers worldwide (Clark 2008, 22). Its first curling club, founded in 1807 in Montreal, remains the oldest active sporting club of any type in North America. Now almost one thousand clubs exist across the provinces, and Canadian teams dominate in world competitions.

In contrast, the United States claims 228 curling clubs in forty-three states. Most of those clubs have been established during the past fifteen years, thanks to the soaring popularity of the sport and an expansionist push by USA Curling, the national organizational body. Increased awareness of this somewhat obscure sport can be traced to curling's inclusion in contemporary winter Olympics, first as a demonstration sport in 1988 and 1992 and then as a medal sport since 1998. The 2018 gold medal win by the US men's team has further increased American interest. Growing participation in curling also can be credited to the sport itself, as it is a lifelong activity, possible to learn and succeed at as an adult, and possible to play successfully despite physical challenges. Adaptive equipment means that a local curling team might have members ranging in age from eight to eighty, with some players using a delivery stick or a wheelchair.

As a result of these forces, US curling has slipped out of its original geographical enclave of northern-tier states, historically from North Dakota to New York, with the greatest density of clubs in Wisconsin and Minnesota. Clubs can now be found in such warm climes as Arizona, California, and Florida. As a Wisconsin-based folklorist, I was fortunate to base my curling career in a state with a long and deep curling heritage. Of Wisconsin's twenty-eight curling clubs, the most of any state in the United States, eleven have celebrated anniversaries ranging from centennials to a quartoseptennial by 2021.

The Home of Curling

Curling is an international pastime that occurs in its fullest form locally, at the club level. I agree with the Ontario journalist Doug Clark's assessment: "The heart of the curling world is the curling club" (2008, 22). Curling clubs are voluntary sports organizations often legally organized in the United States as a charitable nonprofit. Clubs are home bases, where traditions are taught and then compared and shared with curlers from other clubs. Even athletes who compete at the world level are identified by their home clubs. Club culture is like family culture; neophytes learn how to be curlers by observing and absorbing the traditions practiced around them on and off the ice. It is only by leaving home or curling at other clubs that one begins to see the variations in common practices.

Sociability is as important in curling as are the games. In addition to the icehouse where the games occur, a curling club includes a lively clubhouse. Members and guests use the clubhouse areas for different purposes: the viewing area for watching games, the club room with tables and chairs for socializing after games, the kitchen for the preparation of food and drink, and the locker rooms for changing and for storing personal equipment. Most clubs allow members access to the building at any time, providing practice time when ice is free or a meeting space for gatherings. When I visited the Royal Montreal Curling Club on a summer morning, the ice was out for the season, but a group of elder curlers was there for an exercise class. In Arlington, Wisconsin, the curling club is an early-morning coffee spot where members of the club, along with members of the community, drop in for coffee and donuts and a few hands of cribbage before starting the day.

One huge challenge to establishing the social side of curling in the newest curling clubs is that they start out without dedicated facilities. Called "arena clubs," they do not have their own physical buildings, instead playing games at a municipal ice arena at narrowly scheduled times. In these spaces, shared with hockey players and figure skaters, curlers must get off the ice before the Zamboni preps the rink for the next sport's shift, often meaning they do not get a full two hours (or eight ends) of play. There is no clubhouse in which to socialize, no locker rooms in which to store a bottle to share after the game or to personalize lockers with photos of curling teams in playful poses at a bonspiel (a curling tournament), and no kitchen for sharing meals. New curlers make up the majority of these clubs, meaning that they have not served an apprentice role, learning both skills and traditions from masters who have generational roots in the game. In these situations, curling might become a rec-league activity for which players sign up rather than a club that they join, participate in, learn about, and work to maintain as a volunteer. This is part of the threat to maintaining the spirit of curling during this time of expansion.

The Spirit of Curling

The physical core of curling is the local curling club with its space designed to support the spiritual core, which is its sense of camaraderie. The ethos of valuing community as much as competition has been curling's organizing principle for centuries. Its many expressions have shifted over time and between places but are still traceable to the sport's Scottish roots. As a folklorist, I found that experiencing and documenting these variations is one of the many pleasures of membership in this cultural community.

Camaraderie on and off the ice is sometimes referred to as "the spirit of curling," a term that comes from a well-shared essay of the same name, "The Spirit of Curling," attributed to H. T. Ferguson (2011, 10), Madison Curling Club president in 1943 and 1944, when reprinted every year in the club directory but rarely given attribution when modified for other uses by other clubs or curling organizations. One line captures the basic sentiment: "While the main object of the game is to determine the relative skill of the players, the spirit of the game demands good sportsmanship, kindly feeling, and honourable conduct."

"Kindly feelings" on the ice are exhibited by behaviors such as handshakes and the wish of "Good curling" exchanged by all players before the game, with handshakes repeated after the game along with congratulatory comments from both sides. There is no visible or audible rejoicing when an opponent makes a mistake, and acknowledgments like "Nice shot" are expressed to opponents. Games are self-regulated, with players calling their own fouls rather than relying on an umpire or referee. Again, from "The Spirit of Curling": "Curlers play to win, but never to humble their opponents. A true curler never attempts to distract opponents, nor to prevent them from playing their best, and would prefer to lose rather than to win unfairly."

Sociability off the ice is as important as fair play on the ice. Following a game, both teams are expected to sit together at a table and share drinks and talk. Thus, the two-hour game expands into at least a three-hour event with the added postgame visiting. The historical record shows that postgame socializing with libations is a centuries-old part of the game. An entry by the parish minister of Muirkirk about his parishioners, recorded in Sir John Sinclair's *Statistical Account of Scotland (1781—1799)*, reads:

> Their chief amusement in winter is curling, or playing stones on smooth ice. They eagerly vie with one another who shall come nearest the mark, and one part of the parish against another, one description of men against another, one trade or occupation against another, and often one whole parish against another,—earnestly contend for the palm, which is generally all the prize, except that perhaps the victors claim from the vanquished the dinner and bowl of toddy, which, to do them justice, both commonly take together with great cordiality, and generally without any grudge at the fortune of the day. (Sinclair 1793, 612)

Postgame conviviality emigrated from Scotland to Canada, evidenced in the 1807 charter of the Royal Montreal Curling Club. Of its six founding articles, the last is: "The losing party of the day shall pay for a Bowl of Whiskey Toddy to be placed in the middle of the table for those who may have it."

After hundreds of years of precedent, this enshrined practice of drinking with teammates and opponents following the game continues in the United States as well, in various forms. In many clubs, it is the winning team that gets drinks for the losing team, especially in competitive situations such as bonspiels or in places where drinks are not included in membership dues and are purchased at the clubhouse bar. The Detroit Curling Club keeps

A horizontal variation of how brooms might be stacked midgame, Women's Shamrock Bonspiel, Green Bay Curling Club, March 9, 2019. (Photograph by author.)

a framed, handwritten reminder of this tradition inside the icehouse, close to the door teams use to exit into the clubhouse for postgame socializing: "Curling tradition has it that the winner was to provide the loser with a sip from his jug to heal any strain to their friendship. Angus McTavish."

Broomstacking in Curling

One particular drinking tradition, "broomstacking," has an especially wide set of variations that I continue to discover as my curling career expands and I visit other curling clubs. As I learned from my curling mentors, broomstacking is a midgame drinking break in which players' brooms are laid on the ice to hold their place until the game resumes postdrink. It is a practice reserved for especially friendly games, such as an annual grudge match for a tongue-in-cheek trophy and bragging rights or when a club hosts a delegation of curlers from Scotland or Canada on a friendship tour of US clubs. A shorter break involves a shot of liquor, typically whiskey; a longer break involves a glass of beer.

When broomstacking, Madison curlers haphazardly lay their brooms on the ice in the center of the target house nearest the door going into the clubroom. It is done quickly, with no aesthetic care given. The artlessness of this practice became clear when Madison hosted the 2017 men's Scot Tour. For that midgame drinking break, the Scots painstakingly taught the Madison players how to literally stack the brooms, using all eight brooms to form a vertical structure that remained standing while the men went inside to toast one another. That variation suggested that Madison had maintained the essential dimension of broomstacking (the convivial midgame drink) while abandoning the difficult but aesthetically pleasing actual stacking of the brooms.

A vertical variation on how brooms might be stacked midgame, Scottish Men's Curling Tour to USA, Madison Curling Club, January 18, 2017. (Photograph by author.)

And the variations continued to unfold. I was honored to be part of a curling friendship tour to the Maritime Provinces in 2018 through the national women's curling association, the USWCA. At one stop in Nova Scotia, our hosts at the Wolfville Curling Club feted us with a midgame drinking break. Unlike Madison curlers but like the touring Scots, they artfully stacked the brooms of all eight players vertically in the center of the ice sheet's house. But rather than leaving the ice, we stayed there for a shot of maple crème liquor, a local delicacy. I was surprised later when I asked my counterpart on the Wolfville team about broomstacking. She had no idea what I meant, being completely unfamiliar with the term. So, while those curlers conducted a midgame drinking break as a sign of friendship, they did not call it "broomstacking" and indeed had no other term for it.

Starting around 2018, I started to hear the term "broomstacking" used to refer to postgame socializing, as described in this definition, which I found on several clubs' websites, such as that of the Vikingland Curling Club, established in 2005 in Alexandria, Minnesota: "One of the greatest traditions in curling is broomstacking. The term refers to the social get-together after each game. Originally, curlers, after completing a curling game on the pond, would stack their brooms in front of the fire and enjoy beverages with the opponent. This tradition is still alive today and it is expected that you partake in broomstacking after every game."

At first I thought this use might be confined only to newer clubs, which lack deep heritage in the game and often adapt or lose some of the finer points of traditional practices. But I found a similar definition on websites of well-established clubs in the geographic home of American curling, for example this from the Chicago Curling Club (est. 1948): "It isn't just the sport that makes curling attractive. After a game, curlers engage in the traditional 'broomstacking,' a period for socializing with teammates and opponents." Similarly, the Wauwatosa (Wisconsin) Curling Club (est. 1921) website notes: "We enjoy a postgame tradition called broomstacking, where members socialize with their team and their opponents' team."

Yet a third definition came from Utepils Brewing, a Minneapolis brewery, for use in its marketing of Broomstacker Red Lager, naming both the midgame break and the postgame socializing as broomstacking: "Curlers know the game is just a game. Halfway through and at the end, they stack their brooms and have a beer with their opponents. Because there's nothing like having a good beer while you're having a good time."

While I maintain that my preferred definition of "broomstacking" is the correct one, the existence of these variations in how broomstacking is practiced and defined means that this is a living tradition, being adapted locally but still continuing in the spirit of curling. What these changes highlight, though, is that there will be little chance of midgame broomstacking making its way into the newest US curling clubs if these new definitions continue to spread. The very squeezed schedule of ice time that arena clubs face does not lend itself to a midgame break. Without a clubhouse with beer taps and tables, and without assigned lockers in which to store bottles, along with a general prohibition against the drinking of alcohol on such premises, a midgame broomstack in an ice arena is unlikely. Even postgame socializing is threatened, as it requires driving across town to a selected bar, an add-on for which many players don't show. In this type of situation, the sport takes precedence over the spirit, and the treasured balance between the two is tipped. Opinions and stories about what in curling is most important and crucial to maintain do not get shared, resulting in the loss of a key opportunity for tradition transmission.

One small corrective to this loss can occur when the most enthusiastic curlers in new arena clubs travel to heritage clubs to partake in a bonspiel or national competition. The host club's ability to draw on and display deep traditions can expose these journeymen curlers to some of the riches they can take back to their own nascent arena clubs. Despite many challenges, this might be one way for expansion curlers to learn about traditions such as midgame broomstacking and its role in maintaining the spirit of curling.

PUBLIC FOLKLORE AND THE SPIRIT OF CURLING

The curling club analogy to a family holds true especially in its intergenerational structure. Some amazingly hardy curlers continue playing into their eighties or nineties. They are on teams with players whose ages range through all the younger decades. As the elders pass away, their loss is mourned, along with their generational knowledge of what curling was like in earlier decades. When the Madison Curling Club lost one especially honored elder in 2015, a past president of the club decided that we needed to capture our lived heritage before we lost anyone else. He created a History Committee and populated it with handpicked club members, including three people with especially relevant professions: an archivist, a film-maker, and a folklorist. Among other efforts, the History Committee conducted a series of filmed interviews with longtime members of the Madison Curling Club.

As the folklorist on the committee, I was responsible for conducting preliminary and onscreen interviews, extracting stories from sometimes nervous elders about memorable characters they had curled with, wild times at bonspiels, adverse ice conditions in "the old days," and reflections on the future of curling. Our filmmaker hired a professional crew and equipment for the interviews and then edited selected clips. We showed the final high-quality products at an end-of-season Heritage Dinner at the Eastside Club, referencing an earlier era in which the Madison Curling Club held end-of-season celebration dinners and meetings there. Along with providing a fun evening of socializing, these dinners also offered attendees deeper knowledge about our shared curling heritage and traditions. The stories were great, the jokes were hearty, the drinks flowed, and the feeling that we were all part of something special that is worth preserving was reinforced.

Interviews for the annual Heritage Dinner were my first concerted application of my public folklore skill set to curling. Another has been to develop a slide-show presentation about food and drink traditions in curling, which I have given to noncurlers and, during the pandemic, when our season was canceled, to Madison Curling Club members via Zoom. This latter presentation focused especially on broomstacking and what its variations show about curling's evolving culture. A lively typed chat and subsequent group discussion elicited some great stories, facilitated extensive dialogue about the value of our sport's traditions, and revealed efforts that several curlers have been taking to help maintain them. Two club members have a podcast about curling that often features particular traditions; they will have me on next season to discuss broomstacking. Another curler has agreed to share with me four generations of her family's curling history for research. A retired lawyer who had just finished auditing a folklore class at UW–Madison connected his classroom experience with his lived experience, reflecting, "We might just take our own traditions too much for granted." Exactly! Score another point for public folklore fostering cultural self-awareness and supporting a cultural community's burgeoning awareness of its own heritage.

Extra End

The weekend before an early version of this chapter was due to this volume's editors, I curled. To the editors' possible dismay, I was not at home writing but instead was throwing stones, sweeping stones, calling out weights, and trying to outscore opponents. My team did just that and ended up winning the bonspiel. After each game, I sat with opponents from across Wisconsin—from Kettle Moraine Curling Club, Milwaukee Curling Club, Wausau Curling Club. We drank, we ate, we chatted, and we compared ideas and opinions about curling. I heard stories that expressed surprise and disappointment over how a recent bonspiel had not met basic hospitality expectations and how the current one did. A curler in charge of purchasing the pins for her club (an important part of the sport's material culture) gave me a sneak preview of her club's newest pin, and we exchanged plans that our respective clubs were making for upcoming anniversaries: the 175th for her club and the 100th for mine. Another set of conversations focused on how important it is for established curlers to invite new members to bonspiels so they can experience that vital part of the sport. The most heated discussion was about "eight-enders," the reportedly rarer-than-a-hole-in-one accomplishment in which one team scores eight points in an end because all eight of its stones outcount the other team's. Opinions were hot on the questions of whether purposefully trying for an eight-ender goes against the spirit of curling and whether some eight-enders could be considered illegitimate. (We concluded "no" to both.)

Those postgame conversations were culture in process. We, as active members of a cultural group, were reinforcing traditions, exploring boundaries, defining norms, and instructing neophytes. As both a curler and a folklorist, I value that these bonspieling women were passionate about curling, not just the on-ice competition but also the social, structural, cultural, and interpersonal off-ice elements as well. Together we and our fellow curlers are taking our place in the successive generations that have shaped our beloved pastime, incorporating changes and rejecting others according to the heart of the game, the spirit of curling. Whether midgame broomstacking will continue into future generational expressions of that spirit will be an outcome I am incapable of controlling. But, as a curling folklorist, I can continue to work within the community to identify, document, discuss, and respect midgame broomstacking as a quintessential emblem of the spirit of curling.

"We Wanted to Save Something While There Was Still Something Left"

Restoration and Cultural Maintenance at the Oulu Cultural and Heritage Center

Mirva Johnson

A s you drive north on Wisconsin's Highway 53, there is a point where you start to feel like you're finally getting "Up North" as the fields give way to birch and aspen, jack pine and fir. Most of Wisconsin is known for its farmland, but northern Wisconsin is known for its forests. Despite this long-standing reputation, it was the promise of farming that enticed many immigrants to move up north to clear the stump-riddled land left behind by the commercial logging of the late nineteenth century. These settlers formed close-knit communities, and small-scale yeoman farming—a style of farming in which families shared work with neighbors and within the family—was successful in the region for many years (Gough 1997). However, by the mid-twentieth century, a combination of factors made it difficult to continue farming, and many residents left the small towns for different kinds of work in the cities. Some of the towns that once boasted populations of more than a thousand now hover in the hundreds of residents. When you drive down the smaller county roads and through some of these smaller communities today, there are often a couple of vacant buildings in an otherwise well-kept town. However, the decline of small-town America isn't where this story ends.

As these small towns changed, another movement was burgeoning in the field of historic preservation as the number of museums and especially open-air museums began to grow in the 1960s and 1970s. The open-air museum Old World Wisconsin was built during this museum boom, opening its gates in 1976. The museum was designed around a series of farmsteads with buildings chosen from various ethnic communities around the state. One of these communities was Oulu, Wisconsin, where there were many examples of Finnish American vernacular architecture. Decades later, another preservation effort began, but this one initiated within the community rather than outside it. A dedicated group of Oulu residents and volunteers are working to preserve local history and heritage by relocating area buildings to the Oulu Cultural and Heritage Center (OCHC) and restoring them. It is an entirely community-initiated and community-driven project that began with the restoration

of the Palo Homestead by the Lahti family and has since grown, with nearly a dozen buildings relocated to the property and numerous donations of material culture by area residents.
In addition to offering regular visiting hours, the Center hosts a coffee and conversation hour
every Wednesday, talks by local authors, and an annual summer school program in partnership with the South Shore School District. It is in this context that my own relationship with
the OCHC began in May 2016 when I was part of a small team of researchers from the University of Wisconsin–Madison that drove up to conduct linguistic interviews with heritage
speakers of Finnish.

    While in some ways the OCHC is an outdoor museum, it is more than that, serving as a
community center and a volunteer-run sustainer of Oulu heritage. Importantly, it is keeping area buildings within the community, an approach different from that of some previous
efforts to preserve vernacular architecture, such as that seen with Old World Wisconsin.
Barbro Klein has defined heritage as "phenomena in a group's past that are given high symbolic value and therefore, must be protected for the future" (Klein 2000, 25). Building on
this notion in his discussion of the Ulen Museum in Minnesota, Marcus Cederström further adds that "heritage is created by community members through their interpretation
of history, memory, and lived experiences and can tell us what a community values, what a
community hopes to preserve, and how a community hopes to present itself to the future"
(2018, 396). The work being done at the OCHC both protects elements of the community's past and creates the space for community members to meet and actively shape the
ways their community will be remembered by future generations. While there was an
ethnic focus in the selection of buildings to be housed at Old World Wisconsin and in
many other community-level preservation projects of the time, the work being done to
develop the Heritage Center in Oulu today is moving past that ethnic focus to focus on the
locality, creating a cultural center with a mission to preserve the history, traditions, and
natural resources of the area.

Old World Wisconsin's Beginnings

From the start, Old World Wisconsin differed from the leagues of other open-air museums
created in the United States such as Greenfield Village, Colonial Williamsburg, Mount
Vernon, and Monticello—sites that were built around some of the most important places
in an emerging "nation-building" narrative. Old World Wisconsin instead focused on the
vernacular architecture that had been constructed throughout the state by the different
early immigrant groups that colonized Wisconsin. Described as "one of the most magnifi-
cently planned of the American outdoor museums," Old World Wisconsin was a formida-
ble undertaking carried out by a public–private collaboration between individuals at the
Wisconsin Historical Society, the University of Wisconsin, and many communities across
the state (Rentzhog 2007, 269).

    The idea for the project was conceived by the Milwaukee architect and preservationist
Richard W. E. Perrin, who had witnessed the "continuing deterioration and destruction of
the vernacular ethnic architecture of the nineteenth-century immigrants" by the start of
the 1930s and was agitated enough by it to bring his concerns to the Wisconsin State Historical Society (Krugler 2013, 5). He pitched the idea for Wisconsin's own open-air mu-

seum to the Historical Society; it would be organized by different ethnicities because of the diverse background of the immigrants who colonized the state during its early years and offered a useful categorization system for material culture. The site would preserve those old buildings that remained "in which they lived, worked, worshiped, and carried on their other activities of daily life" as tribute to these early immigrants (Rentzhog 2007, 6). Old World Wisconsin was also the first museum to explicitly focus on the multicultural heritage of an area and to organize itself around that principle. It is worth noting that while Old World Wisconsin was created to celebrate heritage-making, it focused on immigrants involved in the state's colonization rather than on the Indigenous population that was already living there and on the agricultural experience rather than the state's already urban-dwelling populations in the late nineteenth century. Thus, while these efforts to focus on the state's multicultural heritage were steps in the direction of inclusion, they fell short of equity.

A team of university personnel and researchers, State Historical Society officials, and both local and nonlocal contractors came together to create Old World Wisconsin. They sought and relocated buildings around Wisconsin to create a six-hundred-acre site reflective of Wisconsin's settlement history. Due to financial difficulties and other constraints, the original plans had to be scaled back, but the final site still had ten complete farms (Norwegian, Danish, Finnish, Polish, German, and "Yankee"), as well as Bohemian, Irish, and English settlement buildings in the town environment (Rentzhog 2007, 272). The Finnish settlement in particular was an example of the collaboration between public and private not only in the identification and relocation of the buildings to create the settlement but also in the relationship sustained between both parties after the fact.

COMMUNITY AND PRESERVATION

The Finnish settlement at Old World Wisconsin consists mostly of buildings relocated from in and around the town of Oulu, Wisconsin, located just north of Highway 2 in Bayfield County. The Finns were one of many immigrant groups to settle Wisconsin's Cutover during the turn of the twentieth century because of the land that was made available as a result of the Homestead Act of 1862 and other legislation. Oulu became a township in 1904 and is one of several towns in northern Wisconsin that was founded largely by immigrants. From the start it was a mostly Finnish community, with nearly a third of the population monolingual Finnish speakers in 1910 (Bureau of the Census 1910). One of these early settlers was John Pudas, originally from Kittilä, Finland, who had a life trajectory similar to that of many other Finnish immigrants to America. He first moved to Minnesota with his wife and young son before relocating to Ironwood, Michigan, to work in the mines. From there he moved his family to a farm in Oulu and built a house that would serve as a church and meeting place until other structures could be built (Pudas 1977).

From 1900 to 1920 there was rapid growth in the region as farming was encouraged and many immigrants moved to settle the area. This rate of growth rapidly decelerated from 1930 to 1940, in part because of the agricultural depression of the 1920s and zoning laws passed by Wisconsin legislation in the 1930s that discouraged farming and strove to encourage tourism and restore the importance of forestry in the region (Gough 1997, 115–49,

195–200). Greater ease of travel and lack of jobs in the community meant that more and more residents were leaving Oulu in search of work. Duane Lahti, a lifelong resident of Oulu, graduated from high school as these shifts were happening: "As the small farms were disappearing here, some of them were still trying to stay active, [but] their kids had moved on. They got out of high school, and it was pretty much an exodus the minute you got out of high school here, you left. To go on to school and then find employment because there was not much here other than manual labor work" (2018).

As fewer people lived in the community, many of the local stores were forced to close over the next few decades, with the Oulu branch of the co-op store closing in 1984 and Harry's Corner Store (the last store in Oulu) closing in 1991 (Krueger 2004). It was during this shift, as young people were leaving the community and the older generation was passing away, that buildings were abandoned. This was not exclusive to Oulu but rather happened in communities across the state and inspired people like Richard Perrin to find a way to salvage the structures and record of the state's diverse vernacular architecture.

Developers from Old World Wisconsin enlisted the help of an Oulu local, Ed Pudas, the youngest son of the early Oulu settler John Pudas, in selecting buildings for the museum's Finnish settlement. Ed was a skilled carpenter and log builder, having worked on the farm at home as well as in the woods and at logging camps. He was also an active member of the community, co-organizing the Gitchee Gumee 4-H club with his siblings Saima and Eli in 1949 (Krueger 2004, 31). Ed wrote about assisting with Old World Wisconsin in his memoir, written a year after the site opened:

We dismantled enough houses and barns from my hometown area to set up two farmsteads there. The Finnish exhibit is now pretty well completed. When I went there to help put up the buildings, we had dismantled and hauled out there, I honed up my broad axes to shape some logs that we needed for replacing the bad ones. Some of the boys there had never seen a broad axe used and were leery about trying. But our boss on the job, Alan Pape, himself had a natural knack for hewing logs with the broad axe. He is a young, strong man well suited to handle a broad axe. I guess he does the hewing work there yet unless he has by this time trained some young man to be a broad axe man. I did not do much hewing. I am too old for that kind of work. (Pudas 1977, sec. 12)

This excerpt underscores the valuable expertise Ed was able to share in his retirement, as well as the fact that those working in the construction and relocation of the buildings were learning by doing, as was the case in many aspects of the Old World Wisconsin project (Krugler 2013, 8). After the relocation was completed, Ed continued collaborating with the university by giving lessons on log building to other college classes and discussing the history of logging in the area and the unique qualities of Finnish log construction, such as dovetail corner joints. This speaks to the strength of the connection cultivated between Ed, the university, and Old World Wisconsin. Ed's legacy also continued with the Oulu Logbuilders, a home-building contractor based in Oulu that was established in 1970 by Ed Pudas and his son Harry Pudas. Today, the fourth generation of log builders that began

The reconstructed Rankinen House at Old World Wisconsin. (Photograph by author.)

with Ed has been contracted to do work as far afield as the New York Catskills. Ed's work is further referenced in several of the town's local history pamphlets, showing that Ed was well respected and valued for his contributions to the project and for the fact that Oulu's history was being preserved at Old World Wisconsin.

Once the buildings were moved and reconstructed, Old World Wisconsin filled them with furniture and other household objects typically found in an early 1900s farmstead. In this way it re-created both the interior and the exterior setting of the buildings, just as the landscape was sculpted to resemble the building's original location. While there are reenactors today at one of Old World Wisconsin's Finnish settlements, for the most part this material culture is being preserved as a snapshot from the past, frozen in time to look as it would have back then if the family had left their property for the day.

This preservation of vernacular architecture and local buildings was not a new notion in Wisconsin. There had been small-scale projects across the state over the years, including the restoration of log farm structures near Mount Horeb and the restoration and reconstruction of Welsh mining structures in Mineral Point in the 1930s (Krugler 2013, 17). Old World Wisconsin, however, was the first operation to relocate significant structures around the state to one location on such a large scale. Since its completion, in 1976, there have been other projects to relocate and preserve ethnic vernacular architecture. One such project, Little Finland, got its start in 1964 after a collaboration similar to that between Old World Wisconsin, community members, and professors and students from the University of

Wisconsin; participants collected items of Finnish American material culture and set up a display of a Finnish American house, which later became a permanent fixture after a complex was constructed for it in Hurley (Little Finland n.d.).

Some thirty years after Ed Pudas's involvement with the construction of Old World Wisconsin, Oulu is again at the center of efforts to preserve the vernacular architecture of the Finnish settlers. However, this time it is about more than just the preservation of buildings, and the focus is not just on Finnish architecture and ethnic history. Rather, there is a community-initiated endeavor both to preserve buildings and material culture locally and to create a gathering place for a community where members can continue creating and celebrating their heritage.

Preserving Oulu's Cultural Landscape

By all accounts, the cultural landscape of Oulu changed dramatically during the last third of the twentieth century. Duane Lahti recounts, "When I was growing up, every one of these one-mile roads had six farms on them. Every forty acres had a farmstead. And they were pretty much all gone" (Lahti 2018). After finishing college and moving back to Oulu, Duane worked in construction and then for the Wisconsin Department of Natural Resources for thirty years as a field biologist and water program supervisor in the Lake Superior Basin. Duane would regularly pass by the Palo Homestead, a property that has been in his family for more than a hundred years: "We used to come and walk by here every day, and I couldn't stand to see the place sitting the way it was" (Lahti 2018).

In the fall of 1997, Duane's aunt suggested that Duane buy the remaining five acres of the property, including the old house and outbuildings, which had been sitting vacant for twenty-six years, since Duane's grandmother had passed away. Duane and his family went to look at the property, thought it could be saved, and decided to buy it. His aunt had told him he could bulldoze the buildings, and Duane replied, "Are you kidding? That's why I'm buying this thing, to restore it" (Lahti 2018).

The family contacted the Wisconsin State Historical Society, asking officials to come up to see whether the restoration project would merit a spot on the State and National Registers of Historic Places. After a visit, officials agreed that it did, given that the house is a valuable remnant of Finnish vernacular architecture. Duane had learned some of his carpentry skills by working in the construction industry, around the farm at home, and in logging camps: "Nobody ever formally taught us how to run a chainsaw or anything, we learned by working" (Lahti and Lahti 2018). He put these skills to use in his work on the buildings, alongside his wife, Barbara, and sons, Steven and Duane Jr. They stripped the walls, repaired the foundation, ran electricity, drilled a new well, put a new roof on, and converted a closet into a bathroom, among other fixes, creating a house that can be lived in comfortably today. They left the logs exposed inside the house to show the full dovetailed corner notch joints. The buildings include objects that were found in the home back in its early days, as well as more modern features such as a microwave and ceiling fans. The sauna/woodshed/shop building and wellhouse were also restored, complete with hand-sawn cedar shingles on the roofs. The property was listed in the National and Wisconsin State Registers of Historic Places on September 12, 2002.

Palo House kitchen in use during the Oulu Cultural and Heritage Center's summer school. (Photograph by author.)

The homestead is by no means frozen in time. The homestead's main house, the Palo House, is very much in use and is sometimes lived in, making it an active hub at the Oulu Cultural and Heritage Center for hosting festivals and for the annual three weeks of day camp–style summer school. It has regular opening hours. Along with colleagues, I have spent several nights in it quite comfortably, and the kitchen is regularly used during the Center's summer school program.

After the building was finished and listed, Oulu celebrated its centennial, in 2004, and the Oulu Historical Society (est. 2003) organized tours of the community, with the Palo Homestead as one of the stops. The Oulu Historical Society was holding its meetings in the restored Palo House, but the house was a bit cramped, and Duane figured the Society could use some more space. It looked into acquiring Barb's great-grandparents' place, the circa 1899 Pudas homestead house. The building was originally built by John Pudas, the father of Ed Pudas, and had been sitting vacant for years in a deteriorated condition. Duane contacted Harry Pudas, Ed's son, who donated the building and worked with the Lahtis and the rest of the Oulu Logbuilders to restore it. After restoring some of the logs, they acquired necessary replacement logs from the Pudas property. Now that it is completed, it is arguably one of the largest and best-preserved examples of Finnish log construction in the United States.

As people heard about the project, Duane was contacted about various buildings that might be of interest. Ultimately, the OCHC grew to include the Northern Co-op building,

The completed Pudas House during the Oulu Cultural and Heritage Center's 2017 Fall Fest.
(Photograph by author.)

the Pedersen Chicken coop, the Fairview schoolhouse, the Bjorni-Korhonen savusauna, the
Saaski millhouse, and the John Aho house, all in addition to the Palo Homestead. These
buildings were all acquired from within and around Oulu and have been brought together
to create an outdoor museum of Oulu-area history, or an "Up North Old World Wisconsin," as Duane jokes. But it isn't just an outdoor museum. Most of the buildings are
connected to a local family and have been donated by that family, often with the family
name included on the identifying plaque. Personal connections are also seen with the
items of material culture that have been donated, such as a loom that was repeatedly disassembled and reassembled as it was transported around the community, tools representative of the early farming and logging in the area, and other items ranging from stoves and
chests to dresses and toys.

Duane comments that after the local elementary school closed in the 1990s, the community "didn't have a gathering place anymore," which, coupled with the exodus of young
people from the area, made it harder to maintain a sense of community (Lahti 2018).
Duane says the OCHC has "become kind of our gathering place now," showing that its
role in the community is far greater than just serving as a museum preserving the region's
vernacular architecture (Lahti 2018). Rather, it very much highlights OCHC's role in
strengthening personal connections among people, objects, and buildings, creating the
space for visitors to engage with history and connections and to create new memories and
stories. Importantly, the Center is not trying to preserve the community festivals and tradi-

tions the way they were but rather is open to adaptation, change, and the creation of new traditions. The OCHC is preserving not only buildings and material culture but also the natural environment of the Oulu area; an example is the development of a wetland restoration project in the summer of 2019 in cooperation with the Bayfield County Land and Water Conservation Department, the Natural Resources Conservation Service, and the US Fish and Wildlife Service (Wisconsin Natural Resources Conservation Service 2019).

The OCHC has collaborated with numerous groups, from local contractors and the local school district, to state and regional historical societies, to researchers at the University of Wisconsin–Madison. In consultation with the OCHC, for example, I created a short film about the history and mission of the Center, focusing on aspects the Center believed important to include and share about its creation and Oulu's history. The film is currently on the OCHC website and on Oulu's page of the Bayfield County Historical Society's website, serving as a documentary and advertisement for the Center. I continue to visit Oulu regularly to conduct linguistic and ethnographic fieldwork, and, alongside others from UW–Madison past and present, we continue to collaborate on grant applications and serve the Center's volunteers. Recently, we assisted Duane and Steven Lahti in securing an American Scandinavian Foundation folk arts apprenticeship to support the transmission of traditional Finnish American log building techniques and restoration of the John Aho House. As part of the grant, we tracked their restoration work and created an exhibit for the OCHC that documented the process.

Collaboration Creates Community

I moved to Wisconsin from the East Coast in 2014, having been raised in northern Virginia as a heritage speaker of Finnish. In discussing how the OCHC is creating community, it is important to acknowledge the role that community plays in my own collaboration. From my first visit, I felt a sense of connection to this community and the individuals I met. Part of it may be that I had had few experiences speaking with others who had also learned Finnish at home rather than through schooling of some kind. So, while I was very much an outsider to this community (new to Wisconsin, Finnish America, rural communities, and the Upper Midwest), I still felt a level of familiarity with the stories they told and the values they shared with me.

After my first couple of trips to conduct linguistic interviews, I asked if I could help with their summer school sessions—in part to thank them for being generous with their time and assistance. They asked me to teach Finnish, and I became one of numerous guest speakers brought to the summer school each year, allowing for a varied curriculum. Since that first summer, in addition to teaching short Finnish lessons, I have also assisted with crafts (ranging from baking Nordic recipes to painting dioramas to making flower crowns) and supervised outdoor games (including kubb, cornhole, and a variation of capture-the-flag that students created during the summer school's first session: farmers and loggers). I prioritize serving the OCHC in whatever ways are most helpful to the organization. Sometimes doing so positions me behind a camera, conducting interviews. Other times I am in front of the classroom teaching Finnish vocabulary. Still other days I am outside supervising and ensuring that games are running smoothly. And sometimes I am writing about the work being done in Oulu that I am fortunate enough to play a part in, because the collaborative work that we do creating public programming cannot be separated from the analytical work that we do, examining how and why public work matters in various contexts and its impact on everyone involved.

In writing this chapter to include more about my own role in this collaboration, I was resistant to centering myself in what I see as a piece intended to share the work and mission of the OCHC. But I would be leaving out a key layer of what it means to create community and do public culture work if I did not reflect on my own place in it all. It comes down to the fact that collaborating with the OCHC has changed me. It has helped me grow as a researcher and decide to become a folklorist, and it has challenged my understanding of my own heritage and what it means to maintain a culture. My first visit to Oulu to conduct interviews came during my first year of graduate school, a time when I was grappling with those all-too-common whispers of imposter syndrome. My return trips to conduct more interviews gave me a stronger sense of purpose and confidence. When I asked to help with the summer school, the request truly grew out of a desire to give back to the OCHC just a little bit of what it had helped me find. In a thank-you card from that first summer school visit, one community member wrote, "You belong to us now, too." That sentence captures how I view my role in this collaboration: as someone responsible for supporting this community whose members have shared so much of themselves and opened their Center as a place where I can also belong. Since that first trip, I and others from UW–Madison have worked with the OCHC to support its programming and restoration work, collaborating on grants and other efforts to support the summer school and the mission of the Center as a whole. The development of my own research has been shaped by my experiences and conversations with volunteers at the OCHC, and, in turn, I aim to create both academic and public-facing products that support and further the efforts of the OCHC's board and numerous volunteers.

CONCLUSION

Creating and maintaining community is necessarily tied to understanding the connections between a community's past, present, and future. This chapter examines Oulu's complex relationship with Old World Wisconsin and contrasts it with the creation of the Oulu Cultural and Heritage Center. Oulu's and Ed Pudas's relationship with Old World Wisconsin served as a kind of foreshadowing for the work being done today. Those who created Old World Wisconsin reached out for both expertise and physical structures from the Oulu community. More than three decades later, the sons and grandsons of those whose expertise was sought are assisting the OCHC's many volunteers in relocating and restoring examples of vernacular architecture more locally. Thus, the Center can be seen as the following generation's local approach to preserving and presenting heritage publicly while building new collaborations and a space for the community to come together. Previously the buildings were being removed from the community, while now the community is working to restore and preserve them locally, creating a site that is very much alive and continuing to change rather than focusing on creating a snapshot from the past as Old World Wisconsin has done. The Center is continuing to grow and is creating a space where the community can come together and celebrate its local heritage. The community is both aware and proud that

Oulu is a part of the Finnish exhibits at Old World Wisconsin, but this was not an explicit motivation for the creation of the OCHC.

It is not unusual for a Wisconsin community to work to preserve its vernacular architecture, especially those communities that have a tie to an ethnic heritage. What is unusual is for that preservation effort to include the relocation and restoration of more than six major structures to create an open-air museum that also serves as an active community center with regular programming designed to celebrate local culture. Cooperative collaborations have been key in the development of the Oulu Cultural and Heritage Center and are creating a space for the continued celebration of an Oulu heritage. The Center is part of a continuous and reciprocal process of co-creation and identity negotiation in dialogue with a network of collaborators: Old World Wisconsin in the past and researchers (like myself) at the University of Wisconsin–Madison today. This dynamic process speaks to how heritage, identity, and community are constantly being created and re-created in dialogue with connections past and present at the Oulu Cultural and Heritage Center.

"A Growing Art"

Traditional Arts and Heritage Rediscovery in Northern Minnesota Scandinavian Communities

SALLIE ANNA STEINER

In 2017, I undertook a contracted fieldwork project in the Lake Superior and Iron Range regions of Northern Minnesota for the Center for the Study of Upper Midwestern Cultures and the Minnesota Arts Board, part of the first round of fieldwork sponsored by the University of Wisconsin–Madison's Sustaining Scandinavian Folk Arts in the Upper Midwest project. My fieldwork brought me into conversation with a diverse array of Finnish, Sámi, Norwegian, Swedish, and Danish American people as I sought to shed more light on the stories and creative expressions of this region. My work with these descendants of Scandinavian immigrants who came to northern Minnesota in the nineteenth and early twentieth centuries led me to consider how crafting is a physical expressive form through which people celebrate, remember, reflect on, and even discover their heritage and identity. In these regards, the simple practice of traditional arts can be transformative to individuals and communities alike, in particular as they strive to retain and reclaim community-based identities.

The people who feature in this fieldwork represent mainly the third and fourth generations of the Nordic diaspora in the Upper Midwest. Some of the people I worked with perform crafts that they learned as children and practiced as part of subsistence lifestyles, like Deb Wiitanen, a third-generation Finnish American homesteader who lived without running water or electricity into the 1990s in rural Embarrass, Minnesota. For Wiitanen, crafts like weaving and felting were part of her family's survival on the Iron Range in northern Minnesota. Her skills are uniquely tailored to the Finnish immigrant experience in that area: rooted in Finnish craft traditions like felting and weaving but filling the needs of northern Minnesota miners, homesteaders, and their descendants, using materials from the local environment. Wiitanen makes a variety of things, including rag rugs, birch bark ornaments, and felted boot liners, and runs a small shop and craft school out of her home. She has also worked for many years as a reenactor at the Minnesota Discovery Center, where she is paid to practice the crafts she grew up with for an audience of learners and tourists. Wiitanen's craft practice straddles the process of transformation from immigrant to ethnic folklore outlined by Robert Klymasz: "content, form, and context are inextricably integrated with one another" such that the craft is deeply enmeshed in Deb Wiitanen's everyday life, and yet there is "a deeper and widened gap between the active, individual performer(s) and the passive spectator or audience" (Klymasz 1973, 136) and a growing objectification seen through the gaze of onlookers such as myself who notice with intrigue this growing divide between traditional customs and cycles and the realities of industrialized, urbanized, and capitalized life. But Deb continues to find a niche for herself and a profitable use for her skills, just as her immigrant grandmothers did when they arrived on the Iron Range and began crafting for their new lives.

The majority of the people I documented in my fieldwork, however, fit more comfortably into Klymasz's (1973) "ethnic folklore" category, in which folk art is practiced in nontraditional contexts that are less framed by traditional milieus and calendric cycles. While the people I worked with had often grown up surrounded by traditional arts, their own Scandinavian craft practices often began in adulthood as a means to understand and reflect on the cultures of their forbearers. Many of the people I profile here have lifelong interests and even professional careers in arts and crafts, which fills their need for reflection on self and place. The Norwegian phenomenologist and craft scholar Mikkel Tin (2013) argues that crafting literally "makes sense" and that "making may be seen as a study, an inquiry, in its own right" that "generates a specific knowledge" and "articulates a meaning that can only partly be conceptualized" (1, 4). The craft practices of the artisans I discuss constitute a practical and bodily inquiry into heritage, which Barbara Kirshenblatt-Gimblett (1995) defines as "a new mode of cultural production in the present that has recourse to the past" (369). The craft practices of these artisans are thus heritage practices undertaken through folk reflexivity—a pondering of traditional arts and the self in light of past heritage and contemporary situation (Steiner 2016, 83)—and form an entry point for personal discovery, community creation, and identity maintenance.

NORTH SHORE SÁMI: RECOVERING HERITAGE

For the artisans I worked with, craft offers a tangible site for the discovery and re-creation of ethnic identity. Taking ownership of ethnic identity in this very hands-on way is a powerful mode of maintaining, remembering, and reestablishing connections to ancestors that have been fractured and complicated by immigration experiences and Americanization. While all the people I worked with voiced a desire to connect with ancestors, the past, and their Scandinavian ethnic identity through craft, for the Sámi American people who featured in my study, performing Sámi handwork was an act of reclamation through which they sought to remember a heritage that their immigrant ancestors had been forced to forget (Jensen 2012). Like nearly all Indigenous groups in their various homelands around the world, Sámi people have faced great hardship and discrimination in the Nordic states and Russia, where they have been denied cultural, linguistic, political, and geographic self-determination and preservation by nation-states and their agents, who represent other ethnic and linguistic groups that dominate the systems of power there (Lehtola 2004, 9–16, 57–91). The prejudices that undergird these hierarchies also migrated with immigrants to Scandinavian American settlements (Jensen and Frandy 2021). Many Sámi people thus sought to escape persecution by actively hiding their roots in the New World or by strategically applying the bureaucratic identity transformations read onto them by American immigration authorities, who sorted people largely on the basis of national origin rather than ethnic identity (DuBois 2019, 56–60).

Many of the Sámi people I worked with during my project had grown up with little concept of or conscious connection to their Sámi heritage, which may have been whispered or joked about among the elders of their families but which was largely hidden and forgotten. People in the Lake Superior–area Sámi community have had to rediscover and re-create a Sámi identity and community for themselves, now two or three generations removed from their immigrant ancestors. The Duluth-based crafter Laurel Sanders told me about her own unfolding discovery of her Sámi roots, which began in earnest after Laurel attended a workshop at the Sami Cultural Center of North America in Duluth:

> My dad had been going through some paperwork and he had some letters from some of his great-aunts that said, "Oh, we went, we traded some fish for reindeer hides, you know, with the cousins, you know, we went over the hills"—so anyways, these letters were really interesting. . . . And then I went to a family reunion, and my cousin had a picture of my great-great-grandma Kersti, and she's in a *gákti* [Sámi traditional dress]. And I went, "What's that?" And she goes—her dad had been the genealogist in the family before my cousin Dorothy— she said, "Oh, dad said we're part Laplander." So that's how I found out.
>
> We're what they call South Sámi—it's the southern part of Norway. . . . The thing with the South Sámi was—they weren't as much reindeer herders, they were farmers and fishers, and so their lifestyle was very similar to the Scandinavians who moved in, so they intermarried and assimilated quite early and easily. . . . So they had assimilated, and then you know, the whole story of, um, passing, you know, when you came here to this country, passing as Norwegian, and all that stuff.
>
> [Sallie: So, growing up, you weren't as much aware of your Sámi background?]
>
> Not at all, no.
>
> [Sallie: It was something you discovered?]
>
> Yeah, it was something that I discovered, about ten, fifteen years ago. I always thought we were Norwegian. It's a very common story. (Sanders 2017)

While Laurel's family roots are in Minnesota, she herself grew up in the Pacific Northwest, where she was good friends with some neighbor children from a Walla Walla Native American family. When she returned to Minnesota, she met and married an Anishinaabe man and lived and raised her children on the Fond du Lac Reservation. In our interview, Laurel drew connections between her lifelong affinity for Native American people and her Sámi heritage. While she was not consciously aware of her Sámi background for most of her life, she expressed to me that her sense of that background went deeper than names and lines printed on a family tree. For her, finding out that she was Sámi was a confirmation of things she had felt her whole life. Laurel told the following joke to express this intangible Sámi sense of the world: "The joke is, 'You might be Sámi if—' Have you heard any of these? You might be Sámi if—every twenty minutes you just *have* to go outside. You just cannot sit inside, and you just have to go outside after twenty minutes being indoors" (Sanders 2017).

Laurel Sanders with some of her craft supplies and finished pieces, including a papoose she made for her grandchild featuring Sámi woven bands and Anishinaabe beading. (Photograph by author.)

Laurel said that in learning about her Sámi heritage, she has really connected with *du-odji*, which is the Sámi term for handcrafts but which for Laurel also refers more conceptually to the idea of making useful, functional things beautiful. "That just made so much sense to me," said Laurel, a lifelong crafter and dabbler in various artistic media. These ideas also resonated with her life on the Fond du Lac Reservation, where Laurel learned to bead, weave, and sew in the Anishinaabe tradition and made powwow costumes for her children. After learning various Sámi traditional arts such as bandweaving, fingerweaving, and pewter thread braiding through self-study and from classes at the Sami Cultural Center in Duluth, Laurel now blends Anishinaabe and Sámi crafts to create unique pieces that express the diverse Indigenous heritage of her family.

Cross-cultural Indigenous connections between Sámi and American Indian people arose again in my conversations with Pam Capin (pron.: *sah-pin*), from Eveleth, Minnesota, who makes and decorates drums and other objects in the Sámi tradition. Pam's own background is Finnish and Croatian, a common creole up in the mining region of Northern Minnesota where Pam lives. Pam grew up being told somewhat ambiguously that she was "Indigenous Finn" and recalls her mother making a distinction between the light-complexioned "Swedish Finns" and the "dark Finns" who made up Pam's own family.

Pam became interested in drums after meeting Mel Mattson, a Finnish-Sámi man who grew up trapping animals and tanning hides in the woods near his home in Palo, Minnesota, where he was known as "Trapper Jack." Throughout his life, Mel worked in collaboration

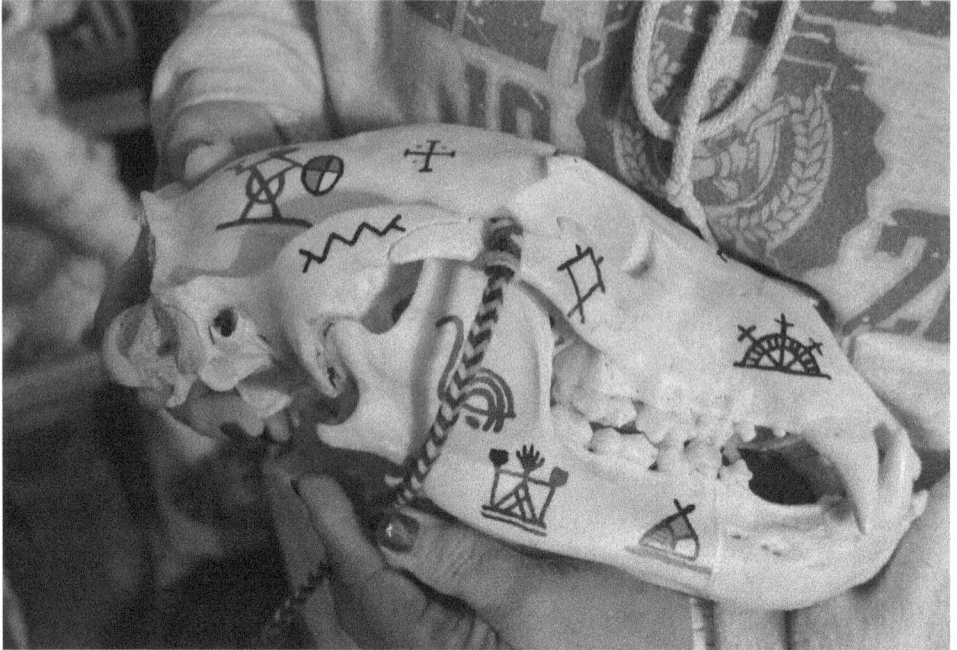

An animal skull painted by Pam Capin. Biegga-Olmmái is visible on the bottom jaw of the skull, holding two shovels or oars, used to shovel up the winds from their domain. Pam uses the symbol of Biegga-Olmmái to represent her friend and mentor Mel Mattson. (Photograph by author.)

with Anishinaabe drum and canoe makers in the local area. He valued the cultures of the Indigenous people of Minnesota and attended drum ceremonies held by his Anishinaabe neighbors. Unfortunately, Mel had suffered several strokes and was not in good enough health to talk with me personally during this fieldwork, and he later passed away in December 2020. However, Mel had taken Pam on as an informal apprentice, and they worked closely together for many years, with Mel constructing the drums and Pam painting them with Sámi motifs and symbols. Mel's traditions, skills, and stories live on in Pam.

In her decorative art, Pam uses Sámi symbols in tandem with one another to create unique personal narratives on the drums and other items she adorns. Pam finds symbols by looking at examples of Sámi sacred items online and mimics their form and composition, but she also adds her own creative interpretation as she uses her craft to meditate and connect spiritually with the objects in her care. Pam often borrows and improvises traditional symbols in unorthodox ways to represent facets of her own life and influences. For example, Pam uses the figure of Biegga-Olmmái (the Wind Man) to represent Mel. By using this symbol on her creations, Pam keeps Mel's spirit with her when she paints.

Drums have a deep spiritual significance in Sámi culture. While emerging outside the bounds of initiated shamanic practices in Sápmi (the Sámi homeland region), Pam and Mel's use of drums is a genuine personal reflection, a way of mediating between and growing closer to themselves, their heritages, and their environment. Pam told me that Mel often practiced drum spirituality by retreating into the woods to play his drums and sing in nature, harkening to the Anishinaabe belief that drums speak to the bearer because they are alive, and thus the bearer needs to go into the woods to listen. Though these practices might at first appear to resemble solitary and individualistic practice, they figure into broader notions of community. These experiences are encouraged in the community; they are interpreted in the community; and they create significant systems of interpretation and relationality for the community through communing with nature.

Legends that circulate around the power of the drum are told in ways that both place value within these traditional mores and help define different subcommunities of neotraditionalists and heritage participants. Pam said she believes that the drums she and Mel made have some kind of power, and she reflected upon how this craft practice has influenced her personal spiritual journey:

> [Drums in Sápmi] are more religious than musical.
> [Sallie: And how is that for you? Is that a part of it for you?]
> Yeah. It is. Since my mother died, I haven't been to church a lot. I used to go to church every so often, not all the time. But since my mother died, I think I've been to church two or three times. More because of the drum making and looking back into that religion. They called it pagan religion, and it is sort of, but it's more nature-based than anything . . . and I like nature. And animals [*Pam gestures to the large collection of stuffed animal moose, bears, and reindeer around her home*]. That's what their religion was based on. And Mel too.
> Mel used to come over every couple weeks on Saturday or Sunday. We were talking about religion and growing up Lutheran. And he looked at me square in the eye and he said, "I'm not a Christian." And I was kind of shocked! 'Cause he used to teach Sunday school and everything, and he said, "I'm not a Christian." He said since he started making the drums and looking into the Sámi religion and culture, he said, "I'm not a Christian anymore." And I started thinking about that as it applied to me, and I started thinking, "I don't know, I'm somewhere in between." I'm sort of both ways. I'm still a member of the Lutheran church, but—I haven't been there in a while. (Capin 2017)

The drums she and Mel worked on took on a powerful presence in Pam's life that transcended simply ethnic identity. Though she admitted she does not fully understand the objects and their power, Pam told of a time she felt a drum manifest its presence:

> Mel used to [take the drums out into nature to play them]. He'd come here, and every new drum he had to try out, so as I was painting the drums, he'd try 'em out. And he'd play different rhythms and then he would say, "This is for so-and-so." And he was drumming, and he said, "This is for your father." And I said, "Mel, my dad died in 1989." And he said, "This is for your father." And I go, "Okay."
> So he's playing this drum, and I was listening to him. About an hour later, the bank called. And I had a loan on the house at the time: I had redone the roof. And they said, "This house isn't yours." And I said, "What do you mean? It's in my name." She said, "No," she said, "Your father never transferred the house to your mother." Because my mother had transferred it to me. She said, "The paperwork was never done, so really the house isn't yours." I said, "My

father's been dead for how many years!" She said, "Nope, we're going to have to redo the whole thing."

So I called Mel and I said, "Mel, please do not drum anymore for my father. You summoned him up!" [*Laughter*] But maybe it was a good thing, because they had to redo the title search and everything was done properly that time. So that might have been a good thing. But that really—I don't know if it freaked me out, but I'm thinking—maybe he's got something here. (Capin 2017)

Pam's spiritual understanding is much like her craft practice: she feels empowered to blend and borrow traditions, creating something that is deep, real, personal, and unique to herself. She does not feel the need to completely understand the forces at work in the Sámi spirituality and craft practices she explores, and she is open and humble about gaps in her knowledge at the same time that she is genuine in her use of these traditions for reflection upon her own ethnic and spiritual identities. Pam thus expresses a "cultural hybridity which exists alongside a disruption or discontinuity" in her performance of Sámi American identity (Jensen 2012, 49). Pam continues the tradition, now passing on what she has learned about Sámi crafts, spirituality, and stories to her two young nieces so that they too will remember this heritage and bring it forward into the future.

SOMETHING OLD, SOMETHING NEW: SCANDINAVIAN HERITAGE REDISCOVERY IN THE AMERICAN CONTEXT

The work of the Swedish American silversmith Brad Nelson from Two Harbors, Minnesota, clearly portrays his cultural pluralism, rooted in his deep respect for and reflection on his own ethnic background and the history of his people. Keeping traditions alive is important to Brad, and he sees himself as a part of carrying immigrant heritage forward and forging American identity:

> I think you have to decide if you want to carry something on or just let it fall away, and because it was always something special for me, I wanted to see it continue. And I feel that way about all different ethnicities: you know, the Native Americans, the Germans and the Poles, and the Dutch. It was kind of fascinating how people came here and settled in their little pockets and kept an assemblance of their former life. And then a generation—my mom and dad's generation came along, and then it was, "We're American." And the language stops. And, you know, some of the traditions and the foods still live on. But it's interesting, the process of becoming American. What do you keep and what do you get rid of? (Nelson 2017)

Brad draws heavily upon Swedish, Norwegian, and Danish styles, techniques, and motifs in his jewelry making. But he also blends a variety of other ethnic styles into his work. He draws heavily from Sámi folk arts, for instance, and has been embraced by members of his local Sámi community. In my visits to Sámi Americans in the area, I often saw them wearing jewelry by Brad that was inspired by Sámi pewter thread braiding, for example. Brad sees himself as partnering with this community to create pieces that meld his own aesthetics with Sámi material culture.

When I started going to Scandinavian shows, the Sámi people were always there. And at that time, they were sort of rediscovering who they are—many people who've come to the United States who were Sámi kind of hid that. But there were always Sámi people coming to these different events. And they would start to buy my jewelry because of the reindeer motif or because of some of the things that spoke to them. And so I kind of became adopted by that group. And I absolutely love the artwork—the bowls, the carvings, the engraving in the antler, the scrimshaw. And then the jewelry of course. So I've been playing with a lot of Sámi-inspired things. Originally in Scandinavia, as I understand it, a lot of the Sámi people themselves were not jewelers. They had Norwegian and Scandinavian artists make jewelry for them to their taste. So maybe I'm one of those people that now makes something for the Sámi taste— though I'm not Sámi myself. And I try not to just make something, you know, *exactly* [in a Sámi way], because I'm not Sámi. I don't claim to make anything Sámi, but it's inspired by things, and it seems to be appreciated and enjoyed by people, so I'm glad for that acceptance. (Nelson 2017)

Like Pam and Laurel, Brad also displays in his craft practice a "double consciousness" in which cultural continuity can be expressed alongside disruption and discontinuity (Jensen 2012, 49). Brad's jewelry and metalwork are made richer by the fact that he uses these mediums to navigate across cultures and time periods, and it is precisely this borrowing that allows him to resurrect old Sámi–Swedish craft relations in the American context. Brad's thoughts on his craft practice harken to a powerful quote from the Sámi American Indian artist David Lawrence Klein Sr., who stated to the ethnographer Ellen Marie Jensen: "I'm Sámi, Cheyenne and Cree Indian, Finnish and French and 100 percent of all of them" (Jensen 2012, 53). If Brad's pendants and brooches could talk, they might have something similar to say.

Brad's adoption of diverse folk art styles is not limited to the arts of Scandinavia. While I was visiting him, he also showed me some buttons he has started to make using heart-shaped jewelry molds he got from India. Brad said the molds reminded him of the heart motifs common in Danish folk art and also of the elephant's foot motif from Hmong *paj ntaub*, an embroidery- and applique-based textile tradition brought to Minnesota and Wisconsin when Hmong people were resettled there as refugees following the Vietnam War. Additionally, he told me about his longtime involvement with Viking reenactment groups in Sweden and showed me a number of reproductions he has created of Viking-era art in metal, stone, and bone. Brad expressed admiration for the world traveling and exploration of the Vikings and noted that at no time in history have people and their cultures ever really stood still: "We are a blending of people from all around the world, in America. Even in the Middle Ages we were too. In Europe, you know. People moved in the migration period, and the Vikings going out and bringing different ideas back, different styles of art, you know—so I don't know if anything ever really belongs to just one group or another group. I think it's all kind of traded around and stirred up and then added more to it, and it's kind of a growing art" (Nelson 2017).

In addition to being inspired by his own ethnic background and those of his neighbors, Brad is also influenced by the land- and waterscape of the Lakeshore region. With his

A Sámi-style *komsekule* by Brad Nelson. This traditional pendant features a Sámi motif at the top, crafted using a pewter thread technique. Lake Superior basalt stones gathered from the beach across the street from Brad's workshop hang from the piece, in addition to the silver hangs that typically adorn *komsekule* pendants in Sápmi. These details give the piece a distinct sense of emerging from a Sámi heritage, experienced within the Lake Superior environment. (Photograph copyright 2017 by Brad Nelson. Used with permission.)

home and workshop situated only a few hundred meters from Lake Superior, Brad often incorporates rocks, driftwood, and manmade items that he finds washed up on the nearby beach into his artistic productions. His work draws from both the cultural and the natural environments in which he lives. For Brad and Pam in particular, relations with nature are critical to their reflexive rediscovery of heritage. Pam, Brad, and many of the other artisans I encountered in my fieldwork used traditional and often nature-based crafts as a medium by which to make sense of their histories, their relationships, and their places in the world.

Conclusion: Fieldwork, Craft Practice, and Community (Re-)Creation

The artisans I worked with all expressed a conscious awareness of personal and communal heritage and of cultural and natural landscape, and their creative expressions represent a conversation between place, community, and heritage in northern Minnesota. Artisans like Laurel, Pam, and Brad use craft as a means to express a deep rootedness in place and identity, as well as to explore, challenge, and transform what those concepts mean for themselves and for their communities.

For Sámi Americans, whose identity transmission was deeply disrupted under the strain of colonization and forced assimilation, craft practices help create and re-create these identities, slowly working to reverse the impacts of cultural disruption. As these artisans craft, they rekindle relationships to each other, to other ethnic groups, and to the animals, plants, and landscapes that make up their local environment. Their craft practices are transformational for them and can also be so for the communities and environments in which they dwell.

Working with individuals engaged in cultural revitalization efforts offers additional rewards beyond what can be accomplished by more conventional folklife surveys meant simply to document the living traditions of the present. Fieldwork in such contexts embraces the creativity present in ethnic and cultural performance as it exists in diaspora and in new relations to other aspects of culture, suggesting the dynamic nature of tradition and problematizing the romanticized notions of cultural authenticity, distinctiveness, and continuity that still underpin much of our professional public infrastructure. These notions have long been critiqued by scholars like Regina Bendix, who examines the ways that authenticity was used to legitimize folklore as a field of study (1997). Today, public folklorists must question the ways we as individuals and our field as a whole all too often cling to these notions in our work, and we must actively reconceptualize how and why we do public folklore work. This is especially true when engaging with communities that are in the midst of revitalization efforts, like the Sámi American community. Cultural practitioners from such communities are not simply working to conserve culture but to creatively and ethically restore, hybridize, and recontextualize traditions in partnership with their Indigenous (and even settler) neighbors facing similar struggles.

Folklorists must reject continuity and "pure" authenticity as prerequisites for legitimacy when conducting field surveys and public presentations in collaboration with communities engaged in revitalization. Folklorists can lend legitimacy to revitalization efforts through our institutional affiliations, our grant writing skills, our curation of public programs, and even through the simple but powerful act of sitting down with someone to document that person's traditions. Perhaps most important, fieldwork and its outcomes provide a model for others to build on as they take up the task of cultural revitalization and reclamation. As Bendix notes, "folkloristic work is by necessity both cultural and political" (1997, 217). Cultural work with people from communities like northern Minnesota's Sámi diaspora does more than just document and preserve; it also engages in a collaborative ethnographic process that can feed back to strengthen the culture-making practices of small and marginalized communities.

The result of that making and sense-making is the emergence of a new kind of heritage and identity among Scandinavian-descended people in northern Minnesota. This heritage is based on the history and ancestors who have come before: on the hard work and perseverance of Swedish, Finnish, and Sámi immigrants to the region. But it is also profoundly shaped by interactions with other immigrant groups—both historical and contemporary—and with the region's Indigenous people, and also by the powerful tides of Lake Superior and the stark, marshy forests of the Iron Range. The "others" present here—people, animals, and environments—are easily visible and tangible in the works of crafters like Laurel, Pam, and Brad. They have *felt* the presence of ancestors and others and have imparted this touch into their own handcrafts as they seek to understand where they come from and who they are. In crafting, people create themselves.

The Art of Survival on the Iron Range

Economic Strategies After the Iron Is Gone

R H O N D A   R .   D A S S

I come from a small town in northern Minnesota. Friends from my hometown have asked me to aid in their efforts to make changes. Understanding how cultural production and traditions can aid in supporting or changing group identity formation, I have been consulted on a number of efforts that have been proposed as ways to ease the transition as the community shifts from a mining existence to relying more on the arts for its economic base. This picturesque town is rich in natural resources but needs help moving from its origins as a mining community and becoming an art community. How can a community transform its identity to provide economic stability? How can a mining town become an art community? We need to have an idea of where it wants to go, what challenges it faces, and how that community developed. This is where folklorists can work with and for communities, by asking questions, documenting cultural traditions, and working to better understand communities and how those communities can help themselves thrive in the face of economic change.

The Iron Range of Minnesota is a unique cultural area. The landscape and resources pulled different settlers than did the other two-thirds of the state. The land is remarkable for its heavily forested landscape and its high density of lakes. It is also well known for the iron-rich pockets or ranges spread out along the Laurentian Divide, a continental ridge delineating watersheds to the north and south. This geography brought different settlers to the region as it was not as hospitable for farming as the southern areas of the state, where the prairie and plains meet. The extreme cold of the northern area also discouraged many settlers until modern technologies were able to tame the cold. Logging camps dotted the landscape first. The mining companies migrated west from areas of Michigan once they had depleted the easily accessible iron resources there. Railroads further opened expansion into the northern parts of the woodlands near the end of the nineteenth century (Walker 1979, 99–103). The settlers of the Iron Range brought their traditions from a number of ethnic communities. Because the mining industry leveraged ethnic divides among the newly arriving immigrants to create competition among low-wage workers, the people, in an environment that forced interdependency, developed distinct cultural differences from the rest of the state and region. The unique traditions and languages have fascinated researchers as much as the landscape has fascinated tourists (Nemanic 2007, 40–42). Near the eastern edge of the Mesabi Iron Range, a mining location first known as Merritt after the brothers who started the operation would become the small town of Biwabik.

When the mining companies came to Minnesota, it was apparent from experiences to the east what would happen to the mining settlements once the resources were depleted. This allowed the towns of the Iron Range to prepare early for the inevitable collapse of the iron-mining industry. The state proactively worked to prepare for this economic eventuality. Economic diversity was proposed for the northern area of the state, which holds three of the largest iron ore deposits—also known as ranges—in North America. After the first fifty years of mining, most of the large natural ore deposits were exhausted. The workforce shrank during the 1930s from more than twelve thousand to two thousand. In 1941, Minnesota's governor Harold Stassen created the Department of Iron Range Resources—more commonly known as the IRRRB for its administrative organization, the Iron Range Resources and Rehabilitation Board. Funds were diverted from taxes on the mining industry and designated for projects that would diversify the region's economic base. The focus of the early efforts was on diversification, but later efforts and funding would go toward supporting research and technologies that would revitalize the iron-mining industry, providing the technologies that would make lower-grade ores viable materials to revitalize the industry in northern Minnesota and maintaining the centrality of the industry for the area's economy until this day (Kellher 1999).

As one drives through the town of Biwabik, one sees little of its mining heritage in the physical appearance of the town except for the large hill to the northwest that is composed of open-pit mining waste, the outlying remains of the mining location houses south of the town proper, and the reddish iron-rich soil along the edges of town. Dotted throughout the town on small well-kept yards are signs that proclaim the town's support for the mining industry. Along the length of the main street's eight blocks are two of the town's three churches, a grocery store tucked underneath the newish city hall/public services building across from the town's only park, and a gas station. There are many empty spaces where buildings have obviously been removed, exposing the prevalent residential side of this small town through the gaps. Banners hang from each of the light posts with the names of local residents who have supported the annual events of the town and a greeting in one of the many ethnic languages of the early settlers of the Range. The red sidewalks and architectural details evident on the main street are more indicative of an alpine village than a mining town. Not part of the original townscape, this appearance resulted from careful IRRRB planning during the 1980s.

The efforts to transform the mining town into a tourist destination have roots going back to the 1960s, when a local group of avid skiers who regularly traveled for skiing decided that the mining waste and some natural hills of the Laurentian Divide presented an opportunity for skiing on the Iron Range. Giants Ridge Ski Area was developed on reclaimed mining land just outside the town of Biwabik, beginning with just one run and a tow rope powered by a car engine. Its location, halfway between the towns of Biwabik and Aurora, allowed the town to distance itself from the tourist-town identity for a while, preferencing to highlight mining origins instead. Unfortunately, the endeavor struggled alongside the struggling town of Biwabik, being as linked to the economics of the mining industry as the town. As the end of the 1970s began to see the closing of numerous mining operations across the Range, Giants Ridge also closed its operations, unsure whether it would ever be able to reopen for another winter of skiing.

Economic diversity was seen as a way to rescue the small towns of the iron area, and tourism was seen as a viable alternative to bring stability to the economics of the area. Biwabik residents were presented with the opportunity to shift their town's identity from that of a mining-centered small town to a tourist-attracting alpine village with the best skiing in northern Minnesota—bolstered by the resources of the IRRRB. This shift brought about the reimagined community appearance with architectural details in keeping with a Bavarian landscape. The first time the World Cup Cross Country Ski Races were held in the United States, the venue was Giant's Ridge. Winter by winter, Giants Ridge continued to struggle, and it was eventually taken over completely by the IRRRB and the state of Minnesota.

With these economic, material, and cultural shifts, residents of Biwabik and the people of the town struggled to clarify their identity—a reality for many even today. Many residents of the Iron Range define their identity by their connection to the history of mining on the Range. It is what brought families to the area; it forced a distinct cultural understanding out of the many diverse immigrant groups pushed to survive in a very inhospitable environment. Mining defined the language and daily activities as well as traditional practices. As the mining operations closed, many young people who were graduating from high school, including my classmates and me, left the area looking for new pathways to employment rather than following in their parents' footsteps into the open-pit mines. How do you stay connected to the mining industry and a mining identity when your future lies elsewhere? Employment within the town was still represented by mining industries even though fewer residents were directly employed in the local mines and more miners were forced to travel to more distant operations to continue in the profession of their parents. Biwabik drifted closer toward being a retirement town when its schools were relocated in 1991 and consolidated with those of the nearby towns of Aurora and Hoyt Lakes. This was an important signal that most of the young people were not remaining in Biwabik and that few young families were moving in. Tourism was one of the few remaining economic opportunities for the town.

The push to become a tourist town was evident not just in the aesthetics of the town but also in an emergent economic focus on the arts. The people of Biwabik launched a Weihnachtfest or winter festival in 1984. Named for the predominantly German settlers from the southern reaches of the state, who were the target market the first Weihnachtfest committee was hoping to attract, the festival fit the Bavarian theme of the town more than the town's actual predominantly Italian and Scandinavian heritage. This festival was designed to highlight the various artistic endeavors of the local peoples and to bring together the arts community for a winter celebration that embraced numerous ethnic traditions. Usually held at the end of November or beginning of December, it is timed to coincide with the start of the Christmas shopping season and the beginning of the skiing season in the north. The festival has a centralized theme but not a centralized location, occupying various buildings throughout the town. The main park and pavilion buildings house several activities, with others taking place in churches, the city hall, the senior/community center, and even outdoor booths. Vendors are encouraged to represent traditional ethnic arts of the alpine regions or their own ethnic origins, but most of the offerings have come to represent the generalized craft fair offerings that can be seen in any blended community across the United States. Although the Weihnachtfest has been a great success for the town, one festival a year does not bring enough tourism to create economic stability.

The people of Biwabik continue to struggle to find economic stability. The focus on mining has shifted back in recent years, despite environmental concerns pushing back against a proposed new use of an old mine site. A new mining-inspired business flourishes on the main street. Carlson's provides the traditional miner's staple food, pasties—a meat-filled pastry adopted from the Cornish mining traditions during the 1800s (Lockwood and Lockwood 1991). While the environmental implications of mining hold up the redevelopment and the economic opportunities many from the area believe it will bring, the town continues to look for ways to survive.

With the focus on utilizing local resources, recreation and the arts have gained support as avenues for economic strength and stability. Although a local issue has temporarily held up the development, the proposed Mesabi Trail would join a network of more than 135 miles of biking/hiking/walking trails in the area. This green initiative replaced the miles of trails that were once dedicated to snowmobiling. As snowfall becomes less predictable and environmental preservation becomes more of a concern, nonmotorized alternatives that can use the same resources in all seasons become desirable for local development. The community was inspired to create activities and celebrations that would bring tourists through this new connection.

The other key investment is looking toward the arts as an avenue for economic strength. These efforts have come primarily from within the business community. The Biwabik Area Commercial Association (BACA) has been at the forefront of the local efforts. The Imagine Biwabik community organization was created to help organize these efforts. Its founder, Kim Sampson, organized efforts to bring varied artists into local businesses to serve the dual purpose of highlighting arts and increasing traffic in local established storefronts. Inclusive of local community members as well as the BACA organization, Imagine Biwabik worked to create specific opportunities to highlight the arts in Biwabik. After internal conflict, Sampson left this project and concentrated her efforts with BACA, and the project shifted drastically, manifesting as an art presentation in the park more on the scale of a farmer's market than an artistic venue. The art was limited to two tables of handcrafted items. Three tables were dedicated to plants and homegrown vegetables. The park setting also presented accessibility challenges as tables were set up in the grass under the large trees providing shade for the vendors but not a clear pathway for visitors.

The community welcomed the Pine Grove Gallery, a stable fixture of support for all of the art efforts around town, in 2009. The fall of 2019 saw the first Honktoberfest celebration after three years of planning and promotions by Sampson. The Bavarian-themed October celebration plays on the town mascot of Honk the Moose. Honk, who wandered the streets of Biwabik in 1915, brought the town its first artistic success in 1935 when a local resident, Kurt Strong, wrote about Honk's escapades in the town, winning a John Newbery Medal for children's literature: "it took me three years to launch Honktoberfest. When I finally got the chance, I had to prove myself. And I did. I have spent three years proving myself to this town and they are finally trusting me and my crazy ideas . . . not that they aren't still a little scared by my crazy ideas, but they are beginning to trust me" (Sampson 2018).

In 2017 funds were awarded to BACA to create a chalet project that would build and rent out small portable chalet-style buildings that would house artists and other small business ventures. The project was to be located in the heart of downtown on a vacant lot directly across from the city's park where a building housing a pizza restaurant had burned to the ground, leaving yet another gap in the main drag. The project was seen as a way to help small businesses grow in the town and to bring more tourism to the main street. The project has encountered a number of delays that revolve around the shifting involvement of individuals in the project. Each change in the committee brings about a return to a discussion on how the chalets should look and how they will be built. There is still support for the mission and the location, but the project continues to be on hold as matching funds and the pandemic have interfered with their completion. Sampson continues to work on this project, hoping that the incubators will bring new enterprises to fruition on the main street.

"The town is open to things," Kim Sampson explains. "They just do not believe anything until they see it once or twice. The 'City,' as in 'City Hall,' does not feel any of this is their place and help very little." New initiatives are met with a "'that's the way we've always done it' mentality. Or we tried that once and it didn't work. Why didn't it work though? A lot of skeptical people. That will never work in Biwabik with no stats to back it up" (Sampson 2018).

Funding has been a challenge for the town of just over nine hundred people, most of whom are over the age of fifty-five. However, outside agencies seem to have more faith in projects proposed for the city than the townspeople. Biwabik has seen continued monetary support from the Iron Range Rehabilitation and Resources Board. "They see value in ideas more than people in town. The Iron Range has a very skeptical/negative vibe," says Sampson. This brings up issues with raising matching funds, which seem to be a major requirement for most of the grants given to support arts initiatives. "I can write grants and get awarded all day long. Getting match money can be tough. We are facing that with the chalet project" (Sampson 2018).

Many projects have seen shifts because other organizations either change membership or have structural or organizational shifts that require organizers to change their original plans. Another recent setback for the chalet project came when the Senior Citizens Center decided to disband and sell off its buildings. The Center had been one of the organizations that had promised to put up matching funding for the chalet project—one of the reasons that BACA was able to obtain the original funding from the IRRRB. "They didn't follow their own Articles of Incorporation as they are dissolving, so all their monies have been forfeited to the City. We don't know if they [the city] will honor [the donation]," says Sampson. "When they had the money, it went to their head, and they had us jumping through hoops to satisfy them. IRRRB did not request as much as they [the city] did.

We are now in our second extension with IRRRB" (Sampson 2018). While regional support continues, it is harder to garner local support.

"Another issue we have had is people are very opinionated as to how the project should look. . . . They do not take the time to look at our models from other cities and basically just make things way more complicated than it needs to be." Some of this is the outcome of the shifting voices that have been a part of the project. While three people have remained at the core of the project, as many as thirty separate individuals have been part of the project at some point, and all want their voices heard. The core is adamant on moving forward before funding is lost and intends to seek more matching funds and complete the project following the original plans. What will this art project mean for the town besides a bit more of the Alpine aesthetic on the main street? "It could help drive the economy, grow artists into brick and mortar stores, and then they are on the tax roll. With Giants Ridge as customers, it can work in this town. It's just hard to get people to see the vision. They are not truly supportive until they see it, and they all have their eggs in the mining basket" (Sampson 2018).

While efforts were under way to bring the arts to Biwabik in new and creative ways to pull more tourism to the town, signs began to pop up all over town—and across the region—stating "Mining Supports Us" or "We Support Mining." These signs were part of a media campaign by the Iron Mining Association of Minnesota (IMA). They were intended to garner support for proposals for projects in the area put forth by mining companies such as PolyMet and Twin Metals, two large international corporations. The signs, however, were displayed by individuals as yard signs or posted on private buildings. The most ironic one I saw was located in an overgrowth of weeds on the garage door of an abandoned home. The attitude of the townspeople was similar to the attitude found across the Iron Range—skepticism until a project is proven.

Trust in the directional vision of organizers is a large portion of creating a successful transition for a community such as Biwabik. In combination with community support, opportunities for funding and human resources provide the foundations for an effective transformation of any town. The town of Biwabik has a small but dedicated population, both within the ten-mile stretch of land that it covers and in the surrounding area, that is committed to staying on the Iron Range and that recognizes the need for change if the town is to survive. Recently the town was successful in acquiring funding to support a main street revitalization project that has the town detoured and deconstructed along the length of its only business district while infrastructure is repaired and aesthetic changes meant to promote visitor retention on the throughway to Giants Ridge Recreation Area are implemented. Major change is on the horizon.

The COVID-19 global pandemic has not stopped people in this highly connected community from supporting one another in any way they can, but it has slowed any progress toward art promotion. As all art events were canceled for an eighteen-month period beginning in the spring of 2020, BACA and Kim Sampson embraced the virtual environment that allowed for activities that the deconstructed main street would not permit. The second annual Honktoberfest went online with a virtual auction for donated goods garnering

Main Street under repair, Biwabik, MN spring 2021. (Photograph by author.)

funds to support the third annual event. This also kept the event in the minds and hearts of the local people. Environmental concerns added to the economic issues facing the nation have shifted any new mining operations that may come to the area (American Rivers n.d.). A recent break in a retaining wall released wastewater from a retaining area into the St. Louis River. Mining entities are facing closer examination of proposed projects with regard to financial planning for the possible future clean-up of such sites. The reconstruction of the main street was delayed due to health concerns but has resumed in the spring of 2021. The chalet project awaits the completion of the streets, but funding has been found. Sampson continues to write grants and to propose new art projects for the town. Kim recently proposed a pet project she has been discussing with me over the past five or more years—a mural that will be featured on the side of one of the buildings on the main street. I have been enlisted as both consultant and artist to help in this project. We are just waiting again for matching funds and clear weather. It's as if the town is poised and waiting to see what will happen next and what will emerge from the chaos of the torn-up streets. I am excited to be there to watch and document, to ask questions of those involved so that we can all better understand how communities can survive in the Northwoods of the Iron Range, and to be involved as my hometown transforms.

As a folklorist and someone connected to the town, I am in a position where I can work with the people who are trying to leverage the arts to revitalize this former mining town. Consulting with BACA and interested residents has already helped to funnel efforts toward projects that use the ethnic heritage of the current residents rather than trying to push an identity that is disconnected from the community members. I look forward to reminding the community of our rich ethnic art heritage and showing them how we can return to these traditions to bring others to the town. I feel that I am able to give back to the community that nurtured me and set me on my journey to becoming a folklorist.

A Fish Sandwich for All

Yvonne R. Lockwood

F irst funded in 1979 by the National Endowment for the Humanities with a Youth Projects Grant, the Folkpatterns program works to support 4-H students "who are interested in learning more about themselves, their families, and their communities" (Kozma 1991, 2). Public folklorists designed the program to engage youth across the state of Michigan in cultural heritage educational activities related to personal and local place-based history and culture (Macdowell and Kozma 2007). In doing so, they have created a variety of lesson plans, guidebooks, activity pages, and other pedagogical materials focusing on folklife and education. For decades, Folkpatterns has worked with 4-Hers, 4-H leaders, folklorists, and community members to help better understand and, in some cases, strengthen community throughout Michigan.

Between 1995 and 1997, Michigan State University Extension's 4-H Folkpatterns program and the Michigan Traditional Arts Program at the Michigan State University Museum conducted a collaborative project on maritime folklore in the Thumb of Michigan.[1] In a state surrounded by the Great Lakes and containing thousands of inland lakes and rivers, maritime culture is a significant aspect of Michigan folklife and was therefore an obvious and important area of focus for the Folkpatterns program.

The folklorist LuAnne G. Kozma directed the project, which included folklorists, 4-H leaders, 4-Hers, and local volunteers, who attended workshops about the ecology, fisheries, culture, and history of the maritime region. Working in teams with a folklorist, they also learned interviewing and other ethnographic techniques to conduct folklore fieldwork, and the participants proceeded to document aspects of local maritime life. At the end of the day, they wrote up their findings, cataloged images and interview tapes, and gave oral presentations about their experience. The result of this research included workshops with 4-H Folkpatterns groups, festival presentations (4-H fairs, Festival of Michigan Folklife, Great Lakes Folk Festival), and publications. The archival and material objects are housed at the Michigan State University Museum (Kozma 1998).

In 1995, a discrete focus of this larger project was Bay Port, a town of about five hundred residents located on Saginaw Bay on the west side of Michigan's Thumb, and specifically the town's Fish Sandwich Festival. During the nineteenth century, the region was considered the lumber capital of the Midwest, and the land was cleared of forests (Lynn 1979, 5). At the turn of the twentieth century, the Thumb was a popular tourist destination with a rail link, dance halls, and beaches, but today the region is rural and somewhat remote. Residents, many of whom are German and Polish in origin, are for the most part agricultural and maritime based. Significant industries are sugar beets (growing and refining), beans, and commercial fishing.

In the early twentieth century, Bay Port was one of the world's largest freshwater fishing ports and the headquarters of the Bay Port Fish Company, which had forty-two full-time commercial fishing tugs at branches around Saginaw Bay and Lake Huron (Lynn 1979, 8). The company directed fish sales, supplied other fishermen with ropes and equipment, and repaired boats and engines. During World War II, according to local legend, local men were exempt from military service in order for the company to continue to supply the nation with fish. Fishermen went each morning in the spring and fall to harvest their catch from nets (pound, later trap nets). It was not uncommon to harvest two to four tons of herring in a single lift. Herring was then the most important catch, and fishermen took 3.5 million tons from Saginaw Bay in the 1930s. Herring was shipped daily by truck and refrigerator express railcars all over the Midwest and South.

Bay Port is still a commercial and recreational fishing center. Although the Bay Port Fish Company is down to a smaller fleet of boats, it is still an active fish supplier, and fish are very much a part of the culture of Bay Port.

It is perhaps not surprising, then, that Bay Port is the home of the fish sandwich, traditionally a batter-dipped breaded fillet, deep fried and garnished with German-style mustard and ketchup, served on a specially made rectangular roll. This sandwich, the focus of the Bay Port Fish Sandwich Festival, turned this small town into a popular tourist destination. This festival is well documented in a variety of local and regional newspapers, but in 1995, as part of the Folkpatterns project on maritime culture, folklorists and 4-Hers began interviewing the many people involved and, of course, eating the fish sandwich. In the years that followed, I kept in contact with Carolyn Engelhard Smith, the daughter of the creators of the fish sandwich, to learn more about the evolution of the sandwich and the festival. This essay examines the festival by presenting background research about the festival, the foodways, and the changing traditions that have been one way that the community of Bay Port has identified itself through food, festivals, and tourism.

I hope to demonstrate the ways in which folklore and education programs can be an important part of public folklore, as well as play a role in which folklorists can work with communities to better understand the community and to purposefully build community. With this particular case study, we see that public work is assisted by good historical research, which in and of itself can be a tool for understanding community building.

BAY PORT, MICHIGAN

Tourism is one of Michigan's largest industries. Competing for tourist dollars, entrepreneurs eagerly commodify their locales and capitalize on local culture. In Michigan, it's not difficult to find Indian tipis (a traditional housing not even used in the region) with all the accoutrements of someone's idea of Woodland Indian life, Paul Bunyans standing aside blue oxen, and Alpine-esque villages with an array of appropriate and inappropriate activities to observe and objects to buy. As a major agricultural and maritime state, Michigan also hosts a cornucopia of food festivals; however, food itself usually plays a smaller role than the festival names imply (Long 2004). The Bay Port festival is one of the most popular. Its fish sandwich illustrates the relationship between place and food, as well as food and identity, and serves as both a unifier and a divider.

The first public appearance of the fish sandwich in Bay Port was in 1949. The local Chamber of Commerce planned a special homecoming event in conjunction with the July Fourth celebration. Henry Engelhard, a member of the Chamber and a co-owner of the Bay Port Fish Company, suggested that such an event should use a hometown product. He made the comparison with Frankenmuth, Michigan, stressing that Bay Port with its fresh fish could do better than Frankenmuth with its chicken.[2]

After gaining the support of the Chamber, Henry contacted a customer in Indiana who received from the Bay Port Fish Company about 250 pounds of herring a day, six days a week, for fish sandwiches. Henry believed that the event planners had an obligation to use Bay Port's fresh fish in an original Bay Port fish sandwich. The customer agreed to travel to Bay Port to get the Engelhard family started with its own fish sandwich, and the Engelhards promised never to divulge the secret ingredients of the batter or the Indiana customer's name.

As a warmup to the July Fourth celebration, Henry's wife, Edna, created a one-pound, batter-dipped, breaded, and deep-fried herring topped with ketchup and German mustard on a specially baked rectangular bun. Edna's family built a stand with wood from their woodlot; Detroit Edison, the electric power provider, had just introduced deep fryers and loaned one for the event. Henry created the slogan "A sandwich so big, it takes two hands to hold it."[3]

After the success of the warmup event, everyone was ready for July Fourth. As an indication of Henry's promotional skills, he had asked his senator to have jets fly over the stand on the day. And it happened! People were very curious about the sandwich. What, they asked, is a fish sandwich? Scholars have pointed out that tourism is based in part on the assumption that the experience offered by the destination site is not available in the tourists' home environment (Cohen 1995, 23; Boissevain 1996, 4). In 1949, fish sandwiches were not common in Michigan, and Bay Port provided a new experience. While nearby hot dog and cotton candy stands had no customers, people stood four-deep waiting for a fish sandwich as Edna, with only one deep fryer, prepared fish. The sandwich was a huge hit. Visitors and locals alike loved it. Locals began making their own fish sandwiches, saying the sandwich didn't need the secret batter. Some even said they had the secret batter recipe. When Henry was confronted with this information, he dismissed it as impossible. He knew locals were trying to imitate the sandwich, but he also knew it could never be duplicated. The Engelhards were invited for a number of repeat performances in nearby towns.

Being practical and resourceful, Edna saw the potential for raising money to help pay for her daughters' schooling. In 1952, she built a stand in their yard along the main street through town. She and her daughters tried offering fish and chips, which didn't sell; customers wanted "the" sandwich. Their customers included tourists, year-round residents, summer cottagers, and sugar beet and bean harvesters, who purchased roasters full. Henry,

Henry Engelhard proudly shows the fish sandwich. (Photograph by LuAnne Gaykowski Kozma.)

the promoter, entertained the waiting customers with information about fish and endless fish stories as he wound his way through the crowd. During sugar beet and bean harvest, the stand often remained open until 5:00 a.m. serving the truck drivers and harvesters.

The lakes, even for those who work in agriculture and sugar refining, are an important part of life in Bay Port. Just like people in many communities throughout the Great Lakes region who depend on the commercial fishing industry, residents of Bay Port rely on the lakes for work, recreation, and food. Of course, the fishing industry has had its ups and downs over the decades. Fishing culture changed in the 1950s and 1960s, because of pollution, the lamprey, the introduction of nonnative species that competed for food, and overfishing. When soldiers returned after World War II, for example, there were more boats in the water and much more fishing. The Engelhards responded to these environmental changes and so the varieties of fish changed, which impacted the fishing industry and the festival.

When herring disappeared from Saginaw Bay in the 1950s, for example, primarily due to overfishing and pollution, the Engelhards turned to white mullet (sucker), a fish with fine lengthwise hook-like bones (Lynn 1979, 10). A special board was devised to cross-cut the bones while leaving the skin and flesh intact. Considered a junk fish, mullet was underused, but in the fish sandwich it became highly prized; the bones were made edible by cross-cutting and deep frying, adding a distinctive nutty flavor.

In 1964, Edna's aging mother required her care, and the last of the Engelhard daughters left for college. The stand closed.

The story picks up in 1978, when again the Chamber of Commerce planned a one-day event to promote Bay Port as a tourist destination. Some members suggested chicken barbecue or a pig roast, but once again Henry argued for fish. Edna agreed to make fish sandwiches only if the Chamber provided her with help and only if she got the fish at cost. Today, the Bay Port Fish Company often donates fish, and the money from the sale of the fish sandwich goes to local food pantries, local charities, and projects in Bay Port.

Despite careful planning, no one anticipated the crowds waiting for the sandwich. By midafternoon they had sold the last of their 1,300 fillets. Mortified, Henry swore this would never happen again, although it is worth noting that in 1992, it did happen again. They ran out of buns and people scoured the neighboring towns, buying everything they found. They ultimately used sliced white bread for the sandwiches. They sold more sandwiches that year than ever before.

Seeing the success of the 1978 event, the Chamber realized the sandwich could make Bay Port a destination and economically benefit the entire area, and it decided to make the festival an annual event. Henry took the role of promoter/publicist, and Edna managed the kitchen crew and the production of the sandwich.

Today, decades later, the festival, still attended by crowds from Canada and the Midwest, is greatly changed. Scholars have noted that as more and more outsiders attend a small-town event, it is not uncommon for the townsfolk to add new activities, because they believe the event is not colorful enough (Boissevain 1996, 12). And so it was with Bay Port. The one-day event became a three-day festival, including a prefestival dance, a parade, the crowning of a festival queen, church bake sales, a firefighters' refreshment stand, music, karaoke, bingo, a petting zoo, and a silent auction. In 1996, for the first time, outside vendors were allowed to sell their wares, which diluted the local character of the festival. Some locals called it a circus. The sandwich, too, changed. In addition to ketchup and mustard, the original sandwich was now offered with tartar sauce, because customers requested it. Hot dog and hamburger buns replaced the specially baked buns. According to lovers of the original sandwich, it was no longer of the same quality. After Edna's death, the recipe for the batter was put in the hands of her oldest daughter. Today, Carolyn, who put the recipe in a safe deposit box, makes the batter for festivals "as needed" while the recipe remains tucked away from prying eyes.

Henry didn't let the changes dampen his enthusiasm. We are familiar with photos of the triumphant fisherman showing off his or her trophy for the camera. In Bay Port, a handpainted sign located near the entrance of the Bay Port Fish Company displays such a trophy: a large fish standing upright on its tail holding a man upside-down by the foot. This is called "Fish Caught the Man." The man represents Henry and, by extension, all those who go to Bay Port for fish and the fish sandwich. As Henry so often claimed, "This is the greatest

Fish caught the man. (Photograph by Yvonne Lockwood.)

event in Michigan! It's the fish they come for. It's the fish that caught the man" (Engelhard 1995). The slogan is a statement of local pride, and Henry's pride and his enthusiasm remained high.

Henry always praised the many volunteers who worked the festival, but he regarded it as his creation. Each year he was in the thick of things. While customers waited for their sandwiches, Henry went up and down the line, asking where people were from and how they had heard about the festival and entertaining them with his fish stories. In 1997, unable to be at the festival because of a stroke, he nonetheless called to ensure that everything was going well. In 1999, too weak to stand and talk to the crowds, he sat in a wheelchair in the midst of the crowd and spoke to waiting customers. In 2000, he was on the telephone from a nursing home micromanaging and inquiring about the fish and bun supply. That same year, Henry was awarded a Michigan Heritage Award, and, according to Carolyn, soon after hearing the news, he passed away. He was ninety-one.

In 2005, fewer mullet were being caught, and more changes took place at the festival. Customers were offered white fish sandwiches made with a commercial batter, or, if they were lucky, mullet with the original batter as long as the supply lasted. According to Carolyn, many like the commercial dressing sold by the Bay Port Fish Company because it is spicy and they consider the original too bland. Portion control became important, and whitefish was a piece rather than a fillet. In 2005, the festival offered plate dinners, but in 2007, the supply of whitefish diminished, and pollack was used instead. In 2019, four different fish were offered: yellow perch, walleye, cod, and mullet. The company was also offering French fries, horseradish, and "all kinds of stuff," according to Carolyn, "to satisfy the people." She also observed that if Henry were alive to witness what was now happening to the fish sandwich, "he'd have a stroke for sure." The number of volunteers had dropped significantly, and people who ordinarily would have volunteered were paid. For the first time, nachos and hot dogs appeared on the fish stand menu. When Carolyn questioned these additions, the response was that not everyone likes fish. Carolyn's response was, then why come to a fish festival? Clearly, the customers have played a role in changing the festival and the sandwich. Lucy Long suggests that festivals draw attention to familiar foods, such as fish, in new contexts, which can lead to a new interpretation of that food (Long 2004, 38–39).

Publicity about the festival is generated today by the local tourist bureau and the Bay Port Fish Company. The bureau distributes brochures describing Bay Port as a quiet, safe, small town with lists of activities for children and adults. Attendees also spread the word on social media, posting photographs and describing their experiences. Before his death, Henry was the primary publicist. His philosophy was "success is determined by taking the hand you are dealt and utilizing it to the best of your ability" (Engelhard 1995). He was dealt a bountiful natural resource in local waters, and he made the best of it.

As the fish sandwich grew in popularity, so too did Henry. He used exaggerated tales and notions of healthful eating to publicize the sandwich, the event, and Bay Port. Visitors are reminded of the occupational and historic connection. His stories communicate a message no advertising firm could project as effectively. Each year he sent out press releases, expanding the magical powers of the fish sandwich, which the local press dutifully reported. A young girl, for example, supposedly advised doctors that the fish sandwich was the only cure for President Eisenhower, who had had a heart attack. An Air Force helicopter was sent to Bay Port in the dead of night for sandwiches. In another story, Queen Elizabeth II sent for fish sandwiches for Prince Charles and Princess Diana, and, according to the narrative, "they lived happily ever after." Henry later stated that he couldn't explain the divorce, but he assumed they must have stopped eating the sandwich. He also told of terrorists who threatened to steal the secret batter recipe and bring the world to its knees. In 1986, a local couple went directly from the church to the festival to celebrate their marriage with a fish sandwich. Beneath the town sign "Bay Port" at the entrance to the town is another sign: "Home of the Fish Sandwich Festival." In 1988, this sign was stolen. Henry's assessment was, "We're convinced it's some crime syndicate as part of a big plot. First, they took our sign and next they might try to get our secret batter recipe. If they'd have got that, we'd be lost. That would have been the end of Bay Port" (Engelhard 1995).

Henry's publicity also included statements about fish as a healthy food choice. Fish, he swore, "will do wonders...whether we're talking about health, happiness, or wealth" (Engelhard 1995). And he told stories to back these claims. When Bay Port was first settled as a fishing community, for example, residents ate only fish, and there were no deaths until the arrival of hunters who, unfortunately, ate game. People who ate two fish sandwiches a year found wealth. One became a great violinist because of increased finger dexterity, and another became a winning football running back. Performing local color and selling rural stereotypes back to the outsiders who craved distinctive and authentic cultural experiences, Henry offered a performance that was effective, legendary, and absolutely integral to the festival.

Henry and Edna were recognized locally, statewide, and nationally for their successful promotion of Bay Port. Henry received awards for leadership in the development of tourism. In 1981, the fish sandwich was featured in *Midwest Living*, a travel magazine, and the *Wall Street Journal*, and Barbara Walters interviewed Henry on *20/20*. In 1986, Governor James Blanchard designated August 2–3 as Bay Port Fish Sandwich Day. The Engelhards hosted national and state dignitaries and politicians and served fish sandwiches at the state capital. While Henry was regarded as the one responsible for the success of the festival, Edna provided the product for the festival. Without her, there might not have been a festival. Although Henry seemed to get all the attention, the community honored Edna, building a pavilion in the center of town in her name. She was one of the creators and sustainers of the festival. Henry was the one out front, meeting the public, officials, journalists, and politicians, while Edna was behind the scenes.

Although Henry's boosterism and performance of stories and jokes enhanced the festival experience, some locals thought these were corny and that Henry was wearing thin. Mention Henry's name and some rolled their eyes. The community, however, was divided about Henry; other locals stated that he was a nice guy who did a lot for the community. In praise of Henry, Ford Williams, co-owner of the Bay Port Fish Company and a former president of the Chamber, said that he was an ambassador for the fish of Bay Port and that the festival put Bay Port on the map. An unofficial survey of locals revealed both positive and negative responses to the festival. The complaints were not unexpected: traffic congestion and noise. The more positive reflections were expressed by volunteers and locals who were involved in festival preparation and implementation. This group benefited from opportunities to socialize and reinforce social networks.

The success of the Fish Sandwich Festival led to other local tourist events, such as "Ye Olde Whitefish Boil" and the annual blessing of the fishing fleet. Lucy Long suggests that the use of such names emphasize foods and activities of the past (Long 2004, 29). These festivals were the brainchild of new residents in the community and do not have a basis in history, although the tourist literature refers to them as "old traditions." These activities are thought to be appropriate to the area, and locals and outsiders attend. Jeremy Boissevain reminds us that "one of the most striking characteristics of tourism is the way it promotes self-awareness, pride, self-confidence, and solidarity," which are especially pronounced when the host community is "remote or in other ways peripheral to tourists" (1996, 6). The annual participation of hundreds of visitors in this out-of-the-way community festival promotes and reinforces local pride as residents celebrate what makes Bay Port special and rediscover their history and that of the local fishing industry. This community festival increases local social capital.

CONCLUSION

The 4-H team that focused on foodways spent hours at the Bay Port Fish Company and with Henry and Carolyn. From Henry and the fishermen, who had gathered, they learned about fish and fishing while Carolyn prepared fish sandwiches. The team documented the history of the Bay Port fish sandwich and its evolution from a family tradition to the heart of a community food festival. When this team returned home, it met with other 4-Hers and planned the annual 4-H fair based on its maritime experience, and leaders developed a curriculum guide for teachers in the Thumb. Although collaboration continued between the MSU Museum staff and the Englehards, this did not include the physical presence of the 4-Hers at the Fish Sandwich Festival. The 4-Hers lived many miles from Bay Port, and because the festival is held on the first weekend of August—several weeks after their workshops—many were unable to participate in this phase of research. However, the work that the 4-Hers did and the work that continued after the 4-Hers left resulted in a variety of publications and presentations. But the fieldwork also highlighted some of the challenges of maintaining a long-running event like the Fish Sandwich Festival.

The reality of the fish sandwich and the festival was lost on many of the newcomers to Bay Port. According to some locals, the newcomers had no knowledge of Bay Port, and so its culture, traditions, and history and information about the festival itself had to be maintained. In talks with the community, the idea of a presentation and an exhibition about the sandwich and the festival was discussed, but it eventually was decided that this would not be a good idea during the festival itself. Instead, discussion turned to an exhibition at the historical society, but, with the lack of funds and interested volunteers, this idea went nowhere. Today, the festival carries on, sustained by the Bay Port Fish Company, the Bayport Chamber of Commerce, a large number of volunteers, and tradition bearers like Carolyn Engelhard Smith. Over the years, the fish has changed, the festival has changed, and the people attending and running the festival have all changed. As folklorists, we and our team of 4-Hers were able to play a small role in documenting some of those changes for future generations. And while a full-on exhibition never came to be, the work of Folkpatterns and many of the projects like the Bay Port maritime project live on and are available through the Michigan State University Museum.

The primary purpose of this research was to document the change of the fish sandwich festival, the change in the sandwich itself, and how these changes impacted the community. In doing so, projects like this one, coupling cultural documentation with educational opportunities for students, like 4-Hers, not only help us understand the reasons why a sandwich and its festival have changed over time but also help create a narrative through which a community can understand itself. In Bay Port, the story of the fish sandwich connects people today with their changing environment and economic realities, with their awareness of the insider-outsider dynamics that shape the festival and the community's sense of identity, and with their sense of place and belonging within the community. Crafting this as a community-driven research project situates ownership over the community's story within community members themselves. As David Fakunkle writes elsewhere in this volume, knowing how to tell your own story uplifts and empowers individuals and communities alike.

And these stories continue to be rewritten. As we have seen before, the environment of the Thumb again is impacting the culture of the peninsula. Recently the Michigan Department of Natural Resources (MDNR), an advocate of recreational fishing, made it illegal for commercial fisheries to fish in water deeper than eighty feet and to take walleye and lake trout, considered reserved for recreational fishermen. This ruling was temporarily overruled in April 2021. Now there are fast-growing numbers of walleye in Saginaw Bay, where the Bay Port Fish Company is located. Not surprisingly, there was walleye at the 2021 festival. When the MDNR reversed its intention to limit commercial fisheries, which included cutting off all fall fishing for whitefish, there was a sigh of relief. This reversal had a large impact on restaurants and tourism. Whitefish is the primary fish of Michigan, and locals declared it their livelihood and lifeline. Though individuals may become attached to certain types of fish, the festival is traditionally bound to the economic and ecological fluctuations that dictate which fish are locally available and economically viable.

The fish sandwich festival has been and still is affected by changes in the environment and other outside forces. In 2020, as the United States dealt with the ongoing COVID-19 pandemic, the festival was canceled outright. In 2021, however, the in-person festival was changed to be curbside-only, allowing attendees to pick up a fish sandwich or a plate dinner without leaving their cars. As some, including Lakon Williams of the Bay Port Fish Company, have pointed out, the new model meant the festival would be without entertainment, arts and crafts, and the many aspects that have come to make the Fish Sandwich Festival an important part of the community (Creenan 2021). This curbside festival reimagined the festival to its most essential core, the sandwich itself and people's access to it—in essence taking the festival out of the festival and returning to the fish sandwich stand of 1949.

The fish sandwich festival has enhanced and strengthened a sense of community, even for the many residents who have lived their entire lives in Bay Port. Revenue earned from the festival, for example, has supported town infrastructure, volleyball and little league fields, a wheelchair-accessible trail, and a college scholarship awarded to the annual festival queen. As we saw during our documentation with the 4-Hers, the informal interaction among and buy-in of all parties at the festival served to explain its success. Fishers claim successful management of the fisheries and show the vitality and cultural significance of their occupation. Entrepreneurial organizers like Henry Engelhard, whose investment in the success of the festival took him to extreme lengths, claimed ownership over the festival. Volunteers who work three long days to make the festival happen also take pride in the success of the festival. Tourists are equally necessary and consume local fish alongside local culture, which legitimizes the value of the community for locals. All parties are necessary, and what we can see through the cooperative documentation effort is that the festival both reflects community and shapes it through expressive cultural practice.

Visitors returning year after year emphasized that one of the attractions, in addition to the fish sandwich, is the commercial fishing, making it possible for them to obtain fish right on the dock. These visitors reinforced the values and ideals of locals. Brochures promote nostalgia for the quiet, safe, comfortable, and wholesome environment for families. Henry used the environment and nature to create a tradition that enhances Bay Port identity. He reminded visitors of the festival's family, occupational, and historic connection. He emphasized that fish is more than just fish and food is more than just food and, in his own sometimes bombastic way, helped remind people of what made Bay Port special.

Fish has become the expression of Bay Port's cultural heritage and local identity (cf. Long 2004, 38). As Henry used to joke, "We speak fish and English" (Engelhard 1995). Public festivals and tourism contribute to defining a local food as regional. The Bay Port fish sandwich became regional through the marketing of the festival that ultimately defined this fish sandwich, and today a facsimile of it is served in many eateries of the Thumb. But there is only one "Bay Port" fish sandwich.

The Bay Port Chamber of Commerce has achieved its goal: the festival has put Bay Port on the map. It has made a huge impact on the local economy, and tourists make Bay Port their destination year after year. As Lakon Williams pointed out to me in a conversation in May 2021, although the sandwich has gone through some changes, mullet with its secret batter is the fish most often ordered today. The fish has, indeed, caught the man, but so has the place.

Notes

An earlier version of this essay appeared in *Repast* 24(1) (2008): 6–10, and was presented at the symposium "Folklore and the Wisconsin Idea: Engaging Public Folklore in the Upper Midwest and Beyond."

1. Michigan's lower peninsula is shaped like a mitten. The mitten's thumb is the area being discussed.

2. Frankenmuth is a small town in mid-Michigan that is known as "Little Bavaria." It was settled by Germans, and the German presence is still strong. Besides its Bavarian-style architecture and the many tourist shops that line the main street, two restaurants, owned by brothers, serve fried chicken dinners with German side dishes. Frankenmuth is known for its chicken dinners.

3. This slogan was originated by Henry and repeated by him many times and reported in many news articles about the festival. Interviews of Henry were conducted by LuAnne Kozma and me in the summer of 1995. I want to acknowledge the assistance of Carolyn Smith, Henry's oldest daughter and archivist of the festival. She provided information on the community, her family's status and history, and the evolution of the sandwich. She also provided access to people and areas and an insider's perspective on the events discussed.

Grocery Stores as Sites for the Study of Material Communication

Ethnographic Guidelines

Ayako Yoshimura

Much about people is communicated through their food sources. Thus grocery stores can serve as rich ethnographic sites that tell us about the past, present, and future of communities. Embedded as they are in people's everyday lives as places that provide food, these stores disclose a great deal about local populations and cultures in terms of race, ethnicity, class, gender, and age group.

These qualities make grocery stores ideal for public folklore projects that aim to teach about local cultures, from K–12 ethnographic programs to community-exploration outings for adults. One successful example was an initiative organized by schoolteacher Mark Wagler and public folklorists Ruth Olson and Anne Pryor (Wisconsin Teachers of Local Culture n.d.). The project was designed to take elementary schoolchildren to neighborhood business establishments to imbibe the diversity of their own culture. In a companion publication titled *Kids' Guide to Local Culture* (2004), grocery stores were recognized as "gathering places" (101), and students were encouraged to understand the sources of their food as part of the social learning experience.

As a material-culture researcher, I wish to elaborate herein on the value of the grocery store for community-based educational projects by providing material-focused ethnographic guidelines. I first discuss two concepts that may be useful in such projects, and afterward proffer a brief sampling from a case study of mine. Although my grocery-store fieldwork was not initially rooted in public folklore, the case study sheds light on the sort of material-centered folkloric information that grocery stores can furnish—which can help people to understand and appreciate their positions in the local community.

THE GROCERY STORE AS LOCUS OF SOCIAL INTERACTION

In *The Great Good Place* (1989), sociologist Ray Oldenburg introduced the term "third place" to refer to public places that foster human sociability, in contrast to the home ("first place") and the workplace ("second place"). Examples of "third places" include pubs, coffeehouses, and hair salons: places at which people gather and create their own social environments.

I argue that grocery stores too are such "third places," because they are loci of social interaction. Examining the food items for sale while observing the interactions among employees and customers, researchers can absorb the folkloric information that stores have to offer. Because of this, folklorists have long studied stores as community centers (Hunt 1979; Beck 1980; Long 1990) and as sites of folklore both verbal (Bauman 1972; Macpherson 1987) and ethnic (Dresser 1971; Stinson 1998; Lockwood and Lockwood 2000).

The work of these folklorists examined small family-run businesses, but I believe that any grocery store—be it family owned or chain, general or ethnic—can function as an ethnographic site for the study of local culture. On many occasions I have overheard in supermarkets conversations suggestive of interpersonal familiarity between customers and butchers, stockers, clerks, and baggers. After all, it is people who create a sense of place, space, and belonging. Any store is a "third place" and therefore qualifies as a research site suitable for public folklore projects that explore local culture.

THE GROCERY STORE AS LOCUS OF MATERIAL COMMUNICATION

It is natural for people to rely on the tangible to make sense of the world around them, as physicality affords a means of expression and communication. For this reason, scholars of material culture seek physical evidence in order to unravel the contexts of human performance and communication (see Prown 1982; Ames 1984; Ward 1984).

For the purpose of researching grocery stores in the context of material communication, it is beneficial to understand a concept from Michael Owen Jones's study of the workplace. Jones (1980, 1987) examined the ways in which people establish work patterns and routines and create comfortable spaces so as to maximize efficiency and minimize stress in their workplaces. Jones called this kind of act "material behavior" (short for "material aspects and manifestations of human behavior") and explained that it "refers to activity involved in producing or responding to the physical dimension of our world" (1997, 202). Thus, rather than looking at grocery stores from the perspective of behavioral economics, researchers can study them from a sociocultural angle: as folkloric places where the practice of business is a joint effort by storekeepers and customers.

Nowadays it is not uncommon for chain grocery stores to launch community-engagement projects by, for instance, selling goods from local producers. Farmers markets are good examples of places that support local growers and manufacturers and that promote direct interaction between producers and consumers. It takes great effort to create a friendly environment that brings satisfaction to all parties while ensuring food safety and economic sustainability. Jess Lamar Reece Holler and colleagues (2018) observed—and helped enact—this in a project that brought an exhibit on Ohio's organic farmers directly to consumers of their goods. Both at their local farmers market and through an online publication (which included interviews with vendors and customers), they learned firsthand what it takes to maintain a safe and economically viable food environment. This exchange enabled producers to hear what consumers expect from them, while consumers could see what great care goes into producing and providing their food.

Another notion helpful in researching stores is that objects themselves communicate human relationships. Anthropologist Christopher Musello chronicled the life of an inherited dry sink that had undergone refurbishments and relocations within a house and explained the ways in which it reflected the relationships among family members and had accumulated multiple meanings through years of use within the family (1992, 54–55). Musello argued that objects take on "multivocal" and "polysemic" qualities from the people who touch, use, and own them over time.

Applying this concept to the researching of grocery stores might seem difficult, as the majority of items found inside are products that are expected to leave the store through sale. However, one can focus on objects that remain at the store, things for employee or customer use. Small independent stores are not alone in harboring "unique" objects ripe for analysis. Cultures vary even across chain and franchise stores, because the employees who staff them are different, as are the people who patronize them. Even standardized supplies allocated by a parent company acquire different histories at each store, because they are handled by different people. Hence seemingly identical objects come to have particular meanings at particular branches. Furthermore, given how seasonal specials and local delicacies differ according to region and local culture, each store requires equipment and routines specific to its locale. Moreover, there is variation in seasonal decor to accord with, for example, local festivals and sporting events. Considering these factors, it is possible to find objects that represent values endemic to each store, regardless of its type.

Folklorists—acting as community liaisons—can encourage public folklore projects for people to learn about the stores that they frequent so as to enhance their appreciation of their own communities or to explore stores that they do not habitually patronize so as to increase awareness of other parts of their locality. A focus on material communication (rather than verbal lore) might provide a convenient point of entry for beginning researchers, while it might enable advanced researchers to glean even deeper understandings of place.

ETHNOGRAPHIC GUIDELINES

With the aforementioned concepts of material communication in mind, a researcher might consider the following when studying a grocery store.

Location

It is important to understand the location of the store in relation to its environs. In what part of town is the store located? How would you describe the neighborhood? Does the store face a busy street? Is it in a shopping district? What other establishments are nearby? Are they related in terms of the population(s) that they serve? What are the sociocultural and socioeconomic profile and history of the area? Answers to these questions will help the researcher to understand the people in the neighborhood.

For example, a corner grocery store in a residential area may function as a quick stop for milk or bread for those in the habit of making weekly trips to a big supermarket to stock up on household provisions. Or people may stop in for snacks and sodas on lunch breaks, or to satisfy late-night cravings. Yet for those with limited mobility, the store may be where they procure daily essentials. When such corner stores are run by immigrants, they tend to carry some ethnic specialty foods that draw other immigrant families in the area.

Chain grocery stores' sizes and inventories may vary from location to location. Some chains, for example, have smaller stores in city centers and larger ones on the outskirts. It is advisable to visit several branches to check for differences among them and then to analyze those differences.

Municipal governments may offer incentives to attract or retain stores in areas classified as "food deserts." In studying such a store, it is important to research the history of the area in terms of food accessibility, because the issue is often associated with income levels, and thus with marginalized communities and vulnerable populations.

The presence in an area of a full-service ethnic grocery store often indicates that a high enough population of the congruent ethnic group(s) resides in or frequents that area. It is useful to check the distribution of ethnic grocery stores to obtain a bigger picture of the ethnic communities in the area. Some ethnic grocery stores may carry general items to serve those in the neighborhood who rely on the store for daily groceries. Others may be situated near big chain grocery stores, which might enable them to focus more fully on specialty foods.

Understanding the history of the area should help the researcher assess the significance of the store's location. Current and past maps of the locale will reveal the course of its development. For example, the construction of highways and exits affects people's mobility and shopping patterns and correlates with the socioeconomic ebb and flow of the area.

Building and Property

The building and its characteristics, along with the property history, provide important information about the community's history. When was the building built, and for what purpose? Were there former owners and/or tenants? What businesses occupied the building in the past? Describe the building in detail: materials used for the exterior and interior, renovations, facade (including signage and decorations). What can you tell about the store from the design of its sign and anything that decorates the storefront? Check the sides and back of the store. How are they used: as resting places for employees (e.g., crates used as chairs), as outside work areas with refuse bins or loading docks, as a parking lot for employees or customers? Do workers have a staff lounge? The ways in which such spaces are used speak to the culture of the workplace.

A chain grocery store might occupy a big concrete building with an extensive parking lot. It might have been built specifically for the company, or it might have been purchased and repurposed (in that case, the facade might still bear traces of a previous store's logo)— such information will intersect with a larger history of chain grocery stores. If a grocery store is in a strip mall, it may be worthwhile to learn the history of all the businesses and their relationships to one another. When stores are in residential–commercial hybrid structures, it can be interesting to find out how the stores were selected and to learn about their rental contracts. If a store is in an individual smaller building, study its history in relation to that of the surrounding area. If the building was originally constructed for a different business, the exterior may retain characteristics of those past businesses, despite possible remodeling and repainting.

Outdoor signs are often eye-catching. The logo, font, colors, and overall design are all important to the success of the business. Is the store's name associated with its location, its genre, an ethnicity, a family name, something else? How is it presented visually on the sign? What kind of image and impression is the sign trying to convey? Such visual effects help to define the store's character.

Interior

As you step inside the store, what are your first impressions? What kind of atmosphere does the store's interior create? Do you notice certain smells? Is the inside well lit? What colors are the walls? Are they decorated with posters or paintings? Are the shelves well organized? How are the products arrayed: according to product type, ethnic group, some other way?

Examine the floorplan and the placement of fixtures, as this will help you understand the flow of people. Are the shelving and product organization aesthetically appealing? Check the location and positioning of the checkout counter, as this informs the ways in which the clerks oversee the store. The clerks welcome customers, but they also need to be alert to problems. Do they have a manual for handling regular business transactions and difficult situations? If so, how is the store's risk-management strategy manifested materially in the interior? For instance, convenience stores often have height-indicator strips at the entrance to estimate the heights of shoplifters or robbers, and it is not unusual for stores to have security gates and cameras.

Signage is also revealing. Some stores may have signs in languages other than English, which may be for the benefit of a population to which the store appeals. Product signs can be handwritten or printed (or printed in a handwritten style), or a combination of the two (e.g., printed signs for staples, handwritten signs for daily and weekly specials). Whether or not the fonts exhibit any character of the store may be worth noting—stylized signs bespeak a level of investment that the store has made in marketing and advertising. Also, it is useful to check whether stores have bulletin boards and whether they circulate free local newsletters, as these yield clues to the kinds of people that come to the stores.

Do the store's carts and baskets bear the store logo or employ its color scheme? The logo may appear on grocery bags also. All these factors contribute to the atmosphere. Some stores have made grocery shopping a brand experience and a status marker. It is worth pondering the ways in which such aspects of marketing affect people's shopping behavior.

Stock

Check merchandise to get an idea of what kinds of customers frequent the store. How much of the stock is devoted to general items as opposed to specialty items (ethnic or otherwise)? Does the store have meat, seafood, and produce sections? Does it have a deli? Does the deli have signature items? What do these selections suggest about the type of clientele that comes to the store?

Nowadays chain grocery stores typically have ethnic food aisles. It is important to study how wide and deep the offerings are, and which cultural groups' foods are represented in these aisles. The existence of such sections does not necessarily mean that the stock is intended principally for immigrants and their descendants; it may simply be indicative of the popularity of ethnic foods in mainstream American culture. Immigrants tend to have preferences for specific brands known in the home countries; therefore, the stock may be more for nonmembers of these ethnic groups, who may not be as selective or knowledgeable about the differences among brands. It requires knowing which brands are favored (or considered passable alternatives) by immigrants to understand at whom these sections are aimed.

The inventory of an ethnic grocery store very much depends upon what export distributors make available, unless demand for a product is so great that it is manufactured in this country. To get a true sense of an ethnic grocery store, it is necessary to scrutinize its selection and variety. Ethnic grocery stores that target the general public carry only a few brands (or American versions instead of imports). Ethnic grocery stores that cater to a population of immigrants and their descendants offer a wide selection from the home countries because those shoppers tend to be faithful to the brands that they know from their homelands.

Another way to gauge the main clientele is by examining the selection of fresh produce and deli items. Some stores offer special selections of meat, seafood, vegetables, fruit, and other items to satisfy the needs of specific populations in the area. Produce and deli items have short shelf lives; so unless there are enough customers to purchase them, stores usually limit their offerings to items that last longer. A store may have special contracts with local suppliers for produce; it may be instructive to inquire about the store's business networks. Also, check if the store prepares deli items in-house or engages local restaurants or caterers as suppliers.

Other things to check include whether the store has organic or "healthy" food aisles (and if it does, of what size and range), whether the store has brands of its own, and whether the store carries local brands or has a local produce section to promote area businesses.

Putting People in the Material Analysis

After observing objects in the store, the researcher can turn to an analysis of material communication and behavior by examining the ways in which people's movements fit into the space. Interview owners, managers, cashiers, stockers, butchers, deli servers, and others about the following: Who owns the business, and who works there? What are the store's work hours and routines? How were they determined? What work is done when the store is closed? When are shelves stocked? When do delivery trucks arrive? Does the store offer weekly or daily specials? If so, what are they, and how are they decided? Does the store, for example, grant discounts to seniors or students? How do the employees feel about working at the store?

A similar set of questions can be asked of the clientele, because customers usually have routines for grocery shopping, and their routines often accord with those of the store. Who comes to the store to shop? When, and how often? What do they come to the store for? Ask questions that will help you better to understand the type of customers: occupations, ethnic backgrounds, genders, ages. Do they live in the neighborhood, or do they come from other parts of town? Among the regular customers is there a nickname for the store? If so, what are the reasons for the name, and what does it reveal about the relationship between the store and the customers or between the employees and the customers? What about the store do the customers like?

Answers to these questions will give the researcher insight into the function and meaning of the store to the owners, workers, and customers, and into their modes of material engagement with the store and its space. In the following section, I provide a glimpse of a case study of material communication that showcases the ways in which the making of place manifests a mutual appreciation between storekeepers and customers.

CASE STUDY: ORIENTAL SHOP

The shop that I researched is a mom-and-pop Asian grocery store in Madison, Wisconsin, called the Oriental Shop. Facing one of the city's main streets, this store functions as a "third place" for many locals and sojourners from Japan. Because of the owner's background, the store has a wide selection of Japanese groceries, and it has stayed in business for more than forty years. I was a regular customer there during the entirety of my residence in Madison (1999–2003 and 2007–15), and I conducted fieldwork that involved observing and interviewing the proprietors and their devoted customers. Through analysis of two aspects of material culture (foodstuffs and store decorations) I examined the dynamic of Japanese folklore in a diasporic setting and the ways in which materials functioned to cultivate personal relationships between the storekeepers and customers (Yoshimura 2009). With this research as a foundation, I later discussed ethnic grocery stores more generally as sites of cultural information (Yoshimura 2011).

The Oriental Shop is not in a conspicuous shopping district, though there are other businesses nearby. There is a Mexican restaurant next door, and a few blocks away are a chain grocery store, an independently owned café, a Chinese restaurant, and a chain hardware store. The store is located near an area called the Greenbush, which historically had many Italian American inhabitants. Indeed, the Oriental Shop is a converted house that once belonged to an Italian American family. The house has a green gable roof with shed dormers. The front is made of brick painted white. A central doorway is flanked by two windows. The name "Oriental Shop" appears in red, painted in what is known as the "Asian font" (the kind used frequently for Chinese takeout menus in the United States). The facade features a wooden relief in the shape of a Shinto shrine gate, also painted red. This announces clearly (to those who recognize the symbolism) that this "oriental" store specializes in Japanese goods. The backyard used to be a vineyard, but it was trimmed to create a small parking lot. Right outside the back door is a modest patch of grass with a flower garden maintained by the owner's friend. This creates a sense of homeyness perfect for eating lunch while sitting on the concrete porch in a nice spring or summer breeze, which is precisely what the owner's husband often does.

Most regular customers are Japanese—usually homemakers responsible for nurturing their families in the Madison area. They have been vocal about their wants, and thanks to the development of the Japanese food export industry, it has become possible in the past two decades for the kind of selection found in the supermarkets of Japan to be obtainable in the United States. The owner will get what the customers want if the items are available through the distributors, and for its size the Oriental Shop's selection of brands and varieties of Japanese food items is impressively vast. The store carries little produce and does not have a deli, but if there are seasonal vegetables or fruits that Japanese people like, the owner will occasionally get some—and they go fast because the regulars snatch them up! Otherwise, she will stock anything with a long shelf life and anything that is freezable. Thanks to her caring customer service, the store retains its long-term faithful customers.

The checkout counter is near the entrance; the location is perfect because it allows the owner to see anyone entering via either the front or back door. There are two shelving units in the middle of the store, perpendicular to the storefront, allowing fresh air to enter while not obscuring the clerk's view of the shoppers. Against the wall on one side are a big refrigerator and freezer aligned so as not to receive direct sunlight.

The store's inside is bright with fluorescent light. Its interior can best be described as homey, with bonsai plants, smiling Buddha statues, and handmade "open" and "closed" signs adorning the front door (made by the owner's gardening friend, who is also a skilled quilter). Popular business lucky charms from Japanese folklore, such as figurines of *maneki-neko* (beckoning cats) and Daruma (papier-mâché dolls modeled after the Chinese Buddhist monk Bodhidharma), are placed facing the entrance to welcome visitors. The walls are white, and parts are covered with large signs advertising noodles or sake.

Behind the counter are two shelves full of small figurines, many of them gifts from customers. They range from tiny happy Buddhas to large ornaments loaded with good-luck symbols. Yet most symbolic of the owner–customer relationship is a cluster of frogs, which consists of ordinary mass-produced items from the North American market—for instance, from the Beanie Babies series. It all started when one customer gave the owner a small frog lucky charm to put in the cash register to wish for business prosperity. When other regular customers found out about this, they sought to express their support as well. Japanese culture has a frog lucky charm that people use to wish for the return of things (treasure, luck, money, love), which plays on two homophonous Japanese words: *kaeru*, one meaning "to return" (帰る・返る) and the other meaning "frog" (蛙). In Japan, frog lucky charms (that is, frogs with such talismanic function) come in a certain shape or with explanatory certificates bestowing this property. But since such charms are not sold in North America, customers contributed any available frog figurines to the cause. In return, the owners display the frog-abilia alongside other gifts inside the store to show their gratitude for their customers' support.

Though this history would not be communicated to a first-time visitor, the store is a personalized space with material manifestations of the kinds of relationships that the storekeepers and customers have jointly nurtured. Surrounded by products that they have selected, business charms that they have positioned, and gifts from appreciative customers and well-wishers, the storekeepers have created a comfortable workplace for themselves. And the place welcomes new customers who will return if they like what the space has to offer. Inside is not merely a business but a collage of human relationships. This explains the homelike ambience of this small Asian enclave.

Conclusion

Certainly not all Madisonians will shop at the Oriental Shop, yet there is still value in their appreciating its presence in the community. It is this that I strove to impart to readers of my original research. The same kind of study could be done for any other store and could be molded into a public folklore project through the addition of an outreach component. People look different, eat different foods, and go to different stores to do their grocery shopping. But people do all this for the same set of reasons (enjoying food, providing for one's family, celebrating special occasions). Folklorists can develop public folklore projects that enable people to realize their common ground by touring local grocery stores to understand their contributions to the community. Such projects will help advocate for cross-cultural understanding and encourage people to respect others' life experiences. Grocery shopping is part of everyday life for most people. Public folklorists seek to connect different groups of people so that we can all appreciate one another. Visiting the "third places" of others raises awareness of how much we actually share.

PART V. ENGAGING WITH THE PAST

Folklorists work in near-constant dialogue with the past, as we look at tradition's winding pathways, at the past as a creative construction of the present, or simply try to better understand historical folklore in context. Long having moved beyond the notion of "tradition bearers" who passively carry the relics of the past forward to new generations, we now engage with the notion of the past and our own heritage as shared productions of the present that meet our contemporary cultural and social needs. Working with the past in creative ways is a creative act of the present, as we continually work to create and re-create ourselves, our histories, our stories, and our traditions.

Working in and with communities, in and with archives, folklorists work historically in a number of ways. We work to improve our understandings of the past to better understand the present, we assist in the creation of cultural histories of marginalized peoples, and we grapple with the complex notion of heritage as a production of the present more than a survival of the past. The chapters in this section look at these dialogues between the past and the present, at heritage and history, at these perpetual negotiations as we draw connections between what once was and what now is.

In his piece on oral history, Troy Reeves focuses on a series of projects he helped develop to serve both internal infrastructural needs on campus and external needs beyond just the campus community. Reeves looks specifically at the mechanisms we use to support the collection of materials, in this case oral histories, that invariably shape how the past is understood in the future.

Mark Louden's work on Pennsylvania German folklife showcases the stark differences between the actual folklore practiced in communities and the fabricated stereotypes held by outsiders that were sold as sensationalist literature for commercial profit. Louden looks at the work of Pennsylvania German folklorists, who strove to work with the deep traditions of Pennsylvania German voices in order to combat the falsehoods surrounding their traditional culture by engaging with the public presentation of that traditional culture.

Rebecca Keyel's chapter considers the use of archives as a publicly oriented process. She details her own use of archives to learn the hands-on techniques used to support American military wartime efforts. Keyel suggests that using archives is a form of craft knowledge—but one too seldom discussed by folklorists—and that the embodied knowledge of re-creation of craft can also be a form of public culture work that links the past to the present.

In her chapter on a legend or hoax involving a petrified French voyageur, Jennifer Gipson explores constructions and contestations of history and historical authority that emerge from public engagement with archives, collections, and their agency over the past. Gipson's work reminds us of how particular moments in history view the past through the lens of their own present, imbuing stories with historical value that lies not in a representation of fact but in creative, fluid, and adapting reflections of folklore belief, disbelief, and fascination rooted in collective anxieties and social and economic contexts.

In Guha Shankar's chapter, we see how the documentation by Alan Lomax and the subsequent collection at the American Folklife Center provides a deep and still relevant set of resources. Shankar walks us through the history of Lomax's work with filmed footage and includes a short case study focusing on how he and a collaborator, James Leary, retrieved and then produced some of Lomax's original footage for a project on folk music in the Upper Midwest. In part, this work reveals the value of archival work and the importance of folklorists continuing to engage with the past in new and creative ways using the technologies of the day.

In his chapter on the use of ebook platforms to represent Icelandic sagas, Colin Gioia Connors's contribution details his production of one such book, effectively using digital technologies to augment contextual information in order to better translate a medieval rendition of the story for a modern audience. Connors examines his own development of the project, acknowledging both the challenges of such a project and its benefits. Such an engagement with history, designed to simulate a more natural storytelling environment, serves the student public and helps show how medieval history is relevant to us today.

While ethnographic documentation is often the stereotypical methodology of folklorists, the chapters in this section remind us of the value and importance of working historically, of engaging with archives and collections, as well as of conducting ethnographic fieldwork, and, in doing so, help illustrate the ongoing relevance of the past as it is continually reimagined into the present to serve a variety of social and cultural needs.

"The Wisconsin Historical Society Gave Me Your Name"

Doing Out-(and In-)reach on Campus, in Wisconsin, and Beyond

Troy Reeves

The Oral Historian of Vatican City?

This chapter's title comes from phone calls and emails I have received as the head of the oral history program at the University of Wisconsin–Madison Archives since 2007. While not all the requests included those exact words, they all had the same gist. Someone in Wisconsin wanted oral history help, and some other someone had pointed them to me.

They found me, primarily because the Wisconsin Historical Society's (WHS) staff doesn't include an oral historian. While the WHS had a robust oral history program in the 1970s and early 1980s, led by Dale Treleven, it was disbanded in the early 1980s ("Wisconsin Historical Society" n.d.). The WHS still collects oral history—primarily thanks to outside or grant funding—continuing to add audio and audio/video interviews to its rich collection on diverse topics such as the Wisconsin Survivors of the Holocaust or the Oscar Mayer Stories project.[1] Because of this fact, I have said that my job is akin to being the oral historian of Vatican City, where in this hypothetical example neither Rome nor Italy has an oral historian.[2]

What steeled my nerves about being the de facto state oral historian was the fact that for seven years (1999–2006) I was Idaho's state oral historian. My official state of Idaho job title was "Historian, Oral." Seriously. In my seven years in Idaho, I gave more than two hundred presentations throughout the Gem State and met with Idahoans to talk about doing oral history or about Idaho State Historical Society's oral history projects. This work began my oral history outreach.

In Wisconsin, conducting oral history outreach was just as necessary. When I came to Madison in February 2007 to be interviewed for the vacant "Head, Oral History Program" position, I stumbled onto the Wisconsin Idea—reading it in a brochure about the UW–Madison Libraries—and used it in my job talk. At the time I offered the standard boilerplate from that document: the boundaries of the campus are the boundaries of the state.

Once I arrived here and learned more about the Wisconsin Idea, I decided that those words, while making for a great soundbite, don't do it justice.

Let me try to explain. Or, let me have Gwen Drury explain. Drury writes: "I began to realize what a huge emphasis our former leaders placed not only on getting information to students and citizens, but also on helping create processes where they could develop strengths and power as citizens, just by getting to know one another. It's what the Wisconsin Idea is about: finding ways to share knowledge with the residents of the state, because knowledge is power; and connecting them with each other, because connection is power. And UW and state leaders wanted Wisconsin citizens to have as much power as they can" (Hathaway n.d.).

It's that Wisconsin Idea that I try to exemplify in my day-to-day work.

And more than that: it's the type of work—sharing knowledge with others to enrich both parties and, when done well, to create new, better history—that all of us in the humanities should do. So, even though my anecdotes in this chapter focus on Wisconsin, we folklorists, oral historians, and ethnographers should strive to do this work everywhere. The Wisconsin Idea should not be limited to "America's Dairyland" but should be instituted beyond our state borders too.

But before we do that, a quick note. My mentor at Idaho State University, emeritus professor Ron Hatzenbuehler, started many a formal presentation with warnings and disclaimers. As an homage to him, I have some too (Reeves 2002). Under "Warnings": There will be name dropping, because one cannot tell an out- (and in-)reach story without discussing the people met, and references to Marvel movies. Under "Disclaimers": this chapter builds on more than a decade of work—some of it written and presented in public, including in a 2017 Wisconsin Humanities Council *Humanities Booyah!* blog post and in a 2017 TEDx talk.

INREACH

Since June 2007, I have advocated to my bosses, and to anyone else who will listen, that one of four primary legs of the proverbial oral history program stool, which I call the "4 Cs"—collecting, curating, communicating, and collaborating—is communication. And particularly during my time in Madison, this includes not only outreach but inreach, which I define as working within the bounds of campus with students, staff, and faculty interested in doing or learning more about oral history.

Inreach has resulted in a laundry list of campus collaborators, of whom I'll share a few briefly before going into more detail about one in particular. First, for example, the George L. Mosse Program in History at UW–Madison has partnered with our program from my first days as program head. Mosse Program leaders John Tortorice and Skye Doney have conducted interviews for our collection and furnished funding or student support to help us make our collections more accessible to people both on and off campus. More recently, I have combined forces with Lyn Korenic and Anna Simon at the Kohler Art Library, as well as with former UW–Madison staffers Tracy Honn and Craig Eley, to include excerpts from an oral history project (Reeves and Lange n.d.) with UW–Madison faculty and alumni involved in the Book Arts—a field of art involving works that use or refer to structural and conceptual properties of a book—in an exhibit at the Chazen Art Museum, which ran in early 2020, coinciding with that institution's fiftieth anniversary.[3] In this case, inreach and outreach combined, as we collaborated on campus to create new exhibitions that are accessible to a wider audience.

Yet another inreach example comes from the folklorists and those overseeing the Center for the Study of Upper Midwestern Cultures (CSUMC). This affinity began even before I arrived in Madison. The best advice I received in the months between accepting the job in Madison and leaving Boise came from Robert McCarl. McCarl taught a class in cultural landscapes at Boise State University, and we connected and collaborated over our shared interest in documenting firefighters' stories.[4] While I cannot recall the advice word for word, my paraphrase of it follows: "Find Jim Leary, tell him I sent you, and offer to buy him a beer. Then shut up and listen."

Ever since, I have tried to build projects or collaborations that bring me into these experts' spheres. Examples include guest lecturing in Jim Leary's or Ruth Olson's classes; helping Chrissy Widmayer and Marcus Cederström write a book chapter (2020) by conducting oral history interviews with Leary and Olson; and volunteering to lead a workshop in their 2017 "Traditions in Dialogue" series, overseen by Cederström, Anna Rue, and Nate Gibson. In addition, I serve as an affiliate at the Center for the Study of Upper Midwestern Culture (CSUMC).

All this has helped me stay a known entity in UW Folklore's universe, which has been vital for at least two reasons, not including the strong connection between folklore and oral history as fields of work and study (Milligan 2012). First, everyone I have met who is either directly or tangentially involved in this universe has become a valued colleague, helping me tap into resources, such as grant possibilities and student staff, that have allowed my program to flourish. Second, each of them offered prototypes of the Wisconsin Idea in action and that our program has tried to emulate.[5]

Last inreach example: when the Libraries invited me to interview for the "Head, Oral History Program" position, I met with the search-and-screen committee, including then UW Digital Collections Center Digital Service librarian Vicki Tobias. Once hired, I ended up working with Tobias, because of a document titled "University of Wisconsin–Madison Audio Preservation Survey and Report" (2007) that she and a graduate student and Archives student staff member, Chris Hartman, had written just before I arrived.

This thorough, sixty-page report offered much grist for my oral history mill—including three pages of analysis and two pages of recommendation—but Tobias and Hartman told me of the participants' interest in working together to build a community around the issues of audio and video access and preservation. That led me to focus on reaching out to them to set up a fall 2007 meeting. From there the A/V Club was born.

The A/V Club's core group—archivists, sound engineers, and librarians from on and off campus—came from UW–Madison's Archives, Mills Music Library, and the Digital Collections Center. We also included members from Wisconsin Public Television, the Wisconsin Historical Society, and the Wisconsin Veterans Museum. Our first goal became to create an A/V clearinghouse, a place where anyone could get A/V access and preservation questions answered.

For several years we held regular meetings, eventually disbanding in 2012. The relationships built and maintained, however, helped us all as we dealt with issues related to A/V access and preservation. From that group, iSchool faculty member Dorothea Salo has built a robust shop, called Recovering Analog and Digital Data, or RADD, that provides A/V advice and support to folks on campus, as well as training and leadership to iSchool students. Also, my University Archives colleague Cat Phan, the digital and image archivist, revived the A/V Club in 2017, and its listserv has offered, yet again, advice and support to those of us working in this field. This "club," along with the other examples already mentioned, stand as our program's attempt at deliberate inreach, building the Wisconsin Idea from the inside.

OUTREACH

In moving from in- to outreach, I start by defining my term. Outreach, for our program, is our effort to offer our oral history services and support to anyone outside UW–Madison's boundaries. I have worked with and learned from dozens of groups around the state and region. I'd like to list some, for they run the gamut from libraries, colleges, historical societies, and museums to community groups and nonprofits. I've worked with libraries in Wild Rose and Sheboygan. The colleges include Carthage and University of Wisconsin–Eau Claire. Under historical societies and museums, I chatted about oral history with the Rock County, Rio, and Kewaskum historical societies. Finally, among the community groups and nonprofits, I consulted with County Health Rankings and Roadmaps and the Robert E. Gard Wisconsin Idea Foundation. This very nonexhaustive list doesn't touch on the many hundreds of individuals I have met with throughout Wisconsin, the region, and the country. For example, we worked with Stuart Levitan regarding his book on Madison during the 1960s (2018).

While I worked with these groups as the oral history "expert," I have delved into outreach opportunities with other oral historians in Madison, Wisconsin, and the Midwest. This work lines up, too, with the Wisconsin Idea, since this work serves not just those on my campus. Two examples follow. First, I convened the Madison Oral History Roundtable (MOHR), which met between August 2008 and September 2016 to discuss issues related directly to the process of conducting oral history interviews. Second, I worked with a few folks from around the region to create a regional group called Midwest Oral Historians (MOH). At our height, we built an email listserv of more than one hundred people from several Midwest states ("Midwest OH Group" n.d.).

But, first and foremost, as de facto Wisconsin State oral historian, I will describe my effort to create a day to celebrate statewide oral history, aptly called Wisconsin Oral History Day (WOHD).

WISCONSIN ORAL HISTORY DAY

I led three WOHDs—in 2008 in Madison, in 2009 in Eau Claire, and in 2010 in Milwaukee—to bring together interested individuals from the campus, the city, the state, and the region to discuss oral history projects and to promote the strong oral history work done by practitioners from each area. The 2010 WOHD stands as the best example. Funded primarily by a Wisconsin Humanities Council mini-grant and attended by more than sixty historians, students, archivists, librarians, and community members, it brought to fruition a dream that started in October 2007, when I wanted to see whether I could live the Wisconsin Idea by bringing the oral history program out into the community.

Holding the 2010 event in Milwaukee—the state's largest city and home to several colleges and universities and several dozen humanities-focused groups—seemed a logical choice. I brought together people from the University of Wisconsin–Milwaukee's (UWM) Department of History and its libraries, including Michael Doylen, Michael Gordon, Jasmine Alinder, and Chia Vang, to serve on its program committee. While the UWM groups and the WHC stood as the primary collaborators, I must list the others—WHS, UW–Madison's Library School Continuing Education Services and its General Library System, UWM's Hmong Diaspora Studies, the Wisconsin Labor History Society, and UW–La Crosse's oral history program—all of which provided both in-kind and financial support, because it did take a village to raise the WOHDs.

While I could offer a play-by-play recitation of WOHD 2010—including our keynote presentation by University of North Texas oral history director Todd Moye—I will focus on just one event, because it's emblematic of the WOHD's programming. This session, titled "Works Concluded and in Progress: Jewish Oral History in Wisconsin," kicked off WOHD. Held at the Jewish Museum Milwaukee (JMM), the panel was moderated by Jonathan Pollack, a Madison Area Technical College history instructor.[6] The panelists included Pollack, JMM's Kathy Bernstein, WHS's Sally Jacobs, and two other Milwaukeeans who had incorporated oral history into their collections or programs.

Pollack's comments touched on the imperative of collecting and preserving oral histories that are unique and relevant and on the growing interest in using these primary sources for teaching and for research. Bernstein described the status of the museum's collection of oral histories of the Milwaukee Jewish community. Jacobs couldn't attend, so I read her presentation, an overview on WHS's Wisconsin Holocaust Survivors Project that showed the online accessibility of the oral history collection, including audio, transcripts, biographies, and photographs.

Two other Milwaukeeans—Leon Cohen, director of the Wisconsin Small Jewish Communities History Project, and Matt Blessing, then the head archivist at Marquette University—rounded out the panel. Cohen discussed plans for the oral histories in the project's collection, as well as plans to design a vehicle for the digital dissemination of the histories on the project's webpage. Blessing presented the challenges and successes of transcribing interviews from the Generation After Oral History Project, sixty-five interviews of Jewish immigrants living in the Milwaukee area that document life in Europe before the Holocaust.

The participants and presenters engaged in questions and answers that underscored the necessity of going out and collecting and presenting oral history responsibly. Presenters and participants alike shared their passion for oral history collections. Technical details and advice were offered, and there was a mutual sense of the challenges involved in finding hidden collections and capturing untold histories before the ravages of time take their toll. The discussion highlighted the need to secure funding to fully realize the educational and research potential that digitization of oral histories and transcripts offer in online environments and to preserve them for the citizens of Wisconsin and the world to discover ("WI Oral History Day" n.d.).

I never held another WOHD after 2010. So, why does this three-year event warrant any prose here? It exemplified the Wisconsin Idea. First, we tried to target all types of Wisconsin citizenry for this conference, such as the historians, students, archivists, librarians, and community members who attended. Along with them, I wanted to attract two other types of people: K–12 educators and the state's many people of color, including Native American community members. Although we could have done more for those two groups, members of the Oneida Nation did participate in 2010. And although no K–12 educators attended, oral history has been and can be a vital part of an educator's learning toolbox, and it can and should be an important tool in decolonization and the continued amplification of all-too-often ignored voices like those of Wisconsin's Indigenous communities.

Another reason: I wanted these events to build a community or network of those interested in oral history. Two attendees—Moye and Pollack—gave feedback to me, noting the variety of attendees and the opportunity offered during the day to either reconnect with colleagues or meet new people. Pollack, for example, bemoaned the fact that he could not stay longer to do "extended networking."

"A Bit of Both": In/Outreach

In the first *Guardians of the Galaxy*, Star Lord (Chris Pratt) answers his own question "What should we do next? Something good, or something bad, or a bit of both?" with "A bit of both." At the OHP, a lot of my work falls into this category, meaning that I try to promote oral history both on and off campus. So, I now offer two subprojects under a multiyear, Internet-based collaboration with our Digital Collections Center, called Campus Voices, to feature "a bit of both."

From 2010 through 2012, I oversaw Campus Voices, creating published pieces from excerpts and images from our collection. The project's mission became to capture, present, and preserve some of the strongest historical stories and memories of UW–Madison, through the people who lived them. Our goals were to digitize and process interviews, photos, and documents related to five historical campus topics; put full content on the UW Digital Collection Center website; and publish online aspects of content, as excerpts or audio clips, on iTunes U, as podcasts at UW Archives website, and as a minimovie on YouTube. While we completed all five projects, including the 1970 TAA Strike, Badger Village, and Women in Science and Engineering, I will offer some depth on two others.

Campus Voices: LGBTQ

Within Campus Voices, two subprojects stand out. The first actually predated the project's official time frame. With help from Vicki Tobias and two campus colleagues, Scott Seyforth and Michele Besant, our program in 2007 started an oral history project to document the stories and memories of the LGBTQ community both on campus and in Madison—going a bit beyond "Campus Voices" in true Wisconsin Idea fashion—from the 1960s to the present. We conducted three interviews that first year; Tobias noted that she "enjoyed getting to know this interesting topic through our first narrators. I hope these interviews lead to a strong LGBTQ oral history collection at the UW–Madison Archives." Well, in the years that have followed, a strong LGBTQ oral history collection has arisen. We now have more than one hundred oral histories, and the collection grows by 5 to 10 per year (LGBT OH Project n.d.).

The project started with five key objectives:

1. Conduct oral histories with longtime members of Madison's LGBTQ community.
2. Build an archive of oral histories, as well as personal and organizational papers, pictures, posters, and pamphlets.
3. Support two growing UW–Madison entities: the LGBT Studies Program and the LGBT library at the LGBT Campus Center.[7]
4. Provide primary-source material for the emerging and burgeoning scholars of LGBTQ history.
5. Reach out to the Madison community to build positive relationships between LGBTQ members and others as well as within the LGBTQ communities.

We endeavored to reach those objectives by building collaborations among interested individuals and organizations on and off campus, continuing to conduct oral history interviews and adding recorded dialogues between community members on current topics or contemporary LGBTQ issues, pursuing funding avenues to professionally process and prepare the recordings as well as the donated material, and building a webpage to offer an overview of the Madison's LGBTQ community history and provide wide access to the project's content (Madison's LGBTQ Community n.d.).

As alluded to earlier, this project has postdated Campus Voices—a few interviews get added every year—and it led to the formation of a permanent collection of material at the University Archives. Thanks to outside funders, including the Mosse Program, the LGBTQ Archive contains oral histories, personal papers, photographs, ephemera, and organizational records related to LGBTQ life in Madison and Dane County from the 1940s to today. From these first oral histories, the collection has grown to include an increasingly diverse array of materials and voices from the LGBTQ community and receives new donations regularly, including an article in a special issue of the *Oral History Review* (Seyforth and Barnes 2016), titled "Listening to and Learning from LGBTQ Lives."

CAMPUS VOICES: STERLING HALL BOMBING OF 1970 AND "UNCIVIL DISOBEDIENCE"

The other subproject, "Sterling Hall Bombing of 1970," arose in early 2010, as the fortieth anniversary of that 1970 event approached.[8] While this Campus Voices subproject focused mainly on extant oral histories in which, during the course of an oral history interview, a narrator had offered memories of the bombing and its aftermath, it led to an interesting, rewarding collaborative sub-subproject that became known as "Uncivil Disobedience." While this ended up a collaborative effort between Mike Lawler and the Wisconsin Story Project and our oral history program, it started when WHS's Sally Jacobs and I learned about Lawler and his storybooth.

Top: Attendees seated before beginning of *Uncivil Disobedience*. *Bottom*: Opening scene of *Uncivil Disobedience*. UW–Madison's Memorial Union, October 2014. (Photograph by author.)

During my first few years in the OHP, Sally and I had bandied about the idea of some type of booth to collect stories; Lawler had already built one. Lawler, who like me came to Wisconsin in the late 2000s, wanted to pursue some project around the bombing, which our program intended to do, too. So, we joined forces, cosponsoring the placement of the WSP's storybooth in Memorial Library in late August 2010, and captured almost one hundred stories about the bombing ("Wisconsin Story Project/Sterling Hall Bombing" n.d.). From there, our program, with Mike's help, conducted more interviews. We also assisted him as he crafted and produced a documentary theater piece, *Uncivil Disobedience*. A staged reading of this play, featuring actors voicing oral history excerpts and other primary-source documents, ran inside Madison's Overture Center for two nights in March 2012 and kicked off the 2014 Oral History Association Annual Meeting, held in Madison.

The storybooth idea really taught me two lessons. First, I discovered the power of nontraditional, facilitated short-form oral history. By gathering many stories on a topic, we could add multiple voices on that subject to our collection. In subsequent years, our program has collected shorter oral histories or facilitated stories on many topics, including campus events that occurred during the Vietnam era, as these events had reached their fiftieth anniversary. I learned a second lesson well after 2010, too. When I started out, I tried to find students who would volunteer to help with these projects. It finally dawned on me that training them to facilitate or interview and paying them for their efforts made it more worthwhile and effective for all involved. Both lessons have let our program add more audio to our collection and enabled us to work with more students using better labor practices.

CONCLUSION: OR, WHY DOES IT MATTER?

In most every presentation, I end by explaining: "Why does oral history matter"? This question needs an answer here, because most of these things I discussed, like the WOHD, did not stand the test of time. I don't think longevity matters: an event or collaboration can be important without being permanent; those two ideas need not be mutually exclusive. In all these cases, whether inreach, outreach, or a "bit of both," they count because our work together has helped people gain knowledge and enriched them (and me). As Gwen Drury said (a mantra made famous in my generation by *Schoolhouse Rock*): knowledge is power. On top of that, again from Drury: community is power. The work I've done helps amplify unheard or ignored voices, to give power to the people by legitimizing their voices, and to create primary sources preserved for posterity. The work has built a community that looks to do collaborative, meaningful, and deliberate oral histories. It's a model everyone can and should follow.

CODA

Like the Marvel movies, I finish with a coda. While I truly relish every opportunity to meet with individuals and groups throughout the city and state, my best days on the job have included this type of correspondence: "I am writing to inquire about the cassette tapes in your archives on which my grandmother's interview is stored. I recently inherited the transcription of the interview from my Grandfather Harold Tarkow. I would very much like to hear the original interview, as I never met my grandmother." This person concluded by inquiring about how to gain access to the audio.

By 2012, we had digitized our analog oral histories. So, I put the audio up in UW–Madison's slice of the "cloud" (Tarkow 1977) and gave her access. Two hours after I sent her an email, she emailed back: "Thank you so much for getting back to me regarding my Grandmother's recorded interview. The files downloaded very easily. It means so much to me to be able to hear her voice for the first time. It's truly a unique and rare gift you and the Oral History Program have given me. Thank you again, Shoshanah Tarkow."

Our oral history program, through our collection's interviews, can bring generations of family members together. Or, and I quote myself here, "sometimes in my job, I get to bring the dead back to life" (University of Wisconsin–Madison Communication 2019). I love meeting with people and groups, whether the meeting was initiated by me or came after someone was directed to me by a third party. I embrace this personal connection to people I interview or help access our oral histories, because it matters most to me.

Notes

1. For more on the Wisconsin Survivors of the Holocaust, see https://www.wisconsinhistory.org /HolocaustSurvivors/. For more on the Oscar Mayer Project, see https://www.oscarmayerstories .com. The Wisconsin Sound Archive also includes WHS oral histories and other audio in its collection: http://content.wisconsinhistory.org/cdm/landingpage/collection/p15932coll11.

2. Okay, this is not exactly true. The Wisconsin Veterans Museum has a full-time oral history archivist, but that position is focused specifically on Wisconsin veterans. So, while it has statewide reach, the position has a narrower focus than mine.

3. For more on Book Arts (and the Kohler Art Library's collection), see https://www.library .wisc.edu/art/collections/artists-book-collection/.

4. For more on McCarl, see https://www.boisestate.edu/sociology/adjunct-faculty/faculty -staff/robert-mccarl/. McCarl and I co-lead a symposium on fire fighting in the Intermountain West. Sadly, no reference to it exists on the Internet; one would need to access the Idaho Oral History Center's program files. To learn about finding aid for the Idaho State Historical Society's "Smokejumping and Forest Fire Fighting Oral History Project," visit https://cdm16281.contentdm .oclc.org/digital/collection/p15073coll1/id/135/rec/2.

5. For just one example, see the following article, which offers an overview of a UW–Madison folklore collaboration: "Ojibwe Birch Bark Canoe Launches in Lake Mendota," College of Letters & Science, UW–Madison, November 20, 2013, http://ls.wisc.edu/news/ojibwe-birch-bark-canoe -launches-in-lake-mendota/.

6. Jon Pollack has published extensively on the Jewish experience in Wisconsin. To learn more about the JMM's oral histories, visit https://jewishmuseummilwaukee.org/archives/oral-histories/. See also the Survivors site, https://www.wisconsinhistory.org/HolocaustSurvivors/.

7. These names were in use in 2007, when I crafted this document. These names are now LGBTQ+ Studies Certificate and the Gender and Sexuality Campus Center.

8. The University Archives holds a wealth of information about the Sterling Hall Bombing, but I recommend starting here: https://www.library.wisc.edu/archives/exhibits/sterling-hall-bombing -of-1970/.

Shoemaker, Frey, and Yoder and the Pennsylvania Dutch Idea

MARK L. LOUDEN

Historians trace the origins of the Wisconsin Idea to a foundational address delivered by University of Wisconsin president Charles Van Hise in 1905, in which he famously proclaimed, "I shall never be content until the beneficent influence of the University reaches every family of the state" (University of Wisconsin–Madison n.d.; see also McCarthy 1912; Carstensen 1956). As the Wisconsin Idea developed, many interpreted the "beneficent influence" to be unidirectional, from the university to the broader community. To be sure, the university is a generator of knowledge that brings tangible benefits to residents of the state and beyond; the pioneering work on vitamin D by the biochemist Harry Steenbock and his colleagues at UW–Madison is one notable example. However, other expressions of the Wisconsin Idea emerge when the laboratory is located not on University of Wisconsin campuses but in homes and communities across the state.

In this chapter, I discuss three folklorists from an earlier generation whose work exemplified the idea that scholarship should have a positive impact outside the ivory tower. Alfred L. Shoemaker (1913–??), J. William Frey (1916–89), and Don Yoder (1921–2015) were three native Pennsylvania Dutchmen who founded the Pennsylvania Dutch Folklore Center (PDFC) at Franklin and Marshall College in Lancaster, Pennsylvania, in 1949 (for biographical information on Shoemaker, see Bronner 1991; on Frey, see Beam 1985; and on Yoder, see Bronner 2016). Under their leadership, the PDFC advanced the nascent interdisciplinary field of Pennsylvania Dutch studies while also engaging the public through a diverse program of outreach that included publications, presentations, and the highly successful Pennsylvania Dutch Folk Festival, today the Kutztown Folk Festival, which celebrated its seventieth anniversary in 2019 (Kutztown Folk Festival n.d.). The impact of Shoemaker, Frey, and Yoder, as scholars writing on the history of folklore in the United States, notably Simon Bronner, have noted, extended far beyond Pennsylvania and its inhabitants of colonial Germanic descent. Indeed, the beneficent influence of what might be called the Pennsylvania Dutch idea endures to this day.

PENNSYLVANIA DUTCH CULTURE

Before discussing the scholarship and outreach of Shoemaker, Frey, and Yoder, a few remarks about the history of the cultural milieu into which the three colleagues were born are in order. The people known as the Pennsylvania Dutch (or Pennsylvania Germans, as scholars more commonly describe them) are the descendants of approximately eighty-one thousand immigrants from German-speaking Europe who settled in the rural hinterlands of southeastern Pennsylvania in the eighteenth century (Louden 2016; Bronner and Brown 2017). Immigration peaked around midcentury and all but ceased at the time of the American Revolution, not resuming again until about two generations later, at which point a distinctive folk culture had developed, at the center of which was a vernacular language similar to the southern German dialects spoken by the founder population with a modest admixture of vocabulary from English. From the outset, as farmers and rural craftspeople who spoke a language that fell between the linguistic chairs of German and English, the Pennsylvania Dutch were derided by Yankees and German Americans as ignorant, superstitious country bumpkins. Pennsylvania Dutch men and women who pursued an advanced education, entered the professions, moved to towns and cities, or married non–Pennsylvania Dutch partners typically sought to distance themselves from their heritage language and culture. The stigma of the "dumb Dutch" is one that is still familiar to Pennsylvanians today (Louden 2016).

When Shoemaker, Frey, and Yoder came of age in the first half of the twentieth century, it appeared that the writing was on the wall for the Pennsylvania Dutch language, the standard-bearer of the culture. The twin forces of industrialization and urbanization conspired to break down the natural barrier between town and country that had for generations insulated distinctive cultural and linguistic minority groups in America, including but not limited to the Pennsylvania Dutch. By the 1930s, the assimilation of Pennsylvania Dutch speakers into the English-monolingual mainstream was such that today, the language is essentially actively used only by members of Amish and Old Order Mennonite communities, the "Plain People," who have very intentionally—and successfully—resisted the pressure to give up their heritage language, which is today an important symbol of their distinctive socioreligious identity. Among the "Church People" (or "Fancy Dutch"), who constituted the historically largest Pennsylvania Dutch subgroup and the one to which Shoemaker, Frey, and Yoder belonged, the transition to English monolingualism is all but complete.

As Pennsylvania Dutch language and culture receded among the Church People in the decades leading up to World War II, the popular curiosity of outsiders about the "peculiar" inhabitants of rural southeastern Pennsylvania increased. The Pennsylvania Dutch soon became a major attraction for tourists from urban areas who could easily reach the "Dutch Country" with their Ford automobiles. Enterprising locals, including some of Pennsylvania Dutch heritage, saw an opportunity to make money and built an industry marketing the folk culture to a curious public. Today, Lancaster County, Pennsylvania, is the destination of millions of tourists from around the world who eagerly consume "Amish stuff."

The most prolific producer of writings about the Pennsylvania Dutch directed at tourists in the 1930s and 1940s was a Harrisburg bookseller-publisher named A. Monroe Aurand Jr. (1895–1956) (Deibler 1988/1989, 1989; Louden 2016, 268–71). Aurand was actually a native speaker of Pennsylvania Dutch, and his pamphlets on language, which are still available today, were not bad. When it came to other aspects of Pennsylvania Dutch culture, Aurand's pamphlets peddled distorted and in some cases outright false images. He was especially fixated on witchcraft and bundling (bed courtship), which he termed "America's greatest indoor sport" (Aurand 1930, 1938, 1942). The first paragraphs from one of Aurand's pamphlets on bundling reflects how he aimed to reach "real lovers of folklore": "WHAT IDEAS DO YOU HOLD RELATIVE TO COURTING IN BED? CAN LOVERS GO TO BED, SAFELY, WHILE WEARING THEIR CLOTHES, AND STILL BE CHASTE? Is it morally wrong for one to go to bed to court—and morally right to sit up all night for the same purpose? The natural love of man for woman, and woman for man, and the almost universal lack of knowledge regarding the widespread custom of clothed, or partly clothed persons— BUNDLING (or courting in bed)—induces us to publish another of our historical accounts for real lovers of folklore" (Aurand 1938, 5).

Aurand, who enjoyed commercial success in what he hawked to visitors to the Dutch Country, drew the ire of Alfred L. Shoemaker, who, along with his colleagues Bill Frey and Don Yoder, began producing their own popularly oriented publications under the auspices of the Pennsylvania Dutch Folklore Center in an effort to set the record straight (Weaver-Zercher 2001, 114–21). Their efforts were not in vain.

SHOEMAKER, FREY, AND YODER AND THE PENNSYLVANIA DUTCH FOLKLORE CENTER

As mentioned earlier, the Pennsylvania Dutch Folklore Center (PDFC) was founded by Shoemaker, Frey, and Yoder at Franklin and Marshall College (F&M) in 1949. It was auspicious for the center to be based at F&M, which had a long tradition as an institution that promoted interest in the history and culture of the region in which it was located and from which most of the students hailed (Bronner 1991, 39). Of the three scholars, Frey arrived at F&M first, in 1944, as the chair of the German department there. Frey had received his graduate training in Germanic linguistics at the University of Illinois, where he completed a 478-page dissertation on Pennsylvania Dutch in 1941, at the age of just twenty-five (Frey 1941). Shoemaker was in the same program as Frey and finished his degree there just one year before his friend and future colleague. Shoemaker's dissertation was notable as it was the first doctoral thesis on Pennsylvania Dutch as spoken by Amish (he conducted his fieldwork in the Arthur, Illinois, settlement; Shoemaker 1940). After a brief time on the faculty of Lafayette College and service in the US Army in Europe in World War II, Shoemaker was appointed to a professorship in American folklore at F&M in 1948. Don Yoder joined F&M's Religion department the following year after completing a doctorate in church history at the University of Chicago.

The PDFC was physically housed in the Fackenthal Library at F&M, which in 1946 had received a huge collection of Pennsylvania Dutch artifacts known as the Unger-Bassler collection. The collection became an important focus of the curatorial and interpretive work of Shoemaker, Frey, and Yoder. From the start, Shoemaker played the leading role in the work of the center, which was modeled after similar institutions that he had personally visited in Europe, including the Swiss Institute for Folklore in Basel and the Irish Folklore Commission in Dublin (Bronner 1998, 288). In 1949, the three colleagues also started publishing a bilingual weekly newspaper, *The Pennsylvania Dutchman*, which three years later became a semimonthly magazine titled *The Dutchman* and eventually the quarterly *Pennsylvania Folklife*, which was published until 1997. The synergy among Shoemaker, Frey, and Yoder was remarkable. In these and the PDFC's various other publications, Shoemaker focused on folklore and material culture, while Frey wrote on language, literature, and music and Yoder wrote on history, religion, and genealogy. Among them, they had the spectrum of Pennsylvania Dutch culture well covered.

The three colleagues placed their greatest priority on offering a corrective to the burgeoning Pennsylvania Dutch–themed tourist industry that was booming in their backyard in Lancaster County. Although their work was grounded in solid scholarship, their most important audience was the general public, including both outsiders and their fellow Pennsylvania Dutch. A search of Pennsylvania newspapers from the late 1940s and early 1950s yields many references to public presentations that Shoemaker, Frey, and Yoder delivered to community groups. Frey also played guitar and sang folksongs he had learned as a boy in eastern York County. Their collective work complemented and intersected with the activities of a number of other grassroots efforts to promote a proper understanding of Pennsylvania Dutch history and culture, including newspaper columns, especially "'S Pennsylfawnisch Deitsch Eck," edited by Preston A. Barba, a professor at Muhlenberg College, for the Allentown *Morning Call*; radio shows; and the growing Grundsow (Groundhog) Lodge movement, which began in 1934 and is still going strong (Donner 2016). By far, the legacy of Shoemaker, Frey, and Yoder and their Pennsylvania Dutch Folklore Center was sealed with their founding of the Pennsylvania Dutch Folk Festival in 1950 in Kutztown, which, known today as the Kutztown Folk Festival, celebrated its seventieth anniversary in 2019 with more than 130,000 attendees and is billed as "the oldest continuously operated folklife festival in America" (Kutztown Folk Festival n.d.).

To see an example of the spirit of the PDFC and the three scholars who led it, it is worth examining one of the pamphlets they brought out in the 1950s. The first part of the introduction to the *1955 Tourist Guide through the Dutch Country*, which was written by Shoemaker, is worth quoting here.

> The words *Pennsylvania Dutch* ordinarily conjure up four pictures in the tourist's mind: quaint, sombre-clad Amish who paint their gates blue to show there is a marriageable daughter in the household; high calibre farmers who paint *hex signs* on their barns to keep away the witches; a bell-don't make bump, hind-end-foremost English; and, above all, the cookingest folk in all of America who serve seven sweets and seven sours three times a day, seven times a week.
>
> Whether one likes it or not, this picture—though far from being factual—has become an integral part of our American folklore. And nothing is likely ever to change any part of it.
>
> This Guide, prepared by the staff of the Pennsylvania Dutch Folklore Center of Franklin and Marshall College, has a twofold purpose: *first*, to direct the tourist through the most interesting parts of the Pennsylvania Dutch country, and *secondly*, to give a brief survey of its colorful folk-culture, a happy mixing of Continental, British, and local American folkways. The Continental influence, pre-Revolutionary in the main, derives from Germany, Switzerland, and little Alsace on the Franco-German border. The "Dutch" in Pennsylvania Dutch has, of course, no connection with Holland. The word "Dutch" has for centuries, both in England

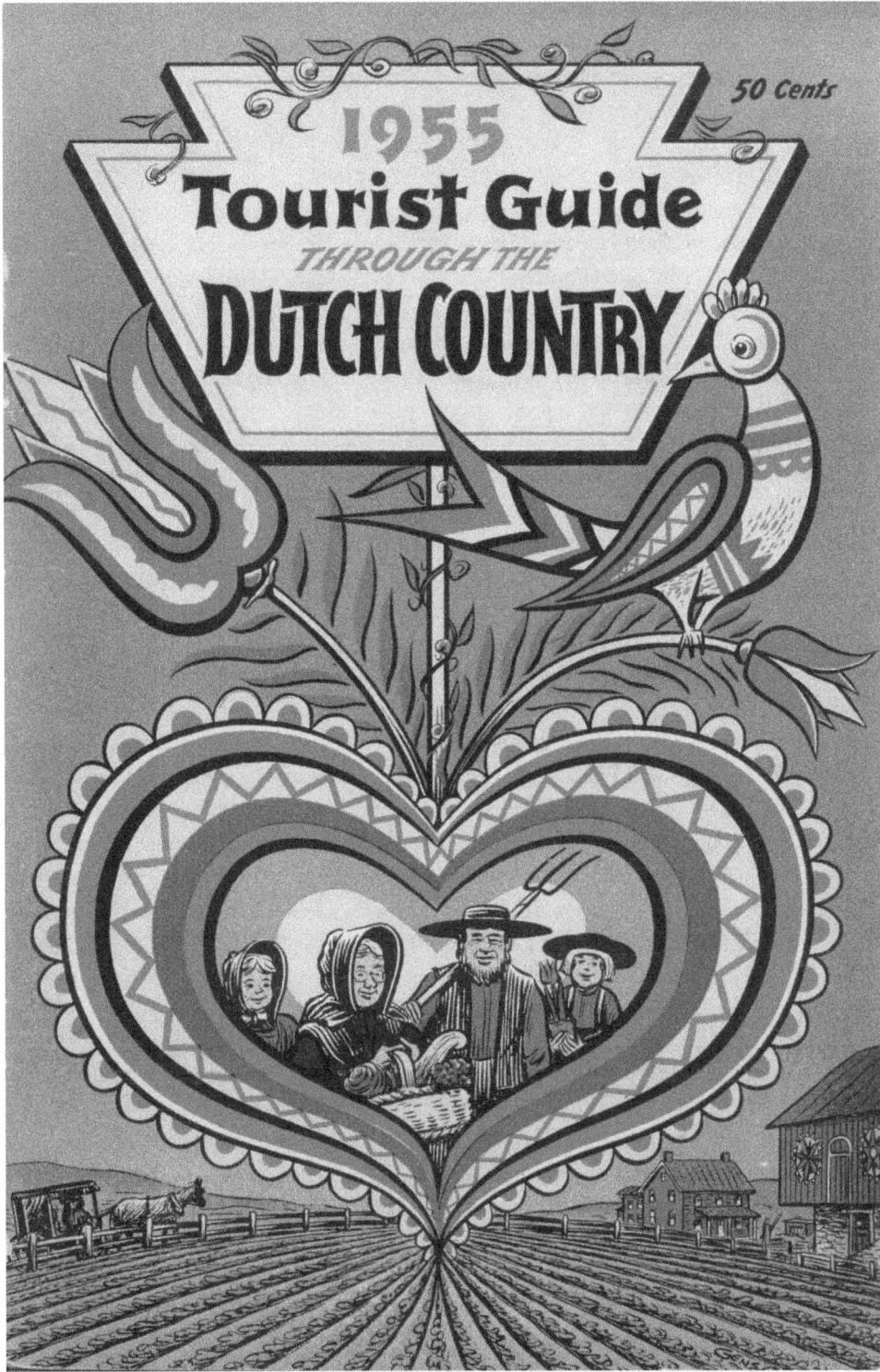

Cover image from *1955 Tourist Guide through the Dutch Country*, by Alfred L. Shoemaker, Don Yoder, et al.

and in the United States, been used synonymously with German. There are a few, particularly those with an eye to learning, who insist on using the term *Pennsylvania German*, "an uncouth name ... one unsanctioned by time or use on man's tongue," Fredric Klees says of it. (Shoemaker and Yoder 1955, 5)

The guide then offers up almost one hundred pages of useful information for the curious visitor, including many excellent photographs. Recognizing the fact that the great majority of tourists would come to the Dutch Country by automobile, Shoemaker and Yoder's *Guide* includes six "tours," self-guided routes that visitors could take at their leisure throughout the Dutch Country, as well as an "Amish Tour" focused on Lancaster County. The guide includes several advertisements for businesses geared to tourists, an element that helped finance the production costs and served the practical purpose of helping visitors to find fuel for themselves and their vehicles, as well as lodging.

Of special interest to scholars and general readers alike in Shoemaker and Yoder's *1955 Guide* are the concise essays by Shoemaker, Yoder, and others on various topics related to Pennsylvania Dutch folklife, including food (with recipes), folk art, language, religion, Plain People (Amish and Mennonites), and customs and holidays. One example is a one-page contribution by Don Yoder titled "The Dutch Folk-Culture," a brilliant summary of the essence of Pennsylvania Dutch culture that is as accurate today as it was when it was written some six decades ago. Like most of the *Guide*'s essays, Yoder's offers a gentle corrective to distortions about the Pennsylvania Dutch peddled by many in the tourist trade.

> One of the most widespread misconceptions about Pennsylvania Dutch culture is that it is something foreign, something alien, something largely unrelated to the general currents of American thought and life. Nothing could be farther from the truth. Our German and Swiss forefathers did not intend to found a "Little Germany" in these hills and valleys where they made their new homes after the trek across the Atlantic. Nor *did* they found a German cultural island divorced from American thinking. True, they settled together in large enough numbers to enable their German language and its everyday daughter "Pennsylvania Dutch" to last into the present generation. But the Americanization process, even in language, began with the immigrant generation. (Shoemaker and Yoder 1955, 43)

As this passage reflects, Yoder recognized that Pennsylvania Dutch culture was fundamentally hybrid and dynamic. It did not constitute some kind of hermetic eighteenth-century Germanic isolate frozen in time in the wilds of southeastern Pennsylvania. He and Frey and Shoemaker soon came to recognize that to do the Pennsylvania Dutch justice, one needed to understand the other cultural groups that were part of the complex tapestry that defined the Commonwealth, including Quakers, Native people, Scotch-Irish, and others. No aspect of Pennsylvania Dutch life was untouched by influences from people whose ancestors were not from Germanic Central Europe, from material culture to foodways to language. This led Shoemaker and Yoder (Frey had to step back from the center due to family responsibilities; his wife was stricken with polio in 1954) to expand the scope of their quarterly journal beyond the Pennsylvania Dutch and to reconstitute the PDFC as the Pennsylvania Folklife Society. The replacement of the term "folklore" with "folklife" (preserved also in the description of the Kutztown festival cited earlier) reflected their desire to emphasize the holistic nature of vernacular cultures like that of the Pennsylvania Dutch (see also Bronner 1998).

Returning to the 1955 *Guide,* and recalling Ammon Monroe Aurand's fixation on bundling, Shoemaker, in the space of a single page, enlightens popular readers on the historical and contemporary reality of bed courtship in an essay on the Amish (Shoemaker and Yoder 1955, 13–14). He begins by quoting the dictionary definition of bundling, followed by a humorous anecdote on the subject attributed to a professor from his alma mater, the University of Illinois. Then Shoemaker the scholar sets the record straight, deftly including references to scholarship (a German-language monograph by a Swedish-Finnish ethnographer, K. Rob. V. Wikman) and his own experience visiting cultural institutions in Europe, all while never losing his reader.

> People usually attribute bundling in New England to two reasons: to the cold winters and the penurious Yankee fathers too tight to supply fuel to keep their daughters warm when their beaus come acourting. Ask any sociologist and he will tell you this is simply not true at all.
>
> Bundling was practiced all over the Continent and England long before the first white settlers ever set foot on American soil. In fact there is a 395-page scholarly treatise on the subject: *Die Einleitung der Ehe* by Karl R. V. Wikman, Åbo Akademi, Åbo, 1937. Judging by the vast ignorance of Americans on bundling, perhaps it would be well to have this treatise translated.
>
> In certain sections of Germany and Switzerland, where the ancestors of the Pennsylvania Dutch came from, bundling is called *fensterlin,* literally "to go windowing." All over Europe the suitor enters his sweetheart's bedroom through a window. If you were to visit the Scandinavian and Dutch Open Air Museums you would even see the architecturally important "Bundling Window."

Shoemaker's treatment of bundling concludes with remarks made by John A. Hostetler (1918–2001), a contemporary of Shoemaker, Frey, and Yoder who was born into an Amish family and later attended college and graduate school, becoming a professor of sociology at Temple University (Kraybill 2001). Hostetler, who founded the interdisciplinary field of Amish studies, shared the concerns of Shoemaker, Frey, and Yoder about what was being served up in popular media about the Pennsylvania Dutch and the Amish in particular, producing accessible publications for tourists that were grounded in scholarship.

John Hostetler's classic, popularly oriented publication on the Amish was *Amish Life,* which first appeared in 1952 and eventually sold more than 700,000 copies. In a section titled "Courting and So Forth," Hostetler describes bundling as follows.

> Even though some writers have explained bundling out of present-day existence, it still remains the accepted form of courting in a few settlements. It is by no means universally practiced, however, and it is only during the past 75 years that the practice has disappeared in other communities. Bundling is defined as a practice where lovers sleep or lie together on the same bed without undressing. However, there is absolutely nothing like the "center board" or the

"bundling bag" described in popularized treatments of the subject. Bundling is a very old custom, stemming from oriental and European practices, and since the Old Order Amish have retained most of the older practices it is quite natural that they should retain bundling. Since most Amish are without the conveniences of electricity and central heating systems, the original reasons for bundling still exist. In almost all localities, however, it is strictly forbidden. (Hostetler 1952, 22–23)

Hostetler thus offers the curious visitor to the Pennsylvania Dutch Country an alternative to the sensationalized accounts found in publications like those of Ammon Monroe Aurand.

Concluding Thoughts

Returning to the Wisconsin Idea, we recall that its emergence is connected with the 1905 speech quoted by Charles Van Hise at the beginning of this essay. In fact, earlier leaders prefigured Van Hise's view that the university should be a source for good not just for faculty and students but also for the state's citizens. One of his predecessors, for example, Thomas C. Chamberlin, who was UW president from 1887 to 1892, once said, "Scholarship for the sake of the scholar is simply refined selfishness. Scholarship for the sake of the state and the people is refined patriotism" (quoted in Carstensen 1956, 184). Even earlier, in 1858, a committee of the Wisconsin Assembly had this to say of its aspirations for the university:

> [The people of Wisconsin] have an unquestioned right to demand that . . . [the university] shall primarily be adapted to popular needs, that its course of instruction shall be arranged to meet as fully as possible, the wants of the greatest number of our citizens. The *farmers, mechanics, miners, merchants, and teachers* of Wisconsin . . . have a right to ask that the bequest of the government shall aid them in securing to themselves and their posterity, such educational advantages as shall fit them for their pursuits in life, and which by an infusion of the intelligence and power, shall elevate those pursuits to a dignity commensurate with their value. (Carstensen 1956, 182)

The enumeration of the beneficiaries of the university's work—"farmers, mechanics, miners, merchants, and teachers"—leads one to wonder whether the research of humanities scholars like folklorists would be valued. Tellingly, the lines immediately preceding the sentence in which President Van Hise expressed his desire to see the "beneficent influence of the University reach[] every family of the state" read as follows:

> The University is a state institution not supported in the interest of or for the professors. They are merely tools in the service of the state. It is not even mainly for the direct benefit of the students who take advantage of its opportunities. It is supported that they may become better fitted to serve the state and the nation. It is supported that the knowledge as well as the achievements of today reach all parts of the state, thus securing larger returns from the soil, the scientific development of mineral resources, the expansion of manufactures, the improvement of the social and economic conditions of the masses, and the enjoyment by the people of the great intellectual and moral experiences of the race. (1905, 4–5)

One would be hard pressed to see how the dispelling of myths surrounding cultural practices such as bed courtship serves any practical purpose akin to, say, enhanced crop yields.
Nor would many consider the expressions of vernacular cultures such as the Pennsylvania
Dutch as exemplary of "the great intellectual and moral experiences of the [human?] race."
In 2015, a spotlight was shone on the Wisconsin Idea when then governor Scott Walker
sought to amend Section 1111.36.01 (2) of Wisconsin Statutes by eliminating key phrases
referring to "improv[ing] the human condition" and "the search for truth" and redefining
the purpose of the University of Wisconsin System to include "meet[ing] the state's workforce needs." The public outcry against these proposed changes prevented them from being adopted, with Governor Walker famously declaring them to be the result of a "drafting
error" (Hamer 2016). Yet many still question the utility of humanistic knowledge beyond
the ivory tower.

Were Alfred Shoemaker, Bill Frey, Don Yoder, and John Hostetler living today, I am
confident they would offer articulate defenses for the value of their outward-facing work,
rooted more generally in the public value of the humanities. In *Humanities World Report
2015*, the report's authors identify a number of tangible benefits of humanities research,
including helping to "create tolerance and understanding between citizens, thereby leading
to social cohesion" and to "enable citizens to understand, preserve, and sometimes challenge their national heritage and culture" (Holm, Jarrick, and Scott 2015, 12). A deeper
knowledge of distinct American subgroups such as the Pennsylvania Dutch helps all of us
understand better what in fact "American" means. The 2015 report's authors also point
out how humanistic work benefits society indirectly, by way of "feed[ing] into other
fields, most obviously the social sciences, but also into medicine, computer science and
engineering/design" (Holm, Jarrick, and Scott 2015, 13). In my own service as a cultural
mediator between Amish people and outsiders, especially in the area of health care, I regularly appreciate the ways in which cultural knowledge that is shared in community meetings held in barns and church basements can improve the ways in which Amish and their
non-Amish neighbors interact with each other.

It is fitting to end this essay with the words of Don Yoder, whose long career was the
very embodiment of the Pennsylvania Dutch idea: "The chief value of folklife studies is
that its data show us the range of human thought, more basically perhaps than history, literature, and other already accepted studies. In showing us what life was like before urbanization and industrialization, we are shown the long roots of the life that we share" (Yoder
2001, 38).

The legacy of folklife scholars like Don Yoder and his colleague-friends Alfred Shoemaker and Bill Frey is one enjoyed by scholars and a curious public alike.

Finding Tradition in the Archives

Craft as Research and Research as Craft

Rebecca J. Keyel

During the first half of the twentieth century, the American Red Cross oversaw a volunteer program that provided handmade clothing for service members and civilians affected by conflict and natural disaster. One of the more popular programs was an effort to hand-knit sweaters and other "comfort items" for active and hospitalized service members. The volunteers making these items had to follow specific guidelines, and by the 1930s, knitting patterns distributed to local chapters included the advice that "one with 'knitting sense'" would know how to suggest volunteers adjust their knitting to make sure it conformed to the guidelines (American Red Cross 1935, 24).

The patterns were referring to the kind of expertise also referred to as "tacit knowledge," "local knowledge," or what the craft scholar Peter Dormer has called "craft knowledge" (1994, 10). Craft knowledge is a way of describing the implicit knowledge that a craftsperson has built up through experience with materials and technique, rather than the more theoretical knowledge of how a craft process works. For example, I may describe the process of knitting as a method of creating fabric using a single string in an interlocking series of loops. The loops are manipulated by using two knitting needles—gently pointed sticks—that the knitter uses to move each loop individually from one to the other. But this description doesn't adequately describe the process or get to the deeper knowledge that a maker has about the materials or the object they are making. This understanding of how the materials interact with the tools used to create them or the vision of what the finished product may look like is the maker's craft knowledge.

This essay examines the ways in which a researcher accumulates and relies on this kind of implicit knowledge as they work. For that reason, I have chosen to use the term "craft knowledge" to describe the way that scholars actually do their research and put that research to work in order to better capture the additional informal knowledge gained through the process of research and writing.

Public folklorists have long pointed out the importance of understanding the folklore of work (Y. Lockwood 1984; Green 1993). Here, I am simply widening the lens to include the work of scholarship itself and to acknowledge explicitly that research requires craft knowledge. I suggest that this craft knowledge is important for scholars to recognize and talk about, but I also suggest that harnessing the craft knowledge of making activities can be a way to help confront what the historian Emily Robinson has called the "absolute alterity of the past" (2010, 518). The physical act of making, of sketching a described scene in a journal or knitting a garment previously rendered only in text, helps ground the object in the present, making it more real and allowing us to interact with it in a way that helps to bridge the gap between unknown and known.

My own experience with experiential making and acquiring craft knowledge began when I was a college sophomore. Alone in my dorm room, I taught myself to knit "in the round"—a technique required to knit socks—from a World War II knitting pattern that had been transcribed and posted online. This experience was in itself an experiment, from learning how to hold the yarn and knitting needles to learning to follow a pattern. A good teacher can explain how to knit, how to hold the yarn so that the tension of the material suspends the needles that aren't currently being worked, but, much like research, it takes craft knowledge to do well.

This experience had several points of connection to the research project that forms the case study for this essay. The project examined how institutions—mainly the American Red Cross—organized thousands of knitters across the United States to hand-knit garments for service members during World Wars I and II. The research project itself had two components. The first was a historical examination of the knitting effort through women's magazines, newspapers, and the archival records of institutions involved with the knitting effort. The second part of the project was an experimental making process that involved hand-knitting a number of the same comfort items, using patterns originally developed by the American Red Cross and the Navy League, the two major players in American knitting efforts during World War I. The goal of this part of the project was to *experience* creating garments similar to those knit during World Wars I and II. The resulting hand-knit objects are useful items for display and study, but the original purpose of this component of the project was the physical act of knitting them.

My decision to bring these two components together was influenced by my own experience as a maker. My own craft knowledge of knitting informed the project because I also knew that actively re-creating the garments would give me a deeper understanding of how they were made. This, in turn, influenced my understanding of how they were designed and how they would have looked and felt when worn on the body. The physical act of knitting each item proved to me that the patterns designed by the Red Cross are straightforward to knit and simple to finish. This means that a beginner who had a limited mastery of knitting would be able to make most of the garments, while a more seasoned knitter could likely finish multiple items more quickly. The physical objects also provided supporting evidence for the historical record. The most visible item of the Red Cross knitting program was the sleeveless sweater. In the original 1917 pattern, these sweaters were constructed with a narrow opening for the neck that would sometimes be too tight (*Pittsburgh Chapter of the American Red Cross* 1922, 96). Soldiers reportedly cut the material, which caused the entire garment to unravel. A new and redesigned pattern was issued in 1918, but I did not find archival evidence to prove that it was to correct the issue. However, the physical differences in the reconstruction proved that the neck of the redesigned pattern was much more elastic and would have been more comfortable to wear.

The different parts of this project also necessitated different approaches to the underlying research. I could not adequately understand the breadth of World War knitting without doing historical research in libraries and archives. Likewise, I could not adequately understand the shape of the garments themselves without making them. These different approaches led to an understanding of the importance of the craft knowledge inherent to research and of the ways in which the physical act of making can inform and enhance the end product.

The core goal of the project was to understand two things: first, why millions of volunteers knit sweaters and other "comfort items" for soldiers during World Wars I and II, and, second, how such a monumental effort was organized. My historical research provided the answer to the second question and a partial explanation for the first. The first question—why did someone in the past do something—is almost impossible to definitively answer, despite all our best efforts at scholarship. What we can do is find the factors that may have led to a decision, the circumstances surrounding an event, or the cultural influences that shaped the final design of the object.

The experiential aspect of my research explored what knitting itself could tell me about the wartime knitting effort in order to approach an understanding of the first question. Why knitting? What could the patterns themselves tell me about how it felt to knit them myself? What could knitting them myself tell me about how the patterns were written? To answer that, I knit fourteen different garments from knitting patterns designed for service members during World Wars I and II. All of these patterns were either designed by the American Red Cross or adapted by the American Red Cross for service members. I used wool yarn that was as close as possible in color and material to what my research told me was available during both wars. I also knit the items with knitting needles made of casein, an early plastic made of milk protein that was readily available in the 1940s and that was used in knitting needles that were recommended in wartime themed knitting patterns (*Knit for Defense* 1941, 4).

Setting these kinds of research parameters required the kind of formal skills learned in a classroom but also required informal skills, acquired through skill transmission and experiential hands-on learning. These were skills that I'd learned not in school but from my grandmother, who in turn had learned to knit from her mother. When I started the making part of the project, I drew on the knitting sense my grandmother had passed on to me and the knitting sense I had acquired from nearly twenty years of leisure knitting.

Much like a knitter, ethnographic researchers have a learning curve. They have to learn how to reach out to potential interviewees, how to use their recording equipment to catch just the right amount of sound, how to read silences in a conversation. They have to learn how to take the gigabytes of digital data and turn them into durable, understandable archives. Archival research also has a learning curve. As a historical researcher working in the digital age, I had to learn how to handle fragile paper and how to read old documents, but I also had to learn how to take study photographs of pages of text so they would be legible later, how to glean the important pieces of a human story from lists of statistics, and how to turn those pieces back into concrete quantifiable data.[1]

These were the data I used to answer the second question posed by the project: how the wartime knitting effort was organized. My initial research into print publications, particularly women's magazines and trade publications, showed that wartime knitting was prevalent in popular culture. Women's magazines of the era wrote glowingly of the patriotic efforts of knitters whose efforts "might save some brave lad from frost bite and amputation" or whose sweater "would keep heart and body warm" (*The Delineator* 1917, 40). Retail trade publications showed that department stores used wartime knitting to sell yarn and large knitting bags, which came into vogue as a visible symbol of one's commitment to patriotism and the war effort (Ghelerter 1989, 64).

Archival records about wartime knitting also made it clear that it was the institutional organization of the American Red Cross that enabled a large-scale hand-knitting campaign to organize knitters across the country to make sweaters and other items. The Red Cross had the military connections, organizational expertise, and professional personnel to work with other volunteer groups to develop and distribute knitting patterns to volunteers *and* to distribute the millions of completed garments to servicemen overseas. After the end of World War I, similar programs continued to mobilize knitters to make sweaters and other items for distribution to hospitalized service members, veterans, and civilians. When World War II began, the American Red Cross ramped up its existing clothing production program to provide clothing for civilians. Eventually, the Red Cross reluctantly authorized a knitting campaign for service members only *after* knitters who were active in local Red Cross chapters threatened to start their own knitting program. Red Cross records made it clear that both organization's own leadership and colleagues within the US military were reluctant to authorize a hand-knitting program, but individual volunteers were writing letters of inquiry to their local chapters almost a year before Pearl Harbor and US entry into the war (Fieser 1941; Smith 1941). This smaller-scale program lasted for the duration of World War II and continued in various forms until 1965.

When I started this project, I had a deep craft knowledge of knitting and a developing craft knowledge of research. Both evolved as I worked, with the completed knitting complementing my research finds. In documenting both aspects of the project, I had to transfer the skills I learned in my ethnographic training and use them to create a kind of personal archive, composed of data from multiple physical archives that I photographed and manipulated and cataloged in digital form.

My basic process went like this. I used a portable digital camera set to take both high-quality "RAW" images and high-quality jpgs, which I then transferred to my computer. When I photographed completed comfort items, I laid them carefully on a white background to try to maintain the color of the original yarn. In archives, when I could, I used a camera stand that allowed me to mount my camera in a fixed position over the document I was photographing. This allowed for clearer photographs that were easier to read and convert into PDFs later. When I couldn't, I stood and used my own body as a makeshift tripod, learning to adjust myself rather than the fragile paper I was photographing. Until I started actually doing in-depth archival research, I did not have the craft knowledge I needed to be able to work effectively. Each technique required its own mastery, its own learned muscle movement.

My craft knowledge of research was developed over time. It took me multiple visits to different archives to fully develop a system for examining and photographing different types of documents and then a system for managing those digital data once I'd gathered them. I examined a range of documents in different settings: government documents held in state historical societies, women's magazines held in university libraries, and knitting patterns held in small museums and libraries. For each visit, I had to carefully think through what I would need for the day's work, from laptop and camera to sack lunch. I found that my experience of these research trips led to an inherent confusion and feeling of unreality, as they were set apart from my regular routine. All the archives and reading rooms I visited had different and special rules and regulations meant to keep the fragile documents safe, and learning to navigate them was a part of the unreality. Typically, researchers are required to divest themselves of most of their belongings before entering an archive's research room, and learning exactly what physical tools I would need to complete the work was another part of the knowledge I had to acquire.

My experiences navigating archives demonstrated that the experiential quality of archival research can be necessary for both practical reasons and affective reasons. Some historians have already explored the affect of archival research, of the physical implications of holding a piece of paper from the past. Robinson has argued that "the archive is the place where historians can literally touch the past, but in doing so are simultaneously made aware of its unreachability. In a maddening paradox, concrete presence conveys unfathomable absence" (2010, 503). The title of her paper "Touching the Void" encapsulates that experience, the "unfathomable absence" of a history that we cannot quite reach but that seems just within our grasp. Similarly, Nicolas Watson has argued that we need to acknowledge the reason that we study the past at all and come to terms with the importance of recognizing our own emotional connection to the past and, more concretely, to our historical work (1999, 61).

Robinson also explores the idea that archival research legitimizes the researcher, that the feeling of having gone and done the work authenticates the historian in her own eyes and in the eyes of her mentors and colleagues (2010, 507). There is also a similar kind of legitimization in doing fieldwork. When a folklorist conducts fieldwork with a craftsperson, learning about the technique a rosemaler uses or where a knitter learned to knit, the researcher is in communication with that unreachable past, with the much more tangible present, and, through the creation of archives, with the future. There is a similar thrill in recording a craftsperson or even a friend, in listening to a story being told and thinking, "Yes! I'm doing it. This is folklore."

The work I completed for the case study that forms the center of this essay is another aspect of this kind of legitimization, but it was to apply my own craft knowledge of hand-knitting to the topic itself. Part of this was to avoid the absurdity of studying knitting, as a knitter, without actually making one of the garments in question. Henry Glassie has argued that "the study of material culture uses objects to approach human thought and action" (1999, 41). Craft practice by its very nature lends itself to a deeper kind of experience of knowing how an object is made. Making an object brings the maker/scholar one step closer to understanding, if not how the maker felt, how the materials and process may have felt in the hand. The experience of making gives the scholar an advantage in understanding the objects themselves; it helps make critical connections that might otherwise not become clear.

Beverly Gordon has argued that understanding textiles "from the 'inside out'" adds to a scholar's critical understanding of the technique and technical ability of an object's maker, as well as to the utility of an object, and suggests that textile production has a particular "kinesthetic" quality that is impossible to convey effectively in words (2002, 4–5). This kinesthetic quality embodies the kind of craft knowledge Dormer discusses. Elizabeth Wayland Barber has described how her attempts to match the weave patterns of a blanket led her to make the object backward, something that allowed her to realize that weaving it correctly would have produced the correct pattern and been easier, a useful piece of knowledge (1995, 22–23). Dress historians have also argued that creating reconstructions of historical garments allows the replicas to be worn and manipulated without damaging fragile fabrics and that the reproductions themselves provide valuable information about the way historical garments were constructed and might have been worn in the past (Davidson and Hodson 2007, 209; Davidson 2019). Similarly, experimental archaeologists use making to test hypotheses about the way tools, clothing, buildings, and the whole array of material culture were produced (Hurcombe 2008). The craft knowledge of a technique allows for a new dimension of understanding of the object.

Knitting is a physical act. It is an immersive experience; it both clears and occupies the mind. Some research suggests that knitting has health benefits similar to meditation, including reduction in blood pressure, relief from chronic pain, and anxiety relief (Corkhill et al. 2014, 39). During the first half of the twentieth century, and likely even earlier, knitting was a common prescription for "jangled nerves" (*Columbia Book of Yarns* 1907; "Knitting as a Nerve Cure" 1911; "Knitting for the Nerves" 1912; Denihoff 1940). During one of her darker periods, Virginia Woolf once called knitting "the saving of life" (Bell 1972, 183). The rhythm of knitting is calming, and it is meaningful. It has a generative quality as the knitter literally creates a garment from a single strand and has a tacit quality that made it ideal for anxious volunteers worried about the state of the world. Knitting for someone else is a physical expression of that meaning to the object and then to the giver. In this process, knitting allowed volunteers to create a meaningful object for someone fighting a long way from home. The Red Cross was able to capitalize on this process and create easy-to-follow, simple directions to guide millions of women in the process of knitting for the war.

The garments themselves were designed to be simple to knit. The sweaters, the most popular garment during both wars, were a single knit length with a collar. Once the long lengths of fabric were finished, they were sewn up the sides to create the garment. This simplicity of design allowed them to be made all in one piece and finished relatively quickly, ensuring a uniform product even though they were made by hand. The simplicity of the directions the Red Cross created both kept skilled knitters working quickly and efficiently and simplified the process for beginners. I used the same patterns to re-create the knit objects. This forced me to look closely at the patterns themselves, in ways that moved beyond close readings of the text and toward our understanding of expressive communication. Knitting from a pattern requires close attention to the way the garment is constructed as the knitter literally creates the garment stitch by individual stitch. Like archives that are constructed document by document, recording by recording, the knitted object functions as a receptacle for the history that came before it. It embodies the knitter's own past, the long tradition of knitting that came before the object was made, and the skills learned formally and informally.

The physicality of reconstruction also means one of the outcomes of this project was physical garments that can be used as a teaching tool or displayed in a gallery. Because they are modern reproductions, they are touchable in ways that historic garments are not, and they can be worn on the body. And, like other elements of material culture, they are a kind of gateway to understanding the world they came from. Only a few of the original Red Cross patterns had accompanying photographs, which means that the reconstructed physical object allows for visual study in a way that a knitting pattern cannot. These finished objects can then be displayed in a variety of venues, from gallery shows to educational programming, and, because they are not historic or fragile, touched and experienced like any other contemporary garment.

This kind of hands-on research has other public implications. Material culture is well suited to public presentation because objects are physical manifestations of culture, both historical and contemporary. In addition, knitting has a relatively low learning curve and remains a popular leisure activity. The advent of YouTube tutorial videos and craft-focused social networking sites like Ravelry means that more and more people are teaching *themselves* to knit. Traditional knowledge transmission is expanding thanks to the availability of technology and the democratization of knowledge. The simplicity of the Red Cross patterns in particular means that, just as they were ideal for novice knitters to make in wartime, they remain simple and straightforward to make for the modern knitter. They therefore make ideal teaching tools to understand both how traditional knowledge is transmitted and the multifaceted role of traditional knowledge in history and contemporary life.

In addition, the wider availability of digitized archived material means that the entry point for citizen scholarship is greater than ever before. When I taught myself to knit in the round from a vintage knitting pattern, I was unknowingly benefiting from the democratization of history. The pattern was made available because the website's owner thought it was important enough to be shared. I was myself participating in this democratization because I knit the pattern and thought about the implications of knitting a historical item and then, many years later, embarked on a research project about wartime knitting. Figuring out the story of wartime knitting relied on analog archives, but the research itself started years before with a digital archive started by an interested knitter.

Access remains a serious barrier to historical research. As important as physically experiencing archives was to me in learning how to research, my research trips were circumscribed by funding, distance, and time. These barriers are even higher for people without the privileges I had as a researcher. Digitizing archives is one way to provide better access to the public at large. Transcribing historical documents for better use by screen readers and other accessibility-related technology is another way to increase access. So too is encouraging other kinds of research, such as hands-on making, that focuses on other skills and leads to new ways of thinking. Learning to knit, to throw a pot, or to build a table requires a different set of skills, but all are work. To do any of those things well, the maker has to have a level of craft knowledge acquired by the process of making and the practice of creating.

The process of knitting is active and experiential. Like other kinds of tactile activities, the experience of actually creating a garment gives the same sense that one is "doing it" that one gets by researching in an archive or recording an interview. The lived experience of making gives the researcher a new insight into the research in part because the researcher has experienced the physicality of creating something from nothing, and from gaining the tacit knowledge that comes from hands-on, experiential learning. Knitting these objects functioned as a way to bridge the gap between observer and participant: to reach into the void of the past and bring it closer to the present. Making objects serves as an interface between the past and present, a way to access the feeling of the past while acknowledging that it is something that we will always have to piece together and view through traditions passed from person to person and through the paper trail of the past.

Note

1. In Art and Design History, "study" photographs are photographs of objects typically used for further study when the original is not available.

Hoaxes, History, Legends, and the Circulation of Stories

The Wisconsin Historical Society and Wisconsin's Petrified French Explorer

Jennifer Gipson

In 1984, the Wisconsin Historical Society (WHS) received a request to "settle an argument about the truth in an old legend" often heard in Northern Wisconsin about remains of an explorer found in a tree by loggers (Inquiry about Petrified Man 1984, 1). Unbeknownst to the writers of this letter, the WHS had a long-standing history of its own with stories of a petrified explorer, usually identified as a French person. While stories of human remains petrified in sap could conceivably have circulated in lore of logging communities, the tale of Wisconsin's petrified man appears to have emerged in 1926 in a struggling, small-town Northern Wisconsin newspaper. The resident satirist "The Rusk County Lyre" (a homonym for "liar") reported the discovery in a felled tree of a petrified French explorer whose remains would be sent to Madison for verification and then repatriated to France. Variants of this story began to circulate in other newspapers, sometimes separated from the Lyre's telling signature, as well as in rumor and oral narrative. Inquiries flooded the overwhelmed WHS, and crowds clamored to see the fabled remains.

If the petrified man's popularity was initially an annoyance to the WHS in 1926, continued public interest rooted him in Wisconsin legendry, lore, history, and archival records, with archivists eventually coming to collect inquiries about him in more recent decades. Today, the WHS's online *Dictionary of Wisconsin History* includes the entry "Petrified Man Hoax" "because we still occasionally receive sincere inquiries about the so-called 'petrified man'" (Wisconsin Historical Society n.d.).

On the one hand, this article explores the history of the petrified man, through a web of textual documents, seen within the collective economic and cultural anxieties that gave rise to them and the cycles of belief, disbelief, and fascination that sustained them. On the other hand, this study, implicitly and sometimes explicitly, constitutes a critical reflection on history, its mediation, its archives, its representations and interpretations, and the role we, as folklorists, play. Indeed, the story of the petrified man first finds fuel in contestations or ridicule of the very institutional authority over knowledge and representations of the past to which many making inquiries of the WHS have appealed. As such, the petrified man points toward a democratization of meaning-making that challenges conventional assumptions about authority and agency and what constitutes history. Beliefs, fictions, even falsifications or forgeries, far from needing to be purged from history, constitute meta-reflections on their own present that can become valuable parts of our past. Ultimately, the deeper "truth" in this old legend depends not on the determination of historical fact but on a testament to the power of stories, the impact of public engagement with the past, and the generative and irrepressible nature of folk belief.

WISCONSIN'S PETRIFIED MAN

On Thursday, January 21, 1926, Ladysmith, Wisconsin's *Rusk County Journal* told of two men from a logging firm who had discovered a petrified French explorer in a felled tree: "There encased in the living trunk of the tree, was the entire body of a man, fully clothed in coarse homespun and buckskins, which fell away when touched. . . . In a pocket of the man's clothes, which were like ashes, was found several decayed bits of paper and a few French gold coins, one of which bears the date, 1664. The only clue to the man's identity was a scrap of official looking paper bearing the name 'Pierre D'Artagnan' and signed 'Jacques Marquette'" (Rusk County Lyre 1926b, 1, 6).

The report speculates that D'Artagnan, chased by Native Americans, hid in a hollow tree, his trapped remains eventually preserved by the sap. "The body," the paper reports, "was brought to this city [Ladysmith,] where it will be shipped to the state university, and it is probable that if present suspicions are verified, it will be offered to France for D'Artagnan was very close to Louis the Great" (Rusk County Lyre 1926b, 6).

In truth, Father Marquette's party exploring the Mississippi in 1673 did not venture near Ladysmith and certainly did not include a D'Artagnan—a captain who had served under Louis XIV but found his greatest fame in the fiction of Alexandre Dumas's nineteenth-century novel *The Three Musketeers*. But the hoax is most visible in the signature of the "Rusk County Lyre."

As this story made the rounds of the newspapers in Wisconsin and beyond, its many variants sometimes amplified these markers of disbelief and sometimes suppressed them. The Prairie du Chien *Courier* of February 2, 1926, omitted the Lyre's signature and inserted the story into a public-interest historical feature on Marquette and Joliet's expedition, tweaking historical details to fit with Ladysmith's petrified man, including the presence of a D'Artagnan in the party (1926, 1, 3). By contrast, the *Eau Claire Leader*'s edition of February 13, 1926, declared the Lyre the greatest "champion fabricator of startling stories and imaginary events since the days when a writer put Paul Bunyan and his big blue ox before fiction readers" (1926d, 2). The *Leader* debunked the story repeatedly in 1926, on February 13, 16, and 27 (1926d, 1926c, 1926a), and on February 27 even mocked the *Wisconsin State Journal* for its reliance on a Minnesota paper for its "news" of Wisconsin (1926a, 8).

Within months, the hoax appears to have entered into vernacular storytelling cycles, much to the chagrin of the WHS, whose frustrated superintendent proclaimed in March: "Somebody in the latitude of Ladysmith has perpetuated one type of practical joke on a large number of people. He did not deceive us, yet we do not for that reason escape a certain amount of annoyance on his account. For, men and women write in to the Histori-cal Society daily to know if the 'petrified man' has yet been received at the Museum, and some have already presented themselves in the character of 'viewers of the remains'" (Schafer 1926, 3).

By May, the *Milwaukee Journal* claimed that the Lyre had supposedly amassed 127 re-prints of his hoax and concluded that the story had run its course: "And so, by unanimous vote, the petrified man was laid to rest" (1926, 31). Yet neither a newspaper's dictates nor the scholarly debunking intervention of the Historical Society superintendent could quash public interest. Indeed, in 1976, "fifty years ago in history" features prompted "a minor del-uge of inquires" (Holzhueter 1979). The petrified man is a powerful reminder that archives and collections are not simply static holdings, that their "official" status does not stomp out traces of unofficial culture.

What gave the petrified man such appeal in the 1920s and propelled him forward into the decades to come? A strikingly similar 1919 story from Minnesota, signed the "LeSueur Lyre," knew no such longevity and provides an instructive contrast. This story also told of the discovery in a hollow tree of petrified remains, this time of a certain Jean LaRue who had fled a Sioux uprising. A note dated 1862 implored anyone finding his remains to repa-triate them and send his money to his family in France. Here, too, reprints omitting the Lyre's signature prompted some to believe the story as fact. The story was sent to Minne-sota's Historical Society, whose staff had apparently already received inquiries from the Wisconsin Historical Society about similar versions of the story in Wisconsin papers (Zeman 2013). While Minnesota's petrified man seems to have vanished again, Wisconsin's took root in state lore, readily reincarnated as legend and hoax, both newspaper fodder and oral narrative, to be engaged with publicly, whether it wished to or not, by the Wisconsin Historical Society for years to come. The reason lies not in the textual artifacts of inquiries or stacks of newspaper clippings about one man's petrified remains but in a shared context. For it was not the chemical properties of sap that cemented the petrified man in a tree but collective anxieties and a history of very real cultural and economic turmoil that fixed the story in the cultural imagination and invited public engagement with the past.

HISTORICAL CONTEXTS AND THE FRENCH CONNECTION

Though the Great War was over and the Great Depression had yet to come, the decline of logging made the mid-1920s a time of economic transition for much of the Western Great Lakes region. Minnesota and Michigan, for example, had a volume and quality of mineral deposits to sustain mining operations that Northern Wisconsin did not. While the logging industry accounted for a staggering quarter of Wisconsin's workers at the end of the nine-teenth century (Edmonds 2009, 41, 43), numbers had dropped precipitously, with only smaller-scale logging continuing in the 1920s. Debates pitted the relative merits of fostering an agricultural economy, as opposed to a hybrid economy of drastically scaled-down log-ging alongside an emerging tourism industry (Jensen 2006, 60–61). But for northernmost Wisconsin counties like Rusk, soil glaciated in the last Ice Age and brutal, prolonged win-ters rendered farming less profitable than in regions even a short distance south. The lure of urban areas and their wider economic opportunity left rural centers scrambling to retain their population. "Small-town residents listened to countless self-congratulatory sermons, and they read innumerable editorials praising village friendliness and cohesion," remarks Glad (2014, 229). In its last months, the *Rusk County Journal* even ran full-page ads spotlighting Ladysmith businesses and opportunities for young people.

While stump-laden land, known as the Cutover, dominated visual landscapes, the figure of the lumberjack flourished in the cognitive landscapes and foundational stories of the region. The greatest lumberjack of them all, Paul Bunyan, embodied the nostalgic spectacle that fashioned the heyday of logging into a golden age of economic prosperity ushered in by the strength of larger-than-life characters and hardened Northwoods pioneers. Log-rolling contests and lumberjack games, great pulls for tourists, allowed the exportation of this performed identity well beyond the rivers of Wisconsin. Old logging equipment became decorative wall hangings. Lumberjack breakfasts appeared at restaurants, and lumberjack stories abounded, solidifying the settler-colonial enterprise of the Northwoods with a heroic epoch of mass appeal that tended to erase or appropriate Native history.

This nostalgic branding and marketing of the Northwoods became central to its economic future. Increases in automobile ownership and improvement of roadways meant that the rural North could tap into another resource, seemingly limitless in summer months, at least. "We can sell our climate and scenery year after year and still retain it forever," remarked a Rhinelander newspaper, the *New North*, on February 21, 1924 (qtd. in Glad 2014, 211), joining a chorus of regional newspapers lauding the natural wonders of lakes, fishing, and clean air and cultural attractions like stylized Native American pow-wows and lumberjack displays. The Burlington *Standard-Democrat* of February 15, 1924, declared Wisconsin "a great natural playground" and an "ideal vacationland" where "the seeker of the 'wilderness places,' can still, with paddle and canoe, go over the trails of the old French voyageurs" (qtd. in Glad 2014, 214n30).

Wisconsin retains a preponderance of French place-names, yet the state's relationship with a legacy of French voyageurs, colonizers, and missionaries often proves conflicted. French settlement after the fur trade was minimized in order to pander to more Anglo-American–friendly renditions of Upper Midwestern history—no small irony given the region's predominantly New Immigrant settlement patterns. As notions of the French fur trade as economic partnership came to overshadow elements of colonization and forced assimilation, Wisconsin settlers acquired moral agency. These elevations of history minimize or obfuscate the negative impacts of Anglo, American, and New Immigrant colonization efforts of Native peoples.

Still, in the economic hardship of the 1920s, French heritage played into the present's idealization of the past, a historical mystique marketable to tourists and a demarcation of regional distinction and settler entitlement over Indigenous lands when brutal forced assimilation policies remained commonplace. On May 28, 1925, the *Rusk County Journal* spotlighted almost two hundred years "as a province of New France" in the first of its twelve-article series "Know Wisconsin First," intended "to make every true Badger love his home and take greater pride in his or her state," but the editors' remarks are just as much about creating a mystique sellable to outsiders: "the story of French explorers has all the lure of romance; its surface is varied, combining beauty of landscape and rich agricultural productiveness" (Hotchkiss and Cannon 1925, 2). In 1926, the petrified man D'Artagnan represented a "concrete" remnant of this settler idyll, when Father Marquette and the fur trader Joliet beheld forests as they explored the Mississippi.

But, far from being frozen in this past, the petrified man spoke to this present. The suggested petrification properties of sap that the Lyre highlights resonated with the frantic search for economically viable by-products from Wisconsin's remaining forests. And human petrification imbues the woods with the very sense of mystery that savvy marketers cultivated for tourists. Wisconsin, especially northern counties, needed French heritage. Thus, repatriating a treasure like the petrified Frenchman seems counterintuitive, culturally and economically. The explanation that D'Artagnan had been a great friend of Louis XIV rings somewhat hollow. Louis XIV died in 1715. And Wisconsin hardly seemed indebted to France. In fact, newspapers reported on negotiations over interest rates on France's postwar debt to the United States (e.g., *Badger State Banner* 1925, 6).

Indeed, the initial rhetorical linchpin of the petrified man's story in Ladysmith lay in almost offhand remark that his remains would be sent to Madison for authentication and then to France. With this, the Lyre nimbly shifted the reader's attention from the story's believability to the imminent displacement of this treasure. Versions published without the Lyre's signature ended on this note, with no marker of the hoax to bring the reader back to disbelief. In fact, the Prairie du Chien *Courier* of February 2, 1926, even reported that the body had already been shipped from Ladysmith to the state university (1)! Thus, the petrified man followed the trajectory of timber and mineral wealth sent to industrialists in urban centers to the south. The prospect of losing the petrified man could draw readers further into belief through what the Internet age might recognize as FOMO, "Fear of Missing Out," that is, of losing the opportunity to see this astounding find and to profit locally from it. In these regards, the story embodies the local and social realities of the 1920s in northern Wisconsin. But the dynamics of belief and disbelief here prove even more complex.

SCIENTIFIC FOLKLORE, AUTHORITY, AND GENRE

The standard tale type index catalogues petrification as a punishment, not an accident (Uther 2004, 235). Nonetheless, Wisconsin's petrified Frenchman had scores of stone predecessors, key to understanding how petrification stories developed a generic rhetoric of their own. Starting in the later decades of the nineteenth century, increased scientific inquiry sparked speculation about basic questions of human existence, demise, and a new array of fantastical natural phenomena reported by scientists, anthropologists, and explorers. Petrification taps into all these anxieties: death and the undecaying body, phenomena from recently colonized territories or remnants of their past, and scientific explanations of once-hidden natural mysteries.

Stories of petrification crossed between oral lore and journalistic fodder. As a young newspaperman, Samuel Clemens noted: "In the fall of 1862 in Nevada and California, the people got to running wild about extraordinary petrifactions and other natural marvels. One could scarcely pick up a paper without finding in it one or two glorified discoveries of this kind. The mania was becoming a little ridiculous" (1875, 239). Clemens, soon to be Mark Twain, wrote his own hoax supposedly to debunk this petrification mania and simultaneously to mock a certain justice of the peace: as Clemens reported, locals, presumably silver miners, planned to blast a petrified Native American from the side of a mountain for Christian burial; however, the judge refused, and streams of curious viewers ensued. On the first score, Twain failed; readers missed clues to the hoax such as the petrified man's hands being held up to his nose in a mocking position. On the second, he succeeded wildly as the judge was inundated with stacks of newspapers' reprints of his story: "I could not have gotten more real comfort out of him without killing him" (1875, 242).

Other petrifications were material hoaxes, relying on many of the same motifs but monetizing the public's desire to see and believe. In 1902, an Indiana workman even sued his employer for custody of supposedly petrified remains that were being displayed for profit and that he had helped to recover (Runyon and Mills 2008, 375–76). In 1869, tapping into interest in Darwin's theories of evolution and doubt of literal biblical interpretations, a New York cigar maker had commissioned the construction of the supposedly petrified Cardiff Giant, bringing paying crowds and sparking many imitations (Rose 2005). An 1896 broadside for a "South Carolina Curiosity," "The Petrified Man" exhibition announces an admission of ten cents, with the spectacle complemented by a tune from "Edison's Latest Improved PHONOGRAPHS" (Buff 1896). Names of doctors certifying the validity of the specimen take up a full third of the advertisement, pointing to another important motif in petrification hoaxes: scientific authentication. However, the authentication, one scholar argues, went beyond science to the validation of the present's uses of the past: a petrified British soldier found by a Confederate veteran provided "a link to South Carolina's glorious Revolutionary past" and a mechanism for transforming Confederate memorialization into an ideology of white supremacy, imperialism, and sometimes entrepreneurialism (Poole 2004, 178–79).

Notions of genre—inherently fluid or sometimes situationally dependent—help us understand the petrified man, not by prescribing fixed labels but by mapping rhetorical strategies. The story has the trappings of a legend, a story that cultivates belief, as Oring (2008, 130) describes the genre. The Lyre deftly fingers strings pulled taunt with a rhetoric of truth: the man's clothes crumble "like ashes"; yet an "official looking paper" remains; physical remains will be held by authorities, inviting authentication. Even pseudo-scientific explanations invite belief (Oring 2008, 151), here details about tree sap and petrification. However, these same features are also common in tall tales, a sort of parody of the legend genre that tests the boundaries of believability to extreme degrees, and also in hoaxes, which present a more purposeful effort to deceive and perpetuate misinformation. I suggest that the petrified man, in his original incarnation, is somewhat of a meta-hoax that flies in the face of the expected rhetoric of petrification stories. The body is "unearthed" far above the ground. Authentication serves not to validate a find for display or increase its monetary value but to trigger repatriation to France. And the state university, as the temporary keepers of petrified remains, also occupies the narrative equivalent of a site of spectacles and freak show–like displays.

At the same time, the story is fluid. As James Fredal observes, "Because the hoax works through an imperfect and permeable framing device to present signs both of belief and doubt, or plausibility and implausibility, the effects of the hoax are similarly unstable and unpredictable and frequently exceed the author's intent" (2014, 79–80). The story of the petrified man exemplifies this fluidity, dependent on receptions and retelling illuminated less by the fixity of generic labels and more by recognizing context-dependent functions of the story's different iterations. While the Lyre's readers in Ladysmith might have experienced the push and pull of belief and disbelief within the story that clearly appeals to collective anxieties, it is difficult to imagine that those already familiar with the Lyre's usual satirical and fantastical fodder would ultimately grant his column credence. That the story then circulated elsewhere as fact created "insider" and "outsider" groups. The delineation between locals in the know and others, even from within Wisconsin, mocked the gullibility on which an emerging tourist economy would depend, all the while giving the economically battered town of Ladysmith much-welcomed publicity and a certain sense of power over other parts of the state, including the governmental seat of power.

As this slippery story circulated and morphed into different forms, the "inside" group grew outside the geographical confines of Ladysmith. On February 24, a short, seemingly satirical note in the *Eau Claire Leader* announced that the French consul in Chicago would be involved and that investigations from Paris would follow to recover D'Artagnan's remains (1926b, 5). On the same page, in a letter signed by the Rusk Country Lyre, the saga of the petrified man unfolds further. The Lyre condemns the *Leader*'s incredulity, insisting that a coonskin cap–clad ghost roams Ladysmith and inviting incredulous Eau Claire reporters speak to the traumatized loggers: "Charpin haunts the Soo depot at Owen and implores travelers not to go to Ladysmith"—perhaps an enticement to do just that (Rusk County Lyre 1926a, 5)?

The petrified man, the Lyre specifies, had actually been displayed briefly in Ladysmith but, while on display, spoke "voicing seventeenth century logic": "This was so far in advance of what we have been getting from official Madison that he has been placed in hiding until next fall, when he will be sent to the executive office, after which more modern ideas on conservation and state governments may be expected. And thus is explained the sudden disappearance of the petrified man, just as the state was becoming interested" (1926a, 5).

If the Lyre offers explanations that tempt belief, justifying why the petrified man is not in Madison, his reasons also make explicit his once-subtle jab at the state capitol, the seat of government and education. The petrified man's ironically advanced logic registers an urban/rural disconnect between Madison—where laws concerning land, forestry, farming, and conservation were being made—and northern parts of the state, like Ladysmith, that were living and dying by these policies.

Conclusions: Publics, Archives, and Power Over the Past

Historians have widely assumed that the Lyre's "little joke backfired" when his lies appeared as truth in some venues (Terrill 1985, 74). But the petrified man's real history is one of success beyond what the Lyre could have orchestrated. The *Rusk County Journal*'s announcement of the Historical Society's superintendent's frustrated dismissal of the petrified man suggests that the attention granted to the story speaks to an inversion of power: "The Rusk County Lyre has even burst into the official archives of the state of Wisconsin. In the following clear-cut analysis the state historical society man proves that the petrified man could not have existed. That has always been somewhat of our own opinion" (*Rusk County Journal* 1926, 1).

From the Lyre's pen came a story whose purposing and repurposing spotlighted the fragility of "truth" and the place of the public, not just industry, the state university, or the state, in deciding what merits note.

In this regard, we can see clearly that the WHS archives are not simply arbiters of the truth of a historical past but rather are keepers of the discursive realities through which various publics express their polyvocal and negotiated realities with one another—whether in seriousness, in jest, in play, or in error. We do not simply create and maintain collections that document the present that later becomes the past. Rather, we create an ongoing diachronic dialogue, through which meaning is perpetually negotiated between the present, the past, and the pasts of the people of the past. That is, the story of the Lyre is not simply one of a hoax or a spurious history. Rather, it is a story that speaks to the ideation of Wisconsinites in the 1920s and how they understood their own past. It is a story that speaks to the historical, economic, and geographical circumstances in which these *kinds* of stories bear cultural resonance. And, as publics continually reengage with the story of the petrified voyageur, it is a story that demonstrates the perpetuation of narratives and their critical role in locales as identity is negotiated and renegotiated over time. In this regard, building and maintaining collections and archives are not simply about the past as much as about the present, as we depend on the stories of the past to manufacture meaning in the present. It is here that we as folklorists, whether working in the public sector, in the private sector, in academia, or elsewhere, can use our experience and expertise to make better sense of the world around us.

The Lyre's story used the detail of authentication by official collections, collections that then archived newspapers' tellings of different versions of this story. Yet we understand as folklorists the limitations of these collections, the way that the circulation of stories follows lines not of veracity but shared values, and how the diversity of voices in communities can work not in harmony but in contest, to mock and play with folklore or stories in ways that challenge a simple dichotomy between truth and mistruth, history and falsehood. This story's various iterations—easily dismissed as historical fallacy or consolidated into a singular hoax—actually speak to a multiplicity of complex historic facts. The larger history here is not that there was a hoax or that it is patently false. Rather, the significance lies in popularization of this story into a joking, generative discourse reflective of insider/outsider dynamics, cycles of folk belief, performance of Northwoods identity, and legitimization of white settlement through the imaginings of French voyageurs and their relationship with the Native people whose land had made logging possible. Folklorists work in the interstices of stories and documents, bringing into the contexts we unearth metanarratives that help us understand the past and contexts of public sentiment, collective anxieties, stories, and belief that shapes material or textual artifacts we see today. Indeed, like many stone curiosities before him, Wisconsin's petrified French explorer can be viewed: we simply must look for the spectacle not in petrified remains but in the protean power of story and the contexts that brought Wisconsin's petrified Frenchman to life and have sustained his story.

Reanimating the Past

Traveling through Michigan with Alan Lomax's 1938 Films

GUHA SHANKAR

T his chapter focuses in the main on the historical and contextual background of
the film footage that makes up the production *Alan Lomax Goes North*, one of the
five multimedia elements (four music CDs, one DVD) in the meticulously conceived and researched multiformat box set of archival recordings *Folksongs of Another
America: Field Recordings from the Upper Midwest, 1937–1946* (Leary 2015). The original elements, the raw footage, for the film were collected by the preeminent folklorist and song
collector Alan Lomax during his field trip to document ethnic folk and traditional music in
Michigan during the period from August to October 1938. They are part of the vast Alan
Lomax collection housed in the American Folklife Center (AFC) at the Library of Congress. Lomax was only twenty-three years old and special assistant in charge at the national
library's Archive of Folk Song but already an established documentarian by the time he
ventured into the Upper Midwest. He subsequently dubbed the region "the most fertile
source" for folk music. The claim can be readily appreciated in light of the numerous musical genres of the dozen cultural and linguistic communities he recorded on several hundred instantaneous disk recordings.

In this chapter, I attempt to illuminate a few of the methodological, intellectual, and theoretical precepts that informed Lomax's earliest known forays into film documentation,
especially in terms of his emergent ethnographic sensibilities, artistry, and humanistic representation of immigrants. Several aspects of his burgeoning development as fieldworker are
ably covered elsewhere—the entire ground of Lomax's journey into the Midwest (Leary
2015; Harvey 2016), the challenges of using audio technologies in fieldwork documentation (Brady 1999). Other important facets lie outside the scope of this chapter but invite
further exploration, including the extent to which his work was influenced by the federal
government's efforts to stitch together social unity during the Depression era via the documentary practices of the Federal Writers Project.[1]

Accordingly, the present attempt is to understand the visual artifact—film and
photograph—that results from an ethnographic intervention into community life as "the
material product of a material apparatus set to work in specific contexts, by specific forces,

Pajo Tomic, Serbian gusle player, filmed and recorded by Alan Lomax in Clairepointe, Detroit, Michigan, August 11, 1938. (Digitized film frame from American Folklife Center Film collection, Library of Congress, 2015.)

for more or less defined purposes" (Tagg 1988). This recognizes the fundamental character of the documentation process and products from historical archival sources as *constructions*, obtained for both the original 1938 footage Lomax produced and the 2013 film that reanimates that material. As to "purpose," these creative constructions seek to provide contemporary audiences a deeper appreciation of the region's immigrant communities, their unique historical traditions and the different aesthetic expressions they long nurtured in the face of numerous obstacles. When done well, they sit squarely within public folklore's commitment to amplifying and championing difference and heterogeneity as the necessary concomitants of a plural society. The related, all-important consideration concerns *representation*—plainly put, do local communities "see themselves" in the constructions ethnographers make of their own historical past and their forebears? In this essay, I first provide the details of the film production process and then turn to a consideration of Lomax's approach to documenting cultural expressions through the medium of film.

Alan Lomax Goes North: Threading a Narrative from the Archival Record

A brief sketch of the institutional context will, I hope, help situate the film project. The Center's holdings of ethnographic field recordings, in the medium of 16mm celluloid film, are neither as extensive nor as widely known as those at the National Anthropological Archives and other public institutions of cultural memory. However, several media producers and scholars have integrated portions of AFC film collections into their film productions and public presentations. These efforts include the AFC alumnus Carl Fleischhauer's pioneering work in compiling and presenting the edited 1960s home movies of Les Stewart, a Nevada rancher, first on a video laserdisc and then in an online presentation of the AFC's field survey of ranching traditions. In 2015, Pete and Toshi Seeger's documentation of Irish music during their 1964 world trip to collect expressive cultural traditions was used by an independent filmmaker from Ireland to illustrate the changes in musical traditions in the country. (As an interesting aside, Pete Seeger credited Lomax, for whom he briefly worked as a volunteer at the Library in the 1950s, with spurring his own interest in filmmaking.) Ken Burns's 2019 documentary series on American roots music, *Country Music*, made use of footage of all types of music captured on film and housed at the Center and the Library.

With specific reference to Lomax's filmed recordings, Irene Chagall's 2014 production focused on children's hand-clapping games, *Let's Get the Rhythm*, uses a snippet of film that shows African American girls, filmed in 1937, in Murrells Inlet, South Carolina. The 2009 CD box set *Alan Lomax in Haiti 1936–1937* is a well-researched compilation by the ethnomusicologist Gage Averill, produced by the record company Dust to Digital. Averill selected the music and documentation for the set from field recordings and other materials in the Center's archive from Lomax and Elizabeth Harold's 1937 field trip to Haiti; Lomax and Harold got married while in Haiti. Included in the box set is a DVD of rare footage of Haitian performance traditions, such as *vodun* and *rara*. In late 2020, the Association of Cultural Equity, Lomax's nonprofit research and publication organization, initiated an effort to remaster and rerelease *Dance and Human History*, a sweeping explication of world dance traditions, rhythm, and movement that was released in 1976.

In that vein, *Alan Lomax Goes North* is the latest effort to draw upon his archival collections. From 2013 to 2015, I worked with Leary on the production of the film, beginning with an initial intensive week-long editing session at the Library of Congress's American Folklife Center (AFC) and then editing and shaping the final version through several subsequent phone and email conversations between us (Leary and Shankar). My own training and experience are in the field of film production and visual anthropology; my day job is senior folklife specialist at the AFC.

Reflecting on the process, I readily admit I had many reservations—of a technical nature—when Leary approached the Center in 2013 and talked to us about editing the footage into a coherent film. My initial impressions of the film footage were not favorable, mostly because the material I had seen at that point was on three-quarter-inch videotape, obviously duplicated from an inferior film print. The footage appeared to be shot on black-and-white film stock or irreversibly faded color stock that could not be restored, or so I thought at the time. Moreover, the frame rate for the transfer to tape had not been properly adjusted to normalize silent, archival film shot at 16 to 18 frames per second (fps) so that movement would appear "normal" when played back or projected at the standard 24fps. Accordingly, people's movement and gestures on the screen were in the comically speeded-up manner that is typical of silent films. In spite of my misgivings, I asked if we could locate a print of the film that would perhaps serve our purposes instead of the videotape. After some searching, Todd Harvey located what appeared to be some semblance of the original materials in the Library's film vaults. When I had the footage pulled from the vaults and transferred to high-definition video (1080p), the results were simply astonishing. Lomax, as it turned out, had employed newly manufactured Kodachrome *color* film stock for his recording forays. The stock was made for the compact, handheld, spring-wound 16mm cameras that were increasingly being employed by field recordists in the 1930s, as opposed to the heavier and bulkier 35mm units. The color was rich and vivid, all these decades later, and the framing and composition of scenes was equally, if not more, impressive. The digitization also opened up access to footage from field trips Lomax and Elizabeth Harold had made to Haiti (as noted earlier) and also to Kentucky and Indiana between 1936 and 1937.

An intriguing possibility is suggested by these earlier films: Whereas Lomax made the trip to Michigan unaccompanied, cutting disks and filming on his own, the footage from those other field trips strongly indicates that Harold participated as recordist. There are no shot logs or explicit notes indicating the person behind the camera, but Lomax and Harold are occasionally glimpsed in several shots. So, the presumption is that the two worked in tandem to film and/or cut disks as circumstances dictated. Harold was a folklorist in her own right and participated in other fieldwork events while she was married to Lomax. One notable example is an interview she conducted with the famed blues singer Reverend Gary Davis, which resulted in a three-hundred-page manuscript, now housed in the Alan Lomax Archive (Harold and Stone n.d.).

As to the Michigan material, the range of ethnic communities Lomax recorded in the state is remarkable, to say the least. When he embarked on his trip in the summer of 1938, he headed west, alone in a Library car, with little else but his recording kit, which consisted of an instantaneous disk-cutting machine, dozens of blank disks, and a 16mm film camera and the stock of color film mentioned previously. He returned to Washington after three months on the road with nearly a thousand recorded songs from communities of Serbian, Finnish, Croatian, Hungarian, Polish, French Canadian, and Italian heritage as well as recordings of African American and Native American performers. Several hundred feet of motion picture images made it back with him, but several rolls of film were stolen on a stop during the expedition and never recovered.

The process for editing the film material into a coherent whole was not uncomplicated. Many elements went into the production, the key ones being the visual record and audio recordings transferred from the analog disk to digital files. Other contextual information was also available in the form of recordings Lomax made of his own voice on the disks. He also took extensive field notes on performers and sometimes described the social situation. With these materials in hand, we wove together film footage and audio recordings, voice-over narration drawn from letters and field notes (featuring the voice of the music historian Bill Malone), and other elements to construct a comprehensive audiovisual document.

The film, which is available online through Mills Music Library Digital Collections, was structured chronologically and composed of fourteen distinct vignettes of musical performances (Leary and Shankar 2015). Narrative coherence was achieved by having the individual sequences follow one another sequentially and mirroring the timeline of Lomax's journey through the state. Individual performers—their ethnic background and the title of the musical piece—were identified by means of intertitles, along with English translations of non-English song lyrics.

The process had several challenges to reckon with. The major task was to simulate synchronous audio recordings of song performances and silent film footage. Lomax's filming process was to have performers sing songs or play instruments while he filmed them, most likely after he had recorded their performance on his phonograph recorder. But his field notes had no information about the filming and what music was being played at any exact moment. Accordingly, the choice of the audio track that I joined to the picture in the Final Cut Pro program on my Macintosh was based solely on reasonable conjecture and our "feeling" as to what song best fit the visuals. Leary's intimate knowledge of the song traditions Lomax recorded was essential to the process of establishing "fake sync" and marrying audio to image. At several points in the editing, the lack of footage of performances proved a real hindrance—maddeningly so! I had to slow down the film frame rate severely in the digital editing system to "cover" a few more seconds of audio track. As is standard editing practice, I also occasionally repeated shots in sequences such as performers' faces and hands in order to squeeze out more on-screen time for visuals.

In my estimation, footage and film achieve one of the key goals of a creative and purposive construction of community life, namely the articulation of unique historical traditions and cultural expressions of immigrant communities. One cogent example is that of the Floriani family, a Croatian *tamburitza* group that also played more popular styles of music. Lomax filmed their performance in the front yard of their home in Ameek, Michigan. It is a town in the "Copper Country," which is a reference to mining, the main industry in that part of the state. In the first part of the clip, we edited together several shots of a mine, under which we added the English-language song "31st Level Blues." The song is about the dangerous job of mine work, an occupation in which many immigrants were engaged. The phrase "31st level" refers to the depths that miners have to descend to do their jobs, and the lyrics amplify the hard toil and weariness of the occupation and the antagonism that characterized relations between mine workers and bosses.[2] In the second part of the clip, the performance style changes abruptly from the sobering account of labor struggles to the traditional Croatian ballad "Majko Moje" (My mother). The song provides evidence of the Florianis' facility as *tamburitza* performers.

LOMAX AND THE CAMERA

To situate my interest in Lomax's work, the film project I became engaged in with Leary spurred my curiosity about his interest in film as documentary medium. I knew little about his first forays into film documentation and was more familiar with the films he had compiled from extant footage toward the middle and end of his career, such as *Dance and Human History*. The compilations were the central content for movement and dance analysis work he and two colleagues, Irmgard Bartenieff and Forrestine Paulay, pioneered in the 1960s under the rubric of "choreometrics," a "monumental work to characterize dance styles and relate them to subsistence and social organization" (Bishop 2001).[3] I was also well familiar with the evocative documentary on African American musical culture in the Mississippi Delta, *The Land Where the Blues Began*, produced by John Bishop, Worth Long, and Lomax in 1979; it was a staple of film festivals and a favorite of folklore colleagues for quite some time. That trip to the Delta was also the last field documentation trip Lomax ever undertook; he later chose to concentrate on academic publishing and research.

To a large extent, it is the footage itself that tells the story of Lomax's fledgling use of the camera, because no formal writing—papers, scenes, essays, articles—on the topic of his *early* (ca. 1937–50) interests in film documentation as method exists. For textual evidence, I have relied on the collected correspondence in the collection, along with the scholar Ronald Cohen's compilation of the same materials (2005). The personal conversations with Anna Lomax Wood, president of the Association for Cultural Equity (and Alan Lomax's daughter), and John Bishop, filmmaker and an occasional collaborator of Lomax's, have been invaluable in helping flesh out details of the young Lomax's orientation to the discipline of filmmaking. By contrast, beginning in the 1960s, Lomax wrote and argued publicly about the utility of the medium to record, analyze, and explicate human behavior, particularly as he and colleagues began developing choreometrics as an arena of analysis and interpretation of human societies (Wood 2018a, 20018b).

The earliest mention of Lomax's own assessment of the utility of the camera as a scientific field recording instrument (and important complement to the phonograph recorder) is in this letter written to his supervisors at the Library in 1937 while he was attempting to conduct fieldwork in Haiti for the Library's Archive of American Folk Song. Predating the trip to the Upper Midwest the following year, the 1937 communiqué is a long diatribe on the local bureaucracy that is torturing him by imposing all manner of barriers on his research. It goes on to implore the Library to intervene and explain to the Haitian government what Lomax intends to do with the camera. This letter is the earliest mention of his attraction to motion picture documentation. I have quoted the relevant passage at length— note the emphasis he places on the scientific method of data collection by means of recording devices.

The camera will be used: 1) To photograph musical instruments and how they are played; 2) to photograph singers in the act of singing; 3) to photograph dances.

All the recent material in regard to the scientific study of music of whatever kind but most particularly of folk and primitive music, stresses the *necessity of moving pictures as supplementary to phonographic recordings* [my emphasis]. In the first place, unless the collector learns to play every instrument that he records, it is impossible to understand the origin or the reason for certain rhythmic and melodic peculiarities of exotic musical instruments, unless one can watch in detail the techniques of their performers. For example, unless one has a film of how the hands are used on the drums here, it will be impossible to understand how the different tones are produced on the drums and the origin (often purely physiological) of certain rhythmic patterns. [Ed. note: For drums, substitute guitar, banjo, or any other instrument.] The same thing is true of the close-ups of the faces of singers in the act of singing, since a study of the use of the lips, teeth, and body in singing often throws light on the characteristics of the songs themselves. (Cohen 2005, 29)

But where to locate Lomax within the roster of the earliest ethnographers who used motion picture documentation in the field in the 1930s? Looking for Lomax's own acknowledgments of his intellectual forebears and models for the deployment of the film camera doesn't yield a lot of results. I have not been able to discern, among the small but growing circle of contemporaries who used the camera to document societies and "human subjects," just who he looked to as models for his film work. Drawing from Homiak's (1995, 1) survey on the topic of early anthropological films, a brief list of documentarians and their areas of focus up to the time of the 1938 field trip to Michigan includes Joseph Dixon, who shot footage of the Crow Indians in Montana (1908); Franz Boas, who filmed Kwakuitl (Fort Ruppert, British Columbia, 1929); Paul Wirz, who documented Lake Sentani Papuans (West Irian, Dutch New Guinea, ca. 1920); Matthew Stirling, who filmed in West Irian (1927), Robert Zingg, who produced footage on the Huichol and Tarahumara (northern Mexico, 1933); and Scudder Mekeel, who filmed the Lakota Sioux (Rosebud Reservation, 1930).

In the same letter, Lomax notes that one of his reasons for using cameras in Haiti is that the preeminent anthropologist Melville Herskovits had traveled to and shot film in the country in 1934, three years before Alan went there. However, there is nothing more mentioned of Herskovits's film documentation as having an influence, decisive or fleeting, on his own work. Other contemporaries of his included Margaret Mead and Gregory Bateson, who were already engaged in their monumental study of Balinese character, society, gender, and temperament (Bateson and Mead 1942). Again, one has to pause when it comes to locating influences: Mead maintained throughout her long and illustrious career that cameras, like other recording devices, are invaluable for empirical documentation because, as she succinctly summed it up, they "provide us with material that can be repeatedly reanalyzed with finer tools and developing theories" (1975, 10). However, while Mead was a strong influence on and a colleague and friend to Lomax for decades, that relationship was not fully established until much later—in the 1940s and 1950s (Wood 2020, personal communication).

So then, given the mention of "recent material" (but which?) in the letter quoted earlier and the relative paucity of other evidence, my provisional claim is that Lomax, along with his contemporaries in the 1930s, was, in a tangible sense, "inventing" or refining the field of ethnographic documentary film by establishing the parameters and writing the grammar of visual anthropology. In the terminology of the discipline, the style of documentation Lomax emphasized in the passage is "observational cinema." Given that this was a nascent and emergent effort at the time of Lomax's documentary career in the late 1930s, the creative tensions between "scientific" and "artistic" approaches to visual documentation of human behavior are apparent in the filmic record.

The essential characteristic and value of the camera as research *instrument* was emphasized by Lomax in his 1937 correspondence. He lays out the case for the centrality of film footage in the emerging field of movement analysis and dance ethnography, which manifested itself in his establishment of choreometrics later in his career. He writes: "Dancing and singing in Haiti are simply two sides of one integrated phenomenon. The types of melodies and rhythms grow out of the dances and at the same time influence the dances in a complicated fashion that I imagine a student better trained than myself could only understand if he had both recordings and moving pictures" (Cohen 2005). Taken together with the emphasis on recording facial expressions, gestures, and bodily postures and on paying close attention to fingering techniques, the focus on documenting observable human behavior is paramount, and he is confident that this can all be achieved by the use of the camera. In this regard, the rationale for using the camera in the field fits with the positivistic and empirical orientation that dominated the recording of human behavior and cultural expression in the early decades of twentieth-century anthropological practice.

In all this writing about the purposive, instrumental uses of the camera and its utility in probing and capturing the human form in action, there's no overt mention made of the aesthetic, poetic aspects of filmmaking. But composition and framing as key aspects of his film style are manifest, nonetheless, and give evidence of Lomax's aesthetic sensibilities in the footage that he shot in Michigan. Lomax's camera work and his scientific aspirations blend sublimely, and there are instances of real visual artistry, as in the scene of Ilona Halinen that he films. She rocks steadily in her chair, occasionally holding her small dog, illuminated by light coming through her parlor window. There is no hint of a performance of a song or interaction with the recordist, but it is deeply observational and poetic at the same time and profound in its intimate depiction of a solitary woman. Bill Malone's narration, drawing on Lomax's field notes, emphasizes her aloneness. The song we used to underpin the scene, "A Little Bird in the Desert Sings Sadly" (Leary 2015, Track 35), is similar in feeling to the visuals.

Another scene is the evocatively framed and filmed question–answer duet between Mose and Exilia Bellaire, French Canadian performers in Baraga. The shots alternate between their expressive weathered and lined faces; they are seated outside their home, their feet counting out a rhythm, and a small boy dances in the background as the light fades slowly. In these and other instances, the depiction of performers—which moves between close-ups of hands plucking the strings of the *gusle* (a Balkan instrument) and/or ballad singers' facial expressions to wider shots that frame the individuals in their spatial context— is also deeply *cinematic*, a principle he carried with him into the later years. As John Szwed notes of the choreometric films that he compiled in the 1960s and 1970s, some thirty years later, Lomax "counted on images more than words [extra-diegetic sounds like narration] to communicate" (2010, 375).

It is also important to note that Lomax, as the assistant in charge of the Archive of American Folk Song, had several goals in capturing empirical data for didactic ends. One goal was to provide disciplinary scholars and academic researchers with the data with which to undertake scholarly analysis and explication of human behavior and cultural expression. He was also working under an imperative—institutional and personal—to create a documentary research record of cultural expressions for the benefit of the cultural communities that were being documented as well as their descendants and neighbors.

The complementary viewpoint to the scientific talk was that the rapid social changes pressed on folk communities by the forces of modernity made it imperative to document and preserve the expressions of cultural formations before they were irretrievably lost. In this and similar formulations, we hear the now (thankfully) bygone anthropological preoccupation with "salvaging" cultures. By contrast, Lomax was a constant and vocal champion of the principle of "cultural equity"—the imperative to heighten popular awareness of the integrity of the creative expressions of folk communities and marginalized cultural groups by making space for their practices to be seen, heard, and appreciated in the public sphere. In service to this progressive, pluralistic ideal, Lomax's considerable talents as recordist and documentarian expanded to the arena of media production and publications throughout his career, and he produced film documentaries along with radio programs and commercial disks well after his first days of fieldwork in the 1930s and up to his death, in 2002.

Long after his passing, sustaining and keeping the cultural expressions he recorded decades ago in circulation for the benefit of present generations is a focus of the Association for Cultural Equity. The organization he founded has worked with folklorist and education specialist Laurie Sommers to develop lesson plans and teaching modules using recordings from his fieldwork and episodes from the film Leary and I produced (Sommers n.d.).

CONCLUSION

At the outset, I raised the notion of representation in the ethnographic process and product as a crucial one for public folklorists, indeed, for all cultural workers, to reckon with. Although my estimation of its effects is based on anecdotal, personal evidence, the responses to the film and to Lomax's impulse to document the folk culture of Michigan all those decades ago has been gratifying. Taken together, the testimonials that have emerged strongly indicate that the question of whether community members "see" themselves and their history reflected in the constructed product can be answered in the affirmative. For one, there was the whole-hearted audience response during a trip Jim Leary and I made in 2013 to premiere the film at FinnFest USA in Houghton, Michigan. The large audience was enthusiastic, and I was particularly moved by the comments of one family who expressed their deep appreciation at being able to view and hear the music of their ancestor.

The Center received similar responses after we made portions of the film available on the Library of Congress website. A correspondent was stuck by the notion that Lomax recorded images, literally from his own front door: "Living here in Calumet Township (Upper Michigan), I've been hearing about the Floriani family and their tamburitza playing for many years. How sweet to see and hear them. And by the way, at the close of that clip, the shot looking down at the railroad trestle above Lake Linden and Torch Lake is less than a mile from my house. To think that the almost-mythical Alan Lomax stood there with his camera, a 10 minute walk from where I'm sitting! Thank you, kiitos, merci, grazie, hvala." Another responded with his appreciation for Lomax's initiative: "How beautiful it was for Mr. Lomax to have the forethought to capture those moments. A national treasure!" The most affecting comment came from the granddaughter of the Bellaires: "I want to thank Mr. Lomax for the awesome history he reproduced here. My grandparents singing and my Dad as a boy dancing, was such a joy. The knowledge of the Library of Congress already having the family history there has made my journey so much easier. May our entire generation as well as more generations to come, have all they need to know of our families' history."

As I step back and consider not just the film but the total production that is Folksongs of Another America, I see it sharing some of the same animating impulses that produced the original documentation, but it is not isomorphic with them. Principally, while instances in which the observable, culturally specific attributes of human behavior that Lomax was keen to capture are apparent, the individual segments and the film as a whole are not much,

if at all, concerned with yielding up analyzable "scientific" data about folk music and musicians. What emerges from the meticulous, exhaustively researched work like this is an imagi-
natively constructed story about the cultural, historical, political, and creative dimensions of
the past that ask us to pay attention to the very fact of its construction. In other words, the
work embodies the texture, tactility, beauty, and extraordinary dimensions of cultural production and folk performance. The reimagined film segments stitch together sounds, images,
and text to direct our attention to the performers' "personality, power and grace amid gritty
surroundings" (Leary 2015, 186).

Notes

1. His father, John Lomax, a noted folksong collector, held the position of honorary consultant
and curator of the Archive of American Folk Song from 1934 to 1948, and Alan accompanied him on
several collecting expeditions in those years. Notably, the senior Lomax went on to serve as an ad-
viser on folklore collecting for two Works Progress Administration initiatives in 1936—the Historical Records Survey and the Federal Writers' Project. He was the FWP's first folklore editor and was
succeeded by Benjamin Botkin in 1938 (Porterfield 1996).

2. For more on labor songs in Michigan's Copper Country, see Virtanen elsewhere in this volume.

3. Choreometrics as a concept and frame of analysis is situated within the ethnographic studies
of dance performance. Johnson and Harvey state that it is "defined as a set of parameters through
which performance style could be observed and compared cross culturally. Working with Imrgard
Bartenieff, Forrestine Paulay and others, Lomax developed a coding system by which specific aspects of dance movement were observed and rated. The cultural geography developed for *Canto-
metrics* [song performance styles], where world cultures were defined and grouped to facilitate
comparative study, was used for choreometrics as well. Lomax and his associates assembled a large
sample of film clips of dance representing these cultural groups. With the coding system that was
developed, dance sequences on the films were rated and compared" (2016, 67).

Translating Context with Digital Media in Medieval Icelandic Literature

Hrafnkels saga and the eSaga Project

COLIN GIOIA CONNORS

Medieval Icelandic literature is challenging to teach because it is challenging to read. Even in translation, medieval sagas of Viking Age heroes are dense and unforgiving. The number of characters one must keep track of boggles the mind, as does the foreign geography, which plays such a fundamental and meaningful part of the storytelling. All these names inevitably dissolve into a mental soup of characters and places named Thor-this and Thor-that.[1] Meanwhile, the story—a nuanced and poetic commentary on justice, who has access to it, and how the intersections of race, gender, class, religion, and privilege affect that access—goes by wholly unappreciated. New readers do not know who is who, where the characters are, and what the rules and social norms are of this society they have only just encountered, and why seemingly minor transgressions can spiral into cyclones of homicidal violence. However, those who spend a decade studying the sagas come to love them, to recognize each and every Thor by name, to track their travels over heath and moor, to comprehend the machinations of their complex feuds, and to cherish the sagas' deeper themes and insightful lessons. The question is: how does one teach Iceland's medieval literature to someone who hasn't got a decade to spare? What if, as is the case in many college classrooms, you have only one week? Or, as is often the case with the public, you have no time at all?

My first teaching job was as a graduate assistant for a large survey course on Scandinavian literature from 1200 to 1900. Each week, the lecturer led students through a half century of literary history while I taught a small section of students basic literary analysis. I became frustrated when I did not have enough class time to give my students all the tools necessary to critically engage with one of our first texts, *The Saga of Hrafnkell Freysgoði*. My students struggled at both the level of *text*—who's who and where's what—and the level of *context*—why the characters did what, and how the text wants the reader to feel about what was done. But there was no time to answer all their questions; at the end of the week, we moved onto the next unit and onto the next fifty years of literary history.

My students' frustrations were the same frustrations experienced by any member of the public who picks a medieval text off the "folklore and mythology" shelf of the local bookstore.

Part and parcel of the lack of textual and contextual understanding of any new reader is an unfamiliarity with the medieval experience of reading. Whereas today reading is generally a solitary and silent experience, reading in the Middle Ages was typically a communal and vocal one (Crosby 1936; Bäuml 1980, 245; Clover 1982, 188–204). An audience would have *listened* to someone else read a saga aloud. The experience was a performative event in which both the reader and the audience contributed to the meaning of the text through performance: the reader by interpreting the text and conveying that interpretation through pacing, volume, affect, and so on; and the audience by reacting to the text as performed by the reader.

One reason newcomers get so easily lost while reading the Icelandic sagas is that the sagas were written for an audience with an insider's knowledge. The sagas therefore lack the kind of contextual clues necessary to explain historical figures, geographies, social norms, and narrative conventions within the text. If only readers today could sit in on a medieval reading, they might not need the text to explain its every detail to them—they might instead glean all the context they needed from the audience beside them. When an audience laughs, cries, or cheers, their reactions signal something about how and why the words of the text are significant. For example, when an imagined medieval Icelandic audience hears that a character has put on *blá klæði* (dark clothes), it immediately falls silent. This happens because "dark clothes" create suspense. The audience, with its insider's knowledge, knows that dark clothes are a narrative device; these words foreshadow that the wearer is on their way to slay an enemy. Such insider knowledge is fundamental to understanding and appreciating the narrative art of the saga; without it, the modern reader may be more distracted than engaged by what otherwise appears to be an irrelevant and ambiguous detail of fashion. But without such an audience alive today to accompany a text and convey its context to first-time readers, how might one craft a text-based narrative experience that would mimic the medieval experience of performance? Surely such an experience would improve the public's ability to appreciate this specific genre of medieval folklore and possibly assist other folklorists in the public presentation of their work.

FOLKLORE AND SAGA STUDIES

Folklorists have long wrestled with how to translate performance to text without losing context and with how to translate one cultural context to another audience. In the case of medieval Icelandic literature, very little context is recorded. Most sagas were written by anonymous scribes who did not date their works, name their patrons, or record their locations. Many of these sagas survive today only as copies of copies of the originals, which are bound into collections of other works, where the context of their creation and use in the Middle Ages is further obscured. How a text was formed and what influences fed into its creation are important questions for the folklorist to ask and vital to answer when investigating historical texts. Most saga scholars now ascribe to what is called the New Traditionalist school, which claims that the sagas are both historiography and narrative art, based on a mix of oral and literary traditions. The challenge, as Carol Clover notes, is defining how that oral tradition operated and how it gave rise to the texts we have today (1986, 37).

Clover coined the term "immanent whole" to refer to an entire epic that is common knowledge to both performer and audience (1986). When oral epics were recorded by folklorists, Clover notes, storytellers were asked to recite the entire epic from beginning to end, a task they were capable of doing but never actually did in performance. Applying this model to the Icelandic case, Clover revived the *þáttr* (episode) theory, which postulated that the sagas existed in the preliterary stage as short folktales that were later cobbled together into longer, written narratives. Clover modifies the theory by proposing that "a whole saga existed at the preliterary stage not as a performed but as an immanent or potential entity, a collectively envisaged 'whole' to which performed parts of *þættir* of various sizes and shapes were understood to belong, no matter what the sequence or the frequency of the presentation" (1986, 34). The narrative events of a saga are only a fraction of what was known and expected to be known, orally or as background knowledge, by saga writers, readers, and audiences alike.

Audience participation and the immanent nature of storytelling in groups is evident in contemporary examples of oral culture as well. Susan Kalcik introduces the term "kernel story" in her analysis of personal narratives in women's support groups (1975). The kernel story might be referenced in conversation or, if invited, told in full. Listeners in the support groups were already familiar with the stories and, depending on their interest, would invite the storyteller to tell them anew. Kalcik's observations demonstrate that even in a variety of storytelling environments, storytellers shape the story by length and structure contingent on contextual needs, such as audience interest. The more intimately the storyteller knows their audience, the more freedom the storyteller has to draw on shared contextual "resources" (Watson and Potter 1962). In other words, the more knowledge of cultural references the storyteller and audience share, the greater the immanent tradition for the oral storyteller to draw upon and manipulate in performance.

Gísli Sigurðsson applied the concept of immanence to the sagas of eastern Iceland and has convincingly argued for an extensive immanent oral culture out of which came Iceland's sagas (2004, 2008). In one example, Gísli examines the character of Þorkell Geitisson, who appears briefly in multiple sagas, at different stages in his life. His character is portrayed consistently in all of these episodes as a wise, peace-loving chieftain who nevertheless often comes out on bottom in contests. Gísli demonstrates that these consistent episodes could not have been generated by one literary work influencing another and that the collection of them together could be told as a rather coherent saga of the man's life. Even though no such textual saga exists, it seems convincing from the available texts that each time a writer included Þorkell Geitisson in a narrative, they were tapping into an immanent saga of the man's life.

Þorkell Geitisson's written name, then, functions as one of Kalcik's kernels. Saga writers dropped Þorkell's name into various manuscripts without any contextualization because they were confident that his life story was well known to their cultural contemporaries. If a medieval reader knew the immanent whole of Þorkell's life—or at least the immanent gist—then who is to say that the medieval reader might not have gone off script while reading to tell Þorkell's story from his own memory, in short or in full, depending on the audience's invitation? Audience participation, or intervention, of course varies from culture to culture, but in many parts of medieval Europe, discussing a text while one read it aloud was a familiar form of education for the elite (Crosby 1936).[2] In the medieval context, the text is not merely a product of the oral tradition but an object used in performance and therefore part of a process of continuing oral tradition. The text supports and is supported by a vast oral tradition whose immanence in performance lends meaning to each written kernel.

TRANSLATING CONTEXT WITH DIGITAL MEDIA

In our present context, however, the text is all that remains. To understand the text today in its medieval context, Gísli builds an immanent saga of Þorkell's life through comparative reconstruction—he reads every medieval text that mentions Þorkell, compares them, and reconstructs what might have been popular knowledge at the time. This is the same method scholars use to recognize other kernels and interpret the meaning behind a narrative device like "dark clothes" (Ranković 2013). Not only is the trope recognizable in other sagas, but the color itself is recognizable in myth and poetry as the color of carrion birds and the goddess of death, Hel (Wolf 2006). The weight of this symbolism and its effect on the saga narrative is, of course, dependent on the immanence of these myths and poems in the reader's mind. But their meaning is further expanded with the knowledge that dark clothes were expensive clothes, requiring vast amounts of expensive blue dyes to create. These associations not only add to the foreshadowing that the wearer intends to kill someone but also suggest that the wearer is proud of their homicidal mission, having donned their best clothes for the occasion. It is one of many potent images in any saga that should spring to mind in every reader or listener, but this great layering of hidden meanings is unlocked today only by reading the entire corpus of medieval Icelandic literature—every saga, every poem, every myth, every homily, and every chronicle. Only then can the modern reader begin to approach the text with anything resembling the medieval audiences' oral knowledge of the immanent context. This necessity to read everything is the *reader's imperative*, to paraphrase John Miles Foley (1991, 53ff.). This pursuit is what scholars dedicate their lives to, but either pedagogically or as an expectation to place upon the public, it is a disaster. The beginner has no hope of understanding even the first sentence until they have finished reading the entire corpus. Instead of the *reader's imperative*, I see it as the *scholar's imperative* to put their expertise to use and provide first-time readers with this context in saga translations. But with so much context and even different types of context to provide, the scholar is quickly confronted with the challenge of how best to provide it. The textual medium is limited both by the types of information it can communicate and by how it communicates them. Flipping back and forth between endless endnotes, for example, disrupts the reader's experience of a text.

Digital media offer more possibilities than print media to handle the fundamental problem of how to translate context. First, digital media are unbound by the cost of the printed page, allowing for more color, more images, and more design possibilities for presentation and layout. More color and more images mean more opportunities for context, and more design possibilities for presentation and layout mean more options for effective communication of that context. Second, digital media allow for the inclusion of contextual elements not possible in print. Audio, video, and interactive maps can combine to produce a multimodal text capable of communicating context through different media. Third, digital media allow for a level of interaction between texts through hyperlinks that simply is not possible with print media. In *Oral Tradition and the Internet*, Foley (2012) finds structural similarities between narrative experiences online and in person and contrasts them with narrative experiences of printed texts. Whereas a printed novel or saga has a definite beginning, middle, and end—and therefore an intended reading order—there is no right or wrong order to navigate a website or to have a conversation. Endnotes upset the reader of a printed text because they upset the hierarchy of the text. Hyperlinks, by contrast, do not upset the Web user because there is no hierarchy to subvert. Hyperlinks are not deviations from an intended path; they are the path itself, ever branching, emergent, nonlinear, and sometimes circular. Web 2.0 is built upon the shared authorship of user-generated content that is constantly being uploaded and therefore constantly changing. Unlike a static printed text, both the path one takes through websites like Wikipedia and YouTube and the content one finds there will never be the same twice. Just as every oral performance is unique, so too is every experience online. While the Internet is not the same as oral tradition, it can mimic it, and that potential can be used to modify a saga to make the digital experience mimic the medieval experience.

In order to better introduce *Hrafnkels saga* to nonspecialists, I decided that an ebook would be best suited to presenting a translation of a medieval saga. An ebook shares the familiar linear structure of a printed book, but it can also integrate some features of the amorphous, hyperlinked, networked structure of the Internet. Most e-readers support common interactive features of printed text, such as the ability to highlight, bookmark, and write on pages, but they also interface with online apps, allowing readers to look up words in the dictionary or on Wikipedia. EPUB 3.0, the industry standard adopted in 2011 and updated to 3.0.1 in 2014, when I started building my ebook, was based on XHTML, which meant that, in theory, anything possible on a website was also possible in an ebook. In practice, however, e-reader apps could read only limited features of XHTML code. No one e-reader could do it all. At the time, Apple's e-reader app, iBooks, supported the most features and was the obvious choice for my ebook—or my esaga, as I began to call it.

iBooks supported a fixed layout, which allowed me to arrange images and notes to the reader in the margins of the page, imitating the marginalia found in medieval manuscripts. Marginalia—including illustrations, captions, chapter summaries, and pull quotes—serve as visual bookmarks and tell stories of their own (Carruthers 2008, 309–24). They were a way of communicating context to the medieval reader, and my use of pull quotes, thumbnail images, and captions in the margins of the esaga continues this medieval tradition. While the small size of a thumbnail limits how much information the image can communicate, the digital platform allows each image to be enlarged to full screen with a tap. Readers may prefer to view photographs of the landscape, for example, in full screen to better contemplate the geographical context they impart to the story. Landscapes, of course, experience natural and cultural changes over time, and therefore photographs are captioned with the history of those changes. Photographs with pickup trucks and hydroelectric dams remind the reader that the photographed landscape is a modern one and that, by inserting these photographs into the text, we actively project an imagined past landscape upon them. This activity is perhaps not unlike the way the medieval audience projected an

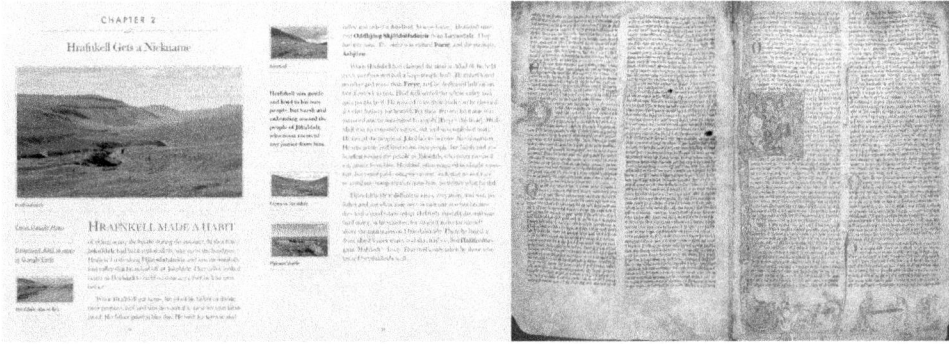

The esaga (*left*) mimics the design of medieval manuscripts (*right*: Flateyjarbók, GKS 1005 fol.) in both form and function. (*Left*: screenshot of author's ebook on iBooks; *right*: Árni Magnússon Institute for Icelandic Studies.)

imagined past Viking Age landscape upon the contemporary landscape visible to their eyes.[3]

In the main text body, bolded and colored text mimics the aesthetics of a manuscript rubric and mimics the effect of input from the audience, such as silence or laughter, to call attention to passages that require contextual in-group knowledge for comprehension. Color signals categories of context: black for people, red for places, and yellow for culture. Tapping, for example, on the bolded yellow words "dark clothes" opens an explanatory pop-up, which links to a glossary that contains all terms, a list of all instances of the term in the text, and a curated list of related terms. Unlike EPUB 2.0, which could support only limited endnotes, EPUB 3.0 with iBooks supports an interactive glossary index that allows users to hyperlink from topic to topic and then to return easily to the main text. A reader might therefore jump ahead to the next use of "dark clothes" in the saga to see if the trope is reinforced or subverted in its next iteration, or the reader might jump to a related glossary entry for "colored clothing" to learn more about material culture. The ebook supports tangential learning within the text by allowing readers to choose their own path and craft a unique learning experience with each reading.

To explore another category of glossed terms, pop-ups for people summarize each character's significance within the saga and across medieval literature and summarize the uniformity or diversity of textual narrative traditions about said character in the Middle Ages. If the reader wants to learn more, the pop-up links to a character map that situates the character genealogically, socially, and geographically, and the glossary links to a curated list of related characters. Should the reader lose track of which Thor is which even after they are introduced in bold and black, every occurrence of every name is hyperlinked to the glossary. Character entries not only help readers remember who's who but also help readers decide which characters are worth remembering and what for. In the case of Hrafnkell's wife, Oddbjörg, the character entry reveals that she is *not* a significant character in this text or any other, insofar as can be determined through comparative reconstruction, because she is not known from any other medieval text. The esaga gives the reader permission to

An interactive map in Google Earth provides place lore and offers readers another path through the text. (Screenshot of author's own custom Google Map file in Google Earth.)

forget Oddbjörg, one name among many in a lengthy list of genealogical character introductions, and instead to focus attention on the names of characters that have greater significance to the story.

Place lore entries also provide important context; they translate place-names, provide photographs, add natural and cultural history, and link to an interactive digital map. Place-names communicate a wealth of immanent medieval lore that adds meaning to the saga narrative. Some qualities, such as the economic and social standing of a residence, might be clearly reflected in a place-name like Aðalból (Manor House), but other qualities, such as natural environment or local history, might not be communicated in any way. When characters travel, for example, the saga text merely lists the names of landmarks to outline their paths. The readers are expected to connect these points in their minds and to make a meaningful interpretation of the route based on their knowledge of the land. For example, one string of place-names reveals that Hrafnkell travels by the longer and safer coastal route, revealing Hrafnkell's complacency, whereas another string of place-names reveals that Sámr travels by the shorter and more dangerous highland route, revealing Sámr's desperation. Place lore entries communicate this context with photographs of the grassy, populated coastlands and the rocky, desert highlands and also by linking to an interactive map on Google Maps/Google Earth, which links these place-names into coherent paths.[4]

Unlike a printed map that is bounded by the scale of the page, the digital map allows one to interact with the map in two significant ways: first, the ability to zoom in and zoom out allows readers to control how they read the map, and second, place lore annotations for each location on the map allow readers to read the saga geographically. These annotations present readers with yet another path through the text; users can navigate through the environments of the narrative independent of the narrative order but inextricably linked to the narrative experiences of characters. Place lore annotations teach readers, for example, to recognize boggy ground by its telltale flora and thereby teach readers the concerns of medieval travelers who measured travel in terms of difficulty as opposed to units of distance. This context helps readers understand narrative events linked to these locations and to understand the landscape as a character unto itself, which can help or hinder human characters. The interactive digital map thus combines the functionality of modern maps with medieval maps—a navigational tool for accurately representing geographic space on the one hand and a teaching tool for learning relationships and narratives on the other.[5] By presenting not only the place-names themselves but also the lore associated with the places, the interactive digital map can both communicate a phenomenological experience of the landscape in medieval terms and mimic the way in which oral traditions are often shared and experienced on location.

The goal, again, was to make the knowledge produced by Old Norse scholars accessible to the English-speaking public in a form that would enhance their reading of Old Norse translations. While iBooks helped me toward this goal, there are some notable shortcomings of this particular platform and of ebooks in general that are worth mentioning. First, iBooks' unique fixed layout, which allowed me to mimic the visual design of a medieval manuscript, means that the font size is unresponsive; it cannot be changed on the reading device. It is optimized for an iPad screen. On a computer screen, the font appears smaller and can be difficult to read for the visually impaired. On an iPhone screen, the font is nearly impossible to read. Second, iBooks is available only on Apple products. While some university libraries have iPads to loan to their students, this proprietary and costly restriction makes the esaga inaccessible to a large number of users. When I published the esaga, in 2015, iBooks was the only platform that could support an interactive glossary—a feature essential for my vision of the translation—but by late 2016, Amazon Kindle, which works on iOS, Android, Mac, and PC, had updated its platform to support an interactive glossary. Rebuilding the esaga for Kindle would solve this proprietary issue, and while I would like to, I have not yet done this. Why not? The third shortcoming: it takes a lot more time to create a hypertext than a text. While the iBooks Author app does not require any coding ability to operate—iBooks Author uses a WYSIWYG interface akin to most word processors—it still takes a lot of time to hyperlink all of the digital features, and this work cannot be easily passed off to an editor. The clerical task of hyperlinking elements cannot be extricated from the academic work of determining how hypertext elements function in relation to the text; this work requires expertise in folklore and Old Norse studies, and it takes time and research to curate an etext with knowledge and scholarly intent. Fourth, I had to translate the text, which also required a huge time investment. The only translations available to me free of copyright were so archaic as to be nearly useless. My only option was to translate the saga for myself, a task that required me to develop additional skills and a unique translation style. A fifth shortcoming, which is endemic to all digital literature, is that of marketing and distribution. Without a physical product to put in bookstores, it can be difficult to get a digital book into the hands of the public.

Beyond these practical shortcomings, it is also worth briefly noting the systemic barriers within academia to the production of such public-serving scholarly works; namely that translations are not considered scholarly works. Despite the considerable amount of original research, interpretative work, and theoretical contributions that go into translation projects, tenure committees largely undervalue translations in relation to peer-reviewed journal articles. The same can be said for the publishing of ebooks and the development of pedagogical tools. Furthermore, these preferences of tenure committees trickle down to graduate students, who, in hopes of landing a tenure-track job one day, can be directly or indirectly dissuaded from submitting nontraditional dissertations. Thus, putting one's labor and expertise toward developments in the pedagogical and public presentation of medieval folklore is a losing bet for the individual academic.

Yet, for all these shortcomings, the question remains: did the esaga succeed? Since I published *The eSaga of Hrafnkell Freysgoði*, in 2015, I have assigned it to students in small seminars and large lectures, and their journal assignments and course evaluations suggest a positive answer. One student wrote in a free-response assignment for a sagas course I taught in 2015: "I find the map very helpful with the text. For example, when Sámr makes the trip through the highlands, the description in the text sounds rather arbitrary, but seeing the journey itself on Google Earth is awesome! Especially being able to see distance— Iceland itself seems pretty darn small, but when you look at the distance, and especially the fact that they travel by horse. . . . I mean, I seriously want to know how long it took to travel that far! And now I understand why Hrafnkell took the coastline to get to the Althing (you know, better weather, access to water, etc.)."

Here is a student who comprehends the saga on the levels of both text and context; the student understands who is doing what, where, and why and has internalized medieval travel concerns, applied this knowledge to the narrative, and become curious to learn more. And all this learning is attributable to the digital apparatus. The pop-ups, digital photography, and interactive maps do not distract or lead the reader astray from the text; they present the reader with unique paths through the text that may be chosen freely on the basis of interest or need, they foster the readers' understanding and appreciation, and they support their tangential learning. And by augmenting the text with the kinds of knowledge that the medieval audience shared orally, the esaga uses digital modes of learning to mimic a medieval performance of the text and makes public the expertise of folklorists. Just as the medieval audience was capable of asking the saga reader to expand upon the text with orally delivered context, the modern audience is capable of asking the esaga to expand upon the text with digitally delivered context. The esaga is the medieval reader, and you are its audience; the story lies somewhere in between.

Notes

I wish to thank the University of Wisconsin Libraries and Department of Information Technology for the technical and financial help they awarded me through the Adopt, Remix, Create (ARC)

Initiative to research and develop The eSaga Project. I also wish to thank the many members of the Sons of Norway District 5 and especially the members of Vennelag Lodge 5-513 in Mount Horeb, Wisconsin, for their financial support through the Melba Huseth Estate Book Grant. Without this combination of funding, I would not have had the opportunity to travel to Iceland and photograph the many saga locations. The esaga is better for their support.

1. Brad Leithauser enumerates this difficulty best: "In *Gisli Sursson's Saga* we meet a man named Thorkel who, on the way to the Thorsnes Assembly, accompanied by Thorbjorn's sons, meets up with Thorstein, the son of Thorolf, who was living at Thorsnes with Thora and their children, Thordis, Thorgrim, and Bork the Stout. But even better, in its hellbent determination to promote domestic confusion, is the man in *Njal's Saga* who 'had two sons, both named Thorhall'" (2001).

2. Clover notes the Land Dayak epic of *Kichagi*, which took W. R. Geddes only sixty-three pages to transcribe but which took nine whole nights to perform because of the audience's frequent questions (1986, 19).

3. The fact that the digital experience mimics the medieval experience does not mean that digital annotations somehow reflect the historical "truth" of the Middle Ages more objectively than textual annotations. Digital annotations do, however, for the reasons outlined, provide more opportunities than textual annotations to communicate the subjective limitations inherent to all translation projects to their readers.

4. For an overview of the retrogressive method used to reconstruct medieval horse trails, see Connors 2014.

5. Cf. Edson 1997, 2007; Foys 2007, 2009.

PART VI. CREATING THE FUTURE

Henry Glassie's influential definition of tradition as the creation of the future out of the past serves as the inspiration for this section. Though folklore is popularly associated with the continuation of the past, folklorists have for decades stressed the role of change and creativity as central to the active transmission of folk cultures. For instance, Barre Toelken's concept of the twin laws of folklore process suggests that folklore has both conservative and dynamic elements to it (1996, 39); Barbro Klein and Mats Widbom (1995) remind us in their subtitle of their classic book on Swedish folk art that "all tradition is change." Folklore must change to adapt to an ever-changing world, and both community members and folklorists alike purposefully employ folklore to strategic ends as we create the future we want.

Whereas the former section grapples with the ways we wrestle with the past, creating and re-creating history and heritage to meet our needs today, this section looks at the creative ways we create the future out of the present. The chapters in this section all discuss how folklore can be an agent of change for the future and about the new realities we aspire to create out of the past through our doings in the present.

In his piece on labor songs, Bucky Halker explores his own work as a musician and scholar in bringing to life deep catalogues of mostly lost labor songs. Serving both scholarly and activist ends, Halker describes his process of locating songs, rearranging them to suit contemporary aural palettes, recording them, and performing them to advance his own activism. By connecting audiences today to labor history, Halker hopes to create stronger activist communities around worker's rights.

Jamie Yuenger's piece is a look at "private-sector folklore," detailing her own creation of a business, StoryKeep, that documents and produces folklore products for families. Yuenger's business model of collaboration, though historically stigmatized in our field because of its profitability, challenges our discipline's models of ethical collaboration and offers viable solutions to systemic problems of underemployment in our field by rethinking how we understand working in communities as folklorists strive to make future careers for themselves in relation to the history of the field.

Joe Salmons's piece involves an interdisciplinary project looking at ethnographic documentation through a linguistic lens in order to understand ethnicity and contemporary performances of that ethnicity. Using Norwegian dialect jokes, Salmons looks at the way dialect is performed in humor and how it deviates from the actual dialects Norwegian native speakers historically used when speaking English. By better understanding the linguistic and cultural aspects of the past and presenting the work publicly, Salmons hopes to counter linguistic stereotyping and discrimination in the future.

Hilary Morgan V. Leathem discusses the complex and ambivalent roles ethnographers have had as "collaborators" in Oaxaca, through processes that led to the extraction of both material and oral culture from Oaxaca, and a legacy in which these ethnographic artifacts were scarcely even accessible to locals. Leathem details a project of locals' own design to produce ground-up and decolonizing ethnographic work designed to empower locally constructed futures (a graphic ethnography produced by locals about cultural sites), which radically alters power dynamics in the processes of public ethnographic representation.

To close the section, Christine Garlough's contribution to this volume looks at her creation of a digital archive of signage from the 2017 Women's March built on an ethics of care. Looking at creative and expressive signage and visual culture used during the march, Garlough highlights examples that illustrate the need to collect both ordinary and exceptional examples of homemade protest signs in order to create historical narratives that advance a vision of equity and justice for future generations.

These chapters look distinctly forward on the way culture work bends toward a more equitable and just world. With these chapters, we find that tradition is not something simply to be documented or preserved but rather a nexus that can be creatively repurposed and reimagined to create the future we wish to live in.

"I Need to Make a Dollar"

On the Road with Working-Class Protest Songs

Bucky Halker

A few years ago I was driving to a concert in southern Illinois and decided to stop in Mowequa, a former coal-mining town on US Highway 51 south of Decatur. Garry Harrison, a fiddler and song collector (Harrison and Burgess 2007) from east central Illinois, told me that a song existed commemorating the 1932 Mowequa mine disaster. I hoped that a visit to the Mowequa mining museum might yield a copy of the song that I could add to my list of coal songs from the state. Unfortunately, the museum was closed. I walked over to the village hall and knocked on the door, which was locked. To my surprise, the woman who opened the door was the mayor, and when I told her of my quest, she happily informed me she had the song in her files and promptly made me a copy. A perfect day of "fieldwork," I thought as I walked back to my car.

Traveling this labor song highway seems perfectly natural now. Combining musical performance, public programming, research, and fieldwork, I have managed to eke out a living, travel hither and yon, and meet and engage with all kinds of people. On my good days, typically after a concert at a library, museum, or union hall, where there's a good crowd and lots of questions and conversation, I believe I might even be helping move the planet forward a bit. I'm doing my best, after all, to take my research into the streets, trekking the world as a public educator.

Becoming this musician–public scholar was hardly predestined and remains a work in progress. I was born in 1954 in Beaver Dam, Wisconsin, "the best town by a dam site." We soon moved to the boreal north, and I spent most of my youth on Lake Superior in Washburn and Ashland, where I graduated from high school in 1972. Other than skiing, my great youthful passion was music. My mother nurtured my enthusiasm, as she played the flute and the piano and required all her children to take music lessons. At the same time, I also loved all the music I heard, from polka and country on the radio to live music in the local taverns and supper clubs.

As it did for many kids, rock and roll changed everything for me. My first memory of television was Elvis gyrating to "Hound Dog." Still, the "British invasion"—the Rolling Stones, Beatles, Animals, and Gerry and the Pacemakers—deserves more credit. Young, hormonally charged boys in Ashland shouted with glee: "No more accordion lessons!" or, in my case, "No more piano lessons." I joined the teenage army that flocked to hear local and regional rock bands. I bought an electric guitar, learned a few chords, and banged out songs like "Get Off My Cloud" and "Louie, Louie." I began writing songs shortly after and played in bands throughout high school.

By the late 1960s, converging national and personal forces altered my political and musical worldview. Antiwar, antidraft, and civil rights unrest, along with the 1968 Democratic convention, forced me to think critically about America. A vaguely defined hippy, antimaterialist, antigovernment, antiwar paradigm came to dominate my thinking. Unintentionally, my dad pushed me in that direction. An alcoholic, prone to domestic violence, he railed against hippies, rock and roll, Indians, Blacks, communists, and anything to the left of Nixon. Joy filled my heart when he relocated himself. A pleasing progressive spirit wafted into our home.

Musically, my ears shifted toward Cream, Janis Joplin, Country Joe and the Fish, B. B. King, Jimi Hendrix, and Neil Young. I found old Folkways records by Leadbelly and Woody Guthrie at the local library and mail ordered blues LPs by Sleepy John Estes, Bessie Smith, Otis Spann, and Mississippi John Hurt. My power trio, aptly named Freedom, did Hendrix and Cream covers, jammed, picked up a couple of blues tunes, banged out my originals, and strummed occasional acoustic numbers. I also discovered "folk music," as it was popularly described. Northland College students Charlie Maguire and Pop Wagner, later key Minneapolis "folkies," led a little scene in town and founded the Ashland Folk Festival. Both commingled politics and music and kindly taught me Guthrie and Leadbelly tunes, including the latter's classic, "Bushwa Blues." I was now a politically oriented singer-songwriter, a "folk" musician, and scored a few solo coffeehouse gigs in Ashland and Washburn.

Scholarships and student loans allowed me to run away to the College of Idaho in Caldwell in 1972. There, I discovered I could think and write in a reasonably intelligent fashion. I majored in history; washed dishes in the cafeteria; dug into the Guthrie songs; corresponded with his former wife, Marjorie; booked the campus coffeehouse; discovered the Industrial Workers of the World (IWW), whose members were sometimes referred to as Wobblies; bought a used Martin guitar; and landed gigs anywhere I could make a few bucks. I finished college with twin passions—the study of history and a drive to perform and to learn about "folk music."

I had no clue how those twin passions might work in a PhD program when I began graduate school at the University of Minnesota in 1976. Fortunately, I enrolled in Hyman Berman's seminar on US labor history and Ellen Stekert's course on American folklore and folksong. Both scholars advocated scholarship in service to the general public. This coincided with the creation of a new democratic model of labor history, one that went beyond the institutional, "top down" approach of the John R. Commons and the Wisconsin School that had defined and dominated the field since the early twentieth century. The school's approach, which paralleled the Wisconsin Idea in its belief that the study and analysis of labor history could be used to solve societal issues, had much to recommend it but narrowly focused on the history and policy of labor institutions and their leadership, paying little attention to the thoughts and actions of the rank and file, ethnic groups, racial minorities, women, and left-of-center labor organizations. By contrast, the new approach to emerge in the sixties followed the lead of the English historian E. P. Thompson and strove to write the history of workers "from the bottom up," consciously rejecting the model of the Wisconsin School (1966).

In that spirit, I was quickly moved to ask, "Why not labor protest songs as source material?" I soon combed secondary sources by Philip Foner, Joyce Kornbluh, Richard Reuss, David Dunaway, Norm Cohen, Archie Green, George Korson, Nels Anderson, and many more. Among the worker music and poetry of the Great Depression, I came across Jim Garland, Florence Reece, and Aunt Molly Jackson; Brookwood Labor College and Commonwealth Labor College; and the more classically trained and oriented Mark Blitzstein, Ellie Siegmeister, and Hans Eisler. Seeking antecedents, I sought out books, newspapers, recordings, poetry chapbooks, and songbooks pertaining to the period 1900–1920, including compositions from the Industrial Workers of the World (IWW), Joe Hill, "Freiheit Poets," and socialists.

Lightbulbs really went off when I scrolled through Gilded Age labor papers and stumbled upon thousands of song-poems.[1] Nearly every paper printed them, many as a regular feature contributed by editors, local labor officials, and rank-and-file members scattered across the country.[2] I also unearthed song-poetry books from the era, most by forgotten working-class songster-bards—Karl Reuber, Phillips Thompson, Michael McGovern ("The Puddler Poet)," and Patrick Fennell ("Shandy Maguire"), to name a few. Here was a trove of working-class art and affirmation of a vital working-class tradition.

The search for and the examination of song-poems, including information on authors, quickly became a key part of my life. Biographical details on Joe Hill or Florence Reece proved easy to locate, but finding similar information for the majority of the song-poets could be difficult.[3] Most song-poems in labor publications from 1865 to 1900 appeared anonymously or with just the writer's name. Fortunately, some entries included the author's residence. I wrote to libraries or historical societies, hoping a sympathetic staff member or a volunteer might unearth information for me. If the author's union local appeared, I might locate the town where it operated and then write my letter. I sought out city directories hoping to find authors' occupations and addresses. My success was mixed, however, particularly if the writers were women, since women typically did not appear in the city directories. Such research is easier today as census data and other materials are accessible online.

In spite of the obstacles, I discovered that the majority of these musical-literary offerings came from everyday workers. Moreover, by tracking geographic locations of writers and papers, I could see the central place of Illinois and Chicago in worker song-poetry. Illinois workers produced hundreds of compositions from 1865 to 1900. How better to do history "from the bottom up" than to examine and assess this work?

Song-poems addressed an array of subjects: strikes, immigration, mining accidents, the eight-hour day, elections, working conditions, boycotts, child labor, wages, local labor issues, unions, and everything else pertaining to unions and workers. Some, especially those written by women, also spoke of nature, children, religion, death, and community. While contributors mirrored labor's progressive cant, a small contingent expressed dislike for the Chinese, for African Americans, and for the new immigrants of the era.

My research and fieldwork methods expanded over time. At the conclusion of a concert at the state museum in Lockport, Illinois, an audience member presented me with a photocopy of sheet music for "Hallelujah, I'm a Bum" by Haywire Mac, a Wobbly and early country musician who had something of a hit with the song in 1928 (McClintock 1972). Not surprisingly, since Illinois was the rail center of the United States and had a large population of migrant workers, Wobblies, railroaders, and hoboes, the song enjoyed wide circulation long before Haywire's recording made the rounds (Sandburg 1927). His was a variant form, depoliticized for the mass market. I often take this copy on the road to illustrate how a labor song might become a "hit" and how the folk transmission process (and politics) results in lyrical variations, a pedagogical tool that blends my research, my music, and my public work.

These gifts became commonplace over the years, something I term "passive fieldwork." For example, I had long sought *UAW-CIO Sings*, a pocket-size songbook from the post–World War II heyday of the United Auto Workers (n.d.). One day, at a Chicago gig, a woman gave me her original copy autographed by the legendary UAW chief Walter Reuther. Similarly, another woman delivered a box of LPs to me that included a Welsh coal miner's choir, Joe Glazer doing IWW songs, and two recordings released by the UAW featuring Ronnie Gilbert, Tommy Makem, Odetta, Billie Holiday, and Cisco Houston.

Early in my research, I performed labor song-poems here and there but shied away from being a "labor bard" per se. I was busy on the singer-songwriter and rock scenes, and the labor music niche was amply populated anyway. Equally important was the matter of how to arrange and perform Gilded Age labor song-poems in a style accessible to audiences and enjoyable to myself. How could I get "inside" these songs, most of which derived from hymns and patriotic music made for group singing?

In the 1980s, I prodded myself into refashioning old labor song-poems to suit my palate. When I moved to Chicago, in 1986, the pace of this process increased swiftly. With a rich labor history, continued labor presence, musical traditions, and a diverse and vibrant music scene, Chicago provided encouragement. I landed in Rogers Park, home of the No Exit and Heartland cafés, two progressive neighborhood bases, and immediately found performance venues. I joined a rootsy "Americana" band that emerged as a local favorite, played Midwestern festivals, and toured from Duluth to Dallas to Winnipeg to Bayfield. Labor organizations soon called me to perform, too. I was almost making a real living, so I cast aside any aspirations for an academic job. Perhaps that was not a good career decision, but the public scholar–musician path was interesting and rewarding.

The next thirty-five years had challenges, especially financial ones. The music scene began a long decline in the early 1990s and never recovered. The recording industry and club scene that previously existed gave way to "DIY" recording, fewer venues, and "pay to play." Having a PhD finally came in handy, as did experience with public programs and a willingness to work with labor. I wrote grants, spoke to general audiences about labor music and labor history, and roused crowds with labor anthems.

I also discovered that labor music had value in Europe, a place where artists still received decent wages. Amerika Haus Frankfurt, part of a network in Germany that received funding through the US Information Service, summoned me for a labor song lecture-performance tour in 1990, just as the Berlin Wall and the German Democratic Republic collapsed. Similar tours followed for years thereafter. Back home, the Illinois State AFL-CIO provided money to research and record a CD of the state's labor songs (Halker 2002). The union invited me to perform at the state convention and gave free copies of the CD to delegates. The Illinois Humanities Council, where I held a part-time job for several years, allowed me to create a speakers' bureau in 1997 that included my labor and folk music programs. I am still a part of the bureau today and have presented nearly two hundred music programs at museums, libraries, union halls, and historical societies in Illinois. I also did similar programs through the Arts Tour program of the Illinois Arts Council Agency. Finally, the City of Chicago Department of Cultural Affairs and a host of funding organizations provided grants to me and to Company of Folk, a nonprofit I cofounded in 2007. These grants supported recording projects devoted to labor songs, along with many other projects related to folk and ethnic music and art in Illinois, many highlighting worker musicians and artists.

To date, I have presented hundreds of concert programs on labor music in Illinois and points beyond. I toured Germany, Switzerland, and Austria for three decades performing labor and original music and appeared on a host of radio and television programs. A Swiss label released several of my recordings, including *Don't Want Your Millions* (1999), a collection of classic and unknown labor songs, and *Welcome to Labor Land* (2002). I played for labor and socialist organizations in Switzerland and Germany, performed at Karl Marx University in Leipzig (when Marx was still on their moniker), and was invited by the Friedrich Ebert Foundation to perform at the 150th anniversary of the German Social Democratic Party in Augsburg in 2012. Labor songs by unknown and famous labor bards floated through bars, colleges, schools, museums, theaters, and concert halls along the way. My musical comrades Ralph Chaplin, Joe Hill, Guthrie, and Leadbelly came along, as did Illinois bards Emily and James Talmadge, Peetie Wheatstraw, Charles Haynes, J. B. Lenoir, Isaac Hanna, and Mrs. S. A. Yates.

A number of labor songs emerged as "standards" in my repertoire. All can be attributed to Illinois and illustrate that state's key role in labor song-poetry. The most obvious candidate is "Solidarity Forever," the anthem of American labor. Ralph Chaplin (1887–1961) composed the lyrics, one of many literary offerings by the Wobbly journalist, bard, and labor activist from Lombard, Illinois (Industrial Workers of the World 1917, 25–26; Chaplin 1948). Appropriately, he borrowed the tune from Julia Ward Howe's Civil War song "The Battle Hymn of the Republic," for which Howe enlisted the melody from "John Brown's Body." Her piece was among the most famous songs in the country, making it an ideal candidate for a labor sing-along. Indeed, seven labor songs from the Gilded Age had adopted the melody (Halker 1991, 87). Chaplin's 1915 composition, however, gained ascendence and in the 1930s became standard fare at labor gatherings, and it remains so today. I pull it out at labor events, funerals for activists, library programs, and union conventions. I sometimes jokingly tell audiences that the song is the "Louie, Louie" of labor songs. I'm weary of playing it, just as I grew tired of the Kingsmen classic in my youth.

I purposely transformed the song when recording it for *Welcome to Labor Land* in 2002, discarding the mandatory strumming, thumpity martial approach of sing-alongs. Oddly, some labor groups leave out verses when printing the lyrics for events. You could argue that's a practical approach for a song with six verses. However, it's the radical verses that get redacted, including the following:

> Is there aught we hold in common with the greedy parasite
> Who would lash us into serfdom and would crush us with his might?
> Is there anything left to us but to organize and fight?
> For the union makes us strong.

Weariness aside, "Solidarity Forever" still has much to recommend. You can teach the song's chorus in short order and rattle the walls. Additionally, Chaplin's lyrics offer a lesson on the labor theory of value at the ideological center of the labor movement for two centuries: "They have taken untold millions that they never toiled to earn." These types of lyrics are particularly useful when performing for public audiences, emphasizing the central place of "labor" in the creation of all wealth.

"Solidarity Forever" is labor's anthem today, but during the Gilded Age that honor belonged to "Hold the Fort." Unfortunately, many versions with differing lyrics exist, so tracing the most popular is problematic. We do know that Midwestern workers sang some form during the Knights of Labor heyday in the 1880s. The Chicago printers James Tallmadge and Emily Tallmadge included their version, titled "Our Battle Song," in their 1886 songbook, *Labor Songs Dedicated to the Knights of Labor*. The Tallmadges followed other song-poets who employed the tune from the gospel hymn "Hold the Fort" written by Phillip Bliss (1838–1876) (Scheips 1971). Bliss wrote the song in 1870 while living in Chicago and serving as the musical portion of an itinerant evangelical team. The song quickly became a hit on the gospel circuit and generated an audience across North America and Europe. Little wonder labor borrowed the melody, as it was simple, singable, and familiar, especially in Illinois.

I've taken this one to exotic places such as Chester, Mt. Vernon, and Watseka, Illinois, as well as to Hamburg, Leipzig, and Erfurt, Germany. The lyrics summon workers to action:

> Hark! the bugle note is sounding
> Over all the land;
> See! the people forth are rushing,
> Oh! the charge is grand.
>
> Storm the fort, you Knights of Labor;
> 'Tis a glorious fight;
> Brawn and brain against injustice—
> God defend the right!
>
> How the mighty host advances,
> Labor leads the van;
> The Knights are rallying by the thousands
> On the labor plan.

Strong entrenched behind their minions,
Sit the money kings;
Slavery grabbers, thieves, and traitors
Join them in their rings.

Who will dare to shun this conflict?
Who would be a slave?
Better die within the trenches
Forward, then, be brave

Finding an arrangement for a solo singer-guitarist proved the difficult part of making this song publicly tasteful. On *Welcome to Labor Land*, I opted for a full-band, rock approach in the studio. In solo concerts I settled into a finger-picking format that mixed melody and rhythm appropriate for hymn-like lyrics. Today, I enjoy the piece as a perfect way to demonstrate how workers thought of their world in the days of the Eight Hour Movement and the Knights of Labor. As one listens, you can hear how religion influenced the music and lyrics of labor, how workers' patriotic sentiments led them to judge the industrial elite as aristocratic "money kings," a treacherous lot of anti-American "slavery grabbers, thieves, and traitors." The song's high moral tone seems distant today but still speaks clearly to audiences and generates discussion.

Peetie Wheatstraw's "304 Blues" strikes a different chord for audiences and for me (Garon 2003). Born William Bunch in 1902, Wheatstraw was a prominent blues guitarist and pianist in the 1930s. Based in East St. Louis, Illinois, he made more than 150 recordings as "Peetie Wheatstraw, the High Sheriff from Hell" or "The Devil's Son-In-Law" prior to his death, in 1941. His lyrics were mostly typical fare, but he sometimes addressed vital issues in his community, including unemployment, public works, and urban renewal. Although he is largely unknown today and his work is confined to reissues on foreign labels, I came across Wheatstraw while researching Illinois folksongs. In "304" I found a gem, a slice-of-life lyric on the difficulties that workers face after getting the pink slip, the "304" form, when a work project comes to an end. "The 304 man makes you cry," and you can also forget about paying the landlord, buying liquor, or holding on to your gal.

Labor anthems elevate listeners and prod them to think about the noble and holy cause of labor, but "304 Blues" effectively highlights the harsh realities of unemployment. I've kept the arrangement simple, circa early Dylanesque strumming and harmonica, but crowds respond enthusiastically to this classic. After one performance for a social studies class, a seventh-grade boy blurted out that he liked the song because he knew girls who didn't like boys without money!

The most emotional responses I receive from any labor song, however, go to "The Dying Miner," a Woody Guthrie song from 1947. Guthrie spent considerable time in Illinois, including visits with Studs Terkel, concerts in Chicago, and a military stint at Scott Field near Belleville, Illinois. He wrote numerous songs during these sojourns, many never recorded and most of which are not part of Guthrie devotees' list of memorable tunes. Nevertheless, since discovering the song more than twenty years ago and revamping it, I have found it a forceful concert piece.

Guthrie's song commemorates a 1947 coal mining disaster that killed 111 miners in Centralia, Illinois. The state was no stranger to mine accidents. A 1909 disaster in Cherry claimed 259 miners, including several children, and later disasters took lives in West Frankfort, Mowequa, and Harco. Each of these accidents also yielded ballads. Such ballads have a long tradition in the United States and Europe, and coal miners were among the most talented labor bards. Notably, Guthrie did not lay claim to the lyrics, which he notes in the song itself: "Every word of this song I took from those words we found around the bodies on that slate rock." Lest we think Guthrie was engaging in the usual folk-singer hyperbole, remember that miners caught underground sometimes lived for several days, giving them time to write notes to loved ones on the slate walls of the mines or on bits of paper. Such was the case in Cherry and Centralia, where many miners wrote moving final words that were recovered during rescue or cleanup operations.

Audiences are noticeably moved by "The Dying Miner," sometimes to tears, and nowhere more so than in Illinois coal-mining towns. After I performed the song at the Centralia Historical Society Museum years ago, relatives of victims shared their stories with me and other audience members. More recently, after a 2018 performance at the library in Nashville, Illinois, six audience members from mining families exchanged memories of mining and mine history. The song works anywhere and provides a convenient way to talk about the tradition of coal-mining songs, the history of mining and accidents, and the efforts of unions to improve the miner's lot.

In concluding, I am once more reminded of Al Gedicks's foundational 1972 essay, "Guerrilla Research: Reversing the Machinery." E. P. Thompson may have spurred us to write workers' stories from the bottom up, but Gedicks charged academics to take their research findings into public forums. He urged scholars to present their work in accessible ways so that people might use it to improve those communities. Of course, many folklorists, historians, and scholars from other disciplines had done this since the early twentieth century. Gedicks and others, however, thought in more radical terms and hoped their approach might yield a grassroots movement to restructure the nation's economic and political foundation. Such thinking resonated with me in my youth, but today my goals for public programming are more modest. When I roll into a burg like Mt. Vernon for an Illinois labor song program, I do not expect anyone to take to the streets thereafter. Rather, I hope people are entertained, learn something new, appreciate the value of working-class art embodied in labor song-poetry, and ponder the meaning of the lyrics. I hope a few might seek out and work to preserve traditions in their own region. Mostly I just hope the program and the pieces I perform stir people to think deeply about the past, present, and future. Simply put, thinking citizens make better citizens.

NOTES

1. See Carmen Beaudoin Bombardier, Kim Chase, Robert Desrosiers, Andy Kolovos, and Lisa Ornstein's chapter in this volume for more on song-poems, or what the authors call "potential music."

2. For a list of papers containing song-poems, see Halker (1991, 217–18).

3. On locating biographical information on nonelites, see Ives (1976).

A Business Model for Folklore

Profitable, Wholehearted, and Cinematic

Jamie Yuenger

I'm going to say something, and I'm only going to say it once: if you are not profitable, you *are not in business.* My first client told me this, a woman who hired me to interview her father-in-law and produce a film dramatizing his life stories. Her business adage on profitability has stayed with me and sustained me. In 2010, I founded the folklore-driven production company StoryKeep. Individuals and families commission the company to create private films, books, and podcasts that celebrate their own family stories, traditions, and identities—their family's folklore. In this chapter, I explore the possibilities and pitfalls of what I term private-sector folklore or business folklore, seen through the lens of my personal and professional experience.

I built a career in business folklore because the options available when I finished school did not suit my personality or vision. For a while, I daydreamed of becoming the director of the Folklore Program at the University of Wisconsin–Madison (UW–Madison), but I could never sincerely imagine myself working in an academic setting. While an undergraduate in folklore, I worked under Anne Pryor at the Wisconsin Arts Board, helping her develop the website Wisconsin Folks. I was fortunate to see up close how my mentors navigated the many ins and outs of academic and public folklore. I wanted a different-looking career, but I had no idea what that might be.

I graduated from UW–Madison in 2004 with a major in Scandinavian studies and two certificates, one in women's studies and the other in folklore. Unable to resist my wanderlust, I spent a postgraduation year traveling solo. I volunteered with human rights organizations, protesting legalized marital rape in Ghana and dowry deaths in India via "bride burnings." I experienced wonders of the world: fist-sized snails in Accra; fresh jasmine flowers strung as necklaces in Chennai; smoky, silent temples in central Bangkok.

In 2005, I returned to the States and took a small-town position directing a tiny nonprofit for gay and lesbian youth in La Crosse, Wisconsin. I felt certain after two weeks that nonprofit work was not my forte. The nonprofit model and seemingly inherent disorganization drove me bonkers. I gave the job a year. In the summer of 2006, I tried my luck at political field organizing. Working out of a dusty office in Stevens Point, Wisconsin, I convinced townspeople to knock on doors for a cause. I worked sixteen hours a day for four months. Despite our efforts, we lost at the ballot in November 2006. I was adrift.

With no job, no apartment, and no partner, I had nothing holding me down. By late November I was eating Thanksgiving dinner with strangers in Brooklyn, New York. I decided to stay in Gotham, and for the next year, I waited tables. The third restaurant where I worked happened to be next door to City Lore, the folklore organization that would eventually be my bridge to a new calling.

I met with Steve Zeitlin, the director of City Lore (The New York Center for Urban Culture). He eventually encouraged me to study radio documentary at the Salt Institute in Portland, Maine. Following my radio studies at Salt, I landed an internship at WNYC, the NPR affiliate in New York City. Two weeks into the gig, I admitted to myself that I was miserable. I had dozens of creative ideas that would never see the light of day in such a hierarchical work environment. Then, sometime in 2009, a friend casually asked me whether I would be willing to interview her father-in-law and record some of the "family stories." I charged her a few hundred dollars and scheduled my first interview with Lou Zandoli. When I entered his house, Lou smiled wide, flashing an impressive gold grill that spanned his entire top teeth. His hands were gigantic and spoke of years of manual labor. After three interviews with Lou, I was struck by lightning: producing private documentaries about family stories was my career calling, my folkloric path. I could combine my years of fieldwork experience with my newly minted documentary know-how and make something meaningful. The disdain I held for organizational hierarchy made a personal enterprise all the more appealing.

After I finished the project with Lou, three other families hired me in quick succession. People were directly buying services and a product that spoke to them. More than a decade later, my company has created more than eighty projects with nearly that many families. I have come to believe that business folklore—what could also be called private-sector folklore—is a viable path for others in the field, those who have a real interest in balancing the work of building a business and the work of folklore.

In this chapter, I share select details of my professional life in hopes that they will inspire some entrepreneurs among us and clarify for everyone what one example of private-sector folklore can look like.

But first . . .

A Short Word about Family Folklore

Each family that contacts StoryKeep has an idea for the "what" and the "who" it wants to capture for posterity. Some people arrive at initial meetings carrying boxes of letters. Susan Brooks handed over two hundred love letters her parents had written to each other during World War II, replete with small stories and grand tales from both the home front and the war abroad. Chris Cory, StoryKeep's film editor, spent dozens of hours reviewing silent film footage from the 1920s that the Ballard family had impressively preserved for nearly a century. On a hot summer afternoon, we filmed Umi Muhammad as she made "Aunt Mazella's poundcake" in the specific manner in which Ms. Mazella had taught her. Phoebe Ford called us in a panic; she was the last one alive who knew her family's stories from nearly seven generations. StoryKeep's archivist cataloged two bank boxes' worth of memorabilia before we set off scoping Phoebe's film project. Members of her family helped settle parts of the American Midwest. One invented a machine that manufactured the pull-away instruction tab on medicine bottles. Another established the first YMCA in India. We eventually included five family trees in the back of Phoebe's accompanying book.

Our clients frequently blend family history, family folklore, and genealogy, seeing little or no difference between the subjects. With my experience in folklore studies, I help people to connect the three, using the dates and names, the letters and diaries, the stories and traditions, and the family tree to tell a meaningful and personal story. For the past couple of decades, Americans have plunged into personal genealogy and family history. It seems that almost everyone has at least one family member building a tree on Ancestry.com. Technological advancements have made it possible to test our DNA at home. It's also on TV! Maybe you have caught an episode of the roots-tracing show *Who Do You Think You Are?* Distinct from these mostly fact-finding endeavors, family folklore is concerned with stories, crafts, traditions, and beliefs that are valuable to the family for what they *say* about the family. At StoryKeep, we find that families most cherish their stories, expressions, personal customs, and keepsakes.

Family folklore was not always a bona fide genre in our field. The first folklorist to focus specifically on family folklore was Mody Boatright, with his 1958 study on family sagas. After Boatright's work, more folklorists began viewing "the family" as an invaluable vessel for folkloric expression. By the 1970s, family folklore began to take off, in response to, as Peggy Yocom notes, the recognition of the importance of a variety of areas of study in the field, including feminist scholarship, personal narratives, contextual studies, and the 1977 TV series *Roots*, based on Alex Haley's novel (1997, 477). In addition, a rather incredible feat was accomplished that proved the centrality of families and folklore. For three summers leading up to and including the Festival of American Folklife in 1976, folklorists recorded family lore with thousands of everyday Americans on the national mall in Washington, DC. The culmination of these vast and varied expressions was the nearly three-hundred-page book *A Celebration of American Family Folklore* (Zeitlin, Kotkin, and Cutting Baker 1982). In it, the authors explain the quirky and embellished nature of family lore: "A family's lore differs from its history. Its stories, photographs, and traditions are personalized and often creative distillations of experience, worked and reworked over time. When a family tells of that glorious moment when a relative just missed the sailing of the Titanic, or a great-grandmother held off a band of outlaws, or a grandfather tricked a border guard on his departure from the old country, the lore is precisely that: a glorious moment carefully selected and elaborated through the years, tailored to the demands of the present" (2).

StoryKeep film, book, and podcast projects attempt to capture these "glorious moments," family tales that we hope speak to living children and grandchildren. As a genre, family folklore is still being actively explored within our field. The *Journal of American Folklore*'s fall 2017 edition focused on family folklore, addressing it with articles on "formation stories and adoptive families" (Sawin) and "constructing and contesting individual and family identity through narrative" (Tye).

What Is "Business Folklore"?

Folklorists generally divide career folklorists into two camps: academic folklorists and public-sector folklorists. We typically think of academic folklorists as researching and teaching folklore and public-sector folklorists as documenting and supporting the conservation, transformation, and presentation of folklore. Of course, many folklorists have found careers outside those two areas, but the significance of these career pathways has been minimized in our field, and the historical and sometimes contentious framing of public and academic folklorists as a disciplinary dichotomy is not simply a relic of the past.

Some folklorists, of course, work in both academic and public folklore over the course of their careers. My own work closely resembles public-sector work, but, as I have stated, it would be more accurate to name it "private-sector" or "business" folklore. Overlaps among these three career paths exist (academic, public, business), but business folklore has often been overlooked as a viable career path for folklorists. Doubtless, the perception (more than the reality) of problematic financial entanglement with those we document has contributed to this neglect. I eagerly invite a broader discussion to debate and dream with colleagues what private-sector folklore *might* encompass and—as much as some might be loath to admit it—how our discipline might benefit from training younger professionals for career paths in the private sector.

It goes without saying that business folklorists spend a great deal of their time running a business, dealing with salaries and benefits, overseeing accounting and bookkeeping, and growing a strategic vision for the business. Running such a business also requires an enormous devotion of energy to creating and marketing a distinct brand and developing services and products for free-market buyers. Certainly, academic and public folklorists "sell" their work as well. Public folklorists create products for varying public audiences, market and brand agencies and nonprofits, do fiscal management, and sell their own value to boards, donors, and politicians. Academics similarly market and brand themselves and their work for other academics, grant funders, publishers, and students. The overlap among these three sectors is substantial. So what makes private-sector folklore unique?

First, business folklore is utterly reliant on customers for the business's existence. Customers are the central axis on which the entire entity turns. Customers—not public funding or grant cycles, not university approval or students, not boards of trustees or donors—determine the ongoing support of the work. The business's brand must communicate an irresistible, compelling message that connects with an intended, buying audience. The business folklorist hones a well-defined message and works tirelessly to spread that message through marketing. Like all other career paths in folklore, business folklorists must build trusting relationships with the people whom they interview, document, and present. A unique factor in business folklore is the direct financial relationship held between the folklorist and the interviewee. The business folklorist's income or salary is being paid directly by the interviewee, as opposed to by an institution. Project pricing, fees, and "money talk" have an impact on business folklorists, their customers, and the folklorist/customer relationship, as well as holistically on the project or product being sold.

The second defining difference of business folklore is financial risks and gains. Business folklorists must take on financial risks. In my case, I worked for nine months to save enough money to start StoryKeep. The company drew zero profit during the first four years—sometimes even less than zero profit. For example, I once quoted a project for $7,000, only to realize halfway into production that my expenses were going to be $6,000 instead of the $4,000 I had estimated. I kept learning too late that my margins were too slim. I worked side jobs to cover my life expenses during that long stretch of time. Five years into the business, I figured out a pricing model that matched both my required income and what a particular sector of the market was willing to pay. In short, what I needed to charge was far higher than what I had originally expected. Only recently has the company provided me with personal financial returns. For me, the payoff has been worth my investment.

In order to reach and speak to the audience I suspected was most willing to pay for Story-Keep projects, I took out a $30,000 business loan to develop critical elements of the brand: a revised logo, a new website, printed collateral, and additional components to brand the business. All this branding and marketing work needed to be managed while doing the actual work of folklore: documentation, interviews, project management, design, research, and presentations. In the past few years, StoryKeep has quoted several major projects. One included a film with a scope of eighteen shoot days in four North American cities, with the goal of producing a documentary running ninety minutes in length. The quote came to $300,000. That single job had a potential profit margin of $50,000. The profit made from that single film project amounted to more income than I had personally made in any previous tax year. I was not certain when I took out the business loan that it was worth the risk. It has been a roller-coaster experience, but I suspect that any folklorists with an entrepreneurial bent will find the tension exciting.

Business folklorists can dream as wide and as high as they allow themselves. The possibility to create "something from nothing" is appealing to many. "Something from nothing" is the landscape in which a business folklorist resides. The personal liberty to fully organize ideas, processes, timelines, teams, creative output, one's own personal time—these benefits cannot be underappreciated. What's more: there's no board, there's no dean. The opportunity to change course midstream or try an entirely new approach when one is desired or warranted is grand. These career privileges are hard to find in academic and public-sector life. If you are willing to claim it, you possess great agency and power as a business folklorist.

My company started by creating audio documentaries, similar to what you might hear on radio shows like *This American Life* or human-interest public radio segments. In 2012, it appeared that prospective customers preferred video to audio works. To meet this need, I brought on a business partner with filmmaking experience and expertise. We did everything ourselves, from camera work to editing to literally packaging DVDs and hand-delivering projects to clients. A few years in, we added books to our repertoire. We did what felt right, tweaking every step of the way. We discussed possible investments such as advertising in the *New Yorker* magazine and attending conferences on genealogy. We made nearly sixty projects together.

After four years into our business partnership, it became clear that my partner and I were envisioning different futures for the company. In 2015, I bought out her half of the business. In a fortnight, I hired a cinematographer, a sound producer, and a video editor to help me complete projects that were mid-production. The sudden addition of StoryKeep team members brought new energy to the work and helped me see new possibilities. For the first time, I understood how the company might begin to scale. I went from enjoying a hobby to truly running a business.

Starting a new venture and keeping it going takes chutzpah—both personal and professional. Many times I wondered: Should I push on? Should I give up? Occasionally, I would receive emails like this one:

> Hi Jamie,
>
> Confession: I've just finally watched the whole video from start to finish. I'm all choked up, realizing how meaningful this film is to me and how beautifully it's been done.
>
> I have been an admirer of StoryKeep since you started the business, but it wasn't until now that I fully grasped the gift that you are giving families.
>
> This film captures the true essence of Mom and Dad and takes us on a journey through their lives. It invokes the tenderness of their early relationship, the ways they have grown together over time, each of their creative sparks and careers, the arrival of Kara and I, and now Ada. I learned new, unexpected things by watching it—when was the last time you sat down with a parent and asked them to tell you the story of their life? Thank you for working with us to create this video, which we will keep with our most precious of family heirlooms.
>
> Warmly,
>
> Elyse

Business folklore provides many of the same experiences that academic and public-sector work does, namely meaningful human interaction, documenting of culture, and the collaborative creation of a finished ethnographic product. Business is ultimately just a vehicle for the work. The question becomes, What vehicle do you want to ride in?

WHOLEHEARTEDNESS AND THE ETHICS OF BUSINESS FOLKLORE

When I started my company, I was nervous about what my mentors and elders in the field would think of me. Would they deem me unethical for making a business out of folklore? Would they find it charming but irrelevant? Or, might a few of them see value and even become inspired by the form I had created for myself? I must admit, I was worried that colleagues would think "business folklore" was inherently unethical. Charging directly for folklore services *and* making a profit somehow seemed "un-folklore"-like. From my particular viewpoint, our field appeared to be dominated by leaders who never got paid enough for their time and talent. Money from all known sources seemed to regularly fall short, get cut, or run out. The more I noticed colleagues talking about "not enough money," the more it appeared to be the culture of our field, our own occupational folklore. Struggling was a badge of honor, even.

The idea of "not enough money" did not appeal to me—but not simply on a personal level. It felt like a professional trap, one partially self-imposed. It made me depressed about our future as a field. I was disheartened when colleagues glorified the long-gone and better days of the past, while offering few ideas for future career opportunities. I certainly do not believe that business folklore is a magic answer to bigger issues at play in declining university and government funding. On the other hand, business might be a door to new ways of thinking, both inside and outside the ivory tower.

If we choose to seriously consider or pursue private-sector folklore, the "airbags" of this unique vehicle must be tested and retested. Work ethics braided into our academic research and public work charge us with prioritizing people and shunning voyeurism. Our primary responsibility is to our collaborators, and this often invites us to integrate our interviewees into the editing and writing processes of our work. The same should be true in private-sector folklore. Here is my most pressing question: What are the particular ethics required when profitability, direct market transactions, and intellectual property enter the field of folklore?

At StoryKeep, we design a project in collaboration with a family. We present the family with a detailed project scope and corresponding price. We explain that any work beyond the agreed-upon scope will be charged additionally, and we tell them the price up-front for scope increases. The client is required to sign the project agreement on the basis of these terms. In essence, we are assigning value to our work as media makers and, in some sense, to their family's folklore.

Along with agreeing to the price, our customers agree not to sell the media that StoryKeep create for them. In turn, StoryKeep does not own their stories and cannot sell the newly created media for further profit. This is the beginning of our financial transparency, a central ethic of business folklore. We regularly talk with our clients about how we see their projects developing. Our feedback process invites families to actively collaborate with us. We want our customers to understand and approve the ways in which we are capturing their stories and presenting them. For films and books, we create three "cuts" or drafts of the work for the client's review. The feedback the client provides can be related to factual information, but very often, it includes feelings about the tone, style, and content of the work. StoryKeep's camera people, sound recordists, editors, and other contractors regularly work on commercial music videos, Netflix series, and narrative films. From experience, I have learned how imperative it is for me to train StoryKeep team members in folklore field ethics. If a producer I interview is enthusiastic about working collaboratively with clients, I know I have found a good match.

During the last five years, StoryKeep's talent pool has grown considerably. As a result, our films, podcasts, and books have become more refined. My cinematographers and sound producers began winning awards. A director of photography began teaching filmmaking at the New School in New York City and for a university in Tokyo. Clients saw that our work surpassed our competitors', not just because of our cinematographers and sound producers but because of the stories we told using my experience in folklore studies as a competitive advantage. In turn, customers were willing to pay more for our product. Our elevated offerings shifted my views on pricing. One day, a producer requested a reasonable but not insignificant raise. I knew she deserved one. To maintain the status quo, I needed to charge our clients more. This slight price increase made me question our overall value to families. What was the *right* price for what we were creating? What if higher prices made our work inaccessible to some families? Our pricing became an ethical dilemma in my mind.

Today, we create high-end productions that only a segment of the population can afford. When I charged less, I could not make enough profit to survive as a business owner. When I charged more, fewer people could afford the product, limiting our clientele to wealthier people. My long-term vision is to capture stories and folklore for families of all stripes. I know that our work has often been used as a tool for family connection and healing. I witness the power of our folklore films when I see a person sit taller, shed a tear, or mend broken bridges after watching our works. It can be extremely powerful, and I believe nearly every family could benefit from a document that honors its existence.

The Future of the Future

In 2021, my team began developing plans for an online academy that would offer a variety of video-based courses on how to document one's personal folklore. In a post–COVID-19 age, many of us are now familiar with meeting and learning online. What might have been an in-person weekend workshop pre-COVID people now warmly accept as a remote course they can follow at their own pace. Moreover, COVID plunged many people into an existential crisis (Ducharme 2020). People's normal lives were put on pause or entirely upended, making many question whether their lives had meaning, purpose, or value. As more of us spent significant time at home and with our families, we reassessed our personal priorities. Many of us found new meaning in our familial and neighborly relationships. StoryKeep's focus on valuing, documenting, and sharing family stories comes at the right time, we think.

Our online platform, StoryKeep Academy, transforms what my team and I have learned from a decade of creating projects for and on behalf of families into a set of ever-growing how-to courses for the general public. The Academy covers topics such as *How to Interview a Loved One on Video, How to Create a Family Cookbook for the Ages, Making Magic Out of Your Family Keepsakes*, and *Cultural Customs, Family Rituals: Documenting Ourselves*.

The prices for StoryKeep online classes are significantly lower than those for our high-end productions, thus making these offerings accessible to a much broader range of individuals. With a new price point, the target customer changes dramatically. Our high-end productions generally start at $75,000, but these online courses will start under $100. Who might find these kinds of online courses valuable? Passionate, self-appointed family historians; recent retirees who have been waiting for an opportunity to make something of their family keepsakes; cultural groups that share their traditions through dance, song, or food and want to expertly capture their expressions; and innovative festival committees. These are potential customers who can benefit from step-by-step, inspired guidance.

The Academy places the focus on a family or cultural member's central role in identifying, documenting, honoring, and sharing his or her own lore. Our role as teacher and guide is to help students with the following:

- Determine the specific aspects of their own folklore they find interesting enough to document and share
- Assess their own capabilities, energy, and time availability
- Create a reasonable work scope based on their interests and capacity
- Provide step-by-step guides for specific projects of interest

- Support their efforts with technical resources
- Offer an online community of like-minded individuals

This new business venture will require marketing investments in the way of online advertisements, developing free webinars that entice people to sign up for a paid course, blogging on related topics, and sending regular newsletters to a growing list of interested prospective customers.

It is satisfying to come full circle and make use of the ten-thousand-plus hours I have spent producing projects for wealthier families. That experience, coupled with my own experience in folklore, helps set our business apart from competitors that offer family documentation. This new business venture empowers anyone with a true interest in his or her own stories and traditions to document and honor them well.

CONCLUSION

The field of folklore has a long and complicated history, dating back to the coining of the term "folk-lore." In the United States, the field as a discipline of study emerged in the mid-nineteenth century and has faced challenges from many directions, contending with racist, sexist, classist, and nationalistic reasons for its study, as individual folklorists in the academy worked to justify and legitimize the study of "the folk" (Baker 1988, 65–69). Public folklore, or at least the tenets of public folklore, existed alongside folklore as far back as the late nineteenth century, but as folklore studies grew more secure in the academy, a new potential career path emerged as interest in folk cultures waxed as we approached the American bicentennial. For years, the two paths seemed to be at odds, sometimes in semipublic debates between luminaries from both sides (Feintuch 1988, 70–74). Today, the distinction has lessened considerably, although this dyad of career avenues has come to define how we conceptualize our discipline's "factory floors." These two career avenues have defined the field. By sharing my own journey as a business folklorist—describing my business model, the necessity of wholeheartedness (a.k.a. ethics) in such work, and the mediums I employ—I argue for acknowledgment, adoption, and encouragement of a third career option: private-sector folklore. I invite seasoned colleagues as well as greenhorn students to consider this unconventional but promising opportunity for the future of folklore.

What other forms of folkloric business can you imagine? I smell culinary possibilities. I hear new beats in ethnomusicology. I feel the textures of material culture shifting.

It has been more than a decade since my friend expressed how critical profit is to business. I have come to wonder—*what is real profit?* If profit includes the making of money but is not limited to the making money, what is it to be truly profitable? Must your customer profit, too? What deeper profit in the work keeps your heart centered and sustained? In answering these questions for myself, I have come to understand what real profit is, what it feels like, what it looks like.

My friend's business adage—*If you are not profitable, you are not in business*—is truer than I could have possibly understood at the outset of founding StoryKeep more than a decade ago. Respect, collaboration, and financial fairness are the building blocks for business folklore, a new structure that might just be a promising possibility for the future of our field.

"Did Ole Really Say That?"

Linguistics, Folklore, and Heritage Languages

JOSEPH SALMONS

Ole "scoffs at George W. Bush's boast of an Ivy League education,
'Yah, vell, aye been to yail too.'"

—James P. Leary, "Dialect Jokes"

This chapter tells a story about how working with folklorists helped me as a linguist get "out of the ivory tower" (to quote a section title from Leary 1998, 15) and begin to do "culture work" as defined in the introduction to this volume. My collaboration was first with Jim Leary in founding the Center for the Study of Upper Midwestern Cultures (CSUMC) and then working with him, Janet Gilmore, and Ruth Olson and others to build and sustain it. I sketch how the model they have developed for public folklore transfers easily to much work in linguistics and to outreach, teaching, and research. The Wisconsin Idea, simply put, is that work at the University of Wisconsin should serve the people of the state. The heart of the Leary–Gilmore model is what has come to be known informally as the "reverse Wisconsin Idea." As Gilmore puts it:

> A public folklorist twist adds a reverse flow to the university's role, allowing knowledge to come into the classroom from outside before it loops back out. This dynamic brings a greater sense of exchange, collective knowledge-building, and social equity between the state's people and the university. Students bring Wisconsin's culturally plural heritage of indigenous people and immigrants from Wisconsin's urban and rural communities into the classroom, where they mingle with students from across the nation and the world. Through off-campus outreach and "public service" in Wisconsin, they similarly connect to the distinctive cultural pluralism within the state's borders that almost always has salient global connections. (2011, 257)

CSUMC has been built on collaboration, largely around this kind of exchange, and it has changed my own work as a linguist learning to do public work. I came to this as someone working on what are now called "heritage languages." These are immigrant languages transmitted to new generations in a new home country or region, just as other cultural practices have been and are transmitted and transformed over generations. That work—historical, structural, and sociolinguistic research on German and closely related languages spoken in the United States—led to the Wisconsin Languages Project (originally the Wisconsin Englishes Project) with Tom Purnell, Eric Raimy, and others (https://wep.csumc.wisc.edu) and then to myriad publications by our research group and students, graduate and undergraduate. We began by documenting heritage languages, first German and Low German (sometimes called a "dialect" but actually another West Germanic language), then expanding to others, as part of an effort to understand the histories of languages and communities in the region. That led naturally to work on how those languages have shaped English in the region today, and that work, in turn, brought us to general work on regional English. (Extensive references are available on the Wisconsin Languages Project website.)

For years now, what we have learned from the people of the state has driven much of that work. To give an early and important example, after a public talk in Dodge County about German spoken in Wisconsin, an audience member asked why contemporary immigrants don't learn English as fast as the Germans in his area had. We know that contemporary immigrants do everything they can to acquire English as fast as possible, but I had no idea about when earlier immigrants had actually learned English. That question led directly to Wilkerson and Salmons (2008), where we found that nineteenth-century German immigrants to Wisconsin often never learned English and that families sometimes remained German monolingual for generations, findings supported by a growing number of follow-on studies with different languages and communities. The evidence directly contradicts the widespread, toxic cliché that "good old immigrants" immediately learned English while newer immigrants don't. Understanding the past can create a better future, we hope: people who realize that their great-grandparents lived here and never learned English are more likely to be understanding of new immigrants who are actively striving to learn it. That effort was helped when the story gained national and international media coverage, including from National Public Radio.

More recently, we have been investigating "tag questions," discussed later in this essay, a project motivated and fed by a long stream of comments and questions in public talks. These projects also led to the development of a course, "Linguistics 237: Language and Immigration in Wisconsin," a writing-intensive course that has produced valuable research, some found on our website as "featured stories." Inspired in part by what I learned from CSUMC and folklorists, this course puts the reverse Wisconsin Idea to work and aims to get students to understand and engage with communities past and present, often the ones they grew up in, on issues of immigrant, refugee, and Indigenous languages, the diversity in the English we hear daily, and language ideology.

In this chapter, I take some classic data, like the joke quoted earlier, and look at them through a linguistic lens to argue that ethnographic documentation can be valuable for linguists. Folkloristic and linguistic research done on documentation can mutually reinforce each other as we understand performative identity in ethnic communities and see that the Wisconsin Idea for culture work can help us examine the past in order to create the future. The features at hand have deep historical roots in immigration to Wisconsin, from which speakers have created new and very different social meanings. These features date from a time when discrimination against Scandinavian immigrants was real but have endured to the present, mostly, it appears, as in-group markers (e.g., in Ole and Lena jokes told within the community). I close by including a word about how we are beginning to connect this to contemporary issues of language ideology and linguistic discrimination.

FOLKLORE AND LINGUISTICS

Dell Hymes opens his essay "The Contribution of Folklore to Sociolinguistic Research" (1971) with these lines: "The folklorist is accustomed (inured might be the word) to having some other discipline, such as linguistics, pointed out to him as important to folklore. I should like to point out the importance of folklore for work in linguistics. Certain lines of folkloristic research, I maintain, are essential to the progress of the trend in linguistic research called 'sociolinguistic'" (42).

At the time, Hymes felt—reasonably—compelled to define the then-new field of sociolinguistics and to justify its existence vis-à-vis generative linguistics. Today, sociolinguistics is a thriving enterprise and mostly no longer seen as diametrically opposed to formal theoretical linguistics.[1] What has not changed is the value of folklore to linguistics. People, it seems, understand that a Venn diagram of folklore and sociolinguistics shows considerable shared space. Ethnographic work generally and work on discourse analysis and on language and identity certainly treat related matters in related ways.

There's a broader and deeper connection. If we use the anthology *Wisconsin Folklore* (Leary 1998) as an example, we see that Leary includes rich material on multilingualism and dialect and the first whole section of the book, "Terms and Talk," is about language, underscoring the close connections between regional culture and language. This includes a lot on a topic that has occupied a set of linguists at Wisconsin for years, namely immigrant influences on regional English, but also a lot of straightforward American dialectology.

As Leary writes: "Each joke performed by a teller in everyday life is part of a complex sociocultural event, a richly human activity of which the texts in this anthology are but dim reflections" (2001, 203). At times, linguists have sometimes avoided what folklorists might call "staged performances" (which linguists often refer to simply as "performance," a usage close to some found in other chapters of this volume) in favor of more "natural" speech, but recent times have brought changes; we increasingly look beyond speech itself to the full context and range of social meanings that connect with speech. Our colleague Tom Purnell (2010) has called this the Hoenigswald-Preston Observation. This triangle has corners for "what people say," "how people react" to it, and "what people say about" those things—but it puts those into the context of both cognition (d) and attitudes and beliefs about each corner. The rest of this chapter looks at performances as examples of mismatches between speech and reactions, attitudes and beliefs about speaking, a particular kind of relationship across all three corners of the triangle.

I'll take three patterns widespread in Ole and Lena jokes, all involving pronunciation, and close with a fourth example that has long intrigued me, namely *yah hey* and its two parts. These examples reflect how and what linguists can learn from folklorists and how and why the collaboration at CSUMC drives public work and academic research.

What Ole Says, Part I: Going to yail, *j* lenition

Now think back to the epigraph from Ole, a joke that hinges on the pronunciation of English affricate /dʒ/ (the first sound in *jail*) as [j] (the first sound in *Yale*), so that Bush's elite college experience lines up with Ole's incarceration—*jail* and *Yale* both pronounced like the latter. This is a phonetic weakening or "lenition" of the usual pronunciation of the English sound. Upper Midwesterners know this stereotype of Norwegian American speech. It goes back to the nineteenth century, including on-stage performances by Gus Heege with names like *Yon Yonson* and *A Yenuine Yentleman*. El Brendel, who made a living as a Swedish dialect comedian, made *yumpin yiminy* one of his catchphrases and recorded a version of a song by that name.[2]

English and Norwegian are closely related, but their sound systems differ in some important ways. My three examples of Norwegian American English ultimately emerge from those differences. For the present case, I need to give a little linguistic detail, but don't worry, this is the only technical passage in the essay. Norwegian lacks some sounds that English has, namely the consonants written in English often as <j> or "soft" <g>, in words like *jail, Jim/gym*, or *edge, fridge*.[3] The post-alveolar affricate, [dʒ] in the phonetic alphabet, doesn't have a close parallel in Norwegian, posing a challenge to Norwegian speakers learning English. The closest equivalent is perhaps the combination of the stops [t, d] and the native fricative /ç/ or perhaps /ʂ/, found in words like *kje* "kid" [¹çeː] or *skje* "spoon" [¹ʂeː] (Kristoffersen 2000, 23). In fact, one guide to English pronunciation identifies the first of these as a common outcome: "Learners from some . . . languages (especially Scandinavians) are apt to articulate /tʃ, dʒ/ with too much lip spreading and overpalatalization, producing sounds resembling [tç, dʝ]" (Cruttenden 2001, 177).

Of course, that's all very far from the glide [j] in words like *year* or *you*, and therein lies the oddity: How did people come to this stereotype? Moen (1988) suggests that a popular song, "My Name Is Yon Yonson and I Come from Wisconsin," might have launched it. Although the history is not clear, the song has been attributed to Gus Heege (Leary 2021). Related and perhaps more plausible is reading the English letter <j> with a Norwegian eye and/or the association of names across the two languages where English has /dʒ/ and Norwegian has /j/, as with *John/Jon* and *Johnson/Jonson*. These correspondences could have created an association of English /dʒ/ with Norwegian /j/. Nonetheless, a long line of descriptions of Norwegian American English going back to the 1920s indicates that this pronunciation was never widely used in the community (e.g., Simley 1930, Haugen 1953, and discussion in Moquin and Salmons 2020), though it can be found today in Scandinavia (Elizabeth Peterson, personal communication). In fact, comments by Simley and others since about this pattern seem motivated by conscious awareness of the feature as a stereotype.

What Ole Says, Part II: Boat of dem, *th* stopping

Sharelle Sånglöf provides a detailed analysis of a set of Ole and Lena jokes, including this one:

> Sven was going for his morning walk one day when he walked past Ole's house and saw a sign that said "Boat For Sale." This confused Sven because he knew that Ole didn't own a boat, so he finally decided to go in and ask Ole about it.

"Hey Ole," said Sven, "I noticed da sign in your yard dat says 'Boat For Sale,' but ya don't even have a boat. All ya have is your old John Deere tractor and combine."

Ole replied, "Yup, and they're boat for sale." (2013, 25)

Again, the joke hinges on a dialect form; pronouncing a standard "th" in *both for sale* would kill the joke. The relevant pattern is called "stopping," pronunciation of "th sounds" as [d] (or [t]), and it is well attested historically (e.g., El Brendel sang "[d]a first [t]ing" for "the first thing"). Simley (1930), Haugen (1953), and others discuss the feature.

Structurally, Norwegian lacks the interdental fricatives [θ, ð] as in *thing* and *this*, respectively. And the history of stopping as a feature brought into English is clear: this is a well-known pattern of speech, still widespread in the Upper Midwest today. It was once directly associated with immigrant heritage—immigrants who spoke German, Polish, Irish English, or other languages had difficulty mastering these sounds, and many speakers used the stops [t, d] when they had trouble with the interdental fricatives. This is found across American English geographically and socially, as noted by Cassidy and Hall in the *Dictionary of American Regional English* (henceforth DARE). They write that stopping is "fairly widespread, especially in the northern urban areas (where it is often characteristic of working-class speech), in the South (especially among Blacks), and in areas such as the Upper Midwest and the Southwest that have had dense settlement by foreign-language speakers" (1985–2017, vol. 1, liii).

In Wisconsin, it was clearly associated with working-class Milwaukee, for example. In the decades since Cassidy and Hall wrote the passage just quoted, things have changed. In an extensive online survey about Wisconsin English, Wilkerson and Salmons (2019) asked about people's perceptions of potential regional features, including this: "Which ones do you mean? Oh, dem over dere." More than 1,700 people started the survey and 1,080 completed it, 80 percent from Wisconsin.[4] Among the respondents, 65 percent recognized this as something people say, and 40 percent associated stopping with Wisconsin speech, but only 4 percent admitted using it themselves. This suggests awareness of it as a regional feature but also stigmatization, which may lead people to deny using it. It was associated by 39 percent with rural speech, by 4 percent with urban speech, by 24 percent with old people, and by 4 percent with young people. This points to a shift from urban to rural associations (a subject of current research) and suggests that it is recessive, losing ground among younger speakers.

Stopping presents something found readily in daily speech and that also appears in stereotypes, but it shows considerable change in its social meaning over time.

What Ole Says, Part III: *bissi, bissi, bissi,* /z/ devoicing

Folklore–linguistics collaboration sometimes pops up somewhat unexpectedly. As I was working on a paper about Norwegian American English (Salmons 2019), I asked Jim Leary whether he knew the Norwegian feature of pronouncing s-sounds for expected z-sounds, what traditionally would be called devoicing of /z/. Leary told a story about a Norwegian woman in Rice Lake who, in response to questions about how she was doing, answered, "bissi, bissi, bissi," that is, "busy, busy, busy."

Structurally, /z/ is a "hole in the pattern" in Norwegian; both languages have /s/ and English has its "voiced" partner /z/, but Norwegian lacks /z/. The same older studies of

Norwegian American English that found *j* lenition to be rare found this to be the single most common feature. Haugen writes, for example: "The most persistent difficulty of Norwegian Americans is the inability to pronounce a proper *z*, especially at the ends of words" (1953, 53). Norwegian American heritage bilinguals do indeed still show this feature, but in phonologically nuanced and interesting ways (Salmons 2019).

Unlike the first two features, perhaps surprisingly, awareness of /z/ devoicing appears to be low, based on performance. As Sånglöf notes, this feature is difficult to portray with "eye dialect" (nonstandard spellings used to signal regional pronunciation), since we so often spell English [z] with <s>, like in *has, is, rows,* and *roads,* all usually pronounced with [z] but spelled with <s>. She notes something that I've also found in dialect writing, namely a double <s>, like *iss,* to represent <is> [ɪs] (2013). Old performances, like El Brendel's recording of *Yumpin Yiminy,* do show this pattern, though inconsistently, so that he sings [vas] for *was* and *jeeper*[s] but also *is* with a [z]. More recently, Wisconsin's Goose Island Ramblers, in their song "No Norwegians in Dickeyville" (written by Bruce Bollerud, himself Norwegian American), play with Norwegian American English. This is especially so in the last verse, where they use stopping and variable merger of /v/ and /w/ (Nor[v]egian and Dickey[w]ille), both common features of Ole and Lena jokes (see opening example), and even deploy a very salient trilled /r/. Still, /z/ is consistently pronounced with [z], not [s].[5]

/z/ devoicing thus provides a bookend to *j* lenition: while lenition was rare in speech, it became a salient stereotype. Using [s] for /z/ was a signature feature of bilingual speech but has mostly been lost from today's performance landscape.

YAH HEY AND TAG QUESTIONS

We have clear historical evidence for each of these three pronunciation features, and they have clear contemporary associations with Wisconsin. My last example differs from those: it's about not pronunciation but rather the iconic Wisconsin phrase *yah hey.* More important, parts of the history are still obscure, and it is an unusual discourse marker, for example, in serving as a greeting and a discourse marker and in being assembled from two other markers, as Elizabeth Peterson points out in correspondence.

Tag questions are elements like *right?* and *you know?* that we use, for example, to elicit confirmation that a listener is listening. After years of talking about the topic and spurred by comments and questions at public talks, those of us involved in Wisconsin Languages began to suspect that they were particularly characteristic of Wisconsin. Wisconsin tags include *ainna?, yah?, or no?, hey?,* and even the iconic Canadian *eh?* These extend to other discourse functions, ways of signaling narrative structure across sentences. Leary had put a joke about tags in the set-up to *So Ole Says to Lena* (2001, 4), in chapter 1, appropriately enough called "Yah, hey":

How would you pronounce Cudahy if it wasn't in Wisconsin?
  Cuda.

If you don't chuckle at reading this, the place name is [kʰʌdəheː], with secondary stress on the final syllable.[6]

DARE recognizes *yah hey* as Upper Midwestern, as an interjection, "used variously, as an affirmation, greeting, or attention-getter" and "esp. Wisconsin, Michigan, Minnesota," reporting it as first attested in Madison, Wisconsin, in 1934.

The affirmative particle *yah* appears in the joke at the beginning of this essay, and Elizabeth Peterson is currently documenting its occurrence and history across various American dialects (2018). DARE points to German, Dutch, Norwegian, Swedish, and Danish as sources and describes its distribution as "scattered but chiefly North, esp North Central, Upper Midwest, Plains States," shown in the DARE upper map included here.

What about the last piece, *hey*? DARE doesn't really show the interrogative particle as associated with Wisconsin at all, as shown in the lower map. In the survey mentioned earlier (Wilkerson and Salmons 2019), we gathered data on tag questions (mostly not yet reported in print), including this: "Seems like it's been cold lately, hey?" In table 1, I've cross-tabulated this against our question about people's perceived awareness of Wisconsin English: "I can usually tell from how they speak whether somebody's from Wisconsin." (I've given only partial results.) That is, the horizontal or "x" axis gives responses to whether the respondent believes he or she can recognize a Wisconsin accent, from strongly agreeing that he or she can to strongly disagreeing (i.e., believing that she or he cannot). The vertical or "y" axis gives reactions to the tag *hey*. The first column, for instance, shows that people who see themselves as aware of Wisconsin English far more strongly associate this tag with Wisconsin than those who don't. The last column underscores that the former group is likely to report using the tag, while the latter do not. Respondents generally associate this feature with old and rural populations and emphatically not with proper English.

These results point to awareness of *hey* as a tag (leaving aside other functions of *hey*, like getting somebody's attention, which would surely score higher). By comparison, the same sentence with *or no?* was regarded by 28 percent of respondents as associated with Wisconsin and *ainna?* by only 18 percent.

In short, Leary's documentation of this joke fills out the picture of *hey* as a Wisconsin feature, one that aligns with other tag questions and discourse markers in regional speech. This enables us to see how research in folklore and linguistics, coupled with public outreach and engagement with communities throughout the region, can help us better understand the ways we communicate with each other through speech, not just directly but also in terms of the social values associated with particular speech patterns and perceptions.

Conclusion

In the end, what Ole said and didn't say stands in a remarkably complex relationship to how Scandinavian Americans actually spoke and still speak in the Upper Midwest. Our pronunciation examples cover the range. Three examples show three possible relationships between what's in Norwegian American English and how such speech is represented:[7]

1. <j> lenition has apparently never been widespread in actual speech but has established itself as a hallmark of performed Norwegianness.
2. <th> stopping is robust in performance and is still found in regional speech, where it has often come to signal ruralness or other traits instead of (just) immigrant heritage.

•yah + varr (Qu. NN1)

•hey interrog exclam 2 + var (Qu. X18)

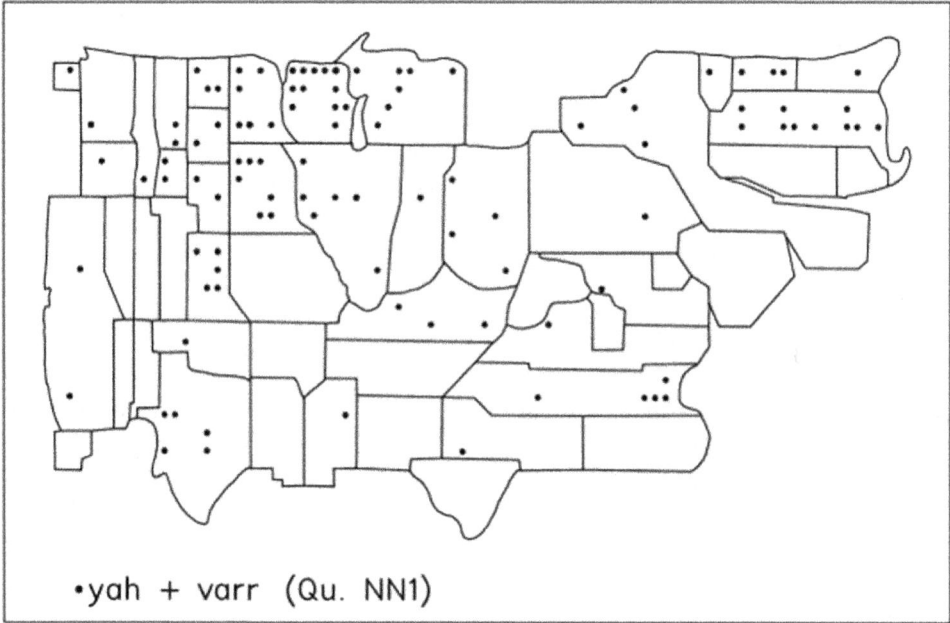

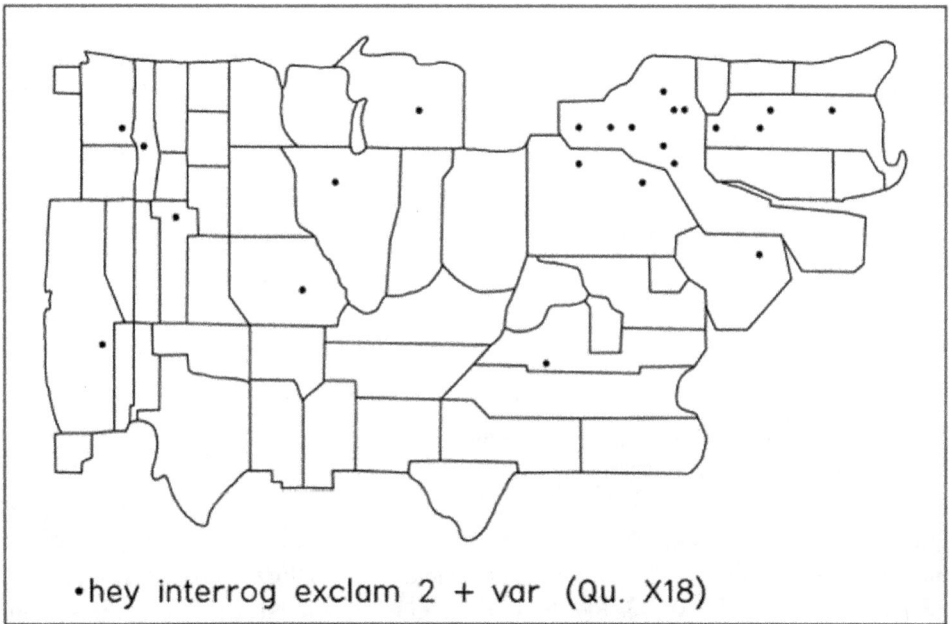

Maps for "yah" and "hey" in American English. (*Dictionary of American Regional English*, 1985–2017.)

Table 1. Reactions to *Hey* as a Tag Question

	"I can usually tell from how they speak whether somebody's from Wisconsin."						
"Seems like it's been cold lately, hey?"	Strongly agree (%)	Agree (%)	Somewhat agree (%)	Neither agree nor disagree (%)	Somewhat disagree (%)	Disagree (%)	Strongly disagree (%)
I associate this with Wisconsin speech.	65.0	46.2	36.3	22.5	30.4	23.0	16.7
I associate this with how old people talk.	23.4	16.6	11.4	7.8	8.7	14.8	16.7
I associate this with how people in rural areas talk.	36.5	24.5	20.9	11.6	17.4	24.6	16.7
I associate this with proper English.	3.6	2.5	1.6	0.78	2.2	1.6	0.0
I say this myself.	31.4	19.7	17.1	14.7	26.1	16.4	0.0

3. /z/ devoicing has long been a clear signal of Norwegian-accented English, and this remains the case today. Yet it has been relatively marginal to stereotyping, present sometimes but sometimes absent.

Our fourth example, though, is the kicker. We have good evidence for two pieces of the puzzle—*yah* and *yah hey*—but Leary's Cudahy joke gives us the missing piece, supported now by survey evidence. We see here how ethnic-immigrant linguistic features are resilient over time, even as their social meanings are constantly renegotiated.

The relationship between actual speech and the representation of speech in performance is not particularly constrained by speech; representations can reflect spontaneous speech or not. Both speech and representations change over time, making the relationship dynamic. Leary is right about performance as "complex sociocultural event, a richly human activity," and, in this case, they tell us things we cannot get simply from actual speech.

These remarks are built on evidence gathered by folklorists, but they provide invaluable linguistic evidence for understanding the emergence of regional speech, informed by more typical linguistic data and, crucially, input from people around the state about speech features and how people see them. And they are spurring new work at present. Recently, linguists on the UW–Madison campus began to work on how to fight language- and dialect-based discrimination and bias on campus and beyond. Awareness of past speech patterns and their social meanings provides context for contemporary regional speech and culture. More important, although I don't know how to operationalize it yet, awareness that can and does change over time gives us hope for addressing current stereotypes and bases for linguistic discrimination. In short, this can parallel the "good old immigrants" example given at the outset of this essay. Again, understanding the linguistic and cultural past can, we hope, help us create a better future.

I close by stressing that CSUMC collaborations have helped me understand not only language and dialect in the Upper Midwest but also, and far more important, how to engage in more meaningful public work, "reversing the Wisconsin Idea." Seeing how folklorists have approached public work and then seeing the resulting documentation have opened doors to new ways of doing public work, and more of it, while also leading to new research projects and teaching opportunities. Most important, and this has become a motto for some of us, this has helped us see that outreach, teaching, and research are all improved when we can integrate them into a single whole enterprise.

Notes

I thank the editors for the invitation to contribute to this volume and the opportunity to acknowledge Jim Leary and Janet Gilmore's contributions and the importance of the chances to collaborate with them. This chapter grew from conversations about the relationships between folklore and linguistics with Monica Macaulay, Cathy Stafford, and Rand Valentine. The arguments and evidence are connected to but distinct from work with Laura Moquin (Moquin and Salmons 2020), which provides linguistic analysis and context. I'm grateful to the following for comments and discussion on this manuscript: Sam[antha] Litty, Monica Macaulay, Laura Moquin, David Natvig, Ruth Olson, Elizabeth Peterson, and Anna Rue. As always with linguistics papers, every glitch in this chapter is my responsibility.

1. I'm always unsatisfied by arguments for such an opposition, in part because of the frequent complaints about Noam Chomsky and generative linguistics, extending from Hymes down to McDowell 2018, that fail to understand or misinterpret the generative enterprise. A challenge today, one in which some of us at Wisconsin are engaged, is to bring the social and the structural aspects of language sciences together, a project that is yielding substantial progress across the field. I wonder whether this in a sense parallels the "public" versus "academic" folklore issue raised in the introduction to this volume.

2. Laura Moquin did the research about El[mer] Brendel, and Moquin and Salmons (2020) present fuller discussion of him and other nineteenth-century performers.

3. Following linguistic conventions, <> indicates spelling, [] reflects phonetic transcription, and // indicates the abstract or phonological analysis.

4. A number of the questions on that survey probe features we first became aware of from discussions in public talks.

5. You can listen to the song at https://www.youtube.com/watch?v=gm5T_tYgxb4; see Leary 2006c on the Ramblers.

6. You can listen to a native pronunciation at http://www.misspronouncer.com/cities/audio /cudahy.mp3.

7. The fourth logical possibility, that a feature is found in neither stereotypes nor actual speech, is simply uninformative.

"Este Lugar Tiene Muchas Historias"

Alternative Forms of Archiving and Community Engagement in Oaxaca, Mexico

Hilary Morgan V. Leathem

Ghosts of Mitleño Histories

It is 9:00 a.m., and I've been invited to help set up an exhibit at Mitla's Frissell Museum, and I am in the midst of preparing *atole*, a traditional corn drink, and a spread of pastries from local bakeries. I was invited there along with three other graduate students from Oaxaca City by the museum's new curator, Macario, who wanted us to be present for the opening.[1] An opening at the Frissell, I should add, was not a typical occurrence in Mitla. Quite the opposite; the museum has a long and markedly contentious history. First opened in the early 1950s by Ervin Frissell, an American businessman, patron, and collector of pre-Hispanic Mexican art, the museum served as a repository for ancient Zapotec artifacts as well as a relatively luxurious residence for Frissell and his wife. Over the decades, the museum gained such a strong reputation as a source for studying Zapotec material culture that it became a focal point for local senses of self and community and, perhaps even more so, a sense of pride. Anyone interested in Zapotec civilization passed through the Frissell; in fact, it housed the most complete collection of Zapotec art and material culture known in the world at the time. To this day, its holdings are said to have been unparalleled—no single institution in the present could boast a similar claim.

This was not to say the museum was an egalitarian space; indeed, locals did not study there but instead were the museum's guards, janitors, and cooks, save for the instance of the role of administrator (Köhler 1995, 71). By contrast, the museum's (small) administrative staff was composed primarily of figures such as Macario—nonresidents, typically non-Indigenous, and never quite integrated into the community. For the most part, Mitleños were not allowed to be experts on their history. Yet community elders told me again and again how proud they were of the museum and remarked upon Frissell's place in the community as a beloved, charitable figure. These stories pointed to the complexity of the power dynamics that structured access to Mitla's history.

Frissell died only a few years after the museum's opening, and, as dictated in his will, it was handed to the American art collector Howard Leigh and then, after Leigh's death, to the archaeologists associated with what is now known as the University of the Americas, or UDLAP, located in Puebla City, Puebla. These archaeologists—including significant figures like Ignacio Bernal, Alfonso Caso, and John Paddock—shepherded Frissell's legacy until the 1990s, and, crucially for Mitleños, they respected one of the key dictates of Frissell's will: the collection, Frissell is said to have written, must not be separated from the building (and thus the town of Mitla) under any circumstances. This statement *mattered* in Mexico. Under Mexican law, any object—whether artifact, oil, or mineral—found in the ground is the property of the state (Ferry 2005). What Frissell was attempting to do, in other words, was to impose his own definition of patrimony in place of the Mexican state's. This suited local community members just fine, as it conformed to the already developed narrative of the Frissell as a distinctly Mitleño institution, despite the imbalances of power it represented. So, when Mexico's National Institute of Anthropology and History (INAH) took possession of Frissell's collection in 2006 and moved it out of the community, Mitleños were mortified. Oaxaca's journalists picked up on their horror and described INAH's actions as a *saquendo*, which is roughly equivalent to the notion of looting, though much more violent. When I first arrived in Mitla in 2008, the Frissell was a ghost building, emptied of its contents and abandoned by its residents, standing only as a reminder of the continued dispossession and disavowal, as one interlocutor put it to me, of the Mitleños' rights to their own heritage and history.

Macario was hired in 2015 by INAH as curator of the Frissell, even though the Frissell's collection remained absent. One friend of mine described the position as "laughable" given the "phantom collection" but also as desirable. "I want that job," he said. "You do nothing but get money. Classic INAH!" Mitleños were understandably aggrieved, wondering why Macario was permitted access to the museum while they were barred from entry. Thus, when Macario invited me to help set up an exhibit at the Frissell in early 2017, I was fascinated by the prospect, and a little confused. What, I wondered, could possibly be on display? And how would the community react? Ambivalently, it turned out.

As I stood laying out the bread, I noticed community members beginning to move around the courtyard, staring at the triangular exhibit panels. The panels parroted a nationalist narrative that glorified the reign of Mexico's second president, Porfirio Díaz, noted for his industrious and combative character (Lomnitz 2001; Overmyer-Velázquez 2006). Although Díaz was from Oaxaca and was half Mixtec, he had no direct or intimate connection to Mitla's history, which the elders quickly began to comment on to each other. Why, they asked, could there not be exhibits about local traditions? Where was their own history? The excitement about the museum's reopening was mixed with skepticism about the exhibition's intentions and confusion at its obvious absences. In the midst of these ambivalences, the *presidente municipal* (mayor) gave an impassioned speech, as is expected at exhibition openings in Oaxaca. "*Este lugar tiene muchas historias.* This place has many histories," he told the community, "and it is very important, no matter what we see here, to remember this." He reflected on the many different past lives of the building, and the different futures these lives had promised Mitla, and on his own experiences as a youth handing the ceramic faces he had dug up to Frissell and his colleague, Howard Leigh.

I begin with this vignette as it highlights the tensions and responsibilities inherent in my research as an ethnographer of heritage in Mitla, a Zapotec and mestizo community in the Mexican state of Oaxaca. The events recounted pose complex and significant questions about the legacy of scholarship in Mitla and the presence and responsibility of the ethnographer, as well as demonstrating the "monumental ambivalence" one is faced with when dealing with communities that are interfacing constantly with heritage experts (Breglia 2006). And alongside the ambivalent constitution of heritage in Mitla and across Mexico, the *legacies* and *relations* of heritage work are equally ambivalent. Inaccessible, asymmetrical, and desirable, narratives regarding Mitla's history and culture are written by outsiders and often not translated into Spanish or shared with the community.

During my fieldwork in Mitla, Oaxaca, I became cognizant of these disparities in power and access to historical knowledge that have haunted the community for more than a century. I grappled with questions such as: How do we return and re-present histories of Mitla to the community in a productive, responsible, and genuine fashion? What are some forms that co-constituted knowledge production can take between researchers and those they work with? Ervin Frissell and Howard Leigh—as well as the folklorist Elsie Clews Parsons, whose work I briefly revisit in what follows—are true products of their time, external stewards of a culture that does not belong to them, no matter their interest or sincerity. And these questions of legacy, responsibility, and access when working with communities are not only pertinent to an ethical ethnography but key to the ways in which we as ethnographers and fieldworkers carry a moral obligation toward improving the lives of those generous enough to assist us.

This chapter explores one way I have attempted to respond to these difficult questions, bringing a detailed ethnographic account of the power imbalances currently at play in Mitla into conversation with an ongoing collaborative project I initiated during my fieldwork. I thus join other folklorists and anthropologists in the endeavor to embrace experimental, collaborative, and multimodal methodologies when working with communities. The project I outline is a graphic ethnography—or "drawing as method"—project I introduced, the goals of which are two-pronged: on the one hand, it hopes to generate interest in history and heritage; on the other, it attempts to invert power by placing the "crafting" of history in the community's hands. Graphic ethnography, I posit, has the potential to be the most democratic of all multimodal and collaborative methodologies. A reciprocal ethnography located in and drawing on current efforts to decolonize disciplines, the project is designed to address these asymmetries of power my vignette emphasized by returning and re-presenting historical knowledge in Mitla.

MITLA IMAGINED AND REIMAGINED:
THE MANY LIVES OF A MONOGRAPH

Before turning to my further discussion, it is useful first to locate Mitla for readers, situating them in the town's ongoing history. San Pablo de Villa Mitla, or simply Mitla, is a town of roughly twelve thousand residents, located forty-five kilometers east of Oaxaca de Juárez, the capital of Oaxaca state in southern Mexico. Much like Oaxaca's itself, Mitla's economy is driven by tourism; the former is home to the UNESCO World Heritage Site of

Monte Albán, monumental Zapotec ruins that perch on the apex of the mountains, whereas Mitla is home to the Mitla Palace and La Fortaleza, a fortress sitting on the town's periphery. Both Monte Albán and Mitla's ruins occupy a stronghold within romanticist imaginaries of Oaxaca's past and have attracted interest since the late nineteenth century from explorers and scholars such as Guillermo Dupaix, Eduard Muhlenpfordt, Désiré Charnay, William Henry Holmes, and Eduard Seler.

Mitleños identify as either indigenous Zapotec (the dominant identification in the community), Mixtec (a neighboring Indigenous community), or mestizo (an ideologically loaded term for a mix of Indigenous and Spanish descent), though the mere mention of Mixtec civilization in Mitla is enough to possibly have one ejected in protest from the town. This is to say that Mitleños are decidedly proud of their Zapotec roots, despite suggestions by archaeologists that the architects of Mitla's palatial ruins may have been their historical adversaries, the Mixtec.[2] While it is true that Mixtec codices, Zapotec *lienzos*, and archaeological data point to strategic marriage alliances between these two civilizations in the precolonial period (Byland and Pohl 1994), I follow the Mitleño assertion that the impressive crimson palatial ruins are Zapotec achievements, bedecked with designs reflecting distinctly Zapotec cosmologies. Despite this tension over whether the most prized religious heritage site in Mitla is actually the work of Mixtec ingenuity, the language of the parents and grandparents of contemporary Mitleños is, without any debate, a part of the Zapotec dialect continuum.

I wish to draw this conflict to the fore, however briefly, since I believe it reflects one of the key issues this chapter is concerned with—the loaded question of who, exactly, gets to control the production of history, as well as the generation and sharing of knowledge. As an ethnographer, I am interested in how Mitleños define themselves, including their particular historical imaginary; I am less concerned with whether what they tell me is in consonance with a set of empirical data gathered from excavations. As archaeologists themselves know, nothing is set in stone, and new data may emerge in the future about the "true creators" of the ruins. Moreover, the bedrock of good ethnography, or "culture work," as Tim Frandy and Marcus Cederström outline here, is trust, respect, and reciprocation, which we must both cultivate and earn. And this fact was impressed upon me by Mitla's mayor at the exhibit opening.

THE MANY LIVES OF A MONOGRAPH

Immediately after wrapping up, the mayor approached Macario; José, a local archaeologist; and me. After exchanging greetings, Macario introduced me as an anthropologist interested in conducting fieldwork in Mitla. "This young woman has come to us all the way from the big city of Chicago," Macario said, gesturing at me.

"The Windy City!" José laughed, hugging his *atole*. Translated into Spanish, it sounded a bit funny.

The mayor beamed and shifted his weight. "It is like Chicago is right out of our stories! *La ciudad de viento*?"

"Indeed," I said. "There is a strong historical connection between Oaxaca and Chicago. I am hoping that I might be able to talk to the community about how they imagine their patrimony and especially hear about the social and emotional relations they have with their heritage sites. You know, how heritage makes them *feel*."

The mayor seemed ecstatic. He grabbed my hand and said, "You will be just like Elsie Clews Parsons! We need another anthropologist; we have not had one for a long time. When she came, she wrote that book. It made people care about Mitla. You can make them care again!"

Parsons and her well-known monograph *Mitla: Town of Souls* (1936) form the second part of my story here today. What was meant to be, I believe, a flattering and well-intentioned statement on the part of the mayor made me feel uncomfortable. I did not want to be compared to an early twentieth-century anthropologist whose legacy of relating to Indigenous communities is, at best, ambivalent (Lévy Zumwalt 1992; Johnson 2018). Also, the mayor's remark seemed to endow me—the outsider—with authority over this ethnographic context. Basic readings of his words might suggest that the mayor was simultaneously affirming the power/knowledge dynamic and establishing me, the "gringo," as someone who knew best. Rather than disentangling and unsettling this particular binary or reconfiguring the relationship between ethnographer and community, the mayor's remark could be regarded as a statement that reproduced and reified asymmetries of power. Yet, perhaps, we might read his words as subversive, instead. The mayor might have been constructing our relationship through the language of legacy—history and heritage—as a mode of recruitment. Positioned as Parsons's inheritor, I was ripped from the familiar and comfy social fabric of life at the University of Chicago and inserted into Mitla's overarching narrative about itself and others. Parsons would be my heritage in the same moment that I came to study their heritage, and this elicited a whole slew of emotions.

The mayor's intentions were, most likely, the latter. This was a strategic recruitment that played on cross-cultural understandings of obligation and responsibility. I was charged with a responsibility. Consequently, I felt both unease and warmth growing out of the invitation and the prospect. In these instances, how do ethnographers reconcile these kinds of invitations with our desires to make fieldwork an egalitarian, collaborative space? The very essence of ethnography is collaborative—all our knowledge is necessarily co-constituted by ourselves and those gracious enough to talk with us. Yet it wasn't until relatively recently that ethnographers systematically responded to or mobilized this methodological reality, at least in Mitla, Oaxaca. Elsie Clews Parsons's monograph evolved over time into a kind of totem across Mitla. Not only was the book just a book, a repository of knowledge, but it also represented her singular authority on the subject matter—in this case, Mitleño history and culture.

And, as it turns out, not only is Parsons's monograph another metonymic figure for these struggles, but also its physical presence in Mitla is inseparable from the Frissell Museum and from Macario himself. After the mayor left us, Macario took me aside and brought me to a small room in the museum. While dimly lit and slightly claustrophobic, the room was bathed with a delicate perfume and brimming with dried, autumnal flower remains, which carpeted the small shrine erected near the wall furthest from us. This room, he explained, was the site of a small Day of the Dead exhibit he had curated for Mitleños a few months ago. More specifically, Macario had drawn specific rituals that Parsons recorded with the aid of a small group of informants, all from the same family, in the 1930s, and presented them to contemporary Mitleños as a pedagogical exhibition, intending to teach them the "correct" way to perform their own rituals. "You don't understand," he told me. "They've told me they don't remember their traditions. They need to relearn. And Parsons' monograph is the premier source of Mitleño culture and history."

"Here let me show you something," he said. Leading me next into his office, Macario pointed to a copy of *Mitla: Town of Souls* that rested on his table. "I had to lock this up! Everyone was fighting over it, and we can't afford to lose it." Notably, the book is out of print, and remaining copies can be very expensive, well out of the reach of the vast majority of working-class Oaxacans. In other words, Macario controlled exclusive access to Parson's monograph, which he characterized as the definitive narrative of Mitla's history. An earlier remark by a friend currently employed by the Museo Textil in downtown Oaxaca struck a chord; they asserted that "the making of heritage in Oaxaca is entirely about struggles over power." What characterizes Oaxacan history—perhaps for the past century at least—is the ways various actors come to dominate and control archaeological, ethnographic, and historical knowledge about the region and its peoples. In so doing, they are able to promulgate a particular narrative that may end up serving one community over others.

Graphic Approaches to Heritage and History

It is this attempt to cultivate public access to history and, more profoundly, a public archaeological orientation *toward* history that I am interested in exploring methodologically here. As this project is still in an early stage, what I will do next is lay out its contours. Through this project, I seek to juxtapose the histories and oral traditions collected in Mitla at the turn of the century with recent accounts and imaginings of history and heritage from community members today. My goal, in the first instance, is to engage younger Mitleños in the collective production of history through putting together a collaborative graphic account for the town that preserves and revitalizes interest in history and heritage. In so doing, I hope to facilitate alternative forms of archiving and documenting, opening up previously shut spaces of knowledge and cultural production.

The project draws extensively on graphic ethnography, an ever-expanding field that includes comics, line drawings, and scribbles once resigned to the dark recesses of our field notebooks (Campbell Galman 2007; Taussig 2011; Causey 2016; Ingold 2016; Flowers 2019). Much as how early anthropologists realized the affinities between literature and ethnography, we are now embracing the ways ethnography is very much like art. This is no surprise. Writes Andrew Causey, "Ethnography and what some call 'art' are not so different. Depicting human life and behavior in either written or visual form is an intense, sensual project based on careful perceptions" (2016, 10). Besides these affinities, ethnography is also like art in that "it travels on its own path and there's usually not much you can do to control it" (16). Ethnography, then, emerges as a vivid, dynamic process, very much alive and further complemented by drawing with and alongside interlocutors.

Working together with Mitleños in their twenties and thirties, I am hosting workshops that focus on identifying, describing, and drawing places of significance to participants and compiling them in a zine that could be distributed among participants and within the community. It is one way that I am trying to help answer the question posed by the Namibian scholar Memory Biwa: "Are there other spaces that we can create where communities themselves can narrate histories of objects?" (Valley 2019). This approach offers many advantages. It is cost-effective, requiring only the expense of printing, which can be done at local stores, and the products can be purchased in turn for a very low cost or distributed *gratis* depending on the resources of the workshop. It also accounts for one potential disadvantage, namely that Internet access is inconsistent in much of the Valley of Oaxaca, whereas there are long histories of low-cost print culture—pioneered, in part, by the well-known Zapotec artist Francisco Toledo. While it lacks the consistent potential for updating of digital archiving, it has the converse power of representing a particular moment in Mitla's cultural history, making it available in Spanish for the community.[3] Drawing thus becomes a way to "arrest" the whirling, sensuous qualities of what we imagine, perceive, and know (Causey 2016, 59). Instead of the ethnographer, once again, waltzing into a community to find new ways of representing culture and history, a communal approach to drawing fragments and disrupts authority. It is perhaps one of the most democratic methodological exercises when it is shared and the community "draws back," since drawing done by the ethnographer alone also poses the risk of being engaged in yet another act of problematic objectification.

I conducted a pilot study on "meaning-mapping" in July 2019 with my colleague Pedro Guillermo Ramón Celis. We asked the Morales Santiago family to illustrate on several pieces of paper places of meaning. The responses from Marco, Elena, Alicia, and Lidia, siblings in their late twenties, varied. Both Elena and Alicia expressed reluctance—they were uncertain why drawing their history would really matter and confessed they felt they could not draw well. Marco was shy about drawing in front of us, so we left him paper and the short prompt asking him to sketch out his own short account of places we (Mitleños, Mexicans, and foreigners) should remember. "What matters the most to you?" we asked. "What histories are important?" Much in the vein of Varick A. Chittenden's work on a registry of "Very Special Places" (2006), Guillermo and I posed this question in order to learn about community values and viewed the drawings as a mode of articulating which places around the town were held in high regard. Usually, decisions on what places "matter" across Mitla are top-down in structure. Heritage experts, often employees of INAH, other cultural organizations, or academics, determine what places best represent history and should thus be preserved. Drawing in this context is bottom-up.

And so it is no surprise that when we picked up the drawings two weeks later, they did *not* reaffirm what INAH and the Mexican government thought mattered. Tourism advertisements depict the sprawling red palatial ruins and their grecas. Quite the opposite, the four graphite illustrations that Marco handed us showed mundane structures or sites of pilgrimage. Elena, Alicia, and Lidia chose to not participate in the exercise, pointing to a gendered dimension to history and heritage-making in Mitla, of which Guillermo and I were previously unaware. I hope to explore these aspects of the project in the future.

There are several interesting patterns that emerge from the drawing exercise, the first being that out of four sketches, Marco bothered to label only a single one: Mitla's Archaeological Zone. Moreover, rather than choosing to represent the palatial ruins from

Marco's drawing of the pillars from the Mitla Archaeological Zone. (Photograph by author.)

Marco's rendering of El Calvario, a sacred building adjacent to the Archaeological Zone. (Photograph by author.)

the civic–ceremonial center—where most tourists and INAH tour guides choose to stage photo ops given the stunning backdrop of vivid red ruins splashed, in deep contrast, against a clear cerulean sky—Marco drew the row of granite pillars from *within* the ruins. The row of pillars is known as the Hall of Columns, and it is steeped in legend. Notably, and quite darkly, hugging a pillar can predict how many years you have left to live.

I find that Marco's choice to represent the Hall of Columns provides social commentary on access to and the policing of history and heritage in Mitla. Like the depiction of the Calvario, the Hall of Columns sits within or atop a sacred heritage site. Spaces of spiritual communion, both sites are either cordoned off by gates or contain gates that limit further entry. In the instance of the Hall of Columns, it is the former—the columns are enveloped by the palatial ruins that are the focal point of Mitla's Archaeological Zone. The zone itself is under the jurisdiction of INAH, which erected metal gates around the periphery of the site in the mid to late 1990s to prevent security breaches and to ensure that tourists could not enter without paying the fee. Simultaneously national and local property and thus a space of contestation and ambivalence where local and institutional stakeholders continuously vie for power, the gates disrupted the normal rhythms of everyday life and left many Mitleños feeling dispossessed when they were told they must suddenly ask others for permission to enter when historically this had never been the case (Leathem 2019). Likewise, the entrance to the inside of the Calvario is gated and often locked. Mitleños climb the steep steps to the Calvario to importune saints and worship ancestors, leaving behind flowers or other offerings. When the gates are locked—and this is entirely haphazard—worshippers are left without access to the sacred space within and must slide their bouquets of flowers beneath the gates. Here again, in other words, are additional instances of restricted entry, not so different from Macario's locking up of Elsie Clews Parsons's monograph. But we also see once again the Mitleño refusal to be restricted; while in a material sense access to history and heritage is complicated, Mitleños like Marco imagine otherwise. By drawing places of meaning that contrast with typical depictions of "what matters" in Mitla, Marco and others disrupt narratives and provide ways to talk candidly about access.

The next step for this project is to scale up from the pilot and begin facilitating community drawing sessions. This will involve hosting workshops for Mitleño youth and, just as in the pilot, asking them to illustrate places of meaning for them in Mitla. Building on these drawings, we expect to create a digital repository for these images, linked through ArcGIS and Google Earth to a live map of Mitla. However, these goals have been somewhat slowed because of the COVID-19 pandemic, which has made both travel and community meetings virtually impossible. We expect to be able to resume developing this project by early 2022, if pandemic conditions continue to improve as predicted in Mexico.

CONCLUDING THOUGHTS

While this is still a developing project, it is my hope that it will—on a small scale at least—transform historical representation, kept away from Mitleños themselves, to the re-presentation of history as a dynamic process made within Mitla and between Mitleños. This is dialogic ethnography, emerging from and developed with community members, who will in turn be able to control access to the knowledge that has been produced about them and to build new spaces dedicated to cultivating local engagement in the process of facilitating this access. This graphic ethnography has the benefit of being collaborative and creative, offering Mitleños opportunities to express or counter historical narratives and representations of what histories matter, as well as *why*. In addition, the project also creates an alternate archive—one that can be both stored and scanned and archived either physically or digitally. As such, notions of heritage and history are returned to the public and represented by those who are inextricably entwined with these pasts—it is Mitleños themselves who can express or counter historical narratives and representations of what—and why—particular histories matter. By attempting to unsettle the ways asymmetries of power enter into our stories from so many angles (Trouillot 1995), multimodal ethnography brings awareness to the troubled formation of knowledge and offers us fresh avenues into public-oriented scholarship.

Notes

1. Unless otherwise indicated, all names in this essay have been changed to protect local identities.

2. One scholar, a notable archaeologist and expert on the Valley of Oaxaca, recounts the moment Mitleños ejected the researchers from the town. After they suggested that Mitla's palatial ruins were the work of Mixtecs who had come to occupy a significant part of Mitla, Mitleños are said to have showed up at her door, armed with ammunition and axes. They asked the archaeologists to leave; bewildered, the researchers did promptly leave Mitla. For more on the Mixtec presence in Mitla's cultural development from the pre-Hispanic era to today, see Robles García (2016).

3. I would endeavor to include Zapotec, but for those born after the 1960s, the language is nearly obsolete. According to Doña Vicky, head of the Morales Santiago family and owner of a successful roadside *lonchería*, language revitalization is currently under way but is only several years old.

Haunting Acknowledgment

Archiving Women's March Folklore and the Political Potential of Care Ethics

Christine Garlough

Even in our most present moments, the past haunts us. Folklorists, keenly attuned to such specters, pay close attention to ways the past inhabits our everyday lives. And sometimes, growing from exigencies in the public sphere, the ways the past demands visibility through community acknowledgment. This was the case on June 10, 2019, during a moving event to recognize Wisconsin as the first state to ratify the Nineteenth Amendment. This event—organized by First Lady Kathy Evers and members of the non-partisan "Committee to Celebrate the Centennial Anniversary of Wisconsin's Ratification of the 19th Amendment," with the aid of the Wisconsin Historical Society—took place at the Wisconsin State Capitol. It was just one component of a broader effort to provide educational materials, toolkits, and activities to highlight Wisconsin's role in the fight for women's suffrage and, at the same time, "acknowledge that the 19th Amendment did not guarantee the right for all women to vote" (Evers 2020). To be sure, this centennial moment was complicated in many ways. After the presidential inauguration of Donald Trump on January 20, 2017, millions of people worldwide participated in Women's Marches, asserting that "women's rights are human rights" and calling attention to the ways issues such as immigration reform, health care reform, LGBTQ rights, and reproductive rights are important aspects of these freedoms. Two years later, a record number of diverse women candidates were elected to the US Senate and US House of Representatives, beginning their terms on January 1, 2019. Yet, in the early summer of 2019, the recently elected Wisconsin governor, Tony Evers, found himself vetoing four abortion bills passed by the Republican-controlled Wisconsin legislature (CBS 2019). Reports from the Global Gender Gap Report suggest that "gender parity will not be attained for 99.5 years" (World Economic Forum 2019, 5). Certainly, while progress for women's rights has been experienced in the past one hundred years, significant challenges remain.

At the Wisconsin Historical Society's Women Suffrage Centennial Celebration, the organizing committee not only acknowledged such challenges but in a Centennial Suffrage Declaration called attention to the ways that the Nineteenth Amendment is "an important but imperfect piece of legislation," neglecting many of the profound political and social struggles faced by women of color and the lack of diversity in the women's suffrage movement (Wisconsin Governor 2019). As First Lady Kathy Evers noted, "The centennial anniversary of the passage of the 19th Amendment is a cause for both celebration and reflection. We celebrate 100 years of allowing women the right to vote, while acknowledging that barriers to voting still exist. As we honor the suffragist movement and plan a celebration to commemorate the centennial, it is important to understand our history and acknowledge that not all women benefitted equally" (Wisconsin Historical Society 2019b). Moreover, the work of women of color, such as Frances Ellen Watkins Harper, Mary Ann Shadd Cary, Zitkala-Ša, Marie Louise Bottineau Baldwin, Mabel Ping-Hua Lee, Maria Guadalupe Evangelina de Lopez, and Aurora Lucero, remains egregiously under-recognized. And a general sense of this troubled history was on display at the Wisconsin Women Suffrage Centennial Celebration, alongside the informational exhibits detailing the local Wisconsin suffrage movement and women's handcrafting of banners, posters, sashes, tunics, and parade floats. Presentations of material culture were accompanied by speeches and video messages by First Lady Kathy Evers, Representative Shelia Stubbs, former Lieutenant Governor Rebecca Kleefisch, and the Honorable Justice Ann Walsh Bradley that called for new ways to reimagine the political and social uplifting of women across Wisconsin (Wisconsin Historical Society 2019a). Adding a performative element, the Suffrage Centennial Celebration Committee and the Wisconsin Historical Society also had invited participants to wear traditional twentieth-century suffrage whites, evoking the memory of influential Wisconsin suffragists including Ada James (Richland Center), Belle Case La Follette (Baraboo and Madison), Carrie Chapman Catt (Ripon), Olympia Brown (Racine), Laura Ross Wolcott (Milwaukee), and Theodora Winton Youmans (Ashippun and Waukesha).

The effect in the Wisconsin Capitol rotunda was haunting. Women in vintage-inspired white gowns and suffrage sashes entreated the audience not to forget the contributions and sacrifices of the suffrage movement but also to remember those still fighting for their place at the polls. This ghostly presence was "pregnant with unfulfilled possibility, with the something to be done that the wavering present is demanding" (Freccero 2013, 336). In this performative evocation, history housed in the archives was repeating itself, but somewhat otherwise. Like the women before them, the Wisconsin Historical Society's Women Suffrage Centennial Celebration Committee recognized that for rhetorical events like ceremonies, parades, and tableaus, costuming oneself as historical, folkloric, or mythological women of note—from Amazonian warriors or Joan of Arc to allegorical figures of Justice, Peace, and Liberty—brought legitimacy to their claims: "Images of strong, determined women, from factory workers to the suffrage herald, revealed the scope of reasons why women needed the vote and announced the profound significance of the cause" (Borda 2002, 39). Such performances remind us that folklore, myth, and rhetoric have always been intertwined and strategically employed in feminist politics in the public sphere. We are haunted by the women who came before us—their challenges and their shortcomings, as well as their triumphs. We ignore such presence at our own peril.

Haunting, of course, has long been a rich area of study for folklorists studying tradition, narrative, and memory (Palleiro 2014). For scholars of archival literature, the notion of haunting also has been influential, as we grapple with the ways archives are shot through with institutional power, memory politics, racial and national imaginaries, and colonial legacies that continue to influence political and social life (Derrida 1996; Ghaddar 2016; Dirckinck-Holmfeld 2019). As a feminist scholar, interested in applied folklore and activism, I am engaged with creating archives that seek to support social justice and develop caring relations as advanced by Caswell and Cifor (2016), Cifor and Gilliland (2016), and Agostinho (2019). This grows from a sense of time as experienced from many directions at once—a sense of time that is haunted. I take to heart the queer theorist Carla Freccero's reminder that "the past is in the present in the form of haunting" (2013, 336) but also embrace rhetoric scholars' call to consider how our future discourses are inventional: "inflected by received opinions and convention, [they] may also recombine and individuate these so as to interrupt the quotidian of ordinary policy and practice" (Farrell 1993, 273). My philosophical orientation toward archiving—also significantly informed by the feminist care ethicist Joan Tronto—seeks to trouble "temptations to forgetting" that limit our ability to address past injustices and avoid an approach to responsibility that "starts with the present and moves to the future with only a glance to the past" (2003, 127). That is, the past's relevance goes beyond the ways it shapes our "present and future options"—we are also accountable to the past as we seek to engage in processes of resolving injustice. For this reason, my focus has been to develop sites, grounded in a logic of care, that actively facilitate *acknowledgment*—communicative acts that grant attention to others, bear witness, and publicly attest, often while invoking a sense of responsibility, ownership, and obligation (Cavell 2005; Hyde 2005; Shulman 2011). These acts inspire opportunities in which individuals begin to care for and feel themselves allied with each other, as well as with a wider, more diverse sense of a public (Garlough 2013). Govier (1999) argues that acknowledgment, in the context of serious wrongdoing, is particularly relevant for the potential of reconciliation between individuals and between groups. In this chapter, I detail the UW digital archives I have designed and explain how they build on ethics-of-care scholarship and advance feminist folklore research. Beyond being a potential source of "radical empathy," as Caswell and Cifor (2016) argue, I consider how digital collections might provide care in pragmatically rhetorical ways: focusing attention and remembrance and providing hands-on educational opportunities for reflection, questions, and conversations. How might this sense of haunting evoke not only the past but questions about our future together? A haunting that is, in fact, a form of care for potential.

To begin, I discuss my philosophical orientation toward creating digital collections of Women's March posters and consider how archiving projects might enact a "feminist ethic of care"—care for individuals, communities, and institutions as well.[1] The potential this holds becomes especially apparent when we consider, for example, the backlash faced by the National Archives after the *Washington Post* disclosed that the Archives had, in an exhibited 2017 Women's March photo, deliberately blurred protest signs that featured language critical of President Trump or referenced women's anatomy, like the words "vagina" or "pussy" (Kennicott 2020). While the National Archives argued that this language was blurred so as "not to engage in current political controversy," prominent historians expressed deep concern about the potential erasure of this protest discourse, some of which addressed the central debates defining the Women's March. And it is not only these central debates that we should be concerned about erasing. I argue that we also should focus on the ways that Women's March poster collections might call attention to histories of excluding BIPOC, Indigenous, LGBTQ, and disability justice concerns—providing evidence for why mainstream feminists' efforts often fall short of solidarity. Following this section, I provide a description of the UW–Madison Women's March Poster Collection and call particular attention to the haunting remnants at a protest's end—the posters calling for care and acknowledgment that have been left behind after the crowds dissipate. Disembodied but still resonating with presence, these crafted pieces of rhetoric, made by hand, tell us something important about how the women's movement might proceed.

UW–Madison Digital Archive's Women's March Poster Collection

My work developing digital feminist archives grows from an embrace of applied folklore methods; that is, I collect, study, and use traditional cultural materials for the purpose of addressing social and political problems. In this sense, the feminist digital archives I cultivate at the University of Wisconsin–Madison are public humanities projects that take seriously the "Wisconsin Idea"—a credo that asserts that our system schools have a responsibility to care for those in Wisconsin by sharing the products of expert research, teaching, and outreach with all. To my mind, this also means confronting legacies of sexism, racism, homophobia, and colonialism that haunt our state and its institutions. To this end, the archives I develop are grounded in "logics of care." Here I extend the scholarship of Tronto (1993, 2013) to consider the potential of archives to contribute to *caring about* (attentiveness), *caring for* (responsibility), *care giving* (competence), *care receiving* (responsiveness), and *caring with* (reciprocity) and to think about the ways that care might improve the health of our democracies (Sevenhuijsen 2003, 2018). These caring practices "include activities that promote social inclusion, social justice, and sustainability and are, therefore, inherently transformative" (Moriggi et al. 2020, 2). One such activity is acts of acknowledgment—"practices of admitting, avowing, or owning a truth, debt, or authority" (Shulman 2011, 4). In previous publications, I have argued that these "acts of acknowledgment" exceed recognition and grow from an ethic of care, calling attention to processes of remembering and forgetting, as well as educating communities and influencing future accountability (Garlough 2013). In developing digital archival spaces devoted to feminist activism, I believe we must heed calls for radical empathy that maintain that "archivists have *affective responsibilities* to other parties and posit that these affective responsibilities should be marked by ... the 'ability to understand and appreciate another person's feelings, experience, etc.'" (Caswell and Cifor 2016, 24–25). Yet, in an effort to engage with increasingly complex conversations about the relationship between care, Transformative Justice, and democratic politics, I would argue that this approach is not enough. That is, knowing something or feeling something does not necessarily mean one acknowledges something publicly in ways that involve action (Shulman 2011; Garlough 2013; brown 2020). In terms of my archival work, this includes acknowledgment of (1) the diversity of issues important to feminist individuals, groups, and allies; (2) how this diversity might complicate solidarity; (3) the range of local and global movements, the people they seek to serve, and the exigencies they address; (4) the scope of precarity in everyday lives; (5) the nuances of approaches between and within Intersectional, Liberal, Radical, Black, Marxist, and Eco feminisms; (6) historical forgetting, exclusion, and misremembrance; (7) claims for rights, justice, and care; (8) agendas for actions; (9) the diversity of peoples involved; and (10) the controversies (internal and external) that fueled debates.

Acknowledgment contributes to care in archival work because, as Tronto notes, "while it is tempting to look toward the future, every indication suggests that those who fail to learn from the past are doomed, not to repeat it, but to think they have escaped it"; that is, we should not privilege future orientations to the extent that it forecloses options for addressing past injustices (2003, 129). Indeed, conceptualizing archives through the framework of "haunting" has been particularly valuable to my understanding of how social, political, and historical memory is protected, ignored, deliberately transformed, controlled, and destroyed (Sekula 1986). I believe that allowing ourselves to be "haunted" is a form of care. Care— encompassing values held and practices done—can provide better understanding, more compassionate human relations, and new ways to imagine being with one another (Sevenhuijsen 2003; Noddings 2013; Tronto 2013; Engster and Hamington 2015; Puig de la Bellacasa 2017; Hamington 2018; Clement [1996] 2019). In archives, an orientation to care "raises specters, and it alters the experience of being in linear time, alters the way we normally separate and sequence the past, the present and the future. These specters or ghosts appear when the trouble they represent and symptomize is no longer being contained or repressed or blocked from view. . . . Haunting . . . is one way . . . we're notified that what's been suppressed or concealed is very much alive and present" (Gordon 2011, 2). This sense of "very present absences" continues to guide my collection of archived feminist materials.

Few folklore scholars have engaged with care ethics scholarship, despite its potential value for understanding aspects of foodways, traditional healing practices, storytelling, or archiving (Garlough 2014). However, through a three-year UW Ethics of Care Initiative, a growing group of folklorists is beginning to build public folklore projects, develop theory and create educational resources around this crucial concept. In terms of my archival work, these projects are helping me further understand the intersections between folklore practices and creative rhetoric that shapes our public sphere. I also am interested in the application of care ethics to academic development practices. Engaging with this scholarship has helped me to reconsider not only the form and function of the archive but also the different set of demands it would place on patrons to "balance their individual gain with their responsibilities to their fellow citizens to care about their society and improve it" (Tronto 2018, 6).

The Women's March Poster Collection is devoted to understanding the ways feminists across the globe use poster work, performance, and material art to address social and political exigencies.[2] This emerging collection is an extension of our work on the South Asian Feminist Poster Collection, a collaborative effort with multiple South Asian feminist organizations and scholars (Olakh, Sahiyar, Jagaran Nepal, and Dr. Manisha Pathak-Shelat from MICA [formerly known as Mudra Institute of Communications, Ahmedabad]).[3] In these sites, there is a strong interest in considering what parts of the collective memory of feminism should be included and how this is to be accomplished because it is clear that records "wield power over the shape and direction of historical scholarship, collective memory, and national identity, over how we know ourselves as individuals, groups, and societies" (Schwartz and Cook 2002, 18). The creation of each collection is nurtured by our work with the UW Digital Collections Center (UWDCC), whose staff has "digitized over two-million objects, developed and implemented technologies to enhance digital collections, and partnered with a variety of content providers to create illustrative and valuable digital resources" (UWDCC n.d.). Both collections contain posters that creatively appropriate folk art, narrative, beliefs, and performances in order to engage audiences in familiar ways, while educating them about topics crucial to feminist politics. Through these collections, we hope to demonstrate the importance of preserving feminist political posters, not only because of their historical significance but also to promote a more nuanced understanding and dialogue about feminist political communication tactics growing from diverse histories of feminist activisms. This approach grows from the sense that posterwork, from the early twentieth century on, has been an effective medium of political communication across the globe (Gronbeck 2008, xxii).

The collection process for these archives is collaborative. For example, the Women's March Poster Collection currently contains more than three hundred of my photos from the 2017 Madison, Wisconsin, Women's March that focus on the range of posters at this event. These photos have been cataloged and coded by two research assistants, Erica Dick and Shani Sun-Hi Long-Meyer, so that accurate metadata are available for the digital collection. In the next year, hundreds of photos of posters from National Women's Marches in Washington, DC, and New York, provided by Professor Erik Bucy's research team at Texas Tech University, will be added. A Wisconsin community project to gather photos of posters and personal narratives of Women's March experiences will begin as well. Finally, in the coming years, a parallel project is slated to begin that will focus on protest materials from the Madison Raging Grannies and Missing and Murdered Indigenous Women's Marches.

These feminist archives featuring posterwork from diverse women's groups preserve and acknowledge a vibrant and ongoing history of this grassroots activism. And as Derrida (1996) notes, such archiving is a "gathering together" that makes a promise or "pledge" to the future, one that "produces as much as it records" (3). Our open-access sites have been designed to provide free materials for researchers, activists, educators, and interested audiences. And, in imagining new feminist interventions, we continue to develop a connected website using the WiscWebCMS system that offers cross-disciplinary curriculum for teachers, activists, and researchers that is linked to the digital archives. This website, created in collaboration with a GWS research team, provides free handouts, lesson plans, and PowerPoint slides that address key political issues, highlight marginalized voices, and provide opportunities to explore social concerns. In this way, we hope educators and activists can (1) give audiences hands-on experiences exploring and analyzing primary data; (2) focus attention and facilitate knowledge building around global feminism and grassroots activism; and (3) offer occasions for acknowledgment that make knowledge public. This seems especially important when dealing with archival material that is haunted by histories of racism, colonial violence, sexism, and heteronormativity. These materials are designed to provoke questions and conversations because the meaning of archived documents is never singular and because the health of our public sphere depends on our ability to speak together about contentious concerns (Farrell 1993; Garlough 2011a; brown 2020).

MADISON, WISCONSIN, WOMEN'S MARCH, 2017

On Saturday, January 21, 2017, I attended the Madison Women's March—as a feminist, as an activist, and as a folklore scholar—curious to see how it would compare to marches for labor rights, immigration rights, and women's rights that I had attended in the United States and South Asia (2008, 2011b, 2013). In Madison, between 75,000 and 100,000 people marched to the State Capitol to voice concerns about policies and social practices endangered by Donald Trump's presidential agenda. This was one of 673 "sister marches" that coincided with the Women's March on Washington and that took place on all seven continents and included more than seven million participants.

Folklorists, of course, have shown a keen interest in researching parades and marches of various kinds, from Mardi Gras celebrations to political demonstrations (Hansen 1988, 2000; Abrahams 2005; Garlough 2011b; Saltzman 2020). And, not surprisingly, folk performances and practices were ever present at the Women's March in Madison. As protesters gathered on State Street, the political and the carnivalesque intertwined in fascinating ways. Participants wearing feathered hot-pink headbands arrived on stilts and spread enormous, gauzy fuchsia wings to embrace fellow protesters. Women sporting handmade "Lady Liberty" tiaras linked arms and joined them in marching down State Street. LGBTQ flags and American flags waved together as protesters marched to the beat of community drummers. Not far behind, a protester hoisted a large Lady Liberty puppet with a pink pussy hat into the air.

Indeed, such handknit pussy hats—forms of craft activism and material folklore—were a well-documented part of the 2017 Women's Marches across the globe (Black 2017; Mandell 2019; Literat and Markus 2020), though as protest strategy they were also critiqued as exclusionary or vagocentric with regard to transgender women, gender nonbinary people, and women of color. As part of the march, a community band played familiar tunes to energize the crowds, and a Mexican folk dancer brought attention to immigration rights issues through her performance.

Most fascinating, to my mind, was one particular folk art form—the poster-sign (Garlough 2014; Rennier 2018). Made in local sites—by family and friends sitting around kitchen tables or by strangers gathering at community centers—these pieces of material art were often constructed with the simplest of materials, such as cardboard, markers, and glue. Forms ranged from posters without pictorial signs, to iconic posters without written language, to multimodal text-image posters. I give closer attention to the process of handcrafting these signs in a book in progress (Garlough, forthcoming) and argue that, in many cases, producing these feminist political posters gained significance because of their implicit and explicit connections to crafting and folk art. For the purposes of this essay, it will suffice to say that this means of protest drew from a wellspring of vernacular cultural forms and popular culture references. Indeed, posters stating, "Girls Just Wanna Have Fundamental Rights," "A Woman's Place Is in the Resistance" (featuring pictures of Princess

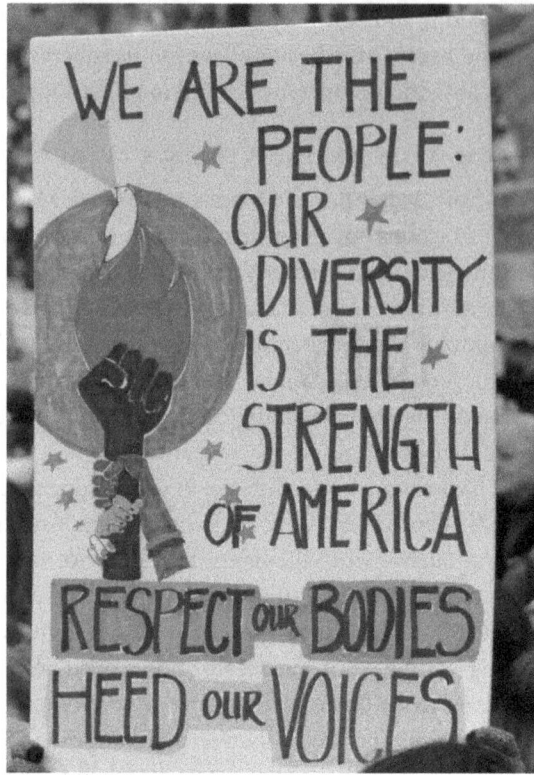

"We Are the People" poster at Madison, Wisconsin, Women's March, 2017. (Photograph by author.)

Leia), and "Resistance Is Fertile" played with familiar cultural forms to create engaging ways to make serious arguments. Themes called for recognition of women's rights as human rights, Intersectional feminism, LGBTQI rights, patriarchal legacies, gender-based violence, sexual harassment, misogyny, reproductive justice, allyship with marginalized groups, and Girl Power, to name but a few. The practice and process of making posters like these, in addition to marching and reflecting on the experience afterward, offered opportunities to invite dialogue about political concerns, personal experiences, and pressing social issues. It held the potential for care (Garlough 2008).

Prospects for Asking for Care and Giving Care after a Politics of Anger

Of the posters I encountered in the UW Women's March digital archive, the one that resonated most deeply was written in black ink on a torn piece of brown cardboard. It simply stated, "I am scared." Propped up against the side of a wall, it was abandoned, disembodied. It soon became the focus of attention for a sea of protestors walking by—wave after wave of differently positioned individuals, if, at the very least, their signs were any indication of what they came to endorse or protest. For me, the question of how this poster might be read

"I Am Scared" poster at Madison, Wisconsin, Women's March, 2017. (Photograph by author.)

remains: this confession, this evocation of precarity, this public admission. In it, there is a turn away from the optimism of moral outrage and toward vulnerability and care.

Scholars sometimes do not pay close enough attention to the remains of protests—what is left over, what is not aesthetically pleasing, what lies in ruins. Yet, in the material artifacts left behind there remains a force. The posters are a remnant of the "energy and activities of the people who made them" (Edensor 2001, 46). Hochberg would argue that the force they manifest "is in their negativity: their appearance marks a void that calls attention to itself" (2012, 66). Abandoned, disembodied posters render haunting "a certain presence known to us and *felt* in its invisibility" (Hochberg 2012, 55). Their ghostly presence leaves behind an emotional trace, "which only lend themselves to speculation and imagination" (Edensor 2001, 48). Whose hands held this sign before the clamor of protest songs and chants died away? What worries troubled the marcher?

"I am scared." The poster's message rose above identity politics to tap into one of the most fundamental of emotions—fear. Unlike other posters, it did not make arguments for a potentially contentious belief or value. Protesters lingering in front of it wondered whether it was a public call for aid and, if so, how to respond, especially when surrounded by signs entreating everyone to love and care and hope? What was its relation to the pathos of this protest context? Who was the owner of the poster, and did the marcher come seeking to "be with" others? How might the protester's embodied presence have changed the ways people responded to the poster? Did the protester receive what she desired? Haunting, uncanny—the ways the personless poster gestured toward a precarity that perhaps implicated us all. In encountering a direct call for help, when do we bear responsibility for responding to care? And what might be the dangers of employing rhetorics of care? How might they be used to justify unwanted paternalism and coercion of groups identified as vulnerable? "I am scared." Did people viewing this poster overidentify with its creator and in an anticipatory resoluteness see, in this absent person, themselves?

"I am scared." Disturbingly blunt. Distinct from the other signs characterized by clever figurative language and cultural appropriation. While implicitly gesturing toward the future, it seemed radically bound to the "right now." And, to my mind, this is what this protest sign does well. It turns away from argumentative, us-versus-them approaches; instead, the "I" statement provides a relational opening for dialogue based on a confession of vulnerability. In two decades of exploring poster art, I have seen very few examples of this kind (Garlough 2014). Rather, claims about vulnerability are most often attributed to others who are perceived as being in need. In contrast, this poster is self-confessional and in many ways reflects discourse found in social media posts from Facebook to Twitter to Instagram. It provides an opening to consider difficult emotions, trauma, and the need for care in the everyday (Cvetkovich, 2003).

"I am scared." This poster resonates affectively in ways that are complex and contradictory, engaging an intricate set of relations between institutional and personal levels. I am not suggesting that the moral outrage found in the vast majority of Women's March posters—or protest posters from around the globe, for that matter—is ineffective. It has its important place and likely always will. However, direct, personless, first-person, affective witnessing seems to have resonance as well—engaging a range of people in productive ways. Perhaps, then, vulnerability that turns from moral outrage, call-out culture, and identity politics may be our best hope in the face of a "politics of anger" that seems to be pervading our public sphere (brown 2020).

FINAL REFLECTIONS

For many feminists, there is a feeling that this moment in history holds a particular significance and resonance. Representation at the polls and in our elected bodies, social inequality, sexual violence and harassment, reproductive health, LGBTQ rights and representation, sexism in the media, the glass ceiling, wage inequality, and the division of domestic labor—all remain deeply problematic. Histories of oppression remain unacknowledged and haunt our public sphere. Feminist grassroots protest spaces that draw on women's folk practices, figures, and narratives allow participants to "play hauntologically" and "acknowledge that multiple perspectives exist . . . and purposefully create spaces . . . where they might emerge and/or insert themselves" (Powell and Shaffer 2008, 2). Haunting, as such, seeks not to "immure but to allow to return, to be visited by a demand, a demand to mourn and a demand to organize" (Freccero 2013, 338). Archives that attend to feminist protest events, like Women's Marches, provide occasions for understanding the potential of feminist protest practices that exhibit care in a variety of ways: caring about, caring for, care giving, care receiving, and caring with (Tronto 2013). Archives, grounded in the same, hold transformative potential when they provide patrons opportunities for *acts of acknowledgment* that exceed recognition and influence future accountability (Garlough 2013). The meaning of the archive

shifts when it addresses confusion with a call for questions, indifference with a commitment to public engagement and discourse, callousness with sense of compassion, exhaus-
tion with focused energy, and coldness with an ethics of care (Cavell 1999).

NOTES

1. The poster collection can be accessed at http://digital.library.wisc.edu/1711.dl/WomensMarch.

2. Women's March Poster Collection, http://digital.library.wisc.edu/1711.dl/WomensMarch.

3. South Asian Feminist Poster Collection, http://uwdc.library.wisc.edu/collections/Gender
Studies.

Works Cited

Aarne, Antti. 1973. *The Types of the Folktale: A Classification and Bibliography.* FF Communications 184. 2nd ed. Helsinki: Suomalainen Tiedeakatemia.

Abrahams, Roger D. 2005. *Everyday Life: A Poetics of Vernacular Practices.* Philadelphia: University of Pennsylvania Press.

Agee, James, and Walker Evans. 1941. *Three Tenant Families/Let Us Now Praise Famous Men.* Boston: Houghton Mifflin.

Agostinho, Daniela. 2019. "Archival Encounters: Rethinking Access and Care in Digital Colonial Archives." *Archival Science* 19(2): 141–65.

Alanen, Arnold. 1975. "The Development and Distribution of Finnish Consumer Cooperatives in Michigan, Minnesota and Wisconsin, 1903–1973." In *The Finnish Experience in the Western Great Lakes Region: New Perspectives,* edited by Michael G. Karni, Matti E. Kaups, and Doublas J. Ollila Jr., 103–30. Turku, Finland: Institute for Migration.

American Council of Learned Societies. 1989. "National Task Force on Scholarship and the Public Humanities." Occasional Paper 11. http://archives.acls.org/op/11_Scholarship_and_Public _Humanities.htm.

American Folklife Center. 2018. "Audio and Moving Image Media Survey and Preservation Plan, Final Report." Unpublished document. January 18.

American Red Cross. 1935. *The American Red Cross Garment Manual Abridged.* May 1935 revision. Red Cross, Folder 494.1 ARC 440-D: Garment Manual Abridged, Box 711, Series 1935–1947, Record Group 200, American National Red Cross Central Decimal Files, National Archives at College Park, MD.

American Rivers. n.d. "St Louis River, Minnesota." https://www.americanrivers.org/river/st-louis -river/.

Ames, Kenneth L. 1984. "Material Culture as Non Verbal Communication: A Historical Case Study." In *American Material Culture: The Shape of Things around Us,* edited by Edith Mayo, 25–47. Bowling Green, OH: Bowling Green State University Popular Press.

Anonymous. 1917. "Agitaattorimatkoilta" (From agitator trips). *Pelto ja Koti* (Farm and home) 6(8): 254–56.

Appleton, Jay. 1975. *The Experience of Landscape.* Ann Arbor: University of Michigan Press.

Arnoldi, MaryJo. 2012. "'From Timbuktu to Washington': Reflections on the 2003 Mali Program at the Smithsonian Folklife Festival." *Africa Today* 59(1): 3–24.

Asplund, Anneli, and Matti Hako, eds. 1981. *Kansanmusiikki.* Helsinki: Suomalaisen Kirjallisuuden Seura.

Associated Press. 2021. "Staffing Shortage at Wisconsin Prisons Has Cost Taxpayers $60M in Overtime Pay." *Wisconsin State Journal*, February 12.

Auerbach, Susan. 1996. *In Good Hands: A Portrait of State Apprenticeship Programs in the Folk and Traditional Arts, 1983–1995*. Washington, DC: National Endowment for the Arts.

Ault, Julie. 1999. "Artist's Project: Dear Friend of the Arts." In *Art Matters: How the Culture Wars Changed America*, edited by Philip Yenawine, Marianne Weems, and Brian Wallis, 32. New York: New York University Press.

Aurand, Ammon Monroe, Jr. 1930. *America's Greatest Indoor Sport: Two-in-a-Bed, or, The Super-Specialist's Handbook on Bundling with the Pennsylvania Dutch*. Harrisburg, PA: Aurand Press.

Aurand, Ammon Monroe, Jr. 1938. *Little Known Facts about Bundling in the New World*. Harrisburg, PA: Aurand Press.

Aurand, Ammon Monroe, Jr. 1942. *The Realness of Witchcraft in America, with Special References to the Pennsylvania Germans and the Conflict of Science vs. Old Time Beliefs and Customs*. Harrisburg, PA: Aurand Press.

Azkue, Resurrección María de. 1905. *Diccionario Vasco-Español-Frances: Dictionnaire Basque-Espagnol-Français*. Bilbao: Dirección Del Autor.

Badger State Banner. 1925. "Reach Agreement on French Debt." September 24, 6.

Baker, Ronald L. 1988. "The Folklorist in the Academy." In *100 Years of American Folklore Studies: A Conceptual History*, edited by William M. Clements, 65–69. Washington, DC: American Folklore Society.

Bakken, Reidar. 2000. *Snikkaren Aslak Olsen Lie: Bygdekunstnar i Valdres og Wisconsin 1798–1886 (Craftsman on Two Continents)*. Oslo: Instituttet for sammenlignende kulturforskning.

Banks, Joanne. 2012. "Storytelling to Access Social Context and Advance Health Equity Research." *Preventive Medicine* 55(5): 394–97.

Banks-Wallace, Joanne. 2002. "Talk That Talk: Storytelling and Analysis Rooted in African American Oral Tradition." *Qualitative Health Research* 12(3): 410–26.

Barber, Elizabeth Wayland. 1995. *Women's Work: The First 20,000 Years: Women, Cloth, and Society in Early Times*. New York: W. W. Norton.

Bateson, Gregory, and Margaret Mead. 1942. *Balinese Character: A Photographic Analysis*. New York: New York Academy of Sciences.

Bauerlein, Mark, and Ellen Grantham. 2009. *National Endowment for the Arts: A History 1965–2008*. Washington, DC: National Endowment for the Arts.

Bauman, Richard. 1972. "The La Have Island General Store: Sociability and Verbal Art in a Nova Scotia Community." *Journal of American Folklore* 85(338): 330–43.

Bäuml, Franz H. 1980. "Varieties and Consequences of Medieval Literacy and Illiteracy." *Speculum* 55(2): 237–65.

Beam, C. Richard. 1985. "Preface." In *A Simple Grammar of Pennsylvania Dutch*, by J. William Frey, iii–xxx. Lancaster, PA: Brookshire Publications.

Beattie, Betsy. 1989. "Community-Building in Uncertain Times: The French-Canadians of Burlington and Colchester." *Vermont History* 57(2): 84–102.

Beattie, Betsy. 1992. "Migrants and Millworkers: The French Canadian Population of Burlington and Colchester, 1860–1870." *Vermont History* 60(2): 96–117.

Beaudoin Bombardier, Carmen, Kim Chase, and Lisa Ornstein. 2018. *A Vermont Franco-American Song Book*. Vol. 1. Middlebury: Vermont Folklife Center and Young Tradition Vermont.

Beck, Jane. 1980. *The General Store in Vermont: An Oral History*. Montpelier: Vermont Historical Society.

Belanus, Betty, and Gregory Hansen. 2000. "From the Guest Editors." *Folklore Forum* 31(2): 1–4.

Bell, Quentin. 1972. *Virginia Woolf: A Biography*. Orlando, FL: Harcourt.

Ben-Amos, Dan. 1971. "Toward a Definition of Folklore in Context." *Journal of American Folklore* 84(331): 3–15.

Bendix, Regina. 1997. *In Search of Authenticity*. Madison: University of Wisconsin Press.

Bergey, Barry. 2002. "Director's Message." *National Heritage Fellowships 2002*. Washington, DC: National Endowment for the Arts.

Bergey, Barry. 2011. *National Endowment for the Arts National Heritage Fellowships 1982–2011, 30th Anniversary*. Washington, DC: National Endowment for the Arts.

Berkovici, Konrad. 1925. *On New Shores*. New York: Century Company.

Bigler, Brian. 2017. Interview with Jared L. Schmidt, Mount Horeb, WI, October 11.

Bigler, Brian, Destinee Udelhoven, and Johnna Buysse. 2019. Interview with Jared L. Schmidt, Mount Horeb, WI, July 2.

Binkiewicz, Donna M. 2004. *Federalizing the Muse: United States Arts Policy and the National Endowment for the Arts 1965–1980*. Chapel Hill: University of North Carolina Press.

Bishop, John. 2001. "Alan Lomax (1915–2002). A Remembrance." *Visual Anthropology Review* 17(2): 13–23.

Black, Shannon. 2017. "KNIT+ RESIST: Placing the Pussyhat Project in the Context of Craft Activism." *Gender, Place & Culture* 24(5): 696–710.

Boatright, Mody. 1958. *The Family Saga and Other Phases of American Folklore*. Urbana: University of Illinois Press.

Bohlman, Philip V. 1979. "Music in the Culture of German Americans in North Central Wisconsin." Master's thesis, University of Illinois.

Boissevain, Jeremy. 1996. *Coping with Tourists*. Providence: Berghahn Books.

Borda, Jennifer L. 2002. "The Woman Suffrage Parades of 1910–1913: Possibilities and Limitations of an Early Feminist Rhetorical Strategy." *Western Journal of Communication (includes Communication Reports)* 66(1): 25–52.

Brady, Erika. 1999. *A Spiral Way: How the Phonograph Changed Ethnography*. Jackson: University of Mississippi Press.

Breglia, Lisa. 2006. *Monumental Ambivalence: The Politics of Heritage*. Austin: University of Texas Press.

Bronner, Simon J. 1991. "A Prophetic Vision of Public and Academic Folklife: Alfred Shoemaker and America's First Department of Folklore." *Folklore Historian* 8:38–55.

Bronner, Simon J. 1998. *Following Tradition: Folklore in the Discourse of American Culture*. Logan: Utah State University Press.

Bronner, Simon J. 2016. "Don Yoder (1921–2015)." *Folklore* 127: 103–6.

Bronner, Simon J., and Joshua R. Brown, eds. 2017. *Pennsylvania Germans: An Interpretive Encyclopedia*. Baltimore: Johns Hopkins University Press.

brown, adrienne maree. 2020. *We Will Not Cancel Us: And Other Dreams of Transformative Justice*. Chico, CA: AK Press.

Buenker, John D. 1998. *The History of Wisconsin*. Vol. 4, *The Progressive Era, 1893–1914*. Madison: Wisconsin Historical Society Press.

Buff, W. M. 1896. "South Carolina Curiosity: The Petrified Man." *Proclamations, Politics, and Commerce: Broadsides from the Colonial Era to the Present at the South Caroliniana Library*. Broadside. University of South Carolina.

Buhle, Mari Jo, and Paul Buhle. 2011. *It Started in Wisconsin: Dispatches from the Front Lines of the New Labor Protest*. London: Verso.

Bureau of the Census. 1910. Department of Commerce and Labor. "Oulu Township, Bayfield, Wisconsin."

Bureau of the Census. 1913. *Thirteenth Census of the United States Taken in the Year 1910. Statistics for Michigan*. Washington, DC: Government Printing Office.

Bureau of Correctional Enterprises. 2003. *150 Years of Inmate Work Programs: Corrections Then and Now*. Madison: Wisconsin Historical Society Press.

Butler, Louise. 2003. "Traditional Crafts in Contemporary Scotland." In *Smithsonian Folklife Festival: Appalachia, Mali, Scotland*, edited by Carla Borden, 88–91. Washington, DC: Smithsonian Institution Center for Folklife and Cultural Heritage.

Byland, Bruce E., and John M. D. Pohl. 1994. *In the Realm of Eight Deer: The Archaeology of the Mixtec Codices*. Norman: University of Oklahoma Press.

Cadaval, Olivia, Sojin Kim, and Diana Baird N'Diaye. 2016. *Curatorial Conversations: Cultural Representation and the Smithsonian Folklife Festival*. Jackson: University of Mississippi Press.

Campbell Galman, Sally. 2007. *Shane, the Lone Ethnographer: A Beginner's Guide to Ethnography*. Lanham, MD: Altamira Press.

Camplin, Erika. 2017. *Prison Food in America*. Washington, DC: Rowman and Littlefield.

Capin, Pam. 2017. Interview with Sallie Anna Steiner, Eveleth, MN, November 19.

Carawan, Guy, Candie Carawan, and Robert Yellin. (1966) 1994. *Ain't You Got a Right to the Tree of Life: The People of Johns Island—Their Faces, Their Words, and Their Songs*. Athens: University of Georgia Press.

Carruthers, Mary J. (1990) 2008. *The Book of Memory: A Study of Memory in Medieval Culture*. 2nd ed. New York: Cambridge University Press.

Carstensen, Vernon. 1956. "The Origin and Early Development of the Wisconsin Idea." *Wisconsin Magazine of History* 39: 181–88.

Casey, Betty. 1981. *International Folk Dancing U.S.A.* Garden City, NY: Doubleday.

Casey, Jeanette L., and James P. Leary. 2016. "Local Centers/Global Sounds: Historic Recordings and Upper Midwestern Musical Vernaculars." Unpublished manuscript. June 1.

Casey, Mike. 2015. "Why Media Preservation Can't Wait: The Gathering Storm." *International Association of Sound & Audiovisual Archives Journal* 44:14–22.

Casey, Mike. 2018. "Hope." *Media Digitization and Preservation Initiative Blog*, Indiana University, June 7. https://blogs.iu.edu/mdpi/2018/06/07/hope/.

Cassidy, Frederic G., and Joan Houston Hall, eds. 1985–2017. *The Dictionary of American Regional English*. Cambridge, MA: Harvard University Press.

Caswell, Michelle, and Marika Cifor. 2016. "From Human Rights to Feminist Ethics: Radical Empathy in the Archives." *Archivaria* 81:23–43.

Causey, Andrew. 2016. *Drawn to See: Drawing as an Ethnographic Method*. Toronto: University of Toronto Press.

Cavell, Stanley. 1999. *The Claim of Reason: Wittgenstein, Skepticism, Morality, and Tragedy*. Oxford: Oxford University Press.

Cavell, Stanley. 2005. *Cities of Words: Pedagogical Letters on a Register of the Moral Life*. Cambridge, MA: Harvard University Press.

CBS. 2019. "Wisconsin's Democratic Governor Vetoes 4 Abortion Bills Passed by Republican-Controlled Legislature." June 21. https://www.cbsnews.com/news/abortion-bills-4-vetoed-by -wisconsin-governor-tony-evers-today-2019-06-21/.

Cederström, B. Marcus. 2018. "'Everyone Can Come and Remember': History and Heritage at the Ulen Museum." *Scandinavian Studies* 90(3): 376–402.

Cederström, B. Marcus. 2021. "Songs of the Finnish Migration from Laulu Aika." Nordic Folklife, University of Wisconsin–Madison, February 26. https://folklife.wisc.edu/2021/02/24/songs-of -the-finnish-migration-from-laulu-aika/.

Cederström, B. Marcus, Thomas A. DuBois, Tim Frandy, and Colin Gioia Connors. 2016. "Heritage Repatriation and Educational Sovereignty at an Ojibwe Public School." *Journal of Folklore and Education* 3:31–41.

Cederström, B. Marcus, Thomas DuBois, Anna Rue, Ralph Tuttila, and Laulu Aika. 2021. "*Songs of the Finnish Migration* with Marcus Cederström, Tom DuBois, and Laulu Aika." Zoom event, FinnFest USA 2021, February 27. https://www.youtube.com/watch?v=mezx8wOCiTo.

Cederström, B. Marcus, Thomas DuBois, Jimmy Träskelin, Sampo Korva, and Katri Haukilahti. 2019. "A Musical Lecture: Displaced Sympathies, Finnish Out- and In-Migration, Then and Now." Performance and lecture, University of Wisconsin–Madison, September 23.

Cederström, B. Marcus, Thomas DuBois, Jimmy Träskelin, Sampo Korva, and Katri Haukilahti. 2020. "*Songs of the Finnish Migration*, Lecture and Musical Performance with Marcus Cederström, Thomas DuBois, Jimmy Träskelin and Tallari." Zoom event, Finnish American Society of Milwaukee, October 25.

Cederström, B. Marcus, Tim Frandy, and Colin Gioia Connors. 2018. "Indigenous Sustainabilities: Decolonization, Education, and Collaboration at the Ojibwe Winter Games." *Journal of Sustainability Education* 18:1–25.

Chamberlin, Thomas. 1890. "The Coming of Age of the State Universities." University of Nebraska Charter Day, Lincoln, Nebraska, February 15.

Chaplin, Ralph. 1948. *The Rough and Tumble Story of an American Radical.* Chicago: University of Chicago Press.

Chase, Kim. 2016. "Winooski—a 'p'tit Canada.'" *Burlington Free Press,* June 10.

Chelf, Jane Harper, Amy M. Deshler, Shauna Hillman, and Ramon Durazo-Arvizu. 2000. "Storytelling: A Strategy for Living and Coping with Cancer." *Cancer Nursing* 23(1): 1–5.

Chicago Curling Club. n.d. "Chicago Curling Club History." https://chicagocurlingclub.org/historyPage .php.

Chittenden, Varick A. 2006. "'Put Your Very Special Place on the North Country Map!': Community Participation in Cultural Landmarking." *Journal of American Folklore* 119(471): 47–65.

Choinière, Michèle, and Deb Flanders. 2005. *Vermont's Native Daughters.* Album. Self-released.

Cifor, Marika, and Anne J. Gilliland. 2016. "Affect and the Archive, Archives and their Affects: An Introduction to the Special Issue." *Archival Science* 16:1–6.

Clark, Doug. 2008. *The Roaring Game: The Sweeping Saga of Curling.* Toronto: Key Porter Books.

Clemens, Samuel L. 1875. *Mark Twain's Sketches, New and Old.* Hartford, CT: American Publishing Company.

Clement, Grace. (1996) 2019. *Care, Autonomy, and Justice: Feminism and the Ethic of Care.* New York: Routledge.

Clover, Carol J. 1982. *The Medieval Saga.* Ithaca, NY: Cornell University Press.

Clover, Carol J. 1986. "The Long Prose Form." *Arkiv för nordisk filologi* 101:10–39.

Cohen, Eric. 1995. "Contemporary Tourism: Trends and Challenges, Sustainable Authenticity or Contrived Post-Modernity." In *Change in Tourism*, edited by Richard Butler and Douglas Pearce, 12–29. New York: Routledge.

Cohen, Ronald. 2003. *Rainbow Quest: The Folk Music Revival and American Society, 1940–1970.* Amherst: University of Massachusetts Press.

Cohen, Ronald, ed. 2005. *Alan Lomax, Assistant in Charge: The Library of Congress Letters, 1935–1945.* New York: Routledge.

Columbia Book of Yarns. 1907. 7th ed. Philadelphia: W. H. Horstmann.

Connors, Colin G. 2014. "Viking-Age Routes, Landscape, and Power in the Mosfell Region." In *Viking-Age Archaeology in Iceland: The Mosfell Archaeological Project,* edited by Davide Zori and Jesse Byock, 207–19. Turnhout, Belgium: Brepols Publishers.

Connors, Colin G. 2015. *The eSaga of Hrafnkell Freysgoði: A New Translation of "Hrafnkels saga Freysgoða."* Apple Inc. iTunes Store. IBA file. https://itunes.apple.com/us/book/id1030596226.

Corkhill, Betsan, Jessica Hemmings, Angela Maddock, and Jill Riley. 2014. "Knitting and Well-being." *Textile: The Journal of Cloth and Culture* 12(1): 34–57.

Council on Library and Information Resources. 2001. *Folk Heritage Collections in Crises.* Washington, DC: Council on Library and Information Resources.

Courier. 1926. "Find Petrified Body of Man in Basswood Tree: May Have Been One of Joliet's Men Who Was Lost." February 2, 1, 3.

Creenan, Robert. 2021. "Bay Port Fish Sandwich Festival to Return This August." *Huron Daily Tribune,* May 3.

Crogan, Neva L., Bronwynne C. Evans, and Robert Bendel. 2008. "Storytelling Intervention for Patients with Cancer: Part 2—Pilot Testing." *Oncology Nursing Forum* 35(2): 265–72.

Crosby, Ruth. 1936. "Oral Delivery in the Middle Ages." *Speculum* 11(1): 88–110.

Cruttenden, Alan. 2001. *Gimson's Pronunciation of English.* 6th ed. London: Arnold.

Cvetkovich, Ann. 2003. *An Archive of Feelings: Trauma, Sexuality, and Lesbian Public Cultures.* Durham, NC: Duke University Press.

Davidson, Hilary. 2019. "The Embodied Turn: Making and Remaking Dress as an Academic Practice." *Fashion Theory* 23(3): 329–62.

Davidson, Hilary, and Anna Hodson. 2007. "Joining Forces: The Intersection of Two Replica Garments." In *Textiles and Text: Re-Establishing the Links between Archival and Object Based Research,* edited by Maria Hayward and Elizabeth Kramer, 204–10. London: Archetype Publications.

de Caro, Frank, ed. 2008. *The Folklore Muse: Poetry, Fiction, and Other Reflections by Folklorists.* Logan: Utah State University Press.

Deibler, Barbara M. 1988/1989. "The Bookish Aurands." *Pennsylvania Portfolio* 6(2): 27–31.

Deibler, Barbara M. 1989. "The Aurands in Print." *Pennsylvania Portfolio* 7(1): 21–25.

Delineator, The. 1917. "Knit Your Bit for The Navy." August, 40–41.

DeMello, Margo. 2009. *Feet and Footwear: A Cultural Encyclopedia.* Santa Barbara, CA: ABC-CLIO.

Denihoff, Alice. 1940. "Women Knit to Aid Warring Countries." *Deseret News,* July 10, 8.

Derrida, Jacques. 1996. *Archive Fever: A Freudian Impression.* Chicago: University of Chicago Press.

Dewhurst, C. Kurt, Patricia Hall, and Charlie Seeman. 2017. *Folklife in Museums: Twenty-First Century Perspectives.* Lanham, MD: Rowman and Littlefield.

Diamond, Heather A., and Ricardo D. Trimillos. 2008. "Interdisciplinary Perspectives on the Folklife Festival." *Journal of American Folklore* 121(479): 3–9.

Dicks, Bella. 2000. *Heritage, Place and Community.* Cardiff: University of Wales Press.

Dirckinck-Holmfeld, Lone. 2019. "Brugerinddragelse i brug og integration af læringsplatforme." *Learning Tech—Tidsskrift for læremidler, didaktik og teknologi* 6:106–33.

Donner, William W. 2016. *Serious Nonsense: Groundhog Lodges, Versammlinge, and Pennsylvania German Heritage.* University Park: Pennsylvania State University Press.

Dormer, Peter. 1994. *The Art of the Maker.* London: Thames and Hudson.

Dorson, Richard M. 1951. "The Great Team of English Folklorists." *Journal of American Folklore* 64(251): 1–10.

Dorson, Richard M. (1952) 2008. *Bloodstoppers and Bearwalkers: Folk Traditions of Michigan's Upper Peninsula*, edited by James P. Leary. Madison: University of Wisconsin Press.

Dorson, Richard M. 1967. *American Negro Folktales*. Greenwich, CT: Fawcett.

Dorson, Richard M. 1968. *The British Folklorists: A History*. London: Routledge and Kegan Paul.

Dregni, Eric. 2011. *Vikings in the Attic: In Search of Nordic America*. Minneapolis: University of Minnesota Press.

Dresser, Norine. 1971. "'Is It Fresh?' An Examination of Jewish-American Shopping Habits." *New York Folklore Quarterly* 27(1): 153–60.

DuBois, Thomas. 2018. "The Migration of a Building: Representation, Replication, and Repatriation of an Emblem of Norwegian, Norwegian American, and Norwegian American-Norwegian Identity." *Scandinavian Studies* 90(3): 331–49.

DuBois, Thomas. 2019. "Recalling—Reconstituting—Migration: Sámi Americans and the Immigrant Experience." In *Transnational Finnish Mobilities: Proceedings of Finnforum IX*, edited by Johanna Leinonen and Auvo Kostiainan, 49–67. Turku: Migration Institute of Finland.

DuBois, Thomas A., and B. Marcus Cederström, eds. 2019. *Songs of the Finnish Migration: A Bilingual Anthology*. Madison: University of Wisconsin Press.

DuBois, Thomas, Jim Leary, Jimmy Träskelin, Sampo Korva, and Katri Haukilahti. 2019. "Created in Finnish America, Preserved in Finland, Returned to the USA: The Collection Work of Simo Westerholm and the Efforts of the University of Wisconsin–Madison to Return It to Americans." Performance and lecture, FinnFest USA 2019, Detroit, MI, September 18–22.

Ducharme, Jamie. 2020. "Why the Covid-19 Pandemic Has Caused a Widespread Existential Crisis." *Time*, December 29.

Dunn, Jon W., Juliet L. Hardest, Tanya Clement, Chris Lacinak, and Amy Rudersdorf. 2018. "Audiovisual Metadata Platform (AMP) Planning Project: Progress Report and Next Steps." March 28. http://hdl.handle.net/2022/21982.

Durocher, Matthew, dir. 2014. *Concentric Circles*. Student film. Houghton: Michigan Technological University Humanities Department.

Eau Claire Leader. 1926a. "D'Artagnan Story Reaches Minnesota Comes Back Again." February 27, 8.

Eau Claire Leader. 1926b. "International Complications." February 24, 5.

Eau Claire Leader. 1926c. "Madison Hears about Stone Man Thinks It Hoax." February 16, 8.

Eau Claire Leader. 1926d. "Petrified Man Story Is a Hoax." February 13, 2. Edensor, Tim. 2001. "Haunting in the Ruins: Matter and Immateriality." *Space and Culture* 11(12): 42–51.

Edmonds, Michael. 2009. *Out of the Northwoods: The Many Lives of Paul Bunyan*. Madison: Wisconsin Historical Society Press.

Edson, Evelyn. 1997. *Mapping Time and Space: How Medieval Mapmakers Viewed Their World*. London: British Library.

Edson, Evelyn. 2007. *The World Map, 1300–1492: The Persistence of Tradition and Transformation*. Baltimore: Johns Hopkins University Press.

Ellingsgard, Nils. 1993. *Norwegian Rose Painting in America: What the Immigrants Brought*. Decorah, IA: Scandinavian University Press.

Ellingsgard, Nils. 1995. "Rosemaling: A Folk Art in Migration." In *Norwegian Folk Art: The Migration of a Tradition*, edited by Marion Nelson, 190–237. New York: Abbeville Press.

Engelhard, Henry. 1995. Field recording with Folkpatterns project. Bay Port, MI.

Engler, Mira. 2000. "Drive-Thru History: Theme Towns in Iowa." In *Take the Next Exit: New Views of the Iowa Landscape*, edited by Robert F. Sayre, 255–76. Ames: University of Iowa Press.

Engster, Daniel, and Maurice Hamington, eds. 2015. *Care Ethics and Political Theory*. Oxford: Oxford University Press.

Evers, Tony. 2020. Exec. Order no. 19. Relating to the Creation of the Committee to Celebrate the Centennial Anniversary of Wisconsin's Ratification of the 19th Amendment. September 30.

Fakunle, David Olawuyi, David Thomas, Kathy A. M. Gonzales, Denise Christina Vidot, and LaShaune P. Johnson. 2021. "What Anansi Did for Us: Storytelling's Value in Equitably Exploring Public Health." *Health Education & Behavior* 48(3): 352–60.

Farrell, Thomas B. 1993. *Norms of Rhetorical Culture*. New Haven, CT: Yale University Press.

Feintuch, Burt. 1988. "The Folklorist and the Public." In *100 Years of American Folklore Studies: A Conceptual History*, edited by William M. Clements, 70–74. Washington, DC: American Folklore Society.

Ferguson, H. T. 2011. "The Spirit of Curling." In *Curling Is in Our Blood: Annual Club Directory*, 10. Madison: Madison Curling Club.

Ferrell, Ann K., and Diane E. Goldstein. Forthcoming. *The Soul of a Folklorist: Expressive Culture, Political Representation, and the Weight of Social Responsibility*. Bloomington: Indiana University Press.

Ferry, Elizabeth Emma. 2005. *Not Ours Alone: Patrimony, Value, and Collectivity in Contemporary Mexico*. New York: Columbia University Press.

Fieser, James. 1941. "March 8, 1941 Letter to Area Managers." Folder 403.4: Armed Forces and Veterans, Series 1935–1947, Record Group 200, American National Red Cross Central Decimal Files, National Archives at College Park, MD.

Flowers, Ebony. 2019. *Hot Comb*. Montreal: Drawn and Quarterly.

Foley, John M. 1991. *Immanent Art: From Structure to Meaning in Traditional Oral Epic*. Bloomington: Indiana University Press.

Foley, John M. 2012. *Oral Tradition and the Internet: Pathways of the Mind*. Urbana: University of Illinois Press.

Foys, Marin K. 2007. *Virtually Anglo-Saxon: Old Media, New Media, and Early Medieval Studies in the Late Age of Print*. Gainesville: University of Florida Press.

Foys, Martin K. 2009. "Digital Mappaemundi: Changing the Way We Work with Medieval World Maps." *Peregrinations: Journal of Medieval Art and Architecture* 2(3): 170–77.

Frandy, Tim. 2015. "Birchbark Canoe Building and Decolonizing Health." *Community Psychologist* 48(1): 25–27.

Frandy, Tim, and B. Marcus Cederström. 2017. "Sustainable Power: Decolonising Sustainability through Anishinaabe Epistemologies and Public Humanities Programming." In *Going Beyond: Perceptions of Sustainability in Heritage Studies*, edited by Marie-Theres Albert, Francesco Bandarin, and Ana Pereira Roders, 217–30. New York: Springer International Publishing.

Freccero, Carla. 2013. "Queer Spectrality: Haunting the Past." In *The Spectralities Reader. Ghosts and Haunting in Contemporary Cultural Theory*, edited by Maria del Pilar Blanco and Esther Peeren, 335–59. New York and London: Bloomsbury.

Fredal, James. 2014. "The Perennial Pleasures of the Hoax." *Philosophy & Rhetoric* 47(1): 73–97.

Frey, J. William. 1941. "The German Dialect of Eastern York County, Pennsylvania." PhD diss., University of Illinois.

Garlough, Christine L. 2008. "On the Political Uses of Folklore: Performance and Grassroots Feminist Activism in India." *Journal of American Folklore* 121(480): 167–91.

Garlough, Christine L. 2011a. "Folklore and the Potential of Acknowledgment: Representing 'India' at the Minnesota Festival of Nations." *Western Folklore* 70(1): 69–98.

Garlough, Christine L. 2011b. "Folklore and Performing Political Protest: Calls of Conscience at the 2011 Wisconsin Labor Protests." *Western Folklore* 70(3/4): 337–70.

Garlough, Christine L. 2013. *Desi Divas: Political Activism in South Asian American Cultural Performances*. Jackson: University Press of Mississippi.

Garlough, Christine L. 2014. "Vernacular Culture and Grassroots Activism: Non-Violent Protest and Progressive Ethos at the 2011 Wisconsin Labour Protests." In *The Political Aesthetics of Global Protest: The Arab Spring and Beyond*, edited by Pnina Werbner, Martin Webb, and Kathryn Spellman-Poots, 263–90. Edinburgh: Edinburgh University Press.

Garlough, Christine L. Forthcoming. *Expressing Care: Acknowledgment, Feminist Politics and Everyday Culture*. Bloomington: Indiana University Press.

Garlough, Christine, and Anne Pryor. 2011. "Fearlessly Sifting and Winnowing: Folklore and the Wisconsin Idea." *Western Folklore* 70(3/4): 243–53.

Garon, Paul. 2003. *The Devil's Son-In-Law: The Story of Peetie Wheatstraw and His Songs*. Chicago: Charles H. Kerr.

Gauvreau Judge, Mark. 2008. "Concert of the Year: A Holy Joy." *Books & Culture*, October 13. http://www.booksandculture.com/articles/webexclusives/2008/october/oct13.html.

Gedicks, Al. 1972. "Guerrilla Research: Reversing the Machinery." *Insurgent Sociologist* 2(3): 26–29.

Ghaddar, Jamila J. 2016. "The Spectre in the Archive: Truth, Reconciliation, and Indigenous Archival Memory." *Archivaria* 82(1): 3–26.

Ghelerter, Donna. 1989. "Knitting in America during the First World War." Master's thesis, SUNY Fashion Institute of Technology.

Gilmore, Janet C. (1989) 1998. "'We Made 'Em to Fit Our Purpose': The Northern Lake Michigan Fishing Skiff Tradition." In *Wisconsin Folklore*, edited by James P. Leary, 457–75. Madison: University of Wisconsin Press.

Gilmore, Janet C. (1986) 1999. *The World of the Oregon Fishboat: A Study in Maritime Folklife*. 2nd ed. Pullman: Washington State University Press.

Gilmore, Janet C. 2009. "Mount Horeb's Oljanna Venden Cunneen. A Norwegian-American Rosemaler 'on the Edge.'" *ARV Nordic Year of Folklore* 65:25–48.

Gilmore, Janet C. 2011. "Teaching Practice through Fieldwork Course Design." *Western Folklore* 70(3/4): 255–85.

Gilmore, Janet C. 2015. "Filling 'An Immense Brain with Very Little in the Brain' for 'Perpetual Memory': Folklore Archiving New and Old." *Journal of Folklore Research* 52(1): 99–138.

Gilmore, Janet C., and James P. Leary. 1986. Eino Okkonen Field Report Records. Wisconsin Folk Art Survey Collection, John Michael Kohler Arts Center, Sheboygan, WI.

Gilmore, Janet C., Nicole Saylor, Mary Hoefferle, and Karen J. Baumann, eds. 2007. "The Ethnic Music in Northern Wisconsin and Michigan Collection." In *Public Folk Arts and Folklife Projects of the Upper Midwest* (Center for the Center of Upper Midwestern Cultures). In *Archival Resources in Wisconsin: Descriptive Finding Aids*, University of Wisconsin Digital Collections. http://digital.library.wisc.edu/1711.dl/wiarchives.uw-csumc-csumc0011cg.

Gísli Sigurðsson. (2002) 2004. *The Medieval Icelandic Saga and Oral Tradition: A Discourse on Method*. Translated by Nicholas Jones. Milman Perry Collection of Oral Literature 2. Cambridge, MA: Harvard University Press.

Gísli Sigurðsson. 2008. "Orality Harnessed: How to Read Written Sagas from an Oral Culture?" In *Oral Art Forms and Their Passage into Writing*, edited by Else Mundal and Jonas Wellendorf, 19–28. University of Copenhagen: Museum Tusculanum Press.

Glad, Paul W. 2014. *War, a New Era, and Depression, 1914–1940*. Madison: Wisconsin Historical Society Press.

Glassie, Henry. 1995. "Tradition." *Journal of American Folklore* 108(430): 395–412.

Glassie, Henry. 1999. *Material Culture*. Bloomington: Indiana University Press.

Glickman, Joel. 1979. Field notes, recording session by Glickman and James P. Leary with Helmer Olavi Wintturi, Herbster, WI, July 31. Ethnic Music in Northern Wisconsin and Michigan Collection, Mills Music Library, University of Wisconsin–Madison. https://search.library.wisc.edu/digital/ACOE4F3MI3P5JL8J.

Golubev, Alexey, and Irina Takala. 2014. *The Search for a Socialist El Dorado: Finnish Immigration to Soviet Karelia*. East Lansing: Michigan State University Press.

Gordon, Avery F. 2011. "Some Thoughts on Haunting and Futurity." *Borderlands* 10(2): 1–21.

Gordon, Beverly. 2002. "The Hand of the Maker: The Importance of Understanding Textiles from the 'Inside Out.'" In *Silk Roads, Other Roads: Proceedings of the 8th Biennial Symposium of the Textile Society of America*. Paper 398. Northampton, MA: Textile Society of America.

Gough, Robert. 1997. *Farming the Cutover: A Social History of Northern Wisconsin*. Lawrence: University Press of Kansas.

Govenar, Alan, dir. 2017. *Extraordinary Ordinary People*. Dallas, TX: Documentary Arts.

Govier, Trudy. 1999. "What Is Acknowledgement and Why Is It Important?" *OSSA Conference Archive* 1. https://scholar.uwindsor.ca/ossaarchive/OSSA3/keynotes/1.

Gradén, Lizette. 2003. *On Parade: Making Heritage in Lindsborg, Kansas*. Uppsala: Acta Universitatis Upsaliensis.

Gradén, Lizette. 2013. "Performing Nordic Spaces in American Museums: Gift Exchange, Volunteerism and Curatorial Practice." In *Performing Nordic Heritage: Everyday Practices and Institutional Culture*, edited by Peter Aronsson and Lizette Gradén, 189–220. Surrey, UK: Ashgate.

Green, Archie. 1993. *Wobblies, Pile Butts, and Other Heroes: Laborlore Explorations*. Urbana: University of Illinois Press.

Green, Archie. 2000. "An Unreconstructed Do-gooder." *Folklore Forum* 31(2): 5–6.

Green, Archie, David Roediger, Franklin Rosemont, and Salvatore Salerno, eds. 2007. *The Big Red Songbook*. Chicago: Charles H. Kerr.

Groce, Nancy. n.d. "History of the American Folklife Center." American Folklife Center. https://www.loc.gov/folklife/AFChist/.

Gronbeck, Bruce E. 2008. "Foreword. Visual Rhetorical Studies: Traces through Time and Space." In *Visual Rhetoric: A Reader in Communication and American Culture*, edited by Lester C. Olson, Cara A. Finnegan, and Diane S. Hope, xxi–xxvi. Los Angeles: SAGE.

Gronow, Pekka. 1982. "Ethnic Recordings: An Introduction." In *Ethnic Recordings in America: A Neglected Heritage*, 1–50. Washington, DC: American Folklife Center, Library of Congress.

Halker, Bucky. 1999. *Don't Want Your Millions*. Chur, Switzerland: Brambus Records.

Halker, Bucky. 2002. *Welcome to Labor Land*. Chur, Switzerland: Brambus Records.

Halker, Bucky. 2017. "Tramp, Tramp, Tramp: The Songs of Joe Hill Around the World." In *Wobblies of the World: A Global History of the IWW*, edited by Peter Cole, David Struthers, and Kenyon Zimmer, 288–98. London: Pluto Press.

Halker, Bucky, and the Complete Unknowns. 2002. *Welcome to Labor Land*. Chicago: Revolting Records.

Halker, Clark "Bucky." 1991. *For Democracy, Workers, and God: Labor Song-Poems and Labor Protest, 1865–1895.* Urbana: University of Illinois Press.

Hall, Jason Y. 2010. "Lobbying for Arts and Culture: From the Culture Wars to the Rise of New Issue." *Journal of Arts Management, Law, and Society* 35(3): 227–38.

Hall, Stephanie A. 1995. *Ethnographic Collections in the Archive of Folk Culture: A Contributor's Guide.* Washington, DC: American Folklife Center.

Hamer, Emily. 2016. "Records Show Walker Wanted to Change Wisconsin Idea." *Badger Herald*, May 27.

Hamer, Emily. 2020. "Staffing Shortages in Wisconsin Prison System Prompt Transfer of 220 Inmates." *Wisconsin State Journal*, December 2.

Hamington, Maurice. 2018. "The Care Ethics Moment: International Innovations." *International Journal of Care and Caring* 2(3): 309–18.

Hansen, Kathryn. 1988. "The Virangana in North Indian History: Myth and Popular Culture." *Economic and Political Weekly* 23(18): WS25–33.

Hansen, Kathryn. 2000. "The Virangana in North Indian History: Myth and Popular Culture." In *Ideals, Images, and Real Lives: Women in Literature and History*, edited by Alice Thorner and Maithreyi Krishnaraj, 257–87. Himayatnagar, India: Sameeksha Trust, Orient Longman Limited.

Hansen, Warren. 1999. *Curling: The History, the Players, the Game.* Toronto: Key Porter Books.

Harold, Ellen, and Peter Stone. n.d. "Reverend Gary Davis." Association for Cultural Equity. http://www.culturalequity.org/alan-lomax/friends/davis.

Harrison, Garry, and Jo Burgess. 2007. *Dear Old Illinois: Traditional Music of Downstate Illinois.* Bloomington, Indiana: Pick Away Press.

Harvey, Todd. 2016. *Michigan I-O.* e-book. Dust to Digital Records.

Hathaway, Carole. n.d. "Celebrating a Shared History." https://www.uwalumni.com/news/celebrating-a-shared-history/.

Hathaway, Edward W. 1989. "Developing a State Archive of Local Music Materials." *Notes* 45(3): 483–94.

Haugen, Einar. 1953. *The Norwegian Language in America.* 2 vols. Philadelphia: University of Pennsylvania Press.

Hawes, Bess Lomax. 1985. *National Heritage Fellowships 1985.* Washington, DC: National Endowment for the Arts.

Hawes, Bess Lomax. (1992) 2007. "Happy Birthday, Dear American Folklore Society: Reflections on the Work and Mission of Folklorists." In *Public Folklore*, edited by Robert Baron and Nick Spitzer, 65–73. Jackson: University Press of Mississippi.

Hawes, Bess Lomax. 2008. *Sing It Pretty: A Memoir.* Urbana: University of Illinois Press.

Heimo, Anne. 2017. "The Italian Hall Tragedy, 1913: A Hundred Years of Remediated Memories." In *The Twentieth Century in European Memory: Transcultural Mediation and Reception*, edited by Tea Sindbæk Andersen and Barbara Törnquist-Pleva, 240–67. Leiden, Netherlands: Brill.

Henderson, Jayne, and Wayne Henderson. 2016. "A Father-Daughter Luthier Duo Builds Souls into Guitars." *All Things Considered.* Interviewer Desire Moses, host Audie Cornish. National Public Radio, October 4.

Hendrickson, John. 2019. Telephone conversation with James P. Leary, September 5.

Hendrickson, William "Bill." 1981. Interviews with James P. Leary, Herbster, WI, January 13 and February 17. Ethnic Music in Northern Wisconsin and Michigan Collection, Mills Music Library, University of Wisconsin–Madison. https://search.library.wisc.edu/digital/ASXYQBFBSX7JLC8N and https://search.library.wisc.edu/digital/AVQ5NBSXXGC2G58Q.

Hendrickson, William "Bill." n.d. "The Way It Was Told to Me in 1897" and "Memories of Bark Point." Unpublished manuscripts.

Hmong Art: Tradition and Change. 1986. Exhibition catalog. John Michael Kohler Arts Center, Sheboygan, WI.

Hochberg, Gil. 2012. "A Poetics of Haunting: From Yizhar's Hirbeh to Yehoshua's Ruins to Koren's Crypts." *Jewish Social Studies: History, Culture, Society* 18(3): 55–69.

Hoeritz, Carol, and Jean Horneck. 2018. Interview with Jared L. Schmidt, Stoughton, WI, December 18.

Holler, Jess Lamar Reece (with Carol Goland, Scott Williams, and Jeremy Purser). 2018. "Growing Right: Pop-Up and Popular Pedagogies for Public Environmental Folklife." *Journal of Folklore and Education* 5(1): 71–91.

Holm, Poul, Arne Jarrick, and Dominic Scott. 2015. *Humanities Report 2015.* London: Palgrave Macmillan UK.

Holmio, Armas K. E. 1967. *Michiganin Suomalaisten Historia.* Hancock, MI: Book Concern.

Holzhueter, Jack. 1979. Response to Inquiry about Petrified Man. January 17. "D'Artagnan." Library reference file, Wisconsin Historical Society.

Holzhueter, John O. 1986. "Aslak Lie and the Challenge of the Artifact." *Wisconsin Magazine of History* 70(1): 2–20.

Homiak, John P. 1995. "Introduction: A Primer on the Film Archives and its Collections." In *Guide to the Collections of the Human Studies Film Archives, 100th Anniversary of Motion Pictures: Commemorative Ethnographic Edition,* edited by Pamela Wintle and John P. Homiak, 1–5. Washington, D.C., National Museum of Natural History, Smithsonian Institution.

Hoog, Ann. 2018. "Documenting Art in Everyday Life." Panel presentation. Society of American Archivists Annual Conference, Washington, DC, August 15.

Horowitz, Yuri. 2020. "Yerevan Magazine Highlights *My Armenia* Cultural Heritage Tourism Experiences for Local Travelers." Center for Folklife and Cultural Heritage. *Smithsonian Folklife Magazine,* August 18.

Hostetler, John A. 1952. *Amish Life.* Scottdale, PA: Herald Press.

Hotchkiss, W. O., and F. A. Cannon. 1925. "Know Wisconsin First." *Rusk County Journal,* May 28, 2.

Houston, Ron. 2018. "Jane Farwell." Society of Folk Dance Historians. https://www.sfdh.us/encyclopedia/farwell_j.html.

Høybye, Mette Terp, Christoffer Johansen, and Tine Tjørnhøj-Thomsen. 2005. "Online Interaction: Effects of Storytelling in an Internet Breast Cancer Support Group." *Psycho-Oncology: Journal of the Psychological, Social and Behavioral Dimensions of Cancer* 14(3): 211–20.

Hunt, Marjorie. 1979. "Folklore in Your Community: The Corner Store." In *Festival of American Folklife 1979* [Program Book], edited by Peter Seitel, 26–27. Washington, DC: Smithsonian Institution.

Hurcombe, Linda. 2008. "Organics from Inorganics: Using Experimental Archaeology as a Research Tool for Studying Perishable Material Culture." *World Archaeology* 40(1): 83–115.

Hyde, Michael J. 2005. *Life-Giving Gift of Acknowledgment.* West Lafayette, IN: Purdue University Press.

Hymes, Dell. 1971. "The Contribution of Folklore to Sociolinguistic Research." *Journal of American Folklore* 84(331): 42–50.

Industrial Workers of the World. 1917. *I.W.W. Songs, Joe Hill Memorial Edition.* Chicago: Industrial Workers of the World.

Ingold, Tim. 2016. *Lines.* London: Routledge.

Inquiry about Petrified Man. 1984. "Dear Sirs." June 14. "D'Artagnan." Library reference file, Wisconsin Historical Society.

Ives, Edward D. 1976. "Common-Man Biography: Some Notes by the Way." In *Folklore Today: A Festschrift for Richard M. Dorson*, edited by Richard Mercer Dorson, Linda Dégh, Henry Glassie, and Felix J. Oinas, 251–64. Bloomington: Indiana University, Research Center for Language and Semiotic Studies.

Ivey, William. 1970. "'The 1913 Disaster': Michigan Local Legend." *Folklore Forum* 3(4): 100–14.

Jabbour, Alan. 1996. "The American Folklife Center: A Twenty-Year Retrospective." 2 parts. *Folklife Center News* 18(1/2; 3/4).

Janus, Edward. 2011. *Creating Dairyland: How Caring for Cows Saved Our Soil, Created Our Landscape, Brought Prosperity to Our State, and Still Shapes Our Way of Life in Wisconsin*. Madison: Wisconsin Historical Society Press.

Jensen, Ellen Marie. 2012. *We Stopped Forgetting: Stories from Sámi Americans*. Kárášjohka, Norway: ČálliidLágádus.

Jensen, Ellen Marie, and Tim Frandy. 2021. "Kulttuurinen pois pyyhkiminen, resilienssi ja jatkuvuus: Kertomuksia saamelaisten muuttoliikkeestä ja nykykulttuurista Yhdysvalloissa." In *Vähemmistöt Muuttajina: Näkökulmia Suomalaisen Muuttoliikehistorian Moninaisuuteen*, edited by Miika Tervonen and Johanna Leinonen, 51–70. Turku: Migration Institute of Finland.

Jensen, George H. 2000. *Storytelling in Alcoholics Anonymous: A Rhetorical Analysis*. Carbondale: Southern Illinois University Press.

Jensen, Joan M. 2006. *Calling This Place Home: Women on the Wisconsin Frontier 1850–1925*. St. Paul: Minnesota State Historical Society Press.

Jensen, Richard. 1995. "The Culture Wars: 1965–1995." *Journal of Social History* 29(Issue Supplement 1): 17–37.

Jervis, Rick. 2017. "Puerto Rican Musical Family Helps Neighbors Where Federal Aid Lags after Maria." *USA Today*, November 8.

Johnson, Adam Fulton. 2018. "Secretsharers: Intersecting Systems of Knowledge and the Politics of Documentation in Southwesternist Anthropology, 1880–1930." PhD diss., University of Michigan.

Johnson, Nancy, and Todd Harvey, eds. (2008) 2016. *Performance Style and Culture Research Guide, Alan Lomax Collection* (AFC 2004/004). American Folklife Center, Library of Congress.

Johnston, Lucy. 2017. *Shoes*. New York: Thames and Hudson.

Jones, Bessie, and Bess Lomax Hawes. 1972. *Step It Down: Games, Plays, Songs, and Stories from the Afro-American Heritage*. New York: Harper & Row.

Jones, Michael Owen. 1980. "A Feeling for Form, as Illustrated by People at Work." In *Folklore on Two Continents: Essays in Honor of Linda Dégh*, edited by Nikolai Burlakoff and Carl Lindahl, 260–69. Bloomington, IN: Trickster Press.

Jones, Michael Owen. 1987. "Aesthetics at Work: Art and Ambience in an Organization." In *Exploring Folk Art: Twenty Years of Thought on Craft, Work, and Aesthetics*, 134–57. Ann Arbor, MI: UMI Research Press.

Jones, Michael Owen. 1993. "A Folklorist's Approach to Organizational Behavior (OB) and Organization Development (OD)." In *Putting Folklore to Use*, edited by Michael Owen Jones, 162–86. Lexington: University of Kentucky Press.

Jones, Michael Owen. 1997. "How Can We Apply Event Analysis to 'Material Behavior,' and Why Should We?" *Western Folklore* 56(3/4): 199–214.

Kalcik, Susan. 1975. "'. . . Like Ann's Gynecologist or the Time I Was Almost Raped': Personal Narratives in Women's Rap Groups." *Journal of American Folklore* 88(347): 3–11.

Karni, Michael G., and Douglas Ollila, eds. 1977. *For the Common Good: Finnish Immigrants and the Radical Response to Industrial America.* Superior, WI: Työmies Society.

Kaunonen, Gary. 2010. *Challenge Accepted: A Finnish Immigrant Response to Industrial America in Michigan's Copper Country.* East Lansing: Michigan State University Press.

Keitumetse, Susan. 2006. "UNESCO 2003 Convention on Intangible Heritage: Practical Implications for Heritage Management Approaches in Africa." *South African Archeological Bulletin* 61(184): 166–71.

Kellher, Bob. 1999. "The History of the IRRB." Minnesota Public Radio, December 6. http://news .minnesota.publicradio.org/features/199912/06_newsroom_irrb-m/history.shtml.

Kemble, Frances Anne. 1961. *Journal of a Residence on a Georgian Plantation in 1838–1839.* Edited by John A Scott. New York: Alfred A. Knopf.

Kennicott, Philip. 2020. "The National Archives Used to Stand for Independence. That Mission Has Been Compromised." *Washington Post*, January 18.

Kerr, John. 1890. *History of Curling—Scotland's Ain Game—and Fifty Years of the Royal Caledonian Curling Club.* Edinburgh: David Douglas.

Keskinen, Suvi. 2019. "Intra-Nordic Differences, Colonial/Racial Histories, and National Narratives: Rewriting Finnish History." *Scandinavian Studies* 91(1/2): 163–81.

keyele. 2010. "Manulani Aluli Meyer on Epistemology." YouTube, October 22. https://www.youtube .com/watch?v=lmJJi1iBdzc.

Kirshenblatt-Gimblett, Barbara. 1991. "Objects of Ethnography." In *Exhibiting Culture: The Poetics and Politics of Museum Display*, edited by Ivan Karp and Steven D. Lavine, 386–443. Washington, DC: Smithsonian Institution Press.

Kirshenblatt-Gimblett, Barbara. 1995. "Theorizing Heritage." *Ethnomusicology* 39(3): 367–80.

Kirshenblatt-Gimblett, Barbara. 1998. *Destination Culture: Tourism, Museum, and Heritage.* Berkeley: University of California Press.

Kitchell Whyte, Bertha. 1971. *Craftsmen of Wisconsin.* Racine, WI: Western Publishing.

Kivisto, Peter, and Johanna Leinonen. 2014. "Ambiguous Identity: Finnish Americans and the Race Question." In *Finns in the United States: A History of Settlement, Dissent, and Integration*, edited by Auvo Kostiainen, 75–87. East Lansing: Michigan State University Press.

Klein, Barbro. 2000. "Folklore, Heritage Politics and Ethnic Diversity: Thinking about the Past and the Future." In *Folklore, Heritage Politics and Ethnic Diversity: A Festschrift for Barbo Klein*, edited by Pertti J. Anttonen, Anna-Leena Siikala, Stein R. Mathisen, and Leif Magnusson, 23–36. Botkyrka, Sweden: Multicultural Centre.

Klein, Barbro and Mats Widbom, eds. 1995. *Swedish Folk Art: All Tradition Is Change.* New York: Harry N. Abrams.

Klymasz, Robert B. 1973. "From Immigrant to Ethnic Folklore: A Canadian View of Process and Transition." *Journal of the Folklore Institute* 10(3): 131–39.

Knit for Defense, Book No. 172—Fifth 4. 1941. Newark, NJ: Chadwick's Red Heart Wools/The Cotton Spool Company.

"Knitting as a Nerve Cure." 1911. *The Medical Brief*, July, 426.

"Knitting for the Nerves." 1912. *Toilettes*, March, 21.

Kodish, Deborah. 2011. "Envisioning Folklore Activism." *Journal of American Folklore* 124(491): 31–60.

Köhler, Ulrich. 1995. "Rectangular Mushroom Stones from Oaxaca, Mexico." *Mexicon* 17(4): 70–73.

Kolehmainen, John I., and George W. Hill. 1951. *Haven in the Woods: The Story of the Finns in Wisconsin.* Madison: State Historical Society of Wisconsin.

Kolovos, Andrew Arthur. 2010. "Archiving Culture: American Folklore Archives in Theory and Practice." PhD diss., Indiana University.

Kolovos, Andy. 2008. "PACT GRAMMY Foundation Archive Survey Report." Unpublished report.

Kostiainen, Auvo. 2014. "Politics of the Left and Right." In *Finns in the United States: A History of Settlement, Dissent, and Integration,* edited by Auvo Kostiainen, 131–55. East Lansing: Michigan State University Press.

Kozma, LuAnne G. 1991. *Folkpatterns Leader's Guide: A Cultural Heritage Project.* East Lansing: Michigan State University Extension and Michigan State University Museum.

Kozma, LuAnne G. 1998. "Learning to Document Maritime Tradition: The 4-H Folkpatterns Maritime Folklife Workshop." In *Michigan Folklife Annual,* edited by Yvonne R. Lockwood and Marsha Macdowell, 48–49. Michigan State University Museum.

Kraybill, Donald B. 2001. "Hostetler, John A. (1918–2001)." *Global Anabaptist Mennonite Encyclopedia Online.* https://gameo.org/index.php?title=Hostetler,_John_A._(1918–2001)&oldid=138868.

Kristoffersen, Gjert. 2000. *The Phonology of Norwegian.* New York: Oxford University Press.

Krueger, Carolyn Maki. 2004. *The Second Fifty Years: The Continuing Story of Oulu, Wisconsin (1950s– 2004).* Bayfield County, WI: Oulu Chapter of the Bayfield County Historical Society.

Krugler, John D. 2013. *Creating Old World Wisconsin: The Struggle to Build an Outdoor History Museum of Ethnic Architecture.* Madison: University of Wisconsin Press.

Kurin, Richard. 1997. *Reflections of a Culture Broker: A View from the Smithsonian.* Washington, DC: Smithsonian Institution.

Kurin, Richard. 1998. *Smithsonian Folklife Festival: Culture of, by, and for the People.* Washington, DC: Smithsonian Institution.

Kurin, Richard. 2011. *Saving Haiti's Heritage: Cultural Recovery After the Earthquake.* Washington, DC: Smithsonian Institution.

Kutztown Folk Festival. n.d. "Festival History." https://www.kutztownfestival.com/about-festival /festival-history.

Lahti, Duane. 2018. Interview with Marcus Cederström and Mirva Johnson, Oulu, WI, November 10.

Lahti, Duane, and Barb Lahti. 2018. Interview with Mirva Johnson, Oulu, WI, June 18.

Lankton, Larry. 1991. *Cradle to Grave: Life, Work, and Death at the Lake Superior Copper Mines.* Oxford: Oxford University Press.

Lankton, Larry. 2007. "American Themes/Keweenaw Stories." In *New Perspectives on Michigan's Copper Country,* edited by Alison K. Hoagland, Erik C. Nordberg, and Terry S. Reynolds, 9–24. Hancock, MI: Quincy Mine Hoist Association.

Larsen, Soren, and Jay T. Johnson. 2017. *Being Together in Place: Indigenous Coexistence in a More Than Human World.* Minneapolis: University of Minnesota Press.

Larson, Evan R., Sara A. Allen, and Chris A. Underwood. 2021. "The Driftless Oaks: A New Network of Tree-Ring Chronologies to Improve Regional Perspectives of Drought in the Upper Midwest, USA." *Progress in Physical Geography* 45(3): 375–406.

Larson, LeRoy. 1975. "Scandinavian-American Folk Dance Music of the Norwegians in Minnesota." PhD diss., University of Minnesota.

Laušević, Mirjana. 2007. *Balkan Fascination.* New York: Oxford University Press.

Lawless, Greg, and Ann Reynolds. 2005. *Keys to Success for Food Co-op Start-ups in Rural Areas: Four Case Studies.* US Department of Agriculture Rural Development Research Report 208. Madison: University of Wisconsin Center for Cooperatives.

Laws, G. Malcolm. 1957. *American Ballads from British Broadsides.* Philadelphia: American Folklore Society.

Leary, James P. 1981a. "Eino Okkonen Field Report." Ethnic Music in Northern Wisconsin and Michigan Collection, Mills Music Library, University of Wisconsin–Madison. https://search .library.wisc.edu/digital/AEthnicMusicWiMi.

Leary, James P. 1981b. *Ethnic Music in Northern Wisconsin and Michigan: A Final Project Report.* Ashland, WI: Northland College.

Leary, James P. 1986. *Accordions in the Cutover: Field Recordings of Ethnic Music from Lake Superior's South Shore.* Mount Horeb: Wisconsin Folklife Center. Double LP and booklet.

Leary, James P. 1987. "Reading the 'Newspaper Dress': An Exposé of Art Moilanen's Musical Tradition." In *Michigan Folklife Reader*, edited by C. Kurt Dewhurst and Yvonne Lockwood, 205–23. East Lansing: Michigan State University Press.

Leary, James P. 1990. "The Legacy of Viola Turpeinen." *Finnish Americana* 8:6–11.

Leary, James P., ed. 1998. *Wisconsin Folklore.* Madison: University of Wisconsin Press.

Leary, James P. 2000. "From a Potato Hole." *Folklore Forum* 31(2): 47–48.

Leary, James P. 2001. *So Ole Says to Lena: Folk Humor of the Upper Midwest.* 2nd ed. Madison: University of Wisconsin Press.

Leary, James P. 2006a. "Dialect Jokes." In *The American Midwest: An Interpretive Encyclopedia*, edited by Andrew Cayton, John Richard Sisson, and Christian K. Zacher, 400–401. Bloomington: Indiana University Press.

Leary, James P. 2006b. "Norwegian Communities." In *Encyclopedia of American Folklife*, vol. 3, edited by Simon J. Bronner, 892–96. Armonk, NY: M. E. Sharpe.

Leary, James P. 2006c. *Polkabilly: How the Goose Island Ramblers Redefined American Folk Music.* Oxford: Oxford University Press.

Leary, James P. 2010. "Yksi Suuri Union: Field Recordings of Finnish American IWW Songs." *Journal of Finnish Studies* 14(1): 6–17.

Leary, James P. 2012. "Accordions and Working-Class Culture along Lake Superior's South Shore." In *The Accordion in the Americas: Klezmer, Polka, Tango, Zydeco, and More!*, edited by Helena Simonett, 136–55. Urbana: University of Illinois Press.

Leary, James P. 2015. *Folksongs of Another America: Field Recordings from the Upper Midwest, 1937–1946.* Madison: University of Wisconsin Press.

Leary, James P. 2019. "Jälkisanat. Lost Treasures Found." In *Songs of the Finnish Migration: A Bilingual Anthology*, edited by Thomas A. DuBois and B. Marcus Cederström, 220–24. Madison: University of Wisconsin Press.

Leary, James P. 2021. "'The Swede from North Dakota': Explicating a Euro-American Folksong." *Ethnologia Scandinavica* 51(1): 23–46.

Leary, James P., and Janet C. Gilmore. 1987. "Cultural Forms, Personal Visions." In *From Hardanger to Harleys: A Survey of Wisconsin Folk Art*, 13–22. Sheboygan, WI: John Michael Kohler Arts Center.

Leary, James P., and Richard March. 1996. *Down Home Dairyland: A Listener's Guide.* Madison: University of Wisconsin–Extension.

Leary, James, P., and Guha Shankar. 2015. *Alan Lomax Goes North.* DVD included with Leary, *Folksongs of Another America.* Madison: University of Wisconsin Press. https://search.library.wisc .edu/digital/AL4BUOBXWV7MEN8F.

Leathem, Hilary Morgan. 2019. "Manifestations That Matter: A Case of Oaxacan Ruin Possession." *Archaeological Review from Cambridge: Beyond the Human* 34(2): 92–110.

Lehto, Steve. 2013. *Death's Door: The Truth behind the Italian Hall Disaster and the Strike of 1913.* 2nd ed. Royal Oak, MI: Momentum Books.

Lehtola, Veli-Pekka. 2004. *The Sámi People: Traditions in Transition.* Fairbanks: University of Alaska Press.

Leithauser, Brad. 2001. "Golden Notebooks." *New York Review of Books,* December 20. https://www.nybooks.com/articles/2001/12/20/golden-notebooks/.

Levin, Amy K. 2007. "Why Local Museums Matter." In *Defining Memory: Local Museums and the Construction of History in America's Changing Communities,* edited by Amy K. Levin, 9–26. Lanham, MD: AltaMira Press.

Levitan, Stuart. 2018. *Madison in the Sixties.* Madison: Wisconsin Historical Society Press.

Lévy-Zumwalt, Rosemary. 1992. *Wealth and Rebellion: Elsie Clews Parsons, Anthropologist and Folklorist.* Urbana: University of Illinois Press.

"LGBT OH Project." n.d. Box 4. Accession 2014-038, Oral History Program Office Files, University Archives, Madison, WI.

Library and Archives Canada. n.d. *Virtual Gramophone: Canadian Historical Sound Recordings.* https://www.bac-lac.gc.ca/eng/discover/films-videos-sound-recordings/virtual-gramophone/Pages/virtual-gramophone.aspx.

Literat, Ioana, and Sandra Markus. 2020. "'Crafting a Way Forward': Online Participation, Craftivism and Civic Engagement in Ravelry's Pussyhat Project Group." *Information, Communication & Society* 23(10): 1411–26.

Little Finland. n.d. "About: National Finnish American Festival." Accessed August 17, 2018. http://www.littlefinland.org/what-we-do.

Lockwood, William G., and Yvonne R. Lockwood. 2000. "Continuity and Adaptation in Arab American Foodways." In *Arab Detroit: From Margin to Mainstream,* edited by Nabeel Abraham and Andrew Shryock, 515–49. Detroit: Wayne State University Press.

Lockwood, Yvonne R. 1984. "The Joy of Labor." *Western Folklore* 43(3): 191, 202–11.

Lockwood, Yvonne R. 1987. "The Sauna: An Expression of Finnish-American Identity." In *Michigan Folklife Reader,* edited by C. Kurt Dewhurst and Yvonne R. Lockwood, 307–20. East Lansing: Michigan State University Press.

Lockwood, Yvonne R., and William G. Lockwood. 1991. "Pasties in Michigan's Upper Peninsula: Foodways, Interethnic Relations, and Regionalism." In *Creative Ethnicity,* edited by Stephen Stern and John A. Cicala, 3–20. Logan: Utah State University Press.

Lomax, John A. 1910. *Cowboy Songs and Other Frontier Ballads.* New York: Sturgis & Walton.

Lomax, John A., and Alan Lomax. 1934. *American Ballads and Folk Songs.* New York: Macmillan.

Lomnitz, Claudio. 2001. *Deep Mexico, Silent Mexico: An Anthropology of Nationalism.* Minneapolis: University of Minnesota Press.

Long, Amos W., Jr. 1990. "The General Store." *Pennsylvania Folklife* 39(3): 98–116.

Long, Lucy. 2004. *Culinary Tourism.* Lexington: University of Kentucky Press.

Louden, Mark L. 2016. *Pennsylvania Dutch: The Story of an American Language.* Baltimore: Johns Hopkins University Press.

Lux, Karen. 1990. *Folk Arts Programming in New York State: A Handbook and Resource Guide.* Syracuse, NY: Regional Council of Historic Agencies.

Lynn, Leslie. 1979. "Bay Port, Great Lakes Fishing Capital." *Chronicle* 14:4–5.

Lyons, Bertram, Rebecca Chandler, and Chris Lacinak. 2015. "Quantifying the Need: A Survey of Existing Sound Recordings in Collections in the United States." *AVPreserve.* https://www.avpreserve.com/wp-content/uploads/2017/07/QuantifyingTheNeed.pdf.

Macdowell, Marsha, and LuAnne G. Kozma. 2007. "Folkpatterns: A Place-Based Youth Cultural Heritage Education Program." *Journal of Museum Education* 32(3): 263–73.

Macpherson, Natalie Dawn. 1987. "Talk, Narrative, and Social Interaction in a Cape Breton General Store." Master's thesis, Memorial University of Newfoundland.

Madison.com. 2012. "Edseth, Olga M." *Madison.com*, September 7. https://madison.com/news /local/obituaries/edseth-olga-m/article_bd49142c-f850-11e1-8d69-001a4bcf887a.html.

"Madison's LGBTQ Community." n.d. University of Wisconsin–Madison Libraries. Accessed May 20, 2021. https://www.library.wisc.edu/archives/exhibits/madisons-lgbt-community-1960s-to -present/.

Mandell, Hinda, ed. 2019. *Crafting Dissent: Handicraft as Protest from the American Revolution to the Pussyhats.* Lanham, MD: Rowman & Littlefield.

Martin, Ann Smart, Cortney Anderson-Kramer, and Jared L. Schmidt. 2020. "The Triumph of Trolls: The Making, Re-making and Commercialization of Heritage Identity." In *Authenticity in North America: Place, Tourism, Heritage, Culture and the Popular Imagination*, edited by Jane Lovell and Sam Hitchmough, 145–60. London: Routledge.

Martin, Philip. 1989. *Rosemaling in the Upper Midwest: A Story of Region and Revival.* Mount Horeb: Wisconsin Folk Museum.

Massey, Doreen. 1995. *A Place in the World.* Oxford: Open University Press.

McAtackney, Laura. 2007. "The Contemporary Politics of Landscape at the Long Kesh/Maze Prison Site, Northern Ireland." In *Envisioning Landscape: Situations and Standpoints in Archaeology and Heritage*, edited by Dan Hicks, Laura McAtackney, and Graham Fairclough, 30–52. Walnut Creek, CA: Left Coast Press.

McCarthy, Charles. 1912. *The Wisconsin Idea.* New York: Macmillan.

McClintock, Harry "Haywire Mac." 1972. *Haywire Mac.* New York: Folkways Records.

McComas Coberly, Lenore. 2005."The Fellowship at Wysong's Clearing." In *Writers Have No Age: Creative Writing for Older Adults*, edited by Lenore McComas Coberly, Jeri McCormick, and Karen Updike, 85–91. Binghamton, NY: Haworth Press.

McDowell, Colin. 1989. *Shoes: Fashion and Fantasy.* New York: Rizzoli International Publications.

McDowell, John Holmes. 2018. "Folklore and Sociolinguistics." *Humanities* 7(1): 9.

Mead, Margaret. 1975. "Visual Anthropology in a Discipline of Words." In *Principles of Visual Anthropology*, edited by Paul Hockings, 3–10. The Hague: Mouton.

"Midwest OH Group." n.d. Box 2, Accession 2014–038, Oral History Program Office Files, University Archives, Madison, WI.

Miller, Doug. 1992. *Interviews with Jane Farwell.* Dodgeville, WI. Transcribed by Amy McFarland. Internal document, Folklore Village.

Milligan, Sarah. 2012. "Intersections of Sister Fields." *Oxford University Press Blog*, October 12. https://blog.oup.com/2012/10/intersections-of-oral-history-folklore/.

Mills Music Library Special Collections. n.d. "History." Mills Music Library, University of Wisconsin–Madison. Accessed June 14, 2021. https://www.library.wisc.edu/music/about-music /history/.

Milwaukee Journal. 1926. "It Was a Corking Yarn and How It Did Travel." May 4, 25, 31.

Moen, Per. 1988. "The English Pronunciation of Norwegian-Americans in Four Midwestern States." *American Studies in Scandinavia* 20:105–121.

Molloy, Courtney L., and Clifford R. Murphy. 2017. *Qualitative Analysis Project Findings: Folk and Traditional Arts Partnership Grants.* Washington, DC: National Endowment for the Arts.

Monroe Evening Times. 1974. "Mineral Point Girl to Holland for Fest." July 25, 4.

Moquin, Laura, and Joseph Salmons. 2020. "Scandinavian-American English over Time: Stereotypes and Regionalization." *Ampersand* 7.

Moriggi, Angela, Katriina Soini, Bettina B. Bock, and Dirk Roep. 2020. "Caring in, for, and with Nature: An Integrative Framework to Understand Green Care Practices." *Sustainability* 12(8): 3361.

Mount Horeb Area Historical Society. 1986. *Mount Horeb—Presettlement to 1986: A History Celebrating Mount Horeb's Quasquicentennial.* Blanchardville, WI: Ski Printers.

Mount Horeb Area Historical Society. 2017. *Creators, Collectors and Communities: Making Ethnic Identity through Objects: An Exhibition Catalogue.* Mount Horeb, WI: Mount Horeb Area Historical Society.

Mount Horeb Area Historical Society. n.d. "Historical Society Acquires Little Norway Artifacts." Accessed June 1, 2021. http://www.mthorebhistory.org/little-norway.html.

Munkel, Arnold. 1974. "Wedding Dance Recording from October 12." https://search.library.wisc.edu/embed/audio/LocalCenters08/eu99-9B2.

Murphy, Clifford R. 2016. "Message from the Director of the Folk and Traditional Arts Program." 2016 National Heritage Fellowships. Washington, DC: National Endowment for the Arts.

Musello, Christopher. 1992. "Objects in Process: Material Culture and Communication." *Southern Folklore* 49(1): 37–59.

Myall, James. 2012. *Franco-Americans in New England: Statistics from the American Community Survey.* State of Maine Legislative Franco-American Task Force. https://digitalcommons.usm.maine.edu/fac-original-research/2/.

National Endowment for the Arts. 2016. "Creating a New Tradition to Honor the NEA National Heritage Fellows." *Art Works Blog,* September 26. https://www.arts.gov/art-works/2016/creating-new-tradition-honor-nea-national-heritage-fellows.

National Endowment for the Arts. 2019. *Living Traditions: A Portfolio Analysis of the National Endowment for the Arts' Folk and Traditional Arts Program.* Washington, DC: National Endowment for the Arts.

National Endowment for the Arts. n.d.(a). "NEA National Heritage Fellowships." Accessed January 11, 2020. https://www.arts.gov/lifetime-honors/nea-national-heritage-fellowships/make-nomination.

National Endowment for the Arts. n.d.(b). *Folk and Traditional Arts Fact Sheet.* Accessed August 1, 2020. https://www.arts.gov/sites/default/files/Folk_FactSheet_7.15.19.pdf.

National Park Service. n.d. "Keweenaw's Copper Story." *Keweenaw National Historical Park.* Accessed July 8, 2020. https://www.nps.gov/kewe/index.htm.

Nelson, Brad. 2017. Interview with Sallie Anna Steiner, Two Harbors, MN, August 8.

Nelson, Marion J. 1989. "Folk Art in Minnesota and the Case of the Norwegian American." In *Circles of Tradition: Folk Arts in Minnesota,* edited by University of Minnesota Art Museum, 24–44. St. Paul: Minnesota Historical Society Press.

Nelson, Marion J. 1995. "Folk Art of Norway." In *Norwegian Folk Art: The Migration of a Tradition,* edited by Marion J. Nelson, 37–72. New York: Abbeville Press.

Nelson-Strauss, Brenda, Samuel Brylawski, and Alan Gevinson. 2012. *The Library of Congress National Recording Preservation Plan.* Library of Congress. Washington, DC: Council on Library and Information Resources.

Nemanic, Mary Lou. 2007. *One Day for Democracy: Independence Day and the Americanization of Iron Range Immigrants.* Athens: Ohio University Press.

Nickel, Adam. 2019. "AV Digitization by the Numbers: Data from UNC-Chapel Hill's Expanding the Reach of Southern Audiovisual Sources Andrew W. Mellon Foundation Grant." *Media Digitization and Preservation Initiative Blog*, December 13. https://blogs.iu.edu/mdpi/2019/12/13/av -digitization-by-the-numbers-data-from-unc-chapel-hills-expanding-the-reach-of-southern -audiovisual-sources-andrew-w-mellon-foundation-grant/.

Noddings, Nel. 2013. *Caring: A Relational Approach to Ethics and Moral Education*. Berkeley: University of California Press.

Nowinski, Joseph, and Stuart Baker. 2012. *The Twelve Step Facilitation Handbook: A Systematic Approach to Recovery from Substance Dependence*. New York: Simon and Schuster.

Okkonen, Wilho H. n.d. "Eino and Helvi Okkonen." *Herbster History*. Accessed June 4, 2021. https://herbsterwisconsin.com/okkonen-eino-and-helvi/.

Oldenburg, Ray. 1989. *The Great Good Place: Cafés, Coffee Shops, Community Centers, Beauty Parlors, General Stores, Bars, Hangouts and How They Get You through the Day*. New York: Paragon House.

Oring, Elliot. 2008. "Legendry and the Rhetoric of Truth." *Journal of American Folklore* 121(480): 127–66.

Österlund-Pötzsch, Susanne. 2003. *American Plus: Etnisk identitet hos finlandssvenska ättlingar i Nordamerika*. Helsinki, Finland: Svenska litteratursällskapet i Finland.

Overmyer-Velázquez, Mark. 2006. *Visions of the Emerald City: Modernity, Tradition, and the Formation of Porfirian Oaxaca, Mexico*. Durham, NC: Duke University Press.

Palleiro, María Inés. 2014. "Haunted Houses and Haunting Girls: Life and Death in Contemporary Argentinian Folk Narrative." In *Vernacular Religion in Everyday Life: Expressions of Belief*, edited by Marion Bowman and Ülo Valk, 211–29. London: Routledge.

Pape, Alan C. 2008. *The Historical, Architectural Analysis, and Restoration Plan for the Aslak Olsen Lie House*. Produced for Folklore Village.

Parrish, Lydia. (1940) 1965. *Slave Songs of the Georgia Sea Islands*. Hatboro, PA: Folklore Associates.

Parsons, Elsie Clews. 1936. *Mitla: Town of Souls*. Chicago: University of Chicago Press.

Patterson, Glenn, and Laura Risk. 2014. "Digitization, Recirculation and Reciprocity: Proactive Archiving for Community and Memory on the Gaspé Coast and Beyond." *MUSICultures* 41(2): 102–32.

Pavlovskaya, Marianna. 2017. "Qualitative GIS." In *International Encyclopedia of Geography: People, the Earth, Environment and Technology*, edited by Douglas Richardson, Noel Castree, Michael F. Goodchild, Audrey Lynn Kobayashi, and Weidong Liu, 1–11. Hoboken, NJ: John Wiley & Sons.

Pawley, Christine. 2010. *Reading Places: Literacy, Democracy, and the Public Library in Cold War America*. Amherst: University of Massachusetts Press.

Pellerin, Martha. 1997. Interview with Gregory Sharrow, Vermont Folklife Center Archive, January 23.

Peterson, Elizabeth. 2018. "Functions and Social Meanings of Agreement Marker *ja* in Sanpete County English." Paper presented at the 9th Workshop on Immigrant Languages in the Americas. University of Wisconsin–Eau Claire, October 25–27.

Pettan, Svanibor, and Jeff Todd Titon. 2019. *Public Ethnomusicology, Education, Archives, and Commerce: An Oxford Handbook of Applied Ethnomusicology*. New York: Oxford University Press.

Pittsburgh Chapter of the American Red Cross. 1922. *Pittsburgh Chapter of the American Red Cross: A History of the Activities of the Chapter from its Organization to January 1, 1921, with an Appendix Containing All Available Names of those who Rendered Red Cross Service During that Period*. Pittsburgh: Pittsburgh Printing Company.

Poole, W. Scott. 2004. *Never Surrender: Confederate Memory and Conservatism in the South Carolina Upcountry*. Athens: University of Georgia Press.

Porterfield, Nolan. 1996. *Last Cavalier: The Life and Times of John A. Lomax, 1867–1948*. Urbana: University of Illinois Press.

Powell, Benjamin D., and Tracy Stephenson Shaffer. 2009. "On the Haunting of Performance Studies." *Liminalities: A Journal of Performance Studies* 5(1): 1–19.

Prown, Jules David. 1982. "Mind in Matter: An Introduction to Material Culture Theory and Method." *Winterthur Portfolio* 17(1): 1–19.

Pryor, Anne. 2004. "Deep Ethnography: Culture at the Core of Curriculum." *Language Arts* 81:396–406.

Pryor, Anne, Debbie Kmetz, Ruth Olson, and Steven A. Ackerman. 2011. "Here at Home: Learning Local Culture Pedagogy through Cultural Tours." In *Through the Schoolhouse Door: Folklore, Community, Curriculum*, edited by Paddy Bowman and Lynne Hamer, 68–98. Logan: Utah State University Press.

Pudas, Ed. 1977. "Autobiography, 1977." Unpublished manuscript.

Puig de la Bellacasa, Maria. 2017. *Matters of Care: Speculative Ethics in More Than Human Worlds*. Minneapolis: University of Minnesota Press.

Puotinen, Arthur E. 1977. "Early Labor Organizations in the Copper Country." In *For the Common Good: Finnish Immigrants and the Radical Response to Industrial America*, edited by Michael G. Karni and Douglas J. Ollila Jr., 119–66. Superior, WI: Työmies Society.

Puotinen, Arthur E. 1979. *Finnish Radicals and Religion in Midwestern Mining Towns, 1865–1914*. New York: Arno Press.

Purnell, Thomas. 2010. "Phonetic Detail in the Perception of Ethnic Varieties of US English." In *A Reader in Sociophonetics*, edited by Dennis Preston and Nancy Niedzielski, 289–326. Berlin: Mouton de Gruyter.

Ranković, Slavica. 2013. "The Temporality of the (Immanent) Saga: Tinkering with Formulas." In *Dating the Sagas: Reviews and Revisions*, edited by Else Mundal, 119–54. Copenhagen: Museum Tusculanum Press.

Reed, Josephine. 2013. "Interview of Sheila Kay Adams." September 12. https://www.arts.gov/honors/heritage/fellows/sheila-kay-adams.

Reed, Josephine. 2015. "Interview of Wayne Henderson." Podcast. National Endowment for the Arts, July 9. https://www.arts.gov/honors/heritage/fellows/wayne-henderson.

Reeves, Troy. 2002. "Beginnings in Oral History: Or How One Man and Two Women Helped Give Birth to an Oral Historian." *Oral History Review* 29(2): 93–95.

Reeves, Troy. 2017a. "What Is(n't) Oral History. Or, the Rise of the 'Oral History of [Fill in the Blank].'" *HumanitiesBooyah*. https://web.archive.org/web/20191211222335/https://www.wisconsinhumanities.org/dont-have-a-cow/.

Reeves, Troy. 2017b. "What's Oral History and Why Does It Matter?" TEDx talk. https://www.youtube.com/watch?v=3trF-14PUsQ.

Reeves, Troy, and Sarah Lange. n.d. "UW–Madison Book Arts: An Oral History." Accessed August 26, 2020. https://www.library.wisc.edu/archives/exhibits/uw-madison-book-arts-an-oral-history/.

Rennier, Michael. 2018. "Protest Signs Are a New Folk-Art." *Dappled Things*. https://dappledthings.org/11013/protest-signs-are-a-new-folk-art/.

Rentzhog, Sten. 2007. *Open Air Museums: The History and Future of a Visionary Idea*. Jamtli Förlag and Carlsson Bokförlag.

Reynolds, William, and James K. Zimmerman. 2015. "Go-Go, the Funky, Percussive Music Invented in Washington, D.C." *Smithsonian Museum of Natural History Blog*, June 9. https://americanhistory.si.edu/blog/go-go-washington-dc.

Robinson, Emily. 2010. "Touching the Void: Affective History and the Impossible." *Rethinking History* 14(4): 503–520.

Robles García, Nelly. 2016. *Mitla: Su desarollo cultural e importancia regional.* Mexico City: Fondo de Cultura Económica.

Rose, Mark. 2005. "When Giants Roamed the Earth: In the Golden Age of Hoaxes, Petrified Men Came to Life." *Archaeology* 58(6). https://archive.archaeology.org/0511/etc/giants.html.

Rosemont, Franklin, ed. 1992. *Juice Is Stranger than Friction: Selected Writings of T-Bone Slim.* Chicago: Charles H. Kerr.

Ross, Ken, and Louis V. Galdieri, dirs. 2013. *1913 Massacre.* Film. 65 minutes. New York: Dreamland Pictures.

Rotto, Beth Hoven. 2013. Interview with Anna Rue, Decorah, IA, August 23.

Royal Montreal Curling Club. 1807. Charter documents. Unpublished.

Rue, Anna. 2014. "From Revival to Remix: Norwegian American Folk Music and Song." PhD diss., University of Wisconsin–Madison.

Rue, Anna. 2018. "'It Breaths Norwegian Life': Heritage Making at Vesterheim Norwegian American Museum." *Scandinavian Studies* 90(3): 350–75.

Runyon, Carl, and Randy K. Mills. 2008. "'The Most Wonderful Thing I Have Ever Seen': Indiana's Contribution to Petrified Man Hoaxes." *Indiana Magazine of History* 104(4): 367–78.

Rusk County Journal. 1926. "State Historian Says Petrified Man Story Is Bunk" 26(44): 1. March 4.

Rusk County Lyre. 1926a. "The Petrified Man." *Eau Claire Leader*, February 24, 5.

Rusk County Lyre. 1926b. "Tells of Unearthing Body of Explorer Near Murry." *Rusk County Journal*, January 21, 1, 6.

Saarela, Tauno, ed. 1997. *Talonpoikainen Sosialisti: Santeri Mäkelä Poliittisena Toimijana ja Kirjailijana.* Helsinki, Finland: Työväen Historian ja Perinteen Tutkimuksen Seura.

Salmons, Joseph. 2019. "The Laryngeal Phonetics and Phonology of Norwegian-American English /s ~ z/." In *Fonologi, sosiolingvistikk og vitenskapsteori: Festskrift til Gjert Kristoffersen*, edited by Jan Kristian Hognestad, Torodd Kinn, and Terje Lohndal, 257–73. Oslo, Norway: Novus.

Saltzman, Rachelle Hope, ed. 2020. *Pussy Hats, Politics, and Public Protest.* Jackson: University Press of Mississippi.

Sampson, Kim. 2018. Interview with Rhonda Dass, Biwabik, MN, July 27.

Sandburg, Carl. 1927. *The American Songbag.* New York: Harcourt, Brace.

Sanders, Laurel. 2017. Interview with Sallie Anna Steiner, Duluth, MN, November 19.

Sånglöf, Sharelle. 2013. "Mock Scandihoovian: The Dialect of Ole and Lena." Master's thesis, University of Uppsala.

Saucier, Joseph. 1910. *Les Montagnards, ou, Tyrolienne des Pyrénées.* St. Louis, MO: Columbia Phonograph Company.

Savoy, Ann Allen, ed. 1984. *Cajun Music: A Reflection of a People.* Vol. 1. Eunice, LA: Bluebird Press.

Sawin, Patricia. 2017. "'Every Kid Is Where They're Supposed to Be, and It's a Miracle': Family Formation Stories among Adoptive Families." *Journal of American Folklore* 130(518): 394–418.

Saylor, Nicole. 2006. "Survey of Public Folklore Collections in the Upper Midwest." Center for the Study of Upper Midwestern Cultures, University of Wisconsin–Madison. https://csumc.wisc.edu/wp-content/uploads/sites/1101/2019/05/NHPRC_final_report_09-2.pdf.

Schafer, Joseph. 1926. "The Petrified Man." *Wisconsin History Bulletin* 12(11): 2–3.

Scheips, Paul. 1971. *Hold the Fort!* Washington, DC: Smithsonian Press.

Schwartz, Joan M., and Terry Cook. 2002. "Archives, Records, and Power: The Making of Modern Memory." *Archival Science* 2(1): 1–19.

See, Scott F. 2013. "Keweenaw National Historical Park: Heritage Partnerships in an Industrial Landscape." PhD diss., Michigan Technological University.

Sekula, Allan. 1986. "The Body and the Archive." *October* 39:3–64.

Sevenhuijsen, Selma. 2003. *Citizenship and the Ethics of Care: Feminist Considerations on Justice, Morality and Politics.* Translated from Dutch by Liz Savage. London: Routledge.

Sevenhuijsen, Selma L. 2018. "Care and Attention." *South African Journal of Higher Education* 32(6): 19–30.

Seyforth, Scott, and Nicole Barnes. 2016. "In People's Faces for Lesbian and Gay Rights." *Oral History Review* 43(1): 81–97.

Sharrow, Gregory. 2012. Unpublished grant proposal narrative.

Sheehy, Daniel. 2000. "Director's Message." National Heritage Fellowships 2000. National Endowment for the Arts, Washington, DC.

Shoemaker, Alfred L. 1940. "Studies on the Pennsylvania German Dialect of the Amish Community in Arthur, Illinois." PhD diss., University of Illinois.

Shoemaker, Alfred L., and Don Yoder, with Alliene Dechant, Edna Eby Heller, and Olive G. Zehner. 1955. *1955 Tourist Guide through the Dutch Country.* Lancaster: Pennsylvania Dutch Folklore Center, Franklin and Marshall College.

Shulman, George. 2011. "Acknowledgment and Disavowal as an Idiom for Theorizing Politics." *Theory & Event* 14(1).

Silvers, Jonathan, dir. 2013. *Red Metal: The Copper Country Strike of 1913.* Arlington, VA: PBS.

Simley, Anne. 1930. "A Study of Norwegian Dialect in Minnesota." *American Speech* 5:469–74.

Sinclair, John, Sir. 1793. *The Statistical Account of Scotland. Drawn Up from the Communications of the Ministers of the Different Parishes.* Vol. 7. Edinburgh: William Creech.

Skloot, Rebecca. 2010. *The Immortal Life of Henrietta Lacks.* New York: Crown.

Smith, Don C. 1941. "June 22, 1941 Letter to Mr Bondy." Folder 422.4: Knitted Articles Able Bodied, Box 658, Series 1935–1947, Record Group 200, American National Red Cross Central Decimal Files, National Archives at College Park, MD.

Smith, Laurajane. 2006. *Uses of Heritage.* London: Routledge.

Smith, Laurajane. 2015. "Theorizing Museums and Heritage Visiting." In *The International Handbook of Museum Studies,* vol. 1, *Museum Theory,* edited by Andrea Witcomb and Kylie Message, 459–84. Hoboken, NJ: Wiley-Blackwell.

Smithsonian. 2016. "Smithsonian Festival Visitor Survey." Unpublished.

Smithsonian. n.d. "Bess Lomax Hawes." Accessed June 1, 2021. https://folklife.si.edu/legacy -honorees/bess-lomax-hawes/smithsonian.

Solberg, Carolyn. 2019. Interview with Nathan Gibson, Stephanie Hoff, Anna Rue, and Meghan Sickel, Decorah, IA, June 19.

Sommers, Laurie. n.d. "Educational Resources." Association for Cultural Equity. http://www .culturalequity.org/resources/for-educators.

Spottswood, Richard K. 1982. "Commercial Ethnic Recordings in the United States." In *Ethnic Recordings in America: A Neglected Heritage,* 51–66. Washington, DC: American Folklife Center.

Stark, Jack. 1995. "The Wisconsin Idea: The University's Service to the State." In *State of Wisconsin 1995–1996 Blue Book,* edited by Wisconsin Legislative Reference Bureau, 2–3. Madison: Wisconsin Legislature Joint Committee on Legislative Organization.

Stefano, Michelle. 2018. "Engaging Collections: AFC Chicago Ethnic Arts Collection Gathering." *Folklife Today Blog,* Library of Congress, October 9. https://blogs.loc.gov/folklife/2018/10 /engaging-collections-afc-chicago-ethnic-arts-collection-gathering.

Stefano, Michelle. 2019. "Folklife at the International Level: Roots of Intangible Cultural Heritage. Part VII, Treasures." *Folklife Today Blog*, Library of Congress, June 20. https://blogs.loc.gov /folklife/2019/06/folklife-at-the-international-level-roots-of-intangible-cultural-heritage-part -vii-treasures/.

Steiner, Sallie Anna. 2016. "Woven Identities: Socioeconomic Change, Women's Agency, and the Making of a Heritage Art in Jølster, Norway." *Journal of Ethnology and Folkloristics* 10(2): 81–101.

Stern, Stephen. 1991. "Introduction." In *Creative Ethnicity: Symbols and Strategies of Contemporary Ethnic Life*, edited by Stephen Stern and John Allan Cicala, xi–xx. Logan: Utah State University Press.

Stewart, Janice S. 1999. *The Folk Arts of Norway*. 3rd ed. Rhinelander, WI: Nordhus Publishers.

Stinson, Craig. 1998. "You Can Get Anything You Want at La Tienda San Jose." In *Wisconsin Folklife: A Celebration of Wisconsin Traditions*, edited by Marshall Cook, 36–39. Madison: Wisconsin Academy of Sciences, Arts and Letters.

Suk, Jiyoun, Aman Abhishek, Yini Zhang, So Yun Ahn, Teresa Correa, Christine Garlough, and Dhavan V. Shah. 2021. "#MeToo, Networked Acknowledgment, and Connective Action: How 'Empowerment through Empathy' Launched a Social Movement." *Social Science Computer Review* 39(2): 276–94.

Suter, John W., ed. 1994. *Working with Folk Materials in New York State: A Manual for Folklorists and Archivists*. Ithaca, NY: New York Folklore Society.

Szwed, John. 2010. *Alan Lomax: The Man Who Recorded the World*. New York: Viking Penguin.

Tagg, John. 1988. *The Burden of Representation: Essays on Photographies and Histories*. Minneapolis: University of Minnesota Press.

Tallmadge, James D., and Emily Tallmadge. 1886. *Labor Songs Dedicated to the Knights of Labor*. Chicago: J. D. Tallmadge.

Tarkow, Elizabeth. 1977. Interview by Laura Smail. OH #0104. Digital audio file and typed transcript. University Archives, Madison, WI.

Tatian, Peter, and Serena Lei. n.d. "Chapter 1: Demographics." Urban Institute. Washington, DC: Our Changing City.

Taussig, Michael. 2011. *I Swear I Saw This: Drawings in Fieldwork Notebooks, Namely My Own*. Chicago: University of Chicago Press.

Teixeira, Samantha. 2018. "Qualitative Geographic Information Systems (GIS): An Untapped Research Approach for Social Work." *Qualitative Social Work* 17(1): 9–23.

Terrill, John M. 1985. *Ladysmith Lore: A Centennial View*. Ladysmith, WI: Ladysmith Centennial Steering Committee.

Teske, Robert T., ed. 1987. *From Hardanger to Harleys: A Survey of Wisconsin Folk Art*. Exhibition catalog. Sheboygan, WI: John Michael Kohler Arts Center.

Teske, Robert T., ed. 1990. *In Tune with Tradition: Wisconsin Folk Musical Instruments*. Exhibition catalog. Cedarburg, WI: Cedarburg Cultural Center.

Teske, Robert T., ed. 1994. *Passed to the Present: Folk Arts along Wisconsin's Ethnic Settlement Trail*. Exhibition catalog. Cedarburg, WI: Cedarburg Cultural Center.

Teske, Robert T., ed. 1998. *Wisconsin Folk Art: A Sesquicentennial Celebration*. Exhibition catalog. Cedarburg, WI: Cedarburg Cultural Center.

Theimer, Kate. 2012. "Archives in Context and as Context." *Journal of Digital Humanities* 1(2). http:// journalofdigitalhumanities.org/1-2/archives-in-context-and-as-context-by-kate-theimer/.

Thompson, E. P. 1966. *The Making of the English Working Class*. London: Vintage Books.

Tikkanen, Oren. 2014. "Challenging Folk Icons: Rewriting Woody and Santeri." Conference paper, Retrospection and Respect: The 1913/14 Mining/Labor Strike Symposium, Michigan Technological University, Houghton, MI, April 12.

Tikkanen, Oren. 2018. Interview with John Prusynski, Laurium, MI, June 20.

Tikkanen, Oren. 2019. Interview with Hilary-Joy Virtanen and Michael Loukinen, Centennial Heights, MI, June 22.

Tin, Mikkel. 2013. "Making and the Sense It Makes." *Techne Series: Research in Sloyd Education and Craft Science* 20(3): 1–4.

Toelken, Barre. 1996. *The Dynamics of Folklore*. Logan: Utah State University Press.

Toelken, Barre. 1998. "The Yellowman Tapes, 1966–1997." *Journal of American Folklore* 111(442): 381–91.

Toelken, Barre. 2003. *The Anguish of Snails: Native American Folklore in the West*. Logan: Utah State University Press.

Toiviainen, Lauri. 2011. *Kanadan Suomalainen Kulttuuriliitto 1971–2011*. Toronto: Finn Cultural Federation Board.

Träskelin, Jimmy. 2019. *Lähtölaulu: A Song of Departure*. Album. Kaustinen, Finland: Kansanmusiikki-instituutti.

Träskelin, Jimmy. 2021. "Tallari History." https://www.tallari.net/en/index.php/yhtye/historia/.

Tronto, Joan C. 1993. *Moral Boundaries: A Political Argument for an Ethic of Care*. New York: Routledge.

Tronto, Joan C. 2003. "Time's Place." *Feminist Theory* 4(2): 119–38.

Tronto, Joan C. 2013. *Caring Democracy: Markets, Equality, and Justice*. New York: New York University Press.

Tronto, Joan C. 2018. "Care as a Political Concept." In *Revisioning The Political: Feminist Reconstructions of Traditional Concepts in Western Political Theory*, edited by Nancy J. Hirschmann and Christine Di Stefano, 139–56. New York: Taylor and Francis.

Trouillot, Michel-Rolph. 1995. *Silencing the Past: Power and the Production of History*. Boston: Beacon.

Twining, Mary A. 2016. *Sea Islands Heritage: Resonances of Africa in Diasporic Communities*. Alpharetta, GA: BookLogix.

Tye, Diane. 2017. "When Mary Went through the Hole: Constructing and Contesting Individual and Family Identity through Narrative." *Journal of American Folklore* 130(518): 419–37.

United Auto Workers. n.d. *UAW-CIO Sings*. Detroit: United Auto Workers, International Education Department.

United Nations Educational, Scientific, and Cultural Organization. n.d. "Guidelines for the Establishment of National 'Living Human Treasures' Systems." Accessed June 27, 2020. https://ich.unesco.org/doc/src/00031-EN.pdf.

University of Wisconsin Digital Collections Center. n.d. "UWDCC." https://www.library.wisc.edu/uwdcc/.

University of Wisconsin–Madison. n.d. "The Wisconsin Idea." Accessed June 1, 2021. https://www.wisc.edu/wisconsin-idea/.

"University of Wisconsin–Madison Audio Preservation Survey and Report." 2007. Box 1, 2014-038, Oral History Program Office Files, University Archives, Madison, WI.

University of Wisconsin–Madison Communication. n.d. "#UWRightNow." Accessed August 27, 2019. https://wayback.archive-it.org/org-131/20120419132841/http://uwrightnow.wisc.edu/user-story/troy-reeves-uw-oral-history-project/.

Utepils Brewing. n.d. "Broomstacker Red Lager." Accessed December 15, 2018. https://utepilsbrewing
.com/beers/broomstacker/#.

Uther, Hans-Jörg. 2004. *The Types of International Folktales: A Classification and Bibliography, Based
on the System of Antti Aarne and Stith Thompson*. Helsinki, Finland: Suomalainen Tiedeakatemia,
Academia Scientiarum Fennica.

Valley, Greer. 2019. "Decolonization Can't Just Be a Metaphor." *Africa Is a Country*, November 12.
https://africasacountry.com/2019/11/decolonization-cant-just-be-a-metaphor.

Van Hise, Charles. 1905. "Address before Press Association." https://www.wisc.edu/pdfs/VanHise
BeneficentAddress.pdf.

Vennum, Thomas, Jr. 1991. "In Tune with Tradition: Wisconsin Folk Musical Instruments, Cedarburg Cultural Center." Review. *Journal of American Folklore* 104(413): 345–48.

Vermont State Advisory Committee. 1983. *Franco-Americans in Vermont: A Civil Rights Perspective*.
Washington, DC: US Commission on Civil Rights.

Vikingland Curling Club. n.d. "Curling Tips." Accessed September 5, 2018. https://www.vikingland
curling.org/learntocurl/curling-tips.

Virtanen, Hilary-Joy. 2010. "What Official History Forgets Lives on in Song: On a Finnish American Parody of 'It's a Long Way to Tipperary.'" *Journal of Finnish Studies* 14(1): 46–52.

Virtanen, Hilary-Joy. 2020. "'Do You Claim Exemption from Draft?' Voicing Dissent through the
World War I Draft Card." In *Home Front in the American Heartland: Local Experiences and Legacies
of World War I*, edited by Patty Sotirin, Steven A. Walton, and Sue Collins, 85–111. Newcastle
upon Tyne, UK: Cambridge Scholars Press.

Wagler, Mark, Ruth Olson, and Anne Pryor. 2004. *Kids' Guide to Local Culture*. Madison, WI: Madison Children's Museum.

Walford, Jonathan. 2007. *The Seductive Shoe: Four Centuries of Fashion Footwear*. London: Thames
and Hudson.

Walker, David A. 1979. *Iron Frontier: The Discovery and Early Development of Minnesota's Three
Ranges*. St. Paul: Minnesota Historical Society Press.

Ward, Daniel Franklin, ed. 1984. *Personal Places: Perspectives on Informal Art Environments*. Bowling
Green, OH: Bowling Green State University Popular Press.

Watson, Jeanne, and Robert J. Potter. 1962. "An Analytic Unit for the Study of Interaction." *Human
Relations* 15:245–63.

Watson, Nicholas. 1999. "Desire for the Past/Afterword." *Studies in the Age of Chaucer* 21(1): 59–97.

Wauwatosa Curling Club. n.d. "About the Wauwatosa Curling Club." Accessed September 5, 2018.
https://wauwatosacurlingclub.com.

Weaver-Zercher, David. 2001. *The Amish in the American Imagination*. Baltimore: Johns Hopkins
University Press.

Widmayer, Christine J., and B. Marcus Cederström. 2020. "The University of Wisconsin–Madison's
Folklore Program and the Wisconsin Idea." In *Folklore in the United States and Canada: An Insti-
tutional History*, edited by Patricia Sawin and Rosemary Lévy Zumwalt, 213–21. Bloomington:
Indiana University Press.

Wilkerson, Miranda, and Joseph Salmons. 2008. "'Good Old Immigrants of Yesteryear' Who Didn't
Learn English: Germans in Wisconsin." *American Speech* 83(3): 259–83.

Wilkerson, Miranda, and Joseph Salmons. 2019. "Leaving Their Mark: How Wisconsin Came to
Sound German." In *English in the German-Speaking World*, edited by Raymond Hickey, 362–84.
Cambridge: Cambridge University Press.

Wilson, Shawn. 2008. *Research Is Ceremony: Indigenous Research Methods*. Halifax, Nova Scotia, Canada: Fernwood.

Winick, Stephen, and Peter Bartis. (1979) 2016. *Folklife and Fieldwork: An Introduction to Cultural Documentation*. Washington, DC: American Folklife Center. https://www.loc.gov/folklife /fieldwork/pdf/FolklifeandFieldwork2016forWeb.pdf.

Wintturi, Helmer Olavi. 1981. "Field notes by James P. Leary." January 7. Ethnic Music in Northern Wisconsin and Michigan Collection, Mills Music Library, University of Wisconsin–Madison. https://search.library.wisc.edu/digital/ASCYYYHNNRZFZG8O.

"WI Oral History Day." n.d. Box 2, Accession 2014-038, Oral History Program Office Files, University Archives, Madison, WI.

Wisconsin Governor. 2019. Wisconsin 19th Amendment Suffrage Centennial Celebration Committee. https://womenvotewi.wi.gov/Pages/home.aspx.

Wisconsin Historical Society. 2019a. "Suffrage Toolkit." https://wisconsinhistory.org/pdfs/whs -womens-suffrage-toolkit.pdf.

Wisconsin Historical Society. 2019b. "Wisconsin Historical Society, First Lady Evers: Launch Suffrage Centennial Video Series." https://my.lwv.org/wisconsin/article/wisconsin-historical -society-first-lady-evers-launch-suffrage-centennial-video-series.

Wisconsin Historical Society. n.d. "Petrified Man Hoax." *Dictionary of Wisconsin History*. Madison: Wisconsin Historical Society. Accessed December 29, 2021. https://www.wisconsinhistory.org /Records/Article/CS1834.

"Wisconsin Historical Society." n.d. Box 2, Accession 2014-038, Oral History Program Office Files, University Archives, Madison, WI.

Wisconsin Natural Resources Conservation Service. 2019. "Bayfield County Success from the Field: Creating Wetland Habitat at the Oulu Cultural and Heritage Center." *Successes from the Field Series*, December. https://www.nrcs.usda.gov/wps/portal/nrcs/detail/wi/newsroom/stories/?cid =nrcseprd1513431.

"Wisconsin Story Project/Sterling Hall Bombing." n.d. File Cabinet, Oral History Program Office Files, University Archives, Madison, WI.

Wisconsin Teachers of Local Culture. n.d. "Park Street Cultural Tour in 2003–2004." Accessed October 18, 2019. https://wtlc.csumc.wisc.edu/park-street-cultural-tour/.

Wolf, Kirsten. 2006. "The Color Blue in Old Norse-Icelandic Literature." *Scripta Islandica* 57:55–78.

Wood, Anna Lomax. 2018a. "Like a Cry from the Heart: An Insider's View of the Genesis of Alan Lomax's Ideas and the Legacy of His Research: Part I." *Ethnomusicology* 62(2): 230–64.

Wood, Anna Lomax. 2018b. "Like a Cry from the Heart: An Insider's View of the Genesis of Alan Lomax's Ideas and the Legacy of His Research: Part II." *Ethnomusicology* 62(3): 403–38.

World Economic Forum. 2019. "Global Gender Gap Report 2020." https://www3.weforum.org /docs/WEF_GGGR_2020.pdf.

World Prison Brief. n.d. "Highest to Lowest: Prison Population Rate." Institute for Crime and Justice Policy Research, Birkbeck, University of London. Accessed January 26, 2020. https://www .prisonstudies.org/highest-to-lowest/prison_population_rate?field_region_taxonomy_tid=All.

Yanarella, Ernest J., and Susan Blankenship. 2006. "Big House on the Rural Landscape: Prison Recruitment as a Policy Tool of Local Economic Development." *Journal of Appalachian Studies* 12(2): 110–39.

Yocom, Peggy. 1997. "Family Folklore." In *Folklore: An Encyclopedia of Beliefs, Customs, Tales, Music, and Art*, edited by Thomas A. Green, 278–84. Santa Barbara, CA: ABC-CLIO.

Yoder, Don. 2001. *Discovering American Folklife: Essays on Folk Culture and the Pennsylvania Dutch.* Mechanicsburg, PA: Stackpole Books.

Yoshimura, Ayako. 2009. "Oriental Shop: An Ethnography of Material Communication Inside an Asian Grocery Store in Madison, Wisconsin." Master's thesis, Memorial University of Newfoundland.

Yoshimura, Ayako. 2011. "Asian American Grocery Stores." In *Encyclopedia of Asian American Folklore and Folklife*, 3 vols., edited by Jonathan H. X. Lee and Kathleen M. Nadeau, 1:21–23. Santa Barbara, CA: ABC-CLIO.

Zaniewski, Kazimierz J., and Carol J. Rosen. 1998. *The Atlas of Ethnic Diversity in Wisconsin.* Madison: University of Wisconsin Press.

Zeitlin, Steven J., Amy Kotkin, and Holly Cutting Baker, eds. 1982. *A Celebration of American Family Folklore: Tales and Traditions from the Smithsonian Collection.* New York: Pantheon.

Zeman, Carrie. 2013. "The Stuff of Legend." *A Thrilling Narrative of Indian Captivity: Dispatches from the Dakota War of 1862.* July 12. https://athrillingnarrative.com/2013/07/12/the-stuff-of-legend/.

Contributors

CARMEN BEAUDOIN BOMBARDIER is a Franco-American performer and cultural educator with a musical career spanning more than forty years.

B. MARCUS CEDERSTRÖM works at the University of Wisconsin–Madison as the community curator of Nordic American folklore. His work focuses on Scandinavian American folklife as well as the intersections of immigration, labor, and creative expression. He also works with Indigenous communities on issues of sustainability, cultural revitalization, and pedagogy.

KIM CHASE is a second-generation, bilingual Franco-American and retired educator.

COLIN GIOIA CONNORS is a lecturer in Scandinavian studies at the University of Washington, where he also produces *Crossing North*, a podcast on Nordic and Baltic society and culture. His research includes landscape archaeology, Old Norse studies, North American Indigenous communities, public folklore, and digital storytelling.

RHONDA R. DASS is full professor in the anthropology department, Minnesota State University, Mankato. She teaches courses on research methods, body art, and museology, as well as a popular course titled "Vampires, Werewolves, and Zombies: The Folklore of Fear." Dass is the founder and director of the American Indigenous studies and museum studies programs at MSU, Mankato.

ROBERT DESROSIERS grew up singing French songs with family and neighbors on Burlington, Vermont's South End.

THOMAS A. DUBOIS is Halls-Bascom Professor of Scandinavian Studies, Folklore, and Religious Studies at the University of Wisconsin–Madison. His research and publications focus on folklore particularly in the Nordic region and North America.

DAVID OLAWUYI FAKUNLE, PHD, is a "mercenary for change," serving as adjunct assistant professor at the University of Florida and associate faculty at the Johns Hopkins

Bloomberg School of Public Health. David is cofounder and CEO of DiscoverME/ RecoverME, an organization using the African oral tradition for healing and growth.

TIM FRANDY is an assistant professor of folk studies at Western Kentucky University whose Indigenous-centered collaborative research includes decolonization, public folklore, and the environmental humanities. Frandy's recent translation of *Inari Sámi Folklore* is the first polyvocal anthology of Sámi oral tradition ever published in English.

CHRISTINE GARLOUGH is a professor of gender and women's studies and head of the folklore program at the University of Wisconsin–Madison. She works with feminist activists in India and the United States who reenvision vernacular culture for rhetorical purposes and explores how care, as a political concept, contributes to social change.

NATHAN D. GIBSON is a folklorist, ethnomusicologist, and the audiovisual preservation archivist for the University of Wisconsin–Madison's General Library System. His work emphasizes curation, preservation, and access to the diverse ethnic musics of the Upper Midwest through the NEH-funded Local Centers/Global Sounds initiative as well as the Nordic Folklife project.

JANET C. GILMORE, University of Wisconsin–Madison, a professor emerita in folklore and landscape architecture, remains active in Center for the Study of Upper Midwestern Cultures public folklore collections projects. Her integrated research, teaching, and outreach incorporate decades of experience in examining maritime folklife, foodways, cultural landscapes, and conservation constructs such as festivals, exhibitions, and archives.

JENNIFER GIPSON studies the historical and ideological intersections of folklore, print, literacy, race, and class, especially in nineteenth-century France and New Orleans. She is particularly interested in how historical narratives generate authority and in the role of literature and folklore in popular beliefs about the past. She holds a PhD from the University of California, Berkeley.

BUCKY HALKER is a freelance historian, musician, and songwriter based in Chicago. For more than forty years, he has been involved in researching, collecting, writing about, recording, and performing American labor songs and poetry, as well as documenting labor lore and folk music in Illinois.

LISA L. HIGGINS directs the Missouri Folk Arts Program, a collaboration between the Missouri Arts Council and the University of Missouri's Museum of Art and Archaeology. She spends most days managing grants to support projects such as Missouri's apprenticeship program. She also helps nonprofits apply for grants to sustain traditional arts.

MIRVA JOHNSON is a PhD candidate in Nordic folklore at the University of Wisconsin–Madison. Her research focuses on the intersections of linguistics and folklore, especially on how language and culture interact in immigrant communities over time. Her work spans heritage language linguistics, Nordic and American migration, and cultural maintenance.

REBECCA J. KEYEL holds a PhD in human ecology (design studies) from the University of Wisconsin–Madison. Her most recent research project examined American women's hand-knitting for servicemen during World Wars I and II and its relationship to labor, patriotism, and the home front.

ANDY KOLOVOS is the Associate Director and Archivist of the Vermont Folklife Center. His professional interests focus on the intersection of ethnographic archives and public folklore practice, fieldwork methods, collaborative research, the ethics of representation and, well, comic books.

JAMES P. LEARY is a folklorist whose collaborative research with diverse peoples has resulted in folklife festivals, public radio programs, films, documentary sound recordings, and publications. An emeritus professor of folklore and Scandinavian studies at the University of Wisconsin–Madison, he cofounded the Center for the Study of Upper Midwestern Cultures.

HILARY MORGAN V. LEATHEM recently obtained their PhD in anthropology from the University of Chicago, where their dissertation examined the moral, emotive, and symbolic dimensions of heritage-making in Oaxaca, Mexico. Previously a Mellon Digital Knowledge Sharing Fellow at the American Philosophical Society, Leathem is currently a visiting fellow at Maynooth University.

YVONNE R. LOCKWOOD is a retired academic specialist and curator emerita of folklife at the Michigan State University Museum. Her research is primarily on the folklife of Finnish Americans and Bosnian Americans, focusing predominantly on ethnicity, material culture, and foodways.

MARK L. LOUDEN is the Alfred L. Shoemaker, J. William Frey, and Don Yoder Professor of Germanic Linguistics and director of the Max Kade Institute for German American Studies at the University of Wisconsin–Madison. His research and public outreach center mostly on the language, faith, and culture of Amish and traditional Mennonites.

RICHARD MARCH is a (now retired) public folklorist. He initiated the folk arts program at the Wisconsin Arts Board and directed it for twenty-six years. Notable accomplishments of the program include folk arts apprenticeships, the Wisconsin Sesquicentennial Folklife Festival, Down Home Dairyland Radio, and the Wisconsin Folks website.

DIANA BAIRD N'DIAYE, PHD, senior curator and cultural heritage specialist at the Smithsonian Institution's Center for Folklife and Cultural Heritage, directs initiatives on

African and African American crafts. Books include the coauthored volume *Curatorial Conversations: Reflections on the Smithsonian Folklife Festival,* awarded Smithsonian Secretary's Research Prize, and the forthcoming book *The Will to Adorn,* on African American style traditions. N'Diaye is a fellow of the American Folklore Society and in 2021 received the Society's Americo Parèdes prize.

LISA ORNSTEIN is a folklorist, archivist, political activist, and professional musician. She served for three years as director of the Centre de valorisation du patrimoine vivant in Quebec and for seventeen years as director of the Acadian Archives at the University of Maine at Fort Kent.

ANNE PRYOR is an independent folklorist and a curler based in Madison, Wisconsin. She consults for the American Scandinavian Foundation and is an honorary fellow with the Folklore Program at UW–Madison. Two past positions of special delight were serving as the state folklorist at the Wisconsin Arts Board and as the board chair for Local Learning. Pryor chairs the Reference Committee for the US Women's Curling Association and the Centennial Committee for the Madison Curling Club, which is 100 years old in 2021.

TROY REEVES is the University of Wisconsin–Madison's oral historian, working inside its University Archives. He oversees the collecting and curating of oral history recordings; he also communicates and collaborates with those interested in oral history and has managed dozens of oral history projects there, including "Madison LGBTQ Community" and "African American Athletes at UW."

ANNA RUE is the associate director of the Center for the Study of Upper Midwestern Cultures and works on the Nordic Folklife project. She holds a master's in American studies from the University of Massachusetts–Boston and a master's and PhD in Scandinavian studies and folklore from the University of Wisconsin–Madison.

JOSEPH SALMONS is the Lester W. J. "Smoky" Seifert Professor of Language Sciences at the University of Wisconsin–Madison. With Jim Leary, he cofounded the Center for the Study of Upper Midwestern Cultures. His research focuses on language change and linguistic theory, especially sound systems, often drawing data from Germanic and Algonquian languages.

NICOLE SAYLOR led the American Folklife Center Archives at the Library of Congress from December 2012 to June 2021, when she became the library's chief of the Digital Innovation Lab. Her AFC team curated an extensive collection of multiformat documentation of traditional arts, cultural expressions, and oral narratives.

CHERYL T. SCHIELE is an arts administrator with twenty years' experience. She currently serves as the folk and traditional arts specialist at the National Endowment for the

Arts, overseeing the National Heritage Fellowships, Folk Arts Partnerships, and National Folklife Network. She has a B.Mus. degree from James Madison University.

CLAIRE SCHMIDT is an associate professor of English at Missouri Valley College, teaching writing and medieval and postcolonial British and World literatures. Her research focuses on the everyday, specifically occupational humor, foodways, and race. Her work includes *If You Don't Laugh You'll Cry: The Occupational Humor of White Wisconsin Prison Workers*.

JARED L. SCHMIDT holds a PhD in folklore studies from the University of Wisconsin–Madison, and a master's of science in anthropology from Minnesota State University, Mankato. His research interests include Nordic folk art, foodways, museum studies, heritage, material culture, occupational folklife, and vampires. He currently resides in Oregon.

GUHA SHANKAR'S work at the American Folklife Center encompasses public programming, documentary production, research, community outreach, and teaching. Among other duties, he codirects the Civil Rights History Project, an oral history documentation effort focusing on the Black freedom struggle, and coordinates Ancestral Voices, a collaborative curation and reparative collection description initiative undertaken with Indigenous communities.

SALLIE ANNA STEINER, PhD, is a folklorist whose research on material culture has focused primarily on Scandinavian and East African communities in Norway and the United States. Dr. Steiner is passionate about public arts work and has worked for museums, libraries, nonprofits, and government arts boards in Minnesota and Wisconsin.

ROBERT T. TESKE served on the faculties of Wayne State University and Western Kentucky University and as an arts specialist with the National Endowment for the Arts Folk Arts Program before joining the staff of the Kohler Arts Center. He subsequently served as the executive director of the Cedarburg Cultural Center and of the Milwaukee County Historical Society.

MARY TWINING BAIRD, author of *Sea Islands Heritage* and *Sea Island Roots* (coedited with K. E. Baird), has published articles on African American quilting, basketry, children's games, and dance. She chaired a seminal conference in 1997 on African American science fiction, fantasy, and horror. She is retired from Clark Atlanta University.

TERRI VAN ORMAN has engaged in arts administration since 2004, at the Ozark Folk Center, the Arkansas Craft School, and, currently, Folklore Village. She has served on the boards of the Arkansas Arts Council and the Arkansas Craft Guild and currently is on the board of the Folk Education Association of America. She has a master's in cultural sustainability from Goucher College.

HILARY-JOY VIRTANEN is an assistant professor of Finnish and Nordic studies at Finlandia University. Much of her research focuses on Finnish ethnicity and its expression through festival, music, dance, and traditional arts. She also works with industrial heritage and laborlore of the Upper Midwest, with an emphasis on copper- and iron-mining districts.

AYAKO YOSHIMURA, Japanese studies librarian at the University of Chicago, has published essays on humor, foodways, and belief traditions. Recent projects include the exhibit *Nikkei South Side: Japanese and Japanese Americans in Hyde Park and Its Vicinity*, and continuing research into dress and identity through kimono wearing.

JAMIE YUENGER is the founder of StoryKeep, a media production company and online course academy that helps families share their personal stories and histories though films, books, and private podcasts. You can view the company's portfolio of recent work and review its online class offerings at www.StoryKeep.com.

Index

Page numbers in italics indicate illustrations. The letter t following a page number denotes a table.